10,000 DREAMS INTERPRETED

10,000 DREAMS INTERPRETED

BARNES
&NOBLE
BOOKS
NEW YORK

This edition published by
BARNES & NOBLE, INC.
by arrangement with
ELEMENT BOOKS LTD

2001 BARNES & NOBLE BOOKS

Printed and bound in the UK by
Butler & Tanner Ltd

ISBN 0-7607-0525-9

9 10 8

Designed and created with The Bridgewater Book Company

ELEMENT BOOKS LIMITED
Managing Editor: Miranda Spicer
Senior Commissioning Editor: Caro Ness
Production Manager: Susan Sutterby
Production Controller: Fiona Harrison

THE BRIDGEWATER BOOK COMPANY
Designers: Jane Lanaway, Kevin Knight, Glyn Bridgewater
Page make-up: Chris Lanaway
Picture Research: Vanessa Fletcher
Studio Photography: Guy Ryecart, Jeremy Thomas
Illustrators: Amanda Cameron, Jane Couldrey, Lorraine Harrison, Ivan Hissey, Katty McMurray, Tony Simpson, Jane Tattersfield, Vikki Yeates
Editor: Viv Croot
Dream Directory compiled by Ingrid Lock

Library of Congress Cataloging in Publication data available

Contents

Preface

THIS GROUNDBREAKING book, 10,000 DREAMS Interpreted, *stands as a milestone in allegorical dream interpretation. The author, Gustavus Hindman Miller, believed that dreams can significantly affect our everyday lives. He was able to communicate to the average man in non-technical terms what a dream can foretell, and he believed that the entries he provided were the keys that would unlock the mysteries of the future.*

In creating this book, Miller selected dreams and subjects that were considered meaningless, and by using the forces around him he strove to find their esoteric or hidden import. His intuitive method for decoding dreams was neither mysterious nor formulaic, but purely instinctive and analytic.

It should be remembered that Miller was writing before Carl Gustav Jung (1875-1961), the great Swiss psychiatrist, had formulated the theories about the significance of dreams which were to permeate modern thinking about dreams and their interpretation. Jung's famous seminar on dream analysis was not conducted until 1928 in Zurich, Switzerland. Miller was therefore a pioneer in the field of dreams, although his path led in a different direction, and his interpretations should be seen in counterpoint rather than in conflict with the modern orthodoxy of Jungian analysis.

FULL COLOR ILLUSTRATIONS TO ENLIVEN AND ILLUMINATE THE TEXT.

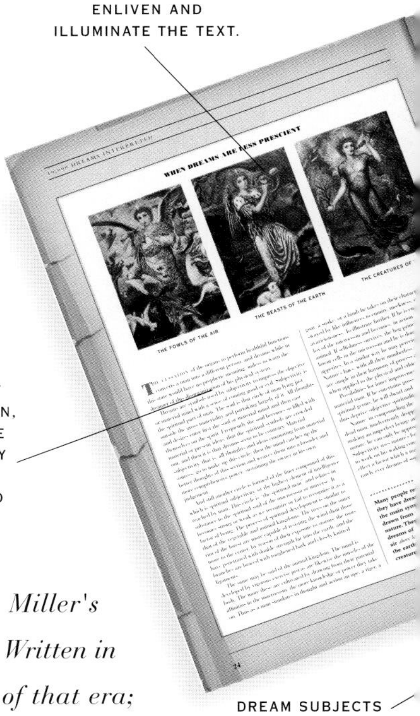

ORIGINAL TEXT OF INTRODUCTION, A GUIDE TO THE INTRIGUING WAY IN WHICH THE AUTHOR'S MIND WORKED.

DREAM SUBJECTS ILLUSTRATED BY ORIGINAL ARTWORK, PHOTOGRAPHY, OR ENGRAVINGS.

UPDATING A CLASSIC

ALTHOUGH RELIABLE in its interpretation of primary dream symbolism, Miller's method was, naturally, influenced by the environment and society he lived in. Written in the early part of the century, many of the entries reflect the mores and attitudes of that era; others are somewhat passé in subject or style for an audience heading into the next century.

However, Miller's main goal and purpose – the use of dream symbols as key to unlock the secrets in your unconscious mind – can never be dated or extraneous. To maintain its relevance, Dr Hans Holzer, one of the world's leading parasychologists, has provided nearly a hundred new entries as well as revised dozens of others to expand and update the original text so that it may continue to be used as a reference guide for discriminating readers.

This updated, illustrated edition is presented as a celebration of Miller's original text; the construction and vocabulary of his language, his spelling imagery and allusions have all been retained to preserve the unique flavor of the original; only a few words and concepts now considered anachronistic or obsolete are explained in the text.

'A dream is an event transpiring in that world belonging to the mind when the objective senses have withdrawn into rest or oblivion.
Then the spiritual man is living alone in the future or ahead of objective life and consequently lives man's future first, developing conditions in a way that enables working man to shape his actions by warnings, so as to make life a perfect existence.'

GUSTAVUS HINDMAN MILLER

How To Use This Book

10,000 DREAMS interpreted is arranged in three parts: the introduction, the main section covering the dreams themselves, and the dream directory. **The Introduction** is the original text written by Gustavus Hindman Miller to explain to his contemporary readership his theories of dreams and their significance and to outline the rationale behind his method of analysis.

The Dreams is the main section of the book. The entries are arranged in 40 thematic chapters, beginning in the Animal Kingdom and finishing in the spiritual realm of Religious Matters and covering most areas of human endeavour and attributes in between. Each entry covers one or more dreams featuring the same subject. When you awake with the memory of a dream in mind, you can look for it in the relevant section; if you dream of dogs, for example, you can review canine dreams grouped together in the domestic animals section of The Animal Kingdom. Here you will be able to read about specific dog dreams and let you eye fall on entries covering similar or related subjects which may throw light on your dream experience.

A system of cross references runs across the bottom of each page, directing the reader to interconnecting entries, dreams about associated subjects, or entries that share the same title but have different meanings, such as poker (the implement) and poker (the card game). To navigate more precisely among the dreams, turn first to part three of the book, The Dream Directory. This lists every dream entry in alphabetical order, so it is simple to look up specific dreams; it also functions as a cross referencing index, covering every aspect of each dream so that you can access it from any approach.

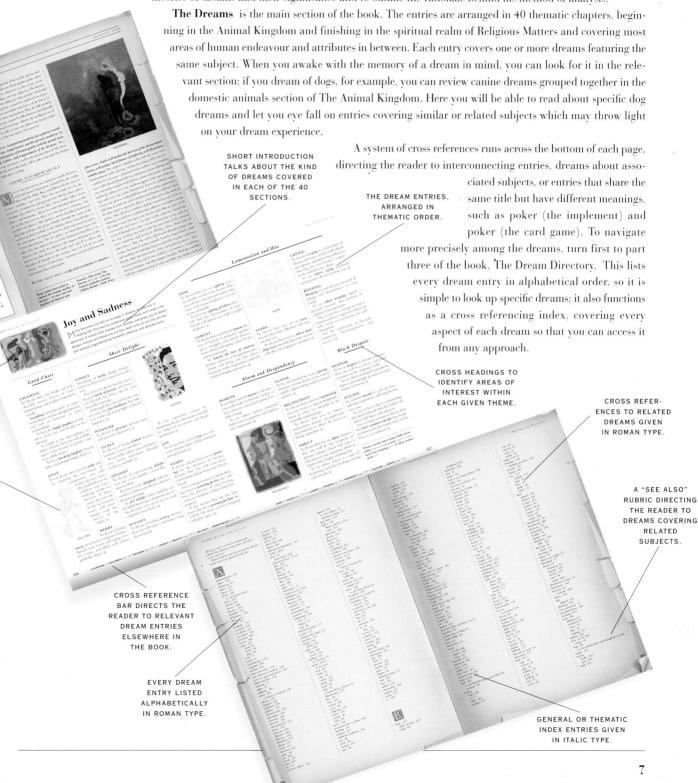

SHORT INTRODUCTION TALKS ABOUT THE KIND OF DREAMS COVERED IN EACH OF THE 40 SECTIONS.
THE DREAM ENTRIES, ARRANGED IN THEMATIC ORDER.
CROSS HEADINGS TO IDENTIFY AREAS OF INTEREST WITHIN EACH GIVEN THEME.
CROSS REFERENCES TO RELATED DREAMS GIVEN IN ROMAN TYPE.
A "SEE ALSO" RUBRIC DIRECTING THE READER TO DREAMS COVERING RELATED SUBJECTS.
CROSS REFERENCE BAR DIRECTS THE READER TO RELEVANT DREAM ENTRIES ELSEWHERE IN THE BOOK.
EVERY DREAM ENTRY LISTED ALPHABETICALLY IN ROMAN TYPE.
GENERAL OR THEMATIC INDEX ENTRIES GIVEN IN ITALIC TYPE.

Introduction

Dreams are rudiments of the great state to come. We dream what is about to happen.

BAILEY

THE BIBLE, as well as other great books of historical and revealed religion, shows traces of a general and substantial belief in dreams. Plato, Goethe, Shakespeare and Napoleon assigned to certain dreams prophetic value. Joseph saw eleven stars of the zodiac bow to himself, the twelfth star. The famine of Egypt was revealed by a vision of fat and lean cattle. The parents of Christ were warned of the cruel edict of Herod, and fled with the Divine Child into Egypt.

Pilate's wife, through the influence of a dream, advised her husband to have nothing to do with the conviction of Christ. But the gross materialism of the day laughed at dreams, as it echoed the voice and verdict of the multitude, "Crucify the Spirit, but let the flesh live." Barabbas, the robber, was set at liberty.

THE ULTIMATUM of all human decrees and wisdom is to gratify the passions of the flesh at the expense of the spirit. The prophets and those who have stood nearest the fountain of universal knowledge used dreams with more frequency than any other mode of divination.

DREAMS IN HISTORY

PROFANE, as well as sacred, history is threaded with incidents of dream prophecy. Ancient history relates that Gennadius was convinced of the immortality of his soul by conversing with an apparition in his dream.

Through the dream of Cecilia Metella, the wife of a consul, the Roman Senate was induced to order the temple of Juno Sospita rebuilt.

The Emperor Marcian dreamed he saw the bow of the Hunnish conqueror break on the same night that Attila died.

Plutarch relates how Augustus, while ill, through the dream of a friend, was persuaded to leave his tent, which a few hours after was captured by the enemy, and the bed whereon he had lain was pierced with the enemies' swords.

If Julius Cæsar had been less incredulous about dreams he would have listened to the warning which Calpurnia, his wife, received in a dream.

Petrarch saw his beloved Laura, in a dream, on the day she died, after which he wrote his beautiful poem "The Triumph of Death."

Crœsus saw his son killed in a dream.

Cicero relates the story of two traveling Arcadians who went to different lodgings – one to an inn, and the other to a private house. During the night the latter dreamed that his friend was begging for help. The dreamer awoke; but, thinking the matter unworthy of notice, went to sleep again. The second time he dreamed his friend appeared, saying it would be too late, for he had already been murdered and his body hid in a cart, under manure. The cart was afterward sought for and the body found. Cicero also wrote, "If the gods love men they will certainly disclose their purposes to them in sleep."

Chrysippus wrote a volume on dreams as divine portent. He refers to the skilled interpretations of dreams as a true divination; but adds that, like all other arts in which men have to proceed on conjecture and on artificial rules, it is not infallible.

A DREAM OF THE EAST

Plato concurred in the general idea prevailing in his day, that there were divine manifestations to the soul in sleep. Condorcet thought and wrote with greater fluency in his dreams than in waking life.

Tartini, a distinguished violinist, composed his "Devil's Sonata" under the inspiration of a dream. Coleridge, through dream influence, composed his "Kubla Khan."

The writers of Greek and Latin classics relate many instances of dream experiences. Homer accorded to some dreams divine origin. During the third and fourth centuries, the supernatural origin of dreams was so generally accepted that the fathers, relying upon the classics and the Bible as authority, made this belief a doctrine of the Christian Church.

Synesius placed dreaming above all methods of divining the future; he thought it the surest, open to both poor and rich alike.

Aristotle wrote: "There is a divination concerning some things in dreams not incredible." Camille Flammarion, in his great book *On Premonitory Dreams and Divination of the Future*, says: "I do not hesitate to affirm at the outset that occurrence of dreams foretelling future events with accuracy must be placed as certain."

Joan of Arc predicted her death.

Cazotte, the French philosopher and transcendentalist, warned Condorcet against the manner of his death.

People dream now, the same as they did in medieval and ancient times.

Dreams are thought to be a direct route connecting the human mind to the spiritual realm. This connective path may be reached by various methods: via simple, sound slumber, through the feverish visions of the sick, or the languorous meditations inspired by an opiate ***above*****.**

DREAMS IN "THE UNKNOWN"

THE FOLLOWING excerpt from *The Unknown**, a recent book by Flammarion, the French astronomer, supplemented with a few of my own thoughts and collections, will answer the purposes intended for this book.

"We may see without eyes and hear without ears, not by unnatural excitement of our sense of vision or of hearing, for these accounts prove the contrary, but by some interior sense, psychic and mental.

"The soul, by its interior vision, may see not only what is passing at a greater distance, but it may also know in advance what is to happen in the future. The future exists potentially, determined by causes which bring to pass successive events.

"POSITIVE OBSERVATION proves the existence of a psychic world, as real as the world known to our physical senses.

"And now, because the soul acts at a distance by some power that belongs to it, are we authorized to conclude that it exists as something real, and that it is not the result of functions of the brain?

"Does light really exist?

"Does heat exist?

"Does sound exist?

"No.

"They are only manifestations produced by movement.

"What we call light is a sensation produced upon our optic nerve by the vibrations of ether, comprising between 400 and 756 trillions per second, undulations that are themselves very obscure.

"What we call heat is a sensation produced by vibrations between 350 and 600 trillions.

"The sun lights up space, as much at midnight as at midday. Its temperature is nearly 270 degrees below zero.

"What we call sound is a sensation produced upon our auditory nerve by silent vibrations of the air, themselves comprising between 32,000 and 36,000 a second.

✣✻✣✻✣✻

"Very many scientific terms represent only results, not causes.

"The soul may be in the same case.

"The observations given in this work, the sensations, the impressions, the visions, things heard, etc., may indicate physical effects produced without the brain.

"Yes, no doubt, but it does not seem so.

"Let us examine one instance.

"Turn back to page 156.

"A young woman, adored by her husband, dies at Moscow. Her father-in-law, at Pulkowo, near St. Petersburg, saw her that same hour by his side. She walked with him along the street; then she disappeared. Surprised, startled, and terrified, he telegraphed to his son, and learned both the sickness and the death of his daughter-in-law.

"We are absolutely obliged to admit that SOMETHING emanated from the dying woman and touched her father-in-law. The thing unknown may have been an ethereal movement, as in the case of light, and may have been only an effect, a product, a result; but this effect must have had a cause, and this cause evidently proceeded from the woman who was dying. Can the constitution of the brain explain this projection? I do not think that any anatomist or physiologist will give this question an affirmative answer. One feels that there is a force unknown, proceeding, not from our physical organization, but from that in us which we think.

"Take another example *(see page 57)*.

"A lady in her own house hears a voice singing. It is the voice of a friend now in a convent, and she faints, because she is sure it is the voice of the dead. At the same moment that friend does really die, twenty miles away from her.

"Does not this give us the impression that one soul holds communication with another?

"Here is another example *(page 163)*:

"The wife of a captain who has gone out to the Indian mutiny sees one night her husband standing before her with his hands pressed to his breast, and a look of suffering on his face. The agitation that she feels convinces her that he is either killed or badly wounded. It was November 14th. The War Office subsequently publishes his death as having taken place on November 15th. She endeavors to have the true date ascertained. The War Office was wrong. He died on the 14th.

"A child six years old stops in the middle of his play and cries out, frightened, 'Mamma, I have seen Mamma.' At that moment his mother was dying far away from him *(page 124)*.

"A young girl at a ball stops short in the middle of a dance and cries, bursting into tears. 'My father is dead; I have just seen him.' At that moment her father died. She did not even know he was ill.

"All these things present themselves to us as indicating not physiological operations of one brain acting on another, but psychic actions of spirit upon spirit. We feel that they indicate to us some power unknown.

"No doubt it is difficult to apportion what belongs to the spirit, the soul, and what belongs to the brain. We can only let ourselves be guided in our judgement and our appreciations by the same feeling that is created in us by the discussion of phenomena. This is how all science has been started. Well, and does not everyone feel that we have here to do with manifestations from beings capable of thought, and not with material physiological facts only?

***from *The Unknown*. Published by Harper & Brothers.**

SATAN WATCHING THE SLEEP OF CHRIST

"This impression is superabundantly confirmed by investigation concerning the unknown faculties of the soul, when active in dreams and somnambulism.

"A brother learns the death of his young sister by a terrible nightmare.

"A young girl sees beforehand, in a dream, the man whom she will marry.

"A mother sees her child lying in a road, covered with blood.

"A lady goes, in a dream, to visit her husband on a distant steamer, and her husband really receives this visit, which is seen by a third person.

"A magnetized lady sees and describes the interior of the body of her dying mother; what she said is confirmed by the autopsy.

"A gentleman sees, in a dream, a lady whom he knows arriving at night in a railroad station, her journey having been undertaken suddenly.

"A magistrate sees three years in advance the commission of a crime, down to its smallest details.

"Several persons report that they have seen towns and landscapes before they ever visited them, and have seen themselves in situations in which they found themselves long after.

"A mother hears her daughter announce her intended marriage six months before it has been thought of.

"Frequent cases of death are foretold with precision.

"A theft is seen by a somnambulist, and the execution of the criminal is foretold.

"A young girl sees her fiancé, or an intimate friend dying (these are frequent cases), etc.

"All these show unknown faculties in the soul. Such at least is my own impression. It seems to me that we cannot reasonably attribute the prevision of the future and mental sight to a nervous action of the brain.

"I think we must either deny these facts or admit that they must have had an intellectual and spiritual cause of the psychic order, and I recommend sceptics who do not desire to be convinced, to deny them outright; to treat them as illusions and cases of a fortuitous coincidence of circumstances. They will find this easier. Uncompromising deniers of facts, rebels against evidence, may be all the more positive, and may declare that the writers of these extraordinary narratives are persons fond of a joke, who have written them to hoax me, and that there have been persons in all ages who have done the same thing to mystify thinkers who have taken up such questions.

"These phenomena prove, I think, that the soul exists, and that it is endowed with faculties at present unknown. That is the logical way of commencing our study, which in the end may lead us to the problem of the after-life and immortality. A thought can be transmitted to the mind of another. There are mental transmissions, communications of thoughts, and psychic currents between human souls. Space appears to be no obstacle in these cases, and time sometimes seems to be annihilated."

Dreams are important in the Christian tradition; Christ himself gained strength from his dreams as he wandered for forty days and nights in the wilderness. Even Satan *above* **dared not interrupt the spiritual trance.**

FRAGMENTARY THOUGHTS FROM DREAM REALMS

MAN IS a little circle of world composed of the infinitesimal atoms thrown off from the great circle or parent world, and fitting into his place in the zone of life. If in the revolutions of the great circle he catches more material he increases his circle to objective or subjective growth; if he absorbs spiritual or mind atoms as they fall from the great body of creative source, he enlarges or contracts his own circle according to the assimilation of the food he receives from the parent.

It is optional with man to obtain spiritual or material manna as it is disseminated throughout existence. To feed on material diet alone, contracts and distorts the circle of the man; but a full comprehension of the needs of the circle, a proper denial of supply to some of the compounds, together with a tender care of other parts, will round out the whole into a perfect physical and mental circle of life.

Dissentious and conflicting results should be avoided in computing the length and breadth of the compounded circle of man's individual world. Objective life is one of the smallest compounds in real life.

Dream life is fuller of meaning and teaching of the inner, or God life, than is the exterior life of man. The mind receives education from communicating with the dream composition in the great circle. Consult with your whole nature or circle before beginning a serious work; partial consultations, or material advice only, often brings defeat of objects sought, when a true home counsel would have brought success and consequent happiness.

Man should live in his subjective realms and study more his relation to other compositions or circles; thus fructifying and making beautiful his own world through intercourse with others who have worked in the great storehouse of subjectivity, and who have climbed already from the basement into the light of spiritual sunshine.

SOME EMPIRICAL EVIDENCE

A FEW YEARS ago a person whom I will designate as "A" related a dream to me as follows: "I take no interest in pugilism or pugilists, but I saw, in a dream, every detail of the Corbett and Fitzsimmons mill, four days before it took place out West. Two nights before the fight I had a second dream in which a favorite horse was running but suddenly, just before the judge's stand was passed, a hitherto unobserved little black horse ran ahead and the crowd shouted in my ears, 'Fitzsimmons wins!"

"B" relates the following as a dream: "I saw the American soldiers, in clay-coloured uniform, bearing the flag of victory two weeks before the Spanish–American war was declared, and of course before any living being could have known the uniform to be adopted. Later I saw, several days before the actual occurrence happened, the destruction of Cervera's fleet by the American navy."

SIGNED "B".

"Just after the South African hostilities began, I saw in a dream a fierce struggle between the British and Boers, in which the former suffered severe losses. A few nights after I had a second dream, in which I saw the contending forces in a long-drawn contest, very disastrous to both, and in which neither could claim a victory. They seemed to be fighting to a frazzle."

SIGNED "C".

"D" related to me at the time of the occurrence of the dream the following: "It had been suggested to me that the two cereals, corn and wheat, were too far apart, and that I ought to buy corn. At noon I lay down on a lounge to await luncheon; I had barely closed my eyes before a voice whispered: 'Don't buy, but sell that corn.' 'What do you mean?' I asked. 'Sell at the present price, and buy at 23⅞.' " The foregoing dream was related to me by a practical, successful businessman who never speculates. I watched the corn market and know it took the turns indicated in the dream.

In this dream we find the dreamer conversing with some strange intelligence possessed of knowledge unknown to objective reason. It could not, therefore, have been the walking thoughts of the dreamer, for he possessed no such information. Was the message superinduced through the energies and activities of the waking mind on the subjective mind? This could not have been, because he had no such thoughts.

WE MUST THEREFORE look to other sources for an explanation. Was it the higher self that manifested to Abraham in the dim ages of the world? Was it the Divine Voice that gave solace to Krishna in his abstraction? Was it the unerring light that preceded Gautama into the strange solitudes of Asia? Was it the Comforter of Jesus in the wilderness and the garden of distress? Or, was it Paul's indwelling spirit of this earthly tabernacle? One thing we may truthfully affirm – that it did not proceed from the rational, objective mind of the rank materialist, who would close all doors to that inner life and consciousness where all true religion finds its birthmark, its hope, its promises and its faith; which, rightly understood, will leave to the horrors of the Roman crucifixion the twin thieves, superstition and scepticism, while the angel of "Goodwill" will go free to solace the world with the fruit and fragrance of enduring power and promise. The steel chains that fasten these hydra-headed crocodiles of sensuous poison around love and destiny can only be severed by the diamond of wisdom and knowledge.

Man cannot contradict the laws of Nature. But, are all the laws of Nature yet understood? Real philosophy seeks rather to solve than to deny.

LYTTON.

SUBJECTIVE INTELLIGENCE, OR THE HIGHER SELF

THE DREAMS described on page 12 and below, except two, cannot be explained by telepathy, because the mental picture cast on the dream mind had not in either instance taken place in waking life. This would account for the dream perception of "E," which did not, in all probability, take place until after the murder had been committed.

The vision of "F" saw the white-robed specter open the door, walk around the room, and finally, taking his position as if to depart, say: "I have taken all you have." No doubt this vision took place at the exact moment of the child's death.

THERE ARE THOUSANDS of similar experiences occurring daily in the lives of honest, healthy, and sane human beings, that rival the psychic manifestations of Indian Yogism or Hebrew records.

Still men go on doubting this true and living subjective intelligence that is constantly wooing for entrance into the soul and is ever vigilant in warning the material life of approaching evils. They prefer the Witch of Endor, and the Black Magicians of ancient Egypt to the higher, or Christ self, that has been seen and heard by the sages and saints of all ages.

To Paul it appeared as a great personal truth whom he was relentlessly persecuting. To many a wayward son or daughter of the present time, it appears as a dead relative or friend, in order to approach the material mind and make its warning more effective.

To those who were interested in the teachings of Christ, but who after his death were inclined to doubt him, this higher self materialized in the form of the Great Master in order to impress on their material minds the spiritual import of his teachings. So, to this day, when doubt and temptation mar the moral instinct, God, through the spiritual self, as Job says, approaches man while in deep sleep upon the bed to impress his instructions that he may change man from his purpose.

DREAM EXAMPLES

A CITIZEN worthy of confidence relates the following dream: "In December 1878, I saw in a dream my brother-in-law, Henry Yarnell, suffering from a bloody knife wound; after this I awoke, but soon fell asleep again. The second time I dreamed of a similar scene, except that the wound was the result of a shotgun. After this I did not go to sleep again. I was much troubled about my dream, and soon started in the direction of my brother-in-law's house. I had not gone far, when I met an acquaintance who promptly informed me that my brother-in-law had been shot."

SIGNED "E".

A WELL-KNOWN resident of Chattanooga, Tenn., formerly of New York City, will vouch for the accuracy of the following incident:

"On February 19, 1878, I was boarding with a family on Christopher Street, New York, while my wife and baby were visiting my parents in the country, a short distance from the city. Our baby was taken sick. The malady developed into brain fever, followed by water on the brain, causing the little one's death.

"At our boarding-place there was at the time a quartette of us grass widowers, as we called ourselves, and in order to pass away the time pleasantly we had organized a 'grass widowers' euchre club.' We used to meet almost every evening after dinner in the dining room, and play until about eleven o'clock, when we would retire. On the above date I dreamed that after playing our usual evening games we took our departure for our rooms, and on the way up the second flight of stairs I heard a slight movement behind me; on looking around I found I was being followed by a tall figure robed in a long, white gown, which came down to the floor. The figure seemed to be that of a man – I would say, about seven feet tall – who followed me up the second flight and along the hallway, entering my room. After coming in the door he made a circle of the room and seemed to be looking for something, and when he approached the door to make his exit he stopped still, and with a gesture of his hand remarked, 'I have taken all you have.' On the following morning, about 9:30 o'clock, I received a telegram from my wife announcing the death of our only baby."

SIGNED "F".

A WELL-KNOWN citizen of Chattanooga, Tenn., relates and vouches for the truth of the following occurrence:

"Several years ago, when a boy, I had a schoolmate and friend, Willie T., between whom and myself there sprung up a mutual feeling of high regard. We were chums in the sense that we were almost constantly together, both at school and at home, and among the partnerships we formed was one of having amateur shadowgraph and panoramic shows in the basement of Willie's home. This much to show the mental and social relationship that existed between us. Some time during this association (I cannot recall the exact night now) I had a strange dream, in which my chum appeared to me with outstretched hand, asking me to shake, saying, 'I shall not see you any more.' With that, the dream lapsed and was over. I thought nothing of the occurrence, and had almost forgotten it, when one day, about a week later, during which time I had not had a glimpse of my chum, while he was out hunting with another friend, W. McC., in following him over a rail fence, the latter's gun was accidentally discharged in Willie's face and neck, resulting in instant death. With this shocking news the memory of the dream I had had came back to me vividly and puzzled me very greatly, and indeed has puzzled me to this day."

SIGNED "G."

The recipients of the above dreams are living today and their names and addresses may be obtained, none of them are credulous fanatics or predisposed to a belief in psychic or spirit phenomena.

THE STRAIGHT LINE

THE SPIRITUAL world always fixes its orbit upon a straight line, while the material world is fonder of curves. We find man struggling through dreadful marshes and deserts of charlatanism in order to get a glimpse into his future, instead of solicitously following the straight line of inner consciousness that connects with the infinite mind, from which, aided by his Church and the healthy action of his own judgement, he may receive those helpful spiritual impressions and messages necessary to solace the longings of the searching soul.

The philosophy of the True Master is the straight line. Pythagoras, Plato and Christ created angles by running vertical lines through the ecclesiastical and hypocritical conventionalities of their day. The new angles and curves thus produced by the bold philosophy of the humble Nazarene have confronted with impregnable firmness during the intervening ages the sophistry of the Pharisees.

In a dream, in a vision of the night, when deep sleep falleth upon men, in slumberings upon the bed; then he openeth the ears of men and sealeth their instruction. That he may withdraw man from his purpose and hide pride from man.

JOB 33:15

Those who live active lives exclude spiritual thought and fill their minds with the fascinations of worldly affairs, pleasure and business, dream with less frequency than those who regard objective matters with lighter concern. The former depend along upon the voluptuous warmth of the world for contentment; they look to money, the presence of someone, or to other external sources for happiness, and are often disappointed; while the latter, with a just appreciation of temporal wants, depend alone upon the inner consciousness for that peace which passeth all carnal understanding.

They are strengthened, as were Buddha and Christ, by suppressing the sensual fires for forty days and nights in the wilderness of trial and temptation. They number a few, and are never disappointed, while the former number millions.

BODY AND SOUL

NATURE IS threefold, so is man; male and female, son or soul. The union of one and two produce the triad or the trinity which underlies the philosophy of the ancients.

Man has a physical or visible body, an atom of the physical or visible earth. He has a soul the exact counterpart of his body, but invisible and subjective; incomplete and imperfect as the external man, or vice versa.

The soul is not only the son or creation of man, but is the real man. It is the inner imperishable double or imprint of what has outwardly and inwardly transpired. All thoughts, desires and actions enter the soul through the objective mind.

The automaton of the body responds as quickly to the bat of the eye as it does to the movement of the whole body. By it the footsteps of man and the very hairs of his head are numbered. Thus it becomes his invisible counterpart. It is therefore the book of life or death, and by it he judges himself or is already judged. When it is complete nothing can be added or taken from its personnel. It is sometimes partly opened to him in his dreams, but in death is clearly revealed.

Man has also a spiritual body, subjective to, and more ethereal than the soul. It is an infinitesimal atom, and is related in substance to the spiritual or infinite mind of the universe. Just as the great physical sun, the center of visible light, life and heat, is striving to purify the foul miasma of the marsh and send its luminous messages of love into the dark crevices of the earth, so the Great Spiritual Sun, of which the former is a visible prototype of reflection, is striving to illuminate with Divine Wisdom the personal soul and mind of man, thus enabling him to become cognizant of the spiritual or Christ presence within.

The heresy and Herod of wanton flesh, degenerate victim of the sensuous filth and fermentation of self-indulgence, is ever striving to exile and suppress, from the wilderness of sin, the warning cry of the Nazarite voice by intriguing with the cunning, incestuous daughters of unholy thoughts and desires.

The objective mind is most active when the body is awake. The subjective influences are most active, and often fill the mind with impressions, while the physical body is asleep. The spiritual intelligence can only intrude itself when the human will is suspended, or passive to external states. A man who lives only on the sensual plane will receive his knowledge through his senses, and will not, while in that state, receive spiritual impressions or warning dreams.

Men and women rarely ever degrade themselves so low that the small voice of the desert does not bring them a message. Sodom and Gomorrah, vile with the debauchery of a nameless crime, were not deserted by the angel of love until the fire which they had lighted in their souls had consumed them. The walls of Jericho did not fall until Rahab, the harlot, had been saved and the inmates had heard for several days the ram's-horn and the tramp of Joshua's infantry.

The evangelist Jonah, the Sam Jones of Hebrew theology, exhorted the adulterous Nineveh many times to repentance before the city fell.

David, while languishing in the seductive embrace of the beautiful Bathsheba, heard the voice of Nathan. Surely God is no respecter of persons, and will speak to all classes if the people will not stiffen their necks or harden their hearts.

Women dream more often and more vividly than men, because their dream composition is less influenced and allied to external environments.

PRESCIENT DREAMS

ALL DREAMS possess an element of warning or prescience; some more than others. This is unknown to the many, but is known to the observing few. There are many people who have no natural taste for music, and who do not know one note from another. There are also those who cannot distinguish one color from another. To the former there is no sound of harmony, and to the latter there is no blending of colors.

They are heard and seen, but there is no artistic recognition of the same. Still it would be absurd to say to either the musician or the artist; your art is false and is only an illusion of the senses.

One man apparently never dreams; another dreams occasionally, and still another more frequently; none attempt to interpret their dream, or to observe what follows; therefore the verdict is, "There is nothing in dreams." (Schopenhauer aptly says: "No man can see over his own height . . . Intellect is invisible to the man who has none.") The first is like the blind man who denies the existence of light, because he does not perceive it. The second and third resemble the color-blind man, who sees but who persists in calling green blue, and vice versa.

A fourth man sees in a dream a friend walking in his room; the vision is so vivid he instantly gets up and strikes a match. After making sure there is no intruder about the room he looks at his watch and goes back to bed. The next day he receives the unwelcome tidings that his friend died at the exact moment of the vision.

At another time he hears in his dream a familiar voice cry out in agony. Soon he hears of a shocking accident or distressing illness befalling the one whose voice he recognized in the dream.

The third man, already referred to, has about the same dream experiences, but calls them strange coincidences.

Again, the fourth man dreams of walking through green fields of corn, grass, or wheat. He notes after such dreams prosperous conditions follow for at least a few days. He also notes, if the area over which he passes is interspersed with rocks or other adverse signs, good and bad follow in the wake of the dream. If he succeeds in climbing a mountain and finds the top barren he will accomplish his object, but the deal will prove unprofitable. If it is green and spring-like in appearance, it will yield good results. If he sees muddy water, sickness, business depression, or causes for jealousy may develop.

A nightmare suggests to the dreamer to be careful of health and diet, to relax his whole body, to sleep with his arms down and keep plenty of fresh air in the room.

He sums up the foregoing with a thousand similar incidents, and is led to believe certain dreams possess an element of warning.

***for authentic records, see Flammarion's *The Unknown*.**

THE THREE TYPES OF DREAMS

THERE ARE three pure types of dreams, namely, subjective, physical, and spiritual. They relate to the past, present, and future, and are influenced by past or subjective, physical and spiritual causes. The latter is always prophetic, especially when it leaves a vivid impression on the conscious mind. The former, too, possess an element of warning and prophecy, though the true meaning is hidden in symbols of allegory. They are due to contingent mental pictures of the past falling upon the conscious mind of the dreamer. Thus he is back at the old home, and finds mother pale and aged, or ruddy and healthy, and the lawn withered or green. It all augurs, according to the aspect the picture assumes, ill or good fortune.

PHYSICAL DREAMS are more or less unimportant. They are usually superinduced by the anxious waking mind, and when this is so they possess no prophetic significance.

Dreams induced by opiates, fevers, mesmerism, and ill health come under this class. A man who gambles is liable to dream of cards; if he dreams of them in deep sleep the warning is to be heeded; but if it comes as a reverie while he sleeps lightly he should regard it as worthless. Such dreams reflect only the present conditions of the body and mind of the dreamer; but as the past and present enter into shaping the future, the reflections thus left on the waking mind should not go by unheeded.

We often observe matters of dress and exterior appearance through mirrors, and we soon make the necessary alterations to put our bodies in harmony with existing formalities. Then, why not study more seriously the mental images reflected from the mirror of the soul upon our minds through the occult processes within us?

Thirdly, the spiritual dreams are brought about by the higher self penetrating the soul realm, and reflecting upon the waking mind approaching events. When we put our animal mind and soul in harmony with our higher self we become one with it, and, therefore, one with the universal mind or will by becoming a part of it. It is through the higher self we reach the infinite. It is through the lower self we fall into the whirlpool of matter.

SPIRITUAL DREAMS

THESE DREAMS are a part of the universal mind until they transpire in the life of man. After this they go to make a part of the personal soul. Whatever has not taken place in the mind, or life of man, belongs exclusively to the impersonal mind. But as soon as a man lives or sees a thing, that thing instantly becomes a part of his soul; hence, the clairvoyant, or mind reader, never perceives beyond the personal ego, as the future belongs exclusively to God or the universal mind, and has no material, subjective existence; therefore, it cannot be known except through the channels of the higher self, which is the Truth or the Word that is constantly striving to manifest itself through the flesh.

Our psychical research people give us conclusive proof of mental telepathy or telegraphy between finite minds. Thus communications or impressions are conveyed many miles from one mind to another. This phenomenon is easier when one or both of the subjects are in a state of somnambulence or sleep.

IN THOUGHT TRANSFERENCE or mind reading it is absolutely necessary to have a positive and a negative subject. Through the same law that mental impressions are telegraphed from one finite mind to another a man may place himself in harmony with the infinite mind and thus receive true and healthful warnings of coming evil or good. Homer, Aristotle, and other writers of the ancient classics thought this not improbable.

The statesman, the poet, the philosopher of the Bible were unanimous in attaching prophetic significance to dreams. Has the law of ethereal vibrations undergone any recent changes to debar or molest the communion of the soul with its spiritual father, any more than it has debarred contact with its material mother or environments?

WE ONLY UNDERSTAND the great laws of nature by effects. We know that vegetation planted in native soil and properly attended with light, heat, and moisture, will grow and yield a certain species of fruit. We may infer how it does this, but we cannot explain the process of transformation any more than we

A FEW QUESTIONS AND SUBJECTIVE ANSWERS REGARDING DREAMS

QUESTION *What is a dream?*
ANSWER A dream is an event transpiring in that world belonging to the mind when the objective senses have withdrawn into rest or oblivion.

Then the spiritual man is living alone in the future or ahead of objective life and consequently lives man's future first, developing conditions in a way that enables waking man to shape his actions by warnings, so as to make life a perfect existence.

QUESTION *What relationship is sustained between the average man and his dreams?*
ANSWER A dream to the average or sensual person, bears the same relation to his objective life that it maintained in the case of the ideal dreamer, but it means pleasures, sufferings, and advancements on a lower or material plane.

QUESTION *Then why is man not always able to correctly interpret his dreams?*
ANSWER Just as words fail sometimes to express ideas, so dreams fail sometimes in their mind pictures to portray coming events.

QUESTION *If they relate to the future, why is it we so often dream of the past?*
ANSWER When a person dreams of past events, those events are warnings of evil or good; sometimes they are stamped so indelibly upon the subjective mind that the least tendency of the waking mind to the past throws these pictures in relief on the dream consciousness.

QUESTION *Why is it that present environments often influence our dreams?*
ANSWER Because the future of man is usually affected by the present, so if he mars the present by wilful wrongs, or makes it bright by right living it will necessarily have influence on his dreams, as they are forecastings of the future.

QUESTION *What is an apparition?*
ANSWER It is the subjective mind stored with the wisdom gained from futurity, and in its strenuous efforts to warn its present habitation – the corporal body – of dangers just ahead, takes on the shape of a dear one as the most effective method of imparting this knowledge.

QUESTION *How does subjectivity deal with time?*
ANSWER There is no past and future to subjectivity. It is all one living present.

QUESTION *If that is so, why can't you tell us accurately of our future as you do of our past?*
ANSWER Because events are like a procession; they pass a few at a time and cast a shadow on subjective minds, and those which have passed before the waking mind are felt by other minds also and necessarily make a more lasting impression on the subjective mind.

QUESTION *To illustrate: A person on retiring or closing his eyes had a face appear to him, the forehead well formed but the lower parts distorted. Explain this phenomenon?*
ANSWER A changed state from perfect sleep or waking possessed him.

Now, the man's face was only the expression of his real thoughts and the state of his business combined. His thoughts were strong and healthy, but his business fagging, hence his own spirit is not a perfect likeness of his own soul, as it takes every atom of earthly composition perfectly normal to reproduce a perfect spirit picture of the soul or mortal man. He would have seen a true likeness of himself had conditions been favorable; thus a man knows when a complete whole is his portion.

Study to make your surroundings always harmonious. Remember that life is only being perfectly carried on when these conditions are in unison.

can explain why certain tropical birds are burnished with glowing colors, and that other birds under the murky skies are gray and brown, while in the Arctic regions they bleach.

In sleep we see, without being awakened, the angry lightning rend the midnight clouds, and hear the explosive thunder hurl its fury at us; but can we explain it any more than our scientist can explain the natural forces of thought, of love and hate, or the subtle intuition of woman?

What of the silhouette or the anthelion of the Scandinavian Alps, and the aerial cities so often seen by explorers and travelers? Do not they defy the law of optics? Must we understand the intricacies of articulation and the forces back of it before we can appropriate speech? Must we discard all belief in an infinite mind because we cannot understand it, and therefore say we are not a part of it because there is no Infinite? Should we discard the belief in the infinitude of number, because we cannot understand it, and therefore say that finite number is not a part of the infinite?

No scientist or naturalist is so grossly stupid as to deny the infinite expansion of numbers? If this be so, it establishes the infinite of number, of which every finite number is a part, and thus we have a parallel in mathematics, the very cornerstone of the exact sciences, for a finite and an infinite mind. It is from the prototype of this infinite of number, namely, the infinite of intelligence, that spiritual dreams proceed. They are, therefore, the reflection of truth upon the dream mind and occur with less frequency than do dreams of the other two classes.

MIXED DREAMS

THERE ARE also mixed dreams, due to a multitude of incidents arising from one or more sources, which being reflected upon the mind at the same instant, produce an incoherent effect similar to that which might be produced by running the same newspaper through two or more presses all of different size type.

Again, if you sit before a mirror when flashlights of faces and other things are reflected simultaneously and instantly removed, you will fail to obtain a well-defined impression of what passed before your mind.

If you should pass on a train, at the speed of two miles a minute, through a forest of flowers and trees, your mind would be unable to distinguish one flower or tree from another.

It is in a similar way dream life and incidents may fall upon the mind.

A woman may dream of receiving a letter, and in the same connection see muddy water, or an arid landscape. Closely following, in waking life, she is astonished to receive a letter in about the same manner of her dream, but the muddy water and the arid landscape are missing.

This is a mixed dream and is due to more than one cause. The first part is literal in its fulfillment, and belongs to the spiritual class; the other part of the dream is subjective, and therefore allegorical in meaning. Together with the letter, it was a forewarning of misfortune.

These dreams are more difficult of interpretation than those belonging to the spiritual type. In such dreams you may see water, letters, houses, money, people and countless other things. The next day you may cross water or receive a letter, the other things you may not see, but annoyance or pleasure will follow.

Again, you may have a similar dream and not receive a letter or cross water in reality, but the waking life will be filled with the other dream pictures and you will experience disappointing or pleasant surprises as are indicated by the letter or water sign in your dream.

ALLEGORICAL DREAMS

I HAVE selected the allegorical type of dreams for the subject of this work. Dreams that are common occurrences are thought by the world to be meaningless.

I have endeavored, through the occult forces in and about me, to find their esoteric or hidden import.

Dreams transpire on the subjective plane. They should therefore be interpreted by subjective intelligence. This, though burdened with many business cares, I have honestly endeavored to do. Through the long hours of many nights I have waited patiently and passively the automatic movement of my hand to write the subjective definitions without receiving a word or a single manifestation of intelligence, and again the mysterious forces would write as fast as my hand could move over the paper.

I will leave it for my readers to draw their own conclusions as to whether automatic writing is the work of extraneous spirits, through the brain and intelligence of the medium, or the result of auto-suggestive influence upon the subjective personality.

It is argued by the materialist, with some degree of strength, that the healthy man does not dream. This is, perhaps, true, in a way, but the whole man comprises the past, present, and future. The past and future always embrace more of the conditions that surround him than the present. The present is only the acute stage, while the chronic stage, considered from a personal view, is the past and future combined.

Man cannot eliminate entirely these states from himself, for, while they are past and future to the personal mind, they are ever present to the higher subjective senses; he is, therefore, never in perfect health unless these states are in harmony with the present. The personal self, in a normal state, cannot free itself from the past or from the anxieties of the future.

THE SPIRIT OF THE NEW CENTURY

The reader should ever keep before his mind the fact that no man ever had the same dream twice. He may have had very similar dreams, but some detail will be missing. Nature seems to abhor duplicates. You could no more find two dreams alike than you could find facsimiles in two blades of grass. A man cannot live two days exactly alike. Different influences and passions will possess him. Consequently, no two dreams can be had under exactly the same influence. Stereotypes are peculiarly the invention of man and not of God or nature.

Since it is impossible to find a man twice in exactly the same mental state, it is equally impossible for him to dream the same dream twice; therefore, it is only possible to approximate dream interpretation by classing them into families. This I have attempted to do in a more comprehensive way than other writers who have preceded me.

DREAM SYMBOLS

All men are acquainted with health and sickness, love and hate, success and failure. Sickness, hate, and failure belong to kindred families, and often ally their forces in such a way that it is hard to say whether the dreamer will fail in love, health, or some business undertaking. But at all times a bad symbol is a warning of evil, though that evil may be minimized or exaggerated, or vice versa, according as signs are good.

Thus, if the dream symbol indicates wealth or fortune to the peasant, his waking life may be gladdened by receiving or seeing a fifty-cent piece, or finding assuring work, while the same symbol to a wealthy man would mean many dollars, or a favorable turn in affairs.

It is the same in physical life. A man may hear the sound of a wagon. He cannot determine by the rattle of the wheels whether it is laden with laundry, groceries, or dry goods. He may judge as to its size and whether it is bearing a heavy or a light burden. When it objectifies he will be able to know its full import and not before. So with dream symbols. We may know they are fraught with evil or good, as in the case of Pilate's wife, but we cannot tell their full meaning until their reflections materialize before the objective sense.

Death is more frequently foretold by dream messages or visions, as explained in another part of this chapter.

During sleep the will is suspended, leaving the mind often a prey to its own fancy. The slightest attack of an enemy may be foretold by the unbridled imagination exaggerating the mental picture into a monstrous shark or snake, when, indeed, a much less portentous sign was cast from the dream mold.

A woman may see a serpent in waking life and through fright lose reason or self-control. She imagines it pursues her when in reality it is going an opposite direction; in a like way dreams may be many times unreal.

The mind loses its reason or will in sleep, but a supersensitive perception is awakened, and, as it regains consciousness from sleep, the sound of a knock on the wall may be magnified into a pistol shot.

The sleeping mind is not only supersensitive as to existing external sounds and lights, but it frequently sees hours and days ahead of the waking mind.

Nor is this contradictory to the laws of nature. The ant housed in the depth of the earth, away from atmospheric changes, knows of the approach of the harvest, and comes forth to lay by his store.

In a like manner, the pet squirrel is a better barometer of the local weather than the weather bureau. With unerring foresight, when a wintry frown nowhere mars the horizon, he is able to apprehend a cold wave twenty-four hours ahead, and build his house accordingly.

A SPIRITUAL AND MATERIAL PARTNERSHIP

So in sleep, man dreams the future by intuitive perception of invisible signs or influences, while awake he reasons it out by cause and effect. The former seems to be the law of the spiritual world, while the latter would appear to be the law of the material world. Man should not depend alone upon either. Together they proclaim the male and female principle of existence and should find harmonious consummation.

In this manner only can man hope to achieve that perfect normal state to which the best thought of the human race is aspiring, where he can create and control influences instead of being created and controlled by them, as the majority of us are at the present day.

God, the highest subjective source of intelligence, may in a dream leave impressions or presentiments on the mind of man, the highest objective source of intelligence.

The physical sun sends its light into the dark corners of the earth, and God, the Spiritual Sun, imparts spiritual light into the passive and receptive soul.

Man, by hiding in a cave, or closing the windows and doors of his house, may shut out all physical light; so he may steep his soul in sensual debauchery until all spiritual light is shut out.

Just as the vital essence of the soil, the mother of nature, may be extracted by abuse, either from omission or commission, until neither the light of the sun, nor the moisture of the heavens will wake the flush of life, so may the spiritual essence be deadened when the soil of the soul is filled with the aged and multiplying weeds of ravishing materiality.

The dream mind is often influenced by the waking mind. When the waking mind dwells upon any subject, the dream mind is more or less influenced by it, and it often assists the waking mind in solving difficult problems. The personal future, embodied in the active states of the universal mind, may affect the dream mind, producing premonitions of death, accidents, and misfortune.

The objective mind rejoices or laments over the aspects of the past and present, while the spiritual mind, striving with the personal future, either laments or rejoices over the prospective conditions.

One is the barometer of the past, while the other is the barometer of the future.

If we study carefully the spiritual impressions left upon the dream mind, through the interpretations of this book, we will be able to shape our future in accordance with spiritual law.

HOW TO DEVELOP THE POWER TO DREAM

Keep the mind clear and as free from material rubbish as is possible and go to sleep in a negative condition (this will, of course, have to be cultivated by the subject). A person can, if he will, completely relax his mind and body to the receptive mood required for dreams to appear as realities, or true explanations of future events.

The importance of a particular symbol may be clear in our dreams, but their full significance is not recognized until we awake. The concept of progress may be experienced as a visitation from an angel *opposite*; horses *below* carry a heavy burden of symbolism and their presence in dreams may be interpreted in many ways.

HORSES

RELATIVE DREAMS

TO DREAM you are conversing with a dead relative, and that relative endeavors to extract a promise from you, warns you of coming distress unless you follow the advice given. Disastrous consequences could be averted if minds could grasp the inner workings and sights of the higher or spiritual self. The voice of relatives is only that higher self taking form to approach more distinctly the mind that lives near the material plane. There is so little congeniality between common or material natures that persons should depend more largely upon their own subjectivity for true contentment and pleasure.

Thus our temporal events will contribute to our spiritual development, and in turn our spiritual knowledge will contribute to our temporal welfare. Without this harmonious interaction of the two great forces in man, the Divine plan of destiny cannot be reached.

This can only be accomplished through the material mind or reason dominating the animal emotions of the heart. In this way we would not covet our neighbor's goods, or grow angry with our brother over trifles.

The house vacated by the selfish appetites of the world would be filled with whispers of spiritual love and wisdom necessary to the mutual welfare and development of body and soul.

A THEORY TO EXPLAIN DREAMS

THE THEORY used in this book to interpret dreams is both simple and rational. By the using of it you will be surprised to find so many of the predictions fulfilled in your waking life. We deal with both the thought and the dream. The thought or sign implied in the object dreamed of and the influence surrounding it are always considered in the interpretation.

Thoughts proceed from the visible mind and dreams from the invisible mind. The average waking mind receives and retains only a few of the lessons of life. It is largely filled with idle and incoherent thoughts that are soon forgotten. The same may be truly said of the dream mind. Many of our day thoughts are day dreams, just as many of our night dreams are night thoughts. Our day deeds of evil or good pierce or soothe the conscience, just as our night symbols of sorrow and joy sadden or please the objective senses. Our day's thoughts are filled with the warnings and presence of the inner mind and our night's thoughts are tinctured and often controlled by our external mind.

Some writer has said: "Everything that exists upon earth has its ethereal counterpart." Christ said: "As a man thinketh so is he." A Hindu proverb says: "Man is a creature of reflection; he becomes that upon which he reflects." A modern metaphysicist says: "Our thoughts are real substance and leave their images upon our personality, they fill our aura with beauty or ugliness according to our intents and purpose in life." Each evil thought or action has its pursuing phantom, each smile or kindly deed its guiding angel, we leave wherever we ignobly stand, a tomb and an epitaph to haunt us through the furnace of conscience and memory.

Closely following in the wake of our multiplying evil thoughts are armies of these ghastly specters pursuing each other with the exact intents and purposes of the mind that gave them being. If we consider well these facts we will be forced into thinking our best thoughts at all times. Thoughts are the subjective and creative force that produces action. Action is the objective effect of thought; hence the character of our daily thoughts is making our failure or success of tomorrow.

CONTRARY DREAMS

THE CONSTANT dwelling of the mind upon certain things distorts their shapes upon subjectivity, thus throwing dreams in exactly opposite channels to the waking reality. Yet the dreamer always feels a sense of being awake in dreams like these, and on awakening experiences no recuperation of mind or body after such contrary dreams. Sleep is not fully sustained while the dreamer is held by material ideas in the subjective state.

TYPES OF MIND

THE IMPERSONAL mind deals with all time and things as ever present. The objective mind is constantly striving to penetrate the spiritual realm, while the spiritual mind is striving to enter matter, hence our actions have their subjective counterparts and their subethereal counterparts. The universal mind, in harmony with the evolutionary plans and laws of the macrocosms, materializes through functions of the microcosm, imparting to each, with its routine of failure and success, its daily objective. The inner or passive dream mind may perceive the subjective types or antitypes many days before they objectify through the microcosm. Their meaning is often wrapt in symbols, but sometimes the actual as it occurs in objective life is conveyed. Our own thought images which have passed before the objective mind may be perceived by the clever mind reader, but those antitypes which are affecting our future, but which have none other but subjective existence, are rarely ever perceived by any one except by the power of the higher self or the spirit within. For this reason we are enjoined by the sages to study self. With the physical mind we only see physical objects, with the subjective mind we see only subjective objects. This was Paul's doctrine and it is the belief of the best psychic thought of this century. By means of our reason – an objective process for divining the future – aided by mathematical and geographical data, we may outline the storm centers and the path of the rain days before they appear in certain localities. After eliminating all contingencies arising from clerical error and counteracting influence, the prognostication is sure of fulfillment.

For centuries** **ahead the astronomer foretells the eclipse of the moon and the sun and the arrival of comets. He does not do this by crossing the borderland dividing the spiritual from the physical world. In a like manner the subjective forces operate under their own planes and know very little even of their own corporal realm, just as our physical senses know little, if anything, of the soul of spiritual habitation. They know that by gross living the sense of conscience may be dulled, or that by right living it may be strengthened. In like manner the subjective mind perceives by its own senses certain invisible types of evil seeking external manifestations in the microcosm. It knows that these forms of error will work harm to the objective mind, and that if persisted in they will pervert all intercourse or interchange of counsel between the two factions of the man. In this there is no spiritual perception of physical objects, any more than there is in mundane life a sense perception of spiritual images and antitypes. The former only sees the forms that manifest on its plane, while the latter can note only those common to its sphere. Each may recognize and feel the violence or good that these manifestations will do to their respective counterparts, but we have no reason to believe that normal objective or subjective states have visional powers beyond their own plane.

The mind of man acting upon the mind of the macrocosm will produce, according as he thinks or acts, antitypes of good or evil in the imagination of the world which is reflected upon the spiritual aura of the microcosm previous to taking on corporal form. While in this state they may be perceived by subjectivity, and thus the images seen are impressed on the dream mind during sleep, or on the passivity of the objective sense.

DREAMS EXAGGERATED

The will is suspended during sleep, so the dream mind is more a prey to excitability than the waking mind.

Thus when images appear upon the dream vision they are frequently distorted into hideous malformations that fill it with fear and excitement.

THE NIGHTMARE

Evil or righteous acts recently committed will more acutely affect the present waking mind than those enacted at a more remote period. In a similar way future disaster or success which is soon to occur will impress the dream mind more vividly than those which are to transpire at a later date. But in the lives of all men there are past incidents which they will never forget, and which will never cease to fill their hearts with pride or remorse. So, too, in their distant future there are important events to transpire which are struggling through tumultuous infinitude to leave their ghastly or smiling impress upon the dream mind. If your mental states are passive you will receive the warnings. There are cases on record which show events have been forecast years ahead of their occurrence.

Not all dreams are pleasant or prognostic. Hideous nightmares *above* **can leave a lasting impression of nameless dread on the unfortunate dreamer.**

Dreams visit everybody, rich or poor, sinner or saint. St Cecilia, the patron saint of music is seen dreaming *overleaf* **of the art of which she is patron.**

THE COMPLEXITY OF INTERPRETATION

WE DO not claim that this book will prove an interpreter of all dreams, or that the keys disclosed will open to you all the mysteries of the future, or even all those surrounding your own personality, but by studying the definitions and the plane upon which they were written, you will be able, through the power of your own spirit, to interpret your own dreams. The combination of dream and dream influences are infinite. They can only be classed and considered as such. They cannot be analyzed in detail or as a whole. In mathematics we have nine digits from which an infinite variety of combinations may be formed and solved by the deducing of the mind.

The symbol O and I exist by reason of NO THING and SOME THING or death and life. The figure one is subject to illimitable expansion. It is without beginning in the infinite of number, as God is without beginning in the infinite of being. As with the vegetable kingdom, the tiny seed or acorn silently working its magical transformation into a plant or tree, and directing its destiny with marvelous intelligence through the torrid and frigid vicissitudes of the seasons; so is man without beginning in the infinitude of his own being or microcosm. Man is both a type and antitype. A type of what pre-existed in the imagination of the world, and an antitype of a future life yet to manifest itself on another plane where the incidents of the one will be subjective, as the events occurring in infancy or in other planes are now subjective. His dreams, thoughts and actions and the influences that produce them and their multiplying combination, cannot be numbered or reproduced any more than you can number the leaves of the forest, or find two exactly similar units among them. Thus the full meaning or interpretation of dreams cannot be fully demonstrated through mental or even spiritual stereotypes. But by the intelligent use of this book you will be able to trace out almost any dream combination and arrive at the true nature of its portent.

A WISE DOCTOR, in preparing medicine for a patient, considers well his age, temperament, and his present condition. So should the interpreter of dreams ponder well the mental state, the health, habits, and temperament of the dreamer. These things no one can know so well as the dreamer himself. He, therefore, with the aid of this book, will be able to interpret his dreams by the light that is in him.

TWO DREAMS ARE NEVER THE SAME, NOR ARE TWO FLOWERS EVER ALIKE

WHATEVER SYMBOL is used to impress the dreamer is the one which is likely to warn him more definitely than any other. No two persons being ever in the same state at the same time, the same symbols would hardly convey identical impressions; neither will the same dream be as effective in all cases of business or love with the same dreamer.

A person's dream perception wavers, much as it does in waking hours. You fail to find the same fragrance in the rose at all times, though the same influences seemingly surround you; and thus it is that different dreams must be used for different persons to convey the same meaning.

Creation, confident of her power to perfect her designs, does not resort to that monotony in her work, which might result were the perception of man, or the petals and fragrance of flowers cast from one stereotype mold of intelligence, beauty, or sweetness. This variety of scheme runs through all creation. You think you have identical dreams, but there is always some variation, even if it be something dreamed immediately over. Nature is no sluggard and is forever changing her compounds, so that there is bound to be change in the details even of dreams. This change would not materially affect that approach of happiness or sorrow in different people, and hence the same dreams are reliable for all.

Persons of the same or similar temperament will be more deeply impressed by a certain dream than would people their opposite; and though the dream cannot be the same in detail yet it is apparently the same, just as two like flowers are called roses, though they are not identical.

If a young woman twenty-five and a girl of fifteen should each have a dream of marriage, the same definition would apply to each, just the same as if they would each approach a flower and smell of it differently. Different influences will possess them unconsciously, though the outward appearance be the same.

A young woman of a certain age is warned in a dream of trouble likely to befall her, while another of similar age and threatened trouble is warned also, but in different symbols, which she fails to grasp and bring back to waking existence, and she thus believes she has had no warning dream.

There are those in the world who lack subjective strength, material or spiritual, and hence they fail to receive dreams, however symbolic, because there is no power within them to retain these impressions.

There are many reasons for this loss: it may be explained by such things as utter material grossness, want of memory, physical weakness uncoupled from extreme nervousness, and total lack of faith in any warning or revelation purporting or coming from the dream consciousness.

To dream at night and the following day have the thing dreamed of actually take place, or come before your notice, is not allegorical. It is the higher or spiritual sense living or grasping the immediate future ahead of the physical mind. The spiritual body is always first to come into contact with the approaching future; it is present with it, while still future to the physical body.

There is no reason why man should not grasp coming events earlier, only he does not cultivate inner sight as he does his outer senses. The allegorical is used because man weakens his spiritual force by catering to the material senses.

He clings to the pleasures and woes of the material world to the exclusion of spirituality.

ST CECILIA DREAMS OF MUSIC

WHEN DREAMS ARE LESS PRESCIENT

THE FOWLS OF THE AIR

THE BEASTS OF THE EARTH

THE CREATURES OF THE SEA

THE CESSATION of the organs to perform healthful functions converts a man into a different person, and dreams while in this state would have no prophetic meaning, unless to warn the dreamer of this disorganization of his physical system.

Dreams are symbols used by subjectivity to impress the objective or material mind with a sense of coming good or evil. Subjectivity is the spiritual part of man. The soul is that circle of man lying just outside the gross materiality and partaking largely of it. All thoughts and desires enter first the soul or material mind and then cast themselves on the spirit. Frequently the soul becomes so filled with material or present ideas, that the spiritual symbols are crowded out, and then it is that dreams seem to be contrary. Material subjectivity, that is, all thoughts and ideas emanating from material sources, go to make up this circle; then the mind catches up the better thoughts of this section and weaves them into a broader and more comprehensive power, sustaining the owner in his own judgement.

And still another circle is formed of the finer compound of this, which is spiritual subjectivity, or the highest element of intelligence reached by man. This circle is "the spiritual man" and relates in substance to the spiritual soul of the macrocosm or universe. It becomes strong or weak as we recognize or fail to recognize it as a factor of being. The process of spiritual development is similar to that of the vegetable and animal kingdoms. The trees on the outer rim of the forest are more capable of resisting the wind than those more to the center, by reason of their exposure to storms; the roots have penetrated with double strength far into the earth, and the branches are braced with toughened bark and closely knitted ligaments.

The same may be said of the animal kingdom. The mind is developed by vigorous exercise just as are likewise the muscles of the body. The more these are cultivated by drawing from their parental affinities in the macrocosm, the more knowledge or power they take on. Thus as a man simulates in thought and action an ape, a tiger, a goat, a snake, or a lamb he takes on their characteristics and is swayed by like influences to enmity, meekness, covetousness, and avariciousness. To illustrate further. If he is cunning he draws on the fox of the microcosm and becomes, in action and thought, like that animal. If selfishness survives, the hog principle is aroused from its latent cells in the microcosm and he is dominated by material appetites. In a similar way he may perceive the spiritual in himself. Nature's laws, with all their numberless and intricate ramifications are simple in their harmony of process and uniformity of purpose when applied to the physical and ethical developments of man.

Possibilities for inner improvements or expansions rest with material man. If he entertains gross desires to the exclusion of spiritual germs, he will dwarf and degrade higher aspirations, and thus deprive subjective spirituality of her rightful possessions.

Nature, in compounding the materials for the creation of the dead man, inadvertently dropped the ingredient sound, hence making an imperfect being; and sound, being thus foreign to his nature, he can only be approached by signs even in dreams. Subjectivity uses nature's forces, while a normal person uses dreams to work on his waking consciousness. As it is impossible to use with effect a factor which a man does not naturally possess, a deaf man rarely ever dreams of sound, or a blind man of light.

Many people report that they have dreams in which the main symbols are drawn from the realms of nature. These may be dreams of the birds of the air *above left*, **the beasts of the earth** *above center*, **or the creatures of the sea** *above right*. **Animal dreams, when examined and interpreted, often indicate that the dreamer is meditating on behavior or attitudes called to mind by the nature of the particular bird, beast, or fish most prominent in the dream.**

COSMIC INTERDEPENDENCY

MAN IS the microcosm or a miniature world. He has a soul and mental firmament, bounded by the stellar dust and the Milky Way, and filled with the mystery of suns, satellites, and stars. These he can study best by the astronomy of induction and introspection. He has also a physical plane, diversified by oceans, lakes, rivers, fertile valleys, waste places, and mountains. All are in cosmic interdependency as they are in the macrocosm. Here rests the mystery of being – the grandest of subjects! The student is no less bewildered and awed than the geologist who gropes blindly through the seams of the earth searching for links in the infinite chain of knowledge, or the astronomer sweeping the heavens of the macrocosm in quest of new phenomena. The two planes are dependent upon each other. It is the smile or disease of the firmament that blesses or diseases the earth. It is likewise the impure firmament of the microcosm that diseases the body and soul. If it reflects the droughts of thought or the various states of evil, deserts will enlarge, forests of infectious, venomous growth will form the habitation of lust and murder.

BEFORE GREAT MORAL or physical revolutions or catastrophes occur, clouds will darken the horizon of the dream mind; storms will gather, lurid flames of lightning will flash their volatile anger. The explosive thunder will recklessly carry on its bombardment; bells will ring, strange knocking will be heard – symbols of a message – phantom forms will be seen, familiar voices will call and plead with you, unknown visitors will threaten you, unearthly struggles with hideous giants and agonies of mind and body will possess you; malformations of the most hideous type will seize your vision; shrouded in sheets of a whitish vapor, evanescent specters, with pallid face and of warning countenance, will cling around you, and contagion and famine will leave their desolate impress upon the flower of health and in the field of plenty. Thus all of us would be nightly warned in our circle or miniature world if we would develop subjective strength to retain the impressions left upon our dream mind. But in spite of all reason and conscience – in spite of the inductive knowledge received through our senses – we go on from day to day, and step by step, feeding our soul on the luscious fruit of the outward senses, until the rank weeds of selfishness have choked out all other forces. Thus the soul is filled with thought images that assume the form of vicious animals, homely visaged fowls, rabid and snarling cats and dogs, leprous and virile serpents, cankerous lizards, slimy intestine worms, hairy and malicious insects. They are generated by greed, envy, jealousy, covetousness, backbiting, amorous longings, and other impure thoughts. With the soul filled with this conglomeration of virus and filth, why doubt a hell and its counterpart conditions, or expect the day or night to bring happiness?

Many artists have tried to capture the strange quality of dreams – at once real and familiar yet bizarre and fantastic. This work, The Dream *above right* is by the French symbolist painter Odilon Redon (1840–1916).

THE DREAM

IF EVIL THOUGHTS will invest the soul with ravenous microbes, good thoughts and deeds will starve and suppress their activity, and create a heaven to supplant them. With this grand and eternal truth in view, man should ever think kindly of those about him, control his temper in word and action, seek his own, think the best of thoughts, study to relieve the worthy poor, seek solace in the depth of being, and let gentleness and meekness characterize his life. Then will he sow the seeds of a present and future heaven. His day thoughts and his night thoughts in harmony will point with unerring forecast to a peaceful end. Spiritual and helpful warnings will fall upon the dream mind, as gently as dew upon the flowers and as softly as a mother's kiss upon the lips of love.

WHEN OUR external lives are guided by the forces within, sweet are the words and messages from our own spirit; for those who are truly blessed are those who seek divine love through the channels of their inner world of consciousness.

THE DREAMS

The Animal Kingdom

Animals of all kinds feature frequently in our dreams, and each has its own particular significance. The following pages explain the significance of dream animals from every part of the kingdom – wild animals, domesticated animals, birds and insects, fish and reptiles – as well as general animal behavior traits.

Zoos and Cages

CAGE

In your dreaming, if you see a ***cage*** full of birds, you will be the happy possessor of immense wealth and many beautiful and charming children. To see only one bird, you will contract a desirable and wealthy marriage. To see no birds at all indicates the loss of a member of the family, either by elopement or death.

To see ***wild animals caged***, denotes that you will triumph over your enemies and misfortunes. If you are in the cage with them, it denotes harrowing scenes from accidents while traveling. ◎

MENAGERIE

To dream of visiting a ***menagerie***, denotes various troubles. ◎

ZOOLOGICAL GARDEN

To dream of visiting ***zoological gardens***, denotes that you will have a varied fortune. Sometimes it seems that enemies will overpower you and again you stand in the front rank of success. You will also gain knowledge by travel and sojourn in foreign countries. ◎

Dreams of animals may include the gentle, bleating sheep *above*, **the cackling macaw** *above right*, **or the mischievous macaque monkey** *opposite top.*

Animal Noises

SHEEP

CACKLING

To hear the *cackling* ***of hens, denotes a sudden shock produced by the news of an unexpected death in your neighborhood. Sickness will cause poverty.*** ❋

BRAY

Hearing an ass *bray*, ***is significant of unwelcome tidings or intrusions.*** ❋

BLEATING

To hear young animals *bleating* ***in your dreams, foretells that you will have new duties and cares, though not necessarily unpleasant ones.*** ❋

Animal Attributes

SNOUTS

To dream of ***snouts***, foretells dangerous seasons for you. Enemies are surrounding you, and difficulties will be numerous. ◎

WINGS

To dream that you have ***wings***, foretells that you will experience grave fears for the safety of someone gone on a long journey away from you.

To see the ***wings of fowls or birds***, denotes that you will finally overcome adversity and rise to wealthy degrees and honor. ◎

MACAW

TAIL

To dream of seeing only the ***tail of a beast***, unusual annoyance is indicated where pleasures seemed assured.

To ***cut off the tail*** of an animal, denotes that you will suffer misfortune by your own carelessness.

To dream that you ***have the tail of a beast*** grown on you, denotes that your evil ways will cause you untold distress, and strange events will cause you perplexity. ◎

ANIMAL HIDE

To dream of the ***hide*** of an animal, denotes profit and permanent employment. ◎

CAGE *see* BIRDS *page 43* ◆ CACKLING *see* HENS *page 39* ◆ BRAY *see* ASS *page 38* ◆ BLEATING *see* LAMB *page 36* ◆
WINGS *see* BIRDS *page 43*

Wild animals stalking through your dreams make a thrilling contribution to the dreamscape; this section covers a wide range of hunters and prey, from majestic big game animals and the big cats of the jungle to sly foxes, cruel wolves, and shy creatures of the woods and forests.

Big Game Beasts

RHINOCEROS

To dream that you see a ***rhinoceros***, foretells that you will have a great loss threatening you, and that you will have secret troubles.

To kill one, shows that you will bravely overcome obstacles. ◎

ELEPHANT

To dream of riding an ***elephant***, denotes that you will possess wealth of the most solid character, and honors which you will wear with dignity. You will rule absolutely in all lines of your business affairs, and your word will be law in the home.

To see many elephants, denotes tremendous prosperity. One ***lone elephant***, signifies that you will live in a small but solid way.

To dream of feeding one, denotes that you will elevate yourself in your community by your kindness. ◎

ANTELOPE

Seeing ***antelopes*** in a dream, foretells that your high ambition may be realized by putting forth energy.

For a young woman to see an ***antelope miss its footing*** and fall from a height denotes that the love she aspires to will prove her undoing. ◎

BUFFALO

If a woman dreams that she kills a lot of ***buffaloes***, she will undertake a stupendous enterprise, but by enforcing will power and leaving off material pleasures, she will win commendation from men, and may receive long wished for favors.

Buffalo, seen in a dream, augurs obstinate and powerful but stupid enemies. They will boldly declare against you, but by diplomacy you will escape much misfortune. ◎

Apes and Monkeys

MACAQUE

APES

This dream brings humiliation and disease to some dear friend.

To see a small ape ***cling to a tree, warns the dreamer to beware; a false person is close to you and will cause unpleasantness in your circle. Deceit goes with this dream.*** ✺

ORANGUTAN

To dream of an orangutan, ***denotes that some person is falsely using your influence to further selfish schemes. For a young woman, it portends an unfaithful lover.*** ✺

MONKEY

To dream of a monkey, ***denotes that deceitful people will flatter you to advance their own interests.***

To see a dead monkey, ***signifies that your worst enemies will soon be removed.***

If a young woman dreams of a monkey, she should insist on an early marriage, as her lover will suspect unfaithfulness.

For a woman to dream of feeding a monkey, ***denotes that she will be betrayed by a flatterer.*** ✺

BEAR

A ***bear*** is significant of overwhelming competition in pursuits of every kind.

To ***kill a bear***, portends extrication from further entanglements.

A young woman who dreams of a bear will have a threatening rival or some misfortune. ◎

KANGAROO

To see a ***kangaroo*** in your dreams, means that you will outwit a wily enemy who seeks to place you in an unfavorable position before the public and the person you are striving to win.

If a ***kangaroo attacks you***, your reputation will be in jeopardy.

If you kill one, you will succeed in spite of enemies and obstacles.

To see a ***kangaroo's hide***, denotes that you are in a fair way to success. ◎

ZEBRA

To dream of a ***zebra***, denotes you will be interested in fleeting enterprises. To see one wild in his native country, foretells that you will pursue a chimerical fancy which will return you unsatisfactory pleasure. ◎

Seals and Polar Bears

SEAL

To dream that you see ***seals***, denotes that you are striving for a place above your power to maintain.

Dreams of seals, usually show that the dreamer has high aspirations and discontent will harass him into struggles to advance his position.

POLAR BEAR

Polar bears in dreams, are prognostic of deceit, as misfortune will approach you in a seeming fair aspect. Your bitterest enemies will wear the garb of friendship. Rivals will supersede you.

To see the skin of one, denotes that you will successfully overcome any opposition. ◎

ELEPHANT *see* **IVORY** *page 70* ◆ **APES** *see* **TREES** *page 64* ◆ **KANGAROO** *see* **ANIMAL HIDE** *page 28* ◆
POLAR BEAR *see* **ANIMAL HIDE** *page 28*

Big Cats

TIGER
To dream of a ***tiger*** advancing toward you, you will be tormented and persecuted by enemies. If it attacks you, failure will bury you in gloom. If you succeed in warding the tiger off, or killing a tiger, you will be extremely successful in all your undertakings.

To see one running away from you, is a sign that you will overcome opposition, and rise to high positions.

To see them in cages, foretells that you will foil your adversaries.

To see rugs of ***tiger skins***, denotes that you are on the way to enjoy luxurious ease and pleasure. ◎

LION
To dream of a ***lion,*** signifies that a great force is driving you.

If you subdue the lion, you will be victorious in any engagement.

If it overpowers you, then you will be open to the successful attack of enemies.

To see ***caged lions***, denotes that your success depends upon your ability to cope with opposition.

To see a man ***controlling a lion***, in its cage or out, denotes success in business and great mental power. You will be favorably regarded by women.

To see ***young lions***, denotes new enterprises, which will bring success if properly attended.

For a young woman to dream of young lions, denotes new and fascinating lovers.

For a woman to dream that she sees ***Daniel in the lion's den***, signifies that by her intellectual qualifications and personal magnetism, she will win fortune and lovers to her highest desire.

To hear the ***roar of a lion***, signifies unexpected advancement and preferment with women.

To see a ***lion's head*** over you, showing his teeth by snarls, you are threatened with defeat in your upward rise to power.

To see a ***lion's skin***, denotes a rise to fortune and happiness.

To ***ride a lion***, denotes courage and persistency in surmounting any difficulties.

To dream that you are defending your children from a lion with a penknife, foretells that enemies will threaten to overpower you, and will well nigh succeed if you allow any artfulness to persuade you for a moment from duty and business obligations. ◎

PANTHER
To see a ***panther*** and experience fright, denotes that contracts in love or business may be canceled unexpectedly, owing to adverse influences working against your honor. But by killing or overpowering it, you will experience joy and be successful in your undertakings. Your surroundings will take on fair prospects.

If one menaces you by its presence, you will have disappointments in business. Other people will likely recede from their promises to you.

If you hear the ***voice of a panther***, and experience terror or fright, you will have unfavorable news, coming in the way of reducing profit or gain, and you may have social discord; no fright forebodes less evil.

A panther, like a cat, seen in a dream, portends evil to the dreamer, unless he kills it. ◎

LYNX
If you dream of seeing a ***lynx***, enemies are undermining your business and disrupting your home affairs.

For a woman, this dream indicates that she has a wary woman rivaling her in the affections of her lover. If she ***kills the lynx***, she will overcome her rival. ◎

LEOPARD
To dream of a ***leopard*** attacking you, denotes that, while the future seemingly promises fair, success holds many difficulties through misplaced confidence.

To kill one, intimates victory in your affairs.

To see one caged, denotes that enemies will surround but fail to injure you.

To see ***leopards in their native place*** trying to escape from you, denotes that you will be embarrassed in business or love, but by persistent efforts you will overcome difficulties.

To dream of a ***leopard's skin***, denotes that your interests will be endangered by a dishonest person who will win your esteem. ◎

LEOPARD

TIGER, LION, LEOPARD *see* **ANIMAL HIDE** *page 28* ◆ **TIGER, LION** *see* **CAGE** *page 28* ◆ **PANTHER** *see* **CATS** *page 40*, **FRIGHTENED** *page 253*, **VOICE** *page 276*

Foxes and Wolves

FOX

To dream of chasing a fox, ***denotes that you are engaging in doubtful speculations and risky love affairs.***

If you see a fox slyly coming into your yard, beware of envious friendships; your reputation is being slyly assailed.

To kill a fox, ***denotes that you will win in every engagement you undertake.*** ❋

WOLF

To dream of a wolf, ***shows that you have a thieving person in your employ, who will also betray secrets.***

To kill one, denotes that you will defeat sly enemies who seek to overshadow you with disgrace.

To hear the howl of a wolf, ***discloses to you a secret alliance to defeat you in honest competition.*** ❋

HYENA

If you see a hyena ***in your dreams, you will meet much disappointment and much ill luck in your undertakings, and your companions will be very uncongenial. If lovers have this dream, they will often be involved in quarrels.***

If one attacks you, your reputation will be set upon by busybodies. ❋

Wilder dreams may include leopards *opposite left* **while rabbits** *right* **inhabit a more restful dream habitat. Hares** *top* **are altogether more troubling.**

Animals of the Field and Forest

HARE

STAG

To see ***stags*** in your dream, foretells that you will have honest and true friends, and will enjoy delightful entertainments. ◎

DEER

This is a favorable dream, denoting pure and deep friendships for the young and a quiet and even life for the married.

To kill a ***deer***, denotes that you will be hounded by enemies. For farmers or business people to dream of ***hunting deer***, denotes failure in their respective pursuits. ◎

FAWN

To dream of seeing a ***fawn***, denotes that you will have true and upright friends. To the young, it indicates faithfulness in love. ◎

REINDEER

To dream of a ***reindeer***, signifies the faithful discharge of duties and remaining staunch to friends in their adversity.

To drive them, foretells that you will have hours of bitter anguish, but friends will attend you. ◎

RACCOON

To dream of a ***raccoon***, denotes that you are being deceived by the friendly appearance of enemies. ◎

MARMOT

To dream of seeing a ***marmot***, denotes that sly enemies are approaching you in the shape of fair women.

For a young woman to dream of a marmot, foretells that temptation will beset her in the future. ◎

PORCUPINE

To see a ***porcupine*** in your dreams, denotes that you will disapprove any new enterprise and repel new friendships with coldness.

For a young woman to dream of a porcupine, portends that she will fear her lover.

To see a ***dead porcupine***, signifies your abolishment of ill feelings and possessions. ◎

RABBIT

To dream of ***rabbits***, foretells favorable turns in conditions, and you will be more pleased with your gains than formerly.

To see ***white rabbits***, denotes faithfulness in love, to the married or single person.

To see rabbits frolicking about, denotes that children will contribute to your joys. ◎

HARE

If you see a ***hare*** escaping from you in a dream, you will lose something valuable in a mysterious way. If you capture one, you will be the victor in a contest.

If you make pets of them, you will have an orderly but unintelligent companion.

A ***dead hare***, betokens death to some friend. Existence will be a prosy affair.

To see ***hares chased by dogs***, denotes trouble and contentions among your friends, and you will concern yourself to bring about friendly relations.

If you dream that you ***shoot a hare***, means that you will be forced to use violent measures to maintain your rightful possessions. ◎

THE WHITE RABBIT

DEER *see* HUNTING *page 174* ◆ HARE *see* DOGS *page 41* ◆ SHOOTING *page 263* ◆ FAWN *see also page 259*

Woodland Animals

BADGER
To dream of a ***badger,*** is a sign of luck after battles with hardships. ◎

SHREW
To dream of a ***shrew***, foretells that you will have a task to keep some friend in a cheerful frame of mind, and that you will unfit yourself for the experiences of everyday existence. ◎

MINK
To dream of a ***mink,*** denotes that you will have sly enemies to overcome.

If you kill one, you will win your desires.

For a young woman to dream that she is partial to ***mink furs***, she will find protection and love in some person who will be inordinately jealous. ◎

WEASEL
To see a ***weasel*** bent on a marauding expedition in your dreams, warns you to beware of the friendships of former enemies, as they will devour you at an unseemly time.

If you destroy them, you will succeed in foiling deep schemes laid for your defeat. ◎

SQUIRREL

SQUIRREL
To dream of seeing ***squirrels***, denotes that pleasant friends will soon visit you. You will advance in your business also.

To kill a squirrel, denotes that you will be unfriendly and disliked.

To pet one, signifies family joy.

To see a dog chasing one, foretells disagreement and unpleasantness among friends. ◎

MOLES
To dream of ***moles,*** indicates secret enemies.

To dream of catching a mole, you will overcome any opposition and rise to prominence. ◎

OTTERS

Otters and Beavers

OTTER
To see ***otters*** diving and sporting in limpid streams, is certain to bring the dreamer waking happiness and good fortune. You will find ideal enjoyment in an early marriage, if you are single; wives may expect unusual tenderness from their spouses after this dream. ◎

BEAVER
To dream of seeing ***beavers,*** foretells that you will obtain comfortable circumstances by patient striving.

If you dream of killing them for their skins, you will be accused of fraud and improper conduct toward the innocent. ◎

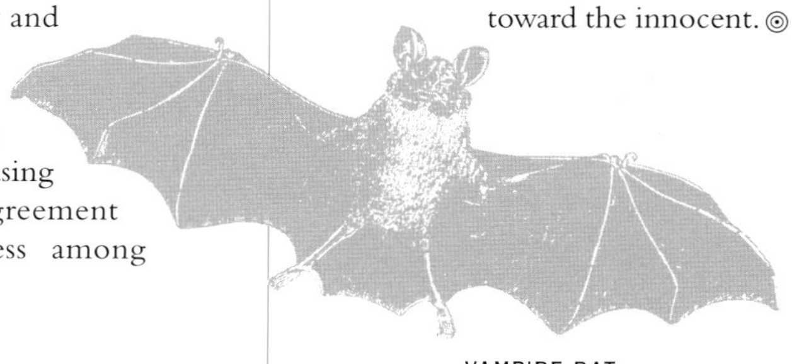

VAMPIRE BAT

Bats

Awful is the fate of the unfortunate dreamer of this ugly animal. Sorrows and calamities from hosts of evil work against you. Death of parents and friends, loss of limbs or sight, may follow after a dream of these ghoulish monsters. A white bat is almost a sure sign of death. Often the death of a child follows this dream. ✻

You may see squirrels *top,* **otters** *left* **and bats** *above* **in your dreams; horses** *opposite top,* **riding** *opposite bottom* **and all things equine are dream subjects that occur frequently in many people's dreams.**

MINK *see* **FURS** *page 157* ◆ **SQUIRREL** *see* **DOGS** *page 41* ◆ **MOLES** *see also page 111* ◆ **BATS** *see* **VAMPIRE** *page 273*

Dreams filled with domesticated animals have quite a different atmosphere. This section is devoted to animals that live peacefully with humanity: placid cattle, anxious sheep, noisy farmyard animals, or beloved pet cats and dogs. The gentle power of horses grants them a special place in people's dreams.

Equestrian Issues

HORSE TRADER

To dream of a ***horse trader***, signifies great profit from perilous ventures.

To dream that you are trading horses, and the trader cheats you, you will lose in trade or love. If you get a better horse than the one you traded, you will better yourself in fortune. ◎

STABLE

To dream of a ***stable***, is a sign of good fortune and advantageous surroundings.

To see a ***stable burning***, denotes successful changes, or it may be seen in actual life. ◎

RIDE

To dream of ***riding***, is unlucky for business or pleasure. Sickness often follows this dream.

If you ***ride slowly***, you will have unsatisfactory results in your undertakings.

Swift riding sometimes means prosperity under hazardous conditions. ◎

RIDING SCHOOL

To attend a ***riding school***, foretells that some friend will act falsely by you, but you will throw off the vexing influence occasioned by it. ◎

HORSESHOE

To dream of a ***horseshoe,*** indicates an advance in business and lucky engagements for women.

To see them broken, ill fortune and sickness are portrayed.

To find a ***horseshoe hanging on the fence***, denotes that your interests will advance beyond your most sanguine expectations.

To pick one up in the road, you will receive profit from a source you know not of. ◎

HORSES

SADDLE

To dream of ***saddles*** is an excellent dream. It foretells news of a pleasant nature, and may also signal unannounced visitors. You are also, probably, about to to take a trip which will prove advantageous. ◎

HARNESS

To dream of possessing a bright, new ***harness***, you will soon prepare for a pleasant journey. ◎

HALTER

To dream that you put a ***halter*** on a young horse, shows that you will manage a very prosperous and clean business. Love matters will shape themselves to suit you.

RIDING

To see other things haltered, denotes that fortune will be withheld from you for a while. You will win it, but with much toil. ◎

BRIDLE

To dream of a ***bridle,*** denotes engagement in some enterprise which will afford much worry, but will eventually terminate in pleasure and gain. If it is old or broken, you will have difficulties to encounter, and the probabilities are that you will go down before them.

A ***blind bridle***, signifies that you will be deceived by some wily enemy, or that some woman will entangle you in an intrigue. ◎

WHIP

To dream of a ***whip***, signifies unhappy dissensions and unfortunate and formidable friendships. ◎

CURRYING A HORSE

To dream of ***currying a horse***, signifies that you will have a great many hard licks to make with both brain and hand before you attain to the heights of your ambition; but if you successfully curry him, you will attain that height, whatever it may be. ◎

HORSE TRADER; HALTER; CURRYING A HORSE *see* HORSE DREAMS *pages 34–5* ◆ STABLE *see* FIRE *page 80*

Horse Dreams

If you dream of seeing or riding a ***white horse***, the indications are favorable for prosperity and pleasurable commingling with congenial friends and fair women. If the white horse is soiled and lean, your confidence will be betrayed by a jealous friend or a woman. If the ***horse is black***, you will be successful in your fortune, but you will practice deception, and will be guilty of assignations. To a woman, this denotes that her husband is unfaithful.

To dream of ***dark horses***, signifies prosperous conditions, but a large amount of discontent. Fleeting pleasures usually follow this dream.

To see yourself riding a ***fine bay horse***, denotes a rise in fortune and gratification of passion. For a woman, it foretells a yielding to importunate advances. She will enjoy material things.

To ride or see passing horses, denotes ease and comfort.

To ride a ***runaway horse***, your interests will be injured by the folly of a friend or employer.

To see a horse running away with others, denotes that you will hear of the illness of friends.

To see ***fine stallions***, is a sign of success and high living, and undue passion will master you.

To see ***brood mares***, denotes congeniality and absence of jealousy between the married and sweethearts.

To ride a ***horse to ford a stream***, you will soon experience some good fortune and will enjoy rich pleasures. If the stream is unsettled or murky, anticipated joys will be somewhat disappointing.

To ***swim on a horse's back*** through a clear and beautiful stream of water, your conception of passionate bliss will be swiftly realized. To a businessman, this dream portends great gain.

To see a ***wounded horse***, foretells the trouble of friends.

To dream of a ***dead horse***, signifies disappointments of various kinds.

To dream of riding a ***horse that bucks***, denotes that your desires will be difficult of consummation. To dream that he throws you, indicates that you will have a strong rival, and your business will suffer slightly through competition.

To dream that a ***horse kicks you***, you will be repulsed by one you love. Your fortune will be embarrassed by ill health.

To dream of ***catching a horse*** to bridle and saddle, or harness it, you will see a great improvement in business of all kinds, and people of all callings will prosper. If you fail to catch it, fortune will play you false.

If you dream of having a ***horse shod***, your success is assured. For a woman, this dream omens a good and faithful husband.

To dream that you ***shoe a horse***, denotes that you will endeavor to and perhaps make doubtful property your own.

To dream of ***race horses***, denotes that you will be surfeited with fast living; but to a farmer, this dream denotes prosperity.

To dream that you ***ride a horse in a race***, you will be prosperous and enjoy life.

To dream of ***killing a horse***, you will injure your friends through selfishness.

To ***ride bareback*** in company with men, you will have honest people to aid you, and your success will be merited. If in company with women, your desires will be loose, and your prosperity will not be so abundant as might be if women did not fill your heart.

To ***curry a horse***, your business interests will not be neglected for frivolous pleasures.

To dream of trimming a ***horse's mane or tail***, denotes that you will be a good financier or farmer. Literary people will be painstaking in their work, and others will look after their interests with solicitude.

To dream of horses, you will amass wealth and enjoy life to its fullest extent.

To see ***spotted horses*** in your dreams, foretells that various enterprises will bring you profit.

SPOTTED HORSES

HORSE DREAMS *see also* **RIDE, HORSESHOE, CURRYING A HORSE, BRIDLE, SADDLE** *page 33,* **TURF, JOCKEY** *page 176,* **TAIL** *page 28,* **VEHICLE** *page 223,* **HILL** *page 90*

POSEIDON'S HORSES

To mount a ***horse bareback***, indicates that you will gain wealth and ease by dint of hard struggles.

To see ***horses pulling vehicles***, denotes wealth with some incumbrance, and love will find obstacles.

If you are ***riding up a hill*** and the horse falls but you gain the top, you will win fortune, though you will have to struggle against enemies and jealousy. If both the horse and you get to the top, your rise will be phenomenal, but substantial.

For a young girl to dream that she rides a ***black horse***, denotes that she should be dealt with by wise authority. Some wishes will be gratified, but at an unexpected time. Black in horses, signifies postponements in anticipations.

To see a ***horse with a tender foot***, denotes that some unexpected unpleasantness will insinuate itself into your otherwise propitious state.

If you attempt to fit a broken shoe which is too small for the horse's foot, you will be charged with making fraudulent deals with unsuspecting parties.

To ride a horse downhill, your affairs will undoubtedly disappoint you. For a young woman to dream that a friend rides behind her on a horse, denotes that she will be foremost in the favors of many prominent and successful men. If she was frightened, she is likely to stir up jealous sensations. If after she alights from the horse it turns into a pig, she will carelessly pass by honorable offers of marriage, preferring freedom until her chances of a desirable marriage are lost. If afterward she sees the pig sliding gracefully along the telegraph wire, she will by intriguing advance her position.

For a young woman to dream that she is riding a ***white horse up and down hills***, often looking back and seeing someone on a black horse pursuing her, denotes that she will have a mixed season of success and sorrow, but through it all a relentless enemy is working to overshadow her with gloom and disappointment.

To see a ***horse in human flesh***, descending on a hammock through the air, and as it nears, your horse is metamorphosed into a man, and he approaches your door and throws something at you which seems to be rubber but turns into great bees, denotes miscarriage of hopes and useless endeavors to regain lost valuables. To see animals in human flesh, signifies great advancement to the dreamer and new friends will be made by modest wearing of well-earned honors. If the human flesh appears diseased or freckled, the miscarriage of well-laid plans is denoted. ◎

Your dream horses may appear as natural as those in real life *opposite* or in symbolic form, as the white horses of the Greek sea god Poseidon that crest the waves of the ocean *above*.

The Equine Family

STALLION

To dream of a ***stallion***, foretells that prosperous conditions are approaching you, in which you will hold a position which will confer honor upon you.

To dream that you ***ride a fine stallion***, denotes that you will rise to position and affluence in a phenomenal way; however, your success will warp your morality and sense of justice.

To see one with the rabies, foretells that wealthy surroundings will cause you to assume arrogance, which will be distasteful to your friends, and your pleasures will be deceitful. ◎

MARE

To dream of seeing ***mares*** in pastures, denotes success in business and congenial companions. If the pasture is barren, it foretells poverty, but warm friends. For a young woman, this omens a happy marriage and beautiful children. ◎

PONY

To see ***ponies*** in your dreams, signifies that moderate speculations will be rewarded with success. ◎

FOAL

To dream of a ***foal,*** indicates new undertakings in which you will be rather fortunate. ◎

STALLION *see* HYDROPHOBIA *page* 110, RIDE *page* 33 ◆ MARE *see* HORSE DREAMS *page* 34

Sheep, Lambs, and Shepherds

SHEEP

To dream of shearing them, denotes that a season of profitable enterprises will shower down upon you.

If you see flocks of ***sheep***, there will be much rejoicing among farmers, and other trades will prosper.

To see them looking scraggy and sick, you will be thrown into despair by the miscarriage of some plan which promised rich returns.

To eat the ***flesh of sheep***, denotes that ill-natured persons will outrage your feelings. ◎

LAMB

To dream of ***lambs*** frolicking in green pastures, betokens chaste friendships and joys. Bounteous and profitable crops to the farmers, and increase of possessions for others.

To see a ***dead lamb***, signifies sadness and desolation.

Blood showing on the white fleece of a lamb, denotes that innocent ones will suffer from betrayal through the wrongdoings of others.

A ***lost lamb***, denotes that wayward people will be under your influence, and you should be careful of your conduct.

To see ***lambskins***, denotes comfort and pleasure usurped from others.

To ***slaughter a lamb*** for domestic uses, signifies that prosperity will be gained through the sacrifice of pleasure and contentment.

To ***eat lamb chops***, denotes illness, and much anxiety over the welfare of children.

To see ***lambs taking nourishment*** from their mothers, denotes happiness through pleasant and intelligent home companions, and many lovable and beautiful children.

If you dream that dogs or wolves ***devour lambs***, innocent people will suffer at the hands of insinuating and designing villains.

If you hear the ***bleating of lambs***, your generosity will be appealed to. ◎

To see them in a winter storm or rain, denotes disappointment in expected enjoyment and betterment of fortune.

To ***own lambs*** in your dreams, signifies that your environments will be pleasant and profitable.

If you ***carry lambs in your arms***, you will be encumbered with happy cares upon which you will lavish a wealth of devotion, and no expense will be regretted in responding to appeals from the objects of your affection.

To ***shear lambs***, shows that you will be cold and mercenary. You will be honest, but inhumane.

For a woman to dream that she is peeling the ***skin of a lamb***, and while doing so, she discovered that it is her child, denotes that she will cause others sorrow which will also rebound to her grief and loss. ◎

RAM

To dream that a ***ram*** pursues you, foretells that some misfortune threatens you.

To see one quietly grazing, denotes that you will have powerful friends, who will use their best efforts for your good. ◎

SHEPHERD

To see ***shepherds*** in your dreams watching their flocks, portends bounteous crops and pleasant relations for the farmer, also much enjoyment and profit for others.

To see them in idleness, foretells sickness and bereavement. ◎

THE RAM WITH THE GOLDEN FLEECE

Kids and Goats

KID

To dream of a ***kid***, denotes that you will not be overscrupulous in your morals or pleasures. You will be likely to bring grief to some loving heart. ◎

GOAT

To dream of ***goats*** wandering around a farm, is significant of seasonable weather and a fine yield of crops.

To see them otherwise, denotes cautious dealings and a steady increase of wealth.

If a ***billy goat*** butts you, beware that enemies do not get possession of your secrets or business plans.

For a woman to dream of ***riding a billy goat***, denotes that she will be held in disrepute because of her coarse and ill-bred conduct.

If a woman dreams that she drinks ***goat's milk***, she will marry for money and will not be disappointed. ◎

SHEEP *see* **EATING** *page 133* ◆ **LAMB** *see* **ANIMAL HIDE** *page 28*, **MEAT, SLAUGHTERHOUSE** *page 135*, **DOGS** *page 41*, **WOLVES** *page 31*, **BLEATING** *page 28*, **RAIN** *page 75*, **STORM** *page 76* ◆ **SHEPHERDS** *see* **IDLE** *page 251* ◆ **GOAT** *see* **MILK** *page 144*

Hogs and Pigs

HOGS

To dream of seeing fat, strong-looking hogs, ***foretells brisk changes in business and safe dealings. Lean hogs predict vexatious affairs and trouble with servants and children.***

To see a sow and litter of pigs, ***denotes abundant crops to the farmer, and advance in the affairs of others.***

To hear hogs squealing, ***denotes unpleasant news from absent friends, and foretells disappointment by death, or failure to realize the amounts you expected in deals of importance.***

To dream of feeding your own hogs, ***denotes an increase in your personal belongings.***

To dream that you are dealing in hogs, ***indicates that you will accumulate considerable property, but that you will have much rough work to perform.*** ❋

PIGS

To dream of fat, healthy pigs, ***denotes reasonable success in affairs. If they are wallowing in mire, you will have hurtful associates, and your engagements will be subject to reproach. This dream will bring to a young woman a jealous and greedy companion though the chances are that he will be wealthy.*** ❋

Dreams of solid domestic animals such as cows, pigs, and goats may seem earthbound, but occasionally animals take on mythic status, such as the ram with the golden fleece *opposite above.*

Cows and Cattle

CATTLE

To dream of seeing good-looking and fat ***cattle*** contentedly grazing in green pastures, denotes prosperity and happiness through a congenial and pleasant companion.

To see ***cattle lean***, shaggy, and poorly fed, you will be likely to toil all your life because of misspent energy and a dislike for detail of work. It is recommended that you correct your habits after this dream.

To see ***cattle stampeding***, means that you will have to exert all the powers of command you have to keep your career in a profitable channel.

To see a ***herd of cows at milking time***, you will be the successful owner of wealth that many have worked to obtain. To a young woman, this means that her affections will not suffer from the one of her choice.

If you dream of ***milking cows*** with udders well filled, great good fortune is in store for you. If the calf has stolen the milk, it signifies that you are about to lose your lover from your neglectful slowness to show your reciprocity, or forfeit your property from neglect of business.

To see ***young calves*** in your dream, you will become a great favorite in society and win the heart of a loyal person. For business, this dream indicates profit from sales. For a lover, the entering into bonds that will be respected. If the calves are poor, look for about the same, except that the object sought will be much harder to obtain.

Long-horned and ***dark, vicious cattle***, denotes enemies. ◎

BULL

To see a ***bull*** pursuing you, portends that business trouble, through the machinations of envious and jealous competitors, will harass you.

If a young woman dreams that she ***meets a bull***, she will have an offer of marriage, but, by declining this offer, she will better her fortune.

To see a ***bull goring*** a person, indicates that misfortune from unwisely using another's possessions will overtake you.

To dream of a ***white bull***, denotes that you will lift yourself up to a higher plane of life than those who persist in making material things their god. It usually denotes gain. ◎

COWS

To dream of seeing ***cows*** waiting for the milking hour, promises abundant fulfillment of hopes and desires. ◎

BULLOCK

This dream denotes that kind friends will surround you, if you are in danger from enemies. Good health is promised you. ◎

CALVES

To dream of ***calves*** peacefully grazing on a velvety lawn, foretells to the young and happy, festive gatherings and enjoyment. Those engaged in seeking wealth will see it rapidly increasing. ◎

OXEN

To see a well-fed ***ox***, signifies that you will become a leading person in your community, and receive much adulation from women.

To see ***fat oxen*** in green pastures, signifies fortune and your rise to positions beyond your expectations. If they are lean, your fortune will dwindle, and your friends will fall away from you.

If you see ***oxen well-matched and yoked***, it betokens a happy and wealthy marriage, or that you are already joined to your true mate.

To see a ***dead ox***, is a sign of bereavement.

If they are drinking from a clear pond, or stream, you will possess some long desired estate; perhaps it will be in the form of a lovely and devoted woman. If a woman, she will win the embraces of her lover. ◎

PIGS *see* **MIRE** *page 90* ◆ **CATTLE, COWS** *see* **MILK** *page 144* ◆ **CALVES** *see* **LAWN** *page 56* ◆ **OXEN** *see* **YOKE** *page 38* ◆ **WATER** *page 78*

Beasts of Burden

ASS

To see an ***ass*** in a dream, you will meet many annoyances, and news or goods will be delayed.

If an ***ass pursues*** you, and you are afraid of it, you will be the victim of scandal or other displeasing reports.

If you unwillingly ride on one, unnecessary quarrels may follow.

MULE

If you dream that you are riding on a ***mule***, it denotes that you are engaging in pursuits which will cause you the greatest anxiety, but if you reach your destination without interruption, you will be recompensed with substantial results.

For a young woman to dream of a ***white mule***, shows that she will marry a wealthy foreigner, or one who, while wealthy, will not be congenial in tastes.

If she dreams of ***mules running loose***, she will have beaux and admirers, but no offer of marriage.

To be ***kicked by a mule***, foretells disappointment in love and marriage.

To see one dead, portends broken engagements and social decline.

DONKEY

To dream of a ***donkey*** braying in your face, denotes that you are about to be publicly insulted by a lewd and unscrupulous person.

To hear the distant braying filling space with melancholy, you will receive wealth and release from unpleasant bonds by the death of some person close to you.

To see ***donkeys carrying burdens***, denotes that, after patience and toil, you will succeed in your undertakings, whether of travel or love.

If you see yourself ***riding on a donkey***, you will visit foreign lands and make many explorations into places difficult of passage.

To see others riding donkeys, denotes a meager inheritance for them and a toiling life.

To dream of seeing many of the old patriarchs traveling on donkeys, shows that the influence of Christians will be thrown against you in your selfish wantonness, causing you to ponder over the rights and duties of one person to another.

To ***drive a donkey***, signifies that all your energies and pluck will be brought into play against a desperate effort on the part of enemies to overthrow you. If you are in love, evil women will cause you trouble.

If you are kicked by this little animal, it shows that you are carrying on illicit connections, from which you will suffer much anxiety from fear of betrayal.

If you lead one by a halter, you will be master of every situation, and lead women into your way of seeing things by flattery.

To see ***children riding and driving donkeys***, signifies health and obedience for them.

To fall or be thrown from one, denotes ill luck and disappointment in secular affairs. Lovers will quarrel and separate.

To see one dead, denotes appetites satiated from licentious excesses.

To dream of ***drinking the milk of a donkey***, denotes that whimsical desires will be gratified, even to the displacement of important duties.

If you see in your dreams a ***strange donkey*** among your stock or on your premises, you will inherit valuables.

To dream of ***coming into the possession of a donkey*** by a present or purchase, you will attain to enviable heights in the business or social world, and if single, will contract a congenial marriage.

To dream of a ***white donkey***, denotes an assured and lasting fortune, which will enable you to pursue the pleasures or studies that lie nearest your heart. For a woman, it signals entrance into that society for which she has long entertained the most ardent desires.

Carrying the Load

LOAD

To dream that you carry a load, ***signifies a long existence filled with labors of love and charity.***

To fall under a load, ***denotes your inability to attain comforts that are necessary to those who look to you for subsistence.***

To see others thus engaged, denotes trials for them in which you will be interested.

BURDEN

To dream that you carry a heavy burden, ***signifies that you will be tied down by oppressive weights of care and injustice, caused from favoritism shown to your enemies by those in power. But to struggle free from it, you will climb to the topmost heights of success.***

YOKE

To dream of seeing a yoke, ***denotes that you will unwillingly conform to the customs and wishes of others.***

To yoke oxen ***in your dreams, signifies that your judgement and counsels will be accepted submissively by those dependent upon you. To fail to yoke them, you will be anxious over some prodigal friend.***

ASS, MULE *see* RIDE *page 33* ◆ DONKEY *see* BRAY *page 28,* RIDE *page 33,* HALTER *page 33,* MILK *page 144* ◆ YOKE *see* OXEN *page 37*

Ships of the Desert

DROMEDARY
To dream of a ***dromedary***, denotes that you will be the recipient of unexpected beneficence, and will wear your new honors with dignity; you will dispense charity with a gracious hand. To lovers, this dream foretells congenial dispositions. ◎

CAMELS
To dream of ***camels*** is good. To see this beast of burden, signifies that you will entertain great patience and fortitude in time of most unbearable anguish and failures that will seemingly sweep every vestige of hope from you.

To ***own a camel***, is a sign that you will possess rich mining property.

To see a ***herd of camels*** on the desert, denotes that assistance will come to you when all human aid seems at a low ebb, and prognosticates a sickness from which you will arise, contrary to all expectations. ◎

Farmyard Fowls

ROOSTER

CHICKENS
To dream of seeing a brood of ***chickens***, denotes worry from many cares, some of which will prove to your profit.

Young or half-grown chickens, signify fortunate enterprises; but to make them so, you will have to exert your physical strength.

If you see ***chickens going to roost***, it signifies that enemies are planning to work you evil.

To eat them, denotes that selfishness will detract from your otherwise good name. Business and love will remain in precarious states. ◎

ROOSTER
To dream of a ***rooster***, foretells that you will be very successful and rise to prominence, but you will allow yourself to become conceited over your fortunate rise.

To see ***roosters fighting***, foretells altercation and rivals. ◎

COCK CROWING
To dream of hearing a ***cock crowing*** in the morning, is significant of good. If you are single, it denotes an early marriage and a luxurious home.

To hear one at night, is despair, and cause for the tears you will have.

To dream of seeing ***cocks fight***, you will leave your family because of quarrels and infidelity. This dream usually announces some unexpected and sorrowful event. The cock warned the Apostle Peter when he was about to perjure himself. It may also warn you in a dream when the meshes of the world are swaying up from "the straight line" of spiritual wisdom. ◎

HENS
To dream of ***hens***, denotes pleasant family reunions with added members. ◎

TURKEY
To dream of seeing ***turkeys***, signifies abundant gain in business, and favorable crops to the farmer.

To see them dressed for the market, denotes improvements in your affairs.

To see them sick or dead, foretells that stringent circumstances will cause your pride to suffer.

To dream that you ***eat turkey***, foretells some joyful occasion approaching.

To see them flying, denotes a rapid transit from obscurity to prominence.

To shoot them as game, is a sign that you will unscrupulously amass wealth. ◎

GEESE
To dream that you are annoyed by the honking of ***geese,*** denotes a death in your family. To see them swimming, denotes that your fortune is gradually increasing.

To see them in grassy places, denotes assured success. If you see them dead, you will suffer loss and displeasure.

For a lover, geese denote the worthiness of his affianced.

If you are picking them, you will come into an estate. To eat them, denotes that your possessions are disputed. ◎

FOWL
To dream of seeing ***fowls***, denotes temporary worry or illness. For a woman to dream of fowls, indicates a short illness or disagreement with her friends. ◎

BROOD
To see a fowl with her ***brood***, denotes that, if you are a woman, your cares will be varied and irksome. Many children will be in your care, and some of them will prove wayward and unruly.

Brood, to others, denotes accumulation of wealth. ◎

Dreams of donkeys *opposite top,* **mules, and burdens may reflect the waking world of work and care; dreams of raucous farmyard fowls** *above left* **foreshadow noisy confrontation.**

CAMELS *see* **BURDEN** *page 38* ◆ **CHICKENS** *see* **POULTRY** *page 136* ◆ **HENS** *see* **CACKLING** *page 28* ◆ **TURKEY** *see* **POULTRY** *page 136,* **SHOOTING** *page 263* ◆ **GEESE** *see* **POULTRY** *page 136*

Cats and Kittens

CATS

CATS

To dream of a ***cat***, denotes ill luck, if you do not succeed in killing it or driving it from your sight. If the cat attacks you, you will have enemies who will go to any extreme to blacken your reputation and to cause you loss of property. But if you succeed in banishing it, you will overcome great obstacles and rise in fortune and fame.

If you meet ***a thin, mean, and dirty-looking cat***, you will have bad news from the absent. Some friend lies at death's door; but if you chase it out of sight, your friend will recover after a long and lingering sickness.

If you hear the scream or ***the mewing of a cat***, some false friend is using all the words and work at his command to do you harm.

If you dream that ***a cat scratches you***, an enemy will succeed in wrenching from you the profits of a deal that you have spent many days bringing to fruition.

If a young woman dreams that she is holding a cat or kitten, she will be influenced into some impropriety through the treachery of others.

To dream of ***a clean white cat***, denotes entanglements which, while seemingly harmless, will prove a source of sorrow and loss of wealth.

When a merchant dreams of a cat, he should put his best energies to work, as his competitors are about to succeed in demolishing his standard of dealing, and he will be forced to other measures if he undersells others and still succeeds.

To dream of seeing ***a cat and snake*** on friendly terms, signifies the beginning of an angry struggle. It denotes that an enemy is being entertained by you with the intention of using him to find out some secret which you believe concerns yourself; uneasy of his confidences given, you will endeavor to disclaim all knowledge of his actions, as you are fearful that things divulged, concerning your private life, may become public. ◎

KITTENS

For a woman to dream of a beautiful fat, ***white kitten***, omens that artful deception will be practiced upon her, which will almost ensnare her to destruction, but her good sense of judgement will prevail in warding off unfortunate conditions.

If the kittens are soiled, or colored and lean, she will be victimized into glaring indiscretions.

To dream of ***kittens***, denotes that abominable small troubles and vexations will pursue you and work your loss, unless you kill the kittens, and then you will overcome these worries.

To see ***snakes kill kittens***, you have enemies who, in seeking to injure you, will work harm to themselves. ◎

Dreams about cats *top left* **are fraught with warnings of deceit and betrayal; dreams of mice** *right,* **the cat's traditional prey, denote the activities of enemies in your life. Dreams of dogs** *opposite* **are altogether less devious. Rats** *opposite top* **are no more welcome in dreams than they are in real life.**

Mice and Mousetraps

MOUSE

For a woman to dream of a mouse, ***denotes that she will have an enemy who will annoy her by artfulness and treachery.*** ❋

MICE

To dream of mice, ***foretells domestic troubles and the insincerity of friends. Business affairs will assume a discouraging tone.***

To kill mice, ***denotes that you will conquer your enemies.***

To let them escape you, is significant of doubtful struggles.

For a young woman to dream of mice, warns her of secret enemies, and that deception is being practiced upon her. If she should see a mouse in her clothing, ***it is a sign of scandal in which she will figure.*** ❋

MOUSETRAP

To see a mousetrap ***in dreams, signifies your need to be careful of character, as wary persons have designs upon you.***

To see it full of mice, you will likely fall into the hands of enemies.

To set a trap, ***you will artfully devise means to overcome your opponents.*** ❋

MOUSE

CAT, KITTENS *see* **SNAKE** *page 54* ◆ **MOUSE** *see* **APPAREL, CLOTHES** *page 154* ◆ **MOUSETRAP** *see* **TRAP** *page 266*

Rats and Rattraps

RAT

RAT

To dream of rats, ***denotes that you will be deceived, and injured by your neighbors. Quarrels with your companions are also foreboded.***

To catch rats, ***means that you will scorn the baseness of others, and worthily outstrip your enemies.***

To kill one, denotes your victory in any contest.

RATTRAP

To dream of falling into a rattrap, ***denotes that you will be victimized and robbed of some valuable object.***

To see an empty one, foretells the absence of slander or competition.

A broken one, denotes that you will be rid of unpleasant associations.

To set one, you will be made aware of the designs of enemies, but the warning will enable you to outwit them.

Canine Dreams

DOGS

To dream of a vicious ***dog***, denotes enemies and unalterable misfortune. To dream that a dog fondles you, indicates the possibility of great gain and constant friends.

To dream of owning ***a dog with fine qualities***, denotes that you will be possessed of solid wealth.

To dream that ***a bloodhound*** is tracking you, you are likely to fall into some temptation, in which there is much danger of your downfall.

To dream of ***small dogs***, indicates that your thoughts and chief pleasures are of a frivolous order.

To dream of ***dogs biting you***, foretells for you a quarrelsome companion either in marriage or business.

Lean, filthy dogs, indicate failure in business; also sickness among children.

To dream of a ***dog show***, is indicative of many and varied favors from fortune.

To hear the ***barking of dogs***, foretells news of a depressing nature. Difficulties are more than likely to follow.

To see ***dogs on the chase*** of foxes and other large game, denotes an unusual briskness in all affairs.

To see ***fancy pet dogs***, signifies a love of show, and that the owner is selfish and narrow. For a young woman, this dream foretells a fop for a sweetheart.

To feel much fright upon seeing a ***large mastiff***, denotes that you will experience inconvenience because of efforts to rise above mediocrity. If a woman dreams this, she will marry a wise and humane man.

To hear the ***growling and snarling of dogs***, indicates that you are at the mercy of designing people, and you will be afflicted with unpleasant home surroundings.

To hear the lonely ***baying of a dog***, foretells a death or a long separation from friends.

To hear dogs ***growling and fighting***, portends that you will be overcome by your enemies, and your life will be filled with depression.

To see ***dogs and cats*** seemingly on friendly terms, and suddenly turning on each other, showing their teeth and a general fight ensuing, you will meet with disaster in love and worldly pursuits, unless you succeed in quelling the row.

If you dream of a friendly ***white dog*** approaching you, it portends for you a victorious engagement, whether in business or love. For a woman, this is an omen of an early marriage.

To dream of a ***many-headed dog***, you are trying to maintain too many branches of business at one time. Success always comes with concentration of energies. A man who wishes to succeed in anything should be warned by this dream.

DOG

To dream of a ***mad dog***, your most strenuous efforts will not bring desired results, and fatal disease may be clutching at your vitals. If a mad dog succeeds in biting you, it is a sign that you or some loved one is on the verge of insanity, and a deplorable tragedy may occur.

To dream of traveling alone, with a ***dog following*** you, foretells staunch friends and successful undertakings.

To dream of ***dogs swimming***, indicates for you an easy stretch to happiness and fortune.

To dream that ***a dog kills a cat*** in your presence, is significant of profitable dealings and some unexpected pleasure.

For ***a dog to kill a snake*** in your presence, is an omen of good luck.

RATTRAP *see* **TRAP** *page 266* ◆ **DOG** *see* **PUPS, MAD DOGS, BULLDOG, HOUNDS, LAP DOG, GREYHOUND** *page 42* ◆ **FOXES** *page 31* ◆ **CATS** *page 40* ◆ **SWIMMING** *page 174* ◆ **SNAKES** *page 54*

Young Dogs

PUPS
To dream of ***pups***, denotes that you will entertain the innocent and hapless, and thereby enjoy pleasure. The dream also shows that friendships will grow stronger, and fortune will increase if the pups are healthy and well formed, and vice versa if they are lean and filthy. ◎

Dangerous Dogs

MAD DOGS
To dream of seeing a ***mad dog***, denotes that enemies will make scurrilous attacks upon you and your friends, but if you succeed in killing the dog, you will overcome adverse opinions and prosper greatly in a financial way. ◎

DREAM DOGS

Special Breeds of Dog

BULLDOG
To dream of entering strange premises and a ***bulldog*** attacking you, you will be in danger of transgressing the laws of your country by using perjury to obtain your desires.

If one meets you in a friendly way, you will rise in life, regardless of adverse criticisms and the seditious interference of enemies. ◎

HOUNDS
To dream of ***hounds*** on a hunt, denotes coming delights and pleasant changes.

For a woman to dream of hounds, she will love a man below her in station.

To dream that hounds are following her, she will have many admirers, but there will be no real love felt for her. ◎

LAPDOG
To dream of a ***lapdog***, foretells that you will be succored by friends in some approaching dilemma. If it be thin and ill-looking, there will be distressing occurrences to detract from your prospects. ◎

GREYHOUND
A ***greyhound*** is a fortunate object to see in your dream. If it is following a young girl, you will be surprised with a legacy from unknown people. If a greyhound is owned by you, it signifies friends where enemies were expected. ◎

HOUNDS

PUPS, MAD DOGS, BULLDOG, HOUNDS, LAPDOG, GREYHOUND *see* DOG *page 41* ◆ HOUNDS *see* HUNTING *page 174*

Birds, with their promise of flight, are powerful symbols in dreams. This section looks at the kinds of birds that flutter through our dreams, from the lofty eagle to the little sparrow, the serene swan to the raucous rook. Insects also feature, as do spiders, so often objects of unreasoning dread in waking life.

Birds in their Little Nests

BIRDS

It is a favorable dream to see ***birds*** of beautiful plumage. A wealthy and happy partner is near, if a woman has dreams of this nature.

Molting and songless birds, denotes merciless and inhuman treatment of the outcast and fallen by people of wealth.

To see a ***wounded bird***, is fateful of deep sorrow caused by erring offspring.

To see ***flying birds***, is a sign of prosperity to the dreamer. All disagreeable environments will vanish before the wave of prospective good.

To ***catch birds***, is not at all bad.

To hear them speak, is owning one's inability to perform tasks that demand great clearness of perception.

To ***kill birds with a gun***, is disaster from dearth of harvest. ◎

BIRD'S NEST

To see an empty ***bird's nest***, denotes gloom and a dull outlook for business. If eggs are in the nest, good results will follow all engagements.

If young ones are in the nest, it denotes successful journeys and satisfactory dealings. If they are lonely and deserted, sorrow and your own folly will cause you anxiety. ◎

Dreams of dogs in general *opposite top* **or specific breeds such as hounds** *opposite bottom* **have their own canine slant. Dreams of birds are many and varied. Feathers** *center* **have many dream connotations, and to dream of the mournful owl** *top* **is a bad portent.**

NEST

To dream of seeing birds' ***nests,*** denotes that you will be interested in an enterprise which will be prosperous. For a young woman, this dream foretells change of abode.

To see an ***empty nest*** indicates sorrow through the absence of a friend.

Hens' nests, foretell that you will be interested in domesticities, and children will be cheerful and obedient.

To dream of a ***nest filled with broken or bad eggs***, portends disappointments and failure. ◎

FEATHER

FEATHER

To dream of seeing ***feathers*** falling around you, denotes your burdens in life will be light and easily borne.

To see ***eagle feathers***, denotes that your aspirations will be realized.

To see ***chicken feathers***, denotes small annoyances.

To dream of buying or selling ***geese or duck feathers***, denotes thrift and fortune.

To dream of ***black feathers***, denotes disappointments and unhappy amours.

For a woman to dream of seeing ***ostrich and other ornamental feathers***, denotes that she will advance in society, but her ways of gaining favor will not bear imitating. ◎

Night Birds

TAWNY OWL

OWL

To hear the solemn, unearthly sound of the muffled voice of the ***owl***, warns dreamers that death creeps closely in the wake of health and joy. Precaution should be taken that life is not ruthlessly exposed to his unyielding grasp. Bad tidings of the absence will surely follow this dream.

To see a ***dead owl***, denotes that you or another will experience a narrow escape from desperate illness or death.

To see an owl, foretells that you will be secretly maligned and be in danger from enemies. ◎

SCREECH OWL

To dream that you hear the shrill, startling notes of the ***screech owl***, denotes that you will be shocked with news of the desperate illness or death of some dear friend. ◎

NIGHTINGALE

To dream that you are listening to the harmonious notes of the ***nightingale***, foretells a pleasing existence, and prosperous and healthy surroundings. This is a most favorable dream to lovers and parents.

To see ***nightingales silent***, foretells slight misunderstandings among friends. ◎

BIRDS *see* **FLYING** *page 268* ◆ **SHOOTING** *page 263* ◆ **BIRD'S NEST** *see* **EGGS** *page 145* ◆ **NEST** *see* **HENS** *page 39* ◆ **EGGS** *page 145* ◆ **FEATHER** *see* **EAGLES** *page 44* ◆ **CHICKEN, GEESE** *page 39* ◆ **DUCKS** *page 45* ◆ **OSTRICH** *page 47*

Birds of Prey

HAWK

EAGLES
To dream that you see an ***eagle*** soaring above you, denotes lofty ambitions which you will struggle fiercely to realize; nevertheless you will gain your desires.

To see one perched on distant heights, denotes that you will possess fame, wealth, and the highest position attainable in your country.

To see ***young eagles*** in their eyrie, signifies your association with people of high standing, and that you will profit from wise counsel from them. You will in time come into a rich legacy.

To dream that you ***kill an eagle***, portends that no obstacles whatever would be allowed to stand before you and the utmost heights of your ambition. You will overcome your enemies and be possessed of untold wealth.

To dream that you are eating the flesh of one, denotes the possession of a powerful will that would not turn aside in ambitious struggles, even for death. You will come immediately into rich possessions.

To see a ***dead eagle*** killed by others than yourself, signifies that high rank and fortune will be wrested from you ruthlessly.

To dream that you ***ride on an eagle's back***, denotes that you will make a long voyage into almost unexplored countries in your search for knowledge and wealth, which you will eventually gain. ◎

HAWK
To dream of a ***hawk***, foretells that you will be cheated in some way by intriguing persons.

To shoot one, foretells that you will surmount obstacles that beset you after many struggles.

For a young woman to ***frighten hawks away*** from her chickens, signifies that she will obtain her most extravagant desires through diligent attention to her affairs. It also denotes that enemies are near you, and they are ready to take advantage of your slightest mistakes. If you succeed in scaring it away before your fowls are injured, this signifies that you will be lucky in your business.

To see a ***dead hawk***, signifies that your enemies will be vanquished.

To dream of ***shooting at a hawk***, you will have a contest with enemies, and will probably win. ◎

FALCON
To dream of a ***falcon***, denotes that your prosperity will make you an object of envy and malice. For a young woman, this denotes that she will be calumniated by a rival. ◎

Carrion Creatures

VULTURES
To dream of ***vultures***, signifies that some scheming person is bent on injuring you, and will not succeed unless you see the vulture wounded or dead.

For a woman to dream of a vulture, signifies that she will be overwhelmed with malicious slander and gossip. ◎

VULTURE

CROW
To dream of seeing a ***crow***, betokens misfortune and grief.

To hear ***crows cawing***, you will be influenced by others to make a bad disposal of property. To a young man, this dream is indicative of his succumbing to the wiles of designing women. ◎

BUZZARD
To dream that you hear a ***buzzard*** talking, foretells that some old scandal will arise and work you injury by your connection with it.

To see one sitting on a railroad, denotes that some accident or loss is about to descend upon you. To see them fly away as you approach, foretells that you will be able to smooth over some scandalous disagreement among your friends, or even one appertaining to yourself.

To see buzzards in a dream, portends generally salacious gossip or that unusual scandal will disturb you. ◎

RAVEN
To dream of a ***raven***, denotes a reverse in fortune and inharmonious surroundings. For a young woman, it is implied in this dream that her lover will betray her. ◎

ROOKS
To dream of ***rooks***, denotes that, while your friends are true, they will not afford you the pleasure and contentment for which you long, as your thoughts and tastes will outstrip their humble conception of life.

A ***dead rook***, denotes sickness or death in your immediate future. ◎

EAGLES *see* RIDE *page 33* ◆ HAWK *see* SHOOTING *page 263,* CHICKENS *page 39* ◆ BUZZARD *see* RAILROAD *page 225*

Thievish Birds

JACKDAW
To see a ***jackdaw***, denotes ill health and quarrels. To catch one, you will outwit enemies.

To kill one, you will come into possession of disputed property. ◎

MAGPIE
To dream of a ***magpie***, denotes much dissatisfaction and quarrels. The dreamer should guard well his conduct and speech after this dream. ◎

JAYBIRD
To dream of a ***jaybird***, foretells pleasant visits from friends and interesting gossips.

To ***catch a jaybird***, denotes pleasant, though unfruitful tasks.

To see a ***dead jaybird***, denotes domestic unhappiness and many vicissitudes. ◎

Water Birds

CRANE
To dream of seeing a flight of ***cranes*** tending northward, indicates gloomy prospects for business. To a woman, it is significant of disappointment.

To see them flying southward, prognosticates a joyful meeting of absent friends, and the continued faithfulness of lovers.

To see them fly to the ground, denotes that events of unusual moment are at hand. ◎

DUCKS
To dream of seeing ***wild ducks*** on a clear stream of water, signifies fortunate journeys, perhaps across the sea.

White ducks around a farm, indicate thrift and a fine harvest.

To ***hunt ducks***, denotes displacement in the employment in the carrying out of plans.

To see them shot, signifies that enemies are meddling with your private affairs.

To see them flying, foretells a brighter future for you. It also denotes marriage, and children in the new home. ◎

SWAN

SWAN
To dream of seeing white ***swans*** floating upon placid waters, foretells prosperous outlooks and delightful experiences.

To see a ***black swan***, denotes illicit pleasure, if near clear water. A ***dead swan***, foretells feelings of satiety and discontentment.

To see them flying, pleasant anticipations will be realized soon. ◎

PELICAN
To dream of a ***pelican***, denotes a mingling of disappointments with success.

To catch one, you will be able to overcome disappointing influences.

To kill one, denotes that you will cruelly set aside the rights of others.

To see ***pelicans flying***, you are threatened with charges, which will impress you with ideas of uncertainty as to good. ◎

GULLS
To dream of ***gulls***, is a prophecy of peaceful dealings with ungenerous persons. Seeing ***dead gulls***, means wide separation for friends. ◎

CRANES

Dreams of hawks *opposite top,* **vultures** *opposite center,* **cranes** *left,* **and swans** *above,* **all have their own special interpretation.**

CRANE *see* **FLYING** *page 268* ◆ **DUCKS** *see* **WATER, POND** *page 78,* **HUNTING** *page 174,* **FLYING** *page 268* ◆ **SWAN** *see* **WATER** *page 78,* **FLYING** *page 268* ◆ **PELICAN** *see* **FLYING** *page 268*

Copycats

PARROT

Parrots chattering in your dreams, signify frivolous employments and idle gossip among your friends.

To see them in repose, denotes a peaceful intermission of family broils.

For a young woman to dream that she ***owns a parrot***, denotes that her lover will come to believe her to be quarrelsome.

To dream that you ***teach a parrot***, you will have trouble in your private affairs. A dead parrot, foretells the loss of social friends. ◎

MOCKINGBIRD

To see or hear a ***mockingbird***, signifies that you will be invited to go on a pleasant visit to friends, and your affairs will move along smoothly and prosperously.

For a woman to see a wounded or dead one, her disagreement with a friend or lover is signified. ◎

Songbirds

PARAKEET

CANARY

To dream of this sweet songster, denotes unexpected pleasures. For the young to dream of possessing a beautiful ***canary***, denotes high-class honors and a successful passage through the literary world, or a happy termination of love's young dream.

To dream that one is given you, indicates a welcome legacy. To ***give away a canary***, denotes that you will suffer disappointment in your dearest wishes.

To dream that one dies, denotes the unfaithfulness of dear friends.

Advancing, fluttering, and singing canaries, in luxurious apartments, denote feasting and a life of exquisite refinements, wealth, and satisfying friendships. If the light is weird or unnaturally bright, it augurs that you are entertaining illusive hopes. Your overconfidence is your worst enemy. A young woman after this dream should beware, lest flattering promises react upon her in disappointment. Fairylike scenes in a dream are peculiarly misleading and treacherous to women. ◎

LARK

To see ***larks*** flying, denotes high aims and purposes, through the attainments of which you will throw off selfishness and cultivate kindly graces of mind.

To hear them singing as they fly, you will be very happy in a new change of abode, and business will flourish.

If you see them fall to the earth and hear them singing as they fall, despairing gloom will overtake you in pleasure's bewildering delights.

A ***wounded or dead lark***, portends sadness or death.

To ***kill a lark***, portends injury to innocence through wantonness.

If they fly around and light on you, fortune will turn her promising countenance toward you.

To catch them in traps, you will honor and love easily.

To see them eating, denotes a plentiful harvest. ◎

Wild Birds

CUCKOO

CUCKOO

To dream of a ***cuckoo***, prognosticates a sudden ending of a happy life, caused by the downfall of a dear friend.

To dream that you ***hear a cuckoo***, denotes the painful illness or the death of some absent loved one, or an accident to someone in your family. ◎

SWALLOW

To dream of ***swallows***, is a sign of peace and domestic harmony.

To see a wounded or dead one, signifies unavoidable sadness. ◎

SPARROW

To dream of ***sparrows***, denotes that you will be surrounded with love and comfort, and this will cause you to listen with kindly interest to tales of woe. Your benevolence will gain you popularity.

To see them distressed or wounded, foretells sadness. ◎

YELLOW BIRD

To see a ***yellow bird*** flitting about in your dreams, foretells that some great event will cast a sickening fear of the future around you.

To see it sick or dead, foretells that you will suffer for another's wild folly. ◎

Cuckoos *left* **are a bad omen in dreams. Parrots and their relatives** *above* **indicate social upheaval. Wood pigeons** *opposite top* **are gentle in your dreams.**

CANARY *see* SINGING *page 167*, WEALTH *page 238* ◆ LARK *see* FLYING *page 268*, SINGING *page 167*, TRAP *page 266*

Doves and Pigeons

DOVES

Dreaming of ***doves*** mating and building their nests, indicates peacefulness of the world and joyous homes, where children render obedience and mercy is extended to all.

To hear the lonely, mournful ***voice of a dove***, portends sorrow and disappointment through the death of one to whom you looked for aid. Often it portends the death of a father.

To see a ***dead dove***, is ominous of a separation of husband and wife, either through death or infidelity.

To see ***white doves***, denotes bountiful harvests and the utmost confidence in the loyalty of friends.

To dream of seeing a flock of white doves, denotes peaceful, innocent pleasures, and fortunate developments in the future.

If one brings you a letter, tidings of a pleasant nature from absent friends are intimated; also a lover's reconciliation is denoted. If the dove seems exhausted, a note of sadness will pervade the reconciliation, or a sad touch may be given the pleasant tidings by mention of an invalid friend; if of business, a slight drop may follow. If the letter bears the message that you are doomed, it foretells that a desperate illness, either your own or that of a relative, may cause a financial misfortune. ◎

PIGEON

To dream of seeing ***pigeons*** and hearing them cooing above their cotes, denotes domestic peace and pleasure-giving children. For a young woman, this dream indicates an early and comfortable union.

If you see them being used in a shooting match, and you participate, it denotes that cruelty in your nature will show in your dealings; you are warned of low and debasing pleasures.

To see them flying, denotes freedom from misunderstandings, and perhaps news from the absent. ◎

WOOD PIGEONS

The Ostrich

To dream of an ostrich, ***denotes that you will secretly amass wealth, but at the same time, maintain degrading intrigues with women.***

To catch one, your resources will enable you to enjoy travel and extensive knowledge. ❋

Game Birds

PARTRIDGE

Partridges seen in your dreams, denote that conditions will be good in your immediate future for the accumulation of property.

To ensnare them, signifies that you will be fortunate in expectations.

To kill them, foretells that you will be successful, but much of your wealth will be given to others.

To eat them, signifies the enjoyment of deserved honors.

To see them flying, denotes that a promising future is before you. ◎

PHEASANT

Dreaming of ***pheasants***, omens good fellowship among your friends.

To ***eat a pheasant***, signifies that the jealousy shown by your wife will cause you to forgo intercourse with your friends.

To ***shoot pheasants***, denotes that you will fail to sacrifice one selfish pleasure in exchange for the comfort of friends. ◎

QUAIL

To see ***quails*** in your dream, is a very favorable omen, if they are alive; if they are dead, you will undergo serious ill luck.

To ***shoot quail***, foretells ill feelings will be shown by friends.

To ***eat quails***, signifies extravagance in your personal living. ◎

Peacocks

For persons dreaming of peacocks, ***there lies below the brilliant and flashing ebb and flow of the stream of pleasure and riches, the slums and sorrow and failure, which threaten to mix with its clearness at the least disturbing influence.***

For a woman to dream that she owns peacocks, ***denotes that she will be deceived in her estimate of a man's honor.***

To hear their harsh voices while looking upon their proudly spread plumage, denotes that some beautiful and well-appearing person will work you discomfort and uneasiness of mind. ❋

DOVE *see* **VOICE** *page 276,* **LETTER** *page 236* ◆ **PIGEON** *see* **SHOOTING** *page 263,* **FLYING** *page 268* ◆ **PARTRIDGE** *see* **TRAP** *page 266,* **POULTRY** *page 136,* **FLYING** *page 268* ◆ **PHEASANT, QUAIL** *see* **POULTRY** *page 136,* **SHOOTING** *page 263,* **GAME** *page 174* ◆ **PEACOCK** *see* **VOICE** *page 276*

Common Insects

ANTS
The dreamer of ***ants*** should expect many petty annoyances during the day; chasing little worries, and finding general dissatisfaction in all things. ◎

BEETLES
To dream of seeing them on your person, denotes poverty and small ills. To kill them is good. ◎

MAY BUGS
To dream of ***May bugs***, denotes an ill-tempered companion where a congenial one was expected. ◎

WEEVIL
To dream of ***weevils*** [types of beetle], portends loss in trade and falseness in love. ◎

BEETLE

BUGS AND BEETLES

Swarmers and Stingers

BEES
Bees signify pleasant and profitable engagements.

For an officer, it brings obedient subjects and healthful environments.

To a preacher, many new members and a praying congregation.

To businessmen, increase in trade.

To parents, much pleasure from dutiful children.

If one stings, loss or injury will bear upon you from a friendly source. ◎

WASP
Wasps, if seen in dreams, denotes that enemies will scourge and spitefully vilify you.

If one stings you, you will feel the effect of envy and hatred.

To kill them, you will be able to throttle your enemies and fearlessly maintain your rights. ◎

HORNET
To dream of a ***hornet***, signals disruption to lifelong friendship, and loss of money.

For a young woman to dream that one stings her, or she is in a nest of them, foretells that many envious women will seek to disparage her before her admirers. ◎

BEE

MOSQUITO
To see ***mosquitoes*** in your dreams, you will strive in vain to remain impregnable to the sly attacks of secret enemies. Your patience and fortune will both suffer from these designing persons.

If you ***kill mosquitoes***, you will eventually overcome obstacles and enjoy fortune and domestic bliss. ◎

Flies and Flytraps

FLIES
To dream of ***flies***, denotes sickness and contagious maladies; also that enemies surround you.

To a young woman, this dream is significant of unhappiness. If she kills or exterminates flies, she will reinstate herself in the love of her intended by her ingenuity. ◎

FLYTRAP
To see a ***flytrap*** in a dream, is signal of malicious designing against you. To see one full of flies, denotes that small embarrassments will ward off greater ones. ◎

FLYPAPER
To dream of ***flypaper***, signifies ill health and disrupted friendships. ◎

MAY BUGS *see* **BUGS** *page 49* ◆ **BEES** *see* **HONEY** *page 148*, **PREACHER** *page 282*, **PARENTS** *page 127*, **STING** *page 112* ◆ **WASP** *see* **STING** *page 112* ◆ **FLIES** *see* **SICKNESS** *page 106* ◆ **FLYTRAP** *see* **TRAP** *page 266*

Spiders and their Webs

SPIDER

To dream of a ***spider***, denotes that you will be careful and energetic in your labors, and fortune will be amassed to pleasing proportions.

To see one ***building its web***, foretells that you will be happy and secure in your own home.

To kill one, signifies quarrels with your wife or sweetheart.

If one bites you, you will be the victim of unfaithfulness and will suffer from enemies in your business.

If you dream that you see ***many spiders*** hanging in their webs around you, foretells most favorable conditions, fortune, good health and friends.

To dream of a ***large spider*** confronting you, signifies that your elevation to fortune will be swift, unless you are in dangerous contact.

To dream that you see a very large spider and a small one coming towards you, denotes that you will be prosperous, and that you will feel for a time that you are immensely successful. If the large one bites you, enemies will steal away your good fortune. If the little one bites you, this signifies that you will be harassed with little spites and jealousies.

To imagine that you are running from a large spider, denotes that you will lose your fortune in slighting opportunities.

If you ***kill the spider***, you will eventually come into fair estate. If it afterwards returns to life and pursues you, you will be oppressed by sickness and wavering fortunes.

For a young woman to dream that she sees ***gold spiders*** crawling around her, foretells that her fortune and prospects for happiness will improve, and new friends will surround her. ◎

SPIDER WEB

To see ***spider webs***, denotes pleasant associations and fortunate ventures. ◎

Lice, Fleas, and Vermin

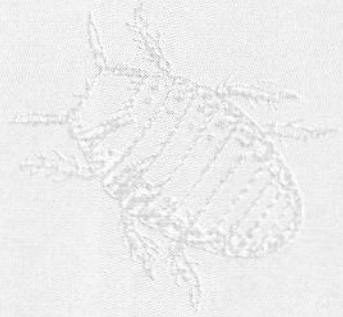

LOUSE

LOUSE

To dream of a louse, ***foretells that you will have uneasy feelings regarding your health, and an enemy will give you exasperating vexation.*** ❊

LICE

A dream of lice ***contains much waking worry and distress. It often implies offensive ailments.***

Lice on stock, ***foretells famine and loss.***

To have lice on your body, denotes that you will conduct yourself unpleasantly with your acquaintances.

To dream of catching lice, ***foretells sickness, and that you will cultivate morbidity.*** ❊

VERMIN

Vermin ***crawling in your dreams, signifies sickness and much trouble. If you succeed in ridding yourself of them, you will be fairly successful, but otherwise death may come to you or your relatives.*** ❊

FLEAS

To dream of fleas, ***indicates that you will be provoked to anger and acts of retaliation by the evil machinations of those who are close to you.***

For a woman to dream that fleas bite her, ***foretells that she will be slandered by pretended friends. To see fleas on her lover, denotes inconstancy.*** ❊

TICKS

To dream you see ticks ***crawling on your flesh, is a sign of impoverished circumstances and ill health. Hasty journeys to sick beds may be made.***

To mash a tick ***on you, denotes that you will be annoyed by treacherous enemies.***

If you see in your dreams large ticks on stock, ***enemies are endeavoring to get possession of your property by foul means.*** ❊

BUGS

To dream of bugs, ***denotes that some disgustingly revolting complication will rise in your daily life. Families will suffer from the carelessness of servants, and sickness may follow.*** ❊

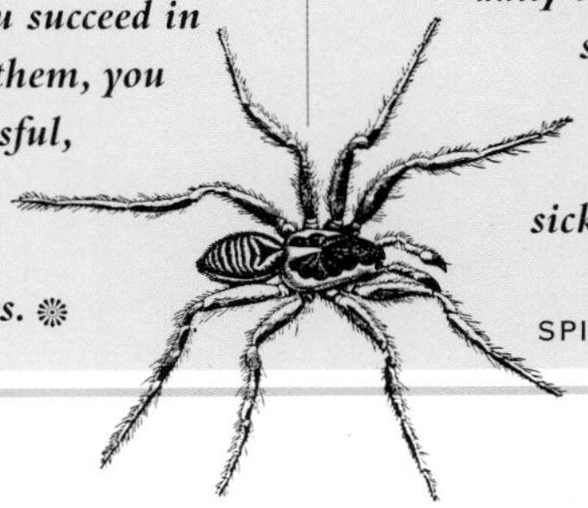

SPIDER

TARANTULA

To see a ***tarantula*** in your dream, signifies that enemies are about to overwhelm you with loss.

To kill one, denotes that you will be successful after much ill luck. ◎

Insects such as beetles and bugs *opposite top left and right,* **bees** *opposite bottom,* **lice** *top,* **and spiders such as the tarantula** *above* **may creep and scuttle through your dreams, but they do not always portend unpleasantness.**

SPIDER *see* **WEB** *page 185,* **BITE** *page 112,* **RUNNING** *page 267,* **GOLD** *page 71* ◆ **FLEAS** *see* **BITE** *page 112* ◆
BUGS *see* **MAY BUGS** *page 48,* **BED BUGS** *page 207*

Idlers and Destroyers

GRASSHOPPER
To dream of seeing ***grasshoppers*** on green vegetables, denotes that enemies threaten your best interests. If on withered grasses, ill health. Disappointing business will be experienced.

If you see grasshoppers between you and the sun, it denotes that you will have a vexatious problem in your immediate business life to settle; but if you use caution, it will adjust itself in your favor. To call people's attention to the grasshopper, shows that you are not discreet in dispatching your private business. ◎

KATYDIDS
To dream of hearing ***katydids*** [large green tree insects resembling grasshoppers], is prognostic of misfortune and unusual dependence on others. If any sick person asks you what katydids are, it foretells that there will be surprising events in your present and future.

For a woman to see them, signifies that she will have a quarrelsome husband or lover. ◎

CRICKET
To hear a ***cricket*** in one's dream, indicates melancholy news, and perhaps the death of some distant friend.

To see them, indicates hard struggles with poverty. ◎

LOCUSTS
To dream of ***locusts***, foretells that discrepancies will be found in your business, for which you will worry and suffer.

For a woman, this dream foretells that she will bestow her affections upon ungenerous people. ◎

SCORPION
To dream of a ***scorpion***, foretells that false friends will improve opportunities to undermine your prosperity. If you fail to kill it, you will suffer loss from an enemy's attack. ◎

Butterflies and Moths

BUTTERFLY

BUTTERFLY
To see a ***butterfly*** among flowers and green grasses, indicates prosperity and fair attainments.

To see them flying about, denotes news from absent friends by letter, or from someone who has seen them. To a young woman, a happy love, culminating in a life union. ◎

CATERPILLAR
To see a ***caterpillar*** in a dream, denotes that low and hypocritical people are in your immediate future, and you will do well to keep clear of deceitful appearances. You may suffer a loss in love or business.

To dream of a caterpillar, foretells that you will be placed in embarrassing situations, and there will be small honor or gain to be expected. ◎

While dreams of butterflies *top* **are happy, dreams of moths** *right* **do not bode as well as might be expected from such fluttery, frivolous inspirations.**

MOTH
If you see a ***moth*** in a dream, small worries will lash you into hurried contracts, which will prove unsatisfactory. Quarrels of a domestic nature are prognosticated. ◎

WHITE MOTH
To dream of a ***white moth***, foretells unavoidable sickness, though you will be tempted to accuse yourself or some other with wrong-doing which you think causes the complaint.

For a woman to see one flying around in the room at night, forebodes unrequited wishes and disposition which will affect the enjoyment of other people.

To see a moth flying and finally setting upon something, or disappearing totally, foreshadows death of friends or relatives. ◎

BUTTERFLIES AND MOTHS

GRASSHOPPER *see* **VEGETABLES** *page 137,* **SUN** *page 84* ◆ **BUTTERFLY** *see* **FLYING** *page 268,* **LETTER** *page 236* ◆ **MOTH** *see* **FLYING** *page 268*

Fish swimming through your dreams are also powerful symbols of a deeper life led in a different medium, a representation of unconscious thought. Reptiles, their land-living cousins, exercise a particularly hypnotic dream power, especially snakes and serpents, at once fascinating and repellent.

Fish and Fishing

FISH

To dream that you see ***fish*** in clear water streams, denotes that you will be favored by the rich and powerful.

Dead fish, signify the loss of wealth and power through some dire calamity.

For a young woman to dream of seeing fish, portends that she will have a handsome and talented lover.

To dream of catching a ***catfish***, denotes that you will be embarrassed by evil designs of enemies, but your luck and presence of mind will tide you safely over the trouble.

To wade in water, ***catching fish***, denotes that you will possess wealth acquired by your own ability and enterprise.

To dream of ***fishing***, denotes energy and economy; but if you do not succeed in catching any, your efforts to obtain honors and wealth will be futile.

Eating fish, denotes warm and lasting attachments. ◎

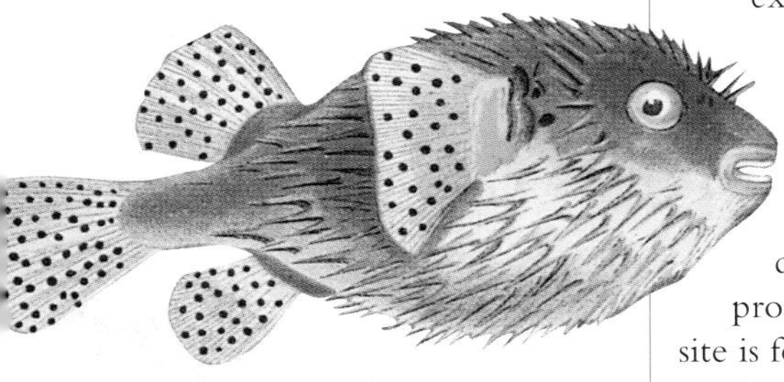

FISH

Dreams of fish *above* **appear to be fortunate overall; dreams of fish hooks** *top right* **and other fishy accessories also portend prosperity through application and enterprise.**

Fishy Activities

FISHERMAN

To dream of a *fisherman*, ***denotes that you are nearing times of greater prosperity than you have yet known.*** ❊

FISHHOOKS

To dream of *fishhooks*, ***denotes that you have opportunities to make yourself a fortune and an honorable name if you rightly apply them.*** ❊

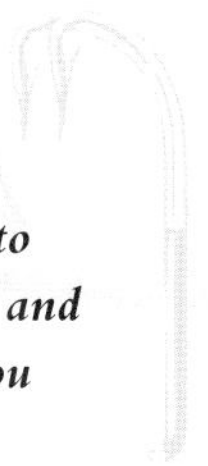

FISHHOOK

FISH MARKET

To visit a *fish market* ***in your dream, brings competence and pleasure.***

To see *decayed fish*, ***foretells that distress will come in the guise of happiness.*** ❊

FISHNET

To dream of a *fishnet*, ***portends numerous small pleasures and gains. A torn one, represents vexatious disappointments.*** ❊

Ornamental Fish

FISHPOND

To dream of a ***fishpond***, denotes illness through dissipation, if muddy. To see one clear and well stocked with fish, portends profitable enterprises and extensive pleasures. To see an ***empty fishpond***, proclaims the near approach of deadly enemies.

For a young woman to fall into a ***clear pond***, omens decided good fortune and reciprocal love. If muddy, the opposite is foretold. ◎

GOLDFISH

To dream of ***goldfish***, is prognostic of many successful and pleasant adventures. For a young woman, this dream is indicative of a wealthy union with a pleasing man. If the ***goldfish are sick*** or dead, heavy disappointments will fall upon her ◎

Salmon and Trout

SALMON

Dreaming of ***salmon***, denotes that much good luck and pleasant duties will employ your time.

For a young woman to eat it, foretells that she will marry a cheerful man, with means to keep her comfortable. ◎

TROUT

To dream of seeing ***trout***, is significant of growing prosperity. To eat some, denotes that you will be happily conditioned.

To catch one with a hook, foretells assured pleasure and competence. If it falls back into the water, you will have a short season of happiness.

To catch them with a seine [a type of net], is a sign of unparalleled prosperity.

To see them in muddy water, shows that your success in love will bring you to grief and disappointments. ◎

FISH *see* **WATER** *page 78*, **ANGLING** *page 174*, **FISH AND SHELLFISH** *page 136* ◆ **FISHERMAN, FISHHOOKS** *see* **ANGLING** *page 174* ◆ **FISHNET** *see* **ANGLING** *page 174*, **NET** *page 185* ◆ **FISHPOND** *see* **POND , WATER** *page 78* ◆ **SALMON** *see* **FISH AND SHELLFISH** *page 136* ◆ **TROUT** *see* **FISH AND SHELLFISH** *page 136*, **ANGLING** *page 174*, **WATER** *page 78*

Slippery Customers

EEL
To dream of an ***eel*** is good if you can maintain your grip on him. Otherwise fortune will be fleeting.

To see an eel in clear water, denotes, for a woman, new but evanescent pleasures.

To see a ***dead eel***, signifies that you will overcome your most maliciously inclined enemies. To lovers, the dream denotes an end to long and hazardous courtship by marriage. ◎

HERRING
To dream of seeing ***herring***, indicates a tight squeeze to escape financial embarrassment, but you will have success later. ◎

Fierce Fish

NEEDLEFISH
To dream of a ***needlefish***, portends a troubled relationship with friends without knowing the causes for the disturbance.

To ***catch a needlefish***, foretells the overcoming of a difficulty that is holding you back. To ***eat a needlefish***, signifies that you have overcome this difficulty. ◎

SHARK
To dream of a ***shark***, denotes formidable enemies.

To see a ***shark pursuing and attacking you***, denotes that unavoidable reverses will sink you into despondent foreboding.

To see them sporting in clear water, foretells that while you are basking in the sunshine of women and prosperity, jealousy is secretly but surely working you disquiet and unhappy fortune.

To see a dead one, denotes reconciliation and renewed prosperity. ◎

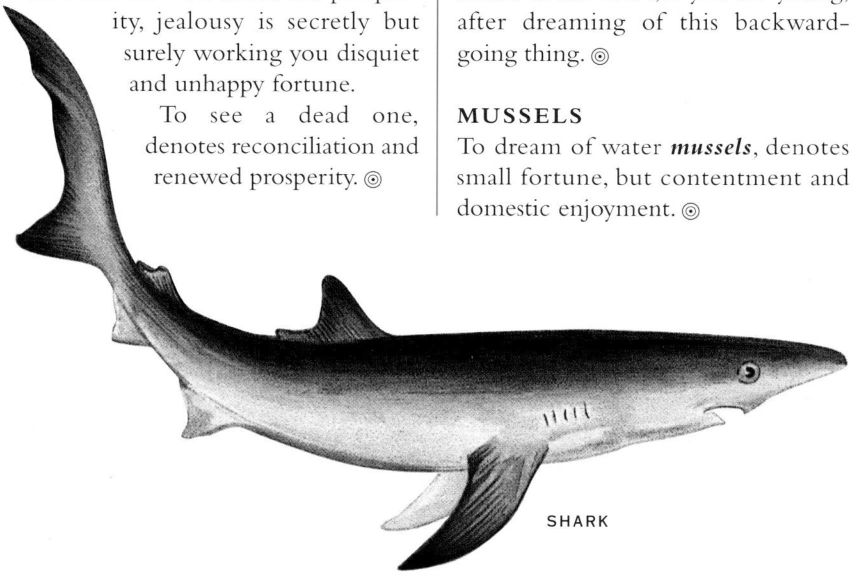

SHARK

Shellfish

CRABS
To dream of ***crabs***, indicates that you will have many complicated affairs, for the solving of which you will be forced to exert the soundest judgement. This dream portends to lovers a long and difficult courtship. ◎

CRAWFISH
Deceit is sure to assail you in your affairs of the heart, if you are young, after dreaming of this backward-going thing. ◎

MUSSELS
To dream of water ***mussels***, denotes small fortune, but contentment and domestic enjoyment. ◎

Sea Mammals

WHALE

DOLPHIN
To dream of a *dolphin*, ***indicates your liability to come under a new government. It is not a very good dream.***

PORPOISE
To see a *porpoise* ***in your dreams, denotes that enemies are thrusting your interest aside, through your own inability to keep people interested in you.***

WHALE
To dream of seeing a *whale* ***approaching a ship, denotes that you will have a struggle between duties, and will be threatened with loss of property.***

If the *whale is demolished*, ***you will happily decide between right and inclination, and will encounter pleasing successes.***

If you see a *whale overturn a ship*, ***you will be thrown into a whirlpool of disasters.***

NEEDLEFISH *see* **ANGLING** *page 174*, **FISH AND SHELLFISH** *page 136*, **WATER** *page 78* ◆
CRABS, MUSSELS *see* **FISH AND SHELLFISH** *page 136* ◆ **WHALE** *see* **SHIP** *page 226*

Reptiles and Serpents

REPTILES
If a ***reptile*** attacks you in a dream, there will be trouble of a serious nature ahead of you. If you succeed in killing it, you will finally overcome obstacles.

To see a ***dead reptile*** come to life, denotes that disputes and disagreements, which were thought to be settled, will be renewed and pushed with bitter animosity.

To handle them without harm to yourself, foretells that you will be oppressed by the ill humor and bitterness of friends, but you will succeed in restoring pleasant relations.

For a young woman to see ***various kinds of reptiles***, she will have many conflicting troubles. Her lover will develop fancies for others. If she is bitten by any of them, she will be superseded by a rival. ◎

SERPENTS
To dream of ***serpents***, is indicative of cultivated morbidity and depressed surroundings. There is usually a disappointment after this dream. ◎

Loathly Worms

WORMS
To dream of ***worms***, denotes that you will be oppressed by the low intriguing of disreputable persons.

For a young woman to dream they crawl on her, foretells that her aspirations will always tend to the material. If she kills or throws them off, she will shake loose from material lethargy and live in morality and spirituality.

To use them in your dreams as ***fish bait***, foretells that by your ingenuity, you will use your enemies to good advantage. ◎

Poisonous Snakes

VIPER
To dream of a ***viper***, foretells that calamities are threatening you.

To dream that a many-hued viper, capable of throwing itself into many pieces or unjointing itself, attacks you, denotes that your enemies are bent on your ruin and will work unitedly, yet apart, to displace you. ◎

BOA CONSTRICTOR
To dream of this, is just about the same as to dream of the devil; it indicates stormy times and much bad fortune. Disenchantment with humanity will follow. To kill a ***boa constrictor*** is good. ◎

ASP
This is an unfortunate dream. Females may lose the respect of honorable and virtuous people. Deadly enemies are at work to defame character. Sweethearts will wrong each other. ◎

Dreams of crabs *opposite left*, **sharks** *opposite bottom*, **and whales** *opposite right* **have their own specific explanation. Dreams of snakes and reptiles are very powerful; to dream of an asp** *right* **brings as much bad luck as it did in reality to the ill-fated Egyptian queen, Cleopatra.**

ADDER
To dream that you see an ***adder*** strike, and a friend, who is dead but seems to be lying down and breathing, rises partly to a sitting position when the adder strikes at him, and then both disappear into some bushes nearby, denotes that you will be greatly distressed over the ill luck of friends, and a loss threatened to yourself.

For a young woman to see an adder, foretells that a deceitful person is going to cause her trouble. If the adder runs from her, she will be able successfully to defend her character in attacks made on her. ◎

CLEOPATRA AND THE ASP

WORMS *see* **FISH** *page 51*, **ANGLING** *page 174* ◆ **VIPER, BOA CONSTRICTOR, ASP, ADDER** *see* **SNAKE DREAMS** *page 54* ◆
BOA CONSTRICTOR *see* **DEVIL** *page 279* ◆ **ADDER** *see* **FRIEND** *page 124*, **DEAD** *page 120*

Snake Dreams

For a woman to dream that a dead ***snake*** is biting her, foretells that she will suffer from malice of a pretended friend.

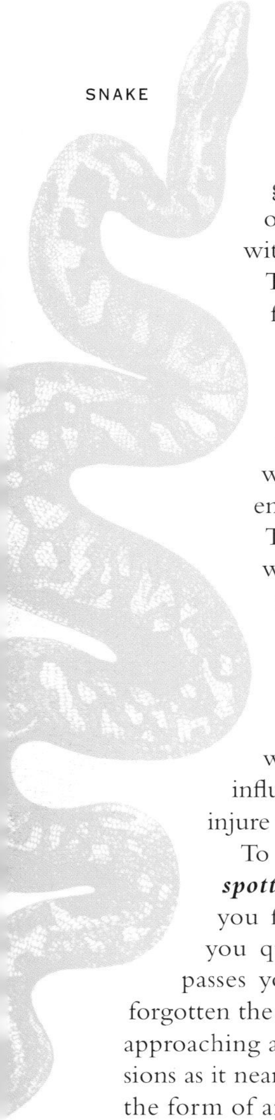

SNAKE

To dream of ***snakes***, is a foreboding of evil in its various forms and stages.

To see them wriggling and falling over others, foretells struggles with fortune and remorse. To kill them, you will feel that you have used every opportunity of advancing your own interests or of respecting those of others. You will enjoy victory over enemies.

To walk over them, you will live in constant fear of sickness, and selfish persons will seek to usurp your place in your companion's life.

If they bite you, you will succumb to evil influences and enemies will injure your business.

To dream that a ***common spotted snake*** approaches you from green herbs, and you quickly step aside as it passes you, and after you had forgotten the incident to again see it approaching and growing in dimensions as it nears you, finally taking on the form of an enormous serpent; if you then, after frantic efforts, succeed in escaping its attack, and altogether lose sight of it, it foretells that you will soon imagine that you are being disobeyed and slighted, and things will go from bad to worse. Sickness, uneasiness, and unkindness will increase to frightful proportions in your mind; but they will adjust themselves to a normal basis, and by putting aside imaginary trouble and masterfully shouldering duties, you will be contended and repaid.

To dream that a ***snake coils itself*** around you and darts its tongue out at you, is a sign that you will be placed in a position where you will be powerless in the hands of enemies, and you will be attacked with sickness.

To dream that you ***handle snakes***, you will use strategy to aid in overthrowing opposition.

To dream that you see ***hairs turn into snakes***, foretells that seemingly insignificant incidents will make distressing cares for you.

If snakes turn into unnatural shapes, you will have troubles which will be dispelled if treated with indifference, calmness, and will power.

To see or ***step on snakes*** while wading or bathing, denotes that there will be trouble where unalloyed pleasure was anticipated.

To see them bite others, foretells that some friend will be injured and criticized by you.

To see ***little snakes***, denotes that you will entertain persons with friendly hospitality who will secretly defame you and work to overthrow your growing prospects.

MENACED BY A SNAKE

ALLIGATOR AND SNAKE

To see children playing with them, is a sign that you will be nonplussed to distinguish your friends from your enemies. For a woman to think that a child places one on the back of her head, and she hears the snake's hisses, foretells that she will be persuaded to yield up some possession seemingly for her good, but she will find out later that she has been inveigled into an intrigue in which enemies will tantalize her.

To see ***snakes raising up their heads*** in a path just behind your friend, denotes that you will discover a conspiracy which has been formed to injure your friend, and also yourself. To think that your friend has them under control, denotes that some powerful agency will be employed in your favor to ward off evil influences.

For a woman to ***hypnotize a snake***, denotes that your rights will be assailed, but you will be protected by law and influential friends. ◎

Snakes and reptiles slither through many dreams; they may even appear together *above*. **Dreams of snakes and reptiles are as many and varied as their interpretations; you may observe snakes from afar** *far left* **or find yourself uncomfortably close to one** *left*; **and crocodiles** *opposite* **may gnash their menacing teeth in fierce warning.**

SNAKE DREAMS *see also* **VIPER, BOA CONSTRICTOR, ASP, ADDER** *page 53,* **BITE** *page 112,* **SERPENTS** *page 53,* **HAIR** *page 102,* **METAMORPHOSIS** *page 275,* **WADING** *page 268,* **CHILDREN** *page 128,* **HISSING** *page 276,* **FRIEND** *page 124,* **HYPNOTIST** *page 170*

Frogs and Toads

FROGS

To dream of catching ***frogs***, denotes carelessness in watching after your health, which may cause no little distress among those of your family.

To see frogs in the grass, denotes that you will have a pleasant and even-tempered friend as your confidant.

To see a ***bullfrog***, denotes, for a woman, marriage with a wealthy widower, but there will be children with him to be cared for.

To see ***frogs in low marshy places***, foretells trouble, but you will overcome it by the kindness of others.

To dream of ***eating frogs***, signifies fleeting joys and very little gain from associating with some people.

To ***hear frogs***, portends that you will go on a visit to friends, but it will in the end prove fruitless of good. ◎

TOAD

To dream of ***toads***, signifies unfortunate adventures. If you are a woman, your good name is threatened with scandal.

To ***kill a toad***, foretells that your judgement will be harshly criticized.

To put your hands on them, you will be instrumental in causing the downfall of a friend. ◎

TADPOLE

To dream of ***tadpoles***, foretells that uncertain speculation will bring cause for uneasiness in business.

For a young woman to see them in clear water, foretells that she will form a relationship with a wealthy but immoral man. ◎

Deadly Reptiles

CROCODILE

As sure as you dream of this creature, you will be deceived by your warmest friends. Enemies will assail you at every turn.

To dream of stepping on a ***crocodile's*** back, you may expect to fall into trouble, from which you will have to struggle mightily to extricate yourself. Heed their warning when dreams of this nature visit you. Avoid giving your confidence even to friends. ◎

ALLIGATOR

To dream of an ***alligator***, unless you kill it, is unfavorable to all persons connected with the dream. It is a dream of caution. ◎

CROCODILE

Slow Movers

SNAIL

To dream that you see ***Snails*** crawling in your dream, signifies that unhealthful conditions are surrounding you.

To step on them, denotes that you will come in contact with disagreeable people. ◎

TURTLE

To dream of seeing ***turtles***, signifies that an unusual incident will cause your enjoyment and improve your business conditions.

To drink ***turtle soup***, denotes that you will find pleasure in compromising intrigue. ◎

Chameleons and Lizards

CHAMELEON

To dream of seeing your sweetheart wearing a ***chameleon*** chained to her, shows that she will prove faithless to you if by changing she can better her fortune. Ordinarily, chameleons signify deceit and self advancement, even though others suffer. ◎

LIZARD

To dream of ***lizards***, foretells attacks upon you by enemies.

If you ***kill a lizard***, you will regain your lost reputation or fortune; but if it should escape, you will meet vexations and crosses in love and business.

For a woman to dream that a ***lizard crawls up her skirt***, or scratches her, she will have much misfortune and sorrow. Her husband will be a victim to invalidism and she will be left a widow, and a little sustenance will be eked out by her own labors. ◎

FROGS *see* GRASS *page 56* ◆ MARSH *page 90* ◆ EATING *page 133* ◆ TADPOLE *see* WATER *page 78* ◆
TURTLE *see* SOUP *page 135* ◆ LIZARD *see* SCRATCH *page 112*

Greenery and Vegetation

Just as characters in dreams change their roles, so does the dream landscape change nightly. This section covers the vegetable factor: green dreams in the green shade of a domestic garden and its glorious flowerbeds; the symmetrical elegance of a landscaped park; the sunny certainties of the farm at harvest time; and the mysterious allure of trees and forests .

Parks and Gardens

PARK

To dream of walking through a well-kept ***park***, denotes enjoyable leisure. If you walk with your lover, you will be comfortably and happily married.

Ill-kept parks, devoid of green grasses and foliage, are ominous of unexpected reverses. ◎

BRIGHT LEAVES

GARDEN

To see a ***garden*** in your dreams, filled with evergreen and flowers, denotes great peace of mind and comfort.

To see ***vegetables***, denotes misery or loss of fortune and calumny. To females, this dream foretells that they will be famous, or exceedingly happy in domestic circles.

To dream of walking with one's lover through a garden where flowering shrubs and plants abound, indicates unalloyed happiness and independent means. ◎

LUSH GREENERY

Grass and Lawns

GRASS

This is a very propitious dream indeed. It gives promise of a happy and well-advanced life to the tradesman, rapid accumulation of wealth, fame to literary and artistic people, and, to all lovers, a safe voyage through the turbulent sea of love.

To see a rugged mountain beyond the ***green expanse of grass***, is momentous of remote trouble.

If in passing through ***green grass***, you pass withered places, it denotes sickness or business embarrassments.

To be a perfect dream, the grass must be clear of obstruction or blemishes. If you dream of ***withered grass***, the reverse is predicted. ◎

LAWNS

To dream of walking upon well-kept ***lawns,*** denotes occasions for joy and great prosperity.

To join a merry party upon a lawn, denotes many secular amusements, and business engagements.

For a young woman to wait upon a ***green lawn*** for the coming of a friend or lover, denotes that her most ardent wishes concerning wealth and marriage will be gratified. If the grass be dead and the ***lawn marshy***, quarrels and separation may be expected.

If you see serpents crawling in the grass before you, betrayal and cruel insinuations will fill you with despair. ◎

LAWN MOWER

To dream of using a ***lawn mower***, means that you will soon engage in a tedious social function. ◎

GARDEN *see* EVERGREEN *page 66* ◆ FLOWERS *page 57* ◆ VEGETABLES *page 137* ◆ LAWN *see* PARTY *page 85* ◆ FRIEND *page 124* ◆ MARSH *page 90* ◆ SERPENTS *page 53* ◆ GRASS *see* MOUNTAIN *page 90*

A SUMMER GARDEN

Garden Tasks and Tools

RAKE

To dream of using a ***rake***, portends that some work which you have left to others will never be accomplished unless you superintend it yourself.

To see a ***broken rake***, denotes that sickness or some accident will bring failure to your plans.

To see ***others raking***, foretells that you will rejoice in the fortunate condition of others. ◎

HOE

To dream of seeing a ***hoe***, denotes that you will have no time for idle pleasures, as there will be others depending upon your work for subsistence.

To dream of ***using a hoe***, indicates that you will enjoy freedom from poverty by directing your energy into safe channels.

For a woman to dream of hoeing, she will be independent of others, as she will be self-supporting.

For lovers, this dream is a sign of faithfulness.

To dream of a foe ***striking at you with a hoe***, foretells that your interest will be threatened by enemies, but with caution you will keep aloof from real danger. ◎

WEEDING

To dream that you are ***weeding***, foretells that you will have difficulty in proceeding with some work which will bring you distinction.

To see ***others weeding***, you will be fearful that enemies will upset your plans. ◎

SPADE

To dream of a kind of shovel called a ***spade***, denotes that you will have work to complete, which will give you much annoyance in the superintending of it. ◎

TROWEL

To dream of a ***trowel***, denotes that you will experience reaction in unfavorable business, and will vanquish poverty.

To see one rusty or broken, unavoidable ill luck is fast approaching you. ◎

A Bouquet of Flowers

FLOWERS

Held in slumber's soft embrace,
She enters realms of flowery grace,
Where tender love and fond caress,
Bids her awake to happiness.

To dream of seeing ***flowers*** blooming in gardens, signifies pleasure and gain, if bright-hued and fresh; white denotes sadness. ***Withered and dead flowers***, signify disappointment and gloomy situations.

For a young woman to receive a ***bouquet of mixed flowers***, foretells that she will have many admirers.

To see the graves or caskets of the dead decorated with ***white flowers***, is unfavorable to pleasure and worldly pursuits.

To see ***flowers blooming*** in barren soil without vestige of foliage, foretells some grievous experience, but your energy and cheerfulness will enable you to climb through these to prominence and happiness. ◎

BOUQUET

To dream of a ***bouque***t beautifully and richly colored, denotes a legacy from some wealthy and unknown relative; also pleasant, joyous gatherings among young folks.

To see a ***withered bouquet***, signifies sickness and death. ◎

WREATH

To dream that you see a ***wreath*** of fresh flowers, denotes that great opportunities for enriching yourself will soon present themselves.

A ***withered wreath***, bears sickness and wounded love.

To see a ***bridal wreath***, foretells a happy ending to uncertain engagements. ◎

Dreams of plants and gardens are usually pleasant and foreshadow agreeable events. You may dream of a lush, jungle-like landscape *opposite* **or a cottage garden in the summer** *above*.

RAKE *see* **BREAK** *page 265* ◆ **SPADE** *see* **CARDS** *page 176* ◆ **TROWEL** *see* **RUST** *page 255* ◆ **FLOWERS** *see* **GRAVE** *page 122* ◆ **WREATH** *see* **WEDDING CLOTHES** *page 131*

Roses all the Way

ROSES
To dream of seeing ***roses***, blooming and fragrant, denotes that some joyful occasion is nearing, and that you will possess the faithful love of your sweetheart.

For a young woman to dream of ***gathering roses***, shows that she will soon have an offer of marriage, which will be much to her liking.

Withered roses, signify the absence of loved ones.

White roses, if seen without sunshine or dew, denotes serious if not fatal illness.

To inhale their fragrance, brings unalloyed pleasure.

For a young woman to dream of ***banks of roses***, and that she is gathering and tying them into bouquets, signifies that she will be made very happy by the offering of some person whom she regards very highly. ◎

DAMASK ROSE
To dream of seeing a ***damask rosebush*** in full foliage and bloom, denotes that a wedding will soon take place in your family, and that great hopes will soon be fulfilled.

For a lover to place ***this rose in your hair***, foretells that you will be deceived. If a woman receives a ***bouquet of damask roses*** in springtime, she will have a faithful lover, but if she receives them in winter, she will cherish blasted hopes. ◎

ROSEBUSH
To see a ***rosebush*** in foliage but no blossoms, denotes that prosperous circumstances are enclosing you. To see a ***dead rosebush***, foretells misfortune and sickness for you or relatives. ◎

BUSH AND RAMBLING ROSES

TENDING FLOWERS

Scented Blossoms

JASMINE
To dream of ***jasmine***, denotes that you are approximating some exquisite pleasure, but that it will be but a fleeting joy. ◎

HONEYSUCKLE
To see or gather ***honeysuckles***, denotes that you will be contentedly prosperous and your marriage will be a singularly happy one. ◎

DAHLIA
To see ***dahlias*** in a dream, if they are fresh and bright, signifies good fortune to the dreamer. ◎

Beautiful scented flowers may be lovely in real life but often carry unfortunate omens in your dreams. You may dream of specific flowers such as roses *left* **or of garden tasks** *above.*

ROSES *see* **PERFUME** *page 98,* **BOUQUET** *page 57* ◆ **DAMASK ROSE** *see* **HAIR** *page 102,* **BOUQUET** *page 57*

Garden Blooms

CHRYSANTHEMUM
To dream that you gather white ***chrysanthemums***, signifies loss and much perplexity; colored ones, betoken pleasant engagements.

To see them in bouquets, denotes that love will be offered you, but that a foolish ambition will cause you to put it aside.

To pass down an avenue of ***white chrysanthemums***, with here and there a yellow one showing among the white, foretells a strange sense of loss and sadness, from which the sensibilities will expand and take on new powers.

If, while looking on these white flowers as you pass, you suddenly feel your spirit leave your body and a voice shouts aloud, "Glory to God, my Creator," it foretells that a crisis is pending in your near future. If some of your friends pass out, and others take up true ideas in connection with spiritual and earthly needs, you will enjoy life in its deepest meaning. Often death is near you in these dreams. ◎

LILY
To dream of a ***lily,*** denotes much chastisement through illness and death.

To see ***lilies growing*** with their rich foliage, denotes early marriage to the young and subsequent separation through death.

To see little children among the flowers, indicates sickness and fragile constitutions to these little ones.

For a young woman to dream of admiring or ***gathering lilies***, denotes much sadness coupled with joy, as the one she loves will have great physical suffering, if not an early dissolution. If she sees them withered, sorrow is even nearer than she could have suspected.

To dream that you breathe the ***fragrance of lilies***, denotes that sorrow will purify and enhance your mental qualities. ◎

WATER LILY
To dream of a ***water lily***, or to see them growing, foretells there will be a close commingling of prosperity and sorrow or bereavement. ◎

MYRTLE
To see ***myrtle*** in foliage and bloom in your dream, denotes that your desires will be gratified, and pleasures will possess you.

For a young woman to dream of wearing a ***sprig of myrtle***, foretells to her an early marriage with a well-to-do and intelligent man.

To see it withered, denotes that she will miss happiness through careless conduct. ◎

HYACINTH
If you dream that you see or gather ***hyacinths***, this indicates that you are about to undergo a painful separation from a friend; however, this will ultimately result in good for you. ◎

Daisies and Dandelions

DAISY
To dream of a bunch of daisies, ***implies sadness; but if you dream of being in a field where these lovely flowers are in bloom, with the sun shining and birds singing, happiness, health, and prosperity will vie each with the other to lead you through the pleasantest avenues of life.***

To dream of seeing them off season, you will be assailed by evil in some guise.

DANDELION
Dandelions ***blossoming in green foliage, foretell happy unions and prosperous surroundings.***

Country Flowers

POPPIES
Poppies seen in dreams, represent a season of seductive pleasures and flattering business, but they all occupy unstable foundations.

If you inhale the odor of one, you will be the victim of artful persuasions and flattery. ◎

VIOLETS
To see ***violets*** in your dreams or to dream that you are gathering them, brings joyous occasions in your life in which you will find favour with some superior person.

For a young woman to gather them, denotes that she will soon meet her future husband.

To see them dry or withered, denotes that her love will be scorned and thrown aside. ◎

MARIGOLD
To dream of seeing ***marigolds***, denotes that contentment with frugality should be your aim. ◎

PRIMROSE
To dream of this little flower starring the grass at your feet, is an omen of joys laden with comfort and peace. ◎

COWSLIPS
To dream of gathering ***cowslips***, portends an unhappy ending of seemingly close and warm friendships; but seeing them growing, denotes a limited competency for lovers. This is a sinister dream.

To see them in full bloom, denotes a crisis in your affairs. The breaking up of happy homes may follow this dream. ◎

CHRYSANTHEMUM *see* **BOUQUET** *page 57,* **GOLD** *page 71* ◆ **LILY** *see* **CHILDREN** *page 128,* **PERFUME** *page 98* ◆
POPPIES *see* **ODOR** *page 98* ◆ **VIOLETS** *see* **HUSBAND** *page 132* ◆ **PRIMROSE** *see* **GRASS** *page 56* ◆ **DAISIES** *see* **FIELDS** *page 60*

Dreams of life on the farm reflect both the idyllic aspect and the sheer hard work necessary to bring the harvest home. This section explains the significance of the various abundant crops and of the tools, skills and processes necessary to transform fields of swaying corn into grain-stuffed granaries.

On the Farm

FARM

To dream that you are living on a ***farm***, denotes that you will be fortunate in all undertakings.

To dream that you are ***buying a farm***, denotes abundant crops to the farmer, a profitable deal of some kind to the business person, and a safe voyage to travelers and sailors.

If you are ***visiting a farm***, it signifies pleasant associations. ◎

FIELDS

To dream of dead corn or stubble ***fields***, indicates to the dreamer dreary prospects for the future.

To see ***green fields***, or ripe with corn or grain, denotes great abundance and happiness to all classes.

To see newly ***plowed fields***, denotes early rise in wealth and fortunate advancement to places of honor.

To see ***fields freshly harrowed*** and ready for planting, denotes that you are soon to benefit by your endeavor and long struggles for success. ◎

PLOWING THE FIELD

Crops and Cereals

CORN AND CORNFIELDS

To dream of husking pied ears of ***corn***, denotes that you will enjoy varied success and pleasure. To see others gathering corn, foretells that you will rejoice in the prosperity of friends or relatives.

To dream of passing through a green and luxurious ***cornfield***, and seeing full ears hanging heavily, denotes great wealth for the farmer. It denotes fine crops and rich harvest, and harmony in the home. To the young, it promises much happiness and true friends; but to see the ears blasted, denotes disappointments and bereavements.

To see ***young corn*** newly plowed, denotes favor with the powerful and coming success. To see it ripe, denotes fame and wealth. To see it cribbed, signifies that your highest desires will be realized.

To see ***shucked corn***, denotes wealthy combines and unstinted favors.

To dream of ***eating green corn***, denotes harmony among friends and happy unions for the young. ◎

RYE

To see ***rye***, is a dream of good, as prosperity envelops your future in brightest promises.

To see ***coffee made of rye***, denotes that your pleasures will be tempered with sound judgement, and your affairs will be managed without disagreeable friction.

To see stock entering rye fields, denotes that you will be prosperous. ◎

Rich Compost

MANURE

To dream of ***seeing*** *manure, is a favorable omen. Much good will follow the dream. Farmers especially will feel a rise in fortune.* ❋

MANURE

DUNGHILL

To dream of a dunghill, ***you will see profits coming in through the most unexpected sources. To the farmer this is a lucky dream, indicating fine seasons and abundant products from soil and stock. For a young woman, it denotes that she will unknowingly marry a man of great wealth.*** ❋

CLOVER

Walking through fields of fragrant ***clover*** is a propitious dream. It brings all objects desired into the reach of the dreamer. Fine crops are portended for the farmer and wealth for the young. ***Blasted fields of clover*** bring harrowing and regretful sighs.

To dream of clover, foretells that prosperity will soon enfold you. For a young woman to dream of seeing a snake crawling through blossoming clover, foretells that she will be early disappointed in love; and her surroundings will be gloomy and discouraging, though to her friends she seems peculiarly fortunate. ◎

BARLEY FIELD

The dreamer will obtain his highest desires, and every effort will be crowned with success. However, as with anything decay denotes loss. ◎

FIELDS *see* **PLOW** *page 62* ◆ **CORN** *see* **EATING** *page 133* ◆ **RYE** *see* **COFFEE** *page 153*

Wheat and Oats

OATS

WHEAT

To see large fields of growing ***wheat*** in your dreams, denotes that your interest will take on encouraging prospects.

If the ***wheat is ripe***, your fortune will be assured and love will be your joyous companion.

To see large, ***clear grains of wheat*** running through the thresher, foretells that prosperity has opened her portals to the fullest for you.

If you see it in sacks or barrels, your determination to reach the apex of success is soon to be crowned with victory and your love matters will be firmly grounded.

If your granary is not well covered and you see its contents getting wet, it foretells that, while you have amassed a fortune, you have not secured your rights and you will see your interests diminishing by the hand of enemies.

If you rub wheat from the head into your hand and eat it, you will labor hard for success and will obtain and make sure of your rights.

To dream that you climb a steep hill covered with wheat and think you are pulling yourself up by the stalks of wheat, denotes that you will enjoy great prosperity and thus be able to distinguish yourself in any chosen pursuit. ◎

OATS

To dream that ***oats*** hold the vision, portends a variety of good things. The farmer will especially advance in fortune and domestic harmony.

To see ***decayed oats***, foretells that sorrow will displace bright hopes. ◎

Hops and Vines

HOPS

To dream of ***hops***, denotes thrift, energy, and the power to grasp and master almost any business proposition. Hops is a favorable dream to all classes, lovers, and tradesmen. ◎

VINE

To dream of ***vines***, is propitious of success and happiness. Good health is in store for those who see flowering vines. If they are dead, you will fail in some momentous enterprise.

To see ***poisonous vines***, foretells that you will be the victim of a plausible scheme and you will impair your health. ◎

VINEYARD

To dream of a ***vineyard***, denotes favorable speculations and auspicious lovemaking.

To visit a vineyard which is not well kept and is filled with bad odors, denotes that disappointment will overshadow your most sanguine anticipations. ◎

Plantation Crops

CANE

To see ***cane*** growing in your dream, foretells favorable advancement towards fortune. To see it cut, denotes absolute failure in all undertakings. ◎

HEMP

To dream of ***hemp***, denotes success in all undertakings, especially large engagements. For a young woman to dream that some accident befalls her through ***cultivating hemp***, foretells the fatal quarrel and separation from her friend. ◎

HEMP SEED

To see ***hemp seed*** in dreams, denotes the near approach of a deep and continued friendship. To the businessman, is shown favorable opportunity for moneymaking. ◎

You may dream of basic farming tasks such as plowing *opposite bottom,* **or making manure** *opposite top,* **of crops such as oats, or of the annual excitement of the *vendange* or wine harvest** *below.*

GATHERING WINE GRAPES

WHEAT *see* **FIELDS** *page 60,* **GRAIN** *page 62,* **EATING** *page 133,* **HILL** *page 90,* **HOPS** *see* **BEER, BREWING** *page 151* ◆ **VINES** *see* **POISON** *page 247* ◆ **VINEYARD** *see* **ODOR** *page 98*

Plowing the Fields

PLOW
To dream of a ***plow***, signifies unusual success, and affairs will reach a pleasing culmination.

To see ***persons plowing***, denotes activity and advancement in knowledge and fortune.

For a young woman to see her lover plowing, indicates that she will have a noble and wealthy husband. Her joys will be deep and lasting.

To plow yourself, denotes rapid increase in property and joys. ◎

SCYTHE
To dream of a ***scythe***, foretells that accidents or sickness will prevent you from attending to your affairs or making journeys.

An ***old or broken scythe***, implies separation from friends, or failure in some business enterprise. ◎

PITCHFORK
Pitchforks in dreams, denote struggles for betterment of fortune and great laboring, either physically or mentally.

To dream that you are attacked by some person using a pitchfork, implies that you will have personal enemies who would not scruple to harm you. ◎

SCYTHE

Sowing the Seed

SEED
To dream of ***seed***, foretells increasing prosperity, though present indications appear unfavorable. ◎

SOWING
To dream that you are ***sowing*** seed, foretells to the farmer fruitful promises, if he sows in newly plowed soil. ◎

GRAIN
Grain is a most fortunate dream, betokening wealth and happiness. For a young woman, it is a dream of fortune. She will meet wealthy and adoring companions. ◎

Bringing in the Sheaves

HARVEST
To dream of ***harvest*** time, is a forerunner of prosperity and pleasure. If the harvest yields are abundant, the indications are good for country and state, as political machinery will grind to advance all conditions.

A ***poor harvest*** is a sign of small profits. ◎

SHEAVES
To dream of ***sheaves***, denotes joyful occasions. Prosperity holds before you a panorama of delightful events, and fields of enterprise and fortunate gain.

To see others sowing, much business activity is portended, which will bring gain to all. ◎

SHEAVES

Dreams of the harvest usually symbolise fruitful activity in life. You may dream of tools such as the scythe *top center,* **harvesting activities** *below,* **seeing the harvest in** *opposite top,* **or of the results of all the hard work such as golden sheaves** *above.*

CUTTING CORN

PLOW *see* **FIELDS** *page 60* ◆ **GRAIN** *see* **CORN AND CORNFIELDS** *page 60,* **THRESHING** *page 63* ◆
HARVEST *see* **REAPERS, GLEANING, THRESHING, BARN** *page 63*

SEEING THE HARVEST IN

Harvest Home

REAPERS
To dream of seeing ***reapers*** busy at work at their task, denotes prosperity and contentment. If they appear to be going through dried stubble, there will be a lack of good crops, and business will consequently fall off.

To see idle ones, denotes that some discouraging event will come in the midst of prosperity.

To see a broken ***reaping machine***, signifies loss of employment, or disappointment in trades. ◎

GLEANING
To dream that you see ***gleaners*** at work at harvest time, denotes prosperous business and, to the farmer, a bountiful yield of crops.

If you are working with the gleaners, you will come into an estate, after some trouble in establishing rights. For a woman, this dream foretells marriage with a stranger. ◎

THRESHING
To dream of ***threshing*** grain, denotes great advancement in business and happiness among families. But if there is an abundance of straw and little grain, unsuccessful enterprises will be undertaken.

To break down or have an accident while threshing, indicates that you will have some great sorrow in the midst of prosperity. ◎

BARN
If well filled with ripe and matured grain, and perfect ears of corn, with fat stock surrounding it, a ***barn*** is an omen of great prosperity. If empty, the reverse may be expected. ◎

Hay, Straw, and Chaff

HAY
If you dream of mowing ***hay***, you will find much that is good in life, and if you are a farmer, your crops will yield abundantly.

To see fields of ***newly cut hay***, is a sign of unusual prosperity.

If you are hauling and putting hay into barns, your fortune is assured, and you will realize great profit from some enterprise.

To see ***loads of hay*** passing through the street, you will meet influential strangers who will add much to your pleasure.

To ***feed hay to stock***, indicates that you will offer aid to someone who will return the favor with love and advancement to higher states. ◎

STRAW
If you dream of ***straw***, this signifies that your life is threatened with emptiness and failure.

To see ***straw piles burning***, is a signal of prosperous times.

To dream that you feed ***straw to stock***, foretells that you will make poor provisions for those depending upon you. ◎

CHAFF
To see ***chaff***, denotes an empty and fruitless undertaking and ill health causing much anxiety.

For a woman to dream of ***piles of chaff***, portends many hours spent in useless and degrading gossip, bringing her into notoriety and causing her to lose her husband who would otherwise have maintained her without work on her part. ◎

REAPERS *see* **HARVEST** *page 62,* **IDLE** *page 251* ◆ **THRESHING** *see* **GRAIN** *page 62* ◆ **BARN** *see* **GRAIN** *page 62* ◆
HAY *see* **FIELDS** *page 60* ◆ **STRAW** *see* **FIRE** *page 80*

Trees have always been seen as potent symbols in the dreamscape. This section looks at individual specimens, specific groups of trees, and trees and bushes en masse in woods and forests. The use and significance of wood and timber, the harvest of the forest, is also examined.

Forests, Trees, and Wood

FORESTS

To dream that you find yourself in a dense ***forest***, denotes loss in trade, unhappy home influences, and quarrels among families. If you are cold and feel hungry, you will be forced to make a long journey to settle some unpleasant affair.

To see a ***forest of stately trees in foliage***, denotes prosperity and pleasures. To literary people, this dream foretells fame and much appreciation from the public.

A young lady relates the following dream and its fulfillment: "I was in a strange forest of what appeared to be coconut trees, with red and yellow berries growing on them. The ground was covered with blasted leaves, and I could hear them crackle under my feet as I wandered about lost. The next afternoon I received a telegram announcing the death of a dear cousin." ◎

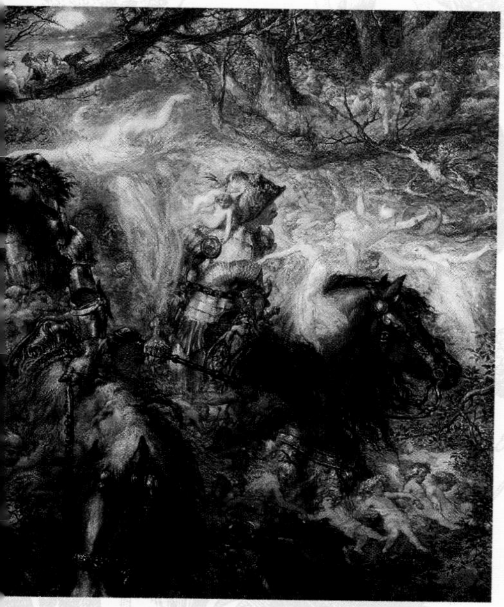

AN ENCHANTED FOREST

TREES

To dream of ***trees*** in new foliage, foretells a happy consummation of hopes and desires. ***Dead trees*** signal sorrow and loss.

To ***climb a tree***, is a sign of swift elevation and preferment.

To cut one down, or pull it up by the roots, denotes that you will waste your energies and wealth foolishly.

To see ***green trees*** newly felled, portends unhappiness coming unexpectedly upon scenes of enjoyment or prosperity. ◎

WOODS

To dream of ***woods***, brings a natural change in your affairs, depending on the nature of the woods. If they appear green, the change will be lucky. If stripped of verdure, it will prove calamitous.

To see ***woods on fire***, denotes that your plans will reach satisfactory maturity. Prosperity will beam with favor upon you.

To dream that you deal in ***firewood***, denotes that you will win fortune by determined struggle. ◎

Root and Branch, Leaf and Blossom

HEDGES

To dream of ***hedges*** of evergreen, denotes joy and profit.

Bare hedges, foretell distress and unwise dealings.

If a young woman dreams of walking beside a ***green hedge*** with her lover, it foretells that her marriage will soon be consummated.

If you dream of being entangled in ***a thorny hedge***, you will be hampered in your business by unruly partners or persons working under you. To lovers, this dream is significant of quarrels and jealousies. ◎

BRANCH

It betokens, if full of fruit and green leaves, wealth and many delightful hours with friends. If they are dried, sorrowful news of the absent. ◎

LEAVES

To dream of ***leaves***, denotes happiness and wonderful improvements in your business.

Withered leaves, indicates that false hopes and gloomy forebodings will harass your spirit into a whirlpool of despondency and loss.

If a young woman dreams of withered leaves, she will be left lonely on the road to conjugality. Death is sometimes implied.

If the leaves are ***green and fresh***, the lucky young woman will come into a legacy and marry a wealthy and prepossessing husband. ◎

BLOSSOMS

To dream of seeing trees and shrubs in ***blossom***, denotes that a time of pleasing prosperity is nearing you. ◎

ROOTS

To dream of seeing ***roots*** of plants or trees, denotes misfortune, as both business and health will go into decline.

To use them as medicine, denotes a warning to you of approaching illness or sorrow. ◎

TREES *see* **CLIMBING** *page 268*, **OAK, WILLOW, PINE TREE, CEDARS, POPLARS, JUNIPER TREE, PALM TREE, BAY TREE** *page 65* ◆ **WOODS** *see* **FIRE** *page 80*, **TIMBER, LUMBER** *page 67* ◆ **HEDGES** *see* **THORNS** *page 67* ◆ **ROOTS** *see* **MEDICINE** *page 116*

Special Trees

OAK

To dream of seeing a forest of ***oak***, signifies great prosperity in all conditions of life.

To see an ***oak full of acorns***, denotes increase and promotion.

If ***blasted oak***, it denotes sudden and shocking surprises.

For sweethearts to dream of oaks, denotes that they will soon begin life together under favorable circumstances. ◎

ACORN

Seeing ***acorns*** in dreams is a portent of pleasant things ahead, and much gain is to be expected.

To pick them from the ground, foretells success after weary labors. For a woman to eat them, denotes that she will rise from a station of labor to a position of ease and pleasure.

To shake them from the trees, denotes that you will rapidly attain your wishes in business or love.

To see ***green-growing acorns***, or to see them scattered over the ground, affairs will change for the better. Decayed or ***blasted acorns*** have import of disappointments and reverses.

To pull them green from the trees, you will injure your interests by haste and indiscretion. ◎

WILLOW

To dream of ***willows***, foretells that you will soon make a sad journey, but you will be consoled in your grief by faithful friends. ◎

PINE TREE

To see a ***pine tree*** in a dream, foretells unvarying success in any undertaking.

Dead pine, for a woman, represents bereavement and cares. ◎

CEDARS

To dream of seeing ***cedars*** green and shapely, denotes pleasing success in an undertaking.

To see them dead or blighted, signifies despair. No object will be attained from seeing them thus. ◎

YEW

YEW TREE

To dream of a ***yew tree***, is a forerunner of illness and disappointment. If a young woman sits under one, she will have many fears to rend her over her fortune and the faithfulness of her lover. If she sees her lover standing by one, she may expect to hear of his illness, or misfortune. To admire one, she will estrange herself from her relatives by a misalliance.

To visit a yew tree and find it dead and stripped of its foliage, predicts a sad death in your family. Property will not console for this loss. ◎

POPLARS

To dream of seeing ***poplars***, is an omen of good, if they are in leaf or bloom.

For a young woman to stand by her lover beneath the blossoms and leaves of a ***tulip poplar***, she will realize her most extravagant hopes. Her lover will be handsome and polished. Wealth and friends will be hers. If they are leafless and withered, she will meet with disappointments. ◎

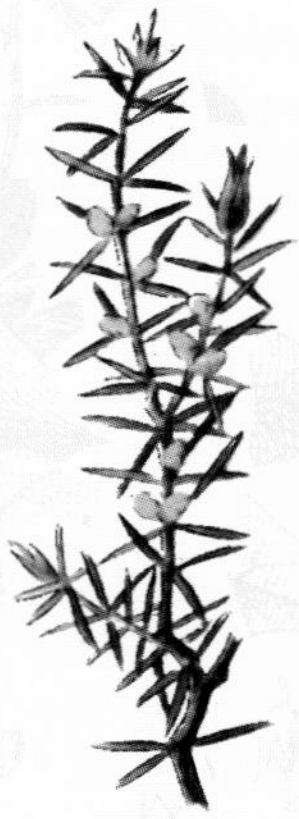

JUNIPER

JUNIPER TREE

To dream of seeing a ***juniper tree***, portends happiness and wealth out of sorrow and depressed conditions. For a young woman, this dream omens a bright future after disappointing love affairs. To the sick, this is an augury of speedy recovery.

To eat or gather the ***berries of a juniper tree***, foretells trouble and sickness. ◎

Palms and Bays

PALM TREE

Palm trees seen in your dreams, are messages of hopeful situations and happiness of a high order.

For a young woman to pass down an ***avenue of palms***, omens a cheerful home and a faithful husband. If the palms are withered, some unexpected sorrowful event will disturb her serenity. ◎

BAY TREE

To dream of a ***bay tree***, a palmy leisure awaits you, in which you will meet many pleasing varieties of diversions. Much knowledge will be repeated in rest from work. It is generally a good dream for everybody. ◎

When you dream of the woods and the trees, you may dream of specific trees such as pine *left*, **yew** *center*, **or juniper** *above*, **or of the mysterious forest in its entirety** *opposite*.

OAK, WILLOW, PINE TREE, CEDARS, POPLARS, JUNIPER TREE, PALM TREE, BAY TREE *see* TREES *page 64* ◆
ACORNS *see* EATING *page 133*, TREES *page 64* ◆ JUNIPER TREE *see* HERBS *page 139*, EATING *page 133*

Evergreens

LAUREL
Dreaming of the ***laurel***, brings success and fame. You will acquire new possessions in love. Enterprises will be laden with gain.

For a young woman to ***wreathe laurel*** about her lover's head denotes that she will have a faithful man, and one of fame to woo her. ◎

MISTLETOE
To dream of ***mistletoe***, foretells happiness and great rejoicing.

To the young, it omens many pleasant pastimes.

If seen with unpromising signs, disappointment will displace pleasure or fortune. ◎

IVY
To dream of seeing ***ivy*** growing on trees or houses, predicts excellent health and increase of fortune. Innumerable joys will succeed this dream. To a young woman, it augurs many prized distinctions. If she sees ivy clinging to the wall in the moonlight, she will have clandestine meetings with young men.

Withered ivy, denotes broken engagements and sadness. ◎

EVERGREEN
This dream denotes boundless resources of wealth, happiness, and learning. It is a free presentiment of prosperity to all classes. ◎

THE MISTLETOE GATHERER

IVY

Mosses and Ferns

MOSS
To dream of ***moss***, denotes that you will fill dependent positions, unless the moss grows in rich soil, when you will be favored with honors. ◎

FERNS
To see ***ferns*** in dreams, foretells that pleasant hours will break up gloomy forebodings.

To see them withered, indicates that much and varied illness in your family connections will cause you grave unrest. ◎

Burrs and Brambles

BRAMBLES
To dream of ***brambles*** entangling you, is a messenger of evil. Lawsuits will go against you, and malignant sickness attack you, or some of your family. ◎

BRIARS
To see yourself caught among ***briars***, forewarns that black enemies are weaving cords of calumny and perjury intricately around you and will cause you great distress; but if you succeed in disengaging yourself from the briars, loyal friends will come to your assistance in every emergency. ◎

BURR
To dream of ***burr***, denotes that you will struggle to free yourself from some unpleasant burden, and will seek a change of surroundings. ◎

LAUREL *see* **WREATH** *page 57* ◆ **IVY** *see* **TREES** *page 64,* **HOUSE** *page 188,* **WALLS** *page 190*

Christmas Greenery

FATHER CHRISTMAS

YULE LOG
To dream of a *yule log,* ***foretells that your joyous anticipations will be realized by your attendance at great festivities.*** ◎

CHRISTMAS TREE
To dream of a Christmas tree, ***denotes joyful occasions and auspicious fortune.***

To see one dismantled, foretells some painful incident following occasions of festivity. ◎

Stings and Pricks

NETTLES
If in your dreams you walk among ***nettles*** without being stung, you will be prosperous.

To be stung by them, you will be discontented with yourself and make others unhappy.

For a young woman to dream of passing through nettles, foretells that she will be offered marriage by different men, and her decision will fill her with anxious foreboding.

To dream of nettles, is portentous of stringent circumstances and disobedience shown to you, either by children or servants. ◎

THORNS
To dream of ***thorns***, is an omen of dissatisfaction, and evil will surround every effort to advancement.

If the thorns are hidden beneath green foliage, your prosperity will be interfered with by secret enemies. ◎

A THORNY PLACE

Working Wood

TIMBER
To see ***timber*** in your dreams, is an augury of prosperous times and peaceful surroundings.

If the timber appears dead, there are great disappointments for you. ◎

LUMBER
To dream of ***lumber***, denotes many difficult tasks, but little remuneration or pleasure.

To see ***piles of lumber*** burning, indicates profit from an unexpected source.

To dream of ***sawing lumber***, denotes unwise transactions in business and unhappiness in general. ◎

STUMPS
To dream of a ***stump***, foretells that you are to have reverses and will depart from your usual mode of living.

To see ***fields of stumps***, signifies that you will be unable to defend yourself from the encroachments of adversity.

To dig or pull them up, is a sign that you will extricate yourself from the environment of poverty by throwing off sentiment and pride, and meeting the realities of life with a determination to overcome whatever opposition you may meet. ◎

WOODPILE
To dream of a ***woodpile***, denotes unsatisfactory business and misunderstandings in love. ◎

STICKS
To dream of ***sticks***, is an unlucky omen. ◎

Sylvan dreams may also include evergreens such as mistletoe *opposite bottom*, **or ivy** *opposite top*. **A dream of thorns** *above* **is as uncomfortable as a bed of such vexatious plants is in reality. Yule logs and Christmas trees** *above left* **always signify good cheer.**

NETTLES *see* **STING** *page 112* ◆ **THORNS** *see* **LEAVES** *page 64* ◆ **LUMBER** *see* **SAW** *page 197* ◆
STUMPS *see* **FIELDS** *page 60*, **DIGGING** *page 193*

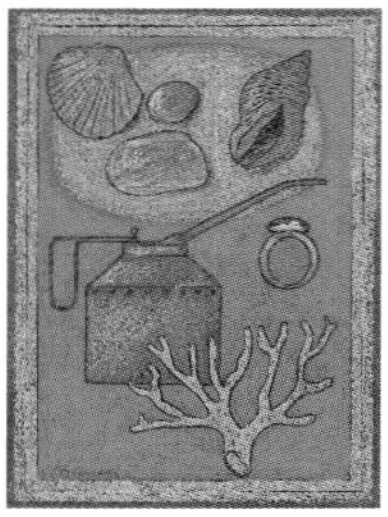

Rocks and Minerals

The Mineral Kingdom also has its place in our dreams. Living rock, burnished metal, cool polished stone all feature as well as more rough-hewn stone and pebbles, industrial elements and chemicals. Glass, which has its own mystery in our waking lives, is also very significant in our dream world.

Rocks and Minerals

MINERAL
To dream of ***minerals***, denotes that your present unpromising outlook will grow directly brighter.

To walk over mineral land, signifies distress, from which you will escape and be bettered in your surroundings. ◎

ROCKS
To dream of ***rocks***, denotes that you will meet reverses, and that there will be discord and general unhappiness.

To climb a ***steep rock***, foretells immediate struggles and disappointing surroundings. ◎

THE STONE BREAKER

Stones, Sand, and Gravel

STONES
To see ***stones*** in your dreams, foretells numberless perplexities and failures.

To walk among rocks or stones, omens that an uneven and rough pathway will be yours for at least awhile.

To make deals in ***ore-bearing rock lands***, you will be successful in business after many lines have been tried. If you fail to profit by the deal, you will have disappointments. If anxiety is greatly felt in closing the trade, you will succeed in buying or selling something that will prove profitable to you.

Small stones or pebbles, imply that little worries and vexations will irritate you.

If you ***throw a stone***, you will have cause to admonish a person.

If you design to ***throw a pebble*** or stone at some belligerent person, it denotes that some evil feared by you will pass because of your untiring attention to right principles. ◎

STONE MASON
To see ***stone masons*** at work while dreaming, foretells disappointment.

To dream that you are a stone mason, portends that your labors will be unfruitful and your companions will be dull and uncongenial. ◎

QUARRY
To dream of being in a ***quarry*** and seeing the workmen busy, denotes that you will advance by hard labor.

An ***idle quarry***, signifies failure, disappointment, and often death. ◎

PEBBLES
For a young woman to dream of a ***pebble***-strewn walk, she will be vexed with many rivals and find that there are others with charms that attract besides her own. She who dreams of pebbles is selfish and should cultivate leniency toward others' faults. ◎

GRAVEL
To dream of ***gravel***, denotes unfruitful schemes and enterprises.

If you see gravel mixed with dirt, it foretells that you will unfortunately speculate and lose good property. ◎

SAND
To dream of ***sand***, is indicative of famine and losses. ◎

POWDER
To see ***powder*** in your dreams, denotes that unscrupulous people are dealing with you. You may detect them through watchfulness. ◎

Dreams of minerals may vary from the solidity of stone *left* to the mysteriously transparent yet distorting power of glass *opposite top*.

ROCKS *see* **CLIMBING** *page 268* ◆ **STONE MASON** *see* **MASON** *page 195* ◆ **GRAVEL** *see* **DIRT** *page 255*

Glass and Crystal

GLASS

To dream that you are looking through ***glass***, denotes that bitter disappointments will cloud your brightest hopes.

To see your ***image in a mirror***, foretells unfaithfulness and neglect in marriage, and fruitless speculations.

To see another face with your own in a mirror, indicates that you are leading a double life. You will deceive your friends.

For a married woman to see her husband in a mirror, is a warning that she will have cause to feel anxiety for her happiness and honor.

If a woman sees men other than husband or lover in a looking glass, she will be discovered in some indiscreet affair that will be humiliating to her and a source of worry to her relations.

For a man to dream of seeing strange women in a mirror, he will ruin his health and business by foolish attachments.

To ***break a mirror***, portends an early and accidental death.

To break ***glass dishes*** or windows, foretells the unfavorable termination to enterprises.

To receive ***cut glass***, denotes that you will be admired for your brilliancy and talent.

To make presents of cut glass ornaments, signifies that you will fail in your undertakings.

To look clearly through a ***glass window***, you will have employment, but will have to work subordinately. If the glass is clouded, you will be unfortunately situated. ◎

GLASS BLOWER

To dream that you see ***glass blowers*** at their work, denotes that you will contemplate change in your business, which will appear for the better, but you will make it at a loss to yourself. ◎

GLASS PANES

PANE OF GLASS

To dream that you handle a ***pane of glass***, denotes that you are dealing in uncertainties. If you break it, your failure will be accentuated.

To talk to a person through a pane of glass, denotes that there are obstacles in your immediate future, and they will cause you no slight inconvenience. ◎

GLASS HOUSE

To see a ***glass house***, foretells that you are likely to be injured by listening to flattery. For a young woman to dream that she is ***living in a glass house***, her coming trouble and threatened loss of reputation is emphasized. ◎

CRYSTAL

This is an unfortunate dream. To dream of ***crystal*** in any form, is a fatal sign of coming depression, either in social relationships or business transactions. Electrical storms often attend this dream, doing damage to town and country.

For a woman to dream of seeing a dining room ***furnished in crystal***, even to the chairs, she will have cause to believe that those whom she holds in high regard no longer deserve this distinction; but she will find out that there were others in the crystal-furnished room who were implicated also in this sinister dream. ◎

GLASS *see* **IMAGE** *page 274,* **MIRROR , FACE** *page 101,* **HUSBAND** *page 132,* **BREAK** *page 265,* **DISHES** *page 209,* **WINDOW** *page 213* ◆
PANE OF GLASS *see* **TALKING** *page 230* ◆ **CRYSTAL** *see* **STORM** *page 76,* **CHAIRS** *page 214*

Ebony, Ivory, Coral, and Shells

EBONY
If you dream of ***ebony*** furniture or other articles of ebony, you will have many distressing disputes and quarrels in your home. ◎

IVORY
To dream of ***ivory***, is favorable to the fortune of the dreamer.

To see huge pieces of ivory being carried, denotes financial success and pleasures unalloyed. ◎

CORAL
To dream of ***coral***, is momentous of enduring friendship that will know no weariness in alleviating your trouble. ***Colored coral*** is meant in this dream.

White coral, foretells unfaithfulness and warning of love. ◎

SHELLS
To walk among and gather ***shells*** in your dream, denotes extravagance. Pleasure will leave you naught but exasperating regrets and memories. ◎

SHELL

UNDERSEA CORAL

Coals and Ashes

COALS
To see bright ***coals*** of fire, denotes pleasure and many pleasant changes.

To dream you handle them yourself, denotes unmitigated joy.

To see ***dead coals***, implies trouble and disappointments. ◎

CHARCOAL
To dream of ***charcoal*** unlighted, denotes miserable situations and bleak unhappiness. If it is burning with glowing coals, there are prospects of great enhancement of fortune and possession of unalloyed joys. ◎

ASHES
Dreaming of ***ashes*** omens woes, and many bitter changes are sure to come to the dreamer. Blasted crops to the farmer. Unsuccessful deals for the trader. Parents will reap the sorrows of wayward children. ◎

SOOT
If you see ***soot*** in your dreams, it means that you will meet with ill success in your affairs. Lovers will be quarrelsome and hard to please. ◎

IVORY *see* **ELEPHANT** *page 29* ◆ **SHELLS** *see* **OYSTER SHELLS** *page 136* ◆ **COALS** *see* **COLLIERY OR COALMINE** *page 195*

DECORATIVE METAL

Noble Stone

JASPER
To dream of seeing ***jasper***, is a happy omen, bringing success and love. For a young woman to ***lose a jasper***, is a sign of disagreement with her lover. ◎

ADAMANT
To dream of ***adamant*** [very hard stone], denotes that you will be troubled and defeated in some desire that you held as your life. ◎

MARBLE
To dream of a ***marble*** quarry, denotes that your life will be a financial success, but that your social surroundings will be devoid of affection.

To dream of ***polishing marble***, you will come into a pleasing inheritance.

To see it broken, you will fall into disfavor among your associates by defying all moral codes. ◎

ALABASTER
To dream of ***alabaster***, foretells success in marriage and all legal affairs.

To break an ***alabaster figure*** or vessel, denotes sorrow and repentance.

For a young woman to lose an ***alabaster box*** containing incense, signifies that she will lose her lover or property through carelessness of her reputation. ◎

Decorative Metal

COPPER
To dream of ***copper***, denotes oppression from those above you in station. ◎

BRASS
To dream of ***brass***, denotes that you will rise rapidly in your profession, but, while rising to an apparently solid elevation, you will secretly fear a downfall of fortune. ◎

PEWTER
To dream of ***pewter***, foretells straitened circumstances. ◎

BRONZE
For a woman to dream of a ***bronze statue***, signifies that she will fail in her efforts to win the person she has determined on for a husband.

If the statue simulates life, or moves, she will be involved in a love affair, but no marriage will occur. Disappointment to some person may follow the dream.

To dream of ***bronze serpents or insects***, foretells that you will be pursued by envy and ruin.

To see ***bronze metals***, denotes that your fortune will be uncertain and unsatisfactory. ◎

Precious Metal

GOLD
If you handle ***gold*** in your dream, you will be unusually successful in all enterprises. For a woman to dream that she receives presents of gold, either money or ornaments, she will marry a wealthy but mercenary man.

To ***find gold***, indicates that your superior abilities will place you easily ahead in the race for honors and wealth.

If you ***lose gold***, you will miss the grandest opportunity of your life through negligence.

To dream of finding a ***gold vein***, denotes that some uneasy honor will be thrust upon you.

If you dream that you contemplate working a ***gold mine***, you will endeavor to usurp the rights of others, and should beware of domestic scandals. ◎

GOLD

SILVER
To dream of ***silver***, is a warning against depending too largely on money for real happiness and contentment.

To find ***silver money***, is indicative of shortcomings in others. Hasty conclusions are too frequently drawn by yourself for your own peace of mind.

To dream of ***silverware***, denotes worries and unsatisfied desires. ◎

Your rocky dreams may include the living beauty of shells *opposite top* **or marine coral** *opposite below*; **dreams of decorative metal** *top left* **and precious metal** *above* **are also frequent.**

MARBLE *see* **QUARRY** *page 68*, **POLISHING** *page 218* ◆ **ALABASTER** *see* **BREAK** *page 265* ◆ **BRONZE** *see* **STATUE** *page 182*, **SERPENTS** *page 53*, **INSECTS** *page 48* ◆ **GOLD** *see* **JEWELRY** *page 162*, **GOLD LEAVES** *page 163*, **COINS** *page 242*, **MONEY** *page 239* ◆ **S'LVER** *see* **COINS** *page 242*

Working Metals

ALLOY
To dream of ***alloy***, denotes that your business will vex you in its complications.

For a woman to dream of alloy, is significant of sorrow and trouble completely hiding pleasure. ◎

ALUMINUM
To dream of ***aluminum***, denotes contentment with any fortune, however small.

For a woman to see her ***aluminum ornaments*** or vessels tarnished, foretells strange and unexpected sorrow and loss will befall her. ◎

IRON
To dream of ***iron***, is a harsh omen of distress.

To feel an ***iron weight*** bearing you down, signifies mental perplexities and material losses.

To ***strike with iron***, denotes selfishness and cruelty to those dependent upon you.

To dream that you ***manufacture iron***, denotes that you will use unjust means to accumulate wealth.

To ***sell iron***, you will have doubtful success, and your friends will not be of noble character.

To see ***old, rusty iron***, signifies poverty and disappointment.

To dream that the ***price of iron*** goes down, you will realize that fortune is a very unsafe factor in your life.

If iron advances, you will see a gleam of hope in a dark prospectus.

To see ***red-hot iron*** in your dreams, denotes failure for you by misapplied energy. ◎

SHEET IRON
To see ***sheet iron*** in your dreams, denotes that you are unfortunately listening to the admonition of others. To walk on it, signifies distasteful engagements. ◎

MOLTEN METAL

LEAD
To dream of ***lead***, foretells poor success in any engagement.

A ***lead mine*** indicates that your friends will look with suspicion on your moneymaking. Your sweetheart will surprise you with her deceit and ill temper.

To dream of ***lead ore***, foretells distress and accidents. Business will assume a gloomy cast.

To ***hunt for lead***, denotes discontentment, and a constant changing of employment.

To ***melt lead***, foretells that by impatience you will bring failure upon yourself and others. ◎

WHITE LEAD
To dream of ***white lead***, denotes that relatives or children are in danger because of your carelessness. Prosperity will be chary of favor.

ZINC
To work with or to see ***zinc*** in your dreams, indicates substantial and energetic progress. Business will assume a brisk tone in its varying departments.

To dream of ***zinc ore***, promises the approach of eventful success. ◎

Liquid Assets

OIL
To dream of anointing with oil, ***foretells events in which you will be the particular moving power.***

Quantities of oil, prognosticate excesses in pleasurable enterprises.

For a man to dream that he deals in oil, ***denotes unsuccessful lovemaking, as he will expect unusual concessions.***

For a woman to dream that she is anointed with oil, ***shows that she will be open to indiscreet advances.*** ✽

TURPENTINE
To dream of turpentine, ***foretells that your near future holds unprofitable and discouraging engagements.***

For a woman to dream that she binds turpentine to the wound of another, shows that she will gain friendships and favor through her benevolent acts. ✽

TAR
If you see tar ***in dreams, it warns you against pitfalls and designs of treacherous enemies.***

To have tar on your hands ***or clothing, denotes sickness and grief.*** ✽

Industrial metals *above* **also have a place in the dream world. Chemicals** *opposite top and bottom* **also trail their vapors across dreams.**

ALUMINUM *see* **ORNAMENT** *page 161* ◆ **IRON** *see* **MANUFACTORY** *page 194,* **RUST** *page 255* ◆
LEAD *see* **MINE AND MINING** *page 195* ◆ **OIL** *see* **SWEET OIL** *page 148* ◆ **TURPENTINE** *see* **WOUND** *page 112* ◆
TAR *see* **HANDS** *page 97,* **CLOTHES** *page 154*

Dangerous Chemicals

ACID

To drink any ***acid*** is an adverse dream, bringing you much anxiety.

For a woman to drink ***acidulous liquors***, denotes that she may ensnare herself with compromising situations; even health may be involved.

To see ***poisonous acids***, means that some treachery against you may be discovered. ◎

VITRIOL

If you see ***vitriol*** [sulphuric acid] in your dreams, it is a token of some innocent person being censured by you.

To throw it on people, shows that you will bear malice towards parties who seek to favor you.

For a young woman to have a jealous rival throw it on her face, foretells that she will be the innocent object to some person's hatred. This dream, for a businessman, denotes enemies and much persecution. ◎

SALTPETER

To dream of ***saltpeter***, denotes that change in your living will add loss to some unconquerable grief. ◎

AMMONIA

Ammonia seen in a dream, means displeasure will be felt by the dreamer at the conduct of a friend. Quarrels and disruptions of friendships will follow this dream.

For a young woman to see ***clear bottles of ammonia***, foretells that she will be deceived in the character and intentions of some person whom she considers friendly. ◎

ALUM

Alum seen in a dream, portends frustration of well-laid plans.

To ***taste alum***, denotes secret remorse over some evil work by you upon some innocent person.

For a woman to dream of quantities of alum, foretells disappointment in her marriage and loss of affection. ◎

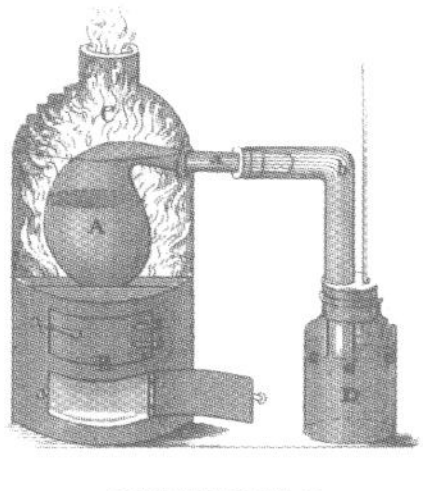

CHEMICALS

PHOSPHORUS

To dream of seeing ***phosphorus***, is indicative of evanescent joys.

For a young woman, it foretells a brilliant but, sadly, brief success with admirers. ◎

SULPHUR

To dream of ***sulphur***, warns you to use much discretion in your dealings, as you are threatened with foul play.

To see ***sulphur burning***, is ominous of great care attendant upon your wealth.

To ***eat sulphur***, indicates good health and consequent pleasure. ◎

MERCURY

To dream of ***mercury***, is significant of unhappy changes through the constant oppression of enemies.

For a woman to be suffering from ***mercurial poisoning***, foretells that she will be deserted by and separated from her family. ◎

Lime

LIME

To dream of ***lime***, foretells that disaster will prostrate you for a time, but you will revive to greater and richer prosperity than before. ◎

LIMEKILN

To dream of a ***limekiln***, foretells that the immediate future holds no favor for speculations in love or business. ◎

THE ALCHEMIST AT WORK

ACID *see* **DRINKING** *page 150,* **POISON** *page 247* ◆ **VITRIOL** *see* **RIVAL** *page 125,* **FACE** *page 101* ◆
AMMONIA *see* **BOTTLE** *page 210* ◆ **SULPHUR** *see* **EATING** *page 133* ◆ **MERCURY** *see* **POISON** *page 247*

Weather and the Elements

This section examines the winds that blow through our dreams and the rain and snow that fall in them. It also looks at the significance of natural disasters caused when wind and rain are unleashed. Fire and water dreams are also examined; water is a very potent symbol and occurs in many shapes and forms in dreams.

Weather and Temperature

WEATHER
To dream of the ***weather***, foretells fluctuating tendencies in fortune. Now you are progressing immensely, to be suddenly confronted with doubts and rumblings of failure.

To think you are reading the reports of a ***weather bureau***, you will change your place of abode after much weary deliberation, but you will be benefited by the change.

To see a ***weather witch***, denotes disagreeable conditions in your family affairs.

To see them conjuring the weather, foretells quarrels in the home and disappointment in business. ◎

BAROMETER
To see a ***barometer*** in a dream, foretells that a change will soon take place in your affairs, which will prove profitable to you.

If it is broken, you will find displeasing incidents in your business, arising unexpectedly. ◎

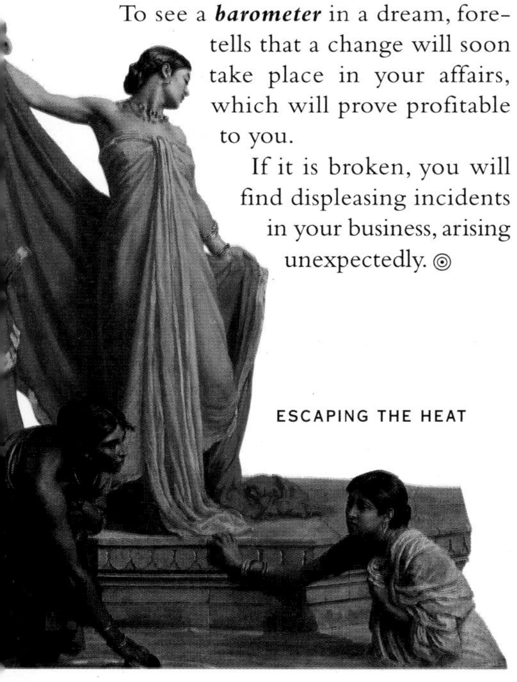

ESCAPING THE HEAT

COLD
To dream of suffering from ***cold***, you are warned to look well to your affairs. There are enemies at work to destroy you. Your health is also menaced. ◎

HEAT
To dream that you are oppressed by ***heat***, denotes failure to carry out designs on account of some friend betraying you. Heat is not a very favorable dream. ◎

The Foggy, Foggy Dew

WET
To dream that you are ***wet***, denotes that a possible pleasure may involve you in loss and disease. You are warned to avoid the blandishments of seemingly well-meaning people.

For a young woman to dream that she is ***soaking wet***, portends that she will be disgracefully implicated in some affair with a married man. ◎

HUMIDITY
To dream that you are overcome with ***humidity***, foretells that you will combat enemies fiercely, but their superior force will submerge you in overwhelming defeat. ◎

CLOUDS
To dream of seeing dark heavy ***clouds***, portends misfortune and bad management. If rain is falling, it denotes trouble and sickness.

To see ***bright transparent clouds*** with the sun shining through them, you will be successful after trouble has been your companion.

To see them with the stars shining, denotes fleeting joys and small advancements. ◎

MIST
To dream that you are enveloped in a ***mist***, denotes uncertain fortunes and domestic happiness. If the mist clears away, your troubles will soon pass.

To see others in a mist, you will profit by the misfortune of others. ◎

FOG
To dream of traveling through a dense ***fog***, denotes much trouble and business worries. To emerge from it, foretells a weary journey, but profitable.

For a young woman to dream of being in a fog, denotes that she will be mixed up in a salacious scandal; but if she gets out of the fog, she will prove her innocence and regain her social standing. ◎

DEW
To feel the ***dew falling*** on you in your dreams, portends that you will be attacked by fever or some malignant disease; but to see the ***dew sparkling*** through the grass in the sunlight, great honors and wealth are about to be heaped upon you. If you are single, a wealthy marriage will soon be your portion. ◎

WEATHER *see* WITCH *page 272* ◆ BAROMETER *see* BREAK *page 265* ◆ WET *see* WATER *page 78,* RAIN *page 75* ◆ CLOUDS *see* SUN, STARS *page 84* ◆ FOG *see* TRAVELING *page 221* ◆ DEW *see* FEVER *page 107,* GRASS *page 56*

The Rainy Season

RAINBOW
To see a ***rainbow*** in a dream, is prognostic of unusual happenings. Affairs will assume a more promising countenance, and crops will give promise of a plentiful yield.

For lovers to see the rainbow, is an omen of much happiness from their union.

To see the rainbow hanging low over green trees, signifies unconditional success in any undertaking. ◎

RAIN
To be out in a clear shower of ***rain***, denotes that pleasure will be enjoyed with the zest of youth, and prosperity will come to you.

If the rain descends from murky clouds, you will feel alarmed over the graveness of your undertakings.

To see and hear rain approaching, and you escape being wet, you will succeed in your plans, and your designs will mature rapidly.

To be sitting in the house and see through the window a ***downpour of rain***, denotes that you will possess fortune, and passionate love will be requited.

To hear the ***patter of rain*** on the roof, denotes a realization of domestic bliss and joy. Fortune will come in a small way.

To dream that your house is leaking during a rain, if the weather is clear, foretells that illicit pleasure will come to you rather unexpectedly, but if it is filthy or muddy, you may expect the reverse, and also exposure.

To find yourself regretting some duty unperformed while ***listening to the rain***, denotes that you will seek pleasure at the expense of another's sense of propriety and justice.

To see it ***rain on others***, foretells that you will exclude friends from your confidence.

For a young woman to dream of getting her clothes wet and soiled while ***out in a rain***, denotes that she will entertain some person indiscreetly, and will suffer the suspicions of friends for the unwise yielding to foolish enjoyments.

To see it raining on farm stock, foretells disappointment in business, and unpleasantness in social circles.

Stormy rains in dreams are always unfortunate. ◎

SHOWER
To dream that you are in a ***shower***, foretells that you will derive exquisite pleasure in the study of creation and the proper placing of selfish pleasures. ◎

PUDDLE
To find yourself stepping into ***puddles*** of clear water in a dream, denotes a vexation, but some redeeming good in the future. If the water be muddy, unpleasantness will go a few rounds with you.

To wet your feet by stepping into puddles, foretells that your pleasure will work you harm afterward. ◎

Air and Wind

AIR
This dream denotes a withering state of things, and bodes no good to the dreamer.

To dream of breathing ***hot air***, suggests that you will be influenced to evil by oppression.

To feel ***cold air*** in your dream, denotes discrepancies in your business affairs, and incompatibility in the sphere of domestic relations.

To feel oppressed with humidity, some curse will fall on you that will prostrate and close down your optimistic views of the future. ◎

ZEPHYR
To dream of soft ***zephyrs*** [soft, gentle breezes], denotes that you will sacrifice fortune to obtain the object of your affection and will find reciprocal affection in your wooing.

If a young woman dreams that she is saddened by the ***whisperings of the zephyrs***, she will have a season of disquietude by the compelled absence of her lover. ◎

WIND
To dream of the ***wind*** blowing softly and sadly upon you, signifies that great fortune will come to you through bereavement.

To hear the ***wind soughing***, denotes that you will wander in estrangement from one whose life is empty without you in it.

To walk briskly against a ***brisk wind***, foretells that you will courageously resist temptations and pursue fortune with a determination not easily put aside.

For the ***wind to blow*** you along against your wishes, portends failure in business undertakings and disappointments in love. If the wind blows you in the direction you wish to go, you will find unexpected and helpful allies, or that you have natural advantages over a rival or competitor. ◎

Calm

To see calm seas, ***denotes the successful ending of a doubtful undertaking.***

To feel calm and happy, is a sign of a long and well-spent life and a vigorous old age. ❋

Heat *opposite* **may be one of the elements affecting your dream climate.**

RAINBOW *see* **TREES** *page 64,* **CLOUDS** *page 74,* **HOUSE** *page 188,* **LEAKING** *page 212,* **WET** *page 74,* **STORM** *page 76* ◆
AIR *see* **HEAT, COLD, HUMIDITY** *page 74* ◆ **ZEPHYR** *see* **WHISPERING** *page 276* ◆ **WIND** *see* **WALKING** *page 267* ◆ **CALM** *see* **SEA** *page 79*

Stormy Weather

GALE
To dream of being caught in a ***gale***, signifies business losses and troubles for working people. ◎

SQUALL
To dream of ***squalls***, foretells disappointing business and unhappiness. ◎

TEMPEST
To dream of ***tempests***, denotes that you will have a siege of calamitous trouble, and friends will treat you with indifference. ◎

THUNDER
To dream of hearing ***thunder***, foretells that you will soon be threatened with reverses in your business.

TAKING SHELTER

To be in a ***thunder shower***, denotes that trouble and grief are close to you.

To hear the terrific ***peals of thunder***, which make the earth quake, portends great loss and disappointment. ◎

STORM
To see and hear a ***storm*** approaching, foretells continued sickness, unfavorable business, and separation from friends, which will cause added distress. If the storm passes, your affliction will not be so heavy. ◎

Lightning Strikes

LIGHTNING
Lightning in your dreams, foreshadows happiness and prosperity of short duration.

THE STORM APPROACHES

If in your dream the ***lightning strikes*** some object near you, and you feel the shock, you will be damaged by the good fortune of a friend, or you may be worried by gossipers and scandalmongers.

To see ***livid lightning*** parting black clouds, omens that sorrow and difficulties will follow close onto fortune.

If it strikes you, this means that unexpected sorrows will overwhelm you in business or love.

To see the ***lightning above your head***, heralds the event of joy and gain.

If you see ***lightning in the south***, fortune will hide herself from you for awhile. If it is in the southwest, luck will come your way. If in the west, your prospects will be brighter than formerly. If in the north, obstacles will have to be removed before your prospects will brighten up. If in the east, you will easily win favors and fortune.

Dreams of lightning from dark and ominous-looking clouds, is always a forerunner of threats of loss and disappointments. Businessmen should stay close to business, and women near their husbands or mothers; children and the sick should be looked after closely. ◎

LIGHTNING ROD
To see a ***lightning rod***, denotes that threatened destruction to some cherished work will confront you.

To see one change into a serpent, foretells that enemies will succeed in their schemes against you.

If the lightning strikes one, there will be an accident or sudden news to give you sorrow.

If you are having one put up, it is a warning to beware how you begin a new enterprise, as you will likely be overtaken by disappointment.

To have them taken down, you will change your plans and thereby further your interests.

To see ***many lightning rods***, indicates a variety of misfortunes. ◎

The climate of dreams has great significance. You may dream of being caught in a rainstorm *above* **or of seeing the dramatic play of lightning** *left;* **in very chilly dreams, you may find yourself ice-skating** *opposite top* **or battling through snowy wastes** *opposite below.*

GALE *see* **WIND** *page 75* ◆ **THUNDER** *see* **SHOWER** *page 75* ◆ **LIGHTNING** *see* **CLOUDS** *page 74,*
LIGHTNING ROD *see* **SERPENT** *page 53*

Ice, Frost, and Snow

ICE SKATING

ICE

To dream of ***ice***, betokens much distress, and evil-minded persons will seek to injure you in your best work.

To see ***ice floating*** in a stream of clear water, denotes that your happiness will be interrupted by ill-tempered and jealous friends.

To dream that you ***walk on ice***, you risk much solid comfort and respect for evanescent joys.

For a young woman to walk on ice, is a warning that only a thin veil hides her from shame.

To dream that you ***make ice***, you will make a failure of your life through egotism and selfishness.

Eating ice, foretells sickness. If you drink ice water, you will bring ill health from dissipation.

Bathing in ***ice water***, denotes that anticipated pleasures will be interrupted with an unforeseen event. ◎

ICICLES

To see ***icicles*** falling from trees, denotes that some distinctive misfortune or trouble will soon vanish.

To see ***icicles*** on the eaves of houses, denotes misery and want of comfort. Ill health is foreboded.

To see icicles on the fence, denotes suffering bodily and mentally.

To see them on trees, forebodes that despondent hopes will grow gloomier.

To see them on evergreens, means that a bright future will be overcast with the shadow of doubtful honors. ◎

FROST

To dream of seeing ***frost*** on a dark gloomy morning, signifies exile to a strange country, but your wanderings will end in peace.

To see frost on a small sunlit landscape, signifies gilded pleasures from which you will be glad to turn later in life, and that by your exemplary conduct, you will succeed in making your circle forget past escapades.

To dream that you see a ***friend in a frost***, denotes a love affair in which your rival will be worsted. For a young woman, this dream signifies the absence of her lover and danger of his waning affections. This dream is bad for all classes in business and love. ◎

HAIL

If you dream of being in a ***hailstorm***, you will meet poor success in any undertaking.

If you watch ***hailstones*** fall through sunshine and rain, you will be harassed by cares for a time, but fortune will soon smile upon you. For a young woman, this dream indicates love after many slights.

To ***hear hail beating*** the house, indicates distressing situations. ◎

SNOW

To see ***snow*** in your dreams, denotes that while you have no real misfortune, there will be the appearance of illness, and unsatisfactory enterprises.

To find yourself in a ***snowstorm***, denotes sorrow and disappointment in failure to enjoy some long expected pleasure. There always follows more or less discouragement after this dream.

If you ***eat snow***, you will fail to realize ideals.

To see ***dirty snow***, foretells that your pride will be humbled, and you will seek reconciliation with some person whom you held in haughty contempt.

If you see it melt, your fears will turn into joy.

To see ***large, white snowflakes*** falling while you are looking through a window, foretells that you will have an angry interview with your sweetheart, and the estrangement will be aggravated by financial depression.

To see ***snow-capped mountains*** in the distance, warns you that your longings and ambitions will bring no worthy advancement.

To see the sun shining through ***landscapes of snow***, foretells that you will conquer adverse fortune and possess yourself of power.

To dream of ***snowballing***, denotes that you will have to struggle with dishonorable issues, and if your judgement is not well grounded, you will suffer defeat.

If ***snowbound*** or lost, there will be constant waves of ill luck breaking in upon you. ◎

THAW

To dream of seeing ice ***thawing***, foretells that some affair which has caused you much worry will soon give you profit and pleasure.

To see the ground thawing after a long freeze, foretells prosperous circumstances. ◎

SNOW CLIMBING

ICE *see* **WALKING** *page 267,* **EATING** *page 133,* **BATH** *page 105* ◆ **ICICLES** *see* **TREES** *page 64,* **HOUSE** *page 188,* **FENCE** *page 191,* **EVERGREEN** *page 66* ◆ **FROST** *see* **MORNING** *page 82,* **FRIEND** *page 124* ◆ **HAIL** *see* **STORM** *page 76,* **HOUSE** *page 188* ◆ **SNOW** *see* **STORM** *page 76,* **EATING** *page 133,* **MOUNTAIN** *page 90,* **SLEIGH** *page 223*

Water

WATER

To dream of ***clear water***, foretells that you will joyfully realize prosperity and pleasure.

If the water is ***muddy***, you will be in danger, and gloom will occupy pleasure's seat.

To see it rise up in your house, denotes that you will struggle to resist evil; but unless you see it subside, you will succumb to dangerous influences.

To find yourself bailing it out, but with feet growing wet, foreshadows that trouble, sickness, and misery will work you a hard task, but you will forestall them by your watchfulness. The same may be applied to muddy water rising in vessels.

To fall into ***muddy water***, is a sign that you will make many bitter mistakes, and will suffer poignant grief therefrom.

To drink muddy water, portends sickness, but drinking it clear and refreshing brings favorable consummation of fair hopes.

To ***sport with water***, denotes a sudden awakening to love and passion.

To have it sprayed on your head, denotes that your passionate awakening to love will meet reciprocal consummation.

The following dream and its allegorical occurrence in actual life is related by a young woman student of dreams:

"Without knowing how, I was (in my dream) on a boat, I waded through clear blue water to a wharf boat, which I found to be snow white, but rough and splintery. The next evening I had a delightful male caller, but he remained beyond the time prescribed by mothers and I was severely censured for it."

In this dream the blue water and fairy white boat were disappointing prospects in the symbol. ◎

WATER CARRIER

To see ***water carriers*** passing in your dreams, denotes that your prospects will be favorable in fortune, and love will prove no laggard in your chase for pleasure.

If you think in your dreams that ***you are a water carrier***, this prognosticates that you will rise above your present position. ◎

Raging Torrents and Calm Waters

FOUNTAIN

To dream that you see a ***clear fountain*** sparkling in the sunlight, denotes vast possessions, ecstatic delights, and many pleasant journeys.

A ***clouded fountain***, denotes the insincerity of associates and unhappy engagements and love affairs.

A ***dry and broken fountain***, indicates death and cessation of pleasures.

For a young woman to seek a ***sparkling fountain*** in the moonlight, signifies ill-advised pleasure which may result in a desertion. ◎

WATERFALL

To dream of a ***waterfall***, foretells that you will secure your wildest desire, and fortune will be exceedingly favorable to your progress. ◎

RAPIDS

To imagine that you are being carried over ***rapids*** in a dream, denotes that you will suffer appalling loss from the neglect of duty and the courting of seductive pleasures. ◎

TORRENT

To dream that you are looking upon a rushing ***torrent***, denotes that you will have unusual trouble and anxiety. ◎

CREEK

To dream of a ***creek***, denotes new experiences and short journeys. If it is overflowing, you will have sharp trouble, but of brief period.

If it is dry, disappointment will be felt by you, and you will see another obtain the things you intrigued to secure. ◎

POND

To see a ***pond*** in your dream, denotes that events will bring no emotion, and fortune will retain a placid outlook.

If the ***pond is muddy***, you will have domestic quarrels. ◎

POND INHABITANTS

LAGOON

To dream of a ***lagoon***, denotes that you will be drawn into a whirlpool of doubt and confusion through misapplication of your intelligence. ◎

CANAL

To see the water of a ***canal*** muddy and stagnant-looking, portends sickness and disorders of the stomach and dark designs of enemies. But if its waters are clear, a placid life and the devotion of friends is before you.

For a young woman to glide in a ***canoe across a canal***, denotes a chaste life and an adoring husband. If she crosses the canal on a bridge over clear water and gathers ferns and other greens on the banks, she will enjoy a life of ceaseless rounds of pleasure and attain to a high social distinction. But if the water be turbid, she will often find herself tangled in meshes of perplexity and will be the victim of nervous troubles. ◎

WATER *see* **HOUSE** *page 188*, **FEET** *page 96*, **WET** *page 74*, **MUD** *page 90*, **HEAT** *page 74* ◆ **FOUNTAIN** *see* **MOON** *page 84* ◆ **POND** *see* **FISHPOND** *page 51*, **MUD** *page 90* ◆ **CANAL** *see* **CANOE** *page 227*, **FERNS** *page 66*, **BRIDGE** *page 192*

Lakes, Rivers, and the Sea

LAKE

For a young woman to dream that she is alone on a turbulent and muddy ***lake***, foretells that many vicissitudes are approaching her, and she will regret former extravagances and disregard of virtuous teaching.

If the water gets into the boat, but by intense struggling she reaches the boathouse safely, it denotes that she will be under wrong persuasion, but will eventually overcome it and rise to honor and distinction. It may predict the illness of someone near her.

If she sees a young couple in the same position as herself, who succeed in rescuing themselves, she will find that some friend has committed indiscretions, but will succeed in reinstating himself in her favor.

To dream of sailing on a ***clear and smooth lake***, with happy and congenial companions, you will have much happiness, and wealth will meet your demands.

A ***muddy lake***, surrounded with bleak rocks and bare trees, denotes unhappy terminations to business and affection.

A muddy lake, surrounded by green trees, portends that the moral in your nature will fortify itself against passionate desires, and overcoming the same will direct your energy into a safe and remunerative channel. If the lake be clear and surrounded by barrenness, a profitable existence will be marred by passionate dissipation.

To see yourself reflected in a ***clear lake***, denotes coming joys and many ardent friends.

To see foliaged trees reflected in the lake, you will enjoy to a satiety love's draught of passion and happiness.

To see slimy and uncanny inhabitants of the lake rise up and menace you, denotes failure and ill health from squandering time, energy, and health on illicit pleasures. You will drain the utmost drop of happiness, and drink deeply of remorse's bitter concoction. ◎

RIVER

If you see a clear, smooth, flowing ***river*** in your dream, you will soon succeed to the enjoyment of delightful pleasures, and prosperity will bear flattering promises.

If the waters are muddy or tumultuous, there will be disagreeable and jealous contentions in your life.

If you are water-bound by the ***overflowing of a river***, there will be temporary embarrassments in your business, or you will suffer uneasiness lest some private escapade will reach public notice and cause your reputation harsh criticisms.

If, while sailing upon a ***clear river***, you see corpses in the bottom, you will find that trouble and gloom will follow swiftly upon present pleasures and fortune.

To see ***empty rivers***, denotes sickness and unusual ill luck. ◎

HIGH TIDE

To dream of ***high tide***, is indicative of favorable progression in your affairs. ◎

WAVES

To dream of ***waves***, is a sign that you hold some vital step in contemplation, which will evolve much knowledge if the waves are clear; but you will make a fatal error if you see them muddy or lashed by a storm. ◎

SEA FOAM

For a woman to dream of ***sea foam***, foretells that indiscriminate and demoralizing pleasures will distract her from the paths of rectitude. If she wears a bridal veil of sea foam, she will engulf herself in material pleasure to the exclusion of true refinement and innate modesty. She will be likely to cause sorrow to some of those dear to her, through their inability to gratify her ambition. ◎

Watery dreams range from the calm of the duckpond *opposite* **to the raging might of the ocean** *above.*

THE SEA

SEA

To dream of hearing the lonely sighing of the ***sea***, foretells that you will be fated to spend a weary and unfruitful life devoid of love and comradeship.

Dreams of the sea, prognosticate unfulfilled anticipations; while pleasures of a material form are enjoyed, there is an inward craving for pleasure that flesh cannot requite.

For a young woman to dream that she glides swiftly over the sea with her lover, means that there will come to her sweet fruition of maidenly hopes, and joy will stand guard at the door of the consummation of changeless marriage vows. ◎

OCEAN

To dream of the ***ocean*** when it is calm, is propitious. The sailor will have a pleasant and profitable voyage. The businessman will enjoy a season of remuneration, and the young man will revel in his sweetheart's charms.

To be ***far out on the ocean***, and hear the waves lash the ship, forebodes disaster in business life, and quarrels and stormy periods in the household.

To be on shore and see the ***waves of the ocean*** foaming against each other, foretells your narrow escape from injury and the designs of enemies.

To dream of seeing the ***ocean so shallow*** as to allow wading or a view of the bottom, signifies prosperity and pleasure with a commingling of sorrow and hardships.

To ***sail on the ocean*** when it is calm, is always propitious. ◎

LAKE *see* **BOAT** *page 226,* **RESCUE** *page 266,* **WATER** *page 78,* **TREES** *page 64* **RIVER** *see* **FLOODS, INUNDATION** *page 81* ◆
SEA FOAM *see* **WEDDING CLOTHES** *page 131* ◆ **OCEAN** *see* **CALM** *page 75,* **SHIP, SAILING** *page 226*

Fire

SMOKE

To dream of ***smoke***, foretells that you will be perplexed with doubts and fears.

To be ***overcome with smoke***, denotes that dangerous persons are victimizing you with flattery. ◎

FIRE

Fire is favorable to the dreamer if he or she does not get burned. Fire experienced in dreams brings continued prosperity to seamen and voyagers, as well as to those on land.

To dream of seeing your ***home burning***, denotes a loving companion, obedient children, and careful servants.

For a businessman to dream that his ***store is burning***, and he is looking on, foretells a great rush in business and profitable results.

To dream that he is ***fighting fire*** and does not get burned, denotes that he will be much worked and worried as to the conduct of his business.

To see the ruins of his store after a fire, forebodes ill luck. He will be almost ready to give up the effort of amassing a handsome fortune and a brilliant business record as useless, but some unforeseen good fortune will bear him up again.

If you dream of ***kindling a fire***, you may expect many pleasant surprises. You will have distant friends to visit.

To see a large ***conflagration***, denotes to sailors a profitable and safe voyage; to men of literary affairs, advancement and honors; to business people, unlimited success. ◎

FLAME

To dream of fighting ***flames,*** foretells that you will have to put forth your best efforts and energy if you are to be successful in amassing wealth. ◎

FIREBRAND

To dream of a ***firebrand***, denotes favorable fortune, if you are not burned or distressed by it. ◎

FIRE DRILL

To dream of a ***fire drill***, denotes disagreement over a financial matter. ◎

FIRE ENGINE

To see a ***fire engine***, denotes worry under extraordinary circumstances, but which will result in good fortune.

To see one broken down, foretells an accident or serious loss.

For a young woman to ride on one, denotes that she will engage in some unladylike and obnoxious affair. ◎

FIREMAN

To see a ***fireman*** in your dreams, signifies the constancy of your friends. For a young woman to see a ***fireman crippled***, or meet with an accident otherwise, implies that grave danger is threatening a close friend. ◎

CONFLAGRATION

To dream of a ***conflagration***, denotes, if no lives are lost, changes in the future which will be beneficial to your interests and happiness. ◎

BURNING

FIRE *see* **HOME** *page 205,* **STORE** *page 203* ◆ **FIREMAN** *see* **CRIPPLED** *page 112*

Natural Disasters

TORNADO AT SEA

TORNADO

If you dream that you are in a tornado, *you will be filled with disappointment and perplexity over the miscarriage of studied plans for swift attainment of fortune*

FLOODS

To dream of a flood *destroying vast areas of country and bearing you on with its muddy debris, denotes sickness, loss in business, and the most unhappy and unsettled situation in the marriage state.*

INUNDATION

To dream of seeing cities or countries submerged in dark, seething waters, denotes great misfortune and loss of life through some dreadful calamity.

To see human beings swept away in an inundation, *portends bereavements and despair, making life gloomy and unprofitable.*

To see a large area inundated with clear water, denotes profit and ease after seemingly hopeless struggles with fortune.

Elemental dreams may include a raging conflagration *opposite* **or a fierce tornado** *above*.

WHIRLPOOL

To dream of a whirlpool, *denotes that great danger is imminent in your business, and unless you are extremely careful, your reputation will be seriously blackened by some disgraceful intrigue.*

WHIRLWIND

To dream that you are in the path of a whirlwind, *foretells that you are confronting a change which threatens to overwhelm you with loss and calamity.*

For a young woman to dream that she is caught in a whirlwind and has trouble to keep her skirts from blowing up and entangling her waist, denotes that she will carry on a secret flirtation and will be horrified to find that scandal has gotten possession of her name, and she will run a close risk of disgrace and ostracism.

EARTHQUAKE

To see or feel the earthquake *in your dream, denotes business failure and much distress from turmoils and wars between nations.*

VOLCANO

To see a volcano *in your dreams, signifies that you will be in violent disputes, which threaten your reputation as a fair-dealing and honest citizen.*

For a young woman to see a volcano in her dreams, it means that her selfishness and greed will lead her into intricate adventures.

HURRICANE

To hear the roar of and see a hurricane *heading toward you with its frightful force, you will undergo torture and suspense, striving to avert failure and ruin in your affairs.*

If you are in a house that is being blown to pieces by a hurricane, and you struggle in the awful gloom to extricate someone from the falling timbers, your life will suffer a change. You will move and remove to distant places, and still find no improvement in domestic or business affairs.

If you dream of looking on debris and havoc wrought by a hurricane, you will come close to trouble, which will be averted by the turn in the affairs of others.

To see people dead and wounded as a result of a hurricane, you will be much distressed over the trouble of others.

DROUGHT

This is an evil dream, denoting warring disputes between nations, and much bloodshed therefrom. Shipwrecks and land disasters will occur, and families will quarrel and separate; sickness will also damage work. Your affairs will go awry as well.

FLOODS *see* **WATER** *page 78* ◆ **INUNDATION** *see* **CITY** *page 220,* **WATER** *page 78* ◆ **WHIRLWIND** *see* **WAIST** *page 94* ◆ **HURRICANE** *see* **STORM** *page 76,* **HOUSE** *page 188,* **DEAD** *page 120*

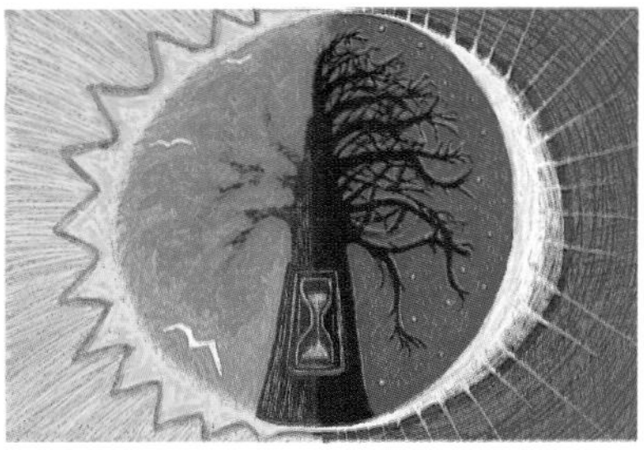

Time and the Seasons

Time also significant in dreams; your dreams may transport you to any time of the day or night, any time of the year; in deepest winter you dream of the hot scents of August; spring nights are chilled by the frosty blasts of January. This section explains the meaning of this, and discusses the dream significance of diaries, clocks, and other time markers.

The Seasons

SPRING

To dream that ***spring*** is advancing, is a sign of fortunate undertakings and cheerful companions.

To dream that you see spring appearing unnaturally, is a foreboding of disquiet and losses. ◎

AUTUMN/FALL

For a woman to dream of ***autumn***, denotes that she will obtain property through the struggles of others.

If she thinks of ***marrying in autumn***, she will make a favorable marriage and have a cheerful home. ◎

WINTER

To dream of ***winter***, is a prognostication of ill health and dreary prospects for the favorable progress of fortune in either business or the domestic sphere. After this dream, your efforts will not yield satisfactory results. ◎

The Time of Day

DAY

To dream of the ***day***, denotes improvements in your situation, and pleasant associations. A gloomy or cloudy day, foretells loss and ill success in new enterprises. ◎

DAYBREAK

To watch the ***daybreak*** in a dream, omens successful undertakings, unless the scene is indistinct and weird; then it may imply disappointment when success in business or love seems assured. ◎

MORNING

To see the ***morning*** dawn clear in your dreams, prognosticates a near approach of fortune and pleasure.

A ***cloudy morning***, portends that weighty affairs will overwhelm you. ◎

AFTERNOON

For a woman to dream of an ***afternoon***, denotes that she will form friendships which will be lasting and entertaining. A ***cloudy, rainy afternoon***, implies disappointment and displeasure. ◎

EVENING

To dream that ***evening*** is about you, denotes unrealized hopes, and you will make unfotunate ventures.

To see stars shining out clear, denotes present distress, but brighter fortune is behind your trouble.

For lovers to ***walk in the evening***, denotes separation by the death of one of them. ◎

EVENING WALK

New Year

To dream of the new year, ***signifies prosperity and connubial anticipations. If you contemplate the new year in weariness, engagements will be entered into auspiciously.*** ✺

Night Thoughts

NIGHT

If you are surrounded by ***night*** in your dreams, you may expect unusual oppression and hardships in business.

If the light seems to be vanishing, conditions which hitherto seemed unfavorable will grow brighter, and your affairs will assume prosperous phases. ◎

DARKNESS

To dream of ***darkness*** overtaking you on a journey, augurs ill for any work you may attempt, unless the sun breaks through before the journey ends; then faults will be overcome.

To dream that you lose your friend or child in the darkness, portends many provocations to wrath. Try to remain under control after dreaming of darkness, for trials in business and love will beset you. ◎

DUSK

This is a dream of sadness; it portends an early decline and unrequited hopes. A dark outlook for trade and pursuits of any nature is prolonged by this dream ◎

AUTUMN *see* **MARRIAGE** *page 130* ◆ **DAY** *see* **CLOUDS** *page 74* ◆ **DAYBREAK** *see* **INDISTINCT** *page 275* ◆ **MORNING** *see* **CLOUDS** *page 74* ◆ **AFTERNOON** *see* **CLOUDS** *page 74*, **RAIN** *page 75* ◆ **EVENING** *see* **STARS** *page 84*, **WALKING** *page 267* ◆ **DARKNESS** *see* **JOURNEY** *page 221*, **FRIEND** *page 124*

A Dream Calendar

JANUARY
To dream of this month, denotes that you will be afflicted with unloved companions or children. ◎

FEBRUARY
To dream of ***February***, denotes continued ill health and gloom, generally. If you happen to see a bright sunshiny day in this month, you will be unexpectedly and happily surprised with some good fortune. ◎

MARCH
To dream of the month of ***March***, portends disappointing returns in business, and some women will be suspicious of your honesty. ◎

APRIL
To dream of the month of ***April***, signifies that much pleasure and profit will be your allotment.

If the weather is miserable, it is a sign of passing ill luck. ◎

MAY
To dream of the month of ***May***, denotes prosperous times, and pleasures for the young.

To dream that nature appears freakish, denotes sudden sorrow and disappointment clouding pleasure. ◎

JUNE
To dream of ***June***, foretells unusual gains in all undertakings.

For a woman to think that vegetation is decaying, or that a drought is devastating the land, she will have sorrow and loss which will be lasting in its effects. ◎

JULY
To dream of this month, denotes that you will be depressed with gloomy outlooks, but, as suddenly, your spirits will rebound to unimagined pleasure and good fortune ◎

Dreams of the evening *opposite* **seems particularly ill omened.**

AUGUST
To dream of the month of ***August***, denotes unfortunate deals, and misunderstandings in love affairs.

For a young woman to dream that she is going to be married in August, is an omen of sorrow in her early wedded life. ◎

SEPTEMBER
To dream of the month of ***September***, portends luck and good fortune. ◎

OCTOBER
To imagine you are in ***October***, is ominous of gratifying success in your undertakings. You will also make new acquaintances which will ripen into lasting friendships. ◎

NOVEMBER
To dream of ***November***, augurs a season of indifferent success in all affairs. ◎

DECEMBER
To dream of ***December***, foretells accumulation of wealth, but loss of friendship. In the affections of some friends, strangers will occupy the position which was formerly held by you. ◎

Tempus Fugit

URGENT
To dream that you are supporting an urgent ***position, is a sign that you will engage in some affair which will need fine financiering to carry it through successfully.***

DELAY
To be delayed ***in a dream, warns you of the scheming of enemies to prevent your progress.***

Marking Time

CLOCK
To dream that you see a ***clock***, denotes danger from a foe.

To hear one strike, you will receive unpleasant news. The death of some friend is implied. ◎

WATCH
To dream of a ***watch***, denotes that you will be prosperous in well-directed speculations.

If you look at the time of one, your efforts will be defeated by rivalry.

If you break one, there will be distress and loss menacing you.

To drop the crystal of one, foretells carelessness or unpleasant companionship.

For a woman to lose one, signifies that domestic disturbances will produce unhappiness.

To imagine you steal one, you will have a violent enemy who will attack your reputation.

To make a present of one, denotes that you will suffer your interest to decline in the pursuance of undignified recreations. ◎

DIARY
To dream of writing a ***diary***, denotes that you will be faulty in your judgement, which will lead to a disastrous outcome.

To dream of ***reading someone else's diary***, denotes that you will soon be reprimanded for an indiscretion. ◎

ALMANAC
To dream of an ***almanac***, means variable fortunes and illusive pleasures.

To be studying the signs, foretells that you will be harassed by small matters taking up your time. ◎

CALENDAR
To dream of keeping a ***calendar***, indicates that you will be very orderly and systematic in your habits throughout the year.

To see a calendar, denotes disappointment in your calculations. ◎

MARCH *see also* **MARCH** *page 168* ◆ **JUNE** *see* **DROUGHT** *page 81* ◆ **AUGUST** *see* **MARRIAGE** *page 130* ◆ **CLOCK** *see* **CHIMES** *page 275* ◆ **WATCH** *see* **BREAK** *page 265*, **STEALING** *page 246*, **GIFT** *see page 240* ◆ **DIARY** *see* **READING** *page 233*, **WRITING** *page 232*

Space, Stars, and Planets

To dream of space and the boundless infinite is at once exhilarating and unnerving. This section explores the major lights, the sun and moon, the stars, planets, and the firmament itself. The moon, an intriguing and powerful object in its own right, appears to exert just as much influence in dreams as it does in reality.

The Sky

SKY
To dream of the ***sky***, signifies distinguished honors and interesting travel with cultured companions, if the sky is clear. Otherwise, it portends blasted expectations and trouble with women.

To see the ***sky turn red***, indicates that public disquiet and rioting may be expected.

FIRMAMENT
To dream of the ***firmament*** filled with stars, denotes many crosses and almost superhuman efforts ere you reach the pinnacle of your ambition. Beware of the snare of enemies in your work.

To see people you know in the firmament, signifies that they are about to commit some unwise act through you, and others must be the innocent sufferers. Great disasters usually follow this dream.

ZENITH
To dream of the ***zenith***, foretells elaborate prosperity, and your choice of suitors will be successful.

Stars, Planets, and Comets

ECLIPSE
To dream of the ***eclipse of the sun***, denotes temporary failure in business and other secular affairs; also disturbances in families.

The ***eclipse of the moon***, portends contagious disease or death.

STARS
To dream of looking upon clear, shining ***stars***, foretells good health and prosperity. If they are dull or red, there is trouble and misfortune ahead.

To see ***a shooting or falling star***, denotes sadness and grief. If you dream that a star falls on you, there will be a bereavement in your family.

If you see stars appearing and vanishing mysteriously, there will soon be strange changes.

To see them rolling around on earth, is a sign of danger.

PLANET
To dream of visiting other ***planets*** or other worlds, means that you will soon be exposed to many new and exciting experiences.

MARS
To dream of ***Mars***, denotes that your life will be made miserable by the cruel treatment of friends. Enemies will endeavor to ruin you.

If you feel yourself drawn up toward the planet, you will develop keen judgement and advance beyond your friends in learning and wealth.

COMET
To dream of this heavenly object, trials of an unexpected nature beset you; but you will rise above them to fame.

For a young person, this dream portends bereavement and sorrow.

The Sun and Moon

SUN
To dream of seeing a clear, shining sunrise, foretells joy and prosperity.

To see the ***sun*** at noontide, denotes the maturity of ambitions and signals unbounded satisfaction.

To see the ***sunset***, is prognostic of joys and wealth passing their zenith, and warns you to care for your interests with renewed vigilance.

A ***sun shining*** through clouds, denotes that troubles and difficulties are losing hold, and prosperity is near.

If the sun appears ***weird, or in an eclipse***, there will be stormy and dangerous times, but these will eventually pass.

MOON
To dream of seeing the ***moon***, with the aspect of the heavens remaining normal, prognosticates success.

A ***weird and uncanny moon***, denotes unpropitious lovemaking, domestic infelicities, and disappointing enterprises of a business character.

To see the ***new moon***, denotes an increase in wealth and congenial partners in marriage.

For a young woman to dream that she appeals to the moon to know her fate, denotes that she will soon be rewarded with marriage to the one of her choice. If she sees ***two moons***, she will lose her lover by being mercenary. If she sees the ***moon grow dim***, she will let the supreme happiness of her life slip for want of womanly tact.

To see a ***blood red moon***, indicates war, and she will see her lover march away in defense of his country.

SKY *see* **TRAVELING** *page 211* ◆ **FIRMAMENT** *see* **ACQUAINTANCE** *page 124* ◆ **STARS** *see* **ILLUMINATIONS** *page 275*, **APPARITION** *page 274* ◆ **SUN** *see* **DAYBREAK** *page 82*, **CLOUDS** *page 74*, **APPARITION** *page 274* ◆ **MOON** *see* **APPARITION** *page 274*

People and Places

Most dreams are peopled with protagonists and take place in a certain setting. This section examines dream people and places. In dreams, people are shown en masse or as individuals, archetypes, or specific characters: crowds or a single human being, heroes or villains. And royalty star regularly, in even the most fervent Republican's dreams.

The Madding Crowd

CROWD

To dream of a large, handsomely dressed ***crowd*** of people at some entertainment, denotes pleasant associations with friends; but anything occurring to mar the pleasure of the guests, denotes distress and loss of friendship, and unhappiness will be found where profit and congenial intercourse were expected. It also denotes dissatisfaction in government and family dissensions.

To see a ***crowd in a church***, denotes that a death will be likely to affect you, or some slight unpleasantness may develop.

To see a ***crowd in a street***, indicates unusual briskness in trade, and a general air of prosperity will surround you.

To try to be heard in a crowd, foretells that you will push your interests ahead of all others.

To see a crowd is usually good, if too many are not wearing black or dull costumes. ◎

PARTY

To dream of an ***unknown party*** of men assaulting you for your money or valuables, denotes that you will have enemies banded together against you. If you escape uninjured, you will overcome any opposition in either business or love.

To dream of attending a ***party of any kind for pleasure***, you will find that life has much good, unless the party is an inharmonious one. ◎

Significant Individuals

MAN

To dream of a ***man***, if handsome, well formed, and supple, denotes that you will enjoy life vastly and come into rich possessions. If he is misshapen and sour-visaged, you will meet disappointments, and many perplexities will involve you.

For a woman to dream of a ***handsome man***, she is likely to have distinction offered her. If he is ugly, she will experience trouble through someone whom she considers a friend. ◎

WOMAN

To dream of ***women***, foreshadows intrigue.

To argue with one, foretells that you will be outwitted and foiled.

To see a ***dark-haired woman*** with blue eyes and a pug nose, definitely determines your withdrawal from a race in which you stood a showing for victory.

If she has brown eyes and a Roman nose, you will be cajoled into a dangerous speculation.

If she has auburn hair with this combination, it adds to your perplexity and anxiety.

If she is a blonde woman, you will find that all your engagements will be pleasant and favorable to your inclinations. ◎

When you dream of people, you may see them in their multitudes or as individuals, such as the old lady *above right*; **such a cheerful person is a hopeful omen in your dreams.**

OLD WOMAN

OLD MAN OR WOMAN

To dream of seeing an ***old man or woman***, denotes that unhappy carers will oppress you, if they appear otherwise than serene. ◎

GIRLS

To dream of seeing a well, bright-looking ***girl***, foretells pleasing prospects and domestic joys. If she is thin and pale, it denotes that you will have an invalid in your family, and much unpleasantness.

For a man to dream that he is a girl, he will be weak-minded, or become an actor and play female parts. ◎

CROWD *see* **CHURCH** *page 189*, **STREET** *page 222* ◆ **PARTY** *see* **STEALING** *page 246* ◆ **MAN** *see* **HANDSOME** *page 100*, **FACE** *page 101* ◆ **WOMAN** *see* **HAIR** *page 102*, **COMPLEXION** *page 101* ◆ **OLD MAN OR WOMAN** *see* **AGE** *page 100* ◆ **GIRLS** *see* **ACTOR AND ACTRESS** *page 169*

Royal Persons and Regalia

KING

To dream of a ***king***, you are struggling with your might, and ambition is your master.

To dream that you are ***crowned king***, you will rise above your comrades and co-workers.

If you are censured by a king, you will be reproved for a neglected duty.

For a young woman to be in the presence of a king, she will marry a man whom she will fear. To receive favors from a king, she will rise to exalted positions and be congenially wedded. ◎

KING

QUEEN

To dream of a ***queen***, foretells successful ventures. If she looks old or haggard, there will be disappointments connected with your pleasures. ◎

EMPEROR

To dream of going abroad and meeting the ***emperor*** of a nation in your travels, denotes that you will make a long journey, which will bring you neither pleasure nor much knowledge. ◎

EMPRESS

To dream of an ***empress***, denotes that you will be exalted to high honors, but you will let pride make you very unpopular.

To dream of an ***empress and an emperor*** is not particularly bad, but brings one no substantial good. ◎

SOVEREIGN

To dream of a ***sovereign***, denotes that you will enjoy increasing prosperity and new friends. ◎

Kings *above* and crowns *right* impart a civilized royal gloss to some dreams, while roguish pirates *opposite* bring wild adventure.

USURPER

To dream that you are a ***usurper***, foretells that you will have trouble in establishing a good title to property.

If others are trying to ***usurp your rights***, there will be a struggle between you and your competitors, but you will eventually win.

For a young woman to have this dream, she will be a party to a spicy rivalry, in which she will win. ◎

CROWN

To dream of a ***crown***, prognosticates a change of mode in the habit of one's life. The dreamer will travel a long distance from home and form new relations. Fatal illness may also be the sad omen of this dream.

To dream that you ***wear a crown***, signifies loss of personal property.

To dream of ***crowning a person***, denotes your own worthiness. ◎

CORONATION

To dream of a ***coronation***, foretells that you will enjoy acquaintances and friendships with prominent people.

For a young woman to be participating in a coronation, foretells that she will come into some surprising favor with distinguished personages. But if the coronation presents disagreeable incoherence in her dreams, then she may expect unsatisfactory states growing out of anticipated pleasure. ◎

SCEPTER

To imagine in your dreams that you wield a ***scepter***, foretells that you will be chosen by friends to positions of trust, and you will not disappoint their estimate of your ability.

To dream that others wield the scepter over you, denotes that you will seek employment under the supervision of others, rather than exert your energies for yourself. ◎

THRONE

If you dream of sitting on a ***throne***, you will rapidly rise to favor and fortune.

If you descend from one, there is much disappointment for you.

To see others on a throne, you will succeed to wealth through the favor of others. ◎

NOBILITY

To dream of associating with the ***nobility***, denotes that your aspirations are not of the right nature, as you prefer show and pleasures to the higher development of the mind.

For a young woman to dream of the nobility, foretells that she will choose a lover for the beauty of his outward appearance, instead of wisely accepting the man of merit for her protector. ◎

PAGE

To see a ***page***, denotes that you will contract a hasty union with one unsuited to you. You will fail to control your romantic impulses.

If a young woman dreams that she ***acts as a page***, it denotes that she is likely to participate in some foolish escapade. ◎

A CROWN OF STARS

QUEEN *see* **HAGGARD** *page 107* ◆ **EMPEROR** *see* **ABROAD** *page 88,* **JOURNEY** *page 221* ◆ **USURPER** *see* **PROPERTY** *page 239* ◆ **CORONATION** *see* **INCOHERENCE** *page 230*

Characters

VIRGIN
To dream of a ***virgin***, denotes that you will have comparative luck in your speculations.

For a married woman to dream that she is a virgin, foretells that she will suffer remorse over her past, and the future will hold no promise.

For a young woman to dream that she is ***no longer a virgin*** foretells that she will run great risk of losing her reputation by being indiscreet.

For a man to dream of illicit association with a virgin, denotes that he will fail to accomplish an enterprise, and much worry will be caused him by the appeals of people. His aspirations will be foiled through unwarranted associations.

GYPSY
If you dream of visiting a ***gypsy*** camp, you will have an offer of importance and will investigate the standing of the parties to your disadvantage.

For a woman to have a ***gypsy tell her fortune***, is an omen of a speedy and unwise marriage. If she is already married, she will be unduly jealous of her husband.

For a man to hold any conversation with a gypsy, he will be likely to lose valuable property.

To dream of ***trading with a gypsy***, you will lose money in speculation.

BELLMAN
Fortune is hurrying after you. Questions of importance will be settled amicably among disputants. To see him looking sad, some sorrowful event or misfortune may soon follow

HERMIT
To dream of a ***hermit***, denotes sadness and loneliness caused by the unfaithfulness of friends.

If you are a hermit yourself, you will pursue research into intricate subjects, and will take great interest in the discussions of the hour.

To find yourself in the ***abode of a hermit***, denotes unselfishness toward enemies and friends alike.

COXCOMB
To dream of a ***coxcomb*** [vain, foolish fellow], denotes a low state of mind. The dreamer should endeavor to elevate his mind.

Extraordinary Characters

ALIEN
To dream of a stranger pleasing you, denotes good health and pleasant surroundings; if he displeases you, look for disappointments.

To dream you are an ***alien***, denotes abiding friendships.

DWARF
If the ***dwarf*** is well formed, it omens that you will never be dwarfed in mind or stature. Health and good constitution will admit of your engaging in many profitable pursuits.

To see ***your friends dwarfed***, denotes their health; and you will have many pleasures through them.

Ugly and hideous dwarfs, always forebode distress.

GIANT
To dream of a ***giant*** appearing suddenly before you, denotes that there will be a great struggle between you and your opponents.

If the giant succeeds in stopping your journey, you will be overcome by your enemy. If he runs from you, prosperity and good health will be yours.

HUNCHBACK
To dream of a ***hunchback***, denotes unexpected reverses.

Villains and Rogues

ROGUE
To think yourself a ***rogue***, foretells that you are about to commit some indiscretion which will give your friends uneasiness of mind. You are likely to suffer from a passing malady.

For a woman to think her husband or lover a rogue, foretells that she will be painfully distressed over neglect shown her by a friend.

ROGUE'S GALLERY
To dream that you are in a ***rogue's gallery***, foretells that you will be associated with people who will fail to appreciate you.

To see your own picture, you will be overawed by a tormenting enemy.

PIRATE

PIRATE
To dream of ***pirates***, denotes that you will be exposed to the evil designs of false friends.

To dream that you are a pirate, denotes that you will fall beneath the society of friends and former equals.

For a young woman to dream that ***her lover is a pirate***, is a sign of his unworthiness and deceitfulness. If she is captured by pirates, she will be induced to leave her home under false pretences.

CROSSBONES
To dream of ***crossbones***, foretells that you will be troubled by the evil influence of others, and prosperity will assume other than promising aspects.

To see crossbones as a monogram on an invitation to a funeral, which was sent out by a secret order, denotes that unnecessary fears will be entertained for some person, and events will transpire that are seemingly harsh, but of good import to the dreamer.

VIRGIN *see* **MARRIAGE** *page 130*, **SEDUCER** *page 126* ◆ **GYPSY** *see* **CAMP** *page 191*, **FORTUNE TELLING** *page 269*, **TRADE** *page 202* ◆ **HERMIT** *see* **ABODE** *page 205* ◆ **DWARF** *see* **FRIEND** *page 124*, **UGLY** *page 100* ◆ **CROSSBONES** *see* **FUNERAL** *page 120*, **SECRET ORDER** *page 271* ◆ **ROGUE** *see* **HUSBAND** *page 132* ◆ **ROGUE'S GALLERY** *see* **PICTURES, PORTRAITS** *page 181*

Where your dreams take place is as important as what happens in them. This section explores the kinds of dreamscapes you might find yourself in and looks at the significance of specific places as well as maps, compasses, and other paraphernalia of geography.

Maps and Geography

GEOGRAPHY

To dream of studying ***geography***, denotes that you will travel much and visit places of renown.

ATLAS

To dream you are looking at an ***atlas***, denotes that you will carefully study interests before making changes or journeys.

COMPASS

To dream of a ***compass***, denotes that you will be forced to struggle in narrow limits, thus making elevation more toilsome but fuller of honor.

To dream of the compass or mariner's needle, foretells that you will be surrounded by prosperous circumstances, and honest people will favor you.

To see one pointing awry, foretells threatened loss and deception.

MAP

To dream of a ***map***, or of studying one, denotes that a change will be contemplated in your business. Some disappointing things will occur, but much profit also will follow the change.

To dream of looking for one, denotes that a sudden discontent with your surroundings will inspire you with new energy, and thus you will rise into better conditions. For a young woman, this dream denotes that she will rise into higher spheres by sheer ambition.

PANORAMA

To dream of a ***panorama***, denotes that you will change your occupation or residence. You should curb your inclinations for change of scene and friends.

DISTANCE

To dream of being a long way from your residence, denotes that you will make a journey soon in which you may meet many strangers who will be instrumental in changing life from good to bad.

To dream of friends at a ***distance***, denotes slight disappointments.

To dream of distance, signifies travel and a long journey. To see men plowing with oxen at a distance, across broad fields, denotes advancing prosperity and honor.

For a man to see strange women in the twilight, at a distance and throwing kisses to him, foretells that he will enter into an engagement with a new acquaintance, which will result in unhappy exposures.

Local Habitation

VILLAGE

To dream that you are in a *village*, ***denotes that you will enjoy good health and find yourself fortunately provided for.***

To revisit the *village home of your youth*, ***denotes that you will have pleasant surprises in store and favorable news from absent friends.***

If the village looks dilapidated, or the dream indistinct, it foretells that trouble and sadness will soon come to you.

NEW YORK SKYLINE

Faraway Places

ABROAD

To dream that you are ***abroad***, or going abroad, foretells that you will soon, in company with a party, make a pleasant trip, and you will find it necessary to absent yourself from your native country for a sojourn in a different climate.

AMERICA

High officials should be careful of affairs of state, others will do well to look after their own person, for some trouble is at hand after this dream.

ASIA

To dream of visiting ***Asia***, is assurance of change, but no material benefits from fortune will follow.

EUROPE

To dream of traveling in ***Europe***, foretells that you will soon go on a long journey, which will avail you in the knowledge you gain of the manners and customs of foreign people. You will also be enabled to forward your financial standing.

For a young woman to feel that she is disappointed with the ***sights of Europe***, omens her inability to appreciate chances for her elevation. She will be likely to disappoint her friends or lover.

MOROCCO

To see ***Morocco*** in your dreams, foretells that you will receive substantial aid from unexpected sources. Your love will be rewarded by faithfulness.

GEOGRAPHY *see* TRAVELING *page 221* ◆ COMPASS *see* MARINER *page 226* ◆ DISTANCE *see* JOURNEY *page 221*, FRIENDS *page 124*, PLOW *page 62*, OXEN *page 37*, FIELDS *page 60*, KISSING *page 125* ◆ VILLAGE *see* HOME *page 205*, INDISTINCTNESS *page 275*

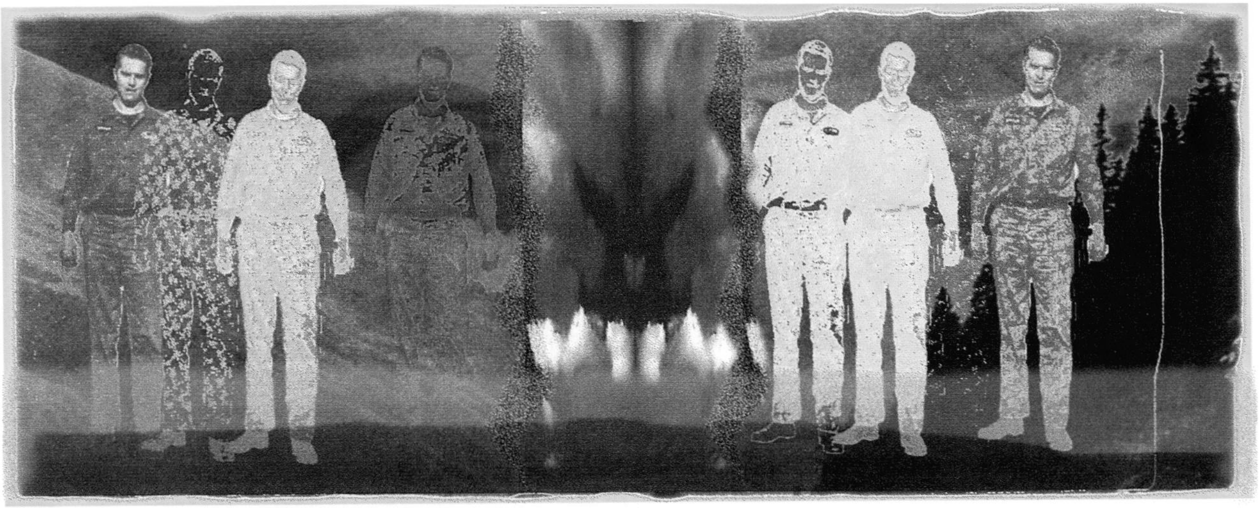

WALKING IN THE OPEN

Wide Open Spaces

ISLAND

To dream that you are on an ***island*** in a clear stream, signifies pleasant journeys and fortunate enterprises. To a woman, this omens a happy marriage.

A ***barren island***, indicates forfeiture of happiness and money through intemperance.

To see an island, denotes comfort and easy circumstances after much striving and worrying to meet honorable obligations.

To see people on an island, denotes a struggle to raise yourself higher in prominent circles. ◎

LAND

To dream of ***land***, when it appears fertile, omens good; but if sterile and rocky, failure and despondency are prognosticated.

To see ***land from the ocean***, denotes that vast avenues of prosperity and happiness will disclose themselves. ◎

COUNTRY

To dream of being in a beautiful and fertile ***country***, where abound rich fields of grain and running streams of pure water, denotes that the very acme of good times is at hand. Wealth will pile in upon you, and you will be able to reign in state in any country.

If the country be ***dry and bare***, you will see and hear of troublous times. Famine and sickness will be in the land. ◎

MEADOW

To dream of ***meadows***, predicts happy reunions under bright promises of future prosperity. ◎

VALLEY

To dream that you find yourself walking through green and pleasant ***valleys***, foretells great improvements in business, and lovers will be happy and congenial.

If the ***valley is barren***, the reverse is predicted. If marshy, illness or vexations may follow. ◎

PRAIRIE

To dream of a ***prairie***, denotes that you will enjoy ease, and even luxury and unobstructed progress.

An ***undulating prairie***, covered with growing grasses and flowers, signifies joyous happenings.

A ***barren prairie***, represents loss and sadness through the absence of friends.

To be lost on one, is a sign of sadness and ill luck. ◎

PLAIN

For a young woman to dream of crossing a ***plain***, denotes that she will be fortunately situated, if the grasses are green and luxuriant; if they are arid, or the grass is dead, she will have much discomfort and loneliness. ◎

DESERT

To dream of wandering through a gloomy and barren ***desert***, denotes famine and uprising of races and great loss of life and property.

For a young woman to find herself ***alone in a desert***, warns that her health and reputation are being jeopardized by her indiscretion. She should be more cautious. ◎

CACTUS

Travel is free in dreams; you may find yourself in a sophisticated urban setting such as New York *opposite top* **or striding through the wide open desert** *top* **among the cactus plants** *above*.

ISLAND *see* **WATER** *page 78* ◆ **LAND** *see* **OCEAN** *page 79* ◆ **COUNTRY** *see* **FIELDS** *page 60*, **GRAIN** *page 62*, **WATER** *page 78* ◆ **MEADOW** *see* **FIELD** *page 60* ◆ **VALLEY** *see* **MARSH** *page 90* ◆ **PRAIRIE** *see* **GRASS** *page 56*, **FLOWERS** *page 57* ◆ **PLAIN** *see* **GRASS** *page 56*

Hills and Mountains

HILLS

To dream of climbing ***hills***, is good if the top is reached, but if you fall back, you will have much envy and contrariness to fight against.

To dream that you see a friend standing like a statue on a hill, denotes that you will advance beyond present pursuits, but will retain former impressions of justice and knowledge, seeking these through every change. If the figure is below you, you will ignore your friends of former days in your future advancement. If it is on a plane or level with you, you will fail in your ambition to reach yourself to seek a change in spite of friendly ties of self-admonition. ◎

MOUNTAIN

For a young woman to dream of crossing a ***mountain*** in company with her cousin and dead brother, who is smiling, denotes that she will have a distinctive change in her life for the better, but there are warnings against allurements and deceitfulness of friends. If she becomes exhausted and refuses to go further, she will be slightly disappointed in not gaining quite so exalted a position as was hoped for by her.

If you ***ascend a mountain*** in your dreams, and the way is pleasant and verdant, you will rise swiftly to wealth and prominence.

If the ***mountain is rugged***, and you fail to reach the top, you may expect reverses in your life, and should strive to overcome all weakness in your nature.

To awaken when you are at a dangerous point in ascending, denotes that you will find affairs taking a flattering turn when they appear gloomy. ◎

Dreams of marshes and mires *above* **may indicate that you are somehow temporarily bogged down in your life. Dreams of bones** *opposite* **are altogether more ominous.**

Swamps, Marshes, and Quagmires

MARSH

SWAMP

To walk through swampy ***places in dreams, foretells that you will be the object of adverse circumstances. Your inheritance will be uncertain, and you will undergo keen disappointments in your love matters.***

To go through a swamp where you see clear water and green growths, indicates that you will take hold of prosperity and singular pleasures, the obtaining of which will be attended with danger and intrigue. ❋

MIRE

To dream of going through mire, ***indicates that your dearest wishes and plans will receive a temporary check by the intervention of unusual changes in your surroundings.*** ❋

BOGS

Bogs, ***denote burdens under whose weight you feel that endeavors to rise are useless. Illness and other worries may oppress you.*** ❋

QUAGMIRE

To dream of being in a quagmire, ***implies your inability to meet obligations. To see others thus situated, denotes that the failures of others will be felt by you. Illness is sometimes indicated by this dream.*** ❋

QUICKSAND

To find yourself in quicksand ***while dreaming, you will meet with loss and deceit.***

If you are unable to overcome it, you will be involved in overwhelming misfortunes.

For a young woman to be rescued by her lover from quicksand, she will possess a worthy and faithful husband, who will still remain her lover. ❋

MUD

To dream that you walk in mud, ***denotes that you will have cause to lose confidence in friendships, and there will be losses and disturbances in family circles.***

If you see others walking in mud, ugly rumors will reach you of some friend or employee. To the farmer, this dream is significant of short crops and unsatifactory gains from stock.

If you see mud on your clothing, ***your reputation is being assailed. To scrape it off, signifies that you will escape the calumny of enemies.*** ❋

MARSH

To dream of walking through marshy ***places, denotes illness resulting from overwork and worry. You will suffer much displeasure from the unwise conduct of a near relative.*** ❋

HILLS *see* **CLIMBING** *page 268,* **FRIEND** *see page 124,* **STATUE** *page 182* ◆ **MOUNTAIN** *see* **DEAD** *page 120,* **BROTHERS** *page 129,* **ASCENDING** *page 286* ◆ **SWAMP** *see* **WATER** *page 78* ◆ **QUICKSAND** *see* **RESCUE** *page 266* ◆ **MUD** *see* **WALKING** *page 267,* **CLOTHES** *page 154,* **STAIN** *page 218* ◆ **MARSH** *see* **WALKING** *page 267*

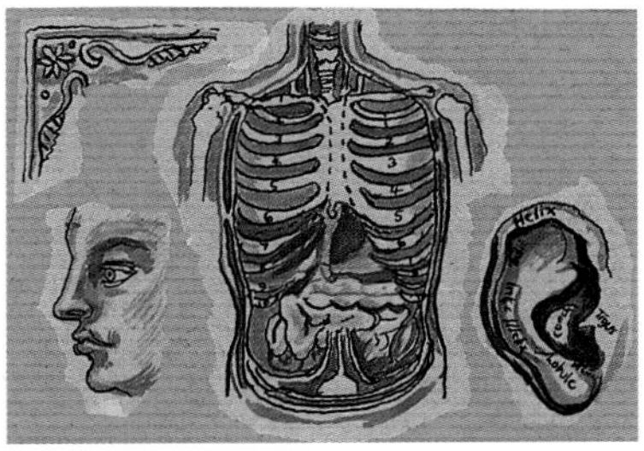

Body and Soul

Everybody knows their own body better than anything else, and so it is not surprising that dreams about the body or parts of it occur frequently. This section covers the whole of the body from head to toe, inside and out – the mechanisms, body systems, and senses – and dreams about looking after or neglecting our bodies.

Body Matters

NAKED

To dream that you are ***naked***, foretells scandal and unwise engagements.

To see others naked, foretells that you will be tempted by designing persons to leave the path of duty. Sickness will be no small factor against your success.

To dream that you suddenly discover your nudity, and are trying to conceal it, denotes that you have sought illicit pleasure contrary to your noblest instincts and are desirous of abandoning those desires.

For a young woman to dream that she ***admires her nudity***, foretells that she will win, but not hold, honest men's regard.

If she thinks herself ill-formed, her reputation will be sullied by scandal.

If she dreams of ***swimming naked*** in clear water, she will enjoy illicit loves, but nature will revenge herself by sickness, or loss of charms.

If she sees naked men swimming in clear water, she will have many admirers. If the water is muddy, a jealous admirer will cause ill-natured gossip. ◎

TATTOO

To see your body appearing ***tattooed***, foretells that some difficulty will cause you to make a long and tedious absence from your home.

To see tattoos on others, foretells that strange loves will make you an object of jealousy.

To dream you are a ***tattooist***, is a sign that you will estrange yourself from friends because of your fancy for some strange experience. ◎

Respire and Perspire

BREATH

To come close in your dreaming to a person with a pure and ***sweet breath***, commendable will be your conduct, and a profitable consummation of business deals will follow.

Fetid breath, indicates sickness and snares.

Losing one's breath, denotes signal failure where success seemed assured. ◎

PERSPIRATION

To dream that you are in ***perspiration***, foretells that you will come out of some difficulty, which has caused much gossip, with new honors. ◎

Bones and Muscles

SKELETON

To dream of seeing a ***skeleton***, is prognostic of illness, misunderstanding, and injury at the hands of others, especially enemies.

To dream that you are a skeleton, is a sign that you are suffering under useless worry, and should cultivate a milder disposition.

If you imagine that a skeleton haunts you, there will soon come to you a shocking accident or death, or the trouble may take the form of financial disaster. ◎

SKULL

To dream of ***skulls*** grinning at you, is a sign of domestic quarrels and jars. Business will feel a shrinkage if you handle them.

To see a ***friend's skull***, denotes that you will receive injury from a friend because of your being preferred to him.

To see your ***own skull***, denotes that you will be the servant of remorse. ◎

BONES

To see your ***bones*** protruding from the flesh, denotes that treachery is working to ensnare you.

To see a ***pile of bones***, indicates that famine and contaminating influences surround you. ◎

MUSCLES

To dream of seeing your ***muscles*** well developed, you will have strange encounters with enemies, but you will succeed in surmounting their evil works, and gain fortune.

If they are rather shrunken, your inability to succeed in your affairs is portended. For a woman, this dream is prophetic of toil and hardships. ◎

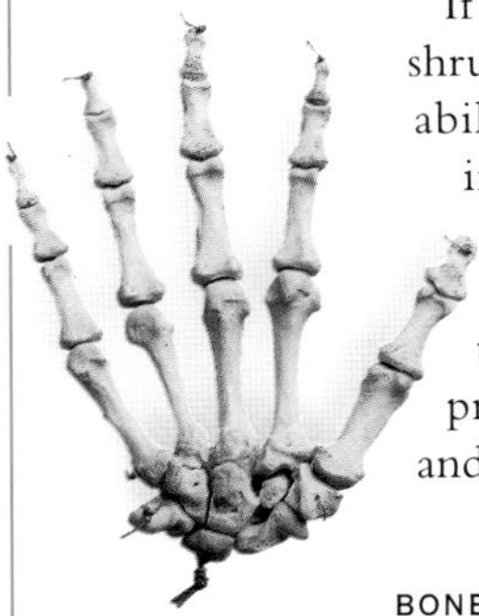

BONES OF THE HAND

NAKED *see* **SWIMMING** *page 174,* **WATER** *page 78* ◆ **SKELETON** *see* **GHOST** *page 275* ◆ **SKULL** *see* **FRIEND** *page 124*

Head and Neck

HEAD
To see a person's ***head*** in your dream, and it is well-shaped and prominent, you will meet persons of power and vast influence who will lend you aid in enterprises of importance.

If you dream of ***your own head***, you are threatened with nervous or brain trouble.

To see a ***head severed*** from its trunk, and bloody, you will meet sickening disappointments, and experience the overthrow of your dearest hopes and anticipations.

To see yourself with ***two or more heads***, foretells a phenomenal and rapid rise in life, but the probabilities are that the rise will not be stable.

To dream that your ***head aches***, denotes that you will be oppressed with worry.

To dream of a ***swollen head***, you will have more good than bad in your life.

To dream of a ***child's head***, there will be much pleasure in store for you and signals financial success.

To dream of the ***head of a beast***, denotes that the nature of your desires will run on a low plane, and only material pleasures will concern you.

To ***wash your head***, you will be sought after by prominent people for your judgement and good counsel. ◎

FOREHEAD
To dream of a fine and smooth ***forehead***, denotes that you will be thought well of for your judgement and fair dealings.

An ***ugly forehead***, denotes displeasure in your private affairs.

To pass your hand over the ***forehead of your child***, indicates sincere praises from friends because of some talent and goodness displayed by your children.

For a young woman to dream of ***kissing the forehead*** of her lover, signifies that he will be displeased with her for gaining notice by indiscreet conduct. ◎

SCRATCHING YOUR HEAD
To dream that you ***scratch your head***, denotes that strangers will annoy you by their flattering attentions, which you will feel are only shown to win favors from you. ◎

BRAIN
To see your own ***brain*** in a dream, denotes that uncongenial surroundings will irritate and dwarf you into an unpleasant companion. To see the ***brains of animals***, foretells that you will suffer mental trouble.

If you eat them, you will gain knowledge, and profit unexpectedly. ◎

NECK
To dream that you see your own ***neck***, foretells that vexatious family relations will interfere with your business.

To admire the ***neck of another***, signifies that your worldly mindedness will cause broken domestic ties.

For a woman to dream that her ***neck is thick***, foretells that she will become querulous and something of a shrew if she fails to control her temper. ◎

A BEAUTIFUL HEAD AND NECK

Jaws and Throat

JAWS
To dream of seeing heavy, misshapen ***jaws***, denotes disagreements, and ill feeling will be shown between friends.

If you dream that you are in the ***jaws of a wild beast***, enemies will work injury to your affairs and happiness. This is a vexatious and perplexing dream.

If your own ***jaws ache with pain***, you will be exposed to climatic changes, and illness may cause you loss in health and finances. ◎

LIPS
To dream of thick, unsightly ***lips***, signifies disagreeable encounters, hasty decisions, and ill tempers in the marriage relation.

Full, sweet, cherry lips, indicate harmony and affluence. To a lover, it augurs reciprocation in love and fidelity.

Thin lips, signify mastery of the most intricate subjects.

Sore or swollen lips, denotes privations and unhealthful desires. ◎

TONGUE
To dream of seeing your own ***tongue***, denotes that you will be looked upon with disfavor by your acquaintances.

To see the tongue of another, foretells that scandal will vilify you.

To dream that your tongue is affected in any way, denotes that your carelessness in talking will get you into trouble. ◎

THROAT
To dream of seeing a well-developed and graceful ***throat***, portends a rise in position.

If you feel that your ***throat is sore***, you will be deceived in your estimation of a friend, and will have anxiety over the discovery. ◎

HEAD *see* **BLOOD** *page 94,* **ACHES** *page 107,* **SWELLING** *page 108,* **CHILDREN** *page 128,* **WASHING** *page 104* ◆ **FOREHEAD** *see* **UGLY** *page 100,* **CHILDREN** *page 128,* **KISSING** *page 125* ◆ **BRAIN** *see* **EATING** *page 133* ◆ **JAWS** *see* **ACHES, PAIN** *page 107* ◆ **LIPS** *see* **SWELLING** *page 108*

Teeth and Dentistry

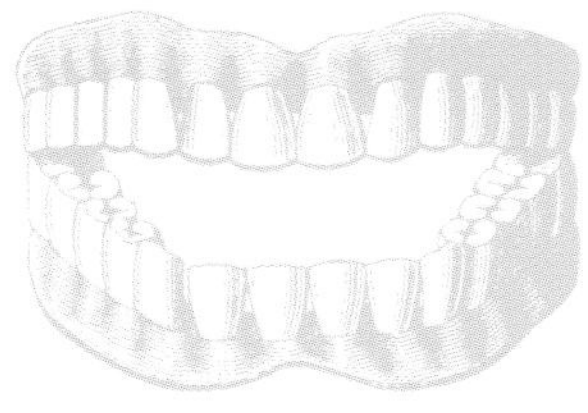

TEETH

TEETH

An ordinary dream of ***teeth***, augurs an unpleasant contact with sickness or disquieting people.

If you dream that your ***teeth are loose***, there will be failures and gloomy tidings.

If the doctor ***pulls your tooth***, you will have desperate illness, if not fatal, it will be lingering.

To have them filled, you will recover lost valuables after much uneasiness.

To clean or ***wash your teeth***, foretells that some great struggle will be demanded of you in order to preserve your fortune.

To dream that you are having a ***set of teeth*** made, denotes that severe crosses will fall upon you, and you will strive to throw them aside.

If you ***lose your teeth***, you will have burdens which will crush your pride and demolish your affairs.

To dream that you have your ***teeth knocked out***, denotes sudden misfortune. Either your business will suffer, or deaths or accidents will come close to you.

To ***examine your teeth***, warns you to be careful of your affairs, as enemies are lurking near you.

If they appear decayed and snaggled, your business or health will suffer from intense strains.

To dream of ***spitting out teeth***, portends personal sickness, or sickness in your immediate family.

Imperfect teeth, is one of the worst dreams. It is full of mishaps for the dreamer. A loss of estates, failure of persons to carry out their plans and desires, bad health, and depressed conditions of the nervous system for even healthy persons.

For ***one tooth to fall out***, foretells disagreeable news; if two, it denotes unhappy states that the dreamer will be plunged into from no carelessness on his part. If three fall out, sickness and accidents of a very serious nature will follow.

Seeing ***all the teeth drop out***, death and famine usually will prevail. If the teeth are decayed and you pull them out, the same; only yourself is prominent in the case.

To dream of tartar or any ***deposit falling off of the teeth*** and leaving them sound and white, is a sign of temporary indisposition, which will pass, leaving you wiser in regard to conduct, and you will find enjoyment in the discharge of duty.

To ***admire your teeth*** for their whiteness and beauty, foretells that pleasant occupations and much happiness will be experienced through the fulfillment of wishes.

To dream that you ***pull one of your teeth*** and lose it, and feel within your mouth with your tongue for the cavity, and failing to find any, have a doctor look for the same, but to no effect, leaving the whole affair enveloped in mystery, denotes that you are about to enter into some engagement which does not exactly please you, and which you decide to ignore, but will later take it up and secretly prosecute it to your own disquieting satisfaction and under the suspicion of friends.

MOLAR

To dream that a ***dentist cleans your teeth*** perfectly, and the next morning you find them rusty, foretells that you will believe your interests secure concerning some person or position, but you will find that they have succumbed to the blandishments of an artful man or woman. ◎

DENTIST

To dream of a ***dentist*** working on your teeth, denotes that you will have occasion to doubt the sincerity and honor of some person with whom you have dealings.

To see him at work on a young woman's teeth, denotes that you will soon be shocked by a scandal in circles near you. ◎

AT THE DENTIST

TOOTHLESS

To dream that you are ***toothless***, denotes your inability to advance your interests, and ill health will cast gloom over your prospects.

To see ***others toothless***, foretells that enemies are trying in vain to calumniate you. ◎

TOOTHPICKS

To dream of ***toothpicks***, foretells that small anxieties and spites will harass you unnecessarily if you give them your attention.

If you use one, you will be a party to a friend's injury. ◎

The head and neck *opposite* are dream subjects open to various interpretations, as are dreams of teeth *top left* and *center*. A visit to the dentist presents a waking nightmare to many people; to dream of one at work *above* may be slightly less frightful.

TEETH *see* **DOCTOR** *page 114,* **WASHING** *page 104,* **ADMIRE** *page 259,* **RUST** *page 255*

The Upper Body

SHOULDER
To dream of seeing naked ***shoulders***, foretells that happy changes will make you look upon the world in a different light than formerly.

To see your own shoulders appearing thin, denotes that you will depend upon the caprices of others for entertainment and pleasure. ◎

BOSOM
For a young woman to dream that her ***bosom*** is wounded, foretells that some affliction is threatening her.

To see it soiled or shrunken, she will have a great disappointment in love, and many rivals will vex her.

If it is white and full, she is soon to be possessed of fortune.

If her lover is slyly observing it through her sheer corset, she is about to come under the soft persuasive influence of a too ardent wooer. ◎

RIB
To dream of seeing ***ribs***, denotes poverty and misery. ◎

WAIST
To dream of a round full ***waist***, denotes that you will be favored by an agreeable dispensation of fortune.

A ***small***, ***unnatural waist***, foretells displeasing success and recriminating disputes. ◎

SHOULDER AND BOSOM

Heart and Blood

HEART
To dream of your ***heart*** paining and suffocating you, there will be trouble in your business. Some mistake of your own will bring loss if not corrected.

Seeing your heart, foretells sickness and failure of energy.

To see the ***heart of an animal***, you will overcome enemies and merit the respect of all.

To ***eat the heart*** of a chicken, denotes that strange desires will cause you to carry out very difficult projects for your advancement. ◎

BLOOD
To dream of bloodstained garments, indicates that you have enemies who seek to tear down a successful career that is opening up before you.

The dreamer should beware of strange friendships after experiencing such a dream.

To see ***blood*** flowing from a wound, physical ailments and worry. Bad business caused from disastrous dealings with foreign combines.

To see ***blood on your hands***, denotes immediate bad luck, if you are not careful of your person and your own affairs. ◎

BLEEDING
To dream of ***bleeding,*** denotes death by horrible accidents and malicious reports about you. Fortune will turn against you. ◎

BLOOD

VEIN
To see your ***veins*** in a dream, ensures you against slander, if they are normal.

To see them bleeding, denotes that you will have a great sorrow from which there will be no escape.

To see veins swollen, indicates that you will rise hastily to distinction and places of trust. ◎

SHOULDER *see* **NAKED** *page 91* ◆ **BOSOM** *see* **WOUND** *page 112* ◆ **HEART** *see* **PAIN** *page 107,* **SUFFOCATING** *page 266,* **EATING** *page 133,* **CHICKENS** *page 39* ◆ **BLOOD** *see* **CLOTHES** *page 154,* **STAIN** *page 218,* **WOUND** *page 112,* **HAND** *page 97*

Stomach, Liver, and Intestines

ABDOMEN
To see your ***abdomen*** in a dream, foretells that you will have great expectations, but you must curb hardheadedness and redouble your energies on your labor, as pleasure is approaching to work you hard.

To see your ***abdomen shriveled***, foretells that you will be persecuted and defiled by false friends.

To see it swollen, denotes tribulations, but you will overcome them and enjoy the fruits of your labor.

To see ***blood oozing from the abdomen***, foretells an accident or tragedy in your family.

The ***abdomen of children*** in an unhealthy state, portends that contagion will pursue you. ◎

PAUNCH
To see a large ***paunch***, denotes wealth and the total absence of refinement.

To see ***a shriveled paunch***, foretells illness and reverses. ◎

BELLY
It is bad to dream of seeing a swollen, mortifying ***belly***; it indicates desperate sickness.

To see anything moving on the belly, prognosticates humiliation and hard labor.

To see a ***healthy belly***, denotes insane desires. ◎

LIVER
To dream of a disordered ***liver***, denotes that a querulous person will be your mate, and fault-finding will occupy his or her time, and disquiet will fill your hours.

To dream of ***eating liver***, indicates that some deceitful person has installed himself or herself in the affection of your sweetheart. ◎

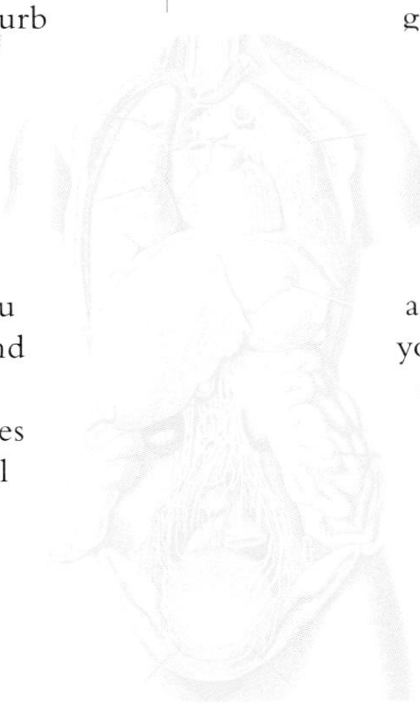

THE INNER SELF

INTESTINES
To dream of seeing ***intestines***, signifies that you are about to be visited by a grave calamity, which will remove some friend.

To see your ***own intestines***, denotes that grave situations are closing around you; sickness of a nature to affect you in your daily communications with others threatens you. Probable loss, with much displeasure, is also denoted.

If in your dreams you think that you lay your intestines upon something, which turns out to be a radiator, and they begin to grow hot and make you very uncomfortable, and you ask others to assist you, and they refuse, it foretells unexpected calamity, which will probably come in the form of a desperate illness or a misfortune for which you will be censured by those formerly your friends. You may have trouble in extricating yourself from an unpromising predicament. ◎

ENTRAILS
To dream of human ***entrails***, denotes horrible misery and despair, shutting out all hope of happiness.

To dream of the ***entrails of a wild beast***, signifies the overthrow of your mortal enemy.

To tear the ***entrails of another***, signifies cruel persecutions to further your own interests.

If you dream of ***your own entrails***, the deepest despair will overwhelm you.

To dream of the ***entrails of your own child***, denotes that the child's or your own dissolution is at hand. ◎

Urinary Tract

KIDNEYS
To dream about your ***kidneys***, foretells that you are threatened with a serious illness, or there will be trouble in marriage relations for you.

If they act too freely, you will be a party to some racy intrigue. If they refuse to perform their work, there will be a sensation, and it will be to your detriment.

If you ***eat kidney stew***, some officious person will cause you disgust in some secret love affair. ◎

BLADDER
To dream of your ***bladder***, denotes heavy trouble in your business if you are not careful of your health and the way you spend your energies.

To see children ***blowing up bladders***, foretells that your expectations will fail to give you much comfort. ◎

URINE
To dream of seeing ***urine***, denotes that ill health will make you disagreeable and unpleasant with your friends.

To dream that you are ***urinating***, is an omen of bad luck and trying seasons of love. ◎

URINAL
If you dream of a ***urinal***, disorder will predominate in your home. ◎

CHILD URINATING

Dreams of the outer part of your body such as shoulders *opposite left* **are to do with romance and the social whirl. Dreams of blood** *opposite* **and the inner self** *above* **are darker. Urinating in your dreams** *above* **is a sign of bad luck.**

ABDOMEN *see* **BLOOD** *page 94*, **CHILDREN** *page 128* ◆ **BELLY** *see* **SWELLING** *page 108* ◆ **LIVER** *see* **EATING** *page 133*, **MEAT** *page 135* ◆ **INTESTINES** *see* **HEAT** *page 74* ◆ **ENTRAILS** *see* **CHILDREN** *page 128* ◆ **KIDNEYS** *see* **EATING** *page 133*, **MEAT** *page 135*

The Lower Body

HIPS

To dream that you admire well-formed ***hips***, denotes that you will be upbraided by your wife.

For a woman to ***admire her hips***, shows that she will be disappointed in love matters.

To notice ***fat hips*** on animals, foretells ease and pleasure.

For a woman to dream that her ***hips are too narrow***, omens sickness and disappointments. If they are too fat, she is in danger of losing her good reputation. ◎

GENITALS

To dream of the male or female ***genitals***, especially if they are diseased or deformed, means that you will soon be tempted into becoming part of a scandalous and illicit affair. If this relationship is undertaken, it will be tempestuous, disruptive, and chaotic.

To dream of ***exposing your genitals***, foretells that your reputation will soon be sullied. ◎

BACK

To dream of seeing a nude ***back***, denotes loss of power. Lending advice or money is dangerous. Sickness often attends this dream.

To see a person turn and walk away from you, you may be sure envy and jealousy are working to do you harm.

To dream of your ***own back***, bodes no good to the dreamer. ◎

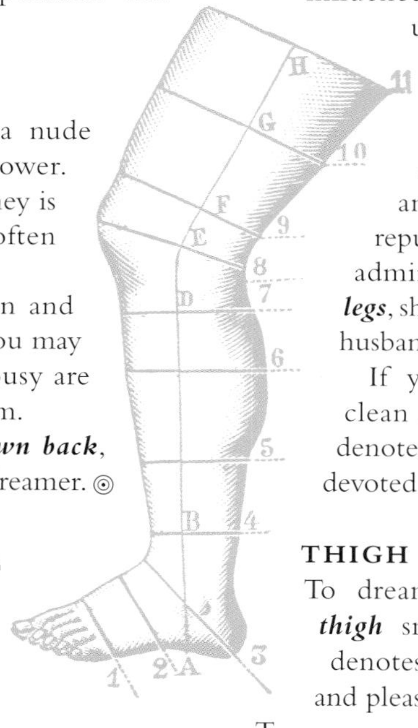

LEG

The extremities play an important role in dream life. Legs *above* in various states of health and shapeliness are frequently seen, and their appearance is open to many interpretations. Hands *opposite* are also very active in dreams.

Legs and Feet

LEGS

If you dream of admiring well-shaped feminine ***legs***, you will lose your judgement, and act very silly over some fair charmer.

To see ***misshapen legs***, denotes unprofitable occupations and ill-tempered comrades.

A ***wounded leg***, foretells losses and agonizing attacks of malaria.

To dream that you have a ***wooden leg***, denotes that you will be mean yourself in a false way to your friends.

If ***ulcers*** are on your legs, it signifies a drain on your income to aid others.

To dream that you have ***three or more legs***, indicates that more enterprises are planned in imagination than will ever benefit you.

If you can't use your legs, it portends poverty.

To have a ***leg amputated***, you will lose valued friends, and the home influence will render life unbearable.

For a young woman to ***admire her own legs***, denotes vanity, and she will be repulsed by the man she admires. If she has ***hairy legs***, she will dominate her husband.

If your own legs are clean and well shaped, it denotes a happy future and devoted friends. ◎

THIGH

To dream of seeing your ***thigh*** smooth and white, denotes unusual good luck and pleasure.

To see ***wounded thighs***, foretells illness and treachery.

For a young woman to admire her thigh, signifies willingness to engage in adventures, and she should heed this as a warning to be careful of her conduct. ◎

KNEE

To dream of ***knees*** is an unfortunate omen.

To dream that your ***knees are too large***, denotes sudden ill luck for you. If they are stiff and pain you, swift and fearful calamity awaits you.

For a women to dream that she has ***well-formed and smooth knees***, predicts that she will have many admirers, but none to woo her in wedlock.

If they are soiled, sickness from dissipation is portended. If they are unshapely, unhappy changes in her fortune will displace ardent hopes. ◎

FEET

To dream of seeing your own ***feet***, is ominous of despair. You will be overcome by the will and temper of another.

To see ***others' feet***, denotes that you will maintain your rights in a pleasant but determined way, and win for yourself a place above the common walks of life.

To dream that you ***wash your feet***, denotes that you will let others take advantage of you.

To dream that your ***feet are hurting*** you, portends trouble of a humiliating character, as they usually are family quarrels.

To see your ***feet swollen and red***, you will make a sudden change in your business by separating from your family. This is an evil dream, as it usually foretells scandal and sensation. ◎

BAREFOOT

To wander in the night ***barefoot*** with torn garments, denotes that you will be crushed in expectation, and evil influences will surround your every effort. ◎

CLOVEN FOOT

To dream of a ***cloven foot***, portends that some unusual ill luck is threatening you, and you will do well to avoid the friendship of strange persons. ◎

HIPS *see* **ADMIRE** *page 259,* **FAT** *page 100* ◆ **BACK** *see* **NAKED** *page 91,* **WALKING** *page 267* ◆ **LEGS** *see* **WOUND** *page 112,* **ULCERS** *page 108,* **AMPUTATION** *page 115,* **ADMIRE** *page 259,* **HAIR** *page 102* ◆ **THIGH** *see* **WOUND** *page112,* **ADMIRE** *page 259* ◆ **FEET** *see* **WASHING** *page 104,* **ACHE** *page 107,* **CORNS** *page 112,* **SWELLING** *page 108* ◆ **BAREFOOT** *see* **NIGHT** *page 82*

Arms and Hands

ARM
To dream of seeing an ***arm*** amputated, means separation or divorce. Mutual dissatisfaction will occur between husband and wife. It is a dream of sinister import. Beware of deceitfulness and fraud. ◎

ELBOWS
To see ***elbows*** in a dream, signifies that arduous labors will devolve upon you, for which you will receive little reimbursement.

For a young woman, this is prognostic of favorable opportunities to make a wealthy marriage. If the ***elbows are soiled***, she will lose a good chance of securing a home by marriage. ◎

HAND
If you see beautiful ***hands*** in your dream, you will enjoy great distinction, and rise rapidly in your calling; but ugly and malformed hands point to disappointments and poverty. To see blood on them, denotes estrangement and unjust censure from members of your family.

If you have an ***injured hand***, some person will succeed to what you are striving most to obtain.

To see a ***detached hand***, indicates a solitary life; that is, people will fail to understand your views and feelings.

To ***burn your hands***, you will overreach the bounds of reason in your struggles for wealth and fame, and lose thereby.

To see your ***hands enlarged***, denotes a quick advancement in your affairs. To see them smaller, the reverse is predicted.

To see your ***hands soiled***, denotes that you will be envious and unjust.

To ***wash your hands***, you will participate in some joyous festivity.

For a woman to admire her own hands, is proof that she will win and hold the sincere regard of the man she prizes above all others. To admire the hands of others, she will be subjected to the whims of a jealous man.

To have a man ***hold her hands***, she will be enticed into illicit engagements. If she lets others kiss her hands, she will have gossips busy.

To handle fire without burning her hands, she will rise to high rank.

To dream that your ***hands are tied***, denotes that you will be involved in difficulties. In loosening them, you will force others to submit to you. ◎

HAIRY HANDS
To dream that your ***hands*** are covered with ***hair*** like that of a beast, signifies that you will intrigue against innocent people, and will find that you have alert enemies who are working to forestall your designs.

To see your ***hands covered with hair***, denotes that you will not become a solid and leading factor in your circle. ◎

SHAKING HANDS
For a young woman to dream that she ***shakes hands*** with some prominent ruler, foretells that she will be surrounded with pleasures and distinction from strangers. If she avails herself of the opportunity, she will stand in high favor with friends. If she finds that she must reach up to shake hands, she will find rivalry and opposition. If she has on gloves, she will overcome these obstacles.

To shake hands with those beneath you, denotes that you will be loved and honored for your kindness and benevolence. If you think you or they have soiled hands, you will find enemies among seeming friends.

For a young woman to dream of shaking hands with a decrepit old man, foretells trouble where amusement was sought.

To dream that you are shaking hands with a person who has wronged you, and he is taking his departure and looks sad, foretells that you will have differences with a close friend and alienation will perhaps follow. You are most assuredly nearing loss of some character. ◎

Fingers and Thumbs

FINGERS
To dream of seeing your ***fingers*** soiled or scratched, with blood exuding, denotes much trouble and suffering. You will despair of making your way through life.

To see beautiful hands, with ***white fingers***, denotes that your love will be requited and that you will become renowned for your benevolence.

To dream that your ***fingers are cut clean off***, you will lose wealth and a legacy by the intervention of enemies. ◎

FINGERNAILS
To dream of soiled ***fingernails***, forebodes disgrace in your family by the wild escapades of the young.

To see ***well-kept nails***, indicates scholarly tastes and some literary attainments; also thrift. ◎

THUMB
To dream of seeing a ***thumb***, foretells that you will be the favorite of artful persons and uncertain fortune.

If you are suffering from a ***sore thumb***, you will lose in business, and your companions will prove disagreeable to you.

To dream that you have ***no thumb***, implies destitution and loneliness. If it seems unnaturally small, you will enjoy pleasure for a time. If abnormally large, your success will be rapid and brilliant.

A ***soiled thumb*** indicates gratification of loose desires. If the thumb has a very long nail, you are liable to fall into evil through seeking strange pleasures. ◎

HAND CLASP

ARM *see* **AMPUTATION** *page 115* ◆ **HAND** *see* **BEAUTY, UGLY** *page 100,* **INJURY** *page 106,* **BURNS** *page 112,* **WASHING** *page 104,* **KISSING** *page 125,* **FIRE** *page 80* ◆ **HAIRY HANDS** *see* **HAIR** *page 102* ◆ **SHAKING HANDS** *see* **OLD MAN** *page 85,* **FAREWELL** *page 258* ◆ **FINGERS** *see* **SCRATCH** *page 112,* **BLOOD** *page 94*

The Nose

NOSE

To see your own ***nose*** in a dream, indicates force of character, and consciousness of your ability to accomplish whatever enterprises you may choose to undertake.

If your nose looks smaller than natural, there will be failure in your affairs. Hair growing on your nose, indicates extraordinary undertakings, and that they will be carried through by sheer force of character or will.

A ***bleeding nose***, is prophetic of disaster, whatever the calling of the dreamer may be. ◎

SNEEZE

To dream that you ***sneeze***, denotes that hasty tidings will cause you to change your plans.

If you see or hear ***others sneeze***, people will bore you with visits. ◎

Scents and Smells

ODOR

To dream of inhaling sweet ***odors***, is a sign of a beautiful woman ministering to your daily life, and successful financiering.

To smell disgusting odors, foretells unpleasant disagreements and unreliable servants. ◎

INCENSE

To dream of burning or smelling ***incense***, denotes that you will be surrounded by good friends and pleasing prospects. ◎

MYRRH

To see ***myrrh*** in a dream signifies that your investments will give satisfaction. For a young woman to dream of myrrh, brings a pleasing surprise to her in the way of a new and wealthy acquaintance. ◎

MUSK

To dream of ***musk***, foretells unexpected occasions of joy, and lovers will agree and cease to be unfaithful. ◎

AROMA

For a young woman to dream of a sweet ***aroma***, denotes that she will soon be the recipient of some pleasure or present. ◎

THE PERFUME MAKER

Perfume

To dream of inhaling perfume, ***is an augury of happy incidents.***

For you to perfume your garments ***and person, denotes that you will seek and obtain adulation.***

Being oppressed by it to intoxication, denotes that excesses in joy will impair your mental qualities.

To spill perfume, ***denotes that you will lose something which affords you pleasure.***

To break a bottle of perfume, ***foretells that your most cherished wishes and desires will end disastrously, even while they promise a happy culmination.***

To dream that you are distilling perfume, ***denotes that your employments and associations will be of the pleasantest character.***

For a young woman to dream of perfuming her bath, ***foretells ecstatic happiness. If she receives it as a gift from a man, she will experience fascinating, but dangerous pleasures.*** ❋

NOSE *see* HAIR *page 102,* BLEEDING *page 94* ◆ PERFUME *see* CLOTHES *page 154,* BOTTLES *page 210,* BATH *page 105*

Eyes and Sight

EYE
To dream of seeing an ***eye***, warns you that watchful enemies are seeking the slightest chance to work injury to your business. This dream indicates to a lover that a rival will usurp him if he is not careful.

To dream of ***brown eyes***, denotes deceit and perfidy. To see ***blue eyes***, denotes weakness in carrying out any intention. To see ***gray eyes***, denotes a love of flattery for the owner.

To dream of ***losing an eye***, or that the eyes are sore, denotes trouble.

To see a ***one-eyed man***, denotes that you will be threatened with loss and trouble, besides which all others will appear insignificant. ◎

EYEBROWS
Eyebrows denote that you will encounter sinister obstacles in your immediate future. ◎

NEARSIGHTED
To dream that you are ***nearsighted***, signifies embarrassing failure and unexpected visits from unwelcome persons. For a young woman, this dream foretells unexpected rivalry.

To dream that your sweetheart is nearsighted, denotes that she will disappoint you. ◎

BLIND
To dream of being ***blind***, denotes a sudden change from affluence to almost abject poverty.

To see others blind, denotes that some worthy person will call on you for aid. ◎

The senses function just as efficiently in the realm of dreams as they do in reality. You may dream you smell the sensuous products of the perfume maker *opposite*, **or you may see a one-eyed creature from mythology** *above*, **or one of the organs of sense such as the ear** *right*.

SQUINTING
To dream that you see some person with ***squinting*** eyes, denotes that you will be annoyed with unpleasant people.

For a man to dream that his sweetheart or some good-looking girl squints her eyes at him, foretells that he is threatened with loss by seeking the favors of women. For a young woman to have this dream about men, she will be in danger of losing her fair reputation. ◎

ONE-EYED
To see ***one-eyed*** creatures in your dreams, is portentous of an overwhelming intimation of secret intriguing against your fortune and happiness. ◎

CYCLOPS, THE ONE-EYED MONSTER

Speech and Muteness

STAMMER
To dream that you ***stammer*** in your conversation, denotes that worry and illness will threaten your enjoyment.

To hear others stammer, foretells that unfriendly persons will delight in annoying you and giving you needless worry. ◎

DUMB
To dream of being ***dumb***, indicates your inability to persuade others into your mode of thinking, and using them for your profit by your glibness of tongue. To the dumb, it denotes false friends. ◎

MUTE
To converse with a ***mute*** in your dreams, foretells that unusual crosses in your life will fit you for higher positions, which will be tendered you.

To dream that you are a mute, portends calamities and unjust persecution. ◎

Hearing

EAR

EARS
If you dream of seeing ***ears***, an evil and designing person is keeping watch over your conversation to work you harm. ◎

HEARING AID
To dream of using a ***hearing aid***, means that you have not paid close enough attention to something which will have significant impact in your life. ◎

NEARSIGHTED, SQUINTING *see* **SWEETHEART** *page 124* ◆ **MUTE** *see* **TALKING** *page 230*

Age and Youth

AGE

To dream of ***age***, portends failures in any kind of undertaking.

To dream of your own age, indicates that perversity of opinion will bring down upon you the indignation of relatives.

For a young woman to dream of being accused of being older than she is, denotes that she will fall into bad companionship, and her denial of stated things will be brought to scorn. To see herself ***looking aged***, intimates possible sickness, or unsatisfactory ventures. If it is her lover she sees aged, she will be in danger of losing him. ◎

YOUNG

To dream of seeing ***young*** people, is a prognostication of reconciliation of family disagreements and favorable times for planning new enterprises.

To dream that you are ***young again***, foretells that you will make mighty efforts to recall lost opportunities, but will nevertheless fail.

For a mother to see her son an infant or small child again, foretells that old wounds will be healed and she will take on her youthful hopes and cheerfulness. If the child seems to be dying, she will fall into ill fortune, and misery will attend her.

To see the ***young in school***, foretells that prosperity and usefulness will envelop you with favors. ◎

YOUNG CHILD

Overweight

FAT

To dream that you are getting ***fat***, denotes that you are about to make a fortunate change in your life.

To see ***others fat***, signifies prosperity. ◎

CORPULENCE

For a person to dream of being ***corpulent***, indicates to the dreamer bountiful increase of wealth and pleasant abiding places.

To see others corpulent, denotes unusual activity and prosperous times.

If a man or woman sees himself or herself looking ***grossly corpulent***, he or she should look well to their moral nature and impulses.

Beware of either concave or convex, telescopically or microscopically drawn pictures of yourself or others, as they forebode evil. ◎

Beauty and Ugliness

THE GILDED BEAUTY OF YOUTH

UGLY

To dream that you are ***ugly***, denotes that you will have a difficulty with your sweetheart, and your prospects will assume a depressed shade.

If a young woman thinks herself ugly, she will conduct herself offensively towards her lover, which will probably cause a break in their pleasant associations. ◎

BEAUTY

Beauty in any form is preeminently good. A ***beautiful woman***, brings pleasure and profitable business.

A well-formed and ***beautiful child***, indicates love reciprocated and a happy union. ◎

HANDSOME

To see yourself ***handsome*** looking in your dreams, you will prove yourself an ingenious flatterer.

To see others appearing handsome, denotes that you will enjoy the confidence of fast people. ◎

MODELS

To dream of a ***model***, foretells that your social affairs will deplete your purse, and quarrels and regrets will follow.

For a young woman to dream that ***she is a model*** or seeking to be one, foretells that she will be entangled in a love affair which will give her trouble through the selfishness of a friend. ◎

YOUNG *see* **MOTHER** *page 128*, **INFANTS** *page 119*, **SON** *page 128*, **SCHOOL** *page 180* ◆
CORPULENCE *see* **APPARITION** *page 274*, **PICTURES** *page 181* ◆ **BEAUTY** *see* **WOMAN** *page85* **CHILDREN** *page 128*

Faces

FACE

FACE

This dream is favorable if you see happy and bright *faces*, but significant of trouble if they are disfigured, ugly, or frowning on you.

To a young person, an ***ugly face*** foretells lovers' quarrels; or for a lover to see the face of his sweetheart looking old, denotes separation and the breaking up of happy associations.

To see a strange and ***weird-looking face***, denotes that enemies and misfortunes surround you.

To dream of seeing your ***own face***, denotes unhappiness; and to the married, threats of divorce will be made.

To see your ***face in a mirror***, denotes displeasure with yourself for not being able to carry out plans for self advancement. You will also lose the esteem of friends. ◎

COUNTENANCE

To dream of a beautiful and ingenuous ***countenance***, you may safely look for some pleasure to fall to your lot in the near future; but to behold an ugly and scowling visage, portends unfavorable transactions. ◎

FRECKLES

For a woman to dream that her face is ***freckled***, denotes that many displeasing incidents will insinuate themselves into her happiness. If she sees them in a mirror, she will be in danger of losing her lover to a rival. ◎

COMPLEXION

To dream that you have a beautiful ***complexion*** is lucky. You will pass through pleasing incidents.

To dream that you have a ***bad and dark complexion***, denotes disappointment and sickness. ◎

BLUSHING

For a young woman to dream of ***blushing***, denotes that she will be worried and humiliated by false accusations. If she sees others blush, she will be given to flippant raillery, which will make her unpleasing to her friends. ◎

ROUGE

To dream of using ***rouge***, denotes that you will practice deceit to obtain your wishes.

To see others with it on their faces, warns you that you are being artfully used to further the designs of some deceitful persons.

If you see it on your hands or clothing, you will be detected in some scheme.

If it comes off of your face, you will be humiliated before some rival, and lose your lover by assuming unnatural manners. ◎

CHALK

For a woman to dream of ***chalking*** her face, denotes that she will scheme to obtain admirers. ◎

LOOKING GLASS

Mirrors

MIRROR

To dream of seeing yourself in a ***mirror***, denotes that you will meet many discouraging issues, and sickness will cause you distress and loss in fortune.

To see a ***broken mirror***, foretells the sudden or violent death of someone related to you.

To see ***others in a mirror***, denotes that others will act unfairly toward you to promote their own interests.

To see ***animals in a mirror***, denotes disappointment and loss in fortune.

For a young woman to ***break a mirror***, foretells unfortunate friendships and an unhappy marriage.

To see her ***lover in a mirror*** looking pale and careworn, denotes death or a broken engagement. If he seems happy, a slight estrangement will arise, but it will be of short duration. ◎

DISTORTING MIRROR

LOOKING GLASS

For a woman to dream of a ***looking glass***, denotes that she is soon to be confronted with shocking deceitfulness and discrepancies; such occurrences may result in tragic scenes or separation. ◎

Dreams of innocent babyhood *opposite bottom* **and the gilded beauty of youth** *opposite center* **are as beguiling as dreams of the looking glass** *left* **and mirror** *above* **are vain and discouraging.**

FACE *see* **UGLY** *page 100* ◆ **SWEETHEART** *page 124,* **AGE** *page 100,* **APPARITION** *page 274* ◆ **COUNTENANCE** *see* **UGLY, BEAUTY** *page 100* ◆ **ROUGE** *see* **HAND** *page 97,* **CLOTHES** *page 154* ◆ **MIRROR** *see* **BREAK** *page 265,* **GLASS** *page 69* ◆ **LOOKING GLASS** *see* **GLASS** *page 69*

Crowning Glory

HAIR
If a woman dreams that she has beautiful ***hair*** and combs it, she will be careless in her personal affairs, and will lose advancement by neglecting mental applications.

HAIR DREAMS

For a man to dream that he is ***thinning his hair***, foreshadows that he will become poor by his generosity, and suffer illness through mental worry.

To see your ***hair turning gray***, foretells death and contagion in the family of some relative or some friend.

To see yourself ***covered with hair***, omens indulgence in vices to such an extent as will debar you from the society of refined people. If a woman, she will resolve herself into a world of her own, claiming the right to act for her own pleasure regardless of moral codes.

If a man dreams that he has ***black, curling hair***, he will deceive people through his pleasing address. He will very likely deceive the women who trust him. If a woman's hair seems black and curly, she will be threatened with seduction.

If you dream of seeing a woman with ***golden hair***, you will prove a fearless lover and be woman's true friend.

To dream that your sweetheart has ***red hair***, you will be denounced by the woman you love for unfaithfulness. Red hair usually suggests changes.

If you dream that you see ***brown hair***, this indicates that you will be unfortunate in choosing a career.

If you see well-kept and neatly ***combed hair***, your fortune will improve.

To dream that you ***cut your hair*** close to the scalp, denotes that you will be generous to lavishness towards a friend. Frugality will be the fruits growing out therefrom.

To see the ***hair growing out*** soft and luxuriant, signifies happiness and luxury.

For a woman to ***compare a white hair with a black one***, which she takes from her head, foretells that she will be likely to hesitate between two offers of seeming fortune, and unless she uses great care, will choose the one that will afford her loss or distress instead of pleasant fortune.

To see ***tangled and unkempt hair***, denotes that life will be a veritable burden, business will fall off, and the marriage yoke will be troublesome to carry.

If a woman is unsuccessful in combing her hair, she will lose a worthy man's name by a needless show of temper and disdain.

For a young woman to dream of women with ***gray hair***, denotes that they will come into her life as rivals in the affection of a male relative, or displace the love of her affianced.

To dream of having your ***hair cut***, denotes serious disappointments.

For a woman to dream that her ***hair is falling out***, and baldness is apparent, she will have to earn her own livelihood, as fortune has passed her by.

For a man or woman to dream that they have hair of ***snowy whiteness***, denotes that they will enjoy a pleasing and fortunate journey through life.

For a man to ***caress the hair*** of a woman, shows that he will enjoy the love and confidence of some worthy woman who will trust him despite the world's condemnation.

To see ***flowers in your hair***, foretells troubles approaching which, when they come, will give you less fear than when viewed from a distance.

For a woman to dream that her hair turns to white flowers, augurs that troubles of a various nature will confront her and she does well if she strengthens her soul with patience, and endeavors to bear her trials with fortitude.

To dream that a lock of your hair ***turns gray and falls out***, is a sign of trouble and disappointment in your affairs. Sickness will cast gloom over bright expectations.

To see one's hair ***turn perfectly white*** in one night, and the face seemingly young, foretells sudden calamity and deep grief. For a young woman to have this dream, signifies that she will lose her lover by a sudden sickness or accident. She will likely come to grief from some indiscretion on her part. She should be careful of her associates. ◎

LOCK OF HAIR

HAIR *see also* **COMBING, HAIRBRUSH, BARBER, HAIRDRESSER, BALD, WIG** *page 103,* **SHAVING, SHAVE, RAZOR, BEARD, MUSTACHE** *page 104,* **FLOWERS** *page 57,* **HAIRY HANDS** *page 97*

Hair Care

COMBING
To dream of ***combing*** one's hair, denotes the illness or death of a friend or relative. Decay of friendship and loss of property is also indicated by this dream. ◎

HAIRBRUSH
To dream of using a ***hairbrush***, denotes that you will suffer misfortune from your mismanagement.

To see old hairbrushes, denotes sickness and ill health. ◎

SHAMPOO
To dream of seeing ***shampooing*** going on, denotes that you will engage in undignified affairs to please others.

To dream that you have your ***own head shampooed***, indicates that you will soon make a secret trip, in which you will have much enjoyment, if you succeed in keeping the real purport from your family or friends. ◎

THE HAIRDRESSER

Hair is an important dream symbol. There are many different hair dreams *opposite left*, **from the single, romantic lock of hair** *opposite* **to an appointment with your dream hairdresser** *above*. **Baldness** *right* **also has its place in your dreams.**

Barbers and Hairdressers

BARBER
To dream of a ***barber***, denotes that success will come through struggling and close attention to business.

For a young woman to dream of a barber, foretells that her fortune will increase, though meagerly. ◎

HAIRDRESSER
Should you visit a ***hairdresser*** in your dreams, you will be connected with a sensation caused by the indiscretion of a good-looking woman. To a woman, this dream means a family disturbance and well-merited censures.

For a woman to dream of having her ***hair colored***, she will narrowly escape the scorn of society, as enemies will seek to blight her reputation. To have her ***hair dressed***, denotes that she will run after frivolous things, and use any means to bend people to her wishes. ◎

YUL BRYNNER AS THE KING OF SIAM

Baldness and Wigs

BALD
To dream that you see a ***baldheaded*** man, denotes that sharpers are about to make a deal adverse to your interests, but by keeping wide awake, you will outwit them.

For a man to dream of a ***baldheaded woman***, ensures him to have a vixen for a wife.

For a young woman to dream of a ***baldheaded man***, is a warning to her to use her intelligence against listening to her next marriage offer.

Baldheaded babies signify a happy home, a loving companion, and obedient children.

A ***bald hill*** or mountain, indicates famine and suffering in various forms. ◎

WIG
To dream you wear a ***wig***, indicates that you will soon make an unpropitious change.

To lose a wig, you will incur the derision and contempt of enemies.

To see others wearing wigs, is a sign of treachery entangling you. ◎

COMBING *see* **HAIR** *page 102* ◆ **HAIRBRUSH** *see* **HAIR** *page 102* ◆ **SHAMPOO** *see* **HAIR** *page 102,* **HEAD** *page 92* ◆ **BARBER** *see* **HAIR** *page 102,* **RAZOR, SHAVE, SHAVING** *page 104* ◆ **HAIRDRESSER** *see* **HAIR** *page 102* ◆ **BALD** *see* **BABY** *page 119,* **HILL, MOUNTAIN** *page 90*

Shaving and Facial Hair

SHAVING
To dream that you are being ***shaved***, portends that you will let impostors defraud you.

To ***shave yourself***, foretells that you will govern your own business and dictate to your household, notwithstanding that the presence of a shrew may cause your quarrels.

If your face appears smooth, you will enjoy quiet, and your conduct will not be questioned by your companions. If it is old and rough, there will be many squalls on the matrimonial sea.

If your ***razor is dull*** and pulls your face, you will give your friends cause to criticize your private life.

If your beard seems ***gray***, you will be absolutely devoid of any sense of justice to those having claims upon you.

For a woman to see ***men shaving***, foretells that her nature will become sullied by indulgence in gross pleasures.

If she dreams of ***being shaved***, she will assume so much masculinity that men will turn from her in disgust. ◎

SHAVE
To merely contemplate getting a ***shave***, in your dream, denotes that you will plan for the successful development of enterprises, but will fail to generate energy sufficient to succeed. ◎

RAZOR
To dream of a ***razor***, portends disagreements and contentions over troubles.

To cut yourself with one, denotes that you will be unlucky in some deal which you are about to make.

Fighting with a razor foretells disappointing business and that someone will keep you harassed almost beyond endurance.

A broken or rusty one, brings unavoidable distress. ◎

BEARD

BEARD
To dream of seeing a ***beard***, denotes that some uncongenial person will oppose his will against yours. There will be a fierce struggle for mastery, and you are likely to lose some money in the combat.

A ***gray beard***, signifies hard luck and quarrels.

To see ***beards on women***, foretells unpleasant associations and lingering illness.

For someone to ***pull your beard***, denotes that you will run a narrow risk if you do not lose property.

To comb and admire it, shows that your vanity will grow with prosperity, making you detestable in the sight of many of your former companions.

For a young woman to ***admire a beard***, intimates her desire to leave celibacy; but she is threatened with an unfortunate marriage. ◎

MUSTACHE
To dream that you have a ***mustache***, denotes that your egotism and effrontery will cause you a poor inheritance in worldly goods, and you will betray women to their sorrow.

If a woman dreams of ***admiring a mustache***, her virtue is in danger, and she should be mindful of her conduct.

If a man dreams that he has his ***mustache shaved***, he will try to turn from evil companions and pleasures, and seek to reinstate himself in former positions of honor. ◎

Grooming in your dreams may find you tending a fine beard *above*, **undergoing a vigorous scrubbing** *right* **or soaking in the tub** *opposite*.

Soap and Washing

SOAP
To dream of ***soap***, foretells that friendships will reveal interesting entertainment. Farmers will have success in their varied affairs.

For a young woman to dream that she is ***making a soap***, omens that a substantial and satisfactory competency will be hers. ◎

BASIN
For a young woman to dream of bathing in a ***basin***, foretells that her womanly graces will win her real friendships and elevations. ◎

WASHBOWL
To dream of a ***washbowl***, signifies that new carers will interest you and afford much enjoyment to others.

To bathe your face and hands in a ***bowl of clear water***, denotes that you will soon consummate passionate wishes which will bind you closely to someone who interested you, but before passion enveloped you.

If the bowl is soiled or broken you will rue an illicit engagement, which will give others pain and afford you small pleasure. ◎

WASHING
To dream that you are ***washing*** yourself, signifies that you pride yourself on the numberless liaisons that you maintain. ◎

WASHING DREAMS

SHAVING *see* **HAIR** *page 102,* **BARBER** *page 103* ◆ **SHAVE** *see* **BARBER** *page 103* ◆ **RAZOR** *see* **BARBER** *page 103,* **CUT** *page 112,* **FIGHT** *page 260,* **RUST** *page 255* ◆ **BEARD** *see* **HAIR** *page 102,* **COMBING** *page 103,* **ADMIRE** *page 259* ◆ **MUSTACHE** *see* **ADMIRE** *page 259* ◆ **BASIN** *see* **BATH** *page 105* ◆ **WASHBOWL** *see* **WATER** *page 78,* **BREAK** *page 265*

Baths and Bathing

BATH

For a young person to dream of taking a ***bath***, means much solicitude for one of the opposite sex, fearing to lose his good opinion through the influence of others.

For a pregnant woman to dream this, denotes miscarriage or accident. For a man, adultery. Dealings of all kinds should be carried on with discretion after this dream.

To go in ***bathing with others***, evil companions should be avoided. Defamation of character is likely to follow. If the water is muddy, evil, death, and enemies are near you. Bathing in a clear sea, denotes expansion of business and satisfying research after knowledge.

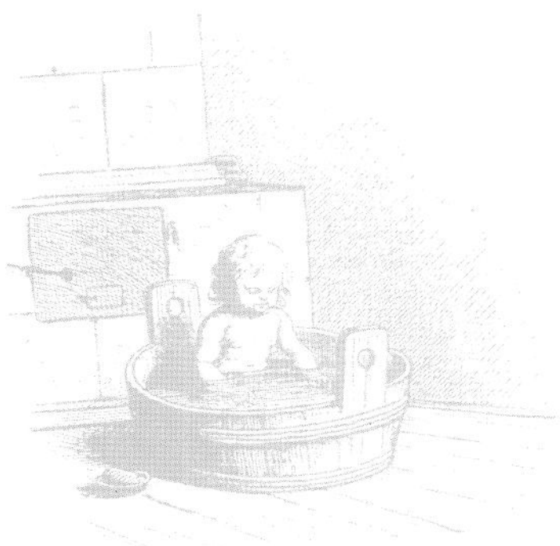

IN THE TUB

For a widow to dream of her bath, she has forgotten her former ties, and is hurrying on to earthly loves. Girls should shun male companions. Men will engage in salacious intrigues.

A ***warm bath*** is generally significant of evil. A ***cold, clear bath*** is the forerunner of joyful tidings and a long period of excellent health. ◎

TURKISH BATHS

To dream of taking a ***Turkish bath***, foretells that you will seek health far from your home and friends, but will have much pleasurable enjoyment.

To see others take a Turkish bath, signifies that pleasant companions will occupy your attention. ◎

Spiritual and Mental Matters

SOUL

To dream of seeing your soul ***leaving your body, signifies that you are in danger of sacrificing yourself to useless designs, which will dwarf your sense of honor and cause you to become mercenary and uncharitable.***

For an artist to see his soul in another, foretells that he will gain distinction if he applies himself to his work and leaves off sentimental roles.

To imagine that another's soul is in you, denotes that you will derive solace and benefit from some stranger who is yet to come into your life.

For a young woman musician to dream that she sees another young woman on the stage clothed in sheer robes, and imagine that it is her own soul in the other person, denotes that she will be outrivaled in some great undertaking.

To dream that you are discussing the immortality of your soul, ***denotes that you will improve opportunities which will aid you in gaining desired knowledge and pleasure of intercourse with intellectual people.*** ❋

MADNESS

To dream of being mad, shows trouble ahead for the dreamer. Sickness, by which you will lose property, is threatened.

To see others suffering under this malady, denotes inconstancy of friends and gloomy ending of bright expectations.

For a young woman to dream of madness, ***foretells disappointment in marriage and wealth.*** ❋

INSANITY

To dream of being insane, ***forebodes disastrous results to some newly undertaken work, or ill health may work sad changes in your prospects.***

To see others insane, denotes disagreeable contact with suffering and appeals from the poverty-stricken. The utmost care should be taken of the health after this dream. ❋

ASYLUM

To dream of an asylum, ***denotes sickness and unlucky dealings, which cannot be overcome without great mental struggle.*** ❋

IDIOT

Idiots ***in a dream, foretell disagreements and losses.***

To dream that you are an idiot, ***you will feel humiliated and downcast over the miscarriage of plans.***

To see idiotic children, ***denotes affliction and unhappy changes.*** ❋

VAPOR BATH

To dream that you are indulging in a ***vapor bath***, you will have fretful people for companions.

If you dream that you are ***emerging from a vapor bath*** then you will find that your cares will be temporary. ◎

TUB

To dream of seeing a ***tub*** full of water, denotes domestic contentment. An ***empty tub***, proclaims unhappiness and waning of fortune.

A ***broken tub***, foretells family disagreements and quarrels. ◎

BATH *see* **WATER** *page 78* ◆ **TUB** *see* **WATER** *page 78,* **BREAK** *page 265* ◆ **IDIOT** *see* **CHILDREN** *page 128*

Sickness and Health

Dreams of sickness and pain are never pleasant but do not always portend the worst; they may be a coded warning that something is going wrong in our lives, but it is rarely as life-threatening as the disease might be in reality. This section covers general symptoms, specific diseases, malfunctions in various body systems as well as dreams of care and cure.

Sickness and Affliction

DISEASE
To dream that you are ***diseased***, denotes a slight attack of illness, or of unpleasant dealings with a relative.

For a young woman to dream that she is ***incurably diseased***, denotes that she will be likely to lead a life of single blessedness. ◎

SICKNESS
To dream of ***sickness***, is a sign of trouble and real sickness in your family. Discord is sure to find entrance into your life also.

To dream of your own sickness, is a warning to be unusually cautious of your person.

To see any of your family ***pale and sick***, foretells that some event will break unexpectedly upon your harmonious hearthstone. Sickness is usually attendant upon this dream. ◎

AFFLICTION
To dream that ***affliction*** lays a heavy hand upon you and calls your energy to a halt, foretells that some disaster is surely approaching you.

To see ***others afflicted***, foretells that you will be surrounded by many ills and misfortunes. ◎

Dreams of illness may find you oppressed by general affliction *above*, **disabled by sudden injury** *right*, **suffering from intense pain such as that of migraine** *opposite top* **or being examined or treated by a doctor** *opposite center*.

Illness and Injury

AFFLICTION

Plague and Epidemic

PLAGUE
To dream of a ***plague*** raging, denotes disappointing returns in business, and your wife or lover will lead you a wretched existence.

If you are ***afflicted with the plague***, you will keep your business out of embarrassment with the greatest maneuvering.

If you are trying to escape it, some trouble, which looks impenetrable, is pursuing you. ◎

EPIDEMIC
To dream of an ***epidemic***, signifies prostration of mental faculties and worry from distasteful tasks. Contagion among relatives or friends is foretold by dreams of this nature. ◎

INJURY
To dream of an ***injury*** being done you, signifies that an unfortunate occurrence will soon grieve and vex you. ◎

INFIRMITIES
To dream of ***infirmities***, denotes misfortune in love and business; enemies are not to be misunderstood, and sickness may follow.

To dream that you see ***others infirm***, denotes that you may have various troubles and disappointments in business. ◎

ILLNESS
For a woman to dream of her own ***illness***, foretells that some unforeseen event will throw her into a frenzy of despair by causing her to miss some anticipated visit or entertainment. ◎

INVALID
To dream of ***invalids***, is a sign of displeasing companions interfering with your interest. To think you are one, portends that you are threatened with displeasing circumstances. ◎

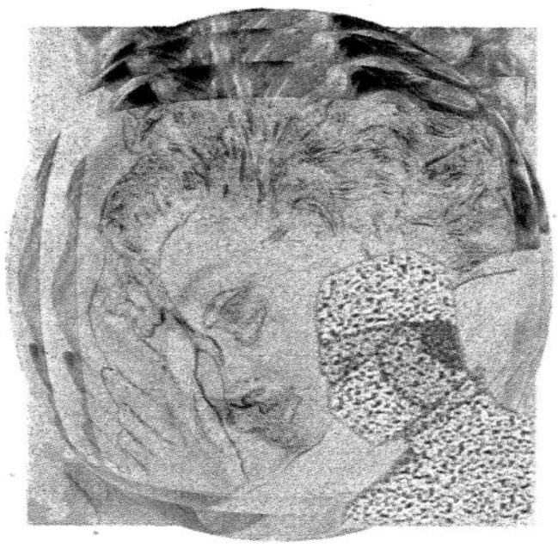

INJURY

PLAGUE *see* **ESCAPE** *page 266* ◆ **INJURY** *see* **CUT, WOUND** *page 112* ◆ **ILLNESS** *see* **SMALLPOX, MEASLES, SCARLET FEVER, CANCER, LOCKJAW, CHOLERA, TYPHOID, HYDROPHOBIA** *page 110,* **JAUNDICE, LEPROSY** *page 111*

Aches and Pains

PAIN
To dream that you are in ***pain***, will make sure your own unhappiness. This dream foretells useless regrets over some trivial transaction.

To dream that you see ***others in pain***, warns you that you are making mistakes in your life. ◎

AGUE
A sickly condition of the dreamer is sometimes implied by this dream. To dream that you are shaking with an ***ague***, signifies that you will suffer from some physical disorder, and that fluctuating opinions of your own affairs may bring you to the borders of prostration.

To see others thus affected, denotes that you will offend people by your supreme indifference to the influences of others. ◎

ACHES
To dream that you have ***aches***, denotes that you are halting too much in your business, and that some other person is profiting by your ideas.

For a young woman to dream that she has ***heartache***, foretells that she will be in sore distress over the laggardly way her love prosecutes his suit. If it is the ***backache***, she will encounter illness through careless exposure. If she has the ***headache***, there will be much disquietude of mind for the risk she has taken to rid herself of rivalry. ◎

AGONY
This is not as good a dream as some would wish you to believe. It portends worry and pleasure intermingled, more of the former than of the latter.

To dream you that you are in ***agony*** over the loss of money, or property, denotes that disturbing and imaginary fears will rack you over the critical condition of affairs, or the illness of some dear relative. ◎

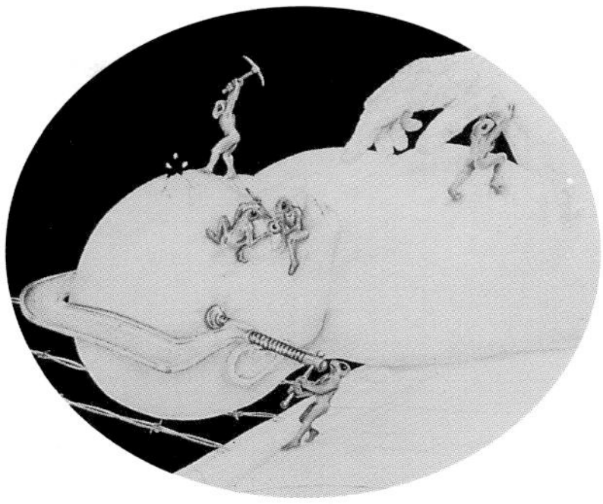

THE AGONY OF MIGRAINE

RHEUMATISM
To feel ***rheumatism*** attacking you in a dream, foretells an unexpected delay in the accomplishment of plans.

To see others so afflicted, brings disappointments. ◎

Fits and Fevers

FEVER
To dream that you are stricken with this malady, signifies that you are worrying over trifling affairs while the best of life is slipping past you, and you should pull yourself into shape and engage in profitable work.

To dream of seeing some of your family sick with ***fever***, denotes temporary illness for some of them. ◎

FITS
To dream of having ***fits***, denotes that you will fall prey to ill health and will lose employment.

To see others in this plight, denotes that you will have much unpleasantness in your circle, caused by quarrels from those under you. ◎

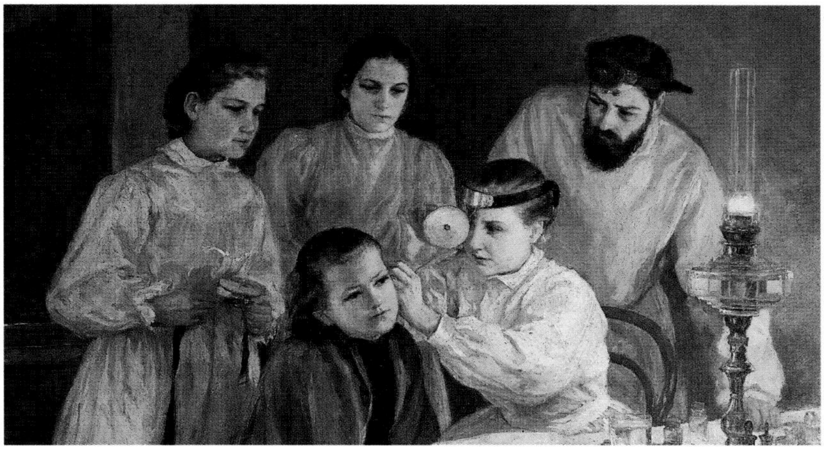

THE DOCTOR'S EXAMINATION

Exhaustion

FEEBLE
To dream of being ***feeble***, denotes unhealthy occupation and mental worry. Seek to make a change for yourself after this dream. ◎

FATIGUE
To feel ***fatigued*** in a dream, foretells ill health or oppression in business. For a young woman to see others fatigued, indicates discouraging progress in health. ◎

HAGGARD
To see a ***haggard*** face in your dreams, denotes misfortune and defeat in love matters.

To see your own face haggard and distressed, denotes trouble over female affairs, which may render you unable to meet business engagements in a healthy manner. ◎

ACHES *see* **HEART** *page 94,* **BACK** *page 96,* **HEAD** *page 92* ◆ **RHEUMATISM** *see* **AFFLICTION** *page 106* ◆ **FEVER** *see* **FAMILY** *page 127* ◆ **HAGGARD** *see* **FACE** *page 101*

Fainting, Palsy, and Paralysis

FAINTING
To dream of ***fainting***, signifies illness in your family and unpleasant news of the absent.

If a young woman dreams of fainting, it denotes that she will fall into ill health and experience disappointment from her careless way of living. ◎

VERTIGO
To dream that you have ***vertigo***, foretells that you will have loss in domestic happiness, and your affairs will be under gloomy outlooks. ◎

PALSY
To dream you are afflicted with ***palsy***, denotes that you are making unstable contracts.

If you see your friend so afflicted, there will be uncertainty as to his faithfulness, and sickness, too, may enter your home.

For lovers to dream that their ***sweethearts have palsy***, signifies that dissatisfaction over some question will mar their happiness. ◎

NUMBNESS
To dream that you feel a ***numbness*** creeping over you, is a sign of illness and disquieting conditions. ◎

PARALYSIS
Paralysis is a bad dream, denoting financial reverses and disappointment in literary attainment. To lovers, it portends a cessation of affections. ◎

In your dreams you may suffer general symptoms such as fainting *above* **or specific illness such as consumption [tuberculosis]** *opposite bottom*. **Unpleasant infestation such as tapeworms** *opposite top* **may also blight your dreams.**

Purging, Swelling, and Splitting

FAINTING

SWELLING
To dream that you see yourself ***swollen,*** denotes that you will amass fortune, but your egotism will interfere with your employment.

To see ***others swollen***, foretells that advancement will meet with envious obstructions. ◎

GANGRENE
To dream that you see anyone afflicted with ***gangrene***, foretells the death of a parent or near relative. ◎

ABSCESS
To dream that you have an ***abscess*** which seems to have reached a chronic stage, you will be overwhelmed with misfortune of your own; at the same time, your deepest sympathies will be enlisted for the sorrows of others. ◎

ULCER
To see an ***ulcer*** in your dream, signifies loss of friends and removal from a loved one. Affairs will remain unsatisfactory.

To dream that you ***have ulcers***, denotes that you will become unpopular with your friends by giving yourself up to foolish pleasures. ◎

RUPTURE
To dream that you are ***ruptured***, denotes that you will have physical disorders or disagreeable contentions. If it be others you see in this condition, you will be in danger of irreconcilable quarrels. ◎

VOMIT
To dream of ***vomiting*** is a sign that you will be afflicted with a malady which will threaten invalidism, or you will be connected with a racy scandal.

To see others vomiting, denotes that you will be made aware of the false pretenses of persons who are trying to engage your aid.

For a woman to dream that she ***vomits a chicken***, and it hops off, denotes that she will be disappointed in some pleasure by the illness of some relative. Unfavorable business and discontent are also predicted.

If it is ***blood that you vomit***, you will find illness a hurried and unexpected visitor. You will be cast down with gloomy forebodings, and children and domesticity in general will ally to work you discomfort. ◎

FLUX
To dream of having ***flux*** [diarrhea], or thinking that you are thus afflicted, denotes that desperate or fatal illness will overtake you or some member of your family.

To see others thus afflicted, implies disappointment in carrying out some enterprise through the neglect of others. Inharmonious states will vex you. ◎

PALSY *see* **AFFLICTION** *page 106* ◆ **GANGRENE** *see* **AFFLICTION** *page 106* ◆
VOMIT *see* **CHICKENS** *page 39*, **BLOOD** *page 94* ◆ **FLUX** *see* **AFFLICTION** *page 106*

Diseases of Excess

INDIGESTION
To dream of ***indigestion***, indicates unhealthy and gloomy surroundings. ◎

GOUT
If you dream of having the ***gout***, you will be sure to be exasperated beyond endurance by the silly conduct of some relative, and suffer small financial loss through the same person. ◎

Infestations

TAPEWORM
To dream that you see a ***tapeworm***, or have one, denotes disagreeable prospects for health or for pleasure. ◎

TAPEWORM

RINGWORMS
To dream of having ***ringworms*** appear on you, you will have a slight illness, and some exasperating difficulty in the near future.

If you see them on others, beggars and appeals for charity will beset you. ◎

Respiratory Problems

COUGH
To dream that you are aggravated by a constant ***cough***, indicates a state of low health, but one from which you will recuperate if care is observed in your habits.

To dream of hearing ***others cough***, indicates that you will be plunged into unpleasant surroundings from which you will ultimately emerge. ◎

CROUP
To dream that your child has the ***croup***, denotes slight illness, but useless fear for its safety. This is generally a good omen of health and domestic harmony. ◎

BRONCHITIS
To dream that you are afflicted with ***bronchitis***, foretells that you will be detained from pursuing your views and plans by unfortunate complications of sickness in your home.

To suffer with bronchitis in a dream, denotes that discouraging prospects of winning desired objects will soon loom up before you. ◎

CONSUMPTION
To dream that you have ***consumption***, denotes that you are exposing yourself to danger. Remain with your friends. ◎

THE CONSUMPTIVE

CROUP *see* **CHILDREN** *page 128* ◆ **BRONCHITIS** *see* **AFFLICTION** *page 106*

THE SICK CHILD

Infectious Illnesses

SMALLPOX
To see people with ***smallpox*** in your dreams, denotes unexpected and shocking sickness, and probably contagion. Such a dream signifies that you will meet failure in accomplishing your designs. ◎

MEASLES
To dream that you have ***measles***, denotes much worry, and anxious care will interfere with your business affairs.

To dream that others have this disease, denotes that you will be troubled over the condition of others. ◎

SCARLET FEVER
To dream of ***scarlet fever***, foretells that you are in danger of sickness, or in the power of an enemy.

To dream that a relative dies suddenly with it, foretells that you will be overcome by villainous treachery. ◎

Cancer

CANCER
To have a ***cancer*** successfully treated in a dream, denotes a sudden rise in circumstance, from obscure poverty to wealthy surroundings.

To dream of a cancer, denotes illness of someone near you, and quarrels with those you love. Depressions may follow to the man of affairs after this dream.

To dream of a cancer, foretells sorrow in its ugliest phase. Love will resolve itself into cold formality, and business transactions will be worrying and profitless. ◎

CANKER
To dream of seeing ***canker*** on anything, is an omen of evil. It foretells death and treacherous companions for the young, sorrow and loneliness to the aged.

Cankerous growths in the flesh, denotes future distinctions, either as head of state or a life on the stage. ◎

Deadly Diseases

LOCKJAW
To dream that you have ***lockjaw***, signifies that there is trouble ahead for you, as some person is going to betray your confidence.

For a woman to see ***others with lockjaw***, foretells that her friends will unconsciously detract from her happiness by assigning her unpleasant tasks to do.

If stock have it, you will lose a friend. ◎

CHOLERA
To dream of this dread disease devastating the country, portends that sickness of virulent type will rage and many disappointments will follow.

To dream that you are attacked by it, denotes your own sickness. ◎

TYPHOID
To dream that you are affected with this malady, is a warning to beware of enemies, and look well to your health.

If you dream that there is an epidemic of ***typhoid***, there will be depression in business, and usual good health will undergo disagreeable changes. ◎

HYDROPHOBIA
To dream that you are afflicted with ***hydrophobia*** [rabies], denotes enemies and a change of business.

If you see others thus afflicted, your work will be interrupted by death or ungrateful dependence.

To dream that an animal with the rabies bites you, means that you will be betrayed by your dearest friend, and much scandal will be brought to light. ◎

Infectious illnesses, especially those of childhood such as measles, may haunt your dreams *above*. **Horrid skin blemishes such as boils and sores** *opposite*, **or unsightly rashes** *opposite top* **offer unpleasant omens.**

SCARLET FEVER *see* **DEATH** *page 120* ◆ **TYPHOID** *see* **EPIDEMIC** *page 106* ◆ **HYDROPHOBIA** *see* **AFFLICTED** *page 106*, **BITE** *page 112*

The skin is the largest organ of our body; it is also our protection from the outside world and the first thing other people notice about us. Dreams of skin disease are often significant of the state of our relationship with other people and the outside world.

Skin Problems

PIMPLE
To dream of your flesh being full of ***pimples***, denotes worry over trifles.

To see others with pimples on them, signifies that you will be troubled with illness and complaints from others.

For a woman to dream that her ***beauty is marred by pimples***, means that her conduct in home or social circles will be criticized by friends and acquaintances. You may have small annoyances to follow this dream. ◎

MOLES
To see ***moles*** or such blemishes on the person, indicates illness and quarrels. ◎

SORES
To dream of seeing ***sores***, denotes that illness will cause you loss and mental distress.

To dress a sore, foretells that your personal wishes and desires will give place to the pleasures of others.

To dream of an infant having a deep sore so that you can see the bone, denotes that distressing and annoying incidents will detract from your plans, and children will be threatened with contagion.

To dream of sores on yourself, portends early decay of health and impaired mentality. Sickness and unsatisfactory business will follow this dream. ◎

BOILS
To dream of a ***boil*** running pus and blood, you will have unpleasant things to meet in your immediate future. It may be that the insincerity of friends will cause you great inconvenience.

To dream of boils on your forehead, is significant of the sickness of someone near you. ◎

WARTS
If you are troubled with ***warts*** on your person in dreams, you will be unable to successfully parry the thrusts made at your honor.

To see them leaving your hands, foretells that you will overcome disagreeable obstructions to fortune.

To see them on others, shows that you have bitter enemies near you.

If you doctor them, you will struggle with energy to ward off threatened danger to you and yours. ◎

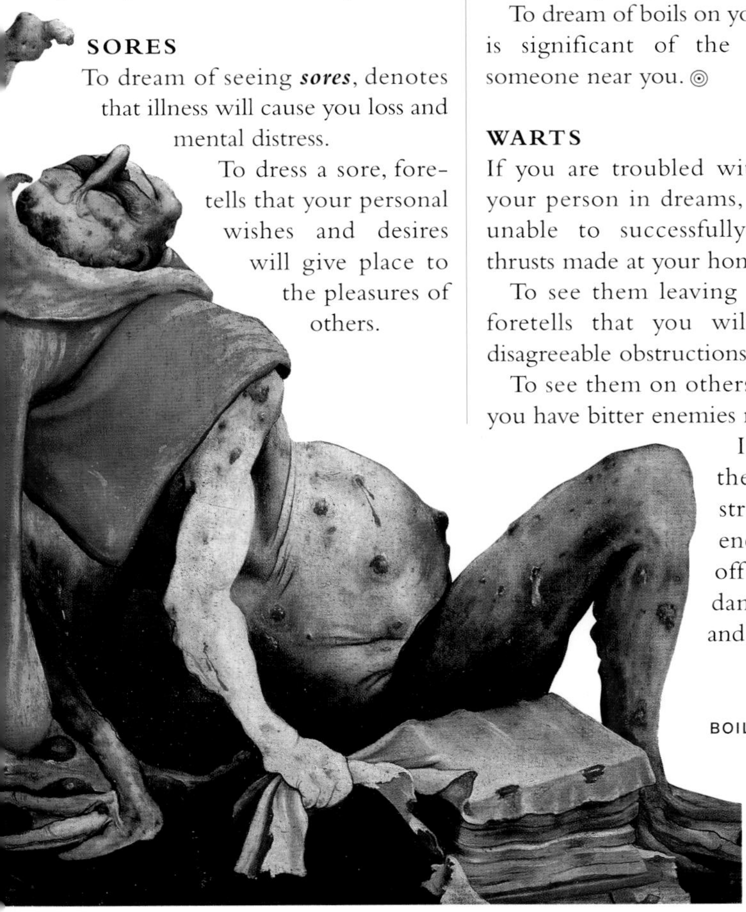

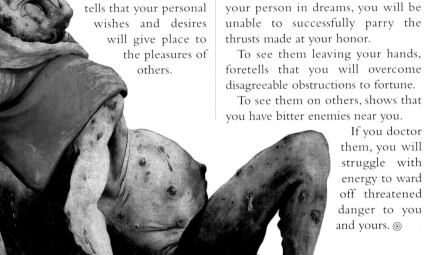

BOILS AND SORES

Itching

HIVES
To dream that your child is afflicted with ***hives***, denotes that it will enjoy good health and be docile.

To see strange children thus afflicted, you will be unduly frightened over the condition of some favorite. ◎

ITCH
To see persons with the ***itch***, and you endeavor to escape contact, you will stand in fear of distressing results when your endeavors will bring pleasant success.

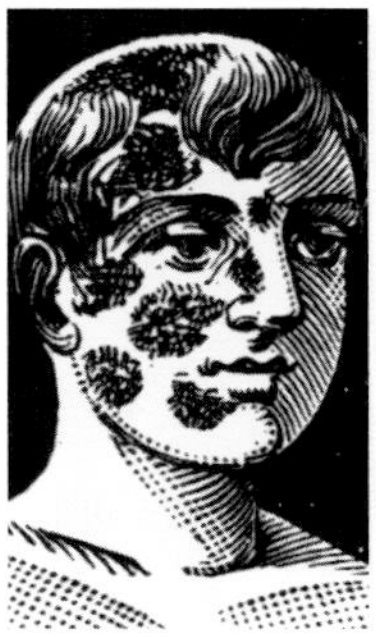

A SKIN PROBLEM

If you dream you have the itch yourself, you will be harshly used, and will defend yourself by incriminating others. For a young woman to have this dream, omens that she will fall into dissolute companionship.

To dream that you itch, denotes unpleasant avocations. ◎

Serious Diseases

JAUNDICE
To dream that you have the ***jaundice***, denotes prosperity after temporary embarrassments.

To see ***others with jaundice***, you will be worried with unpleasant companions and discouraging prospects. ◎

LEPROSY
To dream that you are infected with this dread disease, foretells sickness, by which you will lose money and incur the displeasure of others.

If you see others afflicted thus, you will meet discouraging prospects, and love will turn into indifference. ◎

PIMPLES *see* **ILLNESS** *page 106*, **BEAUTY** *page 100* ◆ **MOLES** *see also* **MOLES** *page 32* ◆ **SORES** *see* **INFANTS** *page 119*, **WOUND** *page 112*, **BONES** *page 91* ◆ **BOILS** *see* **BLOOD** *page 94*, **FOREHEAD** *page 92* ◆ **WARTS** *see* **HANDS** *page 97* ◆ **HIVES** *see* **CHILDREN** *page 128* ◆ **LEPROSY** *see* **DISEASE, SICKNESS** *page 106*

Burns and Cuts

SCALDING
To dream of being ***scalded***, portends that distressing incidents will blot out pleasurable anticipation. ◎

BURNS
Burns stand for tidings of good. To burn your hand in a clear and flowing fire, denotes purity of purpose and the approbation of friends.

To ***burn your feet*** in walking through coals or beds of fire, denotes your ability to accomplish any endeavor, however impossible it may be to others. Your usual good health will remain with you, but, if you are overcome in fire, it represents that your interest will suffer through the treachery of supposed friends. ◎

CUT
To dream of a ***cut***, denotes sickness or that the treachery of a friend will frustrate your cheerfulness. ◎

WOUND
To dream that you are ***wounded***, signals distress and an unfavorable turn in business.

To see others wounded, denotes that injustice will be accorded you by your friends.

To relieve or ***dress a wound***, signifies that you will have occasion to congratulate yourself on your good fortune. ◎

Stings and Splinters

SPLINTER
To dream of ***splinters*** sticking into your flesh, denotes that you will have many vexations from members of your family or from jealous rivals.

If, while you are visiting, you stick a ***splinter in your foot***, you will soon make or receive a visit which will prove extremely unpleasant. Your affairs will go slightly wrong through your continued neglect. ◎

STING
To feel that any insect ***stings you*** in a dream, is a foreboding of evil and unhappiness.

For a young woman to dream that she is stung, is ominous of sorrow and remorse from an unwise overconfidence in men. ◎

SCRATCH
To ***scratch*** others in your dreams, denotes that you will be ill-tempered and fault-finding in your dealings with others.

If you are ***scratched***, you will be injured by the enmity of some deceitful person. ◎

BITE
This dream omens ill. To dream of ***a bite*** implies a wish to undo work that is past undoing. You are also likely to suffer through some enemy. ◎

THE BITE

Lameness

CORNS
To dream that your ***corns*** hurt your feet, denotes that some enemies are undermining you, and you will have much distress; but if you succeed in clearing your feet of corns, you will inherit a large estate from some unknown source.

For a young woman to dream of having ***corns on her feet***, indicates that she will have to bear many crosses and be coldly treated by her sex. ◎

LAME
For a woman to dream of seeing anyone ***lame***, foretells that her pleasures and hopes will be unfruitful and disappointing. ◎

LIMP
To dream that you ***limp*** in your walk, denotes that a small worry will unexpectedly confront you, detracting much from your enjoyment.

To see others ***limping***, signifies that you will be naturally offended at the conduct of a friend. Small failures attend this dream. ◎

CRIPPLED
To dream of the maimed and ***crippled***, denotes famine and distress among the poor, and you should be willing to contribute to their store. It also indicates a temporary dullness in trade. ◎

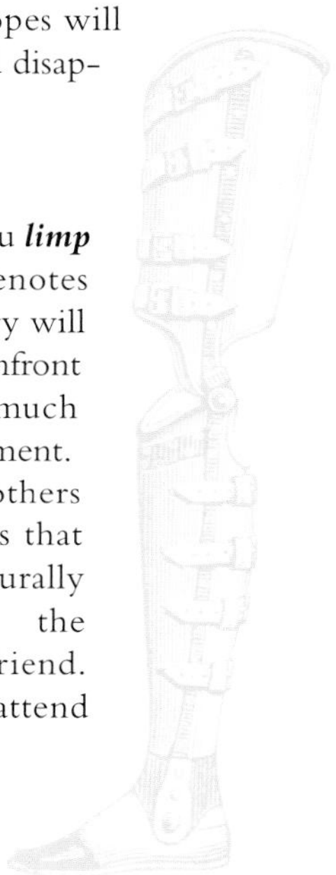

A FALSE LEG

CRUTCHES
To dream that you go on ***crutches***, denotes that you will depend largely on others for your support and advancement.

To see ***others on crutches***, denotes unsatisfactory results from labors. ◎

BURNS *see* **FEET** *page 96*, **COALS** *page 70*, **FIRE** *page 80* ◆ **SPLINTER** *see* **FEET** *page 96* ◆ **STING** *see* **BEE, WASP, HORNET, MOSQUITO** *page 48* ◆ **CORNS** *see* **FEET** *page 96* ◆ **LIMP** *see* **WALKING** *page 267*

Dreams of rescue from injury, care and cure, like dreams of disease, may not portend unalloyed relief and joy. This section covers hospitals and infirmaries, doctors and nurses, surgeons and their implements, medicine and medical tools, old-fashioned remedies, and quack medicine.

Refuge for the Sick

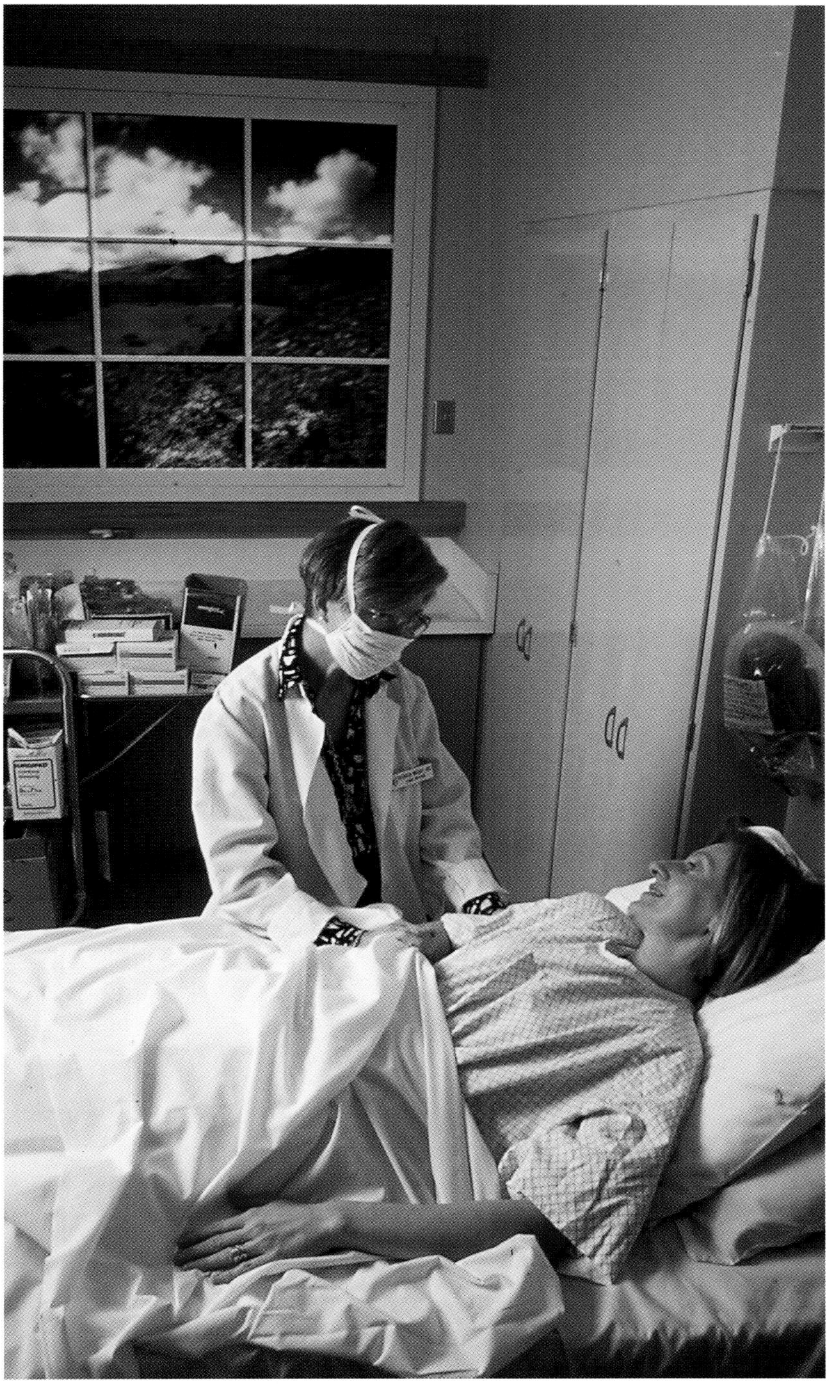

IN HOSPITAL

HOSPITAL

If you dream that you are a patient in a ***hospital***, you will have a contagious disease in your community, and will narrowly escape affliction. If you visit patients there, you will hear distressing news of the absent. ◎

INFIRMARY

To dream that you leave an ***infirmary***, denotes your escape from wily enemies who will cause you much worry. ◎

NURSING CARE

Practical Help

AMBULANCE

To dream of seeing an ***ambulance*** with the siren blaring, omens bad luck and misfortune.

If you are the passenger, you will soon suffer a grave illness. ◎

STRETCHER

To dream that you are using a ***stretcher***, denotes that you will undertake some unpleasant work.

To see a stretcher, foretells disagreeable news. ◎

Dreams of injury may encompass the temporary savagery of a bite *opposite bottom* **or chronic damage such as being crippled and having to wear a false leg** *opposite center*. **However, help may be at hand in your dreams and you may find yourself being examined by a doctor in hospital** *left* **or in your sick bed being looked after by a nurse** *above*.

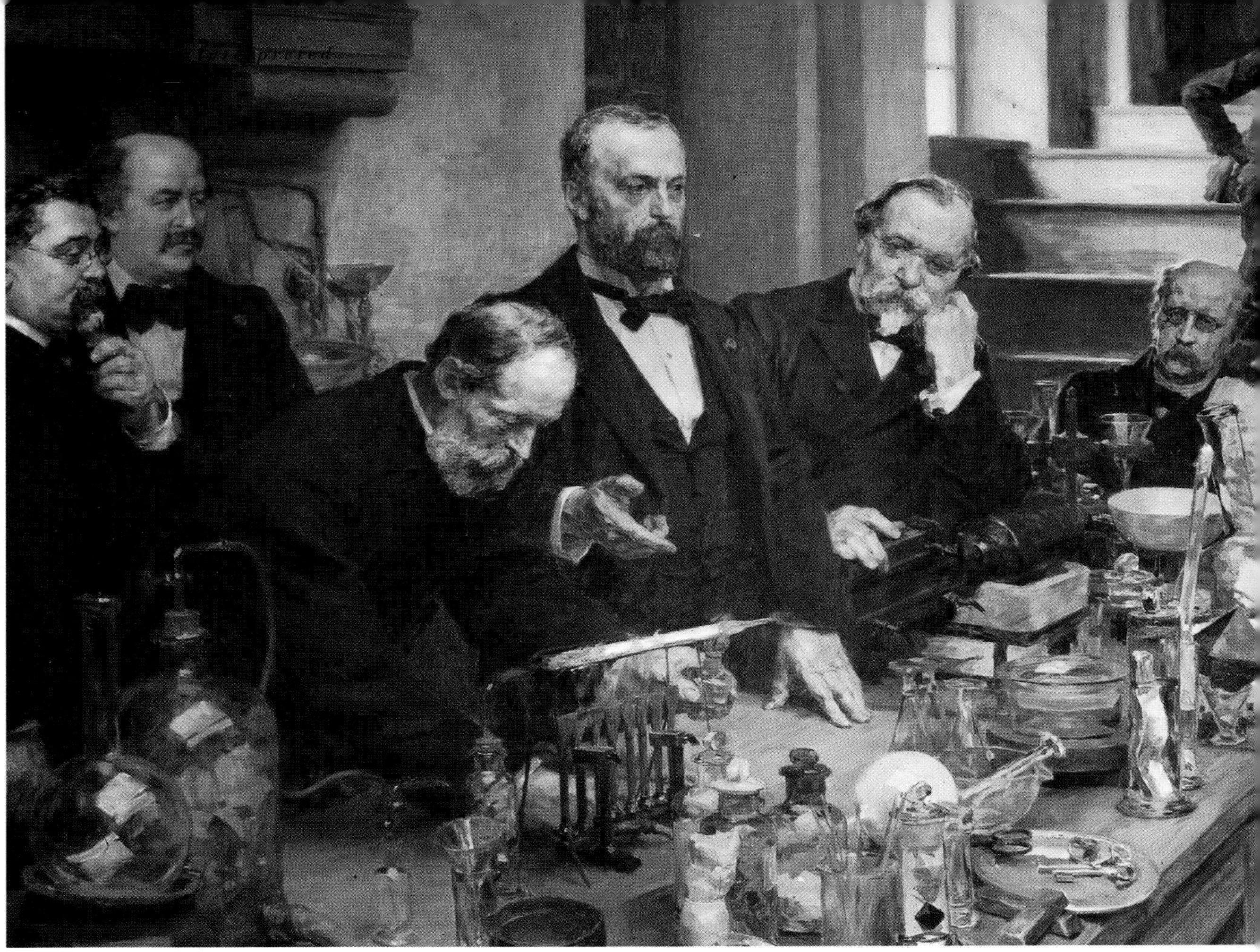

DOCTORS

Doctors and Nurses

PHYSICIAN

For a young woman to dream of a ***physician***, denotes that she is sacrificing her beauty in engaging in frivolous pastimes. If she is sick and thus dreams, she will have sickness or worry, but will soon overcome them, unless the physician appears very anxious, and then her trials may increase, ending in loss and sorrow. ◎

DOCTOR

This is a most auspicious dream, denoting good health and general prosperity, if you dream that you ***meet a doctor*** socially, for you will not then be obliged to spend your money for his services.

If you are young and engaged to ***marry a doctor***, then this dream warns you of deceit.

To dream of a ***doctor*** professionally, signifies discouraging illness and disagreeable differences between members of a family.

To dream that a doctor makes an incision in your flesh, trying to discover blood, but failing in his efforts, denotes that you will be tormented and injured by some evil person, who may try to make you pay out money for his debts. If he finds blood, you will be the loser in some transaction. ◎

NURSE

To dream that a ***nurse*** is retained in your home, foretells distressing illness, or unlucky visiting between friends.

To dream that you see a ***nurse leaving your house***, omens good health in the family.

For a young woman to dream that ***she is a nurse***, denotes that she will gain the esteem of people, through her self-sacrifice.

If she dreams that she parts from a patient, she will yield to the persuasion of deceit. ◎

OCULIST

To dream of consulting an ***oculist***, denotes that you will be dissatisfied with your progress in life, and will use artificial means of advancement. ◎

PSYCHIATRIST

To dream about a ***psychiatrist***, means that you will soon receive some much-needed guidance and advice.

To see yourself as ***a patient of a psychiatrist***, foretells that emotional confusion will soon follow. ◎

DOCTOR *see* **ENGAGEMENT, MARRIAGE** *page 130,* **SURGEON** *page 115,* **BLOOD** *page 94,* **QUACK DOCTOR** *page 117* ◆
NURSE *see* **HOME** *page 205,* **HOUSE** *page 188* ◆ **OCULIST** *see* **EYE** *page 99* ◆ **PSYCHIATRIST** *see* **MADNESS, INSANITY, ASYLUM** *page 105*

Surgery

SURGEON
To dream of a ***surgeon***, denotes that you are threatened by enemies who are close to you in business. For a young woman, this dream promises a serious illness from which she will experience great inconvenience. ◎

AMPUTATION
Ordinary ***amputation*** of limbs, denotes small offices lost; the loss of entire legs or arms, unusual depression in trade. To seamen, storm and loss of property. Afflicted persons should be warned to watchfulness. ◎

SURGICAL INSTRUMENTS
To see ***surgical instruments*** in a dream, foretells that you will feel dissatisfaction at the discreet manner manifested toward you by a friend. ◎

Medical Instruments

SYRINGE

SYRINGE
To dream of a ***syringe***, denotes that a false alarm of the gravity of a relative's condition will reach you.

To see a broken one, foretells that you are approaching a period of ill health or worry over slight mistakes in business. ◎

TRUSS
To see a ***truss*** in your dream, your ill health and unfortunate business arrangement are predicted. ◎

THERMOMETER
To dream of looking at a ***thermometer***, denotes unsatisfactory business and disagreements in the home.

To see a broken one, foreshadows illness.

If the mercury seems to be falling, your affairs will assume a distressing shape. If it is rising, you will be able to throw off bad conditions in your business. ◎

X-RAY MACHINE
To dream of being ***x-rayed***, indicates that someone of some authority will try to uncover a secret of yours, which if revealed will be very harmful to you and your family. You must discover what this secret might be in order to prevent it from being disclosed. ◎

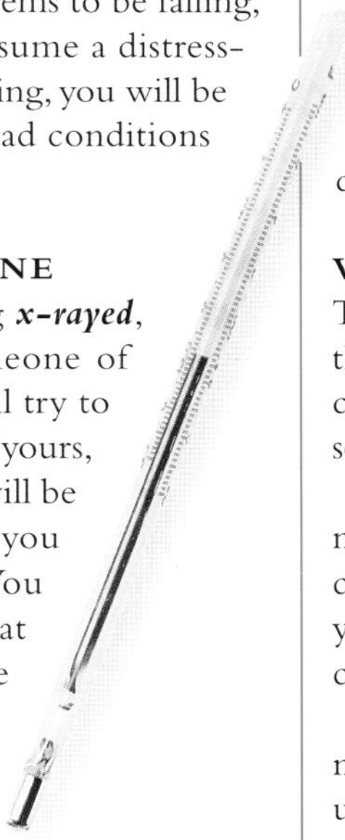

THERMOMETER

STETHOSCOPE
To dream of a ***stethoscope***, foretells calamity to your hopes and enterprises. There will be troubles and recriminations in love. ◎

Diagnosis and Cure

PULSE
To dream of your ***pulse***, is a warning to look after your affairs and health with close care, as both are taking on debilitating conditions.

To dream of feeling the pulse of another, signifies that you are committing depredations in pleasure's domain. ◎

RESUSCITATION
To dream that you are being ***resuscitated***, denotes that you will have heavy losses, but will eventually regain more than you lose, and happiness will attend you.

To ***resuscitate another***, you will form new friendships, which will give you prominence and pleasure. ◎

QUARANTINE
To dream of being in ***quarantine***, denotes that you will be placed in a disagreeable position by the malicious intriguing of enemies. ◎

VACCINATE
To dream of being ***vaccinated***, foretells that your susceptibility to female charms will be played upon to your sorrow.

To dream that others are vaccinated, shows that you will fail to find contentment where it is sought, and your affairs will suffer decline in consequence.

For a young woman to be vaccinated on her leg, foreshadows her undoing through treachery. ◎

In your dreams you may consult with the ablest doctors and physicians *opposite top*. **Specific medical instruments may feature, such as a syringe** *top*, **or a thermometer** *above* **may take the temperature of your dreams.**

AMPUTATION *see* **LEGS** *page 96*, **ARMS** *page 97*, **SAILOR** *page 226*, **STORM** *page 76* ◆ **SYRINGE** *see* **BREAK** *page 265* ◆ **THERMOMETER** *see* **BREAK** *page 265* ◆ **VACCINATE** *see* **LEGS** *page 96*

Modern Medicine

GIVING MEDICINE

MEDICINE

To dream of ***medicine***, if pleasant to the taste, means that trouble will come to you, but in a short time it will work for your good; but if you take ***disgusting medicine***, you will suffer a protracted illness, or some deep sorrow or loss will overcome you.

To ***give medicine to others***, denotes that you will work to injure someone who trusted you. ◎

ANTIBIOTIC MEDICINE

To dream of taking an ***antibiotic***, means that you will soon suffer a temporary illness. However, it will be short and fleeting as long as you attend to it quickly. ◎

QUININE

To dream of ***quinine***, denotes that you will soon be possessed of great happiness, though your prospects for much wealth may be meager.

To take some, foretells improvements in health and energy. You will also make new friends, who will lend you commercial aid. ◎

Pills and Ointments

PILL

To dream that you take ***pills***, denotes that you will have responsibilities to look after, but they will bring you no little comfort and enjoyment.

To give them to others, signifies that you will be criticized for your disagreeableness. ◎

SALVE

To dream of ***salve***, denotes that you will prosper under adverse circumstances and convert enemies into friends. ◎

OINTMENT

To dream of ***ointment***, denotes that you will form friendships which will prove to be both beneficial and pleasing to you.

For a young woman to dream that she ***makes ointment***, denotes that she will be able to command her own affairs, whether they be of a private or public character. ◎

Traditional Remedies

CASTOR OIL

To dream of ***castor oil***, denotes that you will seek to overthrow a friend who is secretly abetting your advancement. ◎

CALOMEL

To dream of ***calomel***, portends that some person is seeking to deceive and injure you through the unconscious abetting of friends.

For a young woman to dream of taking it, foretells that she will be victimized through the artful designs of persons whom she trusts. If it is applied externally, she will close her eyes to deceit in order to enjoy a short season of pleasure. ◎

BRIMSTONE

To dream of ***brimstone***, foretells that discreditable dealings will lose you many friends, if you fail to rectify the mistakes you are making. ◎

BELLADONNA

To dream of ***belladonna*** portends that strategic moves will bring success in commercial circles. Women will find rivals in society; vain and fruitless efforts will be made for places in men's affections.

To dream that you are taking it, denotes misery and failure to meet past debts. ◎

BELLADONNA

MEDICINE *see* **SWEET TASTE** *page 148,* **ILLNESS, SICKNESS, DISEASE, AFFLICTION** *page 106,*
QUACK MEDICINE, PATENT MEDICINE *page 117* ◆ **ANTIBIOTIC MEDICINE,**
PILLS *see* **ILLNESS, SICKNESS, DISEASE, AFFLICTION** *page 106* ◆ **SALVE, OINTMENT** *see* **WOUND** *page 112*

Opiate Drugs

OPIUM

To dream of ***opium***, signifies that strangers will obstruct your chances of improving your fortune, by sly and seductive means.

AN OPIUM SET

LAUDANUM

To dream that you take ***laudanum***, signifies weakness of your own; and that you will have a tendency to be unduly influenced by others. You should cultivate determination.

To prevent others from taking this drug, indicates that you will be the means of conveying great joy and good to people.

To see your ***lover taking laudanum*** through disappointment, signifies unhappy affairs and the loss of a friend.

If you give it, slight ailments will attack some member of your domestic circle.

Drugs and medication of all kinds may cure your dream ailments. You may dream of belladonna *opposite*, **of being unwillingly dosed with traditional medicine** *opposite top*, **escaping from it all in a cloud of opium** *above*, **suffering the painful 'cure' of leeching** *top right* **or succumbing to the wily blandishments of the patent medicine merchant** *right*.

Ancient Remedies

LEECHES

To dream of ***leeches***, foretells that enemies will run over your interests.

If they are applied to you for medicinal purposes, you will have a serious illness in your family (if you escape yourself).

To see them applied to others, denotes sickness or trouble to friends.

If they should bite you, there is danger for you in unexpected places, and you should heed well this warning.

MADSTONE

To see a ***madstone*** applied to a wound from the fangs of some mad animal, denotes that you will endeavor, to the limits of your energy, to shield yourself from the machinations of enemies, which will soon envelop you with the pall of dishonorable defeat.

LEECH

Quackery and Snake Oil

ELIXIR OF LIFE

To dream of the elixir of life, ***denotes that there will come into your environment new pleasures and new possibilities.***

PATENT MEDICINE

To dream that you resort to patent medicine ***in your search for health, denotes that you will use desperate measures in advancing your fortune, but you will succeed, to the disappointment of the envious.***

To dream that you see or manufacture patent medicines, ***you will rise from obscurity to positions above your highest imaginings.***

QUACK DOCTOR

To see a quack doctor ***in your dreams, denotes that you will be alarmed over some illness and its improper treatment.***

QUACK MEDICINE

To dream that you take quack medicine, ***shows that you are growing morbid under some trouble, and should overcome it by industrious application to duty. To read the advertisement of it, foretells that unhappy companions will wrong and distress you.***

THE QUACK AT WORK

LEECHES *see* **MEDICINE** *page 116* ◆ **BITE** *page 112* ◆ **MADSTONE** *see* **WOUND** *page 112* ◆ **QUACK MEDICINE, PATENT MEDICINE** *see* **MEDICINE** *page 116* ◆ **QUACK DOCTOR** *see* **DOCTOR** *page 114*

Birth and Death

Birth and death, the beginnings and endings of life are highly charged symbols. However, to dream of death does not always signify your end in the real world, just as to dream of birth does not necessarily herald a new arrival in your family. This section covers pregnancy, birth and nursing and all the aspects of death from the act of dying to the final resting place.

Pregnancy and Childbirth

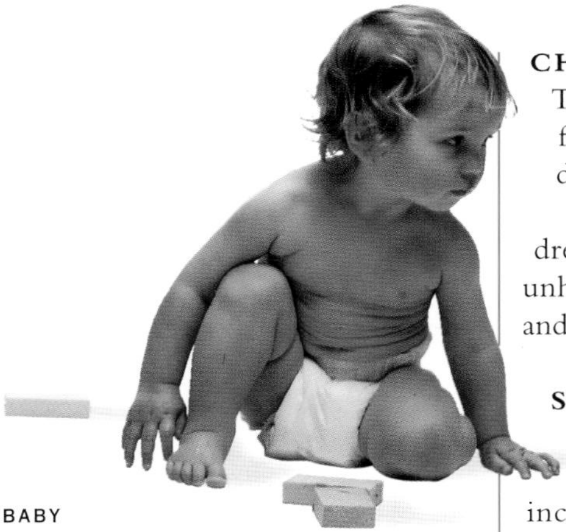

BABY

CHILDBIRTH
To dream of giving ***birth***, denotes fortunate circumstances and safe delivery of a handsome child.

For an unmarried woman to dream of giving birth, denotes unhappy changes from honor to evil and low estates. ◎

STILLBORN
To dream of a ***stillborn*** infant, denotes that some distressing incident will come before your notice. ◎

PREGNANCY
For a woman to dream that she is ***pregnant***, denotes that she will be unhappy with her husband, and her children will be unattractive.

For a virgin, this dream omens scandal and adversity. If a woman is really pregnant and has this dream, it prognosticates a safe delivery and swift recovery of strength. ◎

BIRTH
For a married woman to dream of giving ***birth*** to a child, great joy and a handsome legacy are foretold.

For a single woman, loss of virtue and abandonment by her lover. ◎

MIDWIFE
To see a ***midwife*** in your dreams, signifies unfortunate sickness with a narrow escape from death.

For a young woman to dream of such a person, foretells that distress and calumny will attend her. ◎

Birthdays

BIRTHDAY
To dream of a ***birthday***, is a signal of poverty and falsehood to the young; to the old, long trouble and desolation. ◎

BIRTHDAY PRESENTS
Receiving happy surprises, means a multitude of high accomplishments. Working people will advance in their trades.

Giving ***birthday presents***, denotes small deferences, if given at a fête or reception. ◎

THE BIRTHDAY TEA

PREGNANCY *see* VIRGIN *page 87* ◆ BIRTH *see* SINGLE *page 132,* BABY, TWINS, TRIPLETS, INFANTS *page 119* ◆
MIDWIFE *see* NURSE *page 114* ◆ BIRTHDAY *see* GIFTS *page 240,* RECEPTION *page 173*

Babies and Infants

BABY
To dream of crying ***babies***, is indicative of ill health and disappointments.

A bright, ***clean baby***, denotes love requited, and many warm friends.

A baby walking alone, is a sure sign of independence and a total ignoring of smaller spirits.

If a woman dreams she is ***nursing a baby***, she will be deceived by the one she trusts most.

It is a bad sign to dream that you take your baby if sick with fever. You will have many sorrows of mind. ◎

BABY CARRIAGES
To dream of a ***baby carriage***, denotes that you will have a congenial friend who will devise many pleasurable surprises for you. ◎

TWINS
To dream of seeing ***twins***, foretells security in business, and faithful and loving contentment in the home.

If the twins are sickly, it signifies that you will have disappointment and grief. ◎

TRIPLETS
To dream of seeing ***triplets***, foretells success in affairs when failure was feared.

For a man to dream that his wife has them, signifies a pleasant termination to some affair which has been long in dispute.

To hear newly born ***triplets crying***, signifies disagreements which will be hastily reconciled to your pleasure.

For a young woman to dream that she has triplets, denotes that she will suffer loss and disappointment in love, but will succeed in wealth. ◎

MOTHERHOOD

INFANTS
To dream of seeing a newly born ***infant***, denotes that pleasant surprises are nearing you.

For a young woman to dream that she has an infant, foretells that she will be accused of indulgence in immoral pastime.

To see an ***infant swimming***, portends a fortunate escape from some entanglement. ◎

CRADLE
To dream of a ***cradle***, with a beautiful infant occupying it, portends prosperity and the affections of beautiful children.

To rock your own baby in a cradle, denotes the serious illness of one of the family.

For a young woman to dream of ***rocking a cradle***, is portentous of her downfall. She should beware of gossiping. ◎

Suckling and Nursing

NURSING
For a woman to dream of ***nursing*** her baby, denotes pleasant employment.

For a young woman to dream of nursing a baby, foretells that she will occupy positions of honor and trust.

For a man to dream of seeing his wife nurse their baby, denotes harmony in his pursuits. ◎

WET NURSE
To dream that you are a ***wet nurse***, denotes that you will be widowed or have the care of the aged, or little children.

For a woman to dream that she is a wet nurse, signifies that she will depend on her own labors for sustenance. ◎

SUCKLE
To see the young taking ***suckle***, denotes that contentment and favorable conditions for success are unfolding to you. ◎

CRADLE

The whole experience of pregnancy, childbirth, and infancy is covered in dreams: the baby *opposite top*, **the annual celebration of the birthday** *opposite*, **the the joys of motherhood** *top*, **and the blissful calm of the sleeping baby in its cradle** *above*.

BABY *see* **CRYING** *page 257*, **CRIES** *page 276*, **WALKING** *page 267*, **FEVER** *page 107* ◆ **TRIPLETS** *see* **BIRTH** *page 118*, **CRYING** *page 257*, **CRIES** *page 276* ◆ **INFANTS** *see* **BIRTH** *page 118*, **SWIMMING** *page 174* ◆ **CRADLE** *see* **COT, BED** *page 207*

Death and Dying

DEATH
To dream of seeing any of your ***people dead***, warns you of coming dissolution or sorrow. Disappointments always follow such dreams.

To hear of any friends or relatives being dead, you will soon have bad news from some of them.

Dreams relating to ***death*** or dying, unless they are due to spiritual causes, can be misleading and confusing. A man who thinks intensely fills his aura with thought or subjective images active with the passions that gave them birth; by thinking and acting on other lines, he may supplant these images with others possessed of a different form and nature. In his dreams he may see these images dying, dead, or being buried, and mistake them for friend or enemies. In this way he may, while asleep, see himself or a relative die, when in reality he has been warned that some good thought or deed is to be supplanted by an evil one. To illustrate: If it is a dear friend or relative whom he sees in the agony of death, he is warned against immoral or other improper thought and action, but if it is an enemy or some repulsive object dismantled in death, he may overcome his evil ways.

Often the end or beginning of suspense or trials is foretold by dreams of this nature. They also occur when the dreamer is controlled by imaginary states of evil or good. A man in that state is not himself, but is what the dominating influences make him. He may be warned of approaching conditions or his extrication from the same.

In our dreams we are closer to our real self than in waking life. The hideous or pleasing incidents seen and heard about us in our dreams are all of our own making; they reflect the true state of our soul and body, and we cannot flee from them unless we drive them out of our being by the use of good thoughts and deeds, by the power of the spirit within us. ◎

DYING
To dream of ***dying***, foretells that you are threatened with evil from a source that has contributed to your former advancement and enjoyment.

To see ***others dying***, forebodes general ill luck to you and to your friends.

To dream that you are going to die, denotes that unfortunate inattention to your affairs will depreciate their value. Illness threatens to damage you also.

To see animals in the throes of death, denotes escape from evil influences if the animals be wild or savage.

It is an unlucky dream to see domestic animals dying or in agony.

As these events of good or ill approach you they naturally assume these forms of agonizing death, to impress you more fully with the joyfulness or the gravity of the situation you are about to enter on awakening to material responsibilities, to aid you in the mastery of self which is essential to meeting all conditions with calmness and determination. ◎

DEAD
To dream of the ***dead,*** is usually a dream of warning. If you see and talk with your father, some unlucky transaction is about to be made by you. Be careful how you enter into contracts; enemies are around you. Men and women are warned to look to their reputations after this dream.

To see your mother, warns you to control your inclination to cultivate morbidness and ill will towards your fellow creatures. A brother, or other relative or friend, denotes that you may be called on for charity or aid within a short time.

To dream of seeing the dead, living and happy, signifies that you are letting wrong influences into your life, which will bring material loss if not corrected by the assumption of your own will power.

To dream that you are conversing with a dead relative, and that relative endeavors to extract a promise from you, warns you of coming distress, unless you follow the advice given you. Disastrous consequences could often be averted if minds could grasp the inner workings and sight of the higher or spiritual self. The voice of relatives is only that higher self taking form to approach more distinctly the mind that lives near the material plane. There is so little congeniality between common or material natures that persons should depend upon their own subjectivity for true contentment and pleasure. ◎

Funerals

A COUNTRY FUNERAL

To see a *funeral,* ***denotes an unhappy marriage and sickly offspring.***

To dream of the *funeral of a stranger,* ***denotes unexpected worries.***

To see the *funeral of your child,* ***may denote the health of your family, but very grave disappointment may follow from a friendly source.***

To attend a funeral in black, foretells an early widowhood.

To dream of the funeral of any relative, denotes nervous troubles and family worries.

DEATH *see* **FRIEND** *page 124,* **AGONY** *page 107* ◆ **DYING** *see* **DOMESTIC ANIMALS** *pages 33 to 42,* **AGONY** *page 107,* **WILD** *page 266* ◆ **DEAD** *see* **FATHER, MOTHER** *page 128,* **BROTHERS** *page 129,* **FRIEND** *page 124* ◆ **FUNERAL** *see* **CHILDREN** *page 128*

Funeral Rites

PASSING BELL
To hear a ***passing bell***, unexpected intelligence of the sorrow or illness of the absent is foretold. ◎

BELL

PALLBEARER
To dream of a ***pall-bearer***, indicates that some enemy will provoke your ill feeling by constant attacks on your integrity. If you see a pallbearer, you will antagonize worthy institutions and make yourself obnoxious to friends. ◎

PALL
To dream that you see a ***pall***, denotes that you will have sorrow and misfortune.

If you raise the pall from a corpse, you will doubtless soon mourn the death of one whom you love. ◎

HEARSE
To dream of a ***hearse***, denotes uncongenial relations in the home, and failure to carry on business in a satisfactory manner. It also betokens the death of one near to you, or sickness and sorrow.

If a ***hearse crosses your path***, you will have a bitter enemy to overcome. ◎

BIER
To see one, indicates disastrous losses and the early dissolution of a dear relative.

To see one strewn with flowers in a church, denotes an unfortunate marriage. ◎

Images of death, its rituals and concomitants are well represented in dreams. As well as death in general you may dream of funerals *opposite* **or the melancholy sound of the passing bell** *above*.

Corpses and Coffins

CORPSE
To dream of a ***corpse*** is fatal to happiness, as this dream indicates sorrowful tidings of the absent, and gloomy business prospects. The young will suffer many disappointments, and pleasure will vanish.

To see a ***corpse placed in its casket***, denotes immediate troubles to the dreamer.

To see a ***corpse in black***, denotes the violent death of a friend through some desperate business entanglement.

To see a battlefield strewn with corpses, indicates war and general dissatisfaction between countries and political factions.

To see the ***corpse of an animal***, denotes an unhealthy situation, as to both business and health.

To see the corpse of anyone of your immediate family, indicates death to that person or to some member of the family, or a serious rupture of domestic relations; also unusual business depression. For lovers, it is a sure sign of failure to keep promises of a sacred nature.

To put money on ***the eyes of a corpse*** in your dreams, denotes that you will see unscrupulous enemies robbing you while you are powerless to prevent injury. If you only put it on one eye, you will be able to recover lost property after an almost hopeless struggle.

For a young woman, this dream denotes distress and loss by unfortunately giving her confidence to designing persons.

For a young woman to dream that the proprietor of the store in which she works is a corpse, and that she sees while sitting up with him that his face is clean shaven, foretells that she will fall below the standard of perfection in which she was held by her lover.

If she sees the ***head of the corpse*** falling from the body, she is warned of secret enemies who, in harming her, will also detract from the interest of her employer. Seeing the corpse in the store, foretells that loss and unpleasantness will offset all concerned. There are those who are not conscientiously doing the right thing. There will be a gloomy outlook for peace and prosperous work. ◎

SHROUD
To dream of a ***shroud***, denotes sickness and its attendant distress and anxiety, coupled with the machinations of evil-minded and false friends. Business will threaten decline after this dream.

To see ***shrouded corpses***, denotes a multitude of misfortunes.

To see a shroud removed from a corpse, denotes that quarrels will result in alienation. ◎

COFFIN
This dream is unlucky. You will, if you are a farmer, see your crops blasted and your cattle lean and unhealthy. To businessmen, it means debts whose accumulation they are powerless to avoid. To the young, it denotes unhappy unions and death of loved ones.

If you see your own ***coffin*** in a dream, business defeat and domestic sorrow may be expected.

To dream of a ***coffin moving of itself***, denotes sickness and marriage in close conjunction; sorrow and pleasure intermingled. Death may follow this dream, but there will also be good.

To see your ***corpse in a coffin***, signifies that brave efforts will be crushed in defeat and ignominy.

To dream that you find yourself ***sitting on a coffin*** in a moving hearse, denotes desperate if not fatal illness for you or some person closely allied to you.

Quarrels with the opposite sex are also indicated in this dream. You will remorsefully consider your conduct toward a friend. ◎

PASSING BELL *see* **ALARM BELL** *page 266*, **TOCSIN** *page 275*, **FUNERAL** *page 120* ◆ **HEARSE** *see* **PATH** *page 222* ◆ **BIER** *see* **CHURCH** *page 189*, **FLOWERS** *page 57* ◆ **CORPSE** *see* **MONEY** *page 239*, **EYE** *page 99*, **STORE** *page 203*, **SHAVE** *page 104*, **HEAD** *page 92*, **MORGUE, GRAVE** *page 122*

Through Death's Door

EMBALMING
To see ***embalming*** in process, foretells altered positions in social life and threatened poverty. To dream that you are looking at yourself embalmed, omens unfortunate friendships for you, which will force you into lower classes than those you are accustomed to move in. ◎

CREMATION
To dream of seeing ***bodies cremated***, denotes that enemies will reduce your influence in business circles.

To think ***you are being cremated***, portends distinct failure in enterprises, if you mind any but your own judgement in conducting them. ◎

BURIAL
To attend the ***burial*** of a relative, if the sun is shining on the procession, is a sign of the good health of relations, and perhaps the happy marriage of someone of them is about to occur. But if rain and dismal weather prevail, sickness and bad news of the absent will soon come, and depressions in business circles will be felt.

A burial where there are sad rites performed, or sorrowing faces, is indicative of adverse surroundings or their speedy approach. ◎

MORGUE
To dream that you visit a ***morgue*** searching for someone, denotes that you will be shocked by news of the death of a relative or friend.

If you see many corpses there, much sorrow and trouble will come under your notice. ◎

INQUEST
To dream of an ***inquest***, foretells that you will be unfortunate in your friendships. ◎

A Fine and Private Place

GRAVE
A ***grave*** is an unfortunate dream. Ill luck in business transactions will follow; also sickness is threatened.

To dream that you see a ***newly made grave***, you will have to suffer for the wrongdoings of others.

If you visit a newly made grave, dangers of a serious nature are hanging over you.

To dream of ***walking on graves***, predicts an early death or an unfortunate marriage.

If you look into an ***empty grave***, it denotes disappointment and loss of friends.

If you see a person in a grave with the earth covering him, except the head, some distressing situation will take hold of that person, and loss of property is indicated to the dreamer.

To see your ***own grave***, foretells that enemies are warily seeking to engulf you in disaster, and if you fail to be watchful, they will succeed.

To dream of ***digging a grave*** denotes some uneasiness over some undertaking, as enemies will seek to thwart you; but if you finish the grave, you will overcome opposition.

If the sun is shining, good will come out of seeming embarrassments.

If you return for a corpse to bury it, and when you arrive, the corpse has disappeared, trouble will come to you from obscure quarters.

For a woman to dream that night overtakes her in a graveyard, and she can find no place to sleep but in an ***open grave***, foreshows that she will have much sorrow and disappointment through death or false friends. She may lose in love, and many things seek to work her harm.

To see a graveyard barren, ***except on top of the graves***, signifies much sorrow and despondency for a time, but greater benefits and pleasure awaits you if you properly shoulder your burden.

To see your ***own corpse in a grave***, foreshadows hopeless and despairing oppression. ◎

TOMB
To dream of seeing ***tombs***, denotes there will be sadness and disappointments in business.

Dilapidated tombs, omen death or desperate illness.

To dream of seeing ***your own tomb***, portends your individual sickness or disappointments.

To read the ***inscription on tombs***, foretells unpleasant duties. ◎

MAUSOLEUM
To dream of a ***mausoleum***, indicates the sickness, death, or trouble of some prominent friend.

To find yourself ***inside a mausoleum***, foretells your own illness. ◎

THE CEMETERY

BURIAL *see* **SUN** *page 84*, **PROCESSION** *page 173*, **RAIN** *page 75*, **FACE** *page 100* ◆ **MORGUE** *see* **CORPSE** *page 121* ◆ **GRAVE** *see* **WALKING** *page 267*, **DIGGING** *page 193*, **SUN** *page 84*, **CORPSE** *page 121*, **CHURCHYARD**, **CEMETERY** *page 123*, **NIGHT** *page 82* ◆ **TOMBS** *see* **CHURCHYARD**, **CEMETERY** *page 123*, **INSCRIPTION** *page 232*

Cemetery and Chuchyard

CEMETERY

To dream of being in a beautiful and well-kept ***cemetery***, signifies unexpected news of the recovery of one whom you had mourned as dead, and your good title to lands occupied by usurpers.

To see an old ***bramble-grown and forgotten cemetery***, you will live to see all your loved ones leave you, and you will be left to a stranger's care.

For young people to dream of wandering through the silent avenues of the dead, foreshows that they will meet with tender and loving responses from friends, but will have to meet sorrows that friends are powerless to avert.

Brides dreaming of ***passing a cemetery*** on their way to the wedding ceremony, will be bereft of their husbands by fatal accidents occurring on journeys.

For a mother to carry ***fresh flowers to a cemetery***, indicates that she may expect the continued good health of her family.

For a young widow to visit a cemetery, means she will soon throw aside her weeds for robes of matrimony. If she feels sad and depressed, she will have new cares and regrets.

Old people dreaming of a cemetery, will soon make other journeys where they will find perfect rest.

To see little children gathering flowers and chasing butterflies among the graves, denotes prosperous changes and no graves of any of your friends to weep over. Good health will hold high carnival. ◎

THE CHURCHYARD

CHURCHYARD

To dream of walking in a ***churchyard***, if in winter, denotes that you are to have a long and bitter struggle with poverty. You will reside far from the home of your childhood, and friends will be separated from you.

However, if you see the signs of springtime, you will walk up into pleasant places and enjoy the society of friends.

For lovers to dream of being in a churchyard, means that they will never marry each other, but will see others fill their places. ◎

Grief and Mourning

BEREAVEMENT

To dream of the ***bereavement*** of a child, warns you that your plans will meet with quick frustration; and where you expect success, there will be failure.

Bereavement of relatives or friends, denotes disappointment in well-matured plans and a poor outlook for the future. ◎

MOURNING

To dream that you wear ***mourning*** clothes, omens ill luck and unhappiness.

If others wear it, there will be disturbing influences among your friends causing you unexpected dissatisfaction and loss. To lovers, this dream foretells misunderstanding and probable separation. ◎

After Death

OBITUARY

To dream of writing an ***obituary***, denotes that unpleasant and discordant duties will devolve upon you.

If you read one, news of a distracting nature will soon reach you. ◎

WAKE

To dream that you attend a ***wake***, denotes that you will sacrifice some important engagement to enjoy some ill-favored assignation.

For a young woman to dream that she sees ***her lover at a wake***, foretells that she will listen to the entreaties of passion, and will be persuaded to hazard honor for love. ◎

MEMORIAL

To dream of a ***memorial***, signifies that there will be occasion for you to show patient kindness, as trouble and sickness threaten your relatives. ◎

RESURRECTION

To dream that you are ***resurrected*** from the dead, you will have some great vexation, but will eventually gain your desires.

To see ***others resurrected***, denotes that unfortunate troubles will be lightened by the thoughtfulness of friends. ◎

The final resting place is a frequent dream location, whether it is the melancholy formality of a cemetery *opposite* **or a traditional churchyard complete with lych gate** *above*.

CEMETERY *see* **GRAVE, TOMB, MAUSOLEUM** *page 122,* **BRAMBLES** *page 66,* **WEDDING** *page 131,* **MOTHER** *page 128,* **FLOWERS** *page 57,* **CHIDREN** *page 128,* **BUTTERFLY** *page 50* ◆ **CHURCHYARD** *see* **WINTER** *page 82,* **WALKING** *page 267,* **SPRING** *page 82* ◆ **BEREAVEMENT** *see* **CHILDREN** *page 128,* **FRIEND** *page 124* ◆ **MOURNING** *see* **CLOTHES, APPAREL** *page 154* ◆ **OBITUARY** *see* **WRITING** *page 232,* **READING** *page 233* ◆ **RESURRECTION** *see* **DEAD** *page 120,* **CHRIST** *page 279*

Love and Friendship

Dreams of love and friendship do not always signify joy and happiness. This section covers dreams of friends, acquaintances, and neighbors, as well as lovers both faithful and faithless; the hurt and ecstasy of love; the physical aspects of love and the thrills of seduction and sexual adventure.

Lovers and Friends

LOVE

To dream of loving any object, denotes satisfaction with your present environments.

If you dream that the ***love of others*** fills you with happy forebodings, successful affairs will give you contentment and freedom from the anxious cares of life.

If you find that your ***love fails***, or is not reciprocated, you will become despondent over some conflicting question arising in your mind as to whether it is best to change your mode of living, or to marry and trust fortune for the future advancement of your state.

The ***love of animals***, indicates contentment with what you possess, though you may not think so. For a time, fortune will crown you.

To dream of the ***love of parents***, foretells uprightness in character and progress toward fortune and elevation. ◎

FRIEND

To dream of ***friends*** being well and happy, denotes pleasant tidings of them, or you will soon see them or some of their relatives.

If you see your ***friend troubled*** and haggard, sickness or distress is upon them.

To see your ***friends dark-colored***, denotes unusual sickness or trouble to you or to them.

To see them take the form of animals, signifies that enemies will separate you from your relations.

To see in flaming red your friend who dresses in somber colors, foretells that unpleasant things will transpire, causing you anxiety if not loss, and that friends will be implicated.

To dream that you see a ***friend with a white cloth*** tied over his face, denotes that you will be injured by some person who will endeavor to keep up friendly relations with you. ◎

NEIGHBOR

To see your ***neighbors*** in your dream, denotes that many profitable hours will be lost in useless strife and gossip. If they appear sad or angry, it foretells dissensions and quarrels. ◎

ACQUAINTANCE

To meet an ***acquaintance***, and converse pleasantly with him or her, foretells that your business will run smoothly, and there will be but little discord in your domestic affairs.

If you seem to be disputing, or engaged in loud talk, humiliations and embarrassments will whirl seethingly around you.

If you feel ashamed of ***meeting an acquaintance***, or meet one at an inopportune time, it denotes that you will be guilty of illicitly conducting yourself, and other parties will let the secret out.

For a young woman to think that she has an ***extensive acquaintance***, signifies that she will be the possessor of vast interests, and her love will be worth the winning. If her circle of acquaintances is small, she will be unlucky in gaining social favors. ◎

Hearts and Flowers

AMOROUS

To dream you are ***amorous***, warns you against personal desires and pleasures, as they are threatening to engulf you in scandal.

For a young woman, it portends illicit engagements, unless she chooses staid and moral companions. For a married woman, it foreshadows discontent and desire for pleasure outside the home.

To see others amorous, foretells that you will be persuaded to neglect your moral obligations. To see animals thus, denotes that you will engage in degrading pleasures with fast persons. ◎

VALENTINE

To dream that you are sending ***valentines***, foretells that you will lose opportunities of enriching yourself.

For a young woman to receive one, denotes that she will marry a weak but ardent lover against the counsels of her guardians. ◎

SWEETHEART

To dream that your ***sweetheart*** is affable and of pleasing physique, foretells that you will woo a woman who will prove a joy to your pride and will bring you a good inheritance. If she appears otherwise, you will be discontented with your choice before the marriage vows are consummated.

To dream of her as being sick or in distress, denotes that sadness will be intermixed with joy.

If you dream that your ***sweetheart is a corpse***, you will have a long period of doubt and unfavorable fortune. ◎

FRIEND *see* **HAGGARD** *page 107*, **METAMORPHOSIS** *page 275*, **CLOTHES, APPAREL** *page 154*, **FACE** *page 101* ◆ **NEIGHBOR** *see* **TALKING, DISPUTE** *page 230* ◆ **SWEETHEART** *see* **SICKNESS** *page 106*, **CORPSE** *page 121*, **KISSING** *page 125*

All's Fair in Love

FAITHLESS
To dream that your friends are ***faithless***, denotes that they will hold you in worthy esteem.

For a lover to dream that his sweetheart is faithless, signifies a happy marriage. ◎

COURTSHIP
Bad, bad will be the fate of the woman who dreams of being ***courted***. She will often think that now he will propose, but often she will be disappointed. Disappointments will follow illusory hopes and fleeting pleasures.

For a man to dream of courting, implies that he is not worthy of a companion. ◎

RIVAL
To dream that you have a ***rival***, is a sign that you will be slow in asserting your rights, and will lose favor with people of prominence. For a young woman, this dream is a warning to cherish the love she already holds, as she might unfortunately make a mistake in seeking other bonds.

If you find that a rival has outwitted you, it signifies that you will be negligent in your business, and that you love personal ease to your detriment.

If you imagine that you are the successful rival, it is good for your advancement, and you will find congeniality in your choice of a companion. ◎

BACHELOR
For a man to dream that he is a ***bachelor***, is a warning for him to keep clear of women.

For a woman to dream of a bachelor, denotes love not born of purity. Justice goes awry. Politicians lose honor. ◎

IDEAL
For a young woman to dream of meeting her ***ideal***, foretells a season of uninterrupted pleasure and contentment.

For a bachelor to dream of meeting his ideal, denotes that he will soon experience a favorable change in his affairs. ◎

Kissing and Cuddling

KISSING
To dream that you see children ***kissing***, denotes happy reunions in families and satisfactory work.

To dream that you ***kiss your mother***, you will be very successful in your enterprises, and honored and beloved by your friends.

To ***kiss a brother or sister***, denotes much pleasure in your association.

To ***kiss your sweetheart*** in the dark, denotes dangers and immoral engagements. To kiss her in the light, signifies that honorable intentions occupy your mind always in connection with women.

To ***kiss a strange woman***, denotes loose morals and perverted integrity.

To dream of ***kissing illicitly***, denotes dangerous pastimes. The indulgence of a low passion may bring a tragedy into well-thought-of homes.

To see your rival ***kiss your sweetheart***, you are in danger of losing her esteem.

For married people to ***kiss each other***, denotes that harmony is prized in the home life.

To dream of ***kissing a person on the neck***, denotes passionate inclinations and weak mastery of self.

If you dream of ***kissing an enemy***, you will make an advance toward reconciliation with an angry friend.

For a young woman to dream that some person sees her ***kiss her lover***, indicates that spiteful envy is entertained for her by a false friend.

For her to see her ***lover kiss another***, she will be disappointed in her hopes of marriage. ◎

EMBRACE
To dream of ***embracing*** your husband or wife, as the case may be, in a sorrowing or indifferent way, denotes that you will have dissensions and accusations in your family; also that sickness is threatened.

To ***embrace relatives***, signifies their sickness and unhappiness.

For lovers to dream of embracing, foretells quarrels and disagreements arising from infidelity.

If these dreams take place under auspicious conditions, the reverse may be expected.

If you ***embrace a stranger***, it signifies that you will have an unwelcome guest. ◎

HUGGING
If you dream of ***hugging***, you will be disappointed in love affairs and in business.

For a woman to dream of ***hugging a man***, she will accept advances of a doubtful character from men.

For a married woman to hug others than her husband, will endanger her honor in accepting attentions from others in her husband's absence. ◎

LAP
To dream of sitting on some person's ***lap***, denotes pleasant security from vexing engagements.

If a young woman dreams that she is holding a ***person on her lap***, she will be exposed to unfavorable criticism.

To see a serpent in her lap, foretells that she is threatened with humiliation at the hands of enemies.

If she dreams that she sees a ***cat in her lap***, she will be endangered by a seductive enemy. ◎

FAITHLESS *see* **SWEETHEART** *page 124* ◆ **KISSING** *see* **CHILDREN, MOTHER** *page 128,* **BROTHERS** *page 129,* **SWEETHEART** *page 124,* **NECK** *page 92,* **ENEMY** *page 260* ◆ **EMBRACE** *see* **HUSBAND, WIFE** *page 132* ◆ **LAP** *see* **SERPENT** *page 53,* **CAT** *page 40*

Sex and Seduction

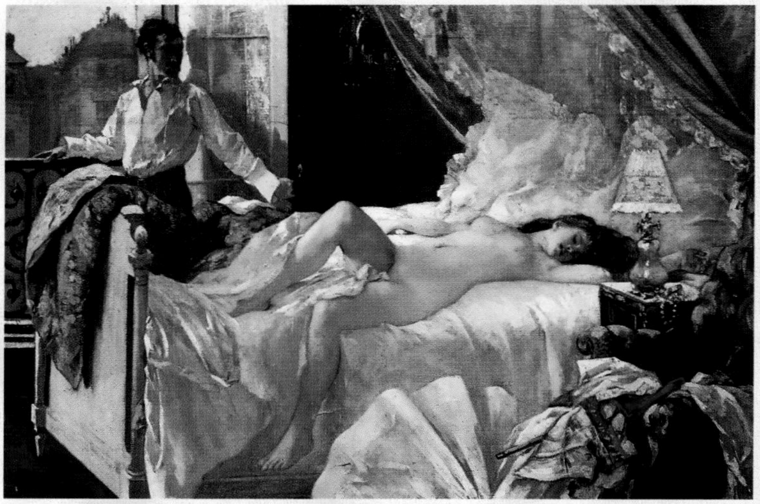

THE BOLD SEDUCER

SEX

To dream that you are having or have had a pleasurable sexual *experience, denotes happiness and contentment in your personal relationships.*

To dream of watching others have intercourse, denotes an inability to be part of a successful, satisfying relationship.

To dream of joyless sexual relationships, *is a warning that you will be contemplating some undertaking which, if carried out, will steep you in disgrace and guilt.*

SEDUCER

For a young woman to dream of being seduced, *foretells that she will be easily influenced by showy persons.*

For a man to dream that he has seduced a girl, is a warning to him to be on his guard, as there are those who will falsely accuse him. If his sweetheart appears shocked or angry under these proposals, he will find that the woman he loves is above reproach. If she consents, he is being used for her pecuniary pleasures.

ADVENTURER

To dream that you are victimized by an adventurer, *proves that you will be an easy prey for flatterers and designing villains. You will be unfortunate in manipulating your affairs to a smooth consistency.*

For a young woman to think she is an adventuress, *portends that she will be too wrapped up in her own conduct to see that she is being flattered into exchanging her favors for disgrace.*

HAREM

To dream that you maintain a harem, *denotes that you are wasting your best energies on low pleasures. Life holds fair promises, if your desires are rightly directed.*

If a woman dreams that she is an inmate of a harem, she will seek pleasure where pleasure is unlawful, as her desires will be toward married men as a rule. If she dreams that she is a favorite of a harem, she will be preferred before others in material pleasures, but the distinction will be fleeting.

CONCUBINE

For a man to dream that he is in company with a concubine, *forecasts that he is in danger of public disgrace, striving to keep from the world his true character and state of business.*

For a woman to dream that she is a concubine, indicates that she will degrade herself by her own improprieties.

For a man to dream that his mistress is untrue, denotes that he has old enemies to encounter. Expected reverses will arise.

HARLOT

To dream of being in the company of a harlot, *denotes ill-chosen pleasures and trouble in your social circles, and business will suffer depression. If you marry one, life will be threatened by an enemy.*

BROTHEL

To dream of being in a brothel, *denotes that you will encounter disgrace through your material indulgence.*

PROSTITUTE

To dream that you are in the company of a prostitute, *denotes that you will incur the righteous scorn of friends for some ill-mannered conduct.*

For a young woman to dream of a prostitute, foretells that she will deceive her lover as to her purity or candor. This dream, to a married woman, brings suspicion of her husband and consequent quarrels.

SEDUCER *see* **SWEETHEART** *page 124* ◆ **CONCUBINE** *see* **FAITHLESS** *page 125* ◆ **HARLOT** *see* **MARRIAGE** *page 130*

Family and Marriage

Dreams of your family and your domestic life are fraught with hidden meaning; it is sometimes difficult to discern this when your dreams are peopled with such familiar faces. This section covers the family tree, individual family members, how families are joined together through matrimony and what happens when marriages end or go wrong.

The Family Tree

FAMILY

To dream of one's ***family*** as harmonious and happy, is significant of health and easy circumstances; but if there is sickness or contentions, it forebodes gloom and disappointment. ◎

GENEALOGICAL TREE

To dream of your ***genealogical tree***, denotes that you will be much burdened with family cares, or will find pleasure in other domains than your own.

To see others studying it, foretells that you will be forced to yield your rights to others.

If any of the branches are missing, it means that you will ignore some of your friends because of their straitened circumstances. ◎

A FAMILY GATHERING

PARENTS

To see your ***parents*** looking cheerful while you are dreaming, denotes harmony and pleasant associates.

If they appear to you after they are dead, it is a warning of approaching trouble, and you should be particular of your dealings.

To see them while they are living, and they seem to be in your home and happy, denotes pleasant changes for you. To a young woman, this usually brings marriage and prosperity. If pale and attired in black, grave disappointments will harass you.

To dream of seeing your ***parents looking robust and contented***, denotes that you are under fortunate environments; your business and love interest will flourish. If they appear indisposed or sad, you will find life's favors passing you by. ◎

GRANDPARENTS

To dream of meeting your ***grandparents*** and conversing with them, you will meet with difficulties that will be hard to surmount; but by following good advice, you will overcome many barriers. ◎

INCREASE

To dream of an ***increase*** in your family, may denote failure in some of your plans, and success to another. ◎

In the field of social relationships, you may find yourself in the delicious disarray of the seducer's bed *opposite top* **or a witness to the wholesome togetherness of the family group** *left.*

PARENTS *see* DEAD *page 120,* HOME *page 205,* LOVE *page 124* ◆ INCREASE *see* PREGNANCY *page 118,* BABY, INFANT *page 119*

Parents and In-Laws

FATHER
To dream of your ***father***, signifies that you are about to be involved in a difficulty, and you will need wise counsel if you are to extricate yourself therefrom.

If he is dead, it denotes that your business is pulling heavily, and you will have to use caution in conducting it.

For a young woman to dream of her ***dead father***, portends that her lover is playing or will play her false. ◎

FATHER-IN-LAW
To dream of your ***father-in-law***, denotes contentions with friends or relatives. To see him well and cheerful, foretells pleasant family relations. ◎

MOTHER
To see your ***mother*** in dreams as she appears in the home, signifies pleasing results from any enterprise.

To hold her in conversation, you will soon have good news from interests you are anxious over.

For a woman to dream of her mother, signifies pleasant duties and connubial bliss.

To see one's ***mother emaciated or dead***, foretells sadness caused by death or dishonor.

To hear your ***mother call you***, denotes that you are derelict in your duties, and that you are pursuing the wrong course in business.

To hear her cry as if in pain, omens her illness, or that some affliction is menacing you. ◎

MOTHER-IN-LAW
To dream of your ***mother-in-law***, denotes that there will be pleasant reconciliations for you after some serious disagreement.

For a woman to dispute with her mother-in-law, she will find that quarrelsome and unfeeling people will give her annoyance. ◎

Children

CHILDREN
To dream of seeing many beautiful ***children*** is portentous of great prosperity and blessings.

For a mother to dream of seeing her ***child sick*** from slight cause, she may see it enjoying robust health, but trifles of another nature may harass her.

To see ***children working*** or studying, denotes peaceful times and general prosperity.

To dream of seeing your ***child desperately ill*** or dead, you have much to fear, for this means that its welfare is sadly threatened.

To dream of your ***dead child***, denotes worry and disappointment in the near future.

To dream of seeing ***disappointed children***, denotes trouble from enemies, and anxious forebodings from the underhanded work of seemingly friendly people.

To ***romp and play with children***, denotes that all your speculation and love enterprises will prevail. ◎

OFFSPRING
To dream of your own ***offspring***, denotes cheerfulness and the merry voices of neighbors and children.

To see the offspring of domestic animals, denotes an increase in prosperity. ◎

Daughters and Sons

DAUGHTER
To dream of your ***daughter***, signifies that many displeasing incidents will give way to pleasure and harmony. If in the dream, she fails to meet your wishes, through any cause, you will suffer vexation and discontent. ◎

DAUGHTER-IN-LAW
To dream of your ***daughter-in-law***, indicates that some unusual occurrence will add to happiness or disquiet, according as she is pleasant or unreasonable. ◎

SON
To dream of your ***son***, if you have one, as being handsome and dutiful, foretells that he will afford you proud satisfaction, and will aspire to high honors. If he is maimed, or suffering from illness or accident, there is trouble ahead for you.

For a mother to dream that her son has fallen to the bottom of a well, and she hears cries, it is a sign of deep grief, losses, and sickness. If she rescues him, threatened danger will pass away unexpectedly. ◎

Family and relatives are the familiar context of daily life just as dreams of children *below* or brothers and sisters *opposite* are a familiar experience to many.

CHILDREN

FAMILY *see* **INCEST** *page 129* ◆ **FATHER** *see* **DEAD** *page 120* ◆ **MOTHER** *see* **HOME** *page 205*, **TALKING** *page 230*, **DEAD** *page 120* , **CALLED** *page 276*, **PAIN** *page 106* ◆ **MOTHER-IN LAW** *see* **DISPUTE** *page 230* ◆ **CHILDREN** *see* **BEAUTY** *page 100*, **SICKNESS** *page 106*, **DEAD** *page 120* ◆ **OFFSPRING** *see* **DOMESTIC ANIMALS** *pages 33 to 42* ◆ **SON** *see* **HANDSOME** *page 100*, **ILLNESS** *page 106*, **WELL** *page 193*, **CRIES** *page 276*, **RESCUE** *page 266*

Brothers and Sisters

BROTHERS
To see your ***brothers***, while dreaming, full of energy, you will have cause to rejoice at your own or their good fortune; but if they are poor and in distress, or begging for assistance, you will be called to a deathbed soon, or some dire loss will overwhelm you or them. ◎

STEPSISTER
To dream of a ***stepsister***, denotes that you will have unavoidable care and annoyance upon you. ◎

BROTHERS AND SISTERS

Aunts and Uncles, Nieces, and Nephews

AUNT
For a young woman to dream of seeing her ***aunt***, denotes that she will receive sharp censure for some action, which will cause her much distress.

If this relative appears smiling and happy, slight differences will soon give way to pleasure. ◎

UNCLE
If you see your ***uncle*** in a dream, you will have news of a sad character soon.

To dream that you see your ***uncle prostrated in mind***, and repeatedly have this dream, prognosticates that you will have trouble with your relations which will result in estrangement, at least for a time.

To see your ***uncle dead***, denotes that you have formidable enemies.

To dream that you have a ***misunderstanding with your uncle***, denotes that your family relations will be unpleasant, and that illness will be continually present. ◎

NIECE
For a woman to dream of her ***niece***, foretells that she will have unexpected trials and much useless worry in the near future. ◎

NEPHEW
To dream of your ***nephew***, denotes that you are soon to come into a pleasing competency, if he is handsome and well looking; otherwise, there will be disappointment and discomfort for you. ◎

COUSIN
Dreaming of one's ***cousin***, denotes disappointment and afflictions. Saddened lives are predicted by this dream.

To dream of an affectionate correspondence with one's cousin, denotes a fatal rupture between families. ◎

Orphans and Adoptions

ORPHAN
Condoling with ***orphans*** in a dream, means that the unhappy cares of others will touch your sympathies and cause you to sacrifice much personal enjoyment.

If the orphans be related to you, new duties will come into your life, causing estrangement from friends and some person held above mere friendly liking. ◎

ADOPTED
To see your ***adopted*** child or parent in your dreams, indicates that you will amass fortune through the schemes and speculations of strangers.

To dream that you or others are ***adopting a child***, indicates that you will make an unfortunate change in your abode. ◎

GUARDIAN
To dream of a ***guardian***, denotes that you will be treated with consideration by your friends.

For a young woman to dream that she is being unkindly dealt with by her guardian, foretells that she will have loss and trouble in the future. ◎

Incest

To dream of incestuous practices, ***denotes that you will fall from honorable places, and will also suffer loss in business.***

BROTHERS *see* **POOR** *page 243*, **BEGGAR** *page 244* ◆ **UNCLE** *see* **DEAD** *page 120* ◆
NEPHEW *see* **HANDSOME** *page 100* ◆ **COUSIN** *see* **LETTER** *page 236* ◆ **ADOPTED** *see* **CHILDREN** *page 128*

Engagement

ENGAGEMENT

For young people to dream that they are ***engaged***, denotes that they will not be much admired.

To dream of ***breaking an engagement***, denotes a hasty and unwise action in some important matters, or disappointments may follow.

To dream of a ***business engagement***, denotes dullness and worries in trade. ◎

Elopement

ELOPEMENT

To dream of ***eloping*** is unfavorable. To the married, it denotes that you hold places you are unworthy to fill; and if your ways are not rectified, your reputation will be at stake. To the unmarried, it foretells disappointments in love and the unfaithfulness of men.

To dream that your ***lover has eloped*** with someone else, denotes his or her unfaithfulness.

To dream of your ***friend eloping*** with one whom you do not approve, denotes that you will soon hear of them contracting a disagreeable marriage. ◎

Marriage

MARRIAGE

For a woman to dream that she ***marries*** an old, decrepit man, with wrinkled face and gray head, denotes that she will have a vast amount of trouble and sickness to encounter. If, while the ceremony is in progress, her lover passes, wearing black and looking at her in a reproachful way, she will be driven to desperation by the coldness and lack of sympathy of a friend.

MARRIAGE

To dream of seeing a marriage, denotes high enjoyment, if the wedding guests attend in pleasing colors and are happy; if they are dressed in black or other somber hues, there will be mourning and sorrow in store for the dreamer.

If you dream of ***contracting a marriage***, you will have unpleasant news from the absent.

If you are an attendant at a wedding, you will experience much pleasure from the thoughtfulness of loved ones, and business affairs will be unusually promising.

To dream of any unfortunate occurrence in connection with a marriage, foretells distress, sickness, or death in your family.

For a young woman to dream that she is a bride, and unhappy or indifferent, foretells disappointments in love, and probably her own sickness. She should be careful of her conduct, as enemies are near her. ◎

WEDLOCK

To dream that you are in the bonds of an unwelcome ***wedlock***, denotes that you will be unfortunately implicated in a disagreeable affair.

For a young woman to dream that she is ***dissatisfied with wedlock***, foretells that her inclinations will persuade her into scandalous escapades.

For a married woman to dream of her wedding day, warns her to fortify her strength and feelings against disappointment and grief. She will also be involved in secret quarrels and jealousies.

For a woman to imagine that she is pleased and securely cared for in wedlock, is a propitious dream. ◎

MARRIAGE LICENSE

For a woman to see a marriage license, foretells that she will soon enter unpleasant bonds, which will humiliate her pride. ◎

ELOPEMENT

ENGAGEMENT *see* **COMMERCE** *page 203*, **RING** *page 161* ◆ **ELOPEMENT** *see* **FRIEND** *page 124* ◆
MARRIAGE *see* **OLD MAN** *page 85*, **WEDDING, BRIDE** *page 131* ◆ **WEDLOCK** *see* **WEDDING** *page 131*

The Wedding

WEDDING

To attend a ***wedding*** in your dream, you will speedily find that there is approaching you an occasion which will cause you bitterness and delayed success.

For a young woman to dream that her ***wedding is a secret***, is decidedly unfavorable to character. It imports her probable downfall.

If she contracts a worldly or ***approved marriage***, it signifies that she will rise in the estimation of those about her, and anticipated promises and joys will not be withheld.

If she thinks in her dream that there are parental objections, she will find that her engagement will create dissatisfaction among her relatives.

For her to dream that her ***lover weds another***, foretells that she will be distressed with needless fears, as her lover will faithfully carry out his promises.

For a person to dream of ***being wedded***, is a sad augury, as death will only be eluded as a miracle. If the wedding is a gay one and there are no ashen, pale-faced, or black-robed ministers enjoining solemn vows, the reverse may be expected.

For a young woman to dream that she sees someone at her wedding dressed in mourning, denotes that she will only have unhappiness in her married life. If at another's wedding, she will be grieved over the unfavorable fortune of some relative or friend. She may experience displeasure or illness where she expected happiness and health.

The pleasure trips of others or her own, after this dream, may be greatly disturbed by unpleasant intrusions or surprises. ◎

NUPTIALS

For a woman to dream of her ***nuptials***, she will soon enter upon new engagements, which will afford her distinction, pleasure, and harmony. ◎

Wedding Material

WEDDING CLOTHES

To see wedding clothes, ***signifies that you will participate in pleasing works and will meet new friends. To see them soiled or in disorder, foretells that you will lose close relations with some much admired person.*** ❋

WEDDING RING

For a woman to dream that her wedding ring ***is bright and shining, foretells that she will be shielded from cares and infidelity.***

If it should be lost or broken, much sadness will come into her life through death and uncongeniality.

To see a wedding ring on the hand of a friend or some other person, denotes that you will hold your vows lightly and will court illicit pleasure. ❋

CONFETTI

To dream of confetti ***obstructing your view in a crowd of merrymakers, denotes that you will lose much by first seeking enjoyment, and later fulfill tasks set by duty.*** ❋

THE WEDDING

The Bride

THE BRIDE

BRIDE

For a young woman to dream that she is a ***bride***, foretells that she will shortly come into an inheritance which will please her exceedingly, if she is pleased in making her ***bridal toilette***. If displeasure is felt, she will suffer disappointment in her anticipations.

To dream that you ***kiss a bride***, denotes a happy reconciliation between friends. For a bride to kiss others, foretells for you many friends and pleasures; to kiss you, denotes that you will enjoy health and find that your sweetheart will inherit unexpected fortune.

To kiss a bride and find that she looks careworn and ill, denotes that you will be pleased with your success and the action of your friends.

If a bride dreams that she is ***indifferent to her husband***, it foretells that many unhappy circumstances will pollute her pleasure. ◎

In dreams, there are as many ways of tying the marital knot as there are in real life. You may dream of the thrill of an elopement *opposite bottom* **or the decorum of a traditional church wedding** *opposite top* **and** *left*. **Whatever the ceremony the bride** *above* **always has pride of place.**

WEDDING *see* **MARRIAGE, WEDLOCK, MARRIAGE LICENSE** *page 130,* **SECRET ORDER** *page 271,* **MOURNING** *page 123* ◆ **WEDDING CLOTHES** *see* **CLOTHES, APPAREL** *page 154,* **VEIL** *page 158* ◆ **WEDDING RING** *see* **RING** *page 161,* **HAND** *page 97,* **FRIEND** *page 124* ◆ **CONFETTI** *see* **CROWD** *page 85* ◆ **BRIDE** *see* **KISSING** *page 125*

Husband and Wife

WIFE
To dream of your ***wife*** denotes unsettled affairs and discord in the home.

To dream that your wife is unusually affable, denotes that you will receive profit from trade.

For a wife to dream that her husband whips her, foretells that unlucky influences will cause harsh criticism and general turmoil. ◎

WIDOW
To dream that you are a ***widow***, foretells that you will have many troubles through malicious persons.

For a man to dream that he ***marries a widow***, denotes that he will see some cherished undertaking crumble down in disappointment. ◎

THE GOOD HUSBAND

HUSBAND
To dream that your ***husband*** is leaving you, and you do not understand why, there will be bitterness between you, but an unexpected reconciliation will ensue. If he mistreats and upbraids you for unfaithfulness, you will hold his regard and confidence, but other worries will ensue and you are warned to be more discreet in receiving attention from men.

If you see him dead, disappointment and sorrow will envelop you.

To see him pale and careworn, sickness will tax you, as some of the family will linger in bed for a time.

To see him gay and handsome, your home will be filled with happiness and bright prospects will be yours. If he is sick, you will be mistreated by him and he will be unfaithful.

To dream that he is in love with another woman, denotes that he will soon tire of his present surroundings and seek pleasure elsewhere.

To be in love with ***another woman's husband*** in your dreams, denotes that you are not happily married, or that you are not happily unmarried, but the chances for happiness are doubtful.

For an unmarried woman to dream that she has a husband, denotes that she is wanting in the graces men admire.

If you see your ***husband depart from you***, and as he recedes from you he grows larger, inharmonious surroundings will prevent immediate congeniality. If disagreeable conclusions are avoided, harmony will be reinstated.

For a woman to dream that she sees her ***husband in a compromising position*** with an unsuspected party, denotes that she will have trouble through the indiscretions of friends. If she dreams that he is killed while with another woman, and a scandal ensues, she will be in danger of separating from her husband or losing property. Unfavorable conditions follow this dream, though the evil is often exaggerated. ◎

COMPANION
To dream of seeing a wife or husband, signifies small anxieties and probable sickness.

To dream of social ***companions***, denotes that light and frivolous pastimes will engage your attention, hindering you from performing your duties.

For a husband or wife to dream that their companion is loving, foretells great happiness around the hearthstone, and bright children. ◎

Unmarried

SINGLE
For married persons to dream that they are ***single***, foretells that their union will not be harmonious, and that constant despondency will confront them. ◎

Marital Strife

BIGAMY
For a man to commit ***bigamy***, denotes loss of manhood and failing mentality. To a woman, it predicts that she will suffer dishonor unless very discreet. ◎

ADULTERY
To dream that you commit ***adultery***, foretells that you will be arraigned for some illegal action.

If a woman has this dream, she will fail to hold her husband's affections, letting her temper and spite overwhelm her at the least provocation.

If it is with her husband's friend, she will be unjustly ignored by her husband. Her rights will be cruelly trampled upon by him. If she thinks she is enticing a youth into this act, she will be in danger of desertion and divorced for her open intriguing. ◎

DIVORCE
To dream of being ***divorced***, denotes that you are not satisfied with your companion, and should cultivate a more congenial atmosphere in the home life. It is a dream of warning.

For women to dream of ***divorce***, denotes that a single life may be theirs through the infidelity of lovers. ◎

The marital relationship is complex and intimate, so dreams about a husband *left* are very significant. Dreams of food may tempt you with a variety of the kind of ingredients that make up a balanced diet *opposite*.

WIFE *see* **WHIP** *page 33* ◆ **WIDOW** *see* **MARRIAGE** *page 130* ◆ **HUSBAND** *see* **FAITHLESS** *page 125*, **DEAD** *page 120*, **HAGGARD** *page 107*, **HANDSOME** *page 100*, **LOVE** *page 124*, **PARTING** *page 258*, **SCANDAL** *page 231* ◆ **COMPANION** *see* **FRIENDS** *page 124*, **CHILDREN** *page 128* ◆ **DIVORCE** *see* **MARRIAGE, WEDLOCK** *page 130*

Food and Drink

Eating and drinking are basic to life, and dreams of food and drink of various kinds are common. In your dreams you may feast or starve, your appetite may be stimulated or satisfied, and your dream menu may bear no relation to your normal diet. This section covers general aspects of eating and drinking and then moves on to specific categories of food and drink.

Hunger and Famine

FAMINE

To dream of a ***famine***, foretells that your business will be unremunerative and that sickness will prove a scourge. This dream is generally bad.

If you dream that you see your enemies perishing by famine, this denotes that you will be successful in competition.

If dreams of famine should break in wild confusion over slumbers, tearing up all heads in anguish, filling every soul with care, hauling down Hope's banners, somber with omens of misfortune and despair, your waking grief more poignant still must grow ere you quench ambition and envy overthrow. ◎

A BALANCED DIET

FAMISH

To dream that you are ***famishing***, foretells that you are meeting disheartening failure in some enterprise which you considered a promising success.

To dream that you see ***others famishing***, brings sorrow to others, as well as to yourself. ◎

STARVING

To dream of being in a ***starving*** condition, portends unfaithful labors and a dearth of friends.

To see others in this condition, omens misery and dissatisfaction with present companions and employment. ◎

HUNGER

To dream that you are ***hungry***, is an unfortunate omen. You will not find comfort and satisfaction in your home; and to lovers, it means an unhappy marriage. ◎

Feast and Plenty

EATING

To dream of ***eating*** alone, signifies loss and melancholy spirits. To eat with others, in contrast denotes personal gain, cheerful environments, and prosperous undertakings.

If your daughter carries away the platter of meat before you ***are done eating***, it foretells that you will have trouble and vexation from those beneath you or dependent upon you. The same would apply to a waiter or waitress. ◎

BANQUET

It is good to dream of a ***banquet***. Friends will wait to do you favors.

To dream of yourself, together with many gaily attired guests, sitting at a banquet eating from costly plates and drinking wine of fabulous price and age, foretells enormous gain in enterprises of every nature, and happiness among friends.

To see inharmonious influences, strange and grotesque faces, or empty tables, is ominous of grave misunderstandings or disappointments. ◎

INDULGENCE

For a woman to dream of ***indulgence***, denotes that she will not escape unfavorable comments on her conduct. ◎

FEAST

To dream of a ***feast***, foretells that pleasant surprises are being planned for you. To see disorder or misconduct at a feast, foretells quarrels or unhappiness through the negligence or sickness of some person.

To arrive ***late at a feast***, denotes that vexing affairs will occupy you. ◎

EPICURE

To dream of sitting at the table with an ***epicure***, denotes that you will enjoy some fine distinction, but that you will be surrounded by people of selfish principles.

To dream that you are an epicure yourself, you will cultivate your mind, body, and taste to the highest polish.

For a woman to dream of trying to ***satisfy an epicure***, signifies that she will have a distinguished husband, but to her he will be a tyrant. ◎

EATING *see* **MEAT** *page 135*, **DAUGHTER** *page 128* ◆ **BANQUET** *see* **DISHES** *page 209*, **WINE** *page 151*

MEALTIME

Eating In and Dining Out

BREAKFAST
This dream is favorable to persons engaged in mental work. To see a ***breakfast*** of fresh milk and eggs and a well-filled dish of ripe fruit, indicates hasty, but favorable changes.

If you are eating alone, it means you will fall into your enemies' trap. If you are eating with others, it is good. ◎

DINNER
To dream that you eat your ***dinner*** alone, denotes that you will often have cause to think seriously of the necessities of life.

For a young woman to dream of taking ***dinner with her lover***, is indicative of a lover's quarrel or a rupture, unless the affair is one of harmonious pleasure, when the reverse may be expected.

To be one of many invited ***guests at a dinner***, denotes that you will soon enjoy the hospitalities of those who are able to extend to you many pleasant courtesies. ◎

MEALS
To dream of ***meals***, denotes that you will let trifling matters interfere with momentous affairs and business engagements. ◎

WAITER
To dream of a ***waiter***, signifies that you will be pleasantly entertained by a friend.

To see a waiter cross or disorderly, means that offensive people will thrust themselves upon your hospitality. ◎

SODA FOUNTAIN
To dream of being at a ***soda fountain***, denotes pleasure and profit after many exasperating experiences.

To dream that you treat others to soda and other delectable iced drinks, indicates that you will be rewarded in your efforts, though the outlook appears full of contradictions. Inharmonious environments and desired results will be forthcoming. ◎

GROCERIES
To dream of general ***groceries***, if they are fresh and clean, is a sign of ease and comfort. ◎

PICNIC
To dream of attending a ***picnic***, foreshadows success and real enjoyment.

Dreams of picnics, brings undivided happiness to the young.

Storms or any interfering elements at a picnic, imply the temporary displacement of assured profit and pleasure in love or business. ◎

A PICNIC

BREAKFAST *see* **MILK** *page 144,* **EGGS** *page 145,* **FRUIT** *page 140* ◆ **DINNER** *see* **INVITE** *page 205* ◆ **PICNIC** *see* **STORM** *page 76*

You may awaken from dreams of main course food such as meat or fish with you appetite apparently satisfied, but such dreams are rarely significant of actual meals. This section looks at high protein dreams and covers meat and butchery in general, specific types of meat and meat dishes, sea fish, freshwater fish, and shellfish.

Meat and Butchery

MEAT

For a woman to dream of ***raw meat***, denotes that she will meet with much discouragement in accomplishing her aims. If she sees ***cooked meat***, it denotes that others will obtain the object for which she will strive. ◎

ROAST

To see or eat ***roast meat*** in a dream, is an omen of domestic infelicity and secret treachery. ◎

BUTCHER

To see a ***butcher*** slaughtering cattle and much blood, you may expect long and fatal sickness in your family.

If you see a butcher cutting meat, your character will be dissected by society to your detriment. Beware of writing letters or documents. ◎

SLAUGHTERHOUSE

To dream of a ***slaughterhouse***, denotes that you will be feared more than loved by your sweetheart or mistress. Your business will divulge a private drain, and there will be unkind insinuations. ◎

CARVING

To dream of ***carving*** a fowl, indicates that you will be poorly off in a worldly way. Companions will cause vexation from continued ill temper.

Carving meat, denotes bad investments; but, if a change is made, prospects will be brighter. ◎

Appetizing food dreams include the conviviality of the family meal *opposite top* **and the alfresco joys of a picnic** *opposite bottom*. **You may also dream of eating a particular food such as meat** *above* **or of preparing meals** *top*.

BASTE

To dream of basting meats while cooking, denotes that you will undermine your own expectations by folly and selfishness. ◎

THE CARNIVORE

Beef and Hash

BEEF

If the ***beef*** is raw and bloody, cancers and tumors of a malignant nature will attack the subject. Be on your guard as to bruises and hurts of any kind.

To see or eat ***cooked beef***, anguish surpassing human aid is before you. Loss of life by horrible means will occur.

Beef properly served under pleasing surroundings, denotes harmonious states in love and business; if otherwise, evil is foreboded, though it may be of a trifling nature. ◎

HASH

To dream you are eating ***hash***, many sorrows and vexations are foretold.

You will probably be troubled with various little jealousies and contentions over mere trifles, and your health will be menaced through worry.

For a woman to dream that she ***cooks hash***, denotes that she will be jealous of her husband, and her children will be a stumbling block to her wantonness. ◎

Soup, Broth, and Gravy

MAKING SOUP

GRAVY

To dream of eating gravy, ***portends failing health and disappointing business.*** ❋

BROTH

Broth ***denotes the sincerity of friends. They will uphold you in all instances. If you need pecuniary aid, it will be forthcoming. To lovers, it promises a strong and lasting attachment.***

To make broth, you will rule your own and others' fate. ❋

SOUP

To dream of soup, ***is a forerunner of good tidings and comfort.***

To see others taking soup, foretells that you will have many good chances to marry.

For a young woman to make soup, ***signifies that she will not be compelled to do menial work in her household, as she will marry a wealthy man.***

If you drink oyster soup ***made of sweet milk, there will be quarrels with some bad luck, but reconciliations will follow.*** ❋

BUTCHER *see* **CATTLE** *page 37*, **BLOOD** *page 94* ◆ **CARVING** *see* **FOWL** *page 39* ◆ **BASTE** *see also* **BASTE** *page 183* ◆
HASH *see* **EATING** *page 133* ◆ **SOUP** *see* **OYSTERS** *page 136*, **MILK** *page 144*

Pork and Ham

PORK
If you eat ***pork*** in your dreams, you will encounter real trouble, but if you only see pork, you will come out of a conflict victoriously. ◎

HAM
To dream of seeing ***hams***, signifies that you are in danger of being treacherously used.

To cut large ***slices of ham***, denotes that all opposition will be successfully met by you.

To ***dress a ham***, signifies that you will be leniently treated by others.

To dream of ***dealing in hams***, prosperity will come to you. Also good health is foreboded.

To ***eat ham***, you will lose something of great value.

To ***smell ham*** cooking, you will be benefited by the enterprises of others. ◎

BACON
To dream of eating ***bacon*** is good, if someone is eating with you and hands are clean.

Rancid bacon, is dullness of perception, and unsatisfactory states will worry you. To dream of ***curing bacon*** is bad, if not clear of salt and smoke. If clear, it is good. ◎

LARD
To dream of ***lard***, signifies that a rise in fortune will soon gratify you. For a woman to find her hand in melted lard, foretells her disappointment in attempting to rise in social circles. ◎

Poultry

POULTRY
To see dressed ***poultry*** in a dream, foretells that extravagant habits will reduce your security in money matters. For a young woman to dream that she is chasing live poultry, foretells that she will devote valuable time to frivolous pleasure. ◎

Fish and Shellfish

SARDINES
To eat sardines ***in a dream, foretells that distressing events will come unexpectedly upon you.***

For a young woman to dream of putting them on the table, denotes that she will be worried with the attentions of a person who is distasteful to her. ✻

OYSTERS
If you dream that you eat oysters, ***it denotes that you will lose all sense of propriety and morality in your pursuit of low pleasures, and it denotes the indulgence of an insatiate thirst for gaining.***

To deal in oysters, denotes that you will not be overmodest in your mode of winning a sweetheart or a fortune.

To see them, denotes easy circumstances, and many children are promised to you. ✻

OYSTER SHELLS
To see oyster shells ***in your dreams, denotes that you will be frustrated in your attempt to secure the fortune of another.*** ✻

LOBSTER
To dream of seeing lobsters, ***denotes that great favors and riches will endow you.***

If you eat them, you will sustain contamination by associating too freely with pleasure-seeking people.

If the lobsters are made into a salad, success will not change your generous nature, but you will enjoy to the fullest your ideas of pleasure.

To order a lobster, you will hold prominent positions and command many subordinates. ✻

CLAMS
To dream of clams, ***denotes dealings with an obstinate but honest person.***

To eat them, foretells enjoyment of another's prosperity.

For a young woman to dream of eating baked clams with her sweetheart, foretells that she will enjoy his money, as well as his confidence. ✻

Tripe and Sausage

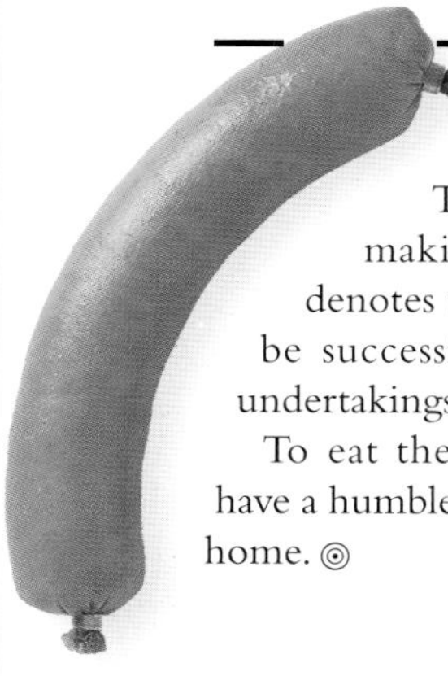

SAUSAGE

SAUSAGE
To dream of making ***sausage***, denotes that you will be successful in many undertakings.

To eat them, you will have a humble but pleasant home. ◎

TRIPE
To see ***tripe*** in a dream, means sickness and danger.

To ***eat tripe***, denotes that you will be disappointed in some serious matter. ◎

Even the humblest of ingredients may flavour your dreams. These may include the frugal sausage *left* **or everyday vegetables such as the turnip** *opposite center* **and the carrot** *opposite top*.

PORK, HAM *see* **PIGS, HOGS** *page 37,* **EATING** *page 133* ◆ **BACON** *see* **PIGS, HOGS,** *page 37,* **EATING** *page 133,* **SALT** *page 139* ◆ **POULTRY** *see* **GEESE, CHICKENS, TURKEY** *page 39,* **DUCKS** *page 45* ◆ **SARDINES** *see* **FISH** *page 51* ◆ **OYSTERS** *see* **EATING** *page 133,* **SOUP** *page 135* ◆ **OYSTER SHELLS** *see* **SHELLS** *page 70* ◆ **LOBSTER** *see* **EATING** *page 133,* **SALAD** *page 138* ◆ **CLAMS** *see* **EATING** *page 133* ◆ **SAUSAGE, TRIPE** *see* **EATING** *page 133*

There appears to be a strong connection between the eating of certain vegetables and the successful pursuit of love. It covers vegetables in general, special types of vegetable - root vegetables, salads, beans and pulses - as well as individual species; it also covers herbs and spices.

Root Vegetables

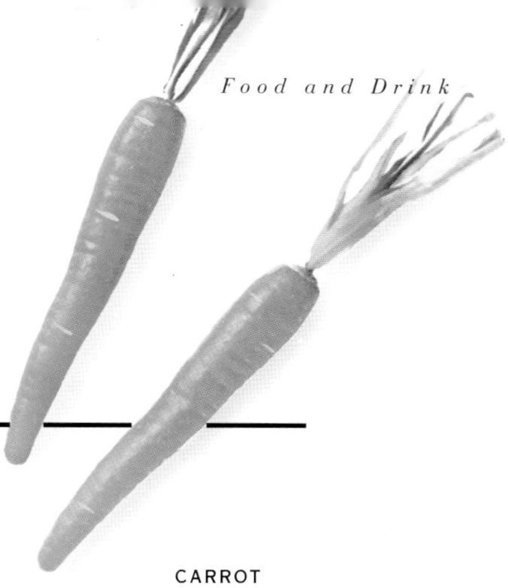

CARROT

VEGETABLES
To dream of eating ***vegetables***, is an omen of strange luck. You will think for a time that you are tremendously successful, but will find, to your sorrow, that you have been grossly imposed upon.

Withered or decayed vegetables, bring unmitigated woe and sadness.

For a young woman to dream that she is ***preparing vegetables*** for dinner, foretells that she will lose the man she desired through pique, but she will win a well-meaning and faithful husband. Her engagements will be somewhat disappointing. ◎

TURNIPS
To see ***turnips*** growing, denotes that your prospects will brighten, and that you will be extremely elated over your success.

TURNIP

To eat them, is a sign of ill health. To pull them up, denotes that you will improve your opportunities and your fortune thereby.

To eat ***turnip greens***, is a sign of bitter disappointment. ***Turnip seed*** is a sign of future advancement.

For a young woman to ***sow turnip seed***, foretells that she will inherit good property and win a handsome husband. ◎

PARSNIPS
To see or eat ***parsnips***, is a favorable omen of successful business or trade, but love will take on unfavorable and gloomy aspects. ◎

POTATOES
Dreaming of ***potatoes***, brings incidents often of good.

Planting them, brings realization of desires.

To dream of digging them, denotes success.

To dream of eating them, you will enjoy substantial gain.

To cook them, signifies congenial employment.

To see them rotting, denotes vanished pleasure and a darkening feature. ◎

Onions and Garlic

ONIONS
Seeing quantities of ***onions*** in your dreams, represents the amount of spite and envy that you will meet, by being successful.

If you eat them, you will overcome all opposition.

If you see them growing, there will be just enough of rivalry in your affairs to make things interesting.

Cooked onions, denote placidity and small gains in business.

To dream that you are ***cutting onions*** and feel the escaping juice in your eyes, denotes that you will be defeated by your rivals. ◎

GARLIC
To dream of passing through a ***garlic*** patch, denotes a rise from penury to prominence and wealth. To a young woman, this denotes that she will marry from a sense of business, and love will not be considered.

To ***eat garlic*** in your dreams, denotes that you will take a sensible view of life and leave its ideals to take care of themselves. ◎

CARROT
To dream of ***carrots***, portends prosperity and health. For a young woman to eat them, denotes that she will contract an early marriage and be the mother of several hardy children. ◎

BEETS
To see them growing abundantly, harvest and peace will obtain in the land; eating them with others, is full of good tidings.

If they are served in soiled or impure dishes, distressful awakenings will disturb you. ◎

Radishes

HORSERADISH
To dream of ***horseradish***, foretells pleasant associations with intellectual and congenial people. Fortune is also expressed in this dream. For a woman, it indicates a rise above her present station.

To ***eat horseradish***, you will be the object of pleasant raillery. ◎

RADISH
To dream of seeing a bed of ***radishes*** growing, is an omen of good luck. Such a dream foretells that your friends will be unusually kind, and your business will prosper.

If you eat them, you will suffer slightly through the thoughtlessness of someone near to you.

To see radishes, or plant them, denotes that your anticipations will be happily realized. ◎

VEGETABLES, PARSNIPS, GARLIC, CARROTS, HORSERADISH, RADISH *see* **EATING** *page 133* ◆ **TURNIP** *see* **EATING** *page 133,* **SEED, SOWING** *page 62* ◆ **POTATOES** *see* **DIGGING** *page 193,* **EATING** *page 133* ◆ **ONIONS** *see* **EATING** *page 133,* **EYE** *page 99* ◆ **BEETS** *see* **EATING** *page 133,* **DISHES** *page 209*

Green Vegetables

CABBAGE
It is bad to dream of ***cabbage***. Disorders may run riot in all forms.

To dream of seeing ***cabbage green***, means unfaithfulness in love and infidelity in wedlock.

To dream that you cut ***heads of cabbage***, denotes that you are tightening the cords of calamity around you by lavish expenditure. ◎

CAULIFLOWER
To dream of eating it, you will be taken to task for neglect of duty. If you see it growing, your prospects will brighten after a period of loss.

For a young woman to see this vegetable in a garden, denotes that she will marry to please her parents and not herself. ◎

CELERY
To dream of seeing fresh, crisp stalks of ***celery***, you will be prosperous and influential beyond your highest hopes.

If you see it decaying, a death in your family will soon occur.

If you eat it, boundless love and affection will be heaped upon you.

For a young woman to eat it with her lover, denotes that she will come into rich possessions. ◎

SALAD
To dream of eating ***salad***, foretells sickness and disagreeable people around you.

For a young woman to dream of making a salad, gives her a sign that her lover will become changeable and quarrelsome. ◎

LETTUCE
To see ***lettuce*** growing green and thrifty, denotes that you will enjoy some greatly desired good, after an unimportant embarrassment.

If you dream that you ***eat lettuce***, illness will separate you from your lover or companion, or perhaps it may be petty jealousy.

For a woman to dream of ***sowing lettuce***, portends that she will be the cause of her own early sickness or death.

To gather it, denotes your superabundant sensitiveness, and that your jealous disposition will cause you unmitigated distress and pain.

To ***buy lettuce***, denotes that you will court your own downfall. ◎

CUCUMBER
This is a dream of plenty, denoting health and prosperity. For the sick to dream of serving ***cucumbers***, denotes their speedy recovery. For the married, a pleasant change. ◎

ASPARAGUS
To dream of ***asparagus***, signifies prosperous surroundings and obedience from servants and children. To eat it, denotes interrupted success. ◎

Olives and Mushrooms

OLIVES
To dream that you go gathering ***olives*** with a merry band of friends, foretells favorable results in business, and delightful surprises.

If you take them from bottles, it foretells conviviality.

To break a ***bottle of olives***, indicates that there will be disappointment on the eve of pleasure.

To eat them, signifies contentment and faithful friends. ◎

MUSHROOM
To see ***mushrooms*** in your dreams, denotes unhealthy desires and unwise haste in amassing wealth, as it may vanish in lawsuits and vain pleasures.

To eat them, signifies humiliation and disgraceful love.

For a young woman to dream of them, foretells her defiance of propriety in her pursuit of foolish pleasures. ◎

Peas, Beans, and Lentils

PEAS
Dreaming of eating ***peas***, augurs robust health and the accumulation of wealth. Much activity is indicated for farmers and their womenfolk.

To see them growing, denotes fortunate enterprises.

To plant them, denotes that your hopes are well grounded and they will be realized.

To gather them, signifies that your plans will culminate in good and you will enjoy the fruits of your labors.

To dream of ***canned peas***, denotes that your brightest hopes will be enthralled in uncertainties for a short season, but they will finally be released by fortune.

To see ***dried peas***, denotes that you are overtaxing your health.

To ***eat dried peas***, foretells that you will, after much success, suffer a slight decrease in pleasure or wealth. ◎

BEANS
This is a bad dream. To see them growing, omens worries and sickness among children.

Dried ***beans***, means much disappointment in worldly affairs. Care should be taken to prevent contagious diseases from spreading.

To dream of eating them, implies the misfortune or illness of a well-loved friend. ◎

LENTILS
If you dream of ***lentils***, it denotes quarrels and unhealthy surroundings. For a young woman, this dream portends dissatisfaction with her lover, but parental advice will cause her to accept the inevitable. ◎

CAULIFLOWER *see* **EATING** *page 133,* **GARDEN** *page 56* ◆ **CELERY, SALAD, ASPARAGUS, BEANS, MUSHROOMS** *see* **EATING** *page 133* ◆ **LETTUCE** *see* **EATING** *page 133,* **SOWING** *page 62* ◆ **OLIVES** *see* **FRIEND** *page 124,* **BOTTLES** *page 210,* **BREAK** *page 265,* **EATING** *page 133* ◆ **PEAS** *see* **SOWING** *page 62,* **EATING** *page 133*

Herbs

ROSEMARY

HERBS
To dream of ***herbs***, denotes that you will have vexatious cares, though some pleasure will ensue.

To dream of ***poisonous herbs***, warns you of enemies.

Balm and other ***useful herbs***, denote satisfaction in business and warm friendships. ◎

PARSLEY
To dream of ***parsley***, denotes hard-earned success; usually, the surroundings of the dreamer are healthful and lively.

To ***eat parsley***, is a sign of good health, but the care of a large family will be your portion. ◎

PEPPERMINT
To dream of ***peppermint***, denotes pleasant entertainments and interesting affairs.

To see it growing, denotes that you will participate in some pleasure in which there will be a dash of romance.

To enjoy drinks in which there is an ***effusion of peppermint***, denotes that you will enjoy assignations with some attractive and fascinating person. To a young woman, this dream warns her against seductive pleasures. ◎

MUSTARD
To see ***mustard*** growing and green, foretells success and joy to the farmer, and to the seafaring, it prognosticates wealth.

To dream that you eat ***mustard seed*** and feel the burning in your mouth, denotes that you will repent bitterly of some hasty action, which has caused you to suffer.

To dream of eating ***green mustard*** cooked, indicates the lavish waste of fortune, and mental strain.

For a young woman to eat ***newly grown mustard***, foretells that she will sacrifice wealth for personal desires. ◎

ROSEMARY
Rosemary, if seen in dreams, denotes that sadness and indifference will cause unhappiness in homes where there is appearance of prosperity. ◎

SAGE
To dream of ***sage***, foretells that thrift and economy will be practiced by your servants or family.

For a woman to think she has too much in her viands, omens that she will regret useless extravagance in love, as well as fortune. ◎

RED SAGE

Spices

SPICE
To dream of ***spice***, foretells that you will probably damage your own reputation in search of pleasure.

For a young woman to dream of ***eating spice***, is an omen of deceitful appearances winning her confidence. ◎

SAFFRON
Saffron seen in a dream, warns you that you are entertaining false hopes, as bitter enemies are interfering secretly with your plans for the future.

To drink a ***tea made from saffron***, foretells that you will have quarrels and alienations in your family. ◎

NUTMEGS
To dream of ***nutmegs***, is a sign of prosperity and pleasant journeyings. ◎

PEPPER
To dream of ***pepper*** burning your tongue, foretells that you will suffer from your acquaintances through your love of gossip.

MUSTARD SEED

To see ***red pepper*** growing, foretells for you a thrifty and an independent partner in the marriage state.

To see piles of ***red pepper pods***, signifies that you will aggressively maintain your rights. To grind ***black pepper***, denotes that you will be victimized by the wiles of ingenious men or women. To see it in stands on the table, omens sharp reproaches or quarrels.

For a young woman to put it on her food, foretells that she will be deceived by her friends. ◎

SALT
Salt is an omen of discordant surroundings when seen in dreams. You will usually find, after dreaming of salt, that everything goes awry, and quarrels and dissatisfaction show themselves in the family circle.

To ***salt meat***, portends that debts and mortgages will harass you.

For a young woman to ***eat salt***, she will be deserted by her lover for a more beautiful and attractive girl, thus causing her deep chagrin. ◎

Herbs and spices have culinary and medicinal uses in the real world, but also carry significance in dreams; dream herbs include rosemary *top left*, **sage** *top right* **or mustard** *left*.

HERBS *see* **POISON** *page 247* ◆ **PARSLEY** *see* **EATING** *page 133* ◆ **PEPPERMINT** *see* **GROWING** *page 62*, **DRINKING** *page 150* ◆ **MUSTARD** *see* **SEED, GROWING** *page 62*, **EATING** *page 133* ◆ **SPICE** *see* **EATING** *page 133* ◆ **SAFFRON** *see* **TEA** *page 153* ◆ **PEPPER** *see* **TONGUE** *page 92* ◆ **SALT** *see* **MEAT** *page 135*, **EATING** *page 133*

Fruit is very significant in the dreamscape and indeed in the human psyche. In the Christian tradition an apple symbolized the fall of humanity, and since that time fruit of all kinds has been laden with meaning. This section covers fruit from many categories and incorportes a subsection on nut dreams.

Fruit and Orchards

FRUIT

To dream of seeing ***fruit*** ripening among its foliage, usually foretells to the dreamer a prosperous future. ***Green fruit*** signifies disappointed efforts or hasty action.

For a young woman to dream of eating ***green fruit***, indicates her degradation and loss of inheritance. Eating fruit is usually unfavorable.

To ***buy or sell fruit***, denotes much business, but not very remunerative.

To see or eat ***ripe fruit***, signifies uncertain fortune and pleasure.

To gather the ripe fruit, is a happy omen of plenty to all classes. ◎

ORCHARD

Dreaming of passing through leafy and blossoming ***orchards*** with your sweetheart, omens a delightful consummation of a long courtship. If the orchard is filled with ripening fruit, it denotes recompense for faithful service to those under masters, and full fruition of designs for the leaders of enterprises. Happy homes, with loyal husbands and obedient children, for wives.

If you are in an orchard and see hogs eating the fallen fruit, it is a sign that you will lose property in trying to claim what are not really your own belongings.

Orchards infested with blight, denote a miserable existence amid joy and wealth.

To be caught in brambles while passing through an orchard, warns you of a jealous rival, or, if married, a private but large row with your partner.

If you dream of seeing a ***barren orchard***, opportunities to rise to higher stations in life will be ignored.

If you see one robbed of its verdure by seeming winter, it denotes that you have been careless of the future in the enjoyment of the present.

To see a ***storm-swept orchard***, brings an unwelcome guest, or duties. ◎

FRUIT SELLER

To dream of a ***fruit seller***, denotes that you will endeavor to recover your loss too rapidly and will engage in unfortunate speculations ◎

Apples, Pears, Cherries, and Plums

CHERRIES

To dream of ***cherries***, denotes that you will gain popularity by your amiability and unselfishness.

To eat them, portends possession of some much desired object.

To see green ones, indicates approaching good fortune. ◎

APPLES

This is a very good dream to the majority of people.

To see red ***apples*** on trees with green foliage, is exceedingly propitious to the dreamer.

To eat them is not as good, unless they be faultless.

A friend who interprets dreams says: "Ripe applies on a tree, denotes that the time has arrived for you to realize your hopes; think over what you intend to do, and go fearlessly ahead. Ripe on the top of the tree, warns you not to aim too high. Applies on the ground imply that false friends and flatterers are working you harm. Decayed applies typify hopeless efforts." ◎

PEARS

To dream of eating ***pears***, denotes poor success and debilitating health.

To admire the golden fruit upon graceful trees, denotes that fortune will wear a more promising aspect than formerly.

To dream of gathering them, denotes that pleasant surprises will follow quickly upon disappointment.

To preserve them, denotes that you will take reverses philosophically.

Baking them, denotes insipid love and friendships. ◎

PLUMS

Plums, if they are green, unless seen on trees, are a sign of personal and relative discomfort.

To see them ripe, denotes joyous occasions, which, however, will be of short duration.

To eat them, denotes flirtations and other evanescent pleasures.

To gather them, you will obtain your desires, but they will not prove so solid as you had imagined.

If you find yourself gathering them up from the ground, and find rotten ones among the good, you will be forced to admit that your expectations are unrealized, and that there is no life filled with pleasure alone. ◎

DAMSON

This is a peculiarly good dream if one is so fortunate as to see these trees lifting their branches loaded with rich purple fruit and dainty foliage; one may expect riches compared with his present estate.

To dream of eating them at any time, forebodes grief. ◎

FRUIT *see* **EATING** *page 133* ◆ **ORCHARD** *see* **BLOSSOMS, LEAVES** *page 64,* **SWEETHEART** *page 124,* **HOGS** *page 37,* **BRAMBLES** *page 66,* **WINTER** *page 82,* **STORM** *page 76* ◆ **CHERRIES** *see* **EATING** *page 133* ◆ **APPLES, PLUMS, DAMSONS** *see* **TREES** *page 64,* **EATING** *page 133* ◆ **PEARS** *see* **EATING** *page 133,* **TREES** *page 64,* **BAKING** *page 146*

Berry Fruits

GOOSEBERRIES
To dream of gathering ***gooseberries***, is a sign of happiness after trouble, and a favorable indication of brighter prospects in one's business affairs.

If you are eating ***green gooseberries***, you will make a mistake in your course to pleasure, and be precipitated into the vortex of sensationalism. Bad results are sure to follow the tasting of green gooseberries.

To see gooseberries in a dream, foretells that you will escape some dreaded work. For a young woman to eat them, foretells that she will be slightly disappointed in her expectations. ◎

STRAWBERRIES
To dream of ***strawberries***, is favorable to advancement and pleasure. You will obtain some long wished for object.

To eat them, denotes requited love.

To deal in them, denotes abundant harvest and happiness. ◎

STRAWBERRY

RASPBERRY
To see ***raspberries*** in a dream, foretells that you are in danger of entanglements which will prove interesting before you escape from them.

For a woman to eat them, means distress over circumstantial evidence in some occurrence causing gossip. ◎

ELDERBERRIES
To dream of seeing ***elderberries*** on bushes with their foliage, denotes domestic bliss and an agreeable country home, with resources for travel and other pleasures.

Elderberries are generally a good dream. ◎

BLACKBERRIES
To dream of ***blackberries***, denotes many ills. To gather them is unlucky. Eating them denotes losses. ◎

MULBERRIES
To see ***mulberries*** in your dreams, denotes that sickness will prevent you from obtaining your desires, and you will be called upon often to relieve suffering.

To eat them, signifies bitter disappointments. ◎

Dreams of delectable fruit make for an appetizing night's sleep. Peaches *top right*, **unless at their ripest, do not live up to their luscious promise; strawberries** *above* **are as sweet in dreams as they are in reality.**

Rhubarb

To dream of rhubarb growing, ***denotes that pleasant entertainments will occupy your time for awhile.***

To cook it, foretells spirited arguments in which you will lose a friend.

To eat it, denotes dissatisfaction with present employment. ❋

Tomatoes

To dream of eating tomatoes, ***signals the approach of good health. To see them growing, denotes domestic enjoyment and happiness.***

For a young woman to see ripe ones, foretells her happiness in the married state. ❋

Peaches and Apricots

PEACHES
Dreaming of seeing or eating ***peaches***, implies the sickness of children, disappointing returns in business, and failure to make anticipated visits of pleasure; but if you see them on trees with foliage, you will secure some desired position or thing after much striving and risking of health and money.

To see ***dried peaches***, denotes that enemies will steal from you.

For a young woman to dream of gathering ***luscious peaches*** from well-filled trees, she will, by her personal charms and qualifications, win a husband rich in worldly goods and wise in travel. If the peaches prove to be green and knotty, she will meet with unkindness from relatives, and ill health will steal away her attractions. ◎

APRICOT
Dreams of seeing ***apricots*** growing, denote that the future, though seemingly rosy hued, holds masked bitterness and sorrow for you.

To eat them signifies the near approach of calamitous influences. If others eat them, your surroundings will be unpleasant and disagreeable to your fancies.

A friend says: "Apricots denote that you have been wasting time over trifles or small things of no value." ◎

GOOSEBERRIES, STRAWBERRIES, RASPBERRY, BLACKBERRIES, MULBERRIES, RHUBARB, APRICOT, TOMATOES *see* EATING *page 133* ◆ ELDERBERRIES *see* LEAVES *page 64* ◆ PEACHES *see* EATING *page 133*, TREES *page 64*

Citrus Fruits

ORANGES

Seeing a number of *orange* trees in a healthy condition, bearing ripe fruit, is a sign of health and prosperous surroundings.

To *eat oranges* is signally bad. Sickness of friends or relatives will be a source of worry to you. Dissatisfaction will pervade the atmosphere in business circles. If they are fine and well-flavored, there will be a slight abatement of ill luck. A young woman is likely to lose her lover, if she dreams of eating oranges. If she dreams of seeing a fine one pitched up high, she will be discreet in choosing a husband from many lovers.

To slip on an *orange peel*, foretells the death of a relative.

To *buy oranges* at your wife's solicitation, and she eats them, denotes that unpleasant complications will resolve themselves into profit. ◎

BRINGING IN THE FRUIT

Tropical Fruits

MELON

To dream of *melons*, denotes ill health and unfortunate ventures in business.

To eat them, signifies that hasty action will cause you anxiety.

To see them growing on green vines, denotes that present troubles will result in good fortune for you. ◎

BANANA

To dream of *bananas*, foretells that you will be mated to an uninteresting and unloved companion.

To dream that you eat them, foretells a tiresome venture in business, and self-inflicted duty.

To see them decaying, you are soon to fall into some disagreeable enterprise.

To trade in them, foretells that non-productive interests will accumulate around you. ◎

LEMONS

To dream of seeing *lemons* on their native trees among rich foliage, denotes jealousy toward some beloved object, but demonstrations will convince you of the absurdity of the charge.

To *eat lemons*, foretells humiliation and disappointments.

Green lemons, denote sickness and contagion.

To see *shriveled lemons*, denotes divorce if married, and separation to lovers. ◎

LEMON

LIMES

To dream of eating *limes,* foretells continued sickness and adverse straits. ◎

POMEGRANATE

Pomegranates, when dreamed of, denote that you will wisely use your talents for the enrichment of the mind, rather than seek those pleasures which destroy morality and health.

If your sweetheart gives you one, you will be lured by artful wiles to very distraction by women's charms, but inner forces will hold you safe from thralldom.

To eat one, signifies that you will yield yourself a captive to the charms of another. ◎

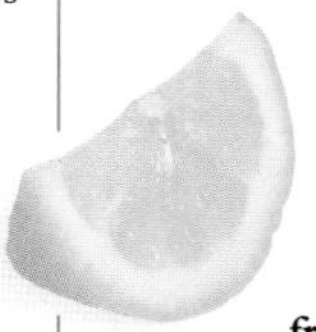

Sour-tasting lemons *left* **bring bitter dreams, whereas a cornucopia of pineapples, grapes, and other luscious fruit** *above* **presages all things good. Dreams of almonds** *opposite left*, **walnuts** *opposite center*, **or gathering nuts of any kind** *opposite bottom* **are excellent omens.**

PINEAPPLE

To dream of *pineapples*, is exceedingly propitious. Success will follow in the near future, if you gather pineapples or eat them.

To dream that you prick your fingers while preparing a pineapple for the table, you will experience considerable vexation over matters which will finally bring pleasure and success. ◎

FIGS

Figs signify a malarious condition of the system, if you are eating them, but are usually favorable to health and profit if you see them growing.

For a young woman to see figs growing, signifies that she will soon wed a wealthy and prominent man. ◎

ORANGE *see* **TREES** *page 64*, **EATING** *page 133*, **WIFE** *page 132* ◆ **LEMONS** *see* **TREES, LEAVES** *page 64*, **EATING** *page 133* ◆ **LIMES** *see* **EATING** *page 133* ◆ **POMEGRANATE** *see* **EATING** *page 133*, **SWEETHEART** *page 124* ◆ **MELONS** *see* **EATING** *page 133*, **VINES** *page 61* ◆ **BANANAS** *see* **EATING** *page 133*, **TRADE** *page 202* ◆ **PINEAPPLE** *see* **EATING** *page 133*, **FINGERS** *page 97* ◆ **FIGS, RAISINS** *see* **EATING** *page 133*

Dates and Grapes

DATES
To dream of seeing them on their parent trees, signifies prosperity and happy union; but to eat them as prepared for commerce, is ominous of want and distress. ◎

RAISINS
To dream of eating ***raisins***, implies that discouragements will darken your hopes when they seem about to be realized. ◎

GRAPES
To eat ***grapes*** in your dream, you will be hardened with many cares; but if you only see them hanging in profuseness among the leaves, you will soon attain to eminent positions and will be able to impart happiness to others. For a young woman, this dream is one of bright promise. She will have her most ardent wish gratified.

To dream of riding on horseback and passing ***muscadine bushes*** and gathering and eating some of their fruit, denotes profitable employment and the realization of great desires. If there arises in your mind a question of the poisonous quality of the fruit you are eating, there will come doubts and fears of success, but they will gradually cease to worry you. ◎

ALMONDS

Nuts

NUTS
To dream of gathering ***nuts,*** augurs successful enterprises and much favor in love.

To eat them, prosperity will aid you in grasping any desired pleasure.

For a woman to dream of nuts, foretells that her fortune will be on blissful heights. ◎

FILBERT
This is a favorable dream, denoting a peaceful and harmonious domestic life and profitable business ventures.

To dream of eating them, signifies to the young, delightful associations and many true friends. ◎

WALNUT
To dream of ***walnuts***, is an omen of prolific joys and favors.

To dream that you crack a ***decayed walnut***, denotes that your expectations will end in bitterness and regrettable collapse.

For a young woman to dream that she has ***walnut stain*** on her hands, foretells that she will see her lover turn his attention to another, and she will entertain only regrets for her past indiscreet conduct. ◎

CHESTNUTS
To dream of handling ***chestnuts***, foretells losses in a business way, but indicates an agreeable companion through life.

Eating them, denotes sorrow for a time, but final happiness.

For a young woman to dream of eating or trying her fortune with them, she will have a well-to-do lover and comparative plenty. ◎

ALMONDS
This is a good omen. It has wealth in store. However, sorrow will go with it for a short while. If the ***almonds*** are defective, your disappointment in obtaining a certain wish will be complete until new conditions are brought about. ◎

COCONUT
Coconuts in dreams, warn you of fatalities in your expectations, as sly enemies are encroaching upon your rights in the guise of ardent friends.

Dead coconut trees are a sign of loss and sorrow. The death of someone near you may follow. ◎

PECANS
To dream of eating this appetizing nut, you will see one of your dearest plans come to full fruition, and seeming failure prove a prosperous source of gain.

To see them growing among leaves, signifies a long, peaceful existence. Failure in love or business will follow in proportion as the ***pecan*** is decayed.

WALNUT

If they are difficult to crack and the fruit is small, you will succeed after much trouble and expense, but returns will be meager. ◎

GATHERING NUTS

DATES *see* **TREES** *page 64,* **EATING** *page 133* ◆ **GRAPES** *see* **EATING** *page 133,* **LEAVES** *page 64,* **RIDE** *page 33,* **HORSE** *page 34-5,* **POISON** *page 247,* **VINES, VINEYARD** *page 61* ◆ **NUTS, FILBERT, PECAN** *see* **EATING** *page 133* ◆ **WALNUT** *see* **STAIN** *page 218,* **HANDS** *page 97* ◆ **COCONUT** *see* **DEAD** *page 120,* **TREES** *page 64* ◆ **CHESTNUTS** *see* **EATING** *page 133,* **FORTUNE TELLING** *page 269* ◆

The cool pleasures of the dairy, if part of your dreamscape, signify a wholesome outcome to plans. This section covers milk, churning, cream, and butter. Cheese is notoriously bad either eaten before dreams or forming part of them. Eggs and omelets are also included here.

In the Dairy

DAIRY

Dairy is a good dream, both to the married and unmarried. ◎

MILK

To dream of drinking ***milk***, denotes abundant harvest to the farmer and pleasure in the home; for a traveler, it foretells a fortunate voyage. This is a very propitious dream for women.

To see ***milk in large quantities***, signifies riches and health.

To dream of ***dealing in milk*** commercially, denotes great increase in fortune.

To ***give milk away***, shows that you will be too benevolent for the good of your own fortune.

To ***spill milk***, denotes that you will experience a slight loss and suffer temporary unhappiness at the hands of friends.

To dream of ***impure milk***, denotes that you will be tormented with petty troubles.

To dream of ***sour milk***, denotes that you will be disturbed over the distress of friends.

To dream of trying unsuccessfully to ***drink milk***, signifies that you will be in danger of losing something of value or the friendship of a highly esteemed person.

To dream of ***hot milk***, foretells a struggle, but the final winning of riches and desires.

To dream of ***bathing in milk***, denotes pleasures and the companionship of congenial friends. ◎

Wholesome dairy dreams may include fresh milk *top*, **cheese making** *right* **and butter** *opposite center*. **Eggs, cooked** *opposite top* **or freshly collected** *opposite bottom* **also have their significance.**

MILKING

To dream of ***milking a cow***, and that the milk flows in great streams from the udder, while the cow is restless and threatening, signifies that you will see great opportunities withheld from you, but which will result in final favor for you. ◎

FRESH MILK

CHURNING

To dream of ***churning***, you will have difficult tasks set before you; but by diligence and industry, you will accomplish them and be very prosperous.

To the farmer, it denotes profit from a plenteous harvest; to a young woman, a thrifty and energetic husband. ◎

CHEESE MAKING

MILK *see* **TRADE** *page 202*, **GIFTS** *page 240*, **DRINKING** *page 150*, **BATHING** *page 105* ◆ **MILKING** *see* **COW** *page 37* ◆ **CHURNING** *see* **BUTTER, CHEESE** *page 145*

Butter and Cream

BUTTER
To dream of eating fresh, golden ***butter***, is a sign of good health and plans well carried out; it will bring unto you possessions, wealth, and knowledge.

To eat ***rancid butter***, denotes a competency acquired through struggles of manual labor.

To ***sell butter***, denotes small gain. ◎

BUTTERMILK
Drinking ***buttermilk***, denotes that sorrow will follow some worldly pleasure, and some imprudence will impair the general health of the dreamer.

To give it away, or feed it to pigs, is worse still.

To dream that you are drinking ***buttermilk made into oyster soup***, denotes that you will be called on to do some very repulsive thing, and ill luck will confront you. There are quarrels brewing and friendships threatened.

If you awaken while you are drinking the soup, by discreet maneuvering you may effect a pleasant understanding of disagreements. ◎

CREAM
To dream of seeing ***cream*** served, denotes that you will be associated with wealth, if you are engaged in business other than farming.

To the farmer, it indicates fine crops and pleasant family relations. To drink cream yourself, denotes immediate good fortune.

To lovers, this is a happy omen, as they will soon be united. ◎

BUTTER

Cheese Dreams

CHEESE
To dream of eating ***cheese***, denotes great disappointments and sorrow. No good of any nature can be hoped for. Cheese is generally a bad dream. ◎

SWISS CHEESE
To dream of ***Swiss cheese***, foretells that you will come into possession of substantial property, and healthful amusements will be enjoyed. ◎

WELSH RABBITS
To dream of preparing or eating ***Welsh rabbits***, denotes that your affairs will assume a complicated state, owing to your attention being absorbed by artful women and enjoyment of neutral fancies. ◎

Eggs and Omelets

A CODDLED EGG

EGGS
To dream of finding a nest of ***eggs***, denotes wealth of a substantial character, happiness among the married, and many children. This dream signifies many and varied love affairs to women.

To ***eat eggs***, denotes that unusual disturbances threaten you in your home.

To see ***broken eggs*** and they are fresh, indicates that fortune is ready to shower upon you her richest gifts. A lofty spirit and high regard for justice will make you beloved by the world.

To dream of ***rotten eggs***, denotes loss of property and degradation.

To see a ***crate of eggs***, denotes that you will engage in profitable speculations.

To dream of being ***spattered with eggs***, denotes that you will sport riches of doubtful origin.

To see ***bird's eggs***, signifies legacies from distant relations, or gain from an unexpected rise in staple products. ◎

OMELET
To see an ***omelet*** being served in your dream, warns you of flattery and deceit, which is about to be used against you.

To eat it, shows that you will be imposed upon by someone seemingly worthy of your confidence. ◎

EGGS

BUTTER *see* **MILK, CHURNING, DAIRY** *page 144,* **EATING** *page 133* ◆ **BUTTERMILK** *see* **MILK** *page 144,* **DRINKING** *page 150,* **GIFTS** *page 240,* **PIGS** *page 37,* **SOUP** *page 135,* **OYSTERS** *page 136* ◆ **CHEESE, WELSH RABBITS** *see* **EATING** *page 133* ◆ **EGGS** *see* **NEST** *page 43,* **BIRDS** *page 43,* **EATING** *page 133* ◆ **OMELET** *see* **EATING** *page 133*

The smell of warm, new-baked bread is just as mouth-watering in your dreams as it is in waking life. Surprisingly, bread, the staff of life, does not always signify a good dream. This section covers bread and baking, pies, cakes, and biscuits. Cereals, rice, and pasta are also included here.

Baking and Flour

VARIETIES OF BREAD

BAKERY

To dream of a ***bakery***, demands caution in making changes in one's career. Pitfalls may reveal themselves on every hand. ◎

BAKING

Baking is unpropitious for a woman. Ill health and the care of many children; meanness and poverty of supporters are indicated. ◎

MAKING CAKES

FLOUR

To dream of ***flour***, denotes a frugal but happy life. For a young woman to dream that she sees flour on herself, denotes that she will be ruled by her husband, and that her life will be full of pleasant cares.

To dream of ***dealing in flour***, denotes hazardous speculations. ◎

CORNMEAL

To see ***cornmeal***, foretells the consummation of ardent wishes.

To eat it made into bread, denotes that you will unwittingly throw obstructions in the way of your own advancement. ◎

Bread in all its varieties *above* **and** *top* **is a staple in dreams as it is in real life. Cakes** *left*, **pies** *opposite top*, **and puddings** *opposite bottom* **offer sweeter fare to the dreaming gourmet.**

BREAD

Daily Bread

BREAD

For a woman to dream of eating ***bread***, denotes that she will be afflicted with children of stubborn will, for whom she will spend many days of useless labor and worry.

To dream of ***baking bread*** with others, indicates an assured competence through life.

To see a lot of ***impure bread***, foretells that want and misery will burden the dreamer. If the bread is good and you have access to it, it is a favorable dream. ◎

RYE BREAD

To see or eat ***rye bread*** in your dreams, foretells that you will have a cheerful and well-appointed home. ◎

LOAVES

To dream of ***loaves*** of bread, denotes frugality. If they be of cake, the dreamer has cause to rejoice over his good fortune, as love and wealth will wait obsequiously upon you.

Broken loaves, bring discontent and bickering between those who love.

To see loaves multiply phenomenally, prognosticates great success. Lovers will be happy in their chosen ones. ◎

CRUST

To dream of a ***crust*** of bread, denotes incompetency, and threatened misery through carelessness in appointed duties. ◎

FLOUR *see* **CORN** *page 60*, **GRAIN, HARVEST** *page 62* ◆ **CORNMEAL** *see* **CORN** *page 60* ◆ **BREAD** *see* **EATING** *page 133* ◆ **RYE BREAD** *see* **RYE** *page 60*, **EATING** *page 133* ◆ **LOAVES** *see* **CAKE** *page 147*, **BREAK** *page 265*

Cakes, Pies, and Puddings

CAKES

Batter or pancakes, denote that the affections of the dreamer are well placed, and a home will be bequeathed to him or her.

To dream of ***sweet cakes***, is gain for the laboring and a favorable opportunity for the enterprising. Those in love will prosper.

Pound cake is significant of much pleasure, from either society or business.

For a young woman to dream of her ***wedding cake***, is the only bad-luck cake in the category. Baking them is not so good an omen as seeing them or eating them. ◎

PANCAKE

To dream of eating ***pancakes***, denotes that you will have excellent success in all enterprises undertaken at this time.

To cook them, denotes that you will be economical and thrifty in your home. ◎

PUDDINGS

To dream of ***puddings*** denotes small returns from large investments, if you only see it.

To eat it, is proof that your affairs will be disappointing.

For a young woman to cook or otherwise ***prepare a pudding***, denotes that her lover will be sensual and worldly minded, and if she marries him, she will see her love and fortune vanish. ◎

PASTRY

To dream of ***pastry***, denotes that you will be deceived by some artful person.

To eat it, implies heartfelt friendships.

If a young woman dreams that she is cooking it, she will fail to deceive others as to her real intentions. ◎

PUDDING

FRUIT PIE

PIES

To dream of eating ***pies***, you will do well to watch your enemies, as they are planning to injure you.

For a young woman to dream of ***making pies***, denotes that she will flirt with men for pastime. She should accept this warning. ◎

Biscuits and Wafers

BISCUITS

Eating or baking ***biscuits***, indicates ill health and family peace ruptured over silly disputes. ◎

WAFER

Wafers, if seen in a dream, purport an encounter with enemies.

To eat one, suggests impoverished fortune.

For a young woman to bake them, denotes that she will be tormented and distressed by fears of remaining in the unmarried state. ◎

Pasta

NOODLES

To dream of ***noodles***, denotes an abnormal appetite and desires. There is little good in this dream. ◎

MACARONI

To dream that you are eating ***macaroni***, denotes small losses.

To see macaroni in large quantities, denotes that you will save money by the strictest economy.

For a young woman, this dream means that a stranger will enter her life. ◎

Rice and Cereals

RICE

Rice is good to see in dreams, as it foretells success and warm friendships. Prosperity to all trades is promised, and the farmer will be blessed with a bounteous harvest.

To dream that you ***eat rice***, signifies happiness and domestic comfort.

To dream that you see ***rice mixed*** with dirt or otherwise impure, denotes sickness and separation from friends.

For a young woman to dream of cooking it, shows that she will soon assume new duties, which will make her happier, and she will enjoy wealth. ◎

OATS

OATMEAL

To dream of eating ***oatmeal***, signifies the enjoyment of worthily earned fortune.

For a young woman to dream of preparing it for the table, denotes that she will soon preside over the destiny of others. ◎

HOMINY

To dream of ***hominy***, denotes that pleasant lovemaking will furnish you with interesting recreation from absorbing study and planning for future progression. ◎

CAKES *see* **SWEET TASTE** *page 148*, **WEDDING** *page 131* ◆ **PANCAKE, PUDDINGS, PIES** *see* **EATING** *page 133* ◆ **BISCUITS, WAFER** *see* **EATING** *page 133*, **BAKING** *page 146* ◆ **NOODLES** *see* **EATING** *page 133* ◆ **RICE** *see* **EATING** *page 133*, **DIRT** *page 255* ◆ **OATMEAL** *see* **OATS** *page 61*, **EATING** *page 133*

In this section of sweet dream tastes, contrast is provided by the bracing sour note of pickles and vinegar. But, as you will discover, not everything that tastes sweet in your dreams promises a pleasant fulfilment in reality. Even in dreams, a sweet tooth can sometimes cause a pang of pain.

Sweet Dreams

SWEET TASTE

To dream of any kind of a ***sweet taste*** in your mouth, denotes that you will be praised for your pleasing conversation and calm demeanor in a time of commotion and distress.

To dream that you are trying to get rid of a sweet taste, foretells that you will oppress and deride your friends, and will incur their displeasure. ◎

SWEET OIL

Sweet oil in dreams, implies that considerate treatment will be withheld from you in some unfortunate occurrence. ◎

Sugar

SUGAR

To dream of ***sugar***, denotes that you will be hard to please in your domestic life and will entertain jealousy while seeing no cause for aught but satisfaction and secure joys. There may be worries, and your strength and temper taxed after this dream.

To ***eat sugar*** in your dreams, you will have unpleasant matters to contend with for a while. But they will result better than expected.

To ***price sugar***, denotes that you are menaced by enemies.

To ***deal in sugar*** and see large quantities of it being delivered to you, you will barely escape a serious loss.

To see a cask of sugar burst and the sugar spill out, foretells a light loss. ◎

SUGAR TONGS

To dream of ***sugar tongs***, foretells that disagreeable tidings of wrongdoings will be received by you. ◎

Sour Tastes

PICKLES

To dream of ***pickles***, denotes that you will follow worthless pursuits if you fail to call energy and judgement to your aid.

For a young woman to dream of ***eating pickles***, foretells an unambitious career.

To dream of pickles, denotes vexation in love, but final triumph.

For a young woman to dream that she is eating them, or is hungry for them, foretells that she will find many rivals, and will be overcome unless she is careful in her private affairs.

Impure pickles, indicate disappointing engagements and lovers' quarrels. ◎

VINEGAR

To dream of ***vinegar*** at all times denotes inharmonious and unfavorable aspects.

To dream of ***drinking vinegar***, denotes that you will be exasperated and worried into assenting to some engagement which will fill you with evil foreboding.

To use vinegar on vegetables, foretells a deepening of already distressing affairs. ◎

BEEHIVE

Sweet dreams may include dreams of honey from the beehive *above*, **candies from a children's "shop"** *opposite bottom* **or, even more delicious, stolen from the store cupboard** *opposite top*.

Jam and Honey

JAM

To dream of ***eating jam***, if it is pure, denotes pleasant surprises and journeys.

To dream of ***making jam***, foretells to a woman a happy home and appreciative friends. ◎

JELLY

If you dream of ***eating jelly***, many pleasant interruptions will take place.

For a woman to dream of ***making jelly***, signifies that she will enjoy pleasant reunions with friends. ◎

MARMALADE

To dream of eating ***marmalade***, denotes sickness and much dissatisfaction. ◎

MOLASSES

To dream of ***molasses***, is a sign that someone is going to extend you pleasant hospitality, and, through its acceptance, you will meet agreeable and fortunate surprises.

To eat it, foretells that you will be discouraged and disappointed in love.

To have it ***smeared on your clothing***, denotes that you will have disagreeable offers of marriage, and probably losses in business. ◎

HONEY

To dream that you see ***honey***, you will be possessed of considerable wealth.

To see ***strained honey***, denotes wealth and ease, but there will be an undercurrent in your life of unlawful gratification of material desires.

To dream of ***eating honey***, foretells that you will attain wealth and love. To lovers, this indicates a swift rush into marital joys.

For a young woman to dream of ***making honey***, denotes unhappy domestic associations. ◎

SWEET OIL *see* OIL *page 72* ◆ SUGAR *see* EATING *page 133*, TRADE *page 202*, CASK *page 210* ◆ PICKLES *see* EATING, HUNGRY *page 133*, SPICE *page 139* ◆ VINEGAR *see* DRINKING *page 150*, VEGETABLES *page 137* ◆ MOLASSES *see* EATING *page 133*, CLOTHES *page 154* ◆ JELLY, MARMALADE, JAM *see* EATING *page 133* ◆ HONEY *see* EATING *page 133*, BEES *page 48*

Chocolates and Candies

CONFECTIONERY
To dream of impure ***confectionery***, denotes that an enemy in the guise of a friend will enter your privacy and disclose secrets to your opponents. ◎

CHOCOLATE
To dream of ***chocolate***, denotes that you will provide abundantly for those who are dependent on you. To see chocolate candy, indicates agreeable companions and employments.

If the chocolate is sour, illness or other disappointments will follow.

To ***drink chocolate***, foretells that you will prosper after a short period of unfavorable reverses. ◎

CANDY
To dream of ***making candy***, denotes profit accruing from industry.

To dream of ***eating crisp, new candy***, implies social pleasures and much lovemaking among the young and old. To dream of ***sour candy*** is a sign of illness, or that disgusting annoyances will grow out of confidences too long kept.

To receive a ***box of bonbons***, signifies to a young person that he or she will be the recipient of much adulation. It generally means prosperity. If you send a box, you will make a proposition, but will meet with disappointment. ◎

COTTON CANDY
To dream of ***eating cotton candy***, foretells a pleasant trip will soon be taken. ◎

LOZENGES
To dream of ***lozenges***, foretells success in small matters. For a woman to eat or throw them away, foretells that her life will be harassed by little spites from the envious. ◎

A VISIT TO THE SWEET SHOP

A SWEET TREAT

Cool Desserts

ICE CREAM
To dream that you are ***eating ice cream***, foretells happy success in affairs already undertaken. To see children eating it, denotes that prosperity and happiness will attend you most favorably.

For a young woman to ***upset her ice cream*** in the presence of her lover or friend, denotes that she will be flirted with because of her unkindness to others.

To see ***sour ice cream***, denotes that some unexpected trouble will interfere with your pleasures. If the ice cream is melted, your anticipated pleasure will reach stagnation before it is realized. ◎

CUSTARD
For a married woman to dream of making or eating ***custard***, indicates that she will be called upon to entertain an unexpected guest. A young woman will meet a stranger, who will in time become a warm friend.

If the custard has a sickening sweet taste, or is insipid, nothing but sorrow will intervene where you had expected a pleasant experience. ◎

CHOCOLATE *see* **DRINKING** *page 150,* **COCOA** *page 153* ◆ **CANDY, COTTON CANDY** *see* **EATING** *page 133,* **SWEET TASTE** *page 148* ◆ **LOZENGES** *see* **EATING** *page 133,* **PILL** *page 116* ◆ **ICE CREAM** *see* **EATING** *page 133,* **CHILDREN** *page 128* ◆ **CUSTARD** *see* **EATING** *page 133,* **SWEET TASTE** *page 148*

Dreams of drink can be double-edged, depending on whether the dreamer is drinking alcoholic or more wholesome beverages. This section covers all aspects of drink and drink related behavior, from thirst to intoxication and from absinthe to cocoa. A small section on smoking and tobacco is included here.

Thirst and Drinking

THIRST

To dream of being ***thirsty***, shows that you are aspiring to things beyond your present reach; but if your thirst is quenched with pleasing drinks, you will obtain your wishes.

To see others thirsty and drinking to slake it, you will enjoy many favors at the hands of wealthy people. ◎

DRINKING

For a woman to dream of hilarious ***drinking***, denotes that she is engaging in affairs that may work to her discredit, though she may now find much pleasure in the same.

If she dreams that she fails to ***drink clear water***, though she uses her best efforts to do so, she will fail to enjoy some pleasure that is insinuatingly offered her. ◎

DRINKING

Inebriation

DRUNKENNESS

This is an unfavorable dream if you are ***drunk*** on heavy liquors, indicating profligacy and loss of employment. You will be disgraced by stooping to forgery or theft.

If ***drunk on wine***, you will be fortunate in trade and lovemaking, and will scale exalted heights in literary pursuits. This dream is always the bearer of aesthetic experiences.

To see others in a drunken condition, foretells for you, and probably others, unhappy states.

Drunkenness in all forms is unreliable as a good dream. All classes are warned by this dream to shift their thoughts into more healthful channels. ◎

INTOXICATION

To dream of ***intoxication***, denotes that you are cultivating your desires for illicit pleasures. ◎

BARMAID

TIPSY

To dream that you are ***tipsy***, denotes that you will cultivate a jovial disposition, and the cares of life will make no serious inroads into your conscience.

To see others tipsy, shows that you are careless as to the demeanour of your associates. ◎

LIQUOR

To dream of buying ***liquor***, denotes selfish usurpation of property upon which you have no legal claim. If you sell it, you will be criticized for niggardly benevolence.

HILARIOUS DRINKING

To drink some, you will come into doubtful possession of wealth, but your generosity will draw around you convivial friends, and women will seek to entrance and hold you.

To see ***liquor in barrels***, denotes prosperity, but an unfavorable tendency toward making home pleasant.

If it is in bottles, fortune will appear in a very tangible form.

For a woman to dream of ***handling or drinking liquor***, foretells for her a happy Bohemian kind of existence. She will be good natured but shallow minded.

To treat others, she will be generous to rivals, and the indifference of lovers or husbands will not seriously offset her pleasures or contentment. ◎

BAR

To dream of tending a ***bar***, denotes that you will resort to some questionable mode of advancement.

Seeing a bar, denotes activity in communities, quick uplifting of fortunes, and the consummation of illicit desires. ◎

Dreams of drinking may include giddy intoxication *top*, **the hard work of tending the bar** *above* **or the more refined pleasures of the wine connoisseur** *left and opposite bottom*.

THIRST *see* DROUGHT *page 81* ◆ DRINKING *see* WATER *page 78* ◆ DRUNKENNESS *see* WINE *page 151* ◆ LIQUOR *see* CASK *page 210* ◆ BAR *see* WAITER *page 134*, BEER *page 151*

Beer and Brewing

BREWING

To dream of being in a vast ***brewing*** establishment, means unjust persecution by public officials, but you will eventually prove your innocence and will rise far above your persecutors.

Brewing seen in any way in your dreams, denotes anxiety at the outset, but projects usually end well in profit and satisfaction. ◎

BEER

Beer is fateful to disappointments, if you dream you are drinking from a bar. To see others drinking beer, the work of designing intriguers will displace your fairest hopes.

To habitués of this beverage, harmonious prospects are foreshadowed, if pleasing, natural, and cleanly conditions survive.

The dream occurrences frequently follow in the actual. ◎

CIDER

To dream of ***cider***, denotes that fortune may be won by you if your time is not squandered upon material pleasure.

To see people drinking it, you will be under the influence of unfaithful friends. ◎

Mixed Drinks

COCKTAIL

To dream that you drink a cocktail, ***denotes that you will deceive your friends as to your inclinations and enjoy the companionship of fast men and women while posing as a serious student and staid home lover. For a woman, this dream portends fast living and an ignoring of morals and set rules.*** ❊

Wine

CORK

To dream of drawing ***corks*** at a banquet, signifies that you will soon enter a state of prosperity, in which you will revel in happiness of the most select kind.

To dream of ***medicine corks***, denotes sickness and wasted energies.

To dream of seeing a ***fishing cork*** resting on clear water, denotes success. If the water is disturbed, you will be annoyed by unprincipled persons.

To dream that you are ***corking bottles***, denotes a well-organized business and system in your living.

For a young woman to dream of drawing ***champagne corks***, indicates that she will have a gay and handsome lover who will lavish much attention and money on her. She should look well to her reputation and listen to the wise warnings of parents after this dream. ◎

CORKSCREW

To dream of seeing a ***corkscrew***, indicates an unsatisfied mind. The dreamer should heed this as a warning to curb his desires, for it is likely they are on dangerous grounds.

To dream of breaking a corkscrew while using it, indicates to the dreamer perilous surroundings. He should use force of will to abandon unhealthful inclinations. ◎

WINE

To dream of ***drinking wine***, forebodes joy and consequent friendships.

To dream of breaking ***bottles of wine***, foretells that your love and passion will border on excess.

To see ***barrels of wine***, prognosticates great luxury.

To pour it from one vessel into another, signifies that your enjoyments will be varied and you will journey to many notable places.

To dream of ***dealing in wine***, denotes that your occupation will be remunerative.

For a young woman to dream of drinking wine, indicates that she will marry a wealthy but withal honorable gentleman. ◎

WINE CELLAR

To dream of a ***wine cellar***, foretells that superior amusements or pleasure will come in your way, to be disposed of at your bidding. ◎

WINEGLASS

To dream of a ***wineglass***, foretells that a disappointment will affect you seriously, as you will fail to see anything pleasing until shocked into the realization of trouble. ◎

THE WINE CELLAR

BREWING *see* **MANUFACTORY** *page 194*, **HOPS** *page 61* ◆ **BEER** *see* **BAR, DRINKING** *page 150* ◆ **CIDER** *see* **DRINKING** *page 150*, **APPLES** *page 140* ◆ **COCKTAIL** *see* **BAR, DRINKING** *page 150* ◆ **CORK** *see* **BANQUET** *page 133*, **MEDICINE** *page 116*, **FISHERMAN** *page 51*, **ANGLING** *page 174*, **WATER** *page 78*, **BOTTLES** *page 210* ◆ **CORKSCREW** *see* **BREAK** *page 265* ◆ **WINE** *see* **DRINKING** *page 150*, **BREAK** *page 265*, **BOTTLES, CASK** *page 210*, **TRADE** *page 202*, **CLARET** *page 152* ◆ **WINE CELLAR** *see* **CELLAR** *page 206* ◆ **WINEGLASS** *see* **GLASS** *page 69*, **GOBLET** *page 210*

Claret, Punch, and Toddy

CLARET
To dream of drinking ***claret***, denotes that you will come under the influence of an ennobling association.

To dream of seeing broken ***bottles of claret***, portends that you will be induced to commit immoralities by the false persuasions of deceitful persons.

CLARET CUP AND PUNCH
To dream of a ***claret cup*** or ***punch***, foretells that you will be much pleased with the attention shown you by new acquaintances.

PUNCH
To dream of drinking the concoction called ***punch***, denotes that you will prefer selfish pleasures to honorable distinction and morality.

TODDY
To dream of taking a ***toddy***, foretells that interesting events will soon change your plan of living.

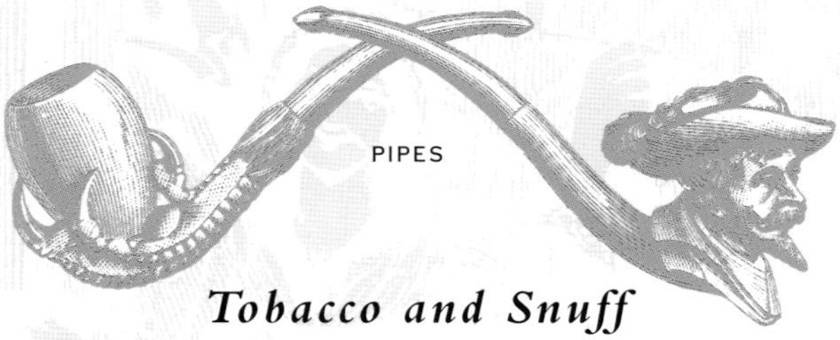

Tobacco and Snuff

PIPE
Pipes ***seen in dreams, are representative of peace and comfort after many struggles.***

Sewer, gas, and such-like pipes, denote unusual thought and prosperity in your community.

Old and broken pipes, signifies ill health and stagnation of business.

To dream that you smoke a pipe, ***denotes that you will enjoy the visit of an old friend, and peaceful settlements of differences will also take place.***

TOBACCO POUCH

TOBACCO
To dream of tobacco, ***denotes success in business affairs, but poor returns in love.***

To use it, warns you against enemies and extravagance.

To see it growing, foretells successful enterprises. To see it dry in the leaf, ensures good crops to farmers, and consequent gain to tradesmen.

To smoke tobacco, ***denotes amiable friendships.***

SNUFF
To dream of snuff, ***signifies that your enemies are seducing the confidence of your friends.***

For a woman to use it in her dreams, foretells complications which will involve her separation from a favored friend.

High Spirits

WHISKY
Whisky is not fraught with much good. Disappointment in some form will likely appear.

To dream of ***whisky in bottles***, denotes that you will be careful of your interests, protecting them with energy and watchfulness, thereby adding to their proportion.

To drink it alone, foretells that you will sacrifice your friends to your selfishness.

To ***destroy whisky***, you will lose your friends by your ungenerous conduct.

To see or drink it, is to strive and reach a desired object after many disappointments. If you only see it, you will never obtain the result hoped and worked for.

RUM
To dream of drinking ***rum***, foretells that you will have wealth, but will lack moral refinement, as you will lean toward gross pleasures.

ABSINTHE
To come under the influence of ***absinthe*** in dreams, denotes that you will lead a merry and foolish pace with innocent companions, and waste your inheritance in prodigal lavishness on the siren, foolish fancy.

BRANDY
To dream of ***brandy***, foretells that, while you may reach heights of distinction and wealth, you will lack the innate refinement which wins true friendship from people whom you most wish to please.

Pipes and tobacco *left*, often partnered with ale and spirits in waking life, also feature in dreams. Elegant tastes are catered for in dreams of after dinner coffee *opposite bottom*.

CLARET *see* **WINE** *page 151*, **BREAK** *page 265*, **BOTTLES** *page 210* ◆ **PUNCH** *see* **DRINKING** *page 150, see also* **PUNCH** *page 260* ◆ **WHISKY** *see* **DRINKING** *page 150*, **BOTTLE** *page 210* ◆ **RUM** *see* **DRINKING** *page 150* ◆ **PIPE** *see* **GAS** *page 212*, **BREAK** *page 265*

Innocent Brews

MINERAL WATER
To dream of drinking ***mineral water***, foretells that fortune will favor your efforts, and you will enjoy your opportunities to satisfy your cravings for certain pleasures. ◎

LEMONADE
If you drink ***lemonade*** in a dream, you will concur with others in signifying some entertainment as a niggardly device to raise funds for the personal enjoyment of others at your expense. ◎

MALT
To dream of ***malt***, betokens a pleasant existence and riches that will advance your station.

To dream of taking ***malted drinks***, denotes that you will interest yourself in some dangerous affair, but will reap much benefit therefrom. ◎

Tea and Cocoa

COCOA
To dream of ***cocoa***, denotes that you will cultivate distasteful friends for your own advancement and pleasure. ◎

TEA
To dream that you are brewing ***tea***, foretells that you will be guilty of indiscreet actions, and will feel deeply remorseful.

To see your friends ***drinking tea***, and you with them, denotes that social pleasures will pall on you, and you will seek to change your feelings by serving others in their sorrow.

To see ***dregs in your tea***, warns you of trouble in love and affairs of a social nature. To ***spill tea***, is a sign of domestic confusion and grief.

To dream that you find your ***tea chest empty***, unfolds much disagreeable gossip and news.

To dream that you are ***thirsty for tea***, denotes that you will be surprised with uninvited guests. ◎

Coffee

COFFEE POT

COFFEE
To dream of drinking coffee, *denotes the disapproval of friends toward your marriage intentions. If you are married, disagreements and frequent quarrels are implied.*

To dream of dealing in coffee, *portends business failures. If selling, sure loss. Buying it, you may with ease retain your credit.*

For a young woman to see or handle coffee, she will be made a byword if she is not discreet in her actions.

To dream of roasting coffee, *for a young woman, denotes escape from evil by luckily marrying a stranger.*

To see ground coffee, *foretells successful struggles with adversity.*

Parched coffee, *warns you of the evil attentions of strangers.*

Green coffee, *denotes that you have bold enemies who will show you no quarter, but will fight for your overthrow.* ❋

COFFEE HOUSE
To see or visit a coffee house *in your dreams, foretells that you will unwisely entertain friendly relations with persons unknown to be your enemies. Designing women may intrigue against your morality and possessions.* ❋

COFFEE MILL
To see a coffee mill *in your dreams, denotes that you are approaching a critical danger, and all your energy and alertness will have to stand up with obduracy to avert its disastrous consequences.*

To hear it grinding, signifies that you will hardily overthrow some evil pitted against your interest. ❋

AFTER DINNER COFFEE

MINERAL WATER *see* **WATER** *page 78,* **DRINKING** *page 150* ◆ **LEMONADE** *see* **DRINKING** *page 150,* **LEMON** *page 142* ◆ **MALT** *see* **DRINKING** *page 150,* **WHISKY** *page 152* ◆ **COCOA** *see* **CHOCOLATE** *page 149* ◆ **TEA** *see* **DRINKING, THIRST** *page 150,* **TEAKETTLE, TEACUPS** *page 211* ◆ **COFFEE** *see* **DRINKING** *page 133,* **TRADE** *page 202*

Clothes and Jewelry

What we wear and how we adorn ourselves determines the first impressions we make on other people. Therefore dreams about clothing (or the lack of it) often have an explanation based on the way we behave socially. This section covers clothes in general, specific items of clothing, boots and shoes, hats, and accessories of all kinds.

Clothes and Apparel

APPAREL

Dreams of ***apparel*** [clothing], denote that enterprises undertaken will be successes or failures, as the apparel seems to be whole and clean, or soiled and threadbare.

To see ***fine apparel***, but out of date, foretells that you will have fortune, but you will scorn progressive ideas.

If you reject out-of-date apparel, you will outgrow pleasant environments and enter into new relations, new enterprises, and new loves, which will transform you into a different person.

To see yourself or others ***appareled in white***, denotes eventful changes, and you will nearly always find the change bearing sadness.

To walk with a person wearing white, proclaims that person's illness or distress, unless it be a young woman or child; then you will have pleasing surroundings for a season at least.

To see yourself or others ***dressed in black***, portends quarrels, disappointments, and disagreeable companions; or, if it refers to business, the business will fall short of expectations.

To see ***yellow apparel***, foretells approaching gaieties and financial progress. Seen as a flitting specter, in an unnatural light, the reverse may be expected. You will be fortunate if you dream of yellow cloth.

To dream of ***blue apparel***, signifies the carrying forward to victory of your aspirations through energetic, insistent efforts. Friends will loyally support you in your efforts.

To dream of ***crimson apparel***, foretells that you will escape formidable enemies by a timely change in your expressed intention.

To see ***green apparel***, is a hopeful sign of prosperity and happiness.

To see ***many-colored apparel***, foretells swift changes, and intermingling of good and bad influences in your future.

To dream of ***misfitting apparel***, intimates crosses in your affections, and that you are likely to make a mistake in some enterprise.

To see old or young in ***appropriate apparel***, denotes that you will undertake some engagement for which you will have no liking, and which will give rise to many cares.

For a woman to dream that she is displeased with her apparel, foretells that she will find many vexatious rivalries in her quest for social distinction.

To admire the ***apparel of others***, denotes that she will have jealous fears of her friends.

To dream of the loss of any article of apparel, denotes disturbances in your business and love affairs.

For a young woman to dream of being attired in a gauzy black costume, foretells that she will undergo chastening sorrow and disappointment.

For a young woman to dream that she meets another attired in a crimson dress and a crepe mourning veil over her face, foretells that she will be outrivaled by one she hardly considers her equal, and bitter disappointment will sour her against women generally.

The dreamer interpreting the dream of apparel should be careful to note whether the objects are looking natural. If the faces are distorted and the light unearthly, though the colors are bright, beware; the miscarriage of some worthy plan will work you harm. There are few dreams in which the element of evil is wanting, as there are few enterprises in waking life from which the element of chance is obviated. ◎

CLOTHES

To dream of seeing ***clothes*** soiled and torn, denotes that deceit will be practiced to your harm. Beware of friendly dealings with strangers.

For a woman to dream that her ***clothing is soiled*** or torn, her virtue will be dragged in the mire if she is not careful of her associates. Clean new clothes, denote prosperity.

To dream that you have ***plenty, or an assortment, of clothes***, is a doubtful omen; you may want the necessaries of life. To a young person, this dream denotes unsatisfied hopes and disappointments. ◎

PAPER DOLL

APPAREL *see* **OLD MAN OR WOMAN** *page 85*, **YOUNG** *page 100*, **ADMIRE** *page 259*, **MOURNING** *page 123* ◆
CLOTHES *see* **STAIN** *page 218*, **ABUNDANCE** *page 238*

FASHIONABLE LADIES

Dressing and Undressing

DRESSING
To dream that you are having trouble in ***dressing***, means that some evil persons will worry and detain you from places of amusement.

If you can't get dressed in time for a train, you will have many annoyances through the carelessness of others. You should depend on your own efforts as far as possible, after these dreams, if you would secure contentment and full success. ◎

UNDRESS
To dream that you are ***undressing***, foretells that scandalous gossip will overshadow you.

For a woman to dream that she sees the ruler of her country undressed, signifies that sadness will overtake anticipated pleasures. She will suffer pain through the apprehension of evil to those dear to her.

To see ***others undressed***, is an omen of stolen pleasures, which will rebound with grief. ◎

WARDROBE
To dream of your ***wardrobe***, denotes that your fortune will be endangered by your attempts to appear richer than you are.

If you imagine you have a ***scant wardrobe***, you will seek association with dangers. ◎

TAILOR
To dream of a ***tailor***, denotes that worries will arise on account of some journey to be made.

To have a ***misunderstanding with a tailor***, shows that you will be disappointed in the outcome of one of your schemes.

For one to take your measure, denotes that you will have quarrels and disagreements. ◎

CLOTHES BRUSH
To see ***clothes brushes***, indicates that a heavy task is pending over you. If you are busy brushing your clothes, you will soon receive reimbursement for laborious work. ◎

Clothes are how we express our personality and style to the rest of the world. In dreams, what we wear may not be to our waking taste. You may dream of an infinite wardrobe to be changed at will, as children do with paper dolls *opposite*; **or you may dream exclusively of high fashion** *above*.

DRESSING *see* **TRAIN** *page 225* ◆ **UNDRESS** *see* **KING, QUEEN, EMPEROR, EMPRESS** *page 86* ◆ **TAILOR** *see* **DISPUTE** *page 230* ◆ **CLOTHES BRUSH** *see* **BRUSHES** *page 215*

Underwear and Nightwear

WHALEBONE
To see or work with ***whalebone*** in your dreams, you will form an alliance which will afford you solid benefit. ◎

CORSET
To dream of a ***corset***, denotes that you will be perplexed as to the meaning of attentions won by you.

If a young woman is vexed over undoing or fastening her corset, she will be strongly inclined to quarrel with her friends under slight provocations. ◎

GIRDLE
To dream of wearing a ***girdle***, and that it presses you, denotes that you will be influenced by designing people.

To see others wearing ***velvet or jeweled girdles***, foretells that you will strive for wealth more than honor.

For a woman to receive one, signifies that honors will be conferred upon her. ◎

NEGLIGEE
To dream of a ***negligee***, signifies that you will lead an adventurous, amorous life with a partner of similar dreams.

To dream that you see a ***negligee in a box***, signifies that you will find relationships of many years still rewarding after much time.

To dream of a woman ***wearing a negligee***, foretells an amorous relationship that will disrupt your life. ◎

PETTICOAT
To dream of seeing new ***petticoats***, denotes that pride in your belongings will make you an object of raillery among your acquaintances.

To see them soiled or torn, portends that your reputation will be in great danger.

If a young woman dreams that she wears ***silken or clean petticoats***, it denotes that she will have a doting but manly husband.

If she suddenly perceives that she has left off her petticoat in dressing, it portends much ill luck and disappointment.

To see her ***petticoat falling*** from its place while she is at some gathering, or while walking, she will have trouble in retaining her lover, and other disappointments may follow. ◎

NIGHTGOWN
If you dream that you are in your ***nightgown***, you will be afflicted with a slight illness.

If you see others thus clad, you will have unpleasant news of absent friends. Business will receive a setback.

If a lover sees his ***sweetheart in her nightgown***, he will be superseded. ◎

CHEMISE

CHEMISE
For a woman to dream of a ***chemise***, denotes that she will hear unfavorable gossip about herself. ◎

Garters and Stockings

STOCKINGS
To dream of ***stockings***, denotes that you will derive pleasure from dissolute companionship.

For a young woman to see her stockings ragged or worn, foretells that she will be guilty of unwise, if not immoral, conduct.

To dream that she puts on ***fancy stockings***, denotes she will be fond of the attention of men, and she should be careful to whom she shows preference.

If ***white stockings*** appear to be on her feet, she is threatened with woeful disappointment or illness. ◎

STOCKINGS

GARTER
For a lover to find his lady's ***garter***, foretells that he will lose prestige with her. He will find rivals.

For a woman to dream that she ***loses her garter***, signifies that her lover will be jealous and suspicious of a handsomer person.

For a married man to dream of a garter, foretells that his wife will hear of his clandestine attachments, and he will have a stormy scene.

For a woman to dream that she is admiring beautiful ***jeweled garters*** on her limbs, denotes that she will be betrayed in her private movements, and her reputation will hang in the balance of public opinion. If she dreams that her lover fastens them on her, she will hold his affections and faith through all adverse criticisms. ◎

GAITERS
To dream of ***gaiters***, foretells pleasant amusements and rivalries. ◎

WHALEBONE *see* WHALE *page 52* ◆ GIRDLE *see* VELVET *page 187*, JEWELS *page 162* ◆ NEGLIGEE *see* BOX *page 211* ◆ PETTICOAT *see* SILK *page 187* ◆ NIGHTGOWN *see* NIGHT *page 82* ◆ GARTER *see* JEWELS *page 162*

Outerwear

PANTS
To dream of ***pants***, foretells that you will be tempted to dishonorable deeds.

If you put them on ***wrong side out***, you will find that a fascination is fastening its hold upon you. ◎

COAT
To dream of wearing another's ***coat***, signifies that you will ask some friend to provide security for you.

To see your ***coat torn***, denotes the loss of a close friend and dreary business prospects.

To see a ***new coat***, portends for you some literary honor.

To ***lose your coat***, you will have to rebuild your fortune lost through being overconfident in speculations. ◎

OVERCOAT
To dream of an ***overcoat***, denotes that you will suffer from contrariness, exhibited by others.

To borrow one, foretells that you will be unfortunate through mistakes made by strangers.

If you see or are wearing a handsome ***new overcoat***, you will be exceedingly fortunate in realizing your wishes. ◎

SHIRTWAIST
For a young woman to dream of a nice, ready-made ***shirtwaist*** (a style of frock), denotes that she will win admiration through her ingenuity and pleasing manners.

To dream that her ***shirtwaist is torn***, she will be censured for her illicit engagements.

If she is ***trying on a shirtwaist***, she will encounter rivalry in love; but if she succeeds in adjusting the waist to her person, she will successfully combat the rivalry and win the object of her love. ◎

Dress dreams may include frivolous chemise *opposite top* **and stockings** *opposite bottom* **or sensible, hard working uniforms** *right*.

SHIRT
To dream of putting on your ***shirt***, is a sign that you will estrange yourself from your sweetheart by your faithless conduct.

To ***lose your shirt***, augurs disgrace in business or love.

A ***torn shirt***, represents misfortune and miserable surroundings.

A ***soiled shirt***, denotes that contagious diseases will confront you. ◎

SHIRT STUDS
To dream of ***shirt studs***, foretells that you will struggle to humor your pride, and will usually be successful. If they are diamonds, and the center one is larger than the others, you will enjoy wealth, or have an easy time, surrounded by congenial friends. ◎

Furs and Ermine

ERMINE
To dream that you wear this beautiful and costly raiment, denotes exaltation, lofty character, and wealth forming a barrier to want and misery.

To see others thus clothed, you will be associated with wealthy people, polished in literature and art.

For a lover to see his sweetheart clothed in ***ermine***, is an omen of purity and faithfulness. If the ermine is soiled, the reverse is indicated. ◎

FURS
To dream of dealing in ***furs***, denotes prosperity and an interest in many concerns.

To be ***dressed in fur,*** signifies your safety from want and poverty.

To see ***fine fur***, denotes honor and riches. For a young woman to dream that she is ***wearing costly furs***, denotes that she will marry a wise man. ◎

Working Clothes

APRON
To dream of an ***apron***, signifies a zigzag course, for a young woman. For a schoolgirl to dream that her apron is loosened or torn, implies bad lessons, and lectures in propriety from parents and teachers. ◎

OVERALLS
For a woman to dream that she sees a man wearing ***overalls***, she will be deceived as to the real character of her lover. If a wife, she will be deceived in her husband's frequent absence, and the real cause will create suspicions of his fidelity. ◎

UNIFORM
To see a ***uniform*** in your dream, denotes that you will have influential friends to aid you in obtaining your desires.

For a young woman to dream that she wears a uniform, foretells that she will luckily confer her favors upon a man who appreciates them and returns love for passion. If she discards it, she will be in danger of public scandal by her notorious love for adventure.

To see people arrayed in ***strange uniforms***, foretells the disruption of friendly relations with some other power by your own government. This may also apply to families or friends.

To see a friend or relative looking sad while dressed in uniform, or as a soldier, predicts ill fortune or continued absence. ◎

IN UNIFORM

PANTS, COAT, OVERCOAT, SHIRTWAIST, SHIRT, SHIRT STUDS *see* **APPAREL** *page 154*, **CLOTHES** *page 154* ◆ **SHIRT** *see* **STAIN** *page 218* ◆ **FURS** *see* **ANIMAL HIDE** *page 28* ◆ **UNIFORM** *see* **SOLDIERS** *page 262*

Veils and Mantillas

VEIL
To dream that you wear a ***veil***, denotes that you will not be perfectly sincere with your lover, and you will be forced to use stratagem to retain him or her.

To see others wearing veils, you will be maligned and defamed by apparent friends.

An ***old or torn veil***, warns you that deceit is being thrown around you with sinister design.

For a young woman to dream that she ***loses her veil***, denotes that her lover sees through her deceitful ways and is likely to retaliate with the same.

To dream of seeing a ***bridal veil***, foretells that you will make a successful change in your immediate future, and much happiness in your position.

For a young woman to dream that she wears a bridal veil, denotes that she will engage in some affair which will afford her lasting profit and enjoyment. If it gets loose, or any accident befalls it, she will be burdened with sadness and pain.

To throw a veil aside, indicates separation or disgrace.

To see ***mourning veils*** in your dreams, signifies distress and trouble, and embarrassment in business. ◎

MANTILLA
To dream of seeing a ***mantilla***, denotes an unwise enterprise which will bring you into unfavorable notice. ◎

Accessories

GLOVES
To dream of wearing new ***gloves***, denotes that you will be cautious and economical in your dealings with others, but not mercenary. You will have lawsuits or business troubles, but will settle them satisfactorily to yourself.

If you wear ***old or ragged gloves***, you will be betrayed and suffer loss.

If you dream that you ***lose your gloves***, you will be deserted and earn your own means of livelihood.

To find a ***pair of gloves***, denotes a marriage or new love affair.

For a man to fasten a ***lady's glove***, indicates that he has, or will have, a woman on his hands who threatens him with exposure.

If you ***pull your glove off***, you will meet with poor success in business or love. ◎

SHAWL
To dream of a ***shawl***, denotes someone will offer flattery and favor.

To ***lose your shawl***, foretells sorrow and discomfort. A young woman is in danger of being jilted by a good-looking man, after this dream. ◎

MUFF
To dream of wearing a ***muff***, denotes that you will be well provided for against the vicissitudes of fortune.

For a lover to see his sweetheart wearing a muff, denotes that a worthier man will usurp his place. ◎

SASH
To dream of wearing a ***sash***, foretells that you will seek to retain the affections of a flirtatious person.

For a young woman to buy one, she will be faithful to her lover, and win esteem by her frank, womanly ways. ◎

GOGGLES
To dream of ***goggles***, is a warning of disreputable companions who will wheedle you into lending your money foolishly.

For a young woman to dream of goggles, means that she will listen to persuasion which will mar her fortune. ◎

Belts and Buckles

BELT
To dream that you have a new style ***belt***, denotes that you are soon to meet and make engagements with a stranger, which will demoralize your prosperity. If it is out of date, you will be meritedly censured for rudeness. ◎

BUCKLE
To dream of ***buckles***, foretells that you will be beset with invitations to places of pleasure, and your affairs will be in danger of chaotic confusion. ◎

Handkerchiefs

HANDKERCHIEFS
To dream of ***handkerchiefs***, denotes flirtations and contingent affairs.

To lose one, omens a broken engagement through no fault of yours.

To see torn ones, foretells that lovers' quarrels will reach such straits that reconciliation will be improbable if not impossible.

To see them soiled, foretells that you will be corrupted by indiscriminate associations.

To see pure white ones in large lots, foretells that you will resist the insistent flattery of unscrupulous persons, and gain entrance into high relations with love and matrimony.

To see them colored, denotes that, while your engagements may not be strictly moral, you will manage them with such ingenuity that they will elude opprobrium.

If you see ***silk handkerchiefs***, it denotes that your pleasing and magnetic personality will shed its radiating cheerfulness upon others, making for yourself a fortunate existence.

For a young woman to wave adieu or a recognition with her handkerchief, or see others doing this, denotes that she will soon make a questionable pleasure trip, or she may knowingly run the gauntlet of disgrace to secure some fancied pleasure. ◎

VEIL *see* BRIDE *page 131,* MOURNING *page 123* ◆ HANDKERCHIEFS *see* STAIN *page 218,* ADIEU *page 258*

Details

POCKET
To dream of your ***pocket***, is a sign of evil demonstrations against you. ◎

EPAULETS
For a man to dream of wearing ***epaulets***, if he is a soldier, denotes his disfavor for a time, but he will finally wear honors.

For a woman to dream that she is introduced to a person wearing epaulets, denotes that she will form unwise attachments, very likely to result in scandal. ◎

COLLAR
To dream of wearing a ***collar***, you will have high honors thrust upon you that you will hardly be worthy of.

For a woman to dream of collars, she will have many admirers, but no sincere ones. She will be likely to remain single for a long while. ◎

PATCH
To dream that you have ***patches*** upon your clothing, denotes that you will show no false pride in the discharge of obligations.

To dream that you see others ***wearing patches***, denotes that want and misery are near.

If a young woman discovers a ***patch on her new dress***, it indicates that she will find trouble facing her when she imagines that her happiest moments are approaching near. If she tries to hide the patches, she will endeavor to keep some ugly trait in her character from her lover. If she is patching, she will assume duties for which she has no liking.

For a woman to do ***family patching***, denotes close and loving bonds in the family, but a scarcity of means is portended. ◎

Accessories such as a pretty parasol *right* **or an extravagant fan** *background* **may also form part of the dream wardrobe.**

Fans and Parasols

FAN
To see a ***fan*** in your dreams, denotes that pleasant news and surprises are awaiting you in the near future.

For a young woman to dream of ***fanning herself***, or that someone is fanning her, gives promise of a new and pleasing acquaintance; if she loses an old fan, she will find that a warm friend is becoming interested in other women. ◎

SUNSHADE
To dream of seeing young girls carrying ***sunshades***, foretells prosperity and exquisite delights.

A broken one, foretells sickness and death to the young. ◎

UMBRELLA
To dream of carrying an ***umbrella***, denotes that trouble and annoyances will beset you.

To see others carrying them, foretells that you will be appealed to for aid by charity.

To borrow one, you will have a misunderstanding, perhaps with a warm friend.

To lend one, portends injury from false friends. To lose one, denotes trouble with someone who holds your confidence.

To see one torn to pieces or broken, foretells that you will be misrepresented and maligned.

To carry a leaky one, denotes that pain and displeasure will be felt by you toward your sweetheart or companions.

To carry a ***new umbrella*** over you in a clear shower or sunshine, omens exquisite pleasure and prosperity. ◎

PARASOL
To dream of a ***parasol***, denotes, for married people, illicit enjoyments.

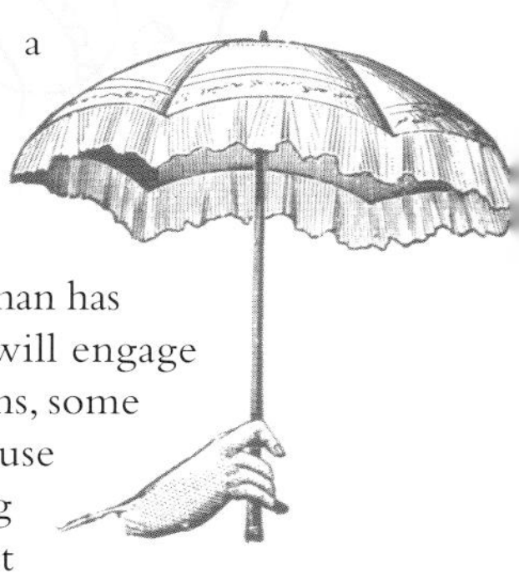

A PARASOL

If a young woman has this dream, she will engage in many flirtations, some of which will cause her interesting disturbances, lest her lover find out her inclinations. ◎

Ribbons and Tassels

RIBBON
Seeing ***ribbons*** floating from the costume of any person in your dreams, indicates that you will have gay and pleasant companions, and practical cares will not trouble you greatly.

For a young woman to dream of ***decorating herself with ribbons***, she will soon have a desirable offer of marriage, but frivolity may cause her to make a mistake.

If she sees other girls ***wearing ribbons***, she will encounter rivalry in her endeavors to secure a husband.

If she buys them, she will have a pleasant and easy place in life.

If she feels angry and displeased about them, she will find that some other woman is dividing her honors and pleasures with her in her social realm. ◎

TASSELS
To see ***tassels*** in a dream, denotes that you will reach the height of your desires.

For a young woman to lose them, denotes that she will undergo some unpleasant experience. ◎

Bags

KNAPSACK
To see a ***knapsack*** while dreaming, denotes that you will find your greatest pleasure away from the associations of friends.

For a woman to dream that she sees an old dilapidated knapsack, means poverty and disagreeableness for her. ◎

EPAULETS *see* **UNIFORM** *page 157*, **SOLDIER** *page 262* ◆ **UMBRELLA** *see* **BORROWING** *page 241*, **LENDING** *page 241*, **BREAK** *page 265*, **LEAKING** *page 212*

Hats and Headgear

HAT

HEADGEAR

To dream of seeing rich ***headgear***, you will become famous and successful.

To see ***old and worn headgear***, you will have to yield up your possessions to others. ◎

BONNET

A ***bonnet***, denotes much gossiping and slanderous insinuations, from which a woman should carefully defend herself.

For a man to see a woman ***tying her bonnet***, denotes unforeseen good luck nearby. His friends will be faithful and true.

A young woman is likely to engage in pleasant and harmless flirtations if her ***bonnet is new*** and of any color except black.

Black bonnets, denote false friends of the opposite sex. ◎

CAP

For a woman to dream of seeing a ***cap***, she will be invited to take part in some festivity.

For a young woman to dream that she sees her ***sweetheart with a cap on***, denotes that she will be bashful and shy in his presence.

To see a ***prisoner's cap***, denotes that your courage is failing you in time of danger.

To see a ***miner's cap***, you will inherit a substantial competency. ◎

HAT

To dream of losing your ***hat***, you may expect unsatisfactory business and failure of persons to keep important engagements.

For a man to dream that he wears ***a new hat***, predicts a change of place and business, which will be very much to his advantage. For a woman to dream that she wears a ***fine new hat***, denotes the attainment of wealth, and she will be the object of much admiration.

For the wind to ***blow your hat off***, denotes sudden changes in affairs, and somewhat for the worse. ◎

HELMET

To dream of seeing a ***helmet***, denotes threatened misery and loss that will be avoided by wise action. ◎

HOOD

For a young woman to dream that she is wearing ***a hood***, is a sign that she will soon attempt to allure some man from the paths of rectitude and bounden duty. ◎

Boots and Shoes

BOOTS

To see your ***boots*** on another, your place will be usurped in the affections of your sweetheart.

To wear ***new boots***, you will be lucky in your dealings. Breadwinners will command higher wages.

Old and torn boots, indicate sickness and snares before you. ◎

SHOES

To dream of seeing your ***shoes*** ragged and soiled, denotes that you will make enemies by your unfeeling criticism.

To have them blackened in your dreams, foretells improvement in your affairs, and some important event will cause you satisfaction.

New shoes, augur changes which will prove beneficial. If they pinch your feet, you will be uncomfortably exposed to the practical joking of the fun-loving companions of your sex.

To find them untied, denotes losses, quarrels, and ill health.

To lose them, is a sign of desertion and divorces.

To dream that your ***shoes have been stolen*** during the night, but you have two pairs of hose, denotes that you will have a loss, but will gain in some other pursuit.

For a young woman to dream that her ***shoes are admired*** while on her feet, warns her to be cautious in allowing newly introduced people, and men of any kind, to approach her in a familiar way. ◎

SHOEMAKER

To see a ***shoemaker*** in your dreams, warns you that indications are unfavorable to your advancement. For a woman to dream that her husband or lover is a shoemaker, foretells that competency will be hers; her wishes will be gratified. ◎

SLIPPERS

To dream of ***slippers***, warns you that you are about to perform an unfortunate alliance or intrigue. You are likely to find favor with a married person which will result in trouble, if not scandal.

To dream that your ***slippers are much admired***, foretells that you will be involved in a flirtation which will suggest disgrace. ◎

WOODEN SHOE

To dream of a ***wooden shoe***, is significant of lonely wanderings and penniless circumstances. Those in love will suffer from unfaithfulness. ◎

SLIPPER

CAP *see* PRISON *page 249*, MINING *page 195* ◆ HAT *see* WIND *page 75* ◆ HELMET *see* UNIFORM *page 157* ◆ SHOES *see* STAIN *page 218*, STEALING *page 246*, ADMIRE *page 259* ◆ SLIPPERS *see* ADMIRE *page 259*

The dreamer's treasure chest overflows with all kinds and all manner of settings. You may dream of fabulous diamonds and rubies or more modest rhinestones and agate, of sophisticated ornament or a simple locket. Most jewel-encrusted dreams indicate fortunate occurrences; only emeralds carry their traditional bad luck with them into your dreams.

Baubles, Bangles, and Beads

CAMEO BROOCH
To dream of a ***cameo brooch***, denotes that some sad occurrence will soon claim your attention. ◎

DIADEM
To dream of a ***diadem***, denotes that some honor will be tendered you for acceptance. ◎

LOCKET
If a young woman dreams that her lover places a ***locket*** around her neck, she will be the recipient of many beautiful offerings, and will soon be wedded, and lovely children will crown her life. If she should ***lose a locket***, death will throw sadness into her life.

If a lover dreams that his sweetheart ***returns his locket***, he will confront disappointing issues. The woman he loves will worry him and conduct herself in a displeasing way toward him.

If a woman dreams that she ***breaks a locket***, she will have a changeable and unstable husband, who will dislike constancy in any form, be it business or affection. ◎

LOCKET

BEADS
To dream of ***beads***, foretells that attention from those in elevated positions will be shown to you.

To ***count beads***, portends immaculate joy and contentment.

To string them, you will obtain the favor of the rich.

To scatter them, signifies loss of station among your acquaintances. ◎

THE NECKLACE

NECKLACE
For a woman to dream of receiving a ***necklace***, omens for her a loving husband and a beautiful home.

To ***lose a necklace***, she will feel the heavy hand of bereavement. ◎

BRACELET
To see in your dreams a ***bracelet*** encircling your arm, which is the gift of a lover or friend, is assurance of an early marriage and a happy union.

If a young woman ***loses her bracelet***, she will meet with sundry losses and vexations.

To find one, good property will come into her possession. ◎

Going from one extreme to the other, you may find your dreams preoccupied with hats *opposite top* **or slippers** *opposite bottom*. **Gems and jewels lend an added sparkle to the dream world. You may dream of a simple locket** *left* **or an elegant necklace** *above*.

RING
To dream of wearing ***rings***, denotes new enterprises in which you will be successful.

A ***broken ring***, foretells quarrels and unhappiness in the married state, and separation to lovers.

For a young woman to ***receive a ring***, denotes that worries over her lover's conduct will cease, as he will devote himself to her pleasures and future interest.

To see ***others with rings***, denotes increasing prosperity and many new friends. ◎

EARRINGS
To see ***earrings*** in dreams, omens that good news and interesting work are before you.

To see them broken, indicates that gossip of a low order will be directed against you. ◎

Ornament

If you wear ornaments ***in dreams, this indicates that you will have a flattering honor conferred upon you.***

If you receive them, you will be fortunate in undertakings. Giving them away, denotes recklessness and lavish extravagance. Losing an ornament, brings the loss of either a lover or a good situation. ◎

LOCKET *see* **NECK** *page 92,* **SWEETHEART** *page 124,* **BREAK** *page 265* ◆ **BEADS** *see* **COUNTING** *page 180* ◆ **NECKLACE** *see* **NECK** *page 92* ◆ **BRACELET** *see* **ARM** *page 97* ◆ **RING** *see* **FINGERS** *page 97,* **BREAK** *page 265* ◆ **EARRINGS** *see* **EARS** *page 99*

Jewelry and Gems

JEWELS
To dream of ***jewels***, denotes much pleasure and riches.

To wear them, brings rank and satisfied ambitions.

If you see others wearing them, distinguished places will be held by you or by some friend.

To dream of ***jeweled garments***, betokens rare good fortune to the dreamer. Inheritance or speculation will raise him to high positions.

If you ***inherit jewelry***, your prosperity will be unusual, but not entirely satisfactory.

To dream of ***giving jewelry away***, warns you that some vital estate is threatening you.

For a young woman to dream that she ***receives jewelry***, indicates much pleasure and desirable marriage. If she dreams that she ***loses jewels***, she will meet people who will flatter and deceive her.

To ***find jewels***, denotes rapid and brilliant advancement in affairs of interest. To ***give jewels away***, you will unconsciously work detriment to yourself.

To buy them, proves that you will be very successful in momentous affairs, especially those pertinent to the heart. ◎

GEMS
To dream of ***gems***, foretells a happy fate in love and business affairs. ◎

JEWELRY
To dream of broken ***jewelry***, denotes keen disappointment in attaining one's highest desires.

If the ***jewelry be cankered***, trusted friends will fail you, and business cares will be on you. ◎

A Dreamer's Jewel Box

DIAMONDS
To dream of owning ***diamonds***, is a very propitious dream. The possession of them signifies that you will receive great honor and recognition from high places.

For a young woman to dream of her lover ***presenting her with diamonds***, foreshows that she will make a great and honorable marriage, which will fill her people with honest pride; but to lose diamonds, and not find them again, is the most unlucky of dreams, foretelling disgrace, want and death.

For a sporting woman to dream of diamonds, foretells for her many prosperous days and magnificent presents. For a speculator, it denotes prosperous transactions. To dream of ***owning diamonds***, portends the same for sporting men and women.

Diamonds are omens of good luck, unless stolen from the bodies of dead persons, when they foretell that your own unfaithfulness will be discovered by your friends. ◎

AMETHYST
Amethyst seen in a dream, represents contentment with fair business.

For a young woman to ***lose an amethyst***, foretells broken engagements and slights in love. ◎

RUBY
To dream of a ***ruby***, foretells that you will be lucky in speculations of business or love.

For a woman to lose one, is a sign of the approaching indifference of her lover. ◎

A DREAM JEWEL BOX

JEWELS *see* **APPAREL** *page 154*, **CLOTHES** *page 154*, **INHERITANCE** *page 240* ◆ **JEWELRY** *see* **BREAK** *page 265*, **CANKER** *page 110* ◆ **DIAMONDS** *see* **STEALING** *page 246*

CLEOPATRA BEDECKED WITH JEWELS

EMERALD
To dream of an ***emerald***, you will inherit property concerning which there will be some trouble with others.

For a lover to see an emerald or emeralds worn on the person of his affianced, warns him that he is about to be discarded for some wealthier suitor.

To dream that you ***buy an emerald***, signifies unfortunate dealings. ◎

PEARLS
To dream of ***pearls***, is a forerunner of good business, trade, and affairs of social nature.

If a young woman dreams that her lover sends her ***gifts of pearls***, she will indeed be most fortunate, as there will be occasions of festivity and pleasure for her, beside a loving and faithful affianced devoid of the jealous inclinations so ruinous to the peace of lovers.

If she loses or ***breaks her pearls***, she will suffer indescribable sadness and sorrow through bereavement or misunderstandings.

To find herself admiring them, she will covet and strive for love or possessions with a pureness of purpose. ◎

AGATE
To see ***agate*** in a dream, signifies that you will enjoy a slight advancement in business affairs. ◎

SARDONYX
To dream of ***sardonyx***, signifies that gloomy surroundings will be cleared away by your energetic overthrow of poverty.

For a woman, this dream denotes an increase in her possessions, unless she loses or throws them away; then it might imply a disregard of opportunities she may have to improve her condition. ◎

SAPPHIRE
To dream of ***sapphire***, is ominous of fortunate gain, and to women, a wise selection in a lover. ◎

TOPAZ
To see ***topaz*** in a dream, signifies that Fortune will be liberal in her favors, and you will have very pleasing companions.

For a woman to lose ***topaz ornaments***, foretells that she will be injured by jealous friends who court her position. To receive one from another besides a relative, foretells that an interesting love affair will occupy her attention. ◎

TURQUOISE
To dream of a ***turquoise***, foretells that you are soon to realize some desire which will please your relatives.

For a woman to have one stolen, foretells that she will meet with crosses in love. If she comes by it dishonestly, she must suffer for yielding to hasty susceptibility in love. ◎

RHINESTONES
To dream of ***rhinestones***, denotes pleasures and favors of short duration.

For a young woman to dream that a ***rhinestone proves to be a diamond***, foretells that she will be surprised to find that some insignificant act on her part will result in good fortune. ◎

BLOODSTONE
To dream of seeing a ***bloodstone***, denotes that you will be unfortunate in your engagements.

For a young woman to receive one as a gift, denotes that she will suffer estrangements from one friend, but will, by this, gain one more worthy. ◎

GOLD LEAVES
To dream of ***gold leaves***, signifies that a flattering future is before you. ◎

In your dreams your jewel box may overflow *opposite* **and you may dazzle every eye, wearing as many fine jewels as the greatest queen** *above*.

EMERALD *see* **ENGAGEMENT** *page 130* ◆ **PEARLS** *see* **GIFTS** *page 240*, **BREAK** *page 265*, **ADMIRE** *page 259* ◆ **TOPAZ** *see* **ORNAMENT** *page 161* ◆ **TURQUOISE** *see* **STEALING** *page 246* ◆ **RHINESTONES** *see* **DIAMONDS** *page 162* ◆ **GOLD LEAVES** *see* **GOLD** *page 71*

Entertainment and Leisure

Having fun in your dreams gives rise to the same sensations as having fun in reality. Dreams filled with the joyous sound of music and the rhythm of dance are in the main indicative of pleasant times to come. Musical dreams appear to link the dream state with harmonious activities in waking life. This section also covers theatrical dreams and formal recreation.

Music

MUSIC

To dream of hearing harmonious ***music***, omens pleasure and prosperity.

Discordant music, foretells troubles with unruly children, and unhappiness in the household. ◎

MUSICAL INSTRUMENTS

To see ***musical instruments***, denotes anticipated pleasures.

If they are broken, the pleasure will be marred by uncongenial companionship. For a young woman, this dream foretells for her the power to make her life what she will. ◎

ORGAN BELLOWS

Keyboard Instruments

THE OCTAVE

ACCORDION

To dream of hearing the music of an ***accordion***, denotes that you will engage in amusement which will win you from sadness and retrospection. You will by this means be enabled to take up your burden more cheerfully.

For a young woman to dream that she is ***playing an accordion***, portends that she will win her lover by some sad occurrence; but, notwithstanding which, the same will confer lasting happiness upon her union. If the accordion gets out of tune, she will be saddened by the illness of trouble of her lover. ◎

PIANO

To dream of seeing a ***piano***, denotes some joyful occasion.

To hear sweet and voluptuous harmony from a piano, signals success and health. If discordant music is being played, you will have many exasperating matters to consider. Sad and plaintive music, foretells sorrowful tidings.

To find your ***piano broken*** and out of tune, portends dissatisfaction with your own accomplishments and disappointment in the failure of your friends or children to win honors.

To see an ***old-fashioned piano***, denotes that you have, in trying moments, neglected the advices and opportunities of the past, and are warned not to do so again.

For a young woman to dream that she is executing difficult but entrancing music, she will succeed in winning an indifferent friend to be a most devoted and loyal lover. ◎

ORGAN

To hear the pealing forth of an ***organ*** in grand anthems, signifies lasting friendships and well-grounded fortune.

To see an ***organ in a church***, denotes despairing separations of families, and death, perhaps, for some of them.

If you dream of rendering harmonious music on an organ, you will be fortunate in the way to worldly comfort, and much social distinction will be given you.

To hear doleful singing and organ accompaniment, denotes that you are nearing a wearisome task, and probable loss of friends or position. ◎

ORGANIST

To see an ***organist*** in your dreams, denotes that a friend will cause you much inconvenience from hasty actions.

For a young woman to dream that she ***is an organist***, foretells that she will be so exacting in love that she will be threatened with desertion. ◎

In musical dreams you may find yourself listening to the sonorous blast of the organ *left*, **reading musical notation** *above* **or admiring the plangent sound of the blues guitar** *opposite*.

MUSICAL INSTRUMENTS *see* **BREAK** *page 265* ◆ **PIANO** *see* **BREAK** *page 265* ◆ **ORGAN** *see* **CHURCH** *page 189*, **HYMNS** *page 168*

String Instruments

HARP
To hear the sad, sweet strains of a ***harp***, denotes the sad ending to what seems pleasing and profitable.

To see a ***broken harp***, betokens illness, or a broken troth between lovers.

To ***play a harp*** yourself, signifies that your nature is too trusting, and you should be more careful in placing your confidence, as well as love matters. ◎

LUTE
To dream of ***playing on a lute***, is auspicious of joyful news from absent friends.

Pleasant occupations follow hearing ***the music of a lute***. ◎

LYRE
To dream of listening to the music of a ***lyre***, foretells chaste pleasure and congenial companionship. Business will run smoothly.

For a young woman to dream of playing on one, denotes that she will enjoy the undivided affection of a worthy man. ◎

BANJO
To dream of a ***banjo***, denotes that pleasant amusements will be enjoyed. ◎

GUITAR
To dream that you have a ***guitar***, or are playing one in a dream, signifies a merry gathering and serious lovemaking.

For a young woman to think it is unstrung or broken, foretells that disappointment in love is sure to overtake her.

Upon hearing the ***weird music of a guitar***, the dreamer should fortify herself against flattery and soft persuasion, for she is in danger of being tempted by a fascinating evil. If the dreamer be a man, he will be courted, and likely to lose his judgement under the wiles of seductive women.

THE GUITARIST

If you ***play on a guitar***, your family affairs will be harmonious. ◎

FIDDLE
To dream of a ***fiddle***, foretells harmony in the home and many joyful occasions abroad. ◎

VIOLIN
To see or hear a ***violin*** in dreams, foretells harmony and peace in the family, and financial affairs will cause no apprehension.

For a young woman to play on one, denotes that she will be honored and receive lavish gifts. If her playing is unsuccessful, she will lose favor and aspire to things she never can possess.

A broken one, indicates sad bereavement and separation. ◎

JEW'S-HARP

To dream of a Jew's-harp, ***foretells that you will experience a slight improvement in your affair. To play one, you will fall in love with a stranger.*** ❋

Brass

HORN
To dream that you hear the sound of a ***horn***, foretells hasty news of a joyful character.

To see ***a broken horn***, denotes death or accident.

To see ***children playing with horns***, denotes congeniality in the home.

For a woman to dream of ***blowing a horn***, foretells that she is more anxious for marriage than her lover. ◎

TRUMPET
To dream of a ***trumpet***, denotes that something of unusual interest is about to befall you.

To ***blow a trumpet***, signifies that you will gain your wishes. ◎

BUGLE
To hear joyous blasts from a ***bugle***, prepare for some unusual happiness, as a harmony of good things for you is being formed by unseen powers.

Blowing a bugle, denotes fortunate dealings. ◎

HARP *see* **BREAK** *page 265* ◆ **GUITAR** *see* **BREAK** *page 265* ◆ **VIOLIN** *see* **BREAK** *page 265* ◆ **HORN** *see* **BREAK** *page 265*, **CHILDREN** *page 128* ◆ **BUGLE** *see* **JOY** *page 256*

Wind Instruments

CLARINET
To dream of a ***clarinet***, foretells that you will indulge in frivolity beneath your usual dignity.

If it is broken, you will incur the displeasure of a close friend. ◎

FLUTE
To dream of hearing notes from a ***flute***, signifies a pleasant meeting with friends from a distance, and profitable engagements.

For a young woman to dream of ***playing a flute***, denotes that she will fall in love because of her lover's engaging manners. ◎

FIFE
To dream of hearing a ***fife***, denotes that there will be an unexpected call on you to defend your honor or that of some person near to you.

To dream that you play one yourself, indicates that whatever else may be said of you, your reputation will remain intact. If a woman has this dream, she will have a soldier husband. ◎

BAGPIPE
This is not a bad dream, unless the music be harsh and the player in rags. ◎

BAGPIPES

Percussion

CYMBAL
Hearing a ***cymbal*** in your dreams, foretells the death of a very aged person of your acquaintance. The sun will shine, but you will see it darkly because of gloom. ◎

GONG
To hear the sound of a ***gong*** while dreaming, denotes a false alarm of illness, or a loss which will vex you excessively. ◎

TAMBOURINE
To dream of a ***tambourine***, signifies that you will have enjoyment in some unusual event which will soon take place. ◎

DRUM
To hear the muffled beating of a ***drum***, denotes that some absent friend is in distress and calls on you for aid.

To see a drum, foretells amiability of character and a great aversion to quarrels and dissensions. It is an omen of prosperity to the sailor, the farmer, and the tradesman alike. ◎

XYLOPHONE
To dream of playing a ***xylophone***, denotes a joyful and happy occasion.

To see a ***broken xylophone***, denotes that, during difficult situations, you have neglected advice and opportunities. You are warned not to do so again. ◎

CLARINET *see* **BREAK** *page 265* ◆ **DRUM** *see* **SOLDIERS** *page 262* ◆ **XYLOPHONE** *see* **BREAK** *page 265*

At the Concert Hall

SINGING

QUARTET
To dream of a ***quartet***, and that you are playing or singing, denotes favorable affairs, jolly companions, and good times.

To see or hear a quartet, foretells that you will aspire to something beyond you. ◎

SYMPHONY
To dream of ***symphonies***, heralds delightful occupations. ◎

ORCHESTRA
Belonging to an ***orchestra*** and playing, foretells pleasant entertainments, and your sweetheart will be faithful and cultivated.

To hear the ***music of an orchestra***, denotes that the knowledge of humanity will at all times prove you to be a much-liked person, and favors will fall unstintedly upon you. ◎

CONCERT
To dream of a ***concert*** of a high musical order, denotes delightful seasons of pleasure, and literary work to the author.

To the businessman, a dream of a concert portends successful trade; and to the young, it signifies unalloyed bliss and faithful loves.

Ordinary concerts which engage ballet singers, denote that disagreeable companions and ungrateful friends will be met with. Business will show a falling off. ◎

The Human Voice

SERENADE
To hear a ***serenade*** in your dreams, you will have pleasant news from absent friends, and your anticipations will not fail you.

If you are one of the serenaders, there are many delights things in your future. ◎

SINGING
To hear ***singing*** in your dreams, betokens a cheerful spirit and happy companions. You are soon to have promising news from the absent.

If you are singing while everything around you gives promise of happiness, jealousy will insinuate a sense of insincerity into your joyfulness. If there are notes of sadness in the song, you will be unpleasantly surprised at the turn your affairs will take.

Ribald songs, signify gruesome and extravagant waste. ◎

BASS VOICE
To dream that you have a ***bass voice***, denotes that you will detect some discrepancy in your business, brought about by the deceit of someone in your employ. For the lover, this foretells estrangements and quarrels. ◎

THE RECITAL

DUET
To dream of hearing a ***duet played***, denotes a peaceful and even existence for lovers; no quarrels, as is customary in this sort of thing. Business people carry on a mild rivalry. To musical people, this denotes competition and wrangling for superiority.

To hear a ***duet sung***, is unpleasant tidings from the absent; but this will not last, as some new pleasure will displace the unpleasantness. ◎

CHOIR
To dream of a ***choir***, foretells that you may expect cheerful surroundings to replace gloom and discontent.

For a young woman to ***sing in a choir***, denotes that she will be miserable over the attention paid others by her lover. ◎

The repertoire of entertaining dreams may include a rousing tune from the bagpipes *opposite*, **a grand recital** *left* **or singing in the choir** *above*.

ORCHESTRA *see* **MUSIC** *page 164*, **MUSICAL INSTRUMENTS** *page 164* ◆ **CONCERT** *see* **BALLET** *page 168* ◆ **SINGING** *see* **JOY** *page 256*, **VOICE** *page 276* ◆ **BASS VOICE** *see* **VOICE** *page 276* ◆ **CHOIR** *see* **CHURCH** *page 189*

Songs and Marches

HYMNS
To dream of hearing ***hymns*** sung, denotes contentment in the home and average prospects in business affairs. ◎

COMIC SONGS
To hear ***comic songs*** in dreams, foretells that you will disregard an opportunity to advance your affairs and enjoy the companionship of the pleasure loving.

To sing one, proves that you will enjoy much pleasure for a time, but difficulties will overtake you. ◎

SHANTY
To dream of a ***shanty***, denotes that you will leave home in the quest of health. This also warns you of decreasing prosperity. ◎

MARCH
To dream of ***marching*** to the strains of music, indicates that you are ambitious to become a soldier or a public official, but you should consider all things well before making a final decision.

For women to dream of seeing ***men marching***, foretells their inclination for men in public positions. They should be careful of their reputations, should they be thrown much with men. ◎

MARINES

Dancing in the Dark

DANCE
For a married person to dream of seeing a crowd of merry children dancing, ***signifies loving, obedient, and intelligent children and a cheerful and comfortable home. To young people, it denotes easy tasks and many pleasures.***

To see older people dancing, ***denotes a brighter outlook for business.***

To dream that you are dancing, denotes that some unexpected good fortune will come to you.

DANCE MASTER
To dream of a dance master, ***foretells that you will neglect important affairs to pursue frivolities.***

For a young woman to dream that her lover is a dance master, ***portends that she will have a friend in accordance with her views of pleasure and life.***

POLKA
To dream of dancing the polka, ***denotes pleasant occupations.***

QUADRILLE
To dream of dancing a quadrille, ***foretells that some pleasant engagements will occupy your time.***

MINUET
To dream of seeing the minuet ***danced, signifies a pleasant existence with congenial companions.***

To dance it yourself, good fortune and domestic joys are foretold.

JIG
To dance a jig, ***denotes cheerful occupations and light pleasures.***

If you see your sweetheart dancing a jig, your companion will be possessed with a merry and hopeful disposition.

To see ballet girls dancing a jig, foretells that you will engage in undignified amusements and follow low desires.

WALTZ
To see the waltz ***danced, foretells that you will have pleasant relations with a cheerful and adventuresome person.***

For a young woman to waltz with her lover, ***denotes that she will be the object of much admiration, but none will seek her for a wife.***

If she sees her lover waltzing with a rival, ***she will overcome obstacles to her desires with strategy.***

If she waltzes with a woman, she will be loved for her virtues and winning ways.

If she sees persons whirling in the waltz as if intoxicated, she will be engulfed so deeply in desire and pleasure that it will be a miracle if she resists the impassioned advances of her lover and male acquaintances.

BALLET
A ballet ***indicates infidelity in the marriage state; also failures in business, and quarrels and jealousies between sweethearts.***

More active dreams may find you marching smartly along with the band *left* **or dancing with your partner** *background.*

HYMNS *see* CHURCH *page 189* ◆ COMIC SONGS *see* COMEDY *page 169* ◆ MARCH *see* SOLDIERS *page 262* ◆ DANCE *see* MERRY *page 256,* CHILDREN *page 128,* OLD MAN OR WOMAN *page 85* ◆ JIG *see* SWEETHEART *page 124,* ◆ WALTZ *see* RIVAL *page 125,* INTOXICATION *page 150*

Just as a theatrical performance or play is an illusion, so dreams about plays and players or the wiles and deceits of the magician or hypnotist are also illusions and rarely signal clearly what they mean. This section also incorporates dreams of the electronic medium, which has a delusional glamor of its own.

Treading the Boards

AMATEUR

To dream of seeing an ***amateur*** actor on the stage, denotes that you will see your hopes pleasantly and satisfactorily fulfilled. If they ***play a tragedy***, evil will be disseminated through your happiness. If there is an indistinctness or distorted images in the dream, you are likely to meet with quick and decided defeat in some enterprise apart from your regular business. ◎

ACTOR AND ACTRESS

To see in your dreams an ***actress***, denotes that your present state will be one of unbroken pleasure and favor.

To see one in distress, you will gladly contribute your means and influence to raise a friend from misfortune and indebtedness.

If you think yourself one, you will have to work for subsistence, but your labors will be pleasantly attended.

If you dream of being in love with one, your inclination and talent will be allied with pleasure and opposed to downright toil.

To see a ***dead actor*** or actress, your good luck will be overwhelmed in violent and insubordinate misery.

To see ***actors wandering and penniless***, foretells that your affairs will undergo a change from promise to threatenings of failure. To those enjoying domestic comforts, it is a warning of revolution and faithless vows.

For a young woman to dream that she is ***engaged to an actor***, or about to marry one, foretells that her fancy will bring remorse after the glamour of pleasure has vanished.

If a man dreams that he is ***sporting with an actress***, it foretells that private broils with his wife or sweetheart will make him more misery than enjoyment. ◎

PLAY

For a young woman to dream that she attends a ***play***, foretells that she will be courted by a genial friend, and will marry to further her prospects and pleasure seeking. If there is trouble in getting to and from the play, or discordant and hideous scenes, she will be confronted with many displeasing surprises. ◎

DRAMA

To see a ***drama***, signifies pleasant reunions with distant friends.

To be bored with the performance of a drama, you will be forced to accept an uncongenial companion at some entertainment or secret affair.

To write one, portends that you will be plunged into distress and debt, to be extricated as if by a miracle. ◎

COMEDY

To dream of being at a ***light play***, denotes that foolish and short-lived pleasures will be indulged in by the dreamer.

To dream of seeing a ***comedy***, is significant of light pleasures and pleasant tasks. ◎

TRAGEDY

To dream of a ***tragedy***, foretells misunderstandings and grievous disappointments.

To dream that you are ***implicated in a tragedy***, portends that a calamity looms which will plunge you into sorrow and peril. ◎

SHAKESPEARE

To dream of ***Shakespeare***, denotes that unhappiness and despondency looms which will work much anxiety to momentous affairs, and love will be stripped of passion's fever.

To dream that you read ***Shakespeare's works***, denotes that you will unalterably attach yourself to literary accomplishments. ◎

Theater and Opera

THEATER

To dream of being at the ***theater*** denotes that you will have much pleasure in the company of new friends. Your affairs will be satisfactory after this dream. If you are one of the players, your pleasures will be short.

If you attend a ***vaudeville theater***, you are in danger of losing property through silly pleasures. If it is a grand opera, you will succeed in your wishes and aspirations.

If you applaud and laugh at a theater, you will sacrifice duty to the gratification of fancy.

To dream of trying to escape from one during a fire or other excitement, foretells that you will engage in some enterprise which will be hazardous.

PANTOMIME

To dream of seeing ***pantomimes***, denotes that your friends will deceive you. If you participate in them, you will have cause of offense. Affairs will not prove satisfactory. ◎

OPERA

To dream of attending an ***opera***, denotes that you will be entertained by friends, and find that your immediate affairs will be favorable. ◎

ACTOR AND ACTRESS *see* **LOVE** *page 124,* **DEAD** *page 120,* **PAUPER** *page 244,* **ENGAGEMENT** *page 130,* **MARRIAGE** *page 130* ◆
DRAMA *see* **WRITING** *page 232* ◆ **THEATER** *see* **LAUGHING** *page 256,* **ESCAPE** *page 266,* **FIRE** *page 80*

Tricks and Deceits

HYPNOTIST
To dream that you are in a ***hypnotic state*** or under the power of others, portends disastrous results, for your enemies will enthrall you; but if you hold others under a spell, you will assert decided will power in governing your surroundings.

For a young woman to dream that she is under strange influences, denotes her immediate exposure to danger, and she should beware.

To dream of seeing ***hypnotic and sleight-of-hand*** performances, signifies worries and perplexities in business and domestic circles, and unhealthy conditions of state.

To dream of seeing a hypnotist trying to hypnotize others, and then turn his attention on you, and fail to do so, indicates that a trouble is hanging above you which friends will not succeed in warding off. Yourself alone can avert the impending danger. ◎

A CARD TRICK

CONJURER
To dream of a ***conjurer***, denotes that unpleasant experiences will beset you in your search for wealth and happiness in life. ◎

LEGERDEMAIN
To dream of practicing ***legerdemain***, or seeing others doing so, signifies that you will be placed in a position where your energy and power of planning will be called into strenuous play to extricate yourself. ◎

A Cast of Characters

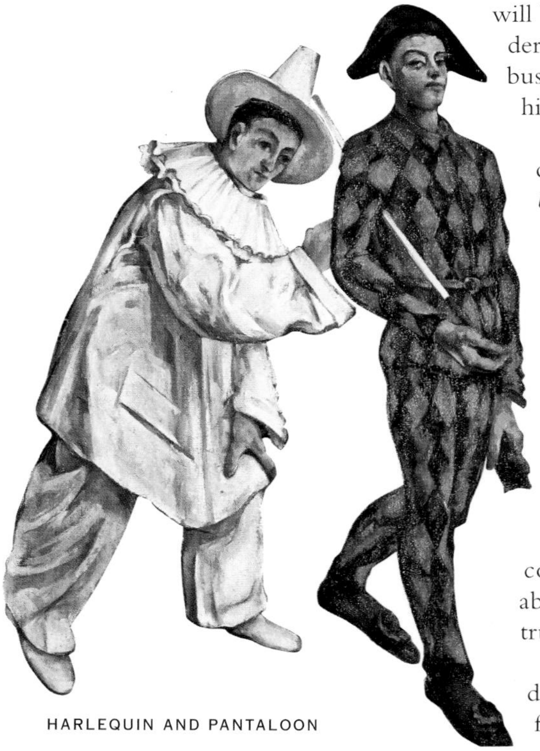

HARLEQUIN AND PANTALOON

HARLEQUIN
If you dream of a ***harlequin***, trouble will beset you.

To dream of a ***harlequin cheating you***, you will find uphill work to identify certain claims that promise profit to you.

To be ***dressed as a harlequin***, denotes passionate error and unwise attacks on strength and purse. Designing women will lure you to paths of sin. ◎

ACROBAT
To dream of seeing ***acrobats***, denotes that you will be prevented from carrying out hazardous schemes by the foolish fear of others.

To see ***yourself acrobating***, you will have a sensation to answer for, and your existence will be made almost unendurable by the guying of your enemies.

To see ***women acrobating***, denotes that your name will be maliciously and slanderously handled. Also your business interests will be hindered.

For a young woman to dream that she sees ***acrobats in tights***, signifies that she will court the favor of men. ◎

VENTRILOQUIST
To dream of a ***ventriloquist***, denotes that some treasonable affair is going to prove detrimental to your interest.

If you think yourself one, you will not conduct yourself honorably toward people who trust you.

For a young woman to dream that she is mystified by the ***voice of a ventriloquist***, foretells that she will be deceived into illicit adventures. ◎

JESTER
To dream of a ***jester***, foretells that you will ignore important things in looking after silly affairs. ◎

CLOWN
To dream of a ***clown***, denotes that you will soon be involved in a frivolous relationship.

To dream of an ***evil clown***, means that someone whom you believe to be trustworthy will prove to be duplicitous.

To dream of a ***sad clown***, means that someone close to you will not take your intentions seriously.

To dream that ***you are a clown***, means that you will soon be humiliated and embarrassed among your peers. ◎

HYPNOTIST see EYES page 99 ◆ LEGERDEMAIN see CARDS page 176 ◆ HARLEQUIN see APPAREL page 154 ◆ ACROBAT see STOCKINGS page 156 ◆ VENTRILOQUIST see VOICE page 276

Recording and Broadcasting

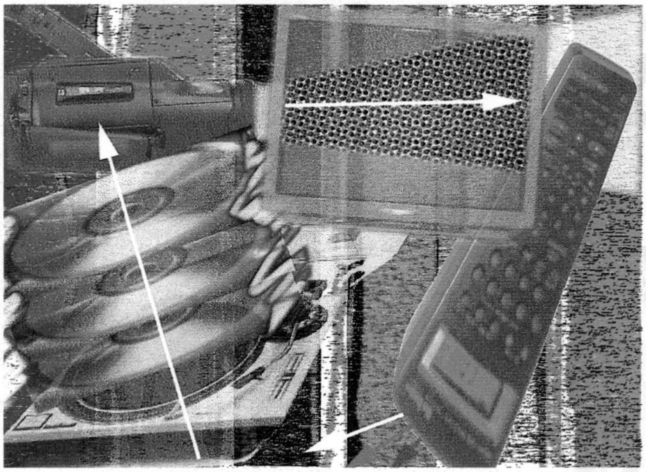

ELECTRONIC MEDIA

RECORD PLAYER
To dream of a *record player,* ***foretells pleasure and prosperity. You will have a peaceful household.***

TAPE RECORDER
To dream of a *tape recorder* ***recording something, means that statements you have uttered in the past will soon come back to haunt you. These words will be used against you in a fashion that will be disruptive to your life, if certain people become privy to the information.***

COMPACT DISC
To dream of a *compact disc,* ***means that you will soon be involved in a new, romantic relationship, which will turn out smoothly.***

CAMCORDER
To dream of using a *camcorder,* ***signifies that an important and exciting event will soon occur in your life.***

RADIO
To dream of listening to a *radio,* ***foretells the advent of some new and pleasing comrade who will lend himself willingly to advance your enjoyment.***

To dream of hearing a *radio playing,* ***foretells pleasure and prosperity.***

TELEVISION
To dream about watching *television* ***and feeling uncomfortable with what you see, foretells that you are being too easily influenced by others.***

To dream that you are *on television,* ***means that you are much too concerned with physical appearances. Your shallowness will lead to heartache.***

REMOTE CONTROL
To dream of using a *remote control,* ***means that you will soon be involved in a manipulative relationship.***

Questions and Answers

RIDDLES
The import of ***riddles*** is confusion and dissatisfaction.

To dream that you are trying to ***solve riddles***, denotes that you will engage in some enterprise which will try your patience and employ your money.

QUIZ
To dream of taking a ***quiz*** or a test, denotes that a very important business opportunity will soon occur.

To ***fail the quiz***, means that a loss will occur to you financially.

To ***score well*** on the quiz, foretells prosperity and peaceful times.

To ***not be able to recall anything*** while you are taking the quiz, means stagnation and an inability to overcome a particular obstacle.

TELEVISION QUIZ SHOW
To see yourself as a contestant on a popular ***television quiz show***, means that you will soon have to answer some very uncomfortable and dubious questions.

If you lose, your reputation will be sullied; if you win, your honor will be retained.

QUIZ SHOW CONTESTANT

Characters who star in your dream theater may include the harlequin *opposite top* **and the clown** *opposite right;* **the quickness of the conjuror's hand** *opposite left* **may deceive your dreaming eye; you may dream of electronic media** *top,* **or see yourself as the contestant on a dream-time TV quiz show above** *above.*

RECORD PLAYER, TAPE RECORDER, COMPACT DISC, RADIO *see* **MUSIC** *page 164* ◆ **QUIZ** *see* **FAILURE** *page 258*

Dreams of public entertainment – at the ball or discotheque, the fairground or carnival – are almost entirely indicative of real pleasures to come. However, just as crowds can be oppressive as well as energizing, and masks can deceive as well as disguise, you should take care when interpreting your dreams of the social whirl.

Music, Dance, and Masquerade

ENTERTAINMENT

To dream of an ***entertainment*** where there is music and dancing, you will have pleasant tidings of the absent, and enjoy health and prosperity. To the young, this is a dream of many and varied pleasures and the high regard of friends. ◎

BALL

A very satisfactory omen, if beautiful and gaily dressed people are dancing to the strains of entrancing music. But if you feel gloomy and distressed at the inattention of others, a death in the family may be expected soon. ◎

DISCOTHEQUE

To dream of being in a ***discotheque***, means that you will soon be distracted, confused and obsessed over a new relationship. ◎

MASQUERADE

To dream of attending a ***masquerade***, denotes that you will indulge in foolish and harmful pleasures to the neglect of business and domestic duties.

For a young woman to dream that she participates in a masquerade, denotes that she will be deceived. ◎

MASK

To dream that you are wearing a ***mask***, denotes temporary trouble, as your conduct toward some dear one will be misinterpreted, and your endeavors to aid that one will be misunderstood, but you will profit by the temporary estrangement.

To see others ***masking***, denotes that you will combat falsehood and envy.

To see a mask in your dreams, denotes that some person will be unfaithful to you, and your affairs will suffer also.

For a young woman to dream that she ***wears a mask***, foretells that she will endeavor to impose upon some friendly person.

If she ***unmasks***, or sees others doing so, she will fail to gain the admiration sought for. She should demean herself modestly after this dream. ◎

In your dreams you can experience in safety all the intrigue and excitement of a masked ball *right* and the heady buzz of a street carnival *opposite*.

AT THE MASQUERADE

ENTERTAINMENT *see* **MUSIC** *page 164*, **DANCE** *page 168* ◆ **MASK** *see* **ORNAMENT** *page 161* ◆ **BALL** *see* **BEAUTY** *page 100*, **MUSIC** *page 164*, **GLOOM** *page 257* ◆ **DISCOTHEQUE** *see* **DANCE** *page 168*

High Days and Holidays

RECEPTION
To dream of attending a ***reception***, denotes that you will have pleasant engagements. Confusion at a reception will work you disquietude. ◎

JUBILEE
To dream of a ***jubilee***, denotes many pleasurable enterprises in which you will be a participant. For a young woman, this is a favorable dream, pointing to matrimony and an increase of temporal blessings.

To dream of a ***religious jubilee***, denotes close but comfortable environments. ◎

HOLIDAY
To dream of a ***holiday***, foretells that interesting strangers will soon partake of your hospitality.

For a young woman to dream that she is ***displeased with a holiday***, denotes that she will be fearful of her own attractions in winning a friend back from a rival. ◎

CARNIVAL
To dream that you are participating in a ***carnival***, portends that you are soon to enjoy some unusual pleasure or recreation.

A ***carnival when masks are used***, or when incongruous or clownish figures are seen, implies discord in the home; business will be unsatisfactory and love unrequited. ◎

FESTIVAL
To dream of being at a ***festival***, denotes indifference to the old realities of life, and a love for those pleasures that make one old before his or her time. You will never want, but will be largely dependent on others. ◎

PROCESSION
To dream of a ***procession***, denotes that alarming fears will possess you relative to the fulfillment of expectations. If it be a funeral procession, sorrow is fast approaching, and will throw a shadow around pleasures.

To see or participate in a ***torch-lit procession***, denotes that you will engage in gaieties which will detract from your real merit. ◎

Fireworks

FIREWORKS
To see ***fireworks***, indicates enjoyment and good health. For a young woman, this dream signifies entertainments and pleasant visiting to distant places. ◎

FIREWORK

ROMAN CANDLE
To see ***Roman candles*** while dreaming, is a sign of speedy attainment of coveted pleasures and positions.

To imagine that you have a loaded candle and find it empty, denotes that you will be disappointed with the possession of some object which you have long striven to obtain. ◎

CARNIVAL

Fairs

FAIR
To dream of being at a ***fair***, denotes that you will have a pleasant and profitable business and a congenial companion.

For a young woman, this dream signifies a jovial and even-tempered man for a life partner. ◎

AMUSEMENT PARK
To see yourself in an ***amusement park***, denotes that you will soon have a vacation.

To dream of actually being on one of the rides, signifies that you will soon be able to enjoy life more and be less inhibited. ◎

CAROUSEL
To dream of riding on a ***carousel***, signifies a period of stagnation in your life.

To dream of seeing others riding a carousel, signifies unfulfilled hopes or desires.

To dream of seeing a carousel in a deserted area, denotes impending doom and unhappiness. ◎

JUBILEE *see* **RELIGION** *page 277* ◆ **CARNIVAL** *see* **MASK** *page 172* ◆ **PROCESSION** *see* **TORCH** *page 216* ◆
ROMAN CANDLE *see* **CANDLES** *page 216* ◆ **CAROUSEL** *see* **RIDE** *page 33*

Sports, Toys, and Games

In your dreams you may well be hurried from sport to sport, and there are many forms of sporting and gaming activity in the dream arena. On the whole, such dreams are good and wholesome; but as many of them reveal your competitive edge, you should take careful heed of them if you find yourself in competition in waking life.

Hunting, Shooting, and Fishing

ANGLING
To dream of ***catching fish*** is good. If you fail to catch any in your dreams, it will be bad for you. ◎

HUNTING
If you dream of ***hunting***, you will struggle for the unattainable.

If you dream that you ***hunt game*** and find it, you will overcome obstacles and gain your desires. ◎

GAME
To dream of ***game***, either of shooting or killing or by other means, denotes fortunate undertakings but selfish motions. If you fail to take game on a hunt, it denotes bad management and loss. ◎

THE HUNTSMAN

Water Sports

DIVING
To dream of ***diving*** in clear water, denotes a favorable termination of some embarrassment. If the water is muddy, you will suffer anxiety at the turn your affairs seem to be taking.

To see ***others diving***, indicates pleasant companions.

For ***lovers to dream of diving***, denotes the consummation of happy dreams and passionate love. ◎

SWIMMING
To dream of ***swimming***, is an augury of success if you find no discomfort in this act. If you feel yourself going down, much dissatisfaction will present itself to you.

For a young woman to dream that she is ***swimming with a girlfriend*** who is an artist in swimming, foretells that she will be loved for her charming disposition, and her little love affairs will be condoned by her friends.

To ***swim underwater***, foretells struggles and anxieties. ◎

Ball Games

BASEBALL
To see a ***baseball*** in your dream, denotes that you will be easily contented, and your cheerfulness will make you a popular companion.

For a young woman to dream that she is ***playing baseball***, means much pleasure for her, but no real profit or comfort. ◎

GOLF
To be playing ***golf*** or watching the game, denotes that pleasant and successive wishing will be indulged in by you.

To see any unpleasantness connected with golf, you will be humiliated by some thoughtless person. ◎

Skating

SKATING
To dream that you are ***skating*** on ice, foretells that you are in danger of losing employment or valuable articles. If you break through the ice while skating, you will have unworthy friends to counsel you.

To see ***others skating***, foretells that disagreeable people will connect your name in scandal with some person who admires you.

To see ***skates***, denotes discord among your associates.

To see young people skating on ***roller skates***, foretells that you will enjoy good health, and feel enthusiastic over the pleasures you are able to contribute to others. ◎

BASEBALL PLAYER

ANGLING *see* FISH *page 51*, FISHERMAN *page 51* ◆ HUNTING *see* PARTRIDGES, PHEASANTS, QUAIL *page 47* ◆ GAME *see* SHOOTING *page 263* ◆ DIVING, SWIMMING *see* WATER *page 78* ◆ SKATING *see* ICE *page 77*

Indoor Sports

BILLIARDS
Billiards, foretell coming troubles to the dreamer; lawsuits and contentions over property. Slander will get in your work to your detriment.

If you see ***table and balls idle***, this denotes that deceitful comrades are undermining you. ◎

BOWLING
If you dream of playing ***bowling***, you will doubtless soon engage in some affair that will bring discredit upon your name, and you will lose your money and true friendship.

To see others engage in this sport, foretells that you will find pleasure in frivolous people and likely lose employment.

For a young woman to play a successful game of bowling, is an omen of light pleasures, but sorrow will attend her later. ◎

NINEPINS
To dream that you play ninepins, signifies that you are foolishly wasting your energy and opportunities. You should be careful in the selection of companions. All phases of this dream are bad. ◎

Boxing

PRIZE FIGHTER
For a young woman to see a ***prize fighter***, foretells that she will have pleasure in fast society, and will give her friends much concern about her reputation. ◎

PRIZE FIGHT
To see a ***prize fight*** in your dreams, denotes that your affairs will give you trouble in controlling them.

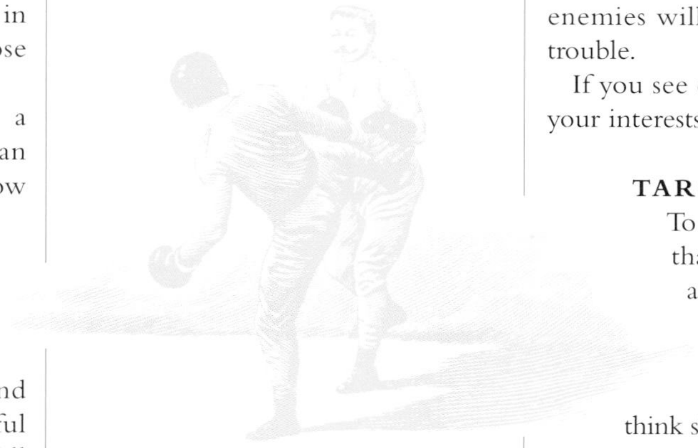

THE BOXERS

Sports Gear

RACKET
To dream of a ***racket***, denotes that you will be foiled in some anticipated pleasure. For a young woman, this dream is ominous of disappointment in not being able to participate in some amusement that has engaged her attention. ◎

JAVELIN
To dream of defending yourself with a ***javelin***, your most private affairs will be searched into to establish claims of dishonesty, and you will prove your innocence after much wrangling.

If you are ***pierced by a javelin***, enemies will succeed in giving you trouble.

If you see others ***carrying javelins***, your interests are threatened. ◎

TARGET
To dream of a ***target***, foretells that you will have some affair demanding your attention from other more pleasant ones.

For a young woman to think she is a target, denotes that her reputation is in danger through the envy of friendly associates. ◎

A Winning Streak

RACE
To dream that you are in a ***race***, foretells that others will aspire to the things you are working to possess; but if you win in the race, you will overcome your competitors. ◎

CHAMPION
To dream of a ***champion***, denotes that you will win the warmest friendship of some person by your dignity and moral conduct. ◎

THE CHAMPION

TROPHY
To see ***trophies*** in a dream, signifies that some pleasure or fortune will come to you through the endeavors of mere acquaintances.

For a woman to ***give away a trophy***, implies doubtful pleasures and fortune. ◎

ROSETTE
To wear them yourself or see ***rosettes*** on others in dreams, is significant of a frivolous waste of time; though you will experience the thrills of pleasure, they will bring disappointments. ◎

GYMNAST
To dream of a ***gymnast***, denotes misfortune in speculation or trade. ◎

Sporting types who run and jump through your dreams may include the huntsman *opposite center*, **the baseball player** *opposite bottom*, **boxers in a prize fight** *above* **and the champion** *left*.

BILLIARDS *see* **TABLE** *page 214* ◆ **PRIZE FIGHTER, PRIZE FIGHT** *see* **FIGHT** *page 260* ◆
JAVELIN *see* **ARROW** *page 264* ◆ **ROSETTE** *see* **ORNAMENT** *page 161*

Taking a Gamble

CLUBS

GAMBLING

To dream that you are ***gambling*** and win, signifies low associations and pleasure at the expense of others.

If you gamble in your dreams and lose, it foretells that your disgraceful conduct will be the undoing of one near to you. ◎

LOTTERY

To dream of a ***lottery***, and that you are taking great interest in the drawing, you will engage in some worthless enterprise, which will cause you to make an unpropitious journey. If you hold the lucky number, you will gain in a speculation which will perplex and give you much anxiety.

To see others ***winning in a lottery***, denotes convivialities and amusements, bringing many friends together.

If you ***lose in a lottery***, you will be the victim of designing persons. Gloomy depressions in your affairs will result.

For a young woman to dream of a lottery in any way, denotes that her careless way of doing things will bring her disappointment, and a husband who will not be altogether reliable or constant.

To dream of a lottery, denotes that you will have unfavorable friendships in business. Your love affairs will produce temporary pleasure. ◎

RAFFLE

If you dream of ***raffling*** any article, you will fall a victim to speculation.

If you are at a ***church raffle***, you will soon find that disappointment is clouding your future. For a young woman, this dream means empty expectations. ◎

SLOT MACHINE

To dream of a ***slot machine***, denotes good fortune; financial gain will come easily to you.

To dream of ***using a slot machine***, denotes that you will soon face financial difficulties. You will try obsessively to correct the situation, but fail. ◎

BETTING

If ***betting*** on races, beware of engaging in new undertakings. Enemies are trying to divert your attention from legitimate business.

Betting at ***gaming tables***, denotes that immoral devices will be used to wring money from you. ◎

WAGER

To dream of making a ***wager***, signifies that you will resort to dishonest means to forward your schemes.

If you ***lose a wager***, you will sustain injury from base connections with those out of your social sphere.

To win one, reinstates you in favor with fortune.

If you are not able to put up a wager, you will be discouraged and prostrated by the adverseness of circumstances. ◎

At the Race Track

TURF

To dream of ***racing turf***, signifies that you will have pleasure and wealth at your command, but your morals will be questioned by your most intimate friends.

To see a green turf, indicates that interesting affairs will hold your attention. ◎

JOCKEY

To dream of a ***jockey***, omens that you will appreciate a gift from an unexpected source. For a young woman to dream that she associates with a jockey, or has one for a lover, indicates that she will win a husband out of her station.

To see one thrown from a horse, signifies that you will be called on for aid by strangers. ◎

Cards and Dice

DICE

To dream of ***dice***, is indicative of unfortunate speculations, and consequent misery and despair. It also foretells contagious sickness.

For a girl to dream that she sees her lover throwing dice, indicates his unworthiness. ◎

CARDS

If playing them in your dreams with others for social pastime, you will meet with fair realization of hopes that have long buoyed you up. Small ills will vanish. But playing for stakes will involve you in difficulties of a serious nature.

If you lose at ***cards***, you will encounter enemies. If you win, you will justify yourself in the eyes of the law, but will have trouble in so doing.

If a young woman dreams that her sweetheart is ***playing at cards***, she will have cause to question his good intentions.

In ***social games***, ***diamonds*** indicate wealth; ***clubs***, that your partner in life will be exacting, and that you may have trouble in explaining your absence at times; ***hearts*** denote fidelity and cozy surroundings; ***spades***, that you will be a widow and encumbered with a large estate. ◎

If you dream of ***spades***, you will be enticed into follies which will bring you grief and misfortune. For a gambler to dream that ***spades are trumps***, means that unfortunate deals will deplete his winnings.

POKER

To play at ***poker***, warns you against evil company; and young women, especially, will lose their moral distinctiveness if they find themselves engaged in this game. ◎

GAMBLING, LOTTERY *see* MONEY *page 239* ◆ RAFFLE *see* CHURCH *page 189* ◆
SLOT MACHINE *see* COINS *page 242* ◆ BETTING *see* RACE *page 175* ◆ TURF *see* RIDE *page 33*
◆ JOCKEY *see* RIDE *page 33,* HORSE DREAMS *page 34* ◆ CARDS *see* SWEETHEART *page 124*

THE CHESS PLAYERS

Dominoes and Board Games

DOMINOES
To dream that you play at ***dominoes***, and lose, you will be affronted by a friend, and much uneasiness for your safety will be entertained by your people, as you will not be discreet in your affairs with women or other matters that engage your attention.

If you are the ***winner of the game***, it foretells that you will be much courted and admired by certain dissolute characters, bringing you selfish pleasures, but much distress to your relatives. ◎

CHECKERS
To dream of playing ***checkers***, you will be involved in difficulties of a serious character, and strange people will come into your life, working you harm.

To dream that you ***win the game***, you will succeed in some doubtful enterprise. ◎

CHESS
To dream of playing ***chess***, denotes stagnation of business, dull companions, and poor health.

If you dream that you ***lose at chess***, worries from mean sources will ensue; but if you win, disagreeable influences may be surmounted. ◎

BACKGAMMON
To dream of playing ***backgammon***, denotes that you will, while visiting, meet with unfriendly hospitality, but will unconsciously win friendships that will endure much straining.

If you are ***defeated in the game***, you will be unfortunate in bestowing your affections, and your affairs will remain in an unsettled condition. ◎

Less physically demanding dreams may center around a chess board *above* **or a party game such as blind man's bluff** *right*.

Blind Man's Bluff

BLIND MAN'S BLUFF
To dream that you are playing at ***blind man's bluff***, denotes that you are about to engage in some weak enterprise which will likely humiliate you, besides losing money for you. ◎

BLINDFOLD
For a woman to dream that she is ***blindfolded***, means that disturbing elements are rising around to distress and trouble her. Disappointment will be felt by others through her. ◎

BLIND MAN'S BLUFF

BLIND MAN'S BLUFF *see* **ORNAMENT** *page 161*, **BLIND** *page 99* ◆ **BLINDFOLD** *see* **HANDKERCHIEF** *page 158*, **BLIND** *page 99*

Dreams of toys can often transport you back to your childhood. However, they are not always indicative of fortune; perhaps they indicate that you are over-attached to childish playthings when you should be concentrating on your actions in the adult world.

Childhood Toys

TOYS
To see ***toys*** in dreams, foretells family joys, if whole and new, but if broken, death will rend your heart with sorrow.

To see children ***at play with toys***, means that a marriage of a happy nature is indicated.

To ***give away toys*** in your dreams, foretells that you will be ignored in a social way by your acquaintances. ◎

TOPS
To dream of a ***top***, denotes that you will be involved in some frivolous difficulties.

To see one ***spinning***, foretells that you will waste your means in childish pleasures.

To see a top, foretells that indiscriminate friendships will involve you in difficulty. ◎

RATTLES
To dream of seeing a baby play with its ***rattle***, omens peaceful contentment in the home, and enterprises will be honorable and full of gain. To a young woman, it augurs an early marriage and tender cares of her own.

To give a baby a rattle, denotes unfortunate investments. ◎

Balloons and Kites

BALLOON
Blighted hopes and adversity come with this dream. Business of every character will sustain an apparent falling off.

To ascend in a ***balloon***, denotes an unfortunate journey. ◎

KITE
To dream of flying a ***kite***, denotes a great show of wealth or business, but with little true soundness to it all.

To see the kite thrown upon the ground, foretells disappointment and failure.

To dream of ***making a kite***, you will speculate largely on small means and seek to win the one you love by misrepresentations.

To see children ***flying kites***, denotes a pleasant and light occupation. If the kite ascends beyond the vision, high hopes and aspirations will resolve themselves into disappointment and loss. ◎

Action Toys

KALEIDOSCOPE
Kaleidoscopes working before you in a dream, portend swift changes with little favorable promise in them. ◎

JUMPING JACK
To dream of a ***jumping jack***, denotes that idleness and trivial pastimes will occupy your thoughts to the exclusion of serious and sustaining plans. ◎

STILTS
To dream of walking on ***stilts***, denotes that your fortune is in an insecure condition.

To fall from them, or feel them break beneath you, you will be precipitated into embarrassments by trusting your affairs to others. ◎

QUOITS
To play at ***quoits*** in dreams, foretells low engagements and loss of good employment. To lose, portends of distressing conditions. ◎

HOOP
To dream of a ***hoop***, foretells that you will form influential friendships. Many will seek counsel of you.

To jump through, or see others ***jumping through hoops***, denotes that you will have discouraging outlooks, but you will overcome them with decisive victory. ◎

THE TOYS

Childhood may be recaptured when images from your old toy box show themselves in your dreams *above.* **Perhaps less welcome are memories of your old school days or dream time visits to your old college or university** *opposite.*

TOYS *see* **CHILDREN** *page 128* ◆ **RATTLES** *see* **BABY** *page 119* ◆ **BALLOON** *see* **FLIGHT** *page 267* ◆ **KITE** *see* **FLYING** *page 268,* **CHILDREN** *page 128*

Education, Arts, and Crafts

Dreams of the life of the mind or the creativity of artistic endeavor are as much a part of the sleeper's repertoire as action dreams. You may dream of revisiting your schooldays or of painting a masterpiece, attaining high educational honors, or putting together a scrap book. Such dreams tend, on the whole, to be promising in both business, social, and romantic fields.

A Little Learning

EDUCATION

To dream that you are anxious to obtain an ***education***, shows that, whatever your circumstances in life may be, there will be a keen desire for knowledge on your part, which will place you on a higher plane than your associates. Fortune will also be more lenient to you.

To dream that you are in ***places of learning***, foretells for you many influential friends. ◎

LEARNING

To dream of ***learning***, denotes that you will take great interest in acquiring knowledge, and if you are economical of your time, you will advance into the literary world.

To enter halls, or ***places of learning***, denotes a rise from obscurity, and finance will be a congenial adherent.

To see ***learned men***, foretells that your companions will be interesting and prominent.

For a woman to dream that she is associated in any way with ***learned people***, she will be ambitious and excel in her endeavors to rise into prominence. ◎

WISDOM

To dream you are possessed of ***wisdom***, signifies that your spirit will be brave under trying circumstances, and you will be able to overcome these trials and rise to prosperous living.

If you think you ***lack wisdom*** in your dreams, it implies that you are wasting your native talents. ◎

Institutes of Education

ACADEMY

To visit an ***academy*** in your dreams, denotes that you will regret opportunities that you have let pass through sheer idleness and indifference.

To think you own, or are an inmate of one, you will find that you are to meet easy defeat of aspirations. You will take on knowledge, but be unable to rightly assimilate and apply it.

For a young woman or any person to ***return to an academy*** after having finished their studies there, signifies that demands will be made which the dreamer may find himself or herself unable to meet. ◎

COLLEGE

To dream of a ***college***, denotes that you are soon to advance to a position long sought after. To dream that you are back in college, foretells that you will receive distinction through some well-favored work. ◎

HIGH SCHOOL

To dream of a ***high school***, foretells ascension to more elevated positions in love, as well as in social and business affairs. For a young woman to be ***suspended from a high school***, foretells that she will have troubles in social circles. ◎

THE ACADEMICS

EDUCATION, LEARNING *see* **SCHOOL** *page 180* ◆ **ACADEMY** *see* **ART GALLERY** *page 181* ◆
HIGH SCHOOL *see* **SCHOOL** *page 180*

School and Classroom

SCHOOL

To dream of attending ***school***, indicates distinction in literary work. If you think you are young and at school as in your youth, you will find that sorrow and reverses will make you sincerely long for the simple trusts and pleasures of days of yore.

To dream of ***teaching a school***, foretells that you will strive for literary attainments, but the bare necessities of life must first be forthcoming.

To visit the ***schoolhouse*** of your childhood days, portends that discontent and discouraging incidents overshadow the present.

To dream of a ***schoolteacher*** denotes that you are likely to enjoy learning and amusements in a quiet way. If you are one, you are likely to reach desired success in literary and other works. ◎

BLACKBOARD

To see in your dreams writing in white chalk on a ***blackboard***, denotes ill tidings of some person prostrated with some severe malady, or that your financial security will be swayed by the panicky condition of commerce. ◎

CHALK

To dream of using ***chalk*** on a board, you will attain public honors, unless it is the blackboard; then it indicates ill luck.

To hold hands full of chalk, disappointment is foretold. ◎

CHALKS

Dreams may revive the scent of chalk dust *above* **and take you back to the classroom or your homework sessions** *top*. **More agreeable may be dreams of being an artist making pictures** *opposite top*, **or of visiting an art gallery** *opposite*.

SCHOOL WORK

History and Maths

HISTORY

To dream that you are reading ***history***, indicates a long and pleasant recreation. ◎

ADDITION

To dream of pondering over ***addition***, denotes that you will have to struggle to overcome difficult situations, which will soon prominently assume formidable shapes in your business transactions.

To find some ***error in addition***, shows that you will be able to overcome enemies by fortunately discerning their intention before they have executed their design.

To dream that you ***add figures with a machine***, foretells that you will have a powerful ally who will save you from much oppression.

If you fail to read the figures, you will lose fortune by blind speculation. ◎

COUNTING

To dream of ***counting*** your children, and they are merry and sweet-looking, denotes that you will have no trouble in controlling them, and they will attain honorable places.

To dream of ***counting money***, you will be lucky and always able to pay your debts; but to count out money to another person, you will meet with loss of some kind. Such will be the case, also, in counting other things. If for yourself, good luck will attend you; if for others, usually bad. ◎

Reference Books

ENCYCLOPEDIA

To dream of seeing or searching through ***encyclopedias***, portends that you will secure literary ability at the cost of prosperity and comfort. ◎

DICTIONARY

To dream that you are referring to a ***dictionary***, signifies that you will depend too much upon the opinion and suggestions of others for the clear management of your own affairs, which could easily be done with proper dispatch if your own will were given play. ◎

SCHOOL *see* WRITING *page 232*, READING *page 233*, CHILDREN *page 128* ◆ ADDITION *see* MONEY *page 239*, TILL *page 242* ◆ COUNTING *see* CHILDREN *page 128*, MONEY *page 239* ◆ ENCYCLOPEDIA *see* LIBRARY *page 233* ◆ DICTIONARY *see* BOOKS *page 233*

Cultural Institutes

MUSEUM

To dream of a ***museum***, denotes that you will pass through many and varied scenes in striving for what appears your rightful position. You will acquire useful knowledge, which will stand you in better light than if you had pursued the usual course of learning. If the museum is distasteful you will have many causes for vexation. ◎

ARTIST AT WORK

ART GALLERY

To visit an ***art gallery***, portends unfortunate unions in domestic circles. You will struggle to put forth an appearance of happiness, but will secretly care for other associations. ◎

Laboratory

To dream of being in a laboratory, ***denotes great energies wasted in unfruitful enterprises when you might succeed in some more practical business.***

If you think yourself an alchemist, and try to discover a process to turn other things into gold, you will entertain far-reaching and interesting projects, but you will fail to reach the apex of your ambition. Wealth will prove a myth, and the woman you love will hold a false position toward you. ❋

Pictures and Images

PICTURES

Pictures appearing before you in dreams, prognosticate deception and the ill will of contemporaries.

To ***make a picture***, denotes that you will engage in some unremunerative enterprise.

To ***destroy pictures***, means that you will be pardoned for using strenuous means to establish your rights.

To buy them, foretells worthless speculation.

To dream of seeing your likeness in a living tree, appearing and disappearing, denotes that you will be prosperous and seemingly contented, but there will be disappointments in reaching out for companionship and reciprocal understanding of any ideas and plans.

To dream of being surrounded with the best efforts of the ***old and modern masters***, denotes that you will have insatiable longings and desires for higher attainments, compared to which your present success will seem to be poverty-stricken and miserable. ◎

ALBUM

To dream of an ***album***, denotes that you will have success and true friends.

For a young woman to dream of looking at ***photographs in an album***, foretells that she will soon have a new lover who will be very agreeable to her. ◎

SCRAPBOOK

To dream of a ***scrapbook***, denotes that disagreeable acquaintances will shortly be made. ◎

PORTFOLIO

To dream of a ***portfolio***, denotes that your employment will not be to your liking, and you will seek a change in your location. ◎

PAINT AND PAINTING

To dream of seeing ***beautiful paintings***, denotes that friends will assume false positions toward you, and you will find that pleasure is illusive.

For a young woman to dream of ***painting a picture***, she will be deceived in her lover, as he will transfer his love to another. ◎

PORTRAITS

To dream of gazing upon the ***portrait*** of some beautiful person, denotes that, while you enjoy pleasure, you can but feel the disquieting and treacherousness of such joys. Your general affairs will suffer loss after dreaming of portraits. ◎

THE ART GALLERY

MUSEUM *see* **STATUES** *page 182* ◆ **ART GALLERY** *see* **ACADEMY** *page 179* ◆ **PICTURES** *see* **PHOTOGRAPHS** *page 182,* **TREES** *page 64* ◆
ALBUM *see* **PHOTOGRAPHS** *page 182,* **CAMERA** *page 182* ◆ **PORTRAITS** *see* **BEAUTY** *page 100*

SCULPTURE BY HENRY MOORE

Photography

PHOTOGRAPHS
If you see ***photographs*** in your dreams, it is a sign of approaching deception.

If you receive the ***photograph of your lover***, you are warned of loyalty, while he tries to so impress you.

For married people to dream of the possession of ***other person's photographs***, foretells unwelcome disclosures of one's conduct.

To dream that you are having your ***own photograph made***, foretells that you will unwarily cause yourself and others trouble. ◎

CAMERA
To dream of a ***camera***, signifies that changes will bring undeserved environments.

For a young woman to dream that she is ***taking pictures with a camera***, foretells that her immediate future will have much that is displeasing, and that a friend will subject her to acute disappointment. ◎

You may dream of high art such as a world-famous sculpture *above* or more domestic and useful crafts such as that of the seamstress *opposite*.

Pottery and Sculpture

POTTER
To dream of a ***potter***, denotes constant employment, with satisfactory results.

For a young woman to see a potter, foretells that she will enjoy pleasant engagements. ◎

POTTER'S FIELD
To see a ***potter's field*** [field where potters discard remnants; paupers' burial place] in your dreams, denotes poverty and misery to distress you.

For a young woman to walk through a potter's field with her lover, she will give up the one she loves in the hope of mercenary gain. ◎

SCULPTOR
To dream of a ***sculptor***, foretells that you will change from your present position to one less lucrative, but more distinguished.

For a woman to dream that her husband or lover is a sculptor, foretells that she will enjoy favors from men of high position. ◎

PUTTY
To dream of working in ***putty***, denotes that hazardous chances will be taken with fortune.

If you put in a ***windowpane with putty***, you will seek fortune with poor results. ◎

CLAY
To dream of ***clay***, denotes isolation of interest and probable insolvency.

To dig in a ***clay bank***, foretells that you will submit to extraordinary demands of enemies. If you dig in an ash bank and find clay, unfortunate surprises will combat progressive enterprises or new work. Your efforts are likely to be misdirected.

Women will find this dream unfavorable in love, social, and business states, and misrepresentations will overwhelm them. ◎

STATUES
To see ***statues*** in dreams, signifies estrangement from a loved one. Lack of energy will cause you disappointment in realizing wishes. ◎

OBELISK
An ***obelisk*** looming up stately and cold in your dreams, is the forerunner of melancholy tidings.

For lovers to stand at the ***base of an obelisk***, denotes fatal disagreements. ◎

PHOTOGRAPHS *see* **PICTURES** *page 181* ◆ **POTTER** *see* **POT** *page 210* ◆ **POTTER'S FIELD** *see* **PAUPER** *page 244*, **BURIAL** *page 122* ◆ **PUTTY** *see* **WINDOW** *page 213* ◆ **CLAY** *see* **DIGGING** *page 193* ◆ **STATUES** *see* **MUSEUM** *page 181*

Materials, textiles, and needlework of all kinds from plain sewing to intricate tapestry reflect a pleasing industry and rewarded worth. Naturally, such dreams are interpreted as symbols of activity or imminent change in the domestic realm, but they are not confined to this arena.

Needlework

EMBROIDERY
If a woman dreams of embroidering, she will be admired for her tact and ability to make the best of everything that comes her way.

For a married man to see ***embroidery***, signifies a new member in his household.

For a lover, this denotes a wise and economical spouse. ◎

TAPESTRY
To dream of seeing rich ***tapestry,*** foretells that luxurious living will be to your liking; and if the tapestries are not worn or ragged, you will be able to gratify your inclinations.

If a young woman dreams that her rooms are ***hung with tapestries***, she will soon wed someone who is rich and above her in standing. ◎

NEEDLEPOINT
To dream of doing ***needlepoint***, means a desire to have the unknown elements of your future filled in with carefully crafted details. Consequently, many questions you have about life will be answered, adversaries will no longer harass you, and friends and family will greatly enjoy your company.

To ***practice needlepoint***, with many different colors of thread, foretells an active social life.

Should you see a ***needlepoint design*** in one color alone, beware, lest fear of change keep you from meeting your appointed destiny.

To find a ***needlepoint cushion***, foretells of new possibilities opening up for you.

For a woman to dream of carrying a ***needlepoint evening bag***, foretells a romantic adventure and change of circumstances. ◎

Crochet and Knitting

CROCHET WORK
To dream of doing ***crochet*** work, foretells your entanglement in some silly affair growing out of a too great curiosity about other people's business. Beware of talking too frankly with overconfidential women. ◎

KNITTING
For a woman to dream of ***knitting***, denotes that she will possess a quiet and peaceful home, where a loving companion and dutiful children delight to give pleasure.

For a man to be in a ***knitting mill***, indicates thrift and a solid rise in prospects.

For a young woman to dream of knitting, is an omen of a hasty but propitious marriage.

For a young woman to dream that she works in a knitting mill, denotes that she will have a worthy and loyal lover. To see the mill in which she works dilapidated, she will meet with reverses in fortune and love. ◎

WOOL
To dream of ***wool***, is a pleasing sign of prosperous opportunities to expand your interests.

To see ***soiled or dirty wool***, foretells that you will seek employment with those who detest your principles. ◎

YARN
To dream of ***yarn***, denotes success in your business and an industrious companion in your home.

For a young woman to dream that she ***works with yarn***, foretells that she will be proudly recognized by a worthy man as his wife. ◎

Plain Sewing

SEWING
To dream of ***sewing*** on new garments, foretells that domestic peace will crown your wishes.

For a young woman to dream that she has ***completed a garment***, denotes that she will soon decide on a husband. ◎

BASTE
For a woman to ***baste*** her sewing, omens much vexation owing to her extravagance. ◎

SEAMSTRESS
To see a ***seamstress*** in a dream, portends that you will be deterred from making pleasant visits by unexpected luck. ◎

NEEDLEWOMAN
To see a ***needlewoman*** in your dreams, portends a foreign influence or agent that will change your circumstances, and foretells a successful domestic life.

Should the needlewoman be actively ***plying her trade***, the forthcoming influence will have a positive effect on your life.

Should the needlewoman be ***asking for work*** from you, contemplate taking action for change before it comes to you unbidden.

Should the needlewoman be ***dunning you for unpaid work***, extreme caution is recommended upon rising. ◎

MENDING
To dream of ***mending*** soiled garments, denotes that you will undertake to right a wrong at an inopportune moment; but if the garment you are working on be clean, you will be successful in adding to your fortune.

For a young woman to dream of mending, foretells that she will be a systematic help to her husband. ◎

THE SEAMSTRESS

EMBROIDERY, TAPESTRY *see* THREAD *page 184* ◆ NEEDLEPOINT *see* THREAD *page 184,* NEEDLE *page 184,* CUSHION *page 215* ◆
WOOL *see* STAIN *page 218* ◆ SEWING *see* APPAREL *page 154,* COMPLETION *page 194* ◆
NEEDLEWOMAN *see* NEEDLE *page 184* ◆ MENDING *see* STAIN *page 218*

Sewing Notions

NEEDLE

To use a ***needle*** in your dream, is a warning of approaching affliction, in which you will suffer keenly the loss of sympathy which is rightfully yours.

To dream of ***threading a needle***, denotes that you will be burdened with the care of others than your own household.

To ***look for a needle***, foretells useless worries.

To ***find a needle***, foretells that you will have friends who will appreciate you.

To break one, signifies loneliness and poverty. ◎

THIMBLE

If you use a ***thimble*** in your dreams, you will have many others to please beside yourself. If a woman, you will have your own position to make.

To lose one, foretells poverty and trouble. To see an old or broken one, denotes that you are about to act unwisely in some momentous affair.

To receive or buy a ***new thimble***, portends new associations in which you will find contentment.

To dream that you use an ***open-end thimble***, but find that it is closed, denotes that you will have trouble, but friends will aid you in escaping its disastrous consequences. ◎

THIMBLE

THREAD

To dream of ***thread***, denotes that your fortune lies beyond intricate paths.

To see ***broken threads***, you will suffer loss through the faithlessness of friends. ◎

SPOOLS

To dream of ***spools*** of thread, indicates some long and arduous tasks, but which when completed will meet your most sanguine expectations. If they are empty, there will be disappointments for you. ◎

BOBBIN

To dream of ***bobbins***, denotes that important work will devolve on you, and your interests will be adversely affected if you are negligent in dispatching the same work. ◎

BUTTONS

To dream of sewing bright shining ***buttons*** on a uniform, betokens to a young woman the warm affection of a fine-looking and wealthy partner in marriage. To a youth, it signifies admittance to military honors and a bright career.

Dull or cloth buttons, denote disappointments, systematic losses, and ill health.

The ***loss of a button***, and the consequent anxiety as to losing a garment, denote prospective losses in trade. ◎

PINS

To dream of ***pins***, augurs differences and quarrels in families.

To a young woman, they warn of unladylike conduct toward her lover.

To dream of ***swallowing a pin***, denotes that accidents will force you into perilous conditions.

To lose one, implies a petty loss or disagreement.

To see a bent or ***rusty pin***, signifies that you will lose esteem because of your careless ways.

To stick one into your flesh, denotes that some person will irritate you. ◎

TAPE

To dream of ***tape***, denotes that your work will be wearisome and unprofitable. For a woman to buy it, foretells that she will find misfortune laying oppression upon her. ◎

Craft-based dreams may include sewing and needlework *right* or specific sewing notions such as thimbles *above* and scissors *above right*. On a less domestic note, rope *opposite top* and twine may entangle you in your dreams.

SCISSORS

To dream of ***scissors*** is an unlucky omen; wives will be jealous and distrustful of their husbands, and sweethearts will quarrel and nag each other into crimination and recrimination. Dullness will overcast business horizons.

To dream that you have ***scissors sharpened***, denotes that you will work to do that which will be repulsive to your feelings.

If you break them, there will be quarrels, and probably separations for you.

To lose them, you will seek to escape from unpleasant tasks. ◎

SCISSORS

SEWING

NEEDLE *see* NEEDLEWOMAN *page 183,* NEEDLEPOINT *page 183* ◆ THREAD *see* WOOL *page 183,* YARN *page 183,* BREAK *page 265* ◆ BUTTONS *see* UNIFORM *page 157* ◆ RUST *see page 255*

Ropes and Twine

JUMPING A ROPE

ROPES

Ropes in dreams, signifies perplexities and complications in affairs, and uncertain lovemaking.

If you climb one, you will overcome enemies.

To ***descend a rope***, brings disappointment.

If you are tied with them, you are likely to yield to love contrary to your judgement.

To break them, signifies your ability to overcome enmity and competition.

To ***tie ropes*** or horses, denotes that you will have power to control others.

To ***walk a rope***, signifies that you will engage in some hazardous speculation, but will surprisingly succeed. To see others walking a rope, you will benefit by the ventures of others.

To ***jump a rope***, foretells that you will startle your associates with a thrilling escapade bordering.

To jump rope with children, shows that you are selfish and overbearing, failing to see that children owe very little duty to inhuman parents.

To ***catch a rope*** with the foot, denotes that, under cheerful conditions, you will be benevolent and tender in your administrations.

To dream that you ***let a rope down*** from an upper window to people below, thinking the proprietors would be adverse to receiving them into the hotel, denotes that you will engage in some affair which will not look exactly proper to your friends, but the same will afford you pleasure and interest. For a young woman, this dream is indicative of pleasures which do not bear the stamp of propriety. ◎

KNOTS

To dream of seeing ***knots***, denotes much worry over the most trifling affairs. If your sweetheart notices another, you will immediately find cause to censure him.

To ***tie a knot***, signifies an independent nature, and you will refuse to be nagged by an ill-disposed lover or friend. ◎

TWINE

To see ***twine*** in your dream, warns you that your business is assuming complications which will be hard to overcome. ◎

Meshes and Webs

MESHES

To dream of being entangled in the ***meshes*** of a net or other like constructions, denotes that enemies will oppress you in time of seeming prosperity. To a young woman, this dream foretells that her environments will bring her into evil and consequent abandonment. If she succeeds in disengaging herself from the meshes, she will narrowly escape slander. ◎

NETS

To dream of ensnaring anything with a ***net***, denotes that you will be unscrupulous in your dealings and deportment with others.

To dream of an ***old or torn net***, denotes that your property has mortgages or attachments, which will cause you trouble. ◎

WEB

To dream of ***webs***, foretells that deceitful friends will work you loss and displeasure. If the web is nonelastic, you will remain firm in withstanding the attacks of the envious persons who are seeking to obtain favors from you. ◎

ROPES *see* **CLIMBING** *page 268*, **BREAK** *page 265*, **JUMPING** *page 267*, **CHILDREN** *page 128*, **FEET** *page 96*, **WINDOW** *page 213* ◆ **TWINE** *see* **YARN** *page 183* ◆ **MESH** *see* **FISH** *page 51* ◆ **NETS** *see* **FISHNET** *page 51* ◆ **WEBS** *see* **SPIDER** *page 49*

Spinning and Weaving

DISTAFF
To dream of a ***distaff***, denotes frugality, with pleasant surroundings. It also signifies that a devotional spirit will be cultivated by you. ◎

WEAVING
To dream that you are ***weaving***, denotes that you will baffle any attempt to defeat you in the struggle for the upbuilding of an honorable fortune.

To see ***others weaving***, shows that you will be surrounded by healthy and energetic conditions. ◎

SPINNING
To dream that you are ***spinning***, you will engage in some enterprise which will be all you could wish. ◎

LOOM
To dream of standing by and seeing a ***loom*** operated by a stranger, denotes much vexation and useless irritation from the talkativeness of those about you. Some disappointment with happy expectations are coupled with this dream.

To see good-looking women attending the loom, denotes unqualified success to those in love. It predicts congenial pursuits to the married. It denotes that you are drawing closer together in taste.

For a woman to dream of weaving on an ***old-time loom***, signifies that she will have a thrifty husband, and beautiful children will fill her life with happy solicitations.

To see an ***idle loom***, denotes a sulky and stubborn person, who will cause you much anxious care. ◎

Flax

FLAX SPINNING
Flax spinning, ***foretells that you will be given to industrious and thrifty habits.*** ❋

FLAX
To see flax ***in a dream, prosperous enterprises are denoted.*** ❋

WEAVERS

Linen and Cotton

LINEN
To see ***linen*** in your dream, augurs prosperity and enjoyment.

If a person appears to you dressed in ***linen garments***, you will shortly be the recipient of joyful tidings in the nature of an inheritance.

If you are appareled in ***clean, fine linen***, your fortune and fullest enjoyment in life is assured. If it be soiled, sorrow and ill luck will be met with occasionally, mingled with the good in your life. ◎

Dreams of textiles may show you weavers at work *above*, **or you may see materials such as rubber** *opposite*.

COTTON
To dream of young, growing ***cotton*** fields, denotes great business and prosperous times. To see cotton ready for gathering, denotes wealth and abundance for farmers.

For manufacturers to dream of cotton, means that they will be benefited by the advancement of this article. For merchants, it denotes a change for the better in their line of business.

To see ***cotton in bales***, is a favorable indication for better times.

To dream that cotton is advancing, denotes an immediate change from low to high prices, and all will be in better circumstances. ◎

Dyes

DYE
To see the ***dyeing*** of cloth or garments in process, means bad or good luck, depending on the color. Blues, reds, and gold, indicate prosperity; black and white, indicate sorrow in all forms. ◎

INDIGO
To see ***indigo*** in a dream, denotes that you will deceive friendly persons in order to cheat them out of their belongings.

To see ***indigo water***, foretells that you will be involved in an ugly love affair. ◎

WEAVING *see* **YARN** *page 183* ◆ **SPINNING** *see* **WOOL** *page 183* ◆ **LINEN** *see* **APPAREL** *page 154* ◆ **COTTON** *see* **FIELDS** *page 60* ◆ **DYE** *see* **CLOTHES** *page 154* ◆ **INDIGO** *see* **WATER** *page 78*

Material Pleasures

VELVET
To dream of ***velvet***, portends very successful enterprises. If you wear it, some distinction will be conferred upon you.

To see ***old velvet***, means that your prosperity will suffer from your extreme pride.

If a young woman dreams that she is clothed in ***velvet garments***, it denotes that she will have honors bestowed upon her, and the choice between several wealthy lovers. ◎

LACE
See to it, if you are a lover, that your sweetheart wears ***lace***, as this dream brings fidelity in love and a rise in position.

If a woman dreams of lace, she will be happy in the realization of her most ambitious desires, and lovers will bow to her edict. No questioning or imperiousness on their part.

If you ***buy lace***, you will conduct an expensive establishment, but wealth will be a solid friend.

If you ***sell laces***, your desires will outrun your resources.

For a young girl to dream of ***making lace***, forecasts that she will win a handsome, wealthy husband. If she dreams of garnishing her ***wedding garments with lace***, she will be favored with lovers who will bow to her charms, but the wedding will be far removed from her. ◎

SILK
To dream of wearing ***silk*** clothes, is a sign of high ambitions being gratified, and friendly relations will be established between those who were estranged.

For a young woman to dream of ***old silk***, denotes that she will have much pride in her ancestors, and will be wooed by a wealthy but elderly person.

If the ***silk is soiled or torn***, she will drag her ancestral pride in the slums of disgrace. ◎

SILKWORM
If you dream of a ***silkworm***, you will engage in a very profitable work, which will also place you in a prominent position.

To see them dead, or cutting through their cocoons, is a sign of reverses and trying times. ◎

GAUZE
To dream of being dressed in ***gauze***, denotes uncertain fortune.

For a lover to dream that he can see his sweetheart clothed in such filmy material, suggests his ability to influence her for good. ◎

Rubber and Leather

RUBBER
To dream of being clothed in ***rubber*** garments, is a sign that you will have honors conferred upon you because of your steady and unchanging stand of purity and morality. If the garments are ragged or torn, you should be cautious in your conduct, as scandal is ready to attack your reputation.

To dream of using ***"rubber" as a slang term***, foretells that you will be easy to please in your choice of pleasure and companions.

If you find that your limbs ***stretch like rubber***, it is a sign that illness is threatening you, and you are likely to use deceit in your wooing and business.

To dream of ***rubber goods***, denotes that your affairs will be conducted on a secret basis, and your friends will fail to understand your conduct in many instances. ◎

RUBBER TIRES

LEATHER
To dream of ***leather***, denotes successful business and favorable engagements with women. You will go into lucky speculations if you dream that you are dressed in leather.

Ornaments of leather, denote faithfulness in love and to the home.

Piles of leather, denote fortune and happiness.

To deal in leather, signifies that no change in the disposition of your engagements is necessary for successful accumulation of wealth. ◎

TANNERY
To dream of a ***tannery***, denotes contagion and other illness. Loss in trade is portended.

To dream that ***you are a tanner***, denotes that you will have to engage in work which is not to your taste, but there will be others dependent upon you.

To buy leather from a tanner, foretells that you will be successful in your undertakings, but will not make many friends. ◎

OILCLOTH
To dream of an ***oilcloth***, is a warning that you will meet coldness and treachery.

To deal in it, denotes uncertain speculations. ◎

VELVET *see* **CLOTHES** *page 154* ◆ **LACE** *see* **SWEETHEART** *page 124*, **WEDDING** *page 131*, **APPAREL** *page 154* ◆ **LEATHER** *see* **ORNAMENT** *page 161*, **ANIMAL HIDE** *page 28* ◆ **TANNERY** *see* **ANIMAL HIDE** *page 28*

Buildings and Structures

The architecture of our dreams is extremely significant, whether you wander through marble halls or squat in a mud hut, dream of individual bricks or great edifices, or find yourself on the rooftops or in a vault. As well as man-made buildings and structures, you may dream of natural structures such as subterranean caves or a towering precipice.

Builders and Buildings

BUILDINGS
To see large and magnificent ***buildings***, with green lawns stretching out before them, is significant of a long life of plenty, and travels and explorations into distant countries.

Small and ***newly built houses***, denote happy homes and profitable undertakings; but, if old and filthy buildings, ill health and decay of lover and business will follow. ◎

ARCHITECT
Architects drawing plans in your dreams, denote a change in your business, which will be likely to result in loss to you.

For a young woman to see an architect, foretells that she will meet rebuffs in her aspirations and maneuvers to make a favorable marriage. ◎

Basic Shelter

SHELTER
To dream that you are building a ***shelter***, signifies that you will escape the evil designs of enemies.

If you are seeking shelter, you will be guilty of cheating, and will try to justify yourself. ◎

HUT
To dream of a ***hut***, denotes indifferent success. To ***sleep in a hut***, denotes ill health and dissatisfaction.

To dream that you see a ***hut in a green pasture***, denotes prosperity, but fluctuating happiness. ◎

Houses and Hotels

HOUSE
To dream of building a ***house***, you will make wise changes in your present affairs.

To dream that you own an ***elegant house***, denotes that you will soon leave your home for a better one, and fortune will be kind to you.

Old and dilapidated houses, denote failure in business or any effort, and declining health. ◎

INN
To dream of an ***inn***, denotes prosperity and pleasures, if the inn is commodious and well furnished.

To be at a ***dilapidated and ill-kept inn***, denotes poor success, mournful tasks, or unhappy journeys. ◎

HOTEL
To dream of living in a ***hotel***, denotes ease and profit.

To visit women in a hotel, means that your life will be rather on a dissolute order.

To dream of seeing a ***fine hotel***, indicates wealth and travel.

If you dream that you are the ***proprietor of a hotel***, you will earn all the fortune you will ever possess.

To ***work in a hotel***, you could find a more remunerative employment than what you have.

To dream of hunting a hotel, you will be baffled in your search for wealth and happiness. ◎

REGISTER
To dream that someone ***registers*** under his or her name at a hotel for you, denotes that you will undertake some work which will be finished by others.

If you register under an assumed name, you will engage in some guilty enterprise which will give you much uneasiness of mind. ◎

Pagodas and Pyramids

PAGODA
To see a ***pagoda*** in your dreams, denotes that you will soon go on a long-desired journey.

If a young woman finds herself in a pagoda with her sweetheart, many unforeseen events will transpire before her union is legalized. An empty one, warns her of separation from her lover. ◎

PYRAMID
To dream of ***pyramids***, denotes that many changes will come to you.

If you scale them, you will journey along before you find the gratification of desires. For a young woman, it prognosticates a husband who is in no sense congenial.

To dream that you are studying the ***mystery of the ancient pyramids***, denotes that you will develop a love for the mysteries of nature, and you will become learned and polished. ◎

Dreams of buildings can vary from the exotic pagoda *background* **to the established church** *opposite*.

BUILDINGS *see* **LAWNS** *page 56* ◆ **SHELTER** *see* **SLEEP** *page 274,* **GRASS** *page 56* ◆ **HOTEL** *see* **CHAMBERMAID** *page 205* ◆ **PYRAMID** *see* **OBELISK** *page 182,* **CLIMBING** *page 268,* **MYSTERY** *page 270*

Mansions and Palaces

MANSION
To dream that you are in a ***mansion*** where there is a haunted chamber, denotes sudden misfortune in the midst of contentment.

To dream of being in a mansion, indicates for you wealthy possessions.

To see a mansion from distant points, foretells future advancement. ◎

PALACE
Wandering through a ***palace*** and noting its grandeur, signifies that your prospects are growing brighter and you will assume new dignity.

To see and hear fine ladies and men dancing and conversing, denotes that you will engage in profitable and pleasing associations.

For a young woman of moderate means to dream that she is a participant in the entertainment, and of equal social standing, is a sign of her advancement through marriage, or the generosity of relatives.

This is often a very deceitful and misleading dream to the young woman of humble circumstances, as it is generally induced in such cases by the unhealthy daydreams of her idle, empty brain. She should strive, after this dream, to live by honest work, and restrain deceitful ambition by observing the fireside counsels of mother and friends. ◎

CASTLE
To dream of being in a ***castle***, you will be possessed of sufficient wealth to make life as you wish. You have prospects of being a great traveler.

To see an ***old and vine-covered castle***, you are likely to become romantic in your tastes, and care should be taken that you do not contract an undesirable marriage or engagement. Business is depressed after this dream.

To dream that you are ***leaving a castle***, you will be robbed of your possessions, or lose your lover or some dear one by death. ◎

Sacred Buildings

CHURCH
To dream of seeing a church ***in the distance, denotes disappointment in pleasures long anticipated.***

To enter one wrapt in gloom, you will participate in a funeral. Dull prospects of better times are portended. ✺

STEEPLE
To see a steeple ***rising from a church, is a harbinger of sickness and reverses.***

A broken one, points to death in your circle of friends.

To climb a steeple, ***foretells that you will have serious difficulties, but will surmount them.***

To fall from one, denotes losses in trade and ill health. ✺

ABBEY
To see an abbey ***in ruins, foretells that your hopes and schemes will fall into ignoble incompletion.***

To dream that a priest bars your entrance into an abbey, denotes that you will be saved from a ruinous state by enemies mistaking your embarrassment for progress.

For a young woman to get into an abbey, foretells her violent illness. If she converses with a priest in an abbey, she will incur the censure of true friends for indiscretion. ✺

CHURCH

CATHEDRAL
To dream of a vast cathedral ***with its dome rising into space, denotes that you will be possessed of an envious nature and unhappy longings for the unattainable, both mental and physical; but if you enter, you will be elevated in life, having for your companions the learned and wise.*** ✺

CHAPEL
To dream of a chapel, ***denotes dissension in social circles and unsettled business.***

To be in a chapel, denotes disappointment and change of business.

For young people to dream of entering a chapel, implies false loves and enemies. Unlucky unions may entangle them. ✺

CLOISTER
To dream of a cloister, ***omens dissatisfaction with present surroundings, and you will soon seek new environments. For a young woman to dream of a cloister, foretells that her life will be made unselfish by the chastening of sorrow.*** ✺

SYNAGOGUE
To dream of a synagogue, ***foretells that you have enemies powerfully barricading your entrance into fortune's realms. If you climb to the top on the outside, you will overcome oppositions and be successful.***

If you read the Hebrew inscription on a synagogue, you will meet disaster, but will eventually rebuild your fortunes with renewed splendor. ✺

MANSION *see* **GHOST** *page 275,* **CHAMBER** *page 206* ◆ **PALACE** *see* **DANCE** *page 168* ◆ **CASTLE** *see* **VINE** *page 61* ◆
CHURCH *see* **GLOOM** *page 257* ◆ **STEEPLE** *see* **BREAK** *page 265,* **CLIMBING** *page 268,* **FALL** *page 265* ◆
ABBEY *see* **RUINS** *page 255,* **PRIEST** *page 280* ◆ **SYNAGOGUE** *see* **INSCRIPTION** *page 232*

Bricks and Walls

WALLS

To dream that you find a ***wall*** obstructing your progress, you will surely succumb to ill-favored influences and lose important victories in your affairs.

To jump over it, you will overcome obstacles and win your desires. To force a breach in a wall, you will succeed in the attainment of your wishes by sheer tenacity of purpose.

To demolish one, you will overthrow your enemies. To build one, foretells that you will carefully lay plans and will solidify your fortune to the exclusion of failure or designing enemies.

For a young woman to walk ***on top of a wall***, shows that her future happiness will soon be made secure. For her to hide behind a wall, denotes that she will form connections that she will be ashamed to acknowledge. If she walks beside a ***base wall***, she will soon have to run the gamut of her attentions, and will likely be deserted at a precarious time. ◎

BRICK

Brick in a dream, indicates unsettled business and disagreements in love affairs. To make them, you will doubtless fail in your efforts to amass great wealth. ◎

Arches, Domes, and Vaults

ARCH

An ***arch*** in a dream, denotes your rise to distinction and the gaining of wealth by persistent effort. To pass under one, foretells that many will seek you who formerly ignored your position.

For a young woman to see a ***fallen arch***, denotes the destruction of her hopes, and she will be miserable in her new situation. ◎

VAULT

To dream of a ***vault***, denotes bereavement and other misfortune.

To see a vault for valuables, signifies that your fortune will surprise many, as your circumstances will appear to be meager.

To see the ***doors of a vault*** open, implies loss and treachery of people whom you trust. ◎

DOME

To dream that you are in the ***dome*** of a building, viewing a strange landscape, signifies a favorable change in your life. You will occupy honorable places among strangers.

To behold a dome from a distance, portends that you will never reach the height of your ambition, and if you are in love, the object of your desires will scorn your attention. ◎

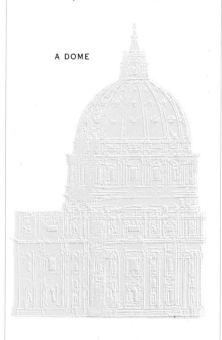

Dream structures may be as permanent as a dome *above* **or as temporary as a tent** *opposite*.

Up on the Roof

ROOF

To find yourself on a ***roof*** in a dream denotes unbounded success.

To become frightened and think that you are falling, signifies that, while you may advance, you will have no firm hold on your position.

To see a ***roof falling in***, you will be threatened with a sudden calamity.

To repair or ***build a roof***, you will rapidly increase your fortune.

To sleep on one, proclaims your security against enemies and false companions. Your health will be robust. ◎

THATCH

To dream that you ***thatch*** a roof with any quickly perishable material, denotes that sorrow and discomfort will surround you.

If you find that a roof which you have thatched with straw is leaking, there will be threatenings of danger; but by your rightly directed energy, they may be averted. ◎

CHIMNEY

To dream of seeing ***chimneys***, denotes that a very displeasing incident will occur in your life. Hasty intelligence of sickness will be borne you.

A ***tumble-down chimney***, denotes sorrow and death in your family.

To see one ***overgrown with ivy*** or with other vines, foretells that happiness will result from sorrow or loss of relatives.

To see a ***fire burning in a chimney***, denotes that much good is approaching you.

To hide in a ***chimney corner***, denotes that distress and doubt will assail you. Business will appear gloomy.

For a young woman to dream that she is going down a chimney, foretells that she will be guilty of some impropriety which will cause consternation among her associates. To ascend a chimney, shows that she will escape trouble which will be planned for her. ◎

WALLS *see* **JUMPING** *page 267* ◆ **VAULT** *see* **TREASURES** *page 238*, **DOOR** *page 213* ◆ **ROOF** *see* **FRIGHTENED** *page 253*, **FALL** *page 265* ◆ **THATCH** *see* **STRAW** *page 63*, **LEAKING** *page 212* ◆ **CHIMNEY** *see* **IVY** *page 66*, **VINE** *page 61*, **FIRE** *page 80*

Porches and Balconies

PORCH

To dream of a ***porch***, denotes that you will engage in new undertakings, and the future will be full of uncertainties.

If a young woman dreams that she is with her lover on a porch, it implies her doubts of someone's intentions.

To dream that you ***build a porch***, you will assume new duties. ◎

VERANDA

To dream of being on a ***veranda***, denotes that you are to be successful in some affair which is giving you anxiety.

For a young woman to be with her lover on a veranda, denotes her early and happy marriage.

To see an ***old veranda***, denotes the decline of hopes, and disappointment in business and love. ◎

BALCONY

For lovers to dream of making sad adieus on a ***balcony***, long and perhaps final separation may follow. A balcony also denotes unpleasant news of absent friends. ◎

CANOPY

To dream of a ***canopy*** or of being beneath one, denotes that false friends are influencing you to undesirable ways of securing gain. You will do well to protect those in your care. ◎

Fences and Gates

PALISADE

To dream of the ***palisades***, denotes that you will alter well-formed plans to please strangers, and by so doing, you will impair your own interests. ◎

RAILING

To dream of seeing ***railings***, denotes that some person is trying to obstruct your pathway in love or business.

To dream of holding on to a railing, foretells that some desperate chance will be taken by you to obtain some object upon which you have set your heart. It may be of love, or of a more material form. ◎

FENCE

To dream of climbing to the top of a ***fence***, denotes that success will crown your efforts.

To ***fall from a fence***, signifies that you will undertake a project for which you are incapable, and you will see your efforts come to naught.

To be ***seated on a fence*** with others, and have it fall under you, denotes an accident in which some person will be badly injured.

To dream that you ***climb through a fence***, signifies that you will use means not altogether legitimate to reach your desires.

To throw the fence down and walk to the other side, indicates that you will, by enterprise and energy, overcome the stubbornest barriers between you and success.

To see stock jumping a fence, if into your enclosure, you will receive aid from unexpected sources; if out of your lot, loss in trade and other affairs may follow.

To dream of ***building a fence***, denotes that you are, by economy and industry, laying a foundation for future wealth.

For a young woman, this dream denotes success in love affairs; or the reverse, if she dreams of the fence falling, or that she falls from it. ◎

GATE

To dream of seeing or passing through a ***gate***, foretells that alarming tidings will reach you soon of the absent. Business affairs are encouraging.

To see a ***closed gate***, inability to overcome present difficulties is predicted. To lock one, denotes successful enterprises and well-chosen friends. A broken one, signifies failure and discordant surroundings.

To be troubled to get through one, or open it, denotes that your most engrossing labors will fail to be remunerative or satisfactory.

To dream that you swing on one, foretells that you will engage in idle and dissolute pleasures. ◎

Temporary Shelter

CAMP

To dream of ***camping*** in the open air, you may expect a change in your affairs; also prepare to make a long and wearisome journey.

If you see a ***camping settlement***, many of your companions will remove to new estates and your own prospects will appear gloomy.

For a young woman to dream that she is in a camp, denotes that her lover will have trouble in getting her to name a day for their wedding, and that he will prove a kind husband. If in a military camp, she will marry the first time she has a chance.

A married woman after dreaming of being in a ***soldier's camp***, is in danger of having her husband's name sullied, and divorce courts may be her destiny. ◎

TENT

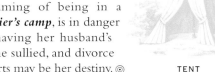

To dream of being in a ***tent***, foretells a change in your affairs.

To see a ***number of tents***, denotes journeys with unpleasant companions.

If the ***tents are torn*** or otherwise dilapidated, there will be trouble for you. ◎

TENT

BALCONY *see* **ADIEU** *page 258* ◆ **FENCE** *see* **CLIMBING** *page 268,* **FALL** *page 265,* **CATTLE** *page 37* ◆ **CAMP** *see* **COUNTRY** *page 89,* **SOLDIERS** *page 262*

Stairs, Ladders, and Other Ways of Going Up

TOWER
To dream of seeing a ***tower***, denotes that you will aspire to high elevations.

If you climb one, you will succeed in your wishes; but if the tower crumbles as you descend, you will be disappointed in your hopes. ◎

STAIRS
To dream of passing up ***stairs***, foretells good fortune and much happiness.

If you ***fall down stairs***, you will be the object of hatred and envy.

To walk down, you will be unlucky in your affairs, and your lovemaking will be unfavorable.

To see ***broad, handsome stairs***, foretells approaching riches and honor.

To see others ***going down stairs***, denotes that unpleasant conditions will take the place of pleasure.

To sit on ***stair steps***, denotes a gradual rise in fortune and delight. ◎

STEPS
To dream that you ascend ***steps***, denotes that fair prospects will relieve former anxiety.

To descend them, you may look for misfortune.

To fall down them, you are threatened with unexpected failure in your affairs. ◎

LADDER
If you dream of a ***ladder*** being raised for you to ascend to some height, your energetic and nervy qualification will raise you into prominence in business affairs.

To ***ascend a ladder***, means prosperity and unstinted happiness.

To fall from one, denotes despondency and unsuccessful transactions to the tradesman, and blasted crops to the farmer.

To see a ***broken ladder***, betokens failure in every instance.

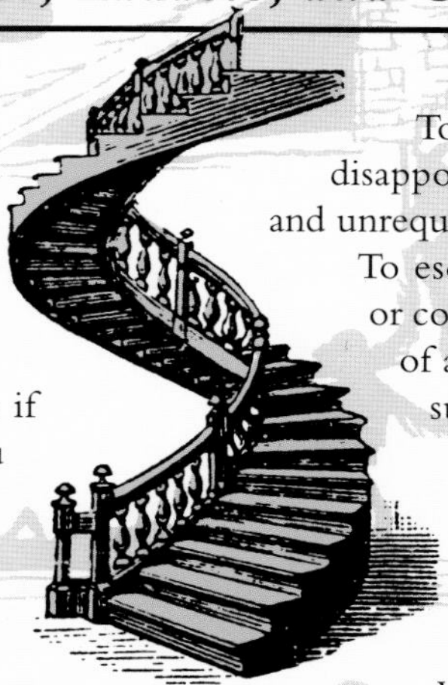

STAIRS

To ***descend a ladder***, is disappointment in business and unrequited desires.

To escape from captivity or confinement by means of a ladder, you will be successful, though many perilous paths may intervene.

To grow dizzy as you ascend a ladder, denotes that you will not wear new honors serenely. You are likely to become haughty and domineering in your newly acquired position. ◎

ESCALATOR
To dream of riding up an ***escalator***, denotes progress in your professional life, albeit a slow one. To dream of riding ***down an escalator***, means that you are not making any advancement in your career.

If you see one not in working condition and are forced to walk up it as if it were stairs, you will fail to receive a promotion. ◎

ELEVATOR
To dream of ascending in an ***elevator***, denotes that you will swiftly rise to a position and wealth; but if you descend in one, your misfortunes will crush and discourage you.

If you see one go down and think you are left, you will narrowly escape disappointment in some undertaking. To see one standing, foretells threatened danger.

To dream of being ***trapped in an elevator***, denotes that a frustrating situation will soon occur. ◎

Piers, Bridges, and Embankments

PIER
To stand upon a ***pier*** in your dream, denotes that you will be brave in your battle for recognition in prosperity's realm, and that you will be admitted to the highest posts of honor.

If you strive to reach a pier and fail, you will lose the distinction you most coveted. ◎

BRIDGE
To see a long ***bridge*** dilapidated, and mysteriously winding into darkness, profound melancholy over the loss of dearest possessions and dismal situations will fall upon you. To the young and those in love, it denotes disappointment in the heart's fondest hopes, as the loved one will fall below your ideal.

To dream that you ***cross a bridge*** safely, portends a final surmounting of difficulties, though the means seem hardly safe to use. Any obstacle or delay denotes disaster.

To see a ***bridge give way*** before you, beware of treachery and false admirers. Affluence comes with clear waters. Sorrowful returns of best efforts are experienced after looking upon or coming in contact with muddy or turbid water in dreams. ◎

EMBANKMENT
To dream that you drive along an ***embankment***, foretells that you will be threatened with trouble and unhappiness. If you continue your drive without unpleasant incidents arising, you will succeed in turning these forebodings to useful account in your advancement.

To dream that you ***ride on horseback along an embankment***, denotes that you will fearlessly meet and overcome all obstacles in your way to wealth and happiness.

To walk along one, you will have a weary struggle for elevation, but will finally reap a successful reward. ◎

TOWER see CLIMBING page 268 ◆ STAIRS see FALL page 265 ◆ STEPS see ASCEND page 268, FALL page 265 ◆
LADDER see ASCEND page 268, FALL page 265, BREAK page 265 ◆ ELEVATOR see ASCEND page 268 ◆
PIER see WATER page 78 ◆ BRIDGE see RIVER page 79 ◆ EMBANKMENT see RIDE page 33

Trenches

DIGGING
To dream of ***digging***, denotes that you will never be in want, but life will be an uphill affair.

To ***dig a hole*** and find any glittering substance, denotes a favorable turn in fortune; but to dig and open up a vast area of hollow mist, you will be harassed with real misfortunes and filled with gloomy forebodings.

Water filling the hole that you dig, denotes that in spite of your most strenuous efforts, things will not bend to your will. ◎

DITCH-DIGGING MACHINE
To dream of a ***ditch-digging machine***, denotes that a past, hidden secret will soon come to light. You must be prepared to confront and deal with this news. ◎

DITCH
To dream of falling in a ***ditch***, denotes degradation and personal loss; but if you jump over it, you will live down any suspicion of wrongdoing. ◎

TRENCHES
To see ***trenches*** in dreams, warns you of distant treachery. You will sustain loss if not careful in undertaking new enterprises or associating with strangers.

To see ***filled trenches***, denotes that many anxieties are gathering. ◎

Heights and Depths

CAVERN OR CAVE
To dream of seeing a ***cavern*** yawning in the weird moonlight before you, foretells that many perplexities will assail you, and advancement will be doubtful because of adversaries. Work and health are threatened.

To be in a ***cave***, foreshadows change. You will be estranged from those dear to you.

For a young woman to walk in a cave with her lover or friend, denotes that she will fall in love with a villain and will suffer the loss of true friends. ◎

GROTTO
To see a ***grotto*** in your dreams, is a sign of incomplete and inconstant friendships. Change from comfortable and simple plenty will make showy poverty unbearable. ◎

PRECIPICE
To dream of standing over a yawning ***precipice***, portends the threatenings of misfortune and calamities.

To ***fall over a precipice***, denotes that you will be engulfed in disaster. ◎

ABYSS
To dream of looking into an ***abyss***, means that you will be confronted by threats of seizure of property, and that there will be quarrels and reproaches of a personal nature which will unfit you to meet the problems of life.

For a woman to be looking into an abyss, foretells that she will burden herself with unwelcome cares. If she falls into it, her disappointment will be complete; but if she crosses or avoids it, she will reinstate herself. ◎

PIT
If you are looking into a ***deep pit*** in your dream, you will run silly risks in business ventures and will draw uneasiness about your wooing.

To ***fall into a pit***, denotes calamity and deep sorrow. To wake as you begin to fall into the pit, brings you out of distress in fairly good shape.

To dream that you are descending into one, signifies that you will knowingly risk health and fortune for greater success. ◎

Subterrania

TUNNEL
To dream of going through a ***tunnel***, is bad for business and love.

To see a ***train coming toward*** you while in a tunnel, foretells ill health and a change in occupation.

To pass through a ***tunnel in a car***, denotes unsatisfactory business, and much unpleasant travel.

To see a ***tunnel caving in***, portends failure and malignant enemies.

To look into one, denotes that you will face a desperate issue. ◎

UNDERGROUND
To dream of being in an ***underground*** habitation, you are in danger of losing reputation and fortune.

An ***underground railway***, foretells that you will engage in some peculiar speculation which will contribute to your distress and anxiety. ◎

Well

WELL
To dream that you are employed in a ***well***, foretells that you will succumb to adversity through your misapplied energies. You will let strange elements direct your course.

To ***fall into a well***, signifies that despair will possess you. For one to cave in, promises that enemies' schemes will overthrow your own.

To see an ***empty well***, denotes that you will be robbed if you allow strangers to share your confidence.

To see one with a pump in it, shows that you will have opportunities to advance your prospects.

To dream of an ***artesian well***, foretells that your splendid resources will gain your admittance into the realms of knowledge and pleasure.

To draw ***water from a well***, denotes the fulfillment of ardent desires. If the water is impure, there will be unpleasantness. ◎

Staircases *opposite top* **are potent dream symbols of life's ups and downs.**

DIGGING *see* **GOLD** *page 71,* **WATER** *page 78* ◆ **DITCH** *see* **FALL** *page 265* ◆ **CAVERN OR CAVE** *see* **MOON** *page 84* ◆ **PRECIPICE** *see* **FALL** *page 265* ◆ **PIT** *see* **FALL** *page 265* ◆ **TUNNEL** *see* **TRAIN** *page 225,* **CAR** *page 224* ◆ **UNDERGROUND** *see* **SUBWAY** *page 225,* **RAILROAD** *page 225* ◆ **WELL** *see* **WATER** *page 78,* **FALL** *page 265*

Work and Industry

To find yourself at work in your dreams may not at first glance offer much respite from the daily grind, but work dreams should be carefully interpreted for their significance in your own field of endeavor. This section looks at dreams concerning industry, domestic service, professional crafts, and office work as well as dreams about tools and implements.

The World of Work

EMPLOYMENT

This is not an auspicious dream. It implies depression in business circles and loss of employment to wage earners. It also denotes bodily illness.

To dream of being ***out of work***, denotes that you will have no fear, as you are always sought out for your conscientious fulfillment of contracts, which makes you a desired help.

Giving ***employment to others***, indicates loss for yourself. All dreams of this nature may be interpreted as the above. ◎

INDUSTRY

WORKSHOP

To see ***workshops*** in your dreams, foretells that you will use extraordinary schemes to undermine your enemies. ◎

WORK

To dream that you are hard at ***work***, denotes that you will win merited success by concentration of energy.

To see others at work, denotes that hopeful conditions will surround you.

To ***look for work***, means that you will be benefited by some unaccountable occurrence. ◎

COMPLETION

To dream of ***completing*** a task or piece of work, denotes that you will have acquired a competency early in life, and that you can spend your days as you like and wherever you please.

MEN AT WORK

To dream of ***completing a journey***, you will have the means to make one whenever you like. ◎

EMPLOYEE

To see one of your ***employees***, denotes crosses and disturbances if he assumes a disagreeable or offensive attitude. If he is pleasant and has communications of interest, you will find no cause for evil or embarrassing conditions upon waking. ◎

LABOR

To dream that you watch domestic animals ***laboring*** under heavy burdens, denotes that you will be prosperous, but unjust to your servants or those employed by you.

To see ***men toiling***, signifies profitable work and robust health. To ***labor yourself***, denotes a favorable outlook for any new enterprise, and bountiful crops if the dreamer is interested in farming. ◎

INDUSTRY

To dream that you are ***industrious***, denotes that you will be unusually active in planning and working out ideas to further your interests, and that you will be successful in your undertakings.

For a lover to dream of being ***industriously at work***, shows that he will succeed in business, and that his companion will advance his position.

To see others busy, is favorable to the dreamer. ◎

MANUFACTORY

To dream of a large ***manufactory***, denotes unusual activity in business circles. ◎

EMPLOYMENT *see* **WAGES** *page 241*, **INCOME** *page 241* ◆ **COMPLETION** *see* **JOURNEY** *page 221* ◆ **LABOR** *see* **BURDEN** *page 38* ◆ **MANUFACTORY** *see* **MACHINERY** *page 198*

Masters and Servants

MASON
To dream that you see a ***mason*** plying his trade, denotes a rise in your circumstances, and a more congenial social atmosphere will surround you.

If you dream of seeing a band of the ***Order of Masons*** in full regalia, it denotes that you will have others besides yourself to protect and keep from the evils of life. ◎

SERVANT
To dream of a ***servant***, is a sign that you will be fortunate, despite gloomy appearances. Anger is likely to precipitate you into useless worries and quarrels.

To discharge one, foretells regrets and losses.

To quarrel with one in your dream, indicates that you will, upon waking, have real cause for censuring someone who is derelict in duty.

To be robbed by one, shows that you have someone near you who does not respect the laws of ownership. ◎

MASTER
To dream that you have a ***master***, is a sign of incompetency on your part to command others, and you will do better work under the leadership of some strong-willed person.

If you ***are a master***, and command many people under you, you will excel in judgement in the fine points of life, and will hold high positions and possess much wealth. ◎

APPRENTICE
To dream that you serve as an ***apprentice***, foretells that you will have a struggle to win a place among your companions. ◎

THE SERVANT

Journeymen and Janitors

JOURNEYMAN
To dream of a ***journeyman***, denotes that you are soon to lose money by useless travels. For a woman, this dream brings pleasant trips, though unexpected ones. ◎

JANITOR
To dream of a ***janitor*** denotes bad management and disobedient children. Unworthy servants will annoy you.

If you ***look for a janitor*** and fail to find him, petty annoyances will disturb your otherwise placid existence. If you find him, you will have pleasant associations with strangers, and your affairs will have no hindrances. ◎

The world of work may show itself in your dreams through laboring men *opposite*, **industry** *opposite top*, **domestic servants** *above*, **or mining** *top*.

Working in a Coalmine

MINERS

COLLIERY OR COAL MINE
To dream of being in a coal mine ***or*** colliery ***and seeing miners, denotes that some evil will assert its power for your downfall; but if you dream of holding a share in a coal mine, it denotes your safe investment in some deal.***

For a young woman to dream of mining coal, foreshows that she will become the wife of a real-estate dealer or dentist. ❁

MINING
To see mining ***in your dreams, denotes that an enemy is seeking your ruin by bringing up past immoralities in your life. You will be likely to make unpleasant journeys, if you stand near the mine.***

If you dream of hunting for mines, you will engage in worthless pursuits. ❁

MINE
To dream of being in a mine, ***denotes failure in affairs.***

To own a mine, ***denotes future wealth.*** ❁

MASON *see* **STONES** *page 68*, **STONE MASON** *page 68*, **SECRET ORDER** *page 271* ◆ **SERVANT** *see* **STEALING** *page 246* ◆
COLLIERY OR COAL MINE *see* **COALS** *page 70* ◆ **MINING** *see* **MINERAL** *page 68*, **ROCKS** *page 68*

The Jolly Miller

MILL

To dream of a mill, *indicates thrift and fortunate undertakings.*

To see a dilapidated mill, *denotes sickness and ill fortune.* ❁

MILLER

To see a miller *in your dreams, signifies that your surroundings will grow more hopeful. For a woman to dream of a miller failing in an attempt to start his mill, foretells that she will be disappointed in her lover's wealth, as she will think him in comfortable circumstances.* ❁

MILLDAM

To dream that you see clear water pouring over a milldam, *foretells pleasant enterprises, of either a business or social nature. If the water is muddy or impure, you will meet with losses, and troubles will arise where pleasure was anticipated.*

If the dam is dry, your business will assume shrunken proportions. ❁

WINDMILL

To see a windmill *in operation in your dreams, foretells abundant accumulation of fortune and marked contentment.*

To see one broken or idle, signifies adversity coming unawares. ❁

MILL

Forging Links

BLACKSMITH AT THE ANVIL

BLACKSMITH

To see a ***blacksmith*** in a dream, means that laborious undertakings will soon work to your advantage. ◎

BELLOWS

Working a ***bellows***, denotes a struggle, but a final triumph over poverty and fate by energy and perseverance.

To dream of seeing a bellows, means that distant friends are longing to see you.

To hear one, occult knowledge will be obtained by the help of powerful means.

One fallen into disuse, portends that you have wasted energies under misguiding impulses. ◎

THE COPPERSMITH

ANVIL

To see a hot iron with sparks flying, is significant of a pleasing work; to the farmer, an abundant crop; favorable indeed to women. Cold or small favors may be expected from those in power. The means of success is in your power, but in order to obtain it, you will have to labor under difficulty.

If in your dream, the ***anvil*** is broken, it foretells that you have, through your own neglect, thrown away promising opportunities that cannot be recalled. ◎

FURNACE

To dream of a ***furnace***, foretells good luck if it is running.

If out of repair, you will have trouble with children or hired help.

To fall into one, portends that some enemy will overpower you in a business struggle. ◎

COPPERSMITH

To dream of a ***coppersmith***, denotes small returns for labor, but withal contentment. ◎

MILL *see* WATER *page 78* ◆ MILLDAM *see* WATERFALL *page 78* ◆ WINDMILL *see* WIND *page 75*, BREAK *page 265* ◆ BLACKSMITH *see* HORSE DREAMS *page 34*, HORSESHOE *page 33* ◆ ANVIL *see* IRON *page 72*, BREAK *page 265* ◆ FURNACE *see* COALS *page 70*, ASHES *page 70*, FALL *page 265* ◆ COPPERSMITH *see* COPPER *page 71*

The Carpenter and his Tools

CARPENTER
To see ***carpenters*** at their labor, foretells that you will engage in honest endeavors to raise your fortune, to the exclusion of selfish pastime or so-called recreation. ◎

CARPENTER'S PLANE
To dream that you use a ***plane***, denotes that your liberality and successful efforts will be highly commended.

To see ***carpenters using their planes***, denotes that you will progress smoothly in your undertakings.

To dream of seeing planes, denotes congeniality and even success. A love of the real, and not the false, is portended by this dream. ◎

SAW
To dream that you use a ***handsaw***, indicates an energetic and busy time, and cheerful home life.

To see ***big saws*** in machinery, foretells that you will superintend a big enterprise, and the same will yield fair returns. For a woman, this dream denotes that she will be esteemed, and her counsels will be heeded.

To dream of ***rusty or broken saws***, denotes failure and accidents.

To ***lose a saw***, you will engage in affairs which will culminate in disaster.

To hear the ***buzz of a saw***, indicates thrift and prosperity.

To find a ***rusty saw***, denotes that you will probably restore your fortune.

To ***carry a saw*** on your back, foretells that you will carry large but profitable responsibilities. ◎

SAWDUST
To dream of ***sawdust***, signifies that grievous mistakes will cause you distress and quarreling in your home. ◎

PLANK
For a young woman to dream that she is walking across muddy water on a rotten ***plank***, denotes that she will feel keenly the indifference shown her by one she loves, or other troubles may arise or her defense of honor may be in danger of collapse. ◎

PALLET
To dream of a ***pallet***, denotes that you will suffer temporary uneasiness over your love affairs. For a young woman, it is a sign of jealous rival. ◎

AUGER
To see ***augers*** in your dreams, is a forecast of labor and toil. ◎

Furniture Making

CHAIR MAKER
To dream of seeing a ***chair maker***, denotes that worry from apparently pleasant labor will confront you. ◎

VARNISHING
To dream of ***varnishing*** anything, denotes that you will seek to win distinction by fraudulent means.

To see others varnishing, foretells that you are threatened with danger from the endeavor of friends to add to their own possessions. ◎

VENEER
To dream that you are ***veneering***, denotes that you will systematically deceive your friends. Your speculations will be of a misleading nature. ◎

STRIPPING FLOORBOARDS

Hardworking dreams may show you the world of the miller *opposite left*, **the blacksmith** *opposite top*, **the coppersmith** *opposite center* **or the carpenter** *right*.

CARPENTER *see* **HAMMER** *page 199* ◆ **SAW** *see* **MACHINERY** *page 198,* **RUST** *page 255,* **BREAK** *page 265* ◆ **PLANK** *see* **WATER** *page 78* ◆ **CHAIR MAKER** *see* **CHAIR** *page 214*

Heavy Engineering

Technology

MACHINERY

To dream of ***machinery***, denotes that you will undertake some project which will give great anxiety, but which will finally result in good for you.

To see ***old machinery***, foretells that enemies will overcome you in your striving to build up your fortune.

To become ***entangled in machinery***, foretells loss in your business, and much unhappiness will follow. Loss from bad deals generally follows this dream. ◎

ENGINE

To dream of an ***engine***, denotes that you will encounter grave difficulties and journeys, but you will have substantial friends to uphold you.

Disabled engines stand for misfortune and loss of relatives. ◎

ENGINEER

To see an ***engineer***, forebodes weary journeys but joyful reunions. ◎

MECHANIC

To dream of a ***mechanic***, denotes a change in your dwelling place and a more active business. Advancement in wages usually follows after seeing mechanics at work on machinery. ◎

DERRICK

Derricks seen in a dream, indicate strife and obstruction in your way to success. ◎

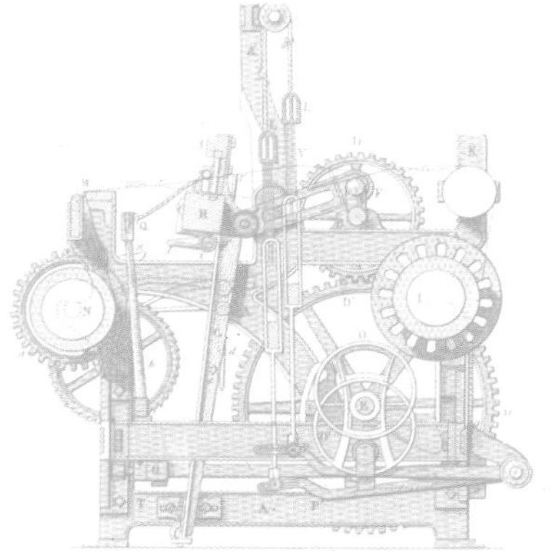

MACHINERY

DYNAMO

To dream of a ***dynamo***, omens successful enterprises if attention is shown to details of business. One out of repair, shows that you are nearing enemies who will involve you in trouble. ◎

STORAGE BATTERY

If you dream of a ***storage battery***, opportune speculations will return you handsome gains. ◎

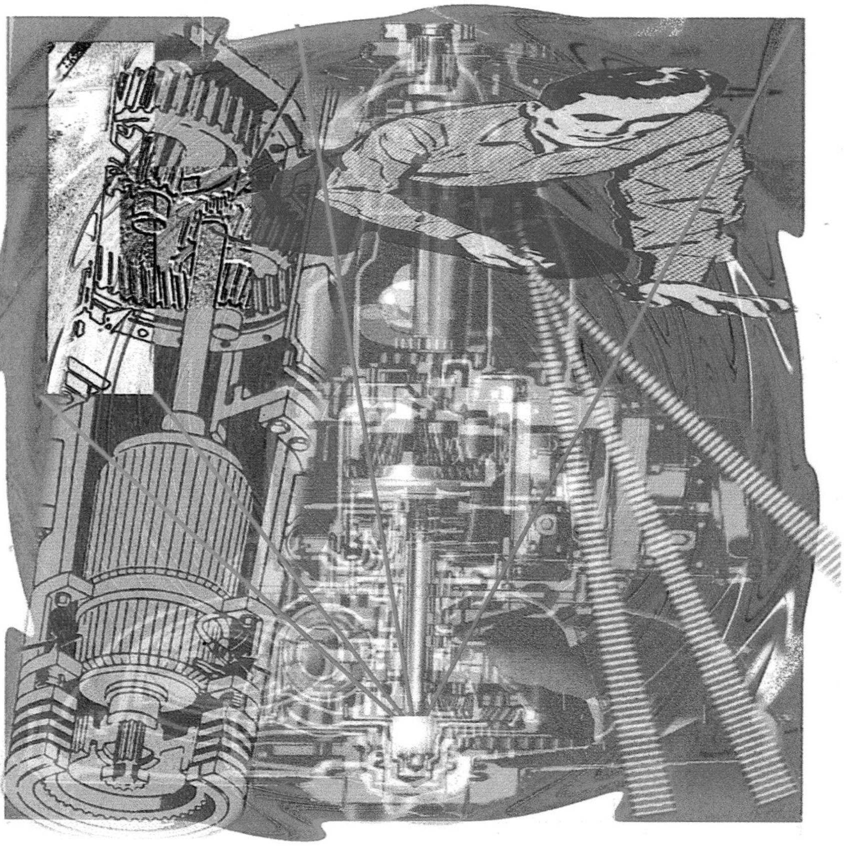

LASER

PUMP

To see a ***pump*** in a dream, denotes that energy and faithfulness to business will produce desired riches. Good health is usually betokened by this dream.

To see a ***broken pump***, signifies that the means of advancing in life will be absorbed by family cares. To the married and the unmarried, it intimates blasted energies.

If you ***work a pump***, your life will be filled with pleasure and profitable undertakings. ◎

LASER

To dream about ***lasers***, means that you are focusing your attentions on superficial problems. This dream is a warning to become more aware of greater concerns or else disaster will ensue. ◎

Heavy machinery *left* **may thunder through your dreams, or the high tech power of lasers** *above* **may bedazzle you. More specifically, you may dream about the right tools for the job, such as the ax** *opposite top*, **the shovel** *opposite center*, **and the tweezers** *opposite bottom*.

MACHINERY *see* MANUFACTORY *page 194*, DANGER *page 266* ◆ ENGINE *see* CARS *page 224*, LOCOMOTIVE *page 225* ◆ PUMP *see* WATER *page 78*, BREAK *page 265*

USING AN AX

Many familiar tools and implements that we see and use in daily life take on a new significance when they feature in our dreams. Mallets, pincers, and tacks take on a glamor and symbolism of their own in the dream world. Knives appear just as unnervingly two-edged – useful yet menacing – in dreams as they are in reality.

Hammers and Mallets

HAMMER

To dream of seeing a ***hammer***, denotes that you will have some discouraging obstacles to overcome in order to firmly establish your fortune. ◎

MALLET

To dream of a ***mallet***, denotes that you will meet unkind treatment from friends on account of your ill health. Disorder in the home is indicated. ◎

Useful Tools

IMPLEMENTS

To dream of ***implements***, denotes unsatisfactory means of accomplishing some work. If the implements are broken, you will be threatened with death or serious illness of relatives or friends, or failure in business. ◎

RAMROD

To dream of a ***ramrod*** denotes unfortunate adventures. You will have cause for grief.

For a young woman to see one bent or broken, foretells that a dear friend or lover will fail her. ◎

SHOVEL

SHOVEL

To see a ***shovel*** in a dream, signifies that laborious but withal pleasant work will be undertaken. A broken or old one, implies frustration of hopes. ◎

HOOK

To dream of a ***hook***, foretells that unhappy obligations will be assumed by you. ◎

PINCERS

To dream of feeling ***pincers*** on your flesh, denotes that you will be burdened with exasperating cares. Any dream of pincers signifies unfortunate incidents. ◎

TWEEZERS

To see ***tweezers*** in a dream, denotes that uncomfortable situations will fill you with discontent, and your companions will abuse you. ◎

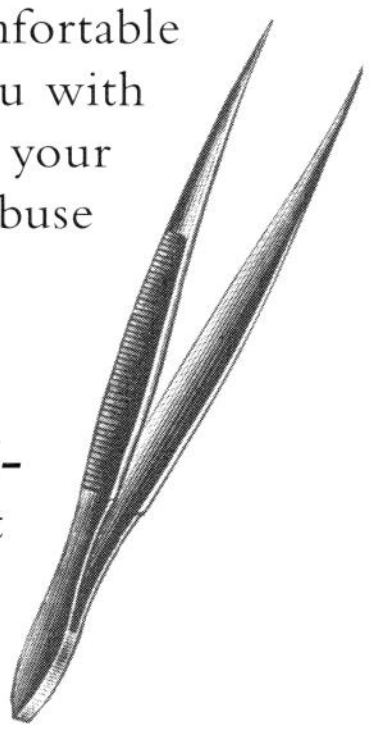

TWEEZERS

YARDSTICK

To dream of a ***yardstick***, foretells that much anxiety will possess you, though your affairs assume unusual activity. ◎

Edged Tools

PICKAX

To dream of a pickax, ***denotes that a relentless enemy is working to overthrow you socially. A broken one, implies disaster to all your interests.*** ◎

AX

Seeing an ax ***in a dream, foretells that what enjoyment you may have will depend on your struggles and energy.***

To see others using an ax, ***foretells that your friends will be energetic and lively, making existence a pleasure when near them.***

For a young woman to see one, portends that her lover will be worthy, but not possessed with much wealth.

A broken or rusty ax, ***indicates illness and loss of money and property.*** ◎

HATCHET

A hatchet ***seen in a dream, denotes that wanton wastefulness will expose you to the evil designs of envious persons.***

If it is rusty or broken, you will have grief over wayward people. ◎

SHEARS

To see shears ***in your dreams, denotes that you will become miserly and disagreeable in your dealings.***

To see them broken, you will lose friends and standing by your eccentric demeanor. ◎

HAMMER *see* **CARPENTER** *page 197*, **NAILS** *page 200* ◆ **MALLET** *see* **CARPENTER** *page 197* ◆ **SHOVEL** *see* **DIGGING** *page 193* ◆ **TWEEZERS** *see* **FINGERS** *page 97* ◆ **AX** *see* **TIMBER** *page 67*, **WOODPILE** *page 67*, **BREAK** *page 265*, **RUST** *page 255* ◆ **HATCHET** *see* **RUST** *page 255*, **BREAK** *page 265* ◆ **SHEARS** *see* **BREAK** *page 265*

Nails and Screws

SCREW

To dream of seeing ***screws***, denotes that tedious tasks must be performed, and peevishness in companions must be combated. It also denotes that you must be economical and painstaking. ◎

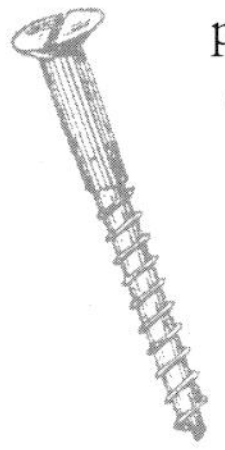

SCREW

TACKS

To dream of ***tacks***, means to you many vexations and quarrels.

For a woman to drive one, foretells that she will master unpleasant rivalry.

If she mashes her finger while driving it, she will be distressed over unpleasant tasks. ◎

NAILS

To see ***nails*** in your dreams, indicates much toil and small recompenses.

To ***deal in nails***, shows that you will engage in honorable work, even if it be lowly.

To see rusty or ***broken nails***, indicates sickness and failure in business. ◎

BOLTS

To dream of ***bolts***, signifies that formidable obstacles will oppose your progress.

If the ***bolts are old or broken*** in the dream, your expectations will be eclipsed by failures. ◎

THE KNIFE GRINDER

Knives and Sharpeners

KNIFE

To dream of a ***knife*** is bad for the dreamer, as it portends separation and quarrels, and losses in affairs of a business character.

To see ***rusty knives***, means dissatisfaction, complaints of those in the home, and separation of lovers.

Sharp knives highly polished, denotes worry. Foes are ever surrounding you.

Broken knives, denote defeat whatever the pursuit, whether in love or business.

To dream that you are wounded with a knife, foretells domestic troubles, in which disobedient children will figure largely. To the unmarried, it denotes that disgrace may follow.

To dream that you ***stab another with a knife***, denotes baseness of character, and you should strive to cultivate a higher sense of right. ◎

KNIFE GRINDER

To dream of a ***knife grinder***, foretells that unwarrantable liberties will be taken with your possessions. For a woman, this omens unhappy unions and much drudgery. ◎

WHETSTONE

To dream of a ***whetstone***, is significant that sharp worries and close attention are needed in your affairs, if you are to avoid difficulties. You are likely to be forced into an uncomfortable journey. ◎

GRINDSTONE

For a person to dream of turning a ***grindstone***, denotes that his dream is prophetic of a life of energy and well-directed efforts bringing handsome competency.

If you are sharpening tools, you will be blessed with a worthy helpmate.

To ***deal in grindstones***, is significant of small but honest gain. ◎

Wires and Magnets

WIRE

To dream of ***wire***, denotes that you will make frequent but short journeys which will be to your disparagement.

Old or rusty wire, signifies that you will be possessed of a bad temper, which will give troubles to your kindred.

To see a ***wire fence*** in your dreams, foretells that you will be cheated in some trade you have in view. ◎

MAGNET

To dream of a ***magnet***, denotes that evil influences will draw you from the path of honor. A woman is probably luring you to ruin.

To a woman, this dream foretells that protection and wealth will be showered upon her. ◎

MAGNET

TACKS *see* **HAMMER** *page 199* ◆ **NAILS** *see* **HAMMER** *page 199*, **RUST** *page 255*, **BREAK** *page 265* ◆
BOLTS *see* **BREAK** *page 265* ◆ **KNIFE** *see* **RUST** *page 255*, **BREAK** *page 265*, **MURDER** *page 247* ◆
WHETSTONE, GRINDSTONE *see* **STONES** *page 68* ◆ **WIRE** *see* **FENCE** *page 191*

Dreaming of the office and its furniture and machinery may make for a dull night's sleeping, but notice should be taken of such seemingly mundane dream subjects; their significance is often much larger than their familiarity at first indicates.

Office Furniture

DESK
To be using a ***desk*** in a dream, denotes that unforeseen ill luck will rise before you.

To see money on your desk, brings you unexpected extrication from private difficulties. ◎

DESK WORK

FILE
To dream that you see a ***file***, signifies that you will transact some business which will prove unsatisfactory in the extreme.

To see files, and to store away bills and other important papers, foretells animated discussions over subjects which bear relation to significant affairs, and which will cause you much unrest and disquiet. Unfavorable predictions for the future are also implied in this dream. ◎

COMPUTER
To see yourself working on a ***computer***, indicates a change in working conditions involving greater responsibility.

To dream of ***not knowing how to use a computer***, means that you will soon be given a project which feels overwhelming. ◎

COPY MACHINE

Typing and Typewriters

TYPE
To see ***type*** in a dream, portends unpleasant transactions with friends.

For a woman to ***clean type***, foretells that she will make fortunate speculations, bringing love and fortune. ◎

TYPEWRITER
To dream of using a ***typewriter***, denotes you will soon be corresponding with a nearly forgotten friend.

In the blue collar dream world you may see the knife grinder *opposite top* **and useful items such as the screw** *opposite top left* **and the magnet** *opposite bottom*. **White collar dreamers may take their work home to dream of desk work** *above*, **the typewriter** *right*, **or the computer** *far right*.

To dream of hearing the tap-tap-tapping noise of ***typewriter keys***, denotes that an urgent situation must be dealt with. This situation is one that you have procrastinated on for too long. ◎

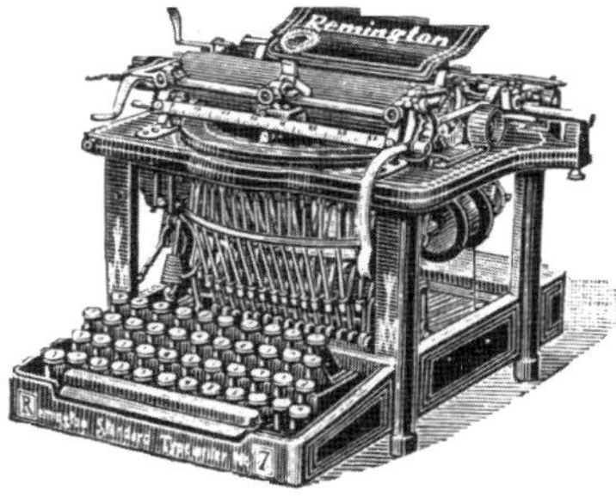

TYPEWRITER

Copy Machinery

COPY MACHINE
To dream of a ***copy machine***, means that someone is trying to steal something from you. The dream is a warning to be more careful in guarding your property or your ideas.

To dream of ***copying something*** with such a machine, indicates uncertainty over how you resolved a situation. ◎

COPYING
To dream of ***copying***, denotes unfavorable workings of well-tried plans.

For a young woman to dream that she is ***copying a letter***, denotes that she will be prejudiced into error by her love for a certain class of people. ◎

DESK *see* **TELEPHONE** *page 237*, **MONEY** *page 239* ◆ **COMPUTER** *see* **FAX MACHINE** *page 237* ◆ **TYPE** *see* **PRINTER** *page 234* ◆ **TYPEWRITER** *see* **WRITING** *page 232*, **TEXT** *page 233* ◆ **COPYING** *see* **LETTER** *page 236*

Trade and Commerce

Dreams of the marketplace brings the competitive business spirit of the waking world into the usually unworldy realm of sleep. This section covers dreams of bustling shops and stores, of the double entry-complexity of accounting ledgers, or honourable business practice and its downside, fraud and cheating.

Buying and Selling

TRADE
To dream of ***trading***, denotes fair success in your enterprise. If you fail in trade, trouble and annoyances will overtake you. ◎

ERRANDS
To go on ***errands*** in your dreams, means congenial associations and mutual agreement in the home circle.

For a young woman to send some person on an errand, denotes that she will lose her lover by her indifference to meet his wishes. ◎

PURCHASES
To dream of ***purchases***, usually means that you will see profit and advancement with pleasure. ◎

AUCTION
To dream of an ***auction*** in a general way, is good. If you hear the auctioneer crying his sales, it means bright prospects and fair treatment from business ventures.

To dream of ***buying at an auction***, signifies close deals to tradesmen, and good luck in livestock to the farmer. Plenty to the housewife, is the omen for women. If there is a feeling of regret about the dream, you are warned to be careful of your business affairs. ◎

TRADER

SOLD
To dream that you have ***sold*** anything, denotes that unfavorable business will worry you. ◎

SAMPLES
To dream of receiving merchandise ***samples***, denotes improvement in your business.

For a traveling man to lose his samples, implies that he will find himself embarrassed in business affairs, or in trouble through love engagements.

For a woman to dream that she is examining samples sent her, denotes that she will have chances to vary her amusements. ◎

Market Forces

MARKET
To dream that you are in a ***market***, denotes thrift and much activity in all occupations.

To see ***an empty market***, indicates depression and gloom.

To see decayed vegetables or meat, denotes losses in business.

For a young woman, a market foretells pleasant changes. ◎

STALL
To dream of a ***stall***, denotes that impossible results from some enterprise will be expected by you. ◎

Dreams of the world of commerce will not take you far from everyday life, but may not be so easily explained as they may seem at first. You may see a market trader *left* **or entrepreneurs balancing their books** *opposite*.

SCALES
To dream of weighing on ***scales***, portends that justice will temper your conduct, and you will see your prosperity widening.

For a young woman to weigh her lover, the indications are that she will find him of solid worth, and faithfulness will balance her love. ◎

WEIGHING
To dream of ***weighing***, denotes that you are approaching a prosperous period; and if you set yourself determinedly toward success, you will victoriously reap the full fruition of your labors.

To weigh others, you will be able to subordinate them to your interest.

For a young woman to weigh with her lover, foretells that he will be ready at all times to comply with her demands. ◎

TRADE *see* **WORK** *page 194*, **LABOR** *page 194* ◆ **PURCHASES** *see* **SHOP** *page 203* ◆ **SAMPLES** *see* **TRAVELING** *page 221* ◆ **MARKET** *see* **VEGETABLES** *page 137*, **MEAT** *page 135*

Stores and Warehouses

SHOP
To dream of a ***shop***, denotes that you will be opposed in every attempt you make for advancement by scheming and jealous friends. ◎

COUNTER
To dream of ***counters***, foretells that active interest will debar idleness from infecting your life with unhealthful desires. To dream of empty and soiled counters, foretells unfortunate engagements which will bring great uneasiness of mind lest your interest be wholly swept away. ◎

STORE
To dream of a ***store*** filled with merchandise, foretells prosperity and advancement.

An empty one, denotes failure of efforts and quarrels.

To dream that your store is burning, is a sign of renewed activity in business and pleasure.

If you find yourself in a department store, it foretells that much pleasure will be derived from various sources of profit.

If you see goods in one, your advancement will be accelerated by your energy and the efforts of friends.

To dream that you sell a pair of soiled, gray cotton gloves to a woman, foretells that your opinion of women will place you in hazardous positions.

If a woman has this dream, her preference for someone of the male sex will not be appreciated very much by him. ◎

WAREHOUSE
To dream of a ***warehouse***, denotes for you a successful enterprise. To see an empty one, is a sign that you will be cheated and foiled in some plan which you have given much thought and maneuvering. ◎

Commerce and Accounts

BALANCING THE BOOKS

COMMERCE
To dream that you are engaged in ***commerce***, denotes that you will handle your opportunities wisely and advantageously. To dream of failures and gloomy outlooks in commercial circles, denotes trouble and ominous threatening of failure in real business life.

To dream of an increase in your business, signifies that you will overcome existing troubles. ◎

ACCOUNTS
To dream of having ***accounts*** presented to you for payment, you will be in a dangerous position. You may have recourse to law to disentangle yourself. If you pay the accounts, you will soon effect a compromise in some serious dispute.

To ***hold accounts*** against others, foretells that disagreeable contingencies will arise in your business, marring the smoothness of its management.

For a young woman bookkeeper to dream of ***footing up accounts***, denotes that she will have trouble in business and in her love affairs, but some worthy person will persuade her to account for his happiness. She will be much respected by her present employers. ◎

LEDGER
To dream of keeping a ***ledger***, you will have perplexities and disappointing conditions to combat.

To dream that you make ***wrong entries*** on your ledge, you will have small disputes and a slight loss will befall you.

To put a ***ledger into a safe***, you will be able to protect your rights under adverse circumstances.

If you get your ***ledger misplaced***, your interests will go awry through neglect of duty.

To dream that your ledger gets ***destroyed by fire***, you will suffer through the carelessness of friends.

To dream that you have a woman to keep your ledger, you will lose money trying to combine pleasure with business.

For a young woman to dream of ledgers, denotes that she will have a solid businessman to make her a proposal of marriage.

To dream that your ***ledger has worthless accounts***, denotes bad management and losses; but if the accounts are good, then your business will assume improved conditions. ◎

VOUCHER
To dream of ***vouchers***, foretells that patient toil will defeat idle scheming to arrest fortune from you.

To sign one, denotes that you have the aid and confidence of those around you, despite the evil workings of enemies.

To lose one, signifies that you will have a struggle for your rights with relatives. ◎

SHOP *see* **PURCHASES** *page 202* ◆ **STORE** *see* **FIRE** *page 80*, **STAIN** *page 218* ◆ **COMMERCE** *see* **TRADE** *page 202*, **FAILURE** *page 258*, **GLOOM** *page 257* ◆ **ACCOUNTS** *see* **MONEY** *page 239* ◆ **LEDGER** *see* **CASHIER** *page 242*, **SAFE** *page 242*, **FIRE** *page 80*

Working Together

PARTNERSHIP
To dream of forming a ***partnership*** with a man, denotes uncertain and fluctuating money affairs. If your partner be a woman, you will engage in some enterprise which you will endeavor to keep hidden from friends.

To dissolve an ***unpleasant partnership***, denotes that things will arrange themselves agreeably to your desires; but if the partnership was pleasant, there will be disquieting news and disagreeable turns in your affairs. ◎

PARTNER
To dream of seeing your ***business partner*** with a basket of crockery on his back, and letting it fall, gets it mixed with other crockery, denotes that your business will sustain a loss through the indiscriminate dealings of your partner. If you reprimand him for it, you will, to some extent, recover the loss. ◎

Bad Business Practice

FRAUD
To dream that you are ***defrauding*** a person, denotes that you will deceive your employer for gain, indulge in degrading pleasures, and fall into disrepute.

If you are defrauded, it signifies the useless attempt of enemies to defame you and cause you loss.

To accuse someone of defrauding you, you will be offered a place of high honor. ◎

MONEY

CHEATED
To dream of being ***cheated*** in business, you will meet designing people who will seek to close your avenues to fortune. ◎

COMPACT DISC

Patents and Inventions

LICENSE
To dream of a ***license***, is an omen of disputes and loss. Married women will exasperate your cheerfulness. ◎

PATENT
To dream of securing a ***patent***, denotes that you will be careful and painstaking with any task you set about to accomplish. If you fail in securing your patent, you will suffer failure for the reason that you are engaging in enterprises for which you have no ability.

If you buy one, you will have occasion to make a tiresome and fruitless journey.

To see one, you will suffer unpleasantness from illness. ◎

INVENTOR
To dream of an ***inventor***, foretells that you will soon achieve some unique work which will add honor to your name. To dream that you are inventing something, or feel interested in some invention, denotes that you will aspire to fortune and will be successful in your designs. ◎

Customs and Exchange

CUSTOMHOUSE
To dream of a ***customhouse***, denotes rivalries and competition in your labors.

To enter a customhouse, foretells that you will strive for, or have offered you, a position that you have long desired.

To leave one, signifies loss of position or trade, or failure to secure some desired object. ◎

EXCHANGE
Exchange denotes profitable dealings in all classes of business. For a young woman to dream that she is exchanging sweethearts with her friend, indicates that she will do well to heed this as advice, as she would be happier with another. ◎

Dreams of the entrepreneurial world may show you such inventions as the compact disc *top*, **or you may see your money disappear into the pockets of a fraudster** *left*. **Cosy dreams of house and home may feature the authoritarian figure of a housekeeper** *opposite*.

PARTNER *see* CROCKERY *page 209* ◆ FRAUD *see* ACCOUNTS *page 203* ◆ EXCHANGE *see* SWEETHEARTS *page 124*

House and Home

Home is where everybody's heart is, and dreams of home are probably the commonest of all dreams. This section covers all things domestic, from the structure and fabric of the house itself, through the kitchen clutter of crockery and gadgets, storage systems, soft furnishings, and lighting to household chores, and even home improvements.

Home Sweet Home

ABODE

To dream that you can't find your ***abode***, you will completely lose faith in the integrity of others.

If you have ***no abode*** in your dreams, you will be unfortunate in your affairs and lose by speculation.

To ***change your abode***, signifies hurried tidings and that hasty journeys will be made by you.

For a young woman to dream that she has left her abode, is significant of slander and falsehoods being perpetrated against her. ◎

HOME

To dream of visiting your old ***home***, you will have good news to rejoice over.

To see your ***old home*** in a dilapidated state, warns you of the sickness or death of a relative. For a young woman, this is a dream of sorrow. She will lose a dear friend.

To ***go home*** and find everything cheery and comfortable, denotes harmony in the present home life and satisfactory results in business. ◎

HOMESICK

To dream of being ***homesick***, foretells that you will lose fortunate opportunities to enjoy travels of interest and pleasant visits. ◎

You're Welcome

INVITE

To dream that you ***invite*** persons to visit you, denotes that some unpleasant event is near, and will cause worry and excitement in your otherwise pleasant surroundings.

If you ***are invited*** to make a visit, you will receive sad news.

For a woman to dream that she is ***invited to attend a party***, she will have pleasant anticipations, but ill luck will mar them. ◎

WELCOME

To dream that you receive a warm ***welcome*** into any society, foretells that you will become distinguished among your acquaintances and will have deference shown you by strangers. Your fortune will approximate anticipation.

To ***accord others welcome***, denotes that your congeniality and warm nature will be your passport into pleasures or any other desired place. ◎

VISIT

If you ***visit*** in your dreams, this foreshadows that you will shortly have some pleasant occasion in your life.

If your ***visit is unpleasant***, your enjoyment will be marred by the action of malicious persons.

For a ***friend to visit you***, denotes that news of a favorable nature will soon reach you. If the friend appears sad and travel worn, there will be a note of displeasure growing out of the visit, or other slight disappointments may follow. If he or she is dressed in black or white and looks pale or ghastly, serious illness or accident are predicted. ◎

HOUSEKEEPER

Domestic Staff

HOUSEKEEPER

To dream that you are a ***housekeeper***, denotes that you will have labors which will occupy your time, and make pleasure an ennobling thing. To employ one, signifies that comparative comfort will be possible for your obtaining. ◎

CHAMBERMAID

To see a ***chambermaid***, denotes bad fortune and that decided changes will be made.

For a man to dream of ***making love to a chambermaid***, shows that he is likely to find himself an object of derision on account of indiscreet conduct and want of tact. ◎

ABODE *see* SHELTER *page 188* ◆ HOME *see* HOUSE *page 188* ◆ INVITE *see* PARTY *page 85* ◆ VISIT *see* TRAVELING *page 221*, FRIEND *page 124* ◆ HOUSEKEEPER *see* HOUSE *page 188*, CHAMBERMAID *see* HOTEL *page 188*, SEX *page 126*

Board and Lodging

RENT
To dream that you rent *a house, is a sign that you will enter into new contracts, which will prove profitable.*

To fail to rent out property, denotes that there will be much inactivity in business.

To pay rent, signifies that your financial interests will be satisfactory.

If you can't pay your rent, it is unlucky for you, as you will see a falling off in trade, and social pleasures will be of little benefit.

LODGER
For a woman to dream that she has lodgers, *foretells that she will be burdened with unpleasant secrets. If one goes away without paying his bills, she will have unexpected trouble with men. For one to pay his bill, omens favor and accumulation of money.*

TENANT
For a landlord to see his tenant *in a dream, denotes that he will have trouble and vexation.*

To imagine you are a tenant, foretells that you will suffer loss in experiments of a business character.

If a tenant pays you money, you will be successful in some engagements.

BOARDINGHOUSE
To dream of a boardinghouse, *foretells that you will suffer entanglement and disorder in your enterprises, and you are likely to change your residence.*

ROOMS IN A HOUSE

Upstairs

CHAMBER
To find yourself in a beautiful and richly furnished ***chamber***, implies sudden fortune, either through legacies from unknown relatives or through speculation.

For a young woman, it denotes that a wealthy stranger will offer her marriage and a fine establishment. If the chamber is plainly furnished, it denotes that a small competency and frugality will be her portion.

ATTIC
To dream that you are in an ***attic***, denotes that you are entertaining hopes which will fail of materialization.

For a young woman to dream that she is ***sleeping in an attic***, foretells that she will fail to find contentment in her present occupation.

GARRET
To dream of climbing to a ***garret***, denotes your inclination to run after theories while leaving the cold realities of life to others less able to bear them than yourself. To the poor, this dream is an omen of easier circumstances.

Your domestic dreams may allow you to wander through the whole house room by room *above*.

Downstairs

CELLAR
To dream of being in a cold, damp ***cellar***, you will be oppressed by doubts. You will lose confidence in all things and suffer gloomy forebodings from which you will fail to escape unless you control your will. It also indicates loss of property.

To see a ***cellar stored with wines*** and table stores, you will be offered a share in profits coming from a doubtful source. If a young woman dreams of this, she will have an offer of marriage from a speculator or gambler.

BASEMENT
To dream that you are in a ***basement***, foretells that you will see prosperous opportunities abating, and with them, pleasure will dwindle into trouble and care.

Bathroom

BATHROOM
To see white roses in a ***bathroom***, and yellow ones in a box, denotes that sickness will interfere with pleasure; but more lasting joys will result from this disappointment.

For a young woman to dream of a bathroom, foretells that her inclinations tend too much toward light pleasures and frivolities.

RENT *see* HOUSE *page 188*, DEBT *page 243* ◆ BOARDINGHOUSE *see* HOTEL *page 188* ◆ CHAMBER *see* CHAMBERMAID *page 205*, ATTIC *see* ROOF *page 190*, SLEEP *page 274* ◆ GARRET *see* CLIMBING *page 268* ◆ CELLAR *see* WINE, WINE CELLAR *page 151* ◆ BATHROOM *see* ROSES *page 58*

Beds and Bedrooms

BEDROOM
To see one newly furnished, denotes a happy change for the dreamer: journeys to distant places and pleasant companions.

BED
A bed, clean and white, denotes surceases of worries. For a woman to dream of making a bed, signifies a new lover and a pleasant occupation.

To dream of being in bed and in a strange room, unexpected friends will visit you. If a sick person dreams of being in bed, complications will arise, and, perhaps, death.

To dream that you are sleeping on a bed in the open air, foretells that you will have delightful experiences, and improving fortune.

To see a friend looking very pale, lying in bed, signifies that strange and woeful complications will oppress your friends, bringing discontent to yourself.

For a mother to dream that her child wets a bed, foretells that she will have unusual anxiety, and sick persons will not reach recovery as early as may be expected. For persons to dream that they wet the bed, denotes sickness, or a tragedy that will interfere with their daily routine of business.

BEDFELLOW
To dream that you do not like your bedfellow, foretells that some person who has claims upon you, will censure and make your surroundings generally unpleasant.

If you have a strange bedfellow, your discontent will worry all who come near you.

If you think you have any kind of animal in bed with you, unbounded ill luck will overhang you.

BEDBUGS
Seen in your dreams, bedbugs indicate continued sickness and unhappy states. Fatalities are intimated if you see many of them.

To see bedbugs simulating death, foretells unhappiness caused by illness.

To mash them, and see water appear instead of blood, denotes alarming but not fatal illness or accident.

To see bedbugs crawling up white walls, and you throw scalding water upon them, denotes that grave illness will distress you, but there will be useless fear of fatality. If the water fails to destroy them, some serious complication with fatal results is not improbable.

MATTRESS
To dream of a mattress, denotes that new duties and responsibilities will shortly be assumed.

To sleep on a new mattress, signifies contentment with present surroundings.

To dream of a mattress factory, denotes that you will be connected in business with thrifty partners and will soon amass wealth.

PILLOW
To dream of a pillow, denotes luxury and comfort.

For a young woman to dream that she makes a pillow, she will have encouraging prospects of a pleasant future.

BLANKET
Blankets in your dream, mean treachery if soiled. If new and white, success where failure is feared; a fatal sickness will be avoided through unseen agencies.

ELECTRIC BLANKET
To dream of an electric blanket, means that comfort and support will soon be necessary.

COUNTERPANE
A counterpane is very good to dream of, if clean and white, denoting pleasant occupations for women; but if it be soiled, you may expect harassing situations. Sickness usually follows.

QUILTS
To dream of quilts, foretells pleasant and comfortable circumstances. For a young woman, this dream foretells that her practical and wise businesslike ways will advance her into the favorable esteem of a man who will seek her for a wife.

If the quilts are clean, but have holes in them, she will win a husband who appreciates her worth, but he will not be most desired by her for a companion.

If the quilts are soiled, she will bear evidence of carelessness in her dress and manners, and thus fail to secure a very upright husband.

COT
To dream of a cot, foretells some affliction, sickness, or accident.

Cots in rows signify that you will not be alone in trouble, as friends will be afflicted also.

BED see SICKNESS page 106, URINE page 95 ◆ BEDBUGS see BUGS page 49 ◆ DEATH page 120 ◆ WATER page 78, WALLS page 190 ◆ MATTRESS see MANUFACTORY page 194 ◆ ELECTRIC BLANKET see ELECTRICITY page 212 ◆ COUNTERPANE, QUILTS see STAIN page 218 ◆ COT see BABY page 119

In the Kitchen

KITCHEN
To dream of a ***kitchen***, denotes that you will be forced to meet emergencies which will depress your spirits.

For a woman to dream that her kitchen is clean and orderly, foretells that she will become the mistress of interesting fortunes. ◎

REFRIGERATOR
To see a ***refrigerator*** in your dreams, portends that your selfishness will offend and injure someone who endeavors to gain an honest livelihood.

To put ice in one, brings the dreamer into disfavor. ◎

FREEZER
To dream of a ***freezer***, denotes that a worrisome situation, which you have found difficult or have tried to avoid coping with, will be resolved. ◎

COOKING
To ***cook*** a meal, denotes that some pleasant duty will devolve on you. Many friends will visit you in the near future. If there is discord or a lack of cheerfulness, you may expect harassing and disappointing events to happen. ◎

COOKING STOVE
To see a ***cooking stove*** in a dream, denotes that much unpleasantness will be modified by your timely interference.

For a young woman to dream of using a cooking stove, foretells that she will be too hasty in showing her appreciation of the attention of some person, and thereby lose a closer friendship. ◎

You may share Alice's vision of a wonderland kitchen *right* **in your dreams. Less dramatic dreams may show you particular pieces of domestic hardware such as a toaster** *above left,* **a piece of porcelain** *opposite top* **or cook's tools in use** *opposite bottom.*

MICROWAVE OVEN
To dream of using a ***microwave oven*** to prepare a dinner, denotes that you will soon have unexpected and unwanted company. ◎

OVEN
For a woman to dream that her baking ***oven*** is red hot, denotes that she will be loved by her own family and friends, for her sweet and unselfish nature. If she is baking, temporary disappointments await her. If the ***oven is broken***, she will undergo many vexations from children and servants. ◎

A DREAM KITCHEN

Kitchen Gadgets

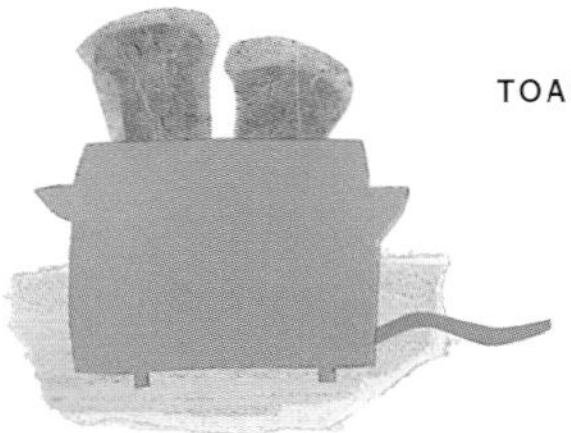

TOASTER

TOASTER
To dream of a ***toaster***, signifies that an unfulfilled wish will soon become reality.◎

MIXER
To dream of an electric ***mixer***, means that you will shortly have a more active social life. ◎

KITCHEN *see* **EATING** *page 133,* **MEALS** *page 134* ◆ **REFRIGERATOR** *see* **ICE** *page 77* ◆ **COOKING** *see* **MEALS** *page 134* ◆ **OVEN** *see* **BAKING** *page 146* ◆ **TOASTER** *see* **BREAD** *page 146*

PORCELAIN PLATE

PORCELAIN
To dream of ***porcelain***, signifies that you will have favorable opportunities of progressing in your affairs.

To see it broken or soiled, denotes that mistakes will be made which will cause grave offense. ◎

CHINA
For a woman to dream of painting or arranging her ***china***, foretells that she will have a pleasant home and be a thrifty and economical matron. ◎

CHINA STORE
For a ***china*** merchant to dream that his ***store*** looks empty, foretells he will have reverses in his business, and withal a gloomy period will follow. ◎

CROCKERY
To dream of having an abundance of nice, clean ***crockery***, denotes that you will be a tidy and economical housekeeper.

To be in a ***crockery store***, indicates, if you are a merchant or businessman, that you will look well to the details of your business and thereby experience profit. To a young woman, this dream denotes that she will marry a sturdy and upright man. An untidy store, with empty shelves, implies loss. ◎

China and Crockery

PLATES
For a woman to dream of ***plates***, denotes that she will practice economy and win a worthy husband. If already married, she will retain her husband's love and respect by the wise ordering of his household. ◎

DISHES
To dream of handling ***dishes***, denotes good fortune; but if from any cause they should be broken, this signifies that fortune will be short-lived for you.

To see shelves of ***polished dishes***, denotes success in marriage.

To dream of dishes, is prognostic of coming success and gain, and you will be able to fully appreciate your good luck. ***Soiled dishes***, represent dissatisfaction and an unpromising future. ◎

DISHWASHER
To dream of using a ***dishwasher***, denotes that a conflict in your personal life or circumstances will shortly be resolved. ◎

Cook's Tools

SPOONS
To see or use *spoons* ***in a dream, denotes favorable signs of advancement. Domestic affairs will afford contentment.***

To think a *spoon is lost*, ***denotes that you will be suspicious of wrongdoing.***

To steal one, is a sign that you will deserve censure for your contemptible meanness in your home.

To dream of *broken or soiled spoons*, ***signifies that you will suffer loss and trouble.*** ❋

LADLE
To see a *ladle* ***in your dreams, denotes that you will be fortunate in the selection of a companion. Children will prove sources of happiness.***

If the *ladle is broken* ***or unclean, you will have a grievous loss.*** ❋

SIEVE
To dream of a *sieve*, ***foretells that some annoying transaction will soon be made by you, which will probably be to your loss. If the meshes are too small, you will have the chance to reverse a decision unfavorable to yourself. If too large, you will eventually lose what you have recently acquired.*** ❋

FORK
To dream of a *fork*, ***denotes that enemies are working for your displacement. For a woman, this dream denotes unhappy domestic relations; for lovers, separation.*** ❋

IN THE KITCHEN

PORCELAIN *see* **BREAK** *page 265*, **STAIN** *page 218* ◆ **CHINA** *see* **PAINT AND PAINTING** *page 181* ◆ **CHINA STORE** *see* **STORE** *page 203* ◆ **CROCKERY** *see* **ABUNDANCE** *page 238*, **STORE** *page 203* ◆ **DISHES** *see* **POLISHING** *page 218*, **STAIN** *page 218* ◆ **SPOONS** *see* **STEALING** *page 246*, **BREAK** *page 265*, **STAIN** *page 218* ◆ **LADLE** *see* **BREAK** *page 265* ◆ **SIEVE** *see* **MESHES** *page 185*

Glasses and Bottles

GLASSES

To dream of ***glasses***, foretells that strangers will cause changes in your affairs. Frauds will be practiced on your credulity.

To dream that you see ***broken glasses***, denotes estrangement caused by fondness for illegal pleasures. ◎

GOBLET

If you dream that you drink water from a silver ***goblet***, you will meet unfavorable business results in the near future.

To see goblets of ancient design, you will receive favors and benefits from strangers.

For a woman to give a man a ***glass goblet*** full of water, denotes illicit pleasures. ◎

CHALICE

To dream of a ***chalice***, denotes that pleasure will be gained by you to the sorrow of others. To break one, foretells your failure to obtain power over some friend. ◎

BOTTLES

Bottles are good to dream of, if well filled with transparent liquid. You will overcome all obstacles in affairs of the heart; prosperous engagements will ensue.

If the ***bottles are empty***, coming trouble will envelop you in meshes of sinister design, from which you will be forced to use strategy to disengage yourself. ◎

THERMOS BOTTLE

To dream of preparing a ***thermos bottle***, foretells that catastrophe or an unfortunate experience will soon occur. ◎

VASE

Jugs, Jars, and Pots

JUG

If you dream of ***jugs*** well filled with transparent liquids, your welfare is being considered by more than yourself. Many true friends will unite to please and profit you. If the jugs are empty, your conduct will estrange you from friends and station.

Broken jugs, indicate sickness and failures in employment.

If you drink ***wine from a jug***, you will enjoy robust health and find pleasure in all circles. Optimistic views will possess you.

To take an ***unpleasant drink from a jug***, omens that disappointment and disgust will follow pleasant anticipations. ◎

JAR

To dream of empty ***jars***, denotes impoverishment and distress.

To see them full, you will be successful.

If you ***buy jars***, your success will be precarious and your burden will be heavy.

If you see ***broken jars***, distressing sickness or deep disappointment awaits you. ◎

JUG

VASE

To dream of a ***vase***, denotes that you will enjoy sweetest pleasure and contentment in your home life.

To drink from a vase, you will soon thrill with the delights of stolen love.

To see a ***broken vase***, foretells early sorrow.

For a young woman to receive one, signifies that she will soon obtain her dearest wish. ◎

VAT

To see a ***vat*** in your dreams, foretells anguish and suffering from the hands of cruel persons, into which you have unwittingly fallen. ◎

CASK

URN

To dream of an ***urn***, foretells that you will prosper in some respects, and in others disfavor will be apparent. If you see broken urns, unhappiness will confront you. ◎

CASK

To see one filled, denotes prosperous times and feastings. If empty, your life will be void of any joy or consolation from outward influences. ◎

PITCHER

To dream of a ***pitcher***, denotes that you will be of a generous and congenial disposition. Success will attend your efforts.

A ***broken pitcher***, denotes loss of friends. ◎

POT

To dream of a ***pot***, foretells that unimportant events will work you vexation.

For a young woman to see a ***boiling pot***, omens busy employment of pleasant and social duties.

To see a broken or rusty one, implies that keen disappointment will be experienced by you. ◎

KEG

To dream of a ***keg***, denotes that you will have a struggle to throw off oppression. Broken ones, indicate separation from family or friends. ◎

Mundane objects such as a glass *top left*, **jug** *center*, **vase** *left*, **cask** *top right*, **basket** *opposite top*, **and even a cupboard** *opposite bottom* **take on a new meaning in dreams.**

GLASSES *see* **BREAK** *page 265* ◆ **GOBLET** *see* **WATER** *page 78*, **SILVER** *page 71*, **GLASS** *page 69* ◆ **CHALICE** *see* **WINE** *page 151* ◆ **JUG** *see* **BREAK** *page 265*, **WINE** *page 151* ◆ **JAR, VASE** *see* **BREAK** *page 265* ◆ **URN** *see* **MILK** *page 144*, **CHURNING** *page 144* ◆ **CASK** *see* **BEER** *page 151* ◆ **PITCHER** *see* **BREAK** *page 265* ◆ **POT** *see* **BREAK** *page 265*, **RUST** *page 255*

Containers and Carriers

PAIL
To dream of full ***pails*** of milk, is a sign of fair prospects and pleasant associations.

An ***empty pail***, is a sign of famine or bad crops.

For a young woman to be ***carrying a pail***, denotes household employment. ◎

TRAY
To see ***trays*** in your dream, denotes that your wealth will be foolishly wasted, and surprises of an unpleasant nature will shock you. If the trays seem to be filled with valuables, surprises will come in the shape of good fortune. ◎

BASKET

BASKET
To dream of seeing or carrying a ***basket***, signifies that you will meet unqualified success, if the basket is full; but ***empty baskets*** indicate discontent and sorrow. ◎

Storage Space

THE CUPBOARD

CUPBOARD
To see a ***cupboard*** in your dream, is significant of pleasure and comfort, and penury and distress, according as the cupboard is clean and full of shining ware, or empty and dirty. ◎

SHELVES
To see empty ***shelves*** in dreams, indicates losses and consequent gloom.

Full shelves, augur happy contentment through the fulfillment of hopes and exertions. ◎

BOX
Opening a goods ***box*** in your dream, signifies untold wealth and that delightful journeys to distant places may be made with happy results. If the box is empty, disappointment in works of all kinds will follow.

To see full ***money boxes***, augurs cessation from business cares and a pleasant retirement. ◎

Spitting Image

CUSPIDOR
To see a cuspidor ***[spittoon] in a dream, signifies that an unworthy attachment will be formed by you, and that your work will be neglected.***

To spit in one, foretells that reflections will be cast upon your conduct. ❁

Teatime

KETTLE
To see ***kettles*** in your dream, denotes great and laborious work before you.

If you see a ***kettle of boiling water***, your struggles will soon end and a change will come to you.

To see a ***broken kettle***, denotes failure after a mighty effort to work out a path to success.

For a young woman to dream of handling ***dark kettles***, foretells disappointment in love and marriage; but a light-colored kettle brings to her absolute freedom from care, and her husband will be handsome and worthy. ◎

TEAKETTLE
To dream you see a ***teakettle***, implies sudden news which will be likely to distress you. For a woman to pour sparkling, cold water from a teakettle, she will have unexpected favor shown her. ◎

TEACUPS
To dream of ***teacups***, foretells that affairs of enjoyment will be attended by you.

For a woman to break or see them broken, omens that her pleasure and good fortune will be marred by a sudden trouble.

To drink wine from one, foretells that fortune and pleasure will be combined in the near future. ◎

PAIL *see* **MILK** *page 144* ◆ **SHELVES** *see* **STORE** *page 203* ◆ **BOX** *see* **MONEY** *page 239*, **CASH BOX** *page 242* ◆ **KETTLE** *see* **TEA** *page 153*, **BREAK** *page 265*, **WATER** *page 78* ◆ **TEAKETTLE** *see* **TEA** *page 153* ◆ **TEACUPS** *see* **TEA** *page 153*, **BREAK** *page 265*, **WINE** *page 151*, **CROCKERY** *page 209*

Open Fires

ANDIRONS
Andirons [firedogs] seen in a dream, denotes good will among friends, if the irons support burning logs; if they are in an empty fireplace, loss of property and death are signified. ◎

MATCH
To dream of ***matches***, denotes prosperity and change.

To ***strike a match*** in the dark, unexpected news and fortune is foreboded. ◎

POKER
To dream of seeing a red-hot ***poker***, or of fighting with one, signifies that you will meet trouble with combative energy. ◎

The Plumbing System

BOILER
To dream of seeing a ***boiler*** out of repair, signifies suffering from bad management or disappointment.

For a woman to dream that she goes into a cellar to see about a boiler, foretells that sickness and losses will surround her. ◎

TANK
To dream of a ***tank***, foretells that you will be prosperous and satisfied beyond your expectations.

To see a ***leaking tank***, denotes loss in your affairs. ◎

CISTERN
To dream of a ***cistern***, denotes that you are in danger of trespassing upon the pleasures and rights of your friends.

To draw from one, foretells that you will enlarge in your pastime and enjoyment in a manner that may be questioned by propriety.

To see an empty one, foretells despairing change from happiness to sorrow. ◎

LEAKING
To dream of seeing a ***leak*** in anything, is usually significant of loss and vexations. ◎

Fuel and Power

GAS
To dream of ***gas***, denotes that you will entertain harmful opinions of others, which will cause you to deal with them unjustly, and you will suffer consequent remorse.

To think you are asphyxiated, denotes trouble which you will needlessly incur through your own wastefulness and negligence.

To try to ***blow gas out***, signifies that you will entertain enemies unconsciously, who will destroy you if you are not wary.

To ***extinguish gas***, denotes that you will ruthlessly destroy your own happiness. To light it, you will easily find a way out of oppressive ill fortune. ◎

ELECTRICITY
To dream of ***electricity***, denotes sudden changes about you, which will not afford you either advancement or pleasure. If you are shocked by it, you will face a deplorable danger.

To see ***live electrical wire***, foretells that enemies will disturb your plans, which have given you much anxiety in forming.

To dream that you can send a package or yourself out over a wire with the same rapidity that a message can be sent, denotes that you will finally overcome obstacles and be able to use your enemies' plans to advance yourself. ◎

BLACKOUT
To dream of a ***blackout*** or an electrical failure, denotes that you will be forgetting something crucial at an inopportune moment. ◎

SWITCH
A dream of a ***switch***, foretells change and misfortune.

A ***broken switch***, foretells disgrace and trouble.

A dream of a ***railroad switch***, denotes that travel will cause you much loss and inconvenience.

To dream of a switch, signifies that you will meet discouragements in momentous affairs. ◎

WIND FARM

Power dreams may show you electricity, perhaps produced by a wind farm *above*. A more depressing image is the window *opposite*, an unremarkable object in life.

ANDIRONS *see* **FIRE** *page 80*, **WOODPILE** *page 67* ◆ **MATCH** *see* **FIRE** *page 80* ◆ **POKER** *see also* **POKER** *page 176* ◆ **BOILER** *see* **CELLAR** *page 206* ◆ **CISTERN** *see* **WATER** *page 78*, **WELL** *page 193* ◆ **ELECTRICITY** *see* **WIRE** *page 200*, **FAX, TELEGRAM** *page 237* ◆ **SWITCH** *see* **BREAK** *page 265*, **RAILROAD** *page 225*

Doors, Doorbells, Keys, and Locks

DOOR
To dream of entering a ***door***, denotes slander and enemies from whom you are trying in vain to escape. This is the same of any door, except the door of your childhood home. If it is this door you dream of entering, this means that your days will be filled with plenty and congeniality.

To dream of ***entering a door*** at night through the rain, denotes, to a woman, unpardonable escapades; to a man, it is significant of a drawing on his resources by unwarranted vice, and also foretells assignations.

To see others go through a ***doorway***, denotes unsuccessful attempts to get your affairs into a paying condition. It also means changes to farmers and the political world. To an author, it foretells that the reading public will reprove his way of stating facts by refusing to read his later works.

To dream that you attempt to ***close a door***, and it falls from its hinges, injuring someone, denotes that malignant evil threatens your friend through your unintentionally wrong advices. If you see another attempt to lock a door, and it falls from its hinges, you will have knowledge of some friend's misfortune and be powerless to aid him. ◎

DOORBELL
To dream you hear or ring a ***doorbell***, foretells unexpected tidings, or a hasty summons to business or to the bedside of a sick relative. ◎

LOCK
To dream of a ***lock***, denotes bewilderment. If the lock works at your command or efforts, you will discover that some person is working you injury. If you are in love, you will find means to aid you in overcoming a rival; you will also make a prosperous journey.

If the ***lock resists your efforts***, you will be derided and scorned in love, and perilous voyages will bring to you no benefit.

To put a lock upon your fiancée's neck and arm, foretells that you are distrustful of her fidelity, but future episodes will disabuse your mind of doubt. ◎

LATCH
To dream of a ***latch***, denotes that you will meet urgent appeals for aid, to which you will respond unkindly. To see a ***broken latch***, foretells disagreements with your dearest friend. Sickness is also foretold in this dream. ◎

KEYHOLE
To dream that you spy upon others through a ***keyhole***, you will damage some person by disclosing confidence. If you catch others ***peeping through a keyhole***, you will have false friends delving into your private matters to advance themselves over you.

To dream that you cannot find the keyhole, you will unconsciously injure a friend. ◎

KEY
To dream of ***keys***, denotes unexpected changes.

If the ***keys are lost***, unpleasant adventures will affect you.

To ***find keys***, brings domestic peace and brisk turns to business.

Broken keys, portend separation through either death or jealousy.

For a young woman to dream of losing the key to any personal ornament, denotes that she will have quarrels with her lover, and will suffer much disquiet therefrom.

If she dreams of ***unlocking a door*** with a key, she will have a new lover and have overconfidence in him. If she locks a door with a key, she will be successful in selecting a husband.

If she ***gives the key away***, she will fail to use judgement in conversation and darken her own reputation thereby. ◎

KNOCKER
To dream of using a ***knocker***, foretells that you will be forced to ask aid and counsel of others. ◎

Windows

THE WINDOW

WINDOW
To see ***windows*** in your dreams, is an augury of a fateful culmination to all your bright hopes. You will see your fairest wish go down in despair. Fruitless endeavors will be your portion after this dream.

To see ***closed windows***, is a representation of desertion. If they are broken, you will be hounded by miserable suspicions of disloyalty from those you love.

To ***sit in a window***, denotes that you will be the victim of folly.

To enter a house ***through a window***, denotes that you will be found out while using dishonorable means to consummate a seemingly honorable purpose.

To escape by one, indicates that you will fall into a trouble whose toils will hold you unmercifully close.

To ***look through a window*** when passing and see strange objects appear, foretells that you will fail in your chosen avocation and lose the respect for which you risked health and contentment. ◎

DOORBELL *see* **CHIMES** *page 275* ◆ **LOCK** *see* **NECK** *page 92,* **ARM** *page 97* ◆ **LATCH** *see* **BREAK** *page 265* ◆ **KEYHOLE** *see* **SPY** *page 271,* **SPYGLASS** *page 237* ◆ **KEYS** *see* **BREAK** *page 265,* **GIFTS** *page 240* ◆ **WINDOW** *see* **BREAK** *page 265,* **GLASS** *page 69,* **HOUSE** *page 188,* **VISIONS** *page 274*

Tables and Table Linen

TABLE

The dream of setting a ***table*** preparatory to a meal, foretells happy unions and prosperous circumstances.

To see ***empty tables***, signifies poverty or disagreements.

To ***clear away the table***, denotes that pleasure will soon assume the form of trouble and indifference.

To ***eat from a table*** without a cloth, foretells that you will be possessed of an independent disposition, and the prosperity or conduct of others will give you no concern.

To see a table walking or moving in some mysterious way, foretells that dissatisfaction will soon enter your life, and you will seek relief in change.

To dream of a ***soiled cloth on a table***, denotes disobedience from servants or children, and quarreling will invariably follow pleasure.

To see a ***broken table***, is ominous of decaying fortune.

To see one standing or sitting on a table, foretells that to obtain their desires they will be guilty of indiscretions.

To see or hear ***table rapping*** or writing, denotes that you will undergo change of feelings toward your friends, and your fortune will be threatened. A loss from the depreciation of relatives or friends is indicated. ◎

NAPKIN

To dream of a ***napkin***, foretells convivial entertainments, in which you will figure prominently.

For a woman to have a dream of ***soiled napkins***, foretells that humiliating affairs will thrust themselves upon her. ◎

You may find yourself sitting comfortably in your dreams either on a chair *top* **or a bench** *right*. **More comfortably you may see yourself surrounded by cushions and carpets** *opposite*.

Chairs and Benches

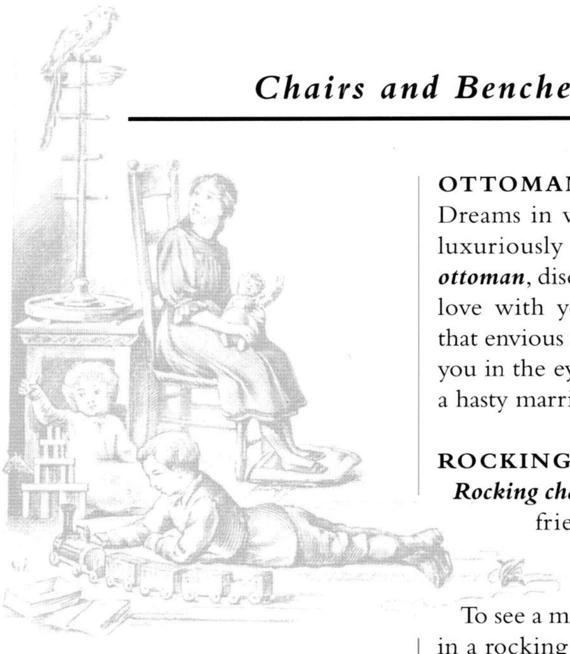

THE CHAIR

SEAT

To think, in a dream, that someone has taken your ***seat***, denotes that you will be tormented by people calling on you for aid.

To give a woman your seat, implies your yielding to some unfair one's artfulness. ◎

CHAIR

To see a ***chair*** in your dream, denotes failure to meet some obligation. If you are not careful, you will also vacate your most profitable places.

To see a friend ***sitting on a chair*** and remaining motionless, signifies news of his death or illness. ◎

BENCH

Distrust debtors and confidants if you dream of sitting on a ***bench***.

If you see others doing so, happy reunions between friends who have been separated through misunderstandings are suggested. ◎

COUCH

To dream of reclining on a ***couch***, indicates that false hopes will be entertained. You should be alert to every change of your affairs, for only in this way will your brightest hopes be realized. ◎

OTTOMAN

Dreams in which you find yourself luxuriously reposing upon an ***ottoman***, discussing the intricacies of love with your sweetheart, foretell that envious rivals will seek to defame you in the eyes of your affianced, and a hasty marriage will be advised. ◎

ROCKING CHAIR

Rocking chairs seen in dreams, bring friendly intercourse and contentment with any environment.

To see a mother, wife, or sweetheart in a rocking chair, is ominous of the sweetest joys that earth affords.

To see ***vacant rocking chairs***, forebodes bereavement or estrangement. The dreamer will surely merit misfortune in some form. ◎

RATTAN CANE

To dream of a ***rattan cane***, foretells that you will depend largely upon the judgement of others, and you should cultivate independence in planning and executing your own affairs. ◎

THE BENCH

TABLE *see* **MEALS** *page 134*, **EATING** *page 133*, **BREAK** *see page 265*, **KNOCKING** *page 276*, **OCCULTIST** *see page 270* ◆ **NAPKIN** *see* **STAIN** *page 218* ◆ **CHAIR** *see* **FRIEND** *page 124*, **CHAIR MAKER** *page 197* ◆ **OTTOMAN** *see* **SWEETHEART** *page 124* ◆ **ROCKING CHAIR** *see* **MOTHER**, *page 128*, **WIFE** *page 132*, **SWEETHEART** *page 124*

Soft Furnishings

CUSHIONS

CURTAINS
To dream of ***curtains***, foretells that unwelcome visitors will cause you worry and unhappiness. ***Soiled or torn curtains*** seen in a dream, mean disgraceful quarrels and reproaches. ◎

CUSHION
To dream of reclining on silken ***cushions***, foretells that your ease will be procured at the expense of others; but to see the cushions, denotes that you will prosper in business and lovemaking alike.

For a young woman to dream of making ***silken cushions***, implies that she will be a bride before many months. ◎

MAT
Keep away from ***mats*** in your dreams, as they will usher you into sorrow and perplexities. ◎

MATTING
To dream of ***matting***, foretells pleasant prospects and cheerful news from the absent. If it is old or torn, you will have vexing things come before you. ◎

CARPET
To see a ***carpet*** in a dream, denotes profit, and wealthy friends to aid you in need.

To ***walk on a carpet***, you will be prosperous and happy.

To dream that you ***buy carpets***, denotes great gain. If selling them, you will have cause to go on a pleasant journey, as well as a profitable one.

For a young woman to dream of carpets, shows that she will own a beautiful home and servants will wait upon her. ◎

A Clean Sweep

BROOM
To dream of brooms, ***denotes thrift and rapid improvement in your fortune, if the brooms are new. If they are seen in use, you will lose in speculation.***

For a woman to lose a broom, ***foretells that she will prove a disagreeable and slovenly wife and housekeeper.***

SWEEPING
To dream of sweeping, ***denote that you will gain favor in the eyes of your husband, and children will find pleasure in the home.***

If you think the floors need sweeping, ***and you from some cause neglect them, there will be distresses and bitter disappointments awaiting you in the approaching days.***

To servants, sweeping is a sign of disagreements and suspicion of the intentions of others.

VACUUM CLEANER
To dream of using a vacuum cleaner, ***denotes that you will soon need to make some decisions concerning a personal or professional relationship. If you do not sort out the situation quickly, complications will arise, causing great confusion.***

BRUSHES
To see miscellaneous brushes, ***foretells a varied line of work, yet withal, rather pleasing and remunerative.***

CURTAINS *see* **STAIN** *page 218,* **WINDOW** *page 213* ◆ **CUSHION** *see* **SILK** *page 187* ◆ **CARPET** *see* **WALKING** *page 267,* **TRADE** *page 202* ◆ **BRUSHES** *see* **HAIR BRUSH** *page 103,* **CLOTHES BRUSH** *page 155*

THE LAMP

Light

LIGHT

If you dream of ***light***, success will attend you. If you dream of weird light, or if the light goes out, you will be disagreeably surprised by some undertaking resulting in nothing.

To see a ***dim light***, indicates partial success. ◎

TORCH

To dream of seeing ***torches***, foretells pleasant amusement and favorable business.

To ***carry a torch***, denotes success in lovemaking or intricate affairs. For one to go out, denotes failure and distress. ◎

Candle Power

WAX TAPER

To dream of lighting ***wax tapers***, denotes that some pleasing occurrence will bring you into association with friends long absent.

To blow them out, signals disappointing times, and sickness will forestall expected opportunities of meeting distinguished friends. ◎

CANDLES

To see them burning with a clear and steady flame, denotes the constancy of those about you and well-grounded fortune.

For a maiden to dream that she is molding ***candles***, denotes that she will have an unexpected offer of marriage and a pleasant visit to distant relatives. If she is ***lighting a candle***, she will meet her lover clandestinely because of parental objections.

If you see a ***candle wasting in a draught***, enemies are circulating detrimental reports about you.

To ***snuff a candle***, portends sorrowful news. Friends are dead or in distressful straits. ◎

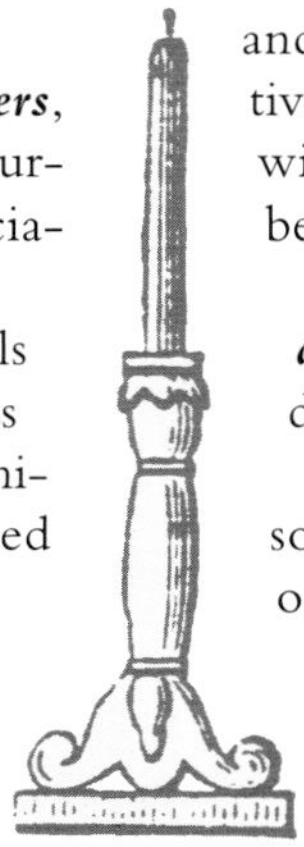

CANDLE

CANDLESTICK

To see a ***candlestick*** in your dreams bearing a whole candle, denotes that a bright future lies before you, and that it will be filled with health, happiness, and loving companions.

If the candlestick is empty, the reverse is denoted. ◎

CHANDELIER

To dream of a ***chandelier***, portends that unhoped for success will make it possible for you to enjoy pleasure and luxury at your caprice.

To see a broken or ill-kept one, denotes that unfortunate speculation will depress your seemingly substantial fortune.

To see the light in one go out, foretells that sickness and distress will cloud a promising future. ◎

Many kinds of light may illuminate your dreams. You may see a wax candle in a candlestick *left*, the soft glow of a traditional table lamp *above* or an old fashioned lantern *opposite*.

CANDLE *see* **FLAME** *page 80* ◆ **CHANDELIER** *see* **BREAK** *page 265* ◆ **LIGHT** *see* **APPARITIONS, VISION** *page 274*

Lamps and Lanterns

LAMPPOST
If you see a ***lamppost*** in your dreams, this means that some stranger will prove your staunchest friend in time of pressing need.

To ***fall against a lamppost***, you will have deception to overcome, or enemies will ensnare you.

To see a ***lamppost across your path***, means that you will have much adversity in your life. ◎

LANTERN
To dream of seeing a ***lantern*** going before you in the darkness, signifies unexpected affluence. If the lantern is suddenly lost to view, then your success will take an unfavorable turn.

To ***carry a lantern*** in your dreams, denotes that your benevolence will win you many friends. If it goes out, you fail to gain the prominence you wish. If you stumble and break it, you will seek to aid others, and in so doing, lose your own station, or be disappointed in some undertaking.

To ***clean a lantern***, signifies that great possibilities are open to you.

To ***lose a lantern***, means business depression, and disquiet in the home.

If you ***buy a lantern***, it signifies fortunate deals.

For a young woman to dream that she ***lights her lover's lantern***, foretells for her a worthy man, and a comfortable home. If she blows it out, by her own imprudence, she will lose a chance of getting married. ◎

LAMP
To see ***lamps*** filled with oil, denotes the demonstration of business activity, from which you will receive gratifying results.

Broken lamps, indicate the death of relatives or friends.

Empty lamps, represent depression and despondency.

To see ***lighted lamps*** burning with a clear flame, indicates a merited rise in fortune and domestic bliss. If they give out a dull, misty radiance, you will have jealousy and envy, coupled with suspicion to combat, in which you will be much pleased to find the right person to attack.

To drop a lighted lamp, foreshadows that your plans and hopes will abruptly turn into failure.

If it explodes, former friends will unite with enemies in damaging your interests.

To ***light a lamp***, denotes that you will soon make a change in your affairs, which will lead to profit.

To ***dream that you carry a lamp***, portends that you will be independent and self-sustaining, preferring your own convictions above others'.

If the light fails, you will meet with unfortunate conclusions, and perhaps the death of friends or relatives.

If you are much affrighted, and throw a bewildering light from your window, enemies will ensnare you with professions of friendship and interest in your achievements.

To dream that you ***ignite your apparel from a lamp***, signifies that you will sustain humiliation from sources from which you expected encouragement and sympathy, and your business will not be fraught with much good. ◎

THE LANTERN

LAMPPOST *see* **PATH** *page 222* ◆ **LANTERN** *see* **TRADE** *page 202* ◆ **LAMP** *see* **OIL** *page 72,* **BREAK** *page 265,* **FLAME** *page 80,* **LIGHT** *page 216,* **AFFRIGHTED** *page 253,* **WINDOW** *page 213,* **APPAREL** *page 154*

Out, Damned Spot

STAIN

To see ***stains*** on your hands or clothing, while dreaming, foretells that trouble over small matters will assail you.

To see a stain on the garments of others or on their flesh, foretells that some person will betray you. ◎

GREASE

To dream you are in ***grease***, is significant of being in the company of disagreeable but polished strangers. ◎

SPONGES

Sponges seen in a dream, denote that deception is being practiced upon you.

To use one in erasing, you will be the victim of folly. ◎

WASHERWOMAN

Washing Day

LAUNDRY

To dream of ***laundering*** clothes, denotes struggles, but a final victory in winning fortune. If the clothes are done satisfactorily, then your endeavors will bring complete happiness. If they come out the reverse, your fortune will fail to procure pleasure.

To see pretty girls at this work, you will seek pleasure out of your rank.

If a ***laundryman*** calls at your house, you are in danger of sickness, or of losing something very valuable.

To see ***laundry wagons***, portends rivalry and contention. ◎

LAUNDROMAT

To dream of washing clothes in a ***laundromat***, foretells that you will soon sever a relationship that has been hostile and welcome one that is supportive. ◎

WASHERWOMAN

A ***washerwoman*** seen in dreams, represents infidelity and a strange adventure. For the businessman or farmer, this dream indicates expanding trade and fine crops. For a woman to dream that **she is a washerwoman**, denotes that she will throw decorum aside in her persistent effort to hold the illegal favor of men. ◎

WASHBOARD

To see a ***washboard*** in your dreams, is indicative of embarrassment. If you see a woman using one, it predicts that you will let women rob you of energy and fortune.

A broken one, portends that you will come to grief and disgraceful deeds through fast living. ◎

IRONING

To dream of ***ironing***, denotes domestic comforts and orderly business.

If a woman dreams that she burns her hand while ironing, it foretells that she will have illness or jealousy to disturb her peace.

If she scorches the clothes, she will have a rival who will cause her much displeasure and suspicions. If the ***iron seems too cold***, she will lack affection in her home. ◎

Home Improvements

POLISHING

If you dream of ***polishing*** any article, high attainments will place you in enviable positions. ◎

DECORATE

To dream of ***decorating*** a place with bright-hued flowers for some festive occasion, is significant of favorable turns in business, and, to the young, of continued rounds of social pleasures and fruitful study. ◎

The domestic drudgery of the washerwoman *above* may have an altogether more exciting significance in your dreams.

PLASTER

To dream of seeing walls plainly ***plastered***, denotes that success will come, but it will not be stable.

To have ***plaster fall upon you***, denotes unmitigated disasters and disclosures.

To see ***plasterers at work***, denotes that you will have a sufficient competency to live above penury. ◎

WHITEWASH

To dream that you are ***whitewashing***, foretells that you will seek to reinstate yourself with friends by ridding yourself of offensive habits and unpleasant companions.

For a young woman, this dream is significant of well-laid plans to deceive others and gain back her lover who has been estranged by her insinuating bearing toward him. ◎

PAINT AND PAINTING

To see ***newly painted*** houses in dreams, foretells that you will succeed with some devised plan.

To have ***paint*** on your clothing, you will be made unhappy by the thoughtless criticisms of others.

To dream that you use the ***paint brush to paint for yourself***, denotes you will be pleased with your present occupation. ◎

STAIN *see* **HAND** *page 97*, **CLOTHES** *page 154* ◆ **LAUNDRY** *see* **CLOTHES** *page 154*, **HOUSE** *page 188*, **WAGON** *page 223* ◆ **WASHBOARD** *see* **BREAK** *page 265* ◆ **IRONING** *see* **BURNS** *page 112*, **HAND** *page 97*, **CLOTHES** *page 154* ◆ **DECORATE** *see also* **DECORATE** *page 259*, **FLOWERS** *page 57* ◆ **PLASTER** *see* **WALLS** *page 199* ◆ **PAINT AND PAINTING** *see also* **PAINT AND PAINTING** *page 181*, **HOUSE** *page 188*, **CLOTHES** *page 154*, **VARNISHING** *page 197*

Public Life

To many of us, dreaming of becoming a public figure is a nightmare; however, not everybody suffers from stage fright in the theater of dreams, and this section covers politics, civic duties and life in the public domain, from local politics to national government, from chairman of the board to the the highest office in the land.

The Electoral Process

INFLUENCE

If you dream of seeing rank or advancement through the ***influence*** of others, your desires will fail to materialize; but if you are in an influential position, your prospects will assume a bright form.

To see friends in high positions, denotes that your comparisons will be congenial, and you will be free from vexations. ◎

OATH

Whenever you take an ***oath*** in your dreams, prepare for dissension and altercations on waking. ◎

VOW

To dream that you are making or listening to ***vows***, foretells that complaints will be made against you of unfaithfulness in business, or some love contract.

To take the ***vows of a church***, denotes that you will bear yourself with unswerving integrity through some difficulty.

To ***break or ignore a vow***, foretells that disastrous consequences will attend your dealings. ◎

ELECTION

To dream that you are at an ***election***, foretells that you will engage in some controversy which will prove detrimental to your social and financial standing. ◎

In your dreams you could talk to presidents, such as John F. Kennedy *above right.*

VOTE

If you dream of casting a ***vote*** on any measure, you will be engulfed in a commotion which will affect your community.

To vote fraudulently, foretells that your dishonesty will overcome your better inclinations. ◎

INAUGURATION

To dream of ***inauguration***, denotes that you will rise to a higher position than you have yet enjoyed.

For a young woman to be disappointed in attending an inauguration, predicts that she will fail to obtain her wishes. ◎

JOHN F. KENNEDY

LEGISLATURE

To dream that you are a member of a ***legislature***, foretells that you will be vain of your possessions and will treat members of your family unkindly. You will have no real advancement. ◎

THE PRESIDENT OF THE UNITED STATES

To dream of talking with the ***President of the United States***, denotes that you are interested in affairs of state, and that you sometimes show a great longings and ambitions to be a politician. ◎

Politics

OFFICE

For a person to dream that he holds ***office***, denotes that his aspirations will sometimes make him undertake dangerous paths, but his boldness will be rewarded with success. If he fails by any means to secure a desired office, he will suffer keen disappointment in his affairs.

To dream that you are ***turned out of office***, signifies loss of valuables. ◎

POLITICIAN

To dream of a ***politician***, denotes displeasing companionship, and incidences where you will lose time and means.

If you engage in political wrangling, it portends that misunderstandings and ill feeling will be shown you by friends.

For a young woman to dream of taking interest in politics, warns her against designing duplicity. ◎

SOCIALIST

To see a ***socialist*** in your dreams, your unenvied position among friends and acquaintances is predicted. Your everyday affairs will be neglected for other imaginary duties. ◎

YANKEE

To dream of a ***Yankee***, foretells that you will remain loyal and true to your promise and duty; but if you are not careful, you will be outwitted in some transaction. ◎

INFLUENCE *see* **FRIEND** *page 124* ◆ **VOW** *see* **CHURCH** *page 189,* **CLERGYMAN** *page 280,* **BREAK** *page 265* ◆ **VOTE** *see* **FRAUD** *page 204* ◆ **PRESIDENT OF THE UNITED STATES** *see* **TALKING** *page 230* ◆ **OFFICE** *see* **FAILURE** *page 258* ◆ **POLITICIAN** *see* **DISPUTE** *page 230*

In Committee

COMMITTEE
To dream of a ***committee***, foretells that you will be surprised into doing some distasteful work.

For one to wait on you, foretells that some unfruitful labor will be assigned to you. ◎

CHAIRMAN
To dream that you see the ***chairman*** of any public body, foretells that you will seek elevation and be recompensed by receiving a high position of trust. To see one looking out of humor, you are threatened with unsatisfactory states.

If you ***are a chairman***, you will be distinguished for your justice and kindness to others. ◎

COUNSELOR
To dream of a ***counselor***, means that you are likely to be possessed of some ability yourself, and you will usually prefer your own judgement to that of others. Be guarded in executing your ideas of right. ◎

Campaigns and Conventions

City Life

CITY HALL
To dream of a city hall, ***denotes contentions and threatened lawsuits.***

To a young woman, this dream is a foreboding of unhappy estrangement from her lover by her failure to keep virtue inviolate. ❋

CITY
To dream that you are in a strange city, ***denotes a sorrowful occasion to change your abode or mode of living.*** ❋

CITY COUNCIL
To dream of a city council, ***foretells that your interests will clash with public institutions and there will be discouraging outlooks for you.*** ❋

CONVENTION
To dream of a ***convention***, denotes unusual activity in business affairs and final engagement in love. An inharmonious or displeasing convention brings you disappointment. ◎

RESIGN
To dream that you ***resign*** any position, signifies that you will unfortunately embark in new enterprises.

To hear of others resigning, denotes that you will have unpleasant tidings. ◎

ADVOCATE
To dream that you ***advocate*** any cause, denotes that you will be faithful to your interests, and endeavor to deal honestly with the public, as your interests affect it, and be loyal to your promises to friends. ◎

CAMPAIGN
To dream of making a political one, signifies your opposition to approved ways of conducting business; you will set up original plans for yourself regardless of enemies working against you. Those in power will lose.

If it is a religious people conducting a ***campaign*** against sin, it denotes that you will be called upon to contribute from your private means to sustain charitable institutions.

For a woman to dream that she is interested in a ***campaign against fallen women***, denotes that she will surmount obstacles and prove courageous in time of need. ◎

THE POLITICAL ARENA

Dreams of people and actions in the the political arena *left* may show you a shadowy world that accurately reflects the machiavellian manipulation and assiduous back-scratching that characterizes politics in real life.

ADVOCATE *see* LAWYER *page 245* ◆ CAMPAIGN *see* RELIGION *page 277,* HARLOT, BROTHEL , PROSTITUTE *page 126*

Travel and Transport

Dreams of travel allow the dreamer to be transported to faraway places, or to roam the world by train, boat, or plane. This section covers dreams of travel for pleasure or profit and looks at the many different modes of transport we use to move us through our dreamscapes.

Setting Out

JOURNEY

To dream that you go on a ***journey***, signifies profit or a disappointment, as the travels are pleasing and successful or as accidents and disagreeable events take active part in your journeying.

To see your friends start cheerfully on a journey, signifies delightful change and more harmonious companions than you have heretofore known. If you see them depart looking sad, it may be many moons before you see them again. Power and loss are implied.

To make a ***long-distant journey*** in a much shorter time than you expected, denotes that you will accomplish some work in a surprisingly short time, which will be satisfactory in a way of reimbursement. ◎

TRAVELING

To dream of ***traveling***, signifies profit and pleasure combined.

To dream of traveling through rough, ***unknown places***, portends dangerous enemies, and perhaps sickness. Over bare or rocky steeps, signifies apparent gain, but loss and disappointment will swiftly follow. If the hills or mountains are fertile and green, you will be eminently prosperous and happy.

To dream that you ***travel alone*** in a car, denotes that you may possibly make an eventful journey, and affairs will be worrying. To travel in a crowded car, foretells fortunate adventures, and new and entertaining companions. ◎

Bags and Baggage

To dream of trunks, *foretells journeys and ill luck. To pack your trunk, denotes that you will soon go on a pleasant trip.*

To see the contents of a trunk *thrown about in disorder, foretells quarrels and a hasty journey from which only dissatisfaction will accrue.*

Empty trunks, *foretell disappointment in love and marriage.*

For a drummer to check his trunk, is an omen of advancement and comfort. If he finds that his trunk is too small for his wares, he will soon hear of his promotion, and his desires will reach gratification.

For a young woman to dream that she tries to unlock her trunk and can't, signifies that she will make an effort to win some wealthy person, but by a misadventure she will lose her change. If she fails to lock her trunk, she will be disappointed in making a desired trip. ✺

LUGGAGE

To dream of luggage, *denotes unpleasant cares. You will be encumbered with people who will prove distasteful to you.*

If you are carrying your own luggage, you will be so full of your own distresses that you will be blinded to the sorrow of others.

To lose your luggage, denotes some unfortunate speculation or family dissensions. To the unmarried, it foretells broken engagements. ✺

PORTER

Seeing a porter *in a dream, denotes decided bad luck and eventful happenings.*

To imagine yourself a porter, *denotes humble circumstances.*

To hire one, you will be able to enjoy whatever success comes to you.

To discharge one, signifies that disagreeable charges will be preferred against you. ✺

LUGGAGE

JOURNEY *see* FRIEND *page 124*, DISTANCE *page 88* ◆ TRAVELING *see* ABROAD *page 88*, HILLS, MOUNTAINS *page 90*, CARS *page 224* ◆ TRUNK *see* LOCK *page 213*

Ways and Paths

WAY
To dream that you lose your ***way***, warns you to disabuse your mind of lucky speculations, as your enterprises threaten failure unless you are painstaking in your management of affairs. ◎

PATH
To dream that you are walking in a narrow and rough ***path***, stumbling over rocks and other obstructions, denotes that you will have a rough encounter with adversity, and feverish excitement will weigh heavily upon you.

To dream that you are trying to ***find your path***, foretells that you will fail to accomplish some work that you have striven to push to desired ends.

To walk through a pathway bordered with green grass and flowers, denotes your freedom from oppressing loves. ◎

PROMENADE
To dream of ***promenading***, foretells that you will engage in energetic and profitable pursuits.

To see others promenading, signifies that you will have rivals in your pursuits. ◎

On the Road

ALLEY
To dream of an ***alley*** denotes that your fortune will not be so pleasing or promising as formerly. Many vexing cares will present themselves to you.

For a young woman to wander through an ***alley after dark***, warns her of disreputable friendships and a stigma on her character. ◎

STREET
To dream that you are walking in a ***street***, foretells ill luck and worries. You will almost despair of reaching your goal you have set up in your aspirations.

To be in a ***familiar street*** in a distant city, and it appears dark, foretells that you will make a journey soon, which will not afford the profit or pleasure contemplated.

If the ***street is brilliantly lighted***, you will engage in pleasure, which will quickly pass, leaving no comfort.

To ***pass down a street*** and feel alarmed lest a thug attack you, denotes that you are venturing upon dangerous ground in advancing your pleasure or business. ◎

ROAD
Traveling over a rough, unknown ***road*** in a dream signifies new undertakings, which will bring little else than grief and loss of time.

If the road is bordered with trees and flowers, there will be some pleasant and unexpected fortune for you. If friends accompany you, you will be successful in building an ideal home, with happy children and faithful wife or husband.

To ***lose the road***, foretells that you will make a mistake in deciding some question of trade, and will suffer loss in consequence. ◎

CURB
To dream of stepping on a ***curb***, denotes your rapid rise in business circles, and that you will be held in high esteem by your friends and public.

For lovers to dream of stepping together on a curb, denotes an early marriage and consequent fidelity; but if in your dream you step or fall from a curb, your fortunes will be reversed. ◎

MILEPOST
To dream that you see or pass a ***milepost***, foretells that you will be assailed by doubtful fears in business or love. To see one down, portends that accidents are threatening to give disorder to your affairs. ◎

CROSSROADS
To dream of ***crossroads***, denotes that you will be unable to hold some former favorable opportunity for reaching your desires.

If you are undecided which one to take, you are likely to let unimportant matters irritate you in a distressing manner. You will be better favored by fortune if you decide on your route.

It may be that, after this dream, you will have some important matter of business or love to decide. ◎

Bon Voyage

PASSENGER
To dream that you see ***passengers*** coming in with their luggage, denotes improvement in your surroundings. If they are leaving, you will lose an opportunity of gaining some desired property.

If you are one of the passengers leaving home, you will be dissatisfied with your present living and will seek to change it. ◎

VOYAGE
To make a ***voyage*** in your dreams, foretells that you will receive some inheritance besides that which your labors win for you.

A ***disastrous voyage***, brings incompetence and false loves. ◎

TOURIST
To dream that you are a ***tourist***, denotes that you will engage in some pleasurable affair which will take you away from your usual residence.

To see ***tourists*** in your dream, indicates brisk but unsettled business and anxiety in love. ◎

PATH *see* WALKING *page 267*, GRASS *page 56*, FLOWERS *page 57* ◆ ALLEY *see* DARKNESS *page 82* ◆ STREET *see* WALKING *page 267*, CITY *page 220*, LIGHT *page 216*, FRIGHTENED *page 253*, ◆ ROAD *see* TREES *page 64*, FLOWERS *page 57*, FRIEND *page 124* ◆ PASSENGER *see* LUGGAGE *page 221*

Wheels in Motion

VEHICLE
To ride in a ***vehicle*** while dreaming, foretells threatened loss or illness.

To be thrown from one, foretells hasty and unpleasant news.

To see a broken one, signals failure in important affairs.

To buy one, you will reinstate yourself in your former position. To sell one, denotes unfavorable change in affairs. ◎

DRIVING
To dream of ***driving*** a carriage, signifies unjust criticism of your seeming extravagance. You will be compelled to do things that appear undignified.

To dream of driving a public cab, denotes menial labor, with little change for advancement. If it is a wagon, you will remain in poverty and unfortunate circumstances for sometime.

If you are driven in these conveyances by others, you will profit by superior knowledge of the world, and will always find some path through difficulties.

If you are a man, you will, in affairs with women, drive your wishes to a speedy consummation. If a woman, you will hold men's hearts at low value after succeeding in getting a hold of them. ◎

STAGE DRIVER
To dream of a ***stage driver***, signifies that you will go on a strange journey in quest of both good fortune and happiness. ◎

WHEELS
To see swiftly rotating ***wheels*** in your dreams, foretell that you will be thrifty and energetic in your business and be successful in pursuits of domestic bliss.

To see ***idle or broken wheels***, proclaims the death or absence of someone in your household. ◎

Vintage Vehicles

CART
To dream of riding in a ***cart***, portends that ill luck and constant work will employ your time if you would keep supplies for your family.

To see a cart, denotes bad news from kindred or friends.

To dream of ***driving a cart***, you will meet with merited success in business and other aspirations.

For lovers to ***ride together in a cart***, they will be true in spite of the machinations of rivals. ◎

CHARIOT
To dream of riding in a ***chariot***, foretells that favorable opportunities will present themselves, resulting in your good if rightly used.

To fall or see others fall from one, denotes displacement from high positions. ◎

CARRIAGE
To see a ***carriage***, implies that you will be gratified, and that you will make visits.

To ride in one, you will have a sickness that will soon pass, and you will enjoy health and advantageous positions.

To dream that you are looking for a carriage, you will have to labor hard, but will eventually be possessed with a fair competency. ◎

GIG
To run a ***gig*** in your dream, you will have to forgo a pleasant journey to entertain unwelcome visitors. Sickness also threatens you. ◎

WAGON
To dream of a ***wagon***, denotes that you will be unhappily mated, and that troubles will prematurely age you.

To dream that you drive a wagon ***down a hill***, is ominous of proceedings which will fill you with disquiet, and which will cause you loss.

To drive one uphill, improves your worldly affairs.

To drive a ***heavily loaded wagon***, denotes that duty will hold you in a moral position, despite your efforts to throw her off.

To drive into muddy water, is a gruesome prognostication, bringing you into a vortex of unhappiness and fearful foreboding.

To see a ***covered wagon***, foretells that you will be encompassed by mysterious treachery, which will retard your advancement.

For a young woman to dream that she drives a wagon near a dangerous embankment, portends that she will be driven into an illicit entanglement, which will fill her with terror, lest she be openly discovered and ostracized. If she drives across a clear stream of water, she will enjoy adventure without bringing opprobium upon herself.

A ***broken wagon***, represents distress and failure. ◎

Snowbound

SLEIGH
To see a *sleigh* ***in your dreams, foretells that you will fail in some love adventure, and incur the displeasure of a friend.***

To ride in one, foretells that injudicious engagements will be entered into by you.

For a young woman to dream of *sleighing,* ***she will find much opposition to her choice of a lover, and her conduct will cause her much ill-favor.*** ❋

VEHICLE *see* **BREAK** *page 265,* **TRADE** *page 202,* **CARS, AUTOMOBILE, LIMOUSINE** *page 224* ◆ **DRIVING** *see* **CAB** *page 224* ◆ **WHEELS** *see* **IDLE** *page 251,* **BREAK** *page 265* ◆ **CART** *see* **RIDE** *page 33,* **HORSE** *pages 34–5* ◆ **CARRIAGE** *see* **RIDE** *page 33* ◆ **WAGON** *see* **HILL** *page 90,* **LOAD** *page 38,* **WATER** *page 78,* **MUD** *page 90,* **EMBANKMENT** *page 192,* **BREAK** *page 265* ◆ **SLEIGH** *see* **SNOW** *page 77,* **RIDE** *page 33*

Dream Cars

CARS
To dream of seeing ***cars***, denotes journeying and changing in quick succession.

To get in one, shows that travel which you held in contemplation will be made under different auspices from those that had been calculated upon.

To miss one, foretells that you will be foiled in an attempt to forward your prospects.

To get out of one, denotes that you will succeed with some interesting schemes which will fill you with self congratulations.

AUTOMOBILE
To dream that you ride in an ***automobile***, denotes that you will be restless under pleasant conditions, and will make a change in your affairs. There is grave danger of impolitic conduct intimated through a dream of this nature.

If one breaks down with you, the enjoyment of a pleasure will not extend to the heights you contemplate.

To find yourself escaping from the path of one, signifies that you will do well to avoid some rival as much as you can honestly allow.

For a young woman to look for one, she will be disappointed in her aims to entice someone into her favor. ◎

LIMOUSINE
To dream of riding in a ***limousine***, means that sudden good fortune will soon be imminent. ◎

GASOLINE
To dream of ***gasoline***, denotes that you have a competency coming to you through a struggling source. ◎

Your dream machine may be a motorbike *above*; **your dream ticket could be for a train leaving Grand Central Station** *opposite*.

Two Wheels

BICYCLE
To dream of riding a ***bicycle*** uphill, signifies bright prospects. Riding it downhill, if the rider be a woman, calls for care regarding her good name and health; misfortune hovers near. ◎

MOTORCYCLE
To dream of riding a ***motorcycle***, denotes that you will be in control of your relationships.

If you are watching someone else ***riding a motorcycle***, it foretells that you are stagnating while others around you will move forward in their personal and professional relationships. ◎

MOTORBIKE

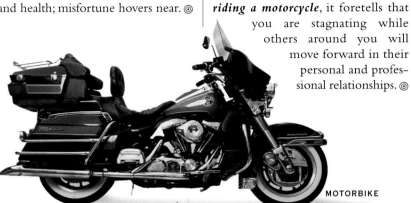

Public Transport

CAB
To ride in a ***cab*** in dreams, is significant of pleasant avocations, and that you will enjoy average prosperity.

To ride in a cab at night with others, indicates that you will have a secret that you will endeavor to keep from your friends.

To dream of ***driving a public cab***, denotes manual labor, with little chance of advancement. ◎

COACH
To dream of riding in a ***coach***, denotes continued losses and depressions in business.

Driving a coach implies removal or business changes. ◎

BUS
To dream of riding on a ***bus***, means that you are making slow and halting progress in your aims and goals.

If the bus is packed with passengers and you are standing, you will find yourself having to compete with many others to succeed.

To dream of traveling on the wrong bus, denotes that you have chosen the wrong path or direction in your life. Carefully evaluate your situation to find the correct road. ◎

STREETCARS
To see ***streetcars*** in your dreams, denotes that some person is actively interested in causing you malicious trouble and disquiet.

To ***ride on a car***, foretells that rivalry and jealousy will enthrall your happiness.

To ***stand on the platform*** of a streetcar while it is running, denotes that you will attempt to carry on an affair that will be extremely dangerous; but if you ride without accident, you will be successful.

If the platform is up high, your danger will be more apparent; but if low, you will barely accomplish your purpose. ◎

TRAILER
To dream of traveling in a ***trailer***, signifies that you will soon embark upon a worrisome journey.

To dream of ***living in a trailer***, signifies a reversal of fortune. ◎

AUTOMOBILE *see* **ESCAPE** *page 266* ◆ **GASOLINE** *see* **OIL** *page 72* ◆ **BICYCLE** *see* **WHEELS** *page 223,* **HILL** *page 90* ◆ **CAB** *see* **DARKNESS** *page 82,* **DRIVING** *page 223* ◆ **COACH** *see* **DRIVING** *page 223* ◆ **BUS** *see* **PASSENGER** *page 222*

On the Rails

TRAIN

To see a ***train of cars*** moving in your dreams, you will soon have cause to make a journey.

To be on a ***train*** and it appears to move smoothly along, though there is no track, denotes that you will be much worried over some affair which will eventually prove a source of profit to you.

To see ***freight trains*** in your dreams, is an omen of changes which will tend to your elevation.

To dream of ***sleeping-cars***, indicate that your struggle to amass wealth is animated by the desire of gratifying selfish and lewd principles which should be mastered and controlled.

To find yourself in a dream, on top of a sleeping car, denotes that you will make a journey with an unpleasant companion, with whom you will spend money and time that could be used in a more profitable and congenial way, and whom you will seek to avoid.

To dream of traveling on ***the wrong train***, denotes that you have chosen the wrong path or direction in your life. Carefully evaluate your situation to find the correct road. ◎

LOCOMOTIVE

To dream of a ***locomotive*** running with great speed, denotes a rapid rise in fortune, and foreign travel.

If the locomotive is disabled, then many vexations will interfere with business affairs, and anticipated journeys will be laid aside through the want of means.

To see one completely demolished, signifies great distress and loss of property.

To hear one coming, denotes news of a foreign nature. Business will assume changes that will mean success to all classes.

To hear it whistle, you will be pleased and surprised at the appearance of a friend who has been absent, or an unexpected offer, which means preferment to you. ◎

RAILROAD

If you dream of a ***railroad***, you will find that your business will need close attention, as enemies are trying to usurp you.

For a young woman to dream of railroads, she will make a journey to visit friends, and will enjoy some distinction.

To see an obstruction on these roads, indicates foul play in your affairs.

To walk the ***crossties of a railroad***, signifies a time of worry and laborious work.

To ***walk the rails***, you may expect to obtain much happiness from your skilful manipulation of affairs.

To see a road inundated with clear water, foretells that pleasure will wipe out misfortune for a time, but it will rise, phoenixlike, again. ◎

SUBWAY

To dream of riding in an ***underground subway***, means that you will soon have many problems disturb you. These problems will involve emotional and psychological turmoil.

To dream of being stuck between ***subway stations***, denotes that you will soon be caught in a moral dilemma. Much patience and thought are required before a decision can be made to resolve the situation. ◎

THE RAILWAY STATION

TRAIN *see* **SLEEP** *page 274* ◆ **LOCOMOTIVE** *see* **WHISTLE** *page 276* ◆ **RAILROAD** *see* **WALKING** *page 267* ◆ **SUBWAY** *see* **UNDERGROUND, TUNNEL** *page 193*

Sailing Away

SAILING
To dream of ***sailing*** on calm waters, foretells easy access to blissful joys, and immunity from poverty and whatever brings misery.

To ***sail on a small vessel***, denotes that your desires will not excel your power of possessing them. ◎

LEEWARD
To dream of sailing ***leeward***, denotes to a sailor a prosperous and merry voyage. To others, a pleasant journey.

SAILOR
To dream of ***sailors***, portends long and exciting journeys.

For a young woman to dream of sailors, is ominous of a separation from her lover through a frivolous flirtation. If she dreams that she is a sailor, she will indulge in some unmaidenly escapade, and be in danger of losing a faithful lover. ◎

MARINER
To dream that you are a ***mariner***, denotes a long journey to distant countries, and much pleasure will be connected with the trip.

If you see your vessel sailing without you, much personal discomfort will be wrought you by rivals. ◎

CREW
To dream of seeing a ***crew*** getting ready to leave port, some unforeseen circumstances will cause you to give up a journey from which you would have gained much.

To see a ***crew working*** to save a ship in a storm, denotes disaster on land and sea. To the young, this dream bodes evil. ◎

Sailing on the sea of dreams *above* may seem just as perilous as life on the real waves of the ocean.

AT SEA

SHIPS
To dream of ***ships***, foretells honor and unexpected elevation to ranks above your mode of life.

To hear of a ***shipwreck***, is ominous of a disastrous turn in affairs. Your female friends will betray you.

To lose your life in one, denotes that you will have an exceeding close call on your life or honor.

To see a ship on her way through a tempestuous storm, foretells that you will be unfortunate in business transactions, and you will be perplexed to find means of hiding some intrigue from the public, as your partner in the affair will threaten you with betrayal.

To see others shipwrecked, you will seek in vain to shelter some friend from disgrace and insolvency. ◎

VESSELS
To dream of ***vessels***, denotes labor and activity. ◎

BOAT
Boat signals forecast bright prospects, if upon clear water. If the water is unsettled and turbulent, cares and unhappy changes threaten the dreamer.

If with a gay party you board a boat without an accident, many favors will be showered upon you.

Unlucky the dreamer who falls overboard while sailing upon stormy waters. ◎

SAILING *see* **LAKE, RIVER, SEA, OCEAN** *page 79*, **CALM** *page 75* ◆ **CREW** *see* **SEAPORT, QUAY** *page 228* ◆ **SHIPS** *see* **WRECK** *page 266*, **STORM** *page 76* ◆ **BOAT** *see* **ROWBOAT** *page 227*, **WATER** *page 78*, **PARTY** *page 85*, **STORM** *page 76*

Ship's Parts

MAST
To dream of seeing the ***masts*** of ships, denotes long and pleasant voyages, the making of many new friends, and the gaining of new possessions.

To see the masts of ***wrecked ships***, denotes sudden changes in your circumstances which will necessitate giving over anticipated pleasures.

If a sailor dreams of a mast, he will soon sail on an eventful trip. ◎

ANCHOR
To dream of an ***anchor***, is favorable to sailors, if seas are calm. To others, it portends separation from friends, change of residence, and foreign travel. Sweethearts are soon to quarrel if either sees an anchor. ◎

RUDDER
To dream of a ***rudder***, you will soon make a pleasant journey to foreign lands, and new friendships will be formed.

A ***broken rudder***, augurs disappointment and sickness. ◎

DECK
To dream of being on the ***deck*** of a ship and that a storm is raging, forebodes that great disasters and unfortunate alliances will overtake you.

If in your dream the sea is calm and the light distinct, your way is clear to success.

For lovers, this dream augurs happiness. ◎

OAR
To dream of handling ***oars***, portends disappointments for you, inasmuch as you will sacrifice your own pleasure for the comfort of others.

To dream that you ***lose an oar***, denotes vain efforts to carry out your designs satisfactorily.

A ***broken oar*** represents interruption in some anticipated pleasure. ◎

CABIN
The ***cabin*** of a ship is a rather unfortunate place to be in, in a dream. A dream of a cabin indicates that some mischief is brewing for you. You will most likely be engaged in a lawsuit, in which you will lose from the instability of your witness. ◎

All Kinds of Boats

ROWBOAT
To dream that you are in a ***rowboat*** with others, denotes that you will derive much pleasure from the companionship of gay and worldly persons. If the boat is capsized, you will suffer financial losses by engaging in seductive enterprises.

If you find yourself defeated in a ***rowing race***, you will lose favors to your rivals with your sweetheart. If you are the victor, you will easily obtain supremacy with women. Your affairs will move agreeably. ◎

CANOE
To paddle a ***canoe*** on a calm stream, denotes your perfect confidence in your own ability to conduct your business in a profitable way.

To row with a sweetheart, means an early marriage and fidelity.

To row on rough waters, you will have to tame a shrew before you attain connubial bliss.

Affairs in the business world will prove disappointing after you dream of rowing in muddy waters.

If the waters are shallow and swift, a hasty courtship or stolen pleasures, from which there can be no lasting good, are indicated.

Shallow, clear, and calm waters in rowing, signifies happiness of a pleasing character, but of short duration.

Water is typical of futurity in the dream realms. If a pleasant immediate future awaits the dreamer, he will come in close proximity with clear water. Or if he emerges from disturbed watery elements into waking life, the near future is filled with crosses for him. ◎

RAFT
To dream of a ***raft***, denotes new locations to engage in enterprises, which will prove successful.

To dream of ***floating on a raft***, denotes uncertain journeys. If you reach your destination, you will surely come into good fortune.

If a raft breaks, or any such mishap befalls it, yourself or some friend will suffer from an accident, or sickness will bear unfortunate results. ◎

LIFEBOAT
To dream of being in a ***lifeboat***, denotes escape from threatened evil.

If you see a ***lifeboat sinking***, friends will contribute to your distress.

To be ***lost in a lifeboat***, you will be overcome with trouble, in which your friends will be included to some extent. If you are saved, you will escape a great calamity. ◎

YACHT
To see a ***yacht*** in a dream, denotes happy recreation away from business and troublesome encumbrances. A stranded one, represents miscarriage of entertaining engagements. ◎

PACKET
To dream of seeing a ***packet*** [cargo ship] coming in, foretells that some pleasant recreation is in store for you.

To see one going out, you will experience slight losses and disappointments. ◎

MAST *see* **SHIPS** *page 226,* **WRECK** *page 266* ◆ **ANCHOR** *see* **SEA** *page 79,* **CALM** *page 75* ◆ **RUDDER** *see* **BREAK** *page 265* ◆ **DECK** *see* **SHIPS** *page 226,* **STORM** *page 76,* **CALM** *page 75,* **LIGHT** *page 216* ◆ **OAR** *see* **BREAK** *page 265* ◆ **ROWBOAT** *see* **BOAT** *page 226* ◆ **CANOE** *see* **WATER** *page 78,* **SWEETHEART** *page 124,* **MUD** *page 90,* **CALM** *page 75* ◆ **RAFT** *see* **FLOATING** *page 268,* **BREAK** *page 265*

Land Ho!

SAFE HARBOR

LIGHTHOUSE
If you see a ***lighthouse*** through a storm, difficulties and grief will assail you, but they will disperse before prosperity and happiness.

To see a lighthouse from a placid sea, denotes calm joys and congenial friends. ◎

DOCKS
To dream of being on ***docks***, denotes that you are about to make an unpropitious journey. Accidents will threaten you. If you are there, wandering alone, and darkness overtakes you, you will meet with deadly enemies; but if the sun be shining, you will escape threatening dangers. ◎

QUAY
To dream of a ***quay***, denotes that you will contemplate making a long tour in the near future.

To see vessels while standing on the quay, denotes the fruition of wishes and designs. ◎

FERRY
To wait at a ***ferry*** for a boat and see the waters swift and muddy, you will be baffled in your highest wishes and designs by unforeseen circumstances.

To ***cross a ferry*** while the water is calm and clear, you will be very lucky in carrying out your plans, and fortune will crown you. ◎

SEAPORT
To dream of visiting a ***seaport***, denotes that you will have opportunities of traveling and acquiring knowledge, but there will be some who will object to your anticipated tours. ◎

Air Travel

AIRPLANE
To dream of seeing an ***airplane*** in flight and then disappearing, denotes that you will escape an unhappy or confining situation.

To see an airplane moving in your dreams, suggests that you will soon have cause to make a journey.

To dream of ***flying in an airplane***, foretells that you will make satisfactory progress in your future speculations.

To dream of being in an ***airplane accident***, foretells gloomy returns for much disturbing and worrisome planning. ◎

PARACHUTE
To dream of a ***parachute*** floating to the ground, foretells a desire to extricate yourself from a personal or business relationship.

To dream of ***jumping with a parachute***, denotes major change in your personal life. You will soon be removing yourself from an unwanted relationship.

To dream that the ***parachute fails to open***, means that great heartache and sadness will ensue. ◎

HELICOPTER
To dream of a ***helicopter*** hovering above you, signifies that a visitor is likely to arrive soon. If the helicopter seems to be aggressive or dangerous, the visitor will be a threatening and menacing one.

To dream of hearing the ***peculiar chopper noise***, indicates that you will soon be making a short journey. ◎

AIRPLANE

Space Travel

ROCKET
To dream of a ***rocket***, indicates that you are currently frustrated with your personal relationship. You are restless and in need of some movement or advancement in your relationship.

To see yourself as manning the ***rocketship***, means that you will take control over your difficulties.

To see a ***rocket launch***, means that your frustrations over your personal relationship will soon be resolved happily.

To see a ***rocket ascending*** in your dream, foretells sudden and unexpected elevation, successful wooing, and faithful keeping of the marriage vows.

To see them falling, unhappy unions may be expected. ◎

SPACE
To dream that you are traveling in outer ***space***, means that you will soon be freeing yourself from a confining situation. You will experience a newfound sense of independence and freedom. ◎

SPACE ALIENS
To dream of encountering ***space aliens***, means that you will meet people whom you consider bizarre and strange. You will at first feel uncomfortable with them, but they will soon become very positive influences in your life. ◎

LIGHTHOUSE *see* **LIGHT** *page 216,* **BEACON LIGHT** *page 230* ◆ **DOCKS** *see* **DARKNESS** *page 82* ◆ **QUAY** *see* **VESSELS** *page 226,* **VISIT** *page 205* ◆ **AIRPLANE** *see* **FLYING** *page 268* ◆ **PARACHUTE** *see* **JUMPING** *page 267,* **FAILURE** *page 258* ◆ **HELICOPTER** *see* **NOISE** *page 276* ◆ **ROCKET** *see* **FIREWORK** *page 173,* **ASCENDING** *page 268* ◆ **SPACE** *see* **SUN, MOON, PLANET, COMET** *page 84* ◆ **SPACE ALIENS** *see* **ALIEN** *page 87*

Media and Messages

Dreams are often considered to be messages sent to us during sleep, and dreaming of the medium as well as the message seems to impart an extra power. This section covers communication by sign, speech, the written word, books and newspapers, post, electronic means, and the use of optical instruments that can help us to see more clearly.

Numbers and Figures

FISHING FOR NUMBERS

NUMBERS

To dream of ***numbers***, denotes that unsettled conditions in business will cause you uneasiness and dissatisfaction. ◎

FIGURES

To dream of ***figures***, indicates great mental distress and wrong. You will be the loser in a big deal if you are not careful of your actions and conversation. ◎

A GEOMETRIC LANDSCAPE

Boats *opposite top left* **and planes** *opposite right* **may transport you in your dreams. Signs, symbols and figures** *above* **and circles** *right* **all carry their own coded meanings in dreams.**

Signs, Shapes, and Symbols

CIPHER

To dream of reading ***cipher***, indicates that you are interested in literary researches, and by constant study you will become well acquainted with the habits and lives of the ancients. ◎

HIEROGLYPHS

Hieroglyphs seen in a dream, foretell that wavering judgement in some vital matter may cause you great distress and money loss. To be able to read them, denotes that your success in overcoming some evil is foretold. ◎

CIRCLE

To dream of a ***circle***, denotes that your affairs will deceive you in their proportions of gain.

For a young woman to dream of a circle, warns her of indiscreet involvement to the exclusion of marriage. ◎

CROSS

To dream of seeing a ***cross***, indicates trouble ahead for you. Shape your affairs accordingly.

To dream of seeing a person ***bearing a cross***, you will be called on by missionaries to aid in charities. ◎

FORM

To see anything ***ill formed***, denotes disappointment. To have a ***beautiful form***, denotes favorable conditions to health and business. ◎

SIDE

To dream of seeing only the ***side*** of any object, denotes that some person is going to treat your honest proposals with indifference.

To dream that your side pains you, there will be vexation in your affairs that will gall your endurance.

To dream that you have a fleshy, healthy side, you will be successful in courtship and business. ◎

CORNER

This is an unfavorable dream if the dreamer is frightened and secretes himself in a ***corner*** for safety.

To see persons talking in a corner, denotes that enemies are seeking to destroy you. The chances are that someone whom you consider a friend will prove a traitor to your interest. ◎

TRIANGLE

To dream of a ***triangle***, foretells separation from friends, and love affairs will terminate in disagreements. ◎

WEDGE

To dream of a ***wedge***, denotes that you will have trouble in some business arrangements which will be the cause of your separation from relatives. Separation of lovers or friends may also be implied. ◎

NUMBERS, FIGURES *see* **COUNTING, ADDITION** *page 180* ◆ **CROSS** *see* **CRUCIFIX, CRUCIFIXION** *page 279* ◆
FORM *see* **BEAUTY, UGLY** *page 100* ◆ **SIDE** *see* **PAIN** *page 107* ◆ **CORNER** *see* **FRIGHTENED** *page 253,* **TALKING** *page 230,* **GOSSIP** *page 231*

Clear Signals

FLAG

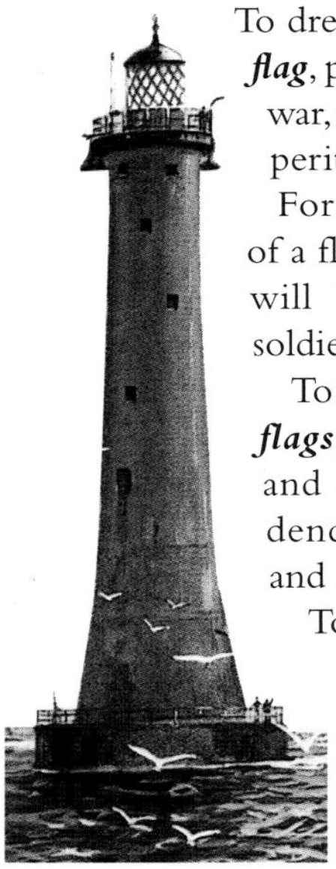

THE SAILOR'S BEACON

To dream of your national *flag*, portends victory if at war, and if at peace, prosperity.

For a woman to dream of a flag, denotes that she will be ensnared by a soldier.

To dream of ***foreign flags***, denotes ruptures and a breach of confidence between nations and friends.

To dream of being ***signaled by a flag***, denotes that you should be careful of your health and name, as both are threatened.

BEACON LIGHT

For a sailor to see a ***beacon light***, portends fair seas and a prosperous voyage.

For persons in distress, warm, unbroken attachments will arise among the young.

To the sick, speedy recovery and continued health. Business will gain new impetus.

To see it go out in time of storm or distress, indicates reverses at the time when you thought Fortune was deciding in your favor.

Beacon lights *above* **may signal to you in your dreams; you may hear again the eloquence of such masters of oratory as Martin Luther King** *right* **or listen to the simple tales and fables of childhood** *opposite*.

Plain Speaking

TALKING

To dream of talking, ***denotes that you will soon hear of the sickness of relatives, and there will be worries in your affairs.***

To hear others talking loudly, foretells that you will be accused of interfering in the affairs of others. To think they are talking about you, denotes that you are menaced with illness and disfavor.

ORATOR

Being under the spell of an orator's ***eloquence, denotes that you will heed the voice of flattery to your own detriment, as you will be persuaded into offering aid to unworthy people.***

If a young woman falls in love with an orator, it is proof that in her loves she will be affected by outward show.

ELOQUENT

If you think you are eloquent ***of speech in your dreams, there will be pleasant news for you concerning one in whose interest you are working.***

To fail in impressing others with your eloquence, ***there will be much disorder in your affairs.***

INCOHERENCE

To dream of incoherence, ***usually denotes extreme nervousness and excitement through the oppression of changing events.***

DISPUTE

To dream of holding disputes ***over trifles, indicates bad health and unfairness in judging others.***

To dream of disputing with learned people, shows that you have some latent ability, but are a little sluggish in developing it.

SWEARING

To dream of swearing, ***denotes some unpleasant obstruction in business. A lover will have cause to suspect the faithfulness of his affianced after this dream.***

To dream that you are swearing before your family, denotes that disagreements will soon be brought about by your unloyal conduct.

INVECTIVE

To dream of using invectives, ***warns you of passionate outbursts of anger, which may estrange you from close companions.***

To hear others using them, foretells that enemies are closing you in to apparent wrong and deceits.

MARTIN LUTHER KING

FLAG *see* **STANDARD-BEARER, BANNER** *page 262,* **ABROAD** *page 88* ◆ **BEACON LIGHT** *see* **LIGHT** *page 216,* **SAILOR** *page 226,* **STORM** *page 76* ◆ **TALKING** *see* **NOISE** *page 276* ◆ **ELOQUENCE** *see* **FAILURE** *page 258* ◆ **SWEARING** *see* **FAMILY** *page 127,* **OATH** *page 219,* **PROFANITY** *page 250* ◆ **INVECTIVE** *see* **BLASPHEMY** *page 250,* **CALUMNY** *page 231*

Scandal

SCANDAL

To dream that you are an object of ***scandal***, denotes that you are not particular to select good and true companions, but rather enjoy having fast men and women contribute to your pleasure. Trade and business of any character will suffer dullness after this dream.

For a young woman to dream that she ***discusses a scandal***, foretells that she will confer favors, which should be sacred, to someone who will deceiver her into believing that he is honorably inclined. Marriage rarely follows swiftly after dreaming of scandal. ◎

THE TALE OF RED RIDING HOOD

Instructive Tales

FABLES

To dream of reading or telling ***fables***, denotes pleasant tasks and a literary turn of mind. To the young, it signifies romantic attachments.

To hear or tell ***religious fables***, denotes that the dreamer will become very devotional. ◎

ANECDOTE

To dream of relating an ***anecdote***, signifies that you will greatly prefer gay companionship to that of intellect, and that your affairs will prove as unstable as yourself.

For a young woman to hear anecdotes related, denotes that she will be one of a merry party of pleasure seekers. ◎

PARABLES

To dream of ***parables***, denotes that you will be undecided as to the best course to pursue in dissenting to some business complication. To the lover or young woman, this is a prophecy of misunderstandings and disloyalty. ◎

Gossip and Slander

GOSSIP

To dream of being interested in common ***gossip***, you will undergo some humiliating trouble caused by overconfidence in transient friendships.

If you are the ***object of gossip***, you may expect some pleasurable surprise. ◎

SLANDER

To dream that you are ***slandered***, is a sign of your untruthful dealings with ignorance.

If you ***slander anyone***, this means that you will feel the loss of friends through selfishness. ◎

CALUMNY

To dream that you are the subject of ***calumny***, denotes that your interests will suffer at the hands of evil-minded gossips.

For a young woman, it warns her to be careful of her conduct, as her movements are being critically observed by persons who claim to be her friends. ◎

Foreign Tongues

LATIN

To dream of studying this language, denotes victory and distinction in your efforts to sustain your opinion on subjects of grave interest to the public welfare. ◎

GREEK

To dream of reading ***Greek***, denotes that your ideas will be discussed and finally accepted and put into practical use. To fail to read it, denotes that technical difficulties are in your way. ◎

ENGLISH

To dream, if you are a foreigner, of meeting ***English*** people, denotes that you will have to suffer through the selfish designs of others. ◎

INTERPRETER

To dream of an ***interpreter***, denotes that you will undertake affairs which will fail in profit. ◎

FABLES *see* **READING** *page 233,* **RELIGION** *page 277* ◆ **PARABLES** *see* **CHRIST** *page 279* ◆ **GOSSIP** *see* **TALKING** *page 230* ◆ **GREEK** *see* **READING** *page 233*

Writing

WRITING

To dream that you are ***writing***, foretells that you will make a mistake which will almost prove your undoing.

To see writing, denotes that you will be upbraided for your careless conduct, and a lawsuit may cause you embarrassment.

To try to read ***strange writings***, signifies that you will escape enemies only by making no new speculation after this dream. ◎

INSCRIPTION

To dream that you see an ***inscription***, foretells that you will shortly receive unpleasant communications. If you are reading them on tombs, you will be distressed by sickness of a grave nature. To write one, you will lose a valued friend. ◎

Paper or Parchment

PAPER OR PARCHMENT

If you have occasion in your dreams to refer to, or handle, any ***paper or parchment***, you will be threatened with losses. They are likely to be in the nature of a lawsuit. For a young woman, it means that she will be angry with her lover and that she fears the opinion of acquaintances. Beware, if you are married, of disagreements in the precincts of the home. ◎

BOOK OF KELLS

Pens and Ink

PEN

To dream of a ***pen***, foretells that you are unfortunately being led into serious complications by your love of adventure. If the pen refuses to write, you will be charged with a serious breach of morality. ◎

PENCIL

To dream of ***pencils***, denotes favorable occupations. For a young woman to write with one, foretells that she will be fortunate in marriage, if she does not rub out words; in that case, she will be disappointed in her lover. ◎

PEN

BALLPOINT PEN

To dream of using a ***ballpoint pen***, means that you will soon write a letter to a dear old friend to whom you have not spoken for many years. ◎

INK

If you see ***ink*** spilled over your clothing, many small and spiteful meannesses will be wrought you through envy.

If a young woman sees ink, she will be slandered by a rival.

To dream that you have ***ink on your fingers***, you will be jealous and seek to injure someone unless you exercise your better nature. If it is red ink, you will be involved in serious trouble.

To dream that you ***make ink***, you will engage in a low and debasing business, and you will fall into disreputable associations.

To see ***bottles of ink*** in your dreams, indicates enemies and unsuccessful interests. ◎

INKSTAND

Empty ***inkstands*** denote that you will narrowly escape public denunciation for some supposed injustice.

If you see them filled with ink, and if you are not cautious, enemies will succeed in calumniation. ◎

QUILLS

To dream of ***quills***, denotes, to the literarily inclined, a season of success.

To dream of them as ornaments, signifies a rushing trade, and some remuneration.

For a young woman to be putting a quill on her hat, denotes that she will attempt many conquests, and her success will depend upon her charms. ◎

Calligraphy

HANDWRITING

To dream that you see and recognize your own ***handwriting***, foretells that malicious enemies will use your expressed opinion to foil you in advancing to some competed position. ◎

COPPERPLATE

Copperplate seen in a dream, is a warning of discordant views causing unhappiness between members of the same household. ◎

Dreams of communication may see you writing with a pen *above*, **studying ancient manuscripts** *left*, **reading** *opposite top* **or browsing in a library or bookstore** *opposite*.

WRITING *see* **READING** *page 233* ◆ **INK** *see* **CLOTHES** *page 154*, **FINGER** *page 97*, **BOTTLES** *page 210* ◆ **QUILLS** *see* **FEATHER** *page 43*, **ORNAMENT** *page 161*, **HAT** *page 160*

The Written Word

TEXT

To dream of hearing a minister reading his ***text***, denotes that quarrels will lead to separation with some friend.

To dream that you are in a dispute about a text, foretells unfortunate adventures for you.

If you try to recall a text, you will meet with unexpected difficulties.

If you are repeating and pondering over one, you will have great obstacles to overcome if you gain your desires. ◎

READING

AUTHOR

For an ***author*** to dream that his manuscript has been rejected by the publisher, denotes some doubt at first, but finally his work will be accepted as authentic and original.

To dream of seeing an author over his work, perusing it with anxiety, denotes that you will be worried over some literary work, either your own or that of some other person. ◎

MANUSCRIPT

To dream of a ***manuscript*** in an unfinished state, forebodes disappointment. If finished and clearly written, great hopes will be realized.

If you are at ***work on a manuscript***, you will have many fears for some cherished hope; but if you keep the blurs out of your work, you will succeed in your undertakings.

If it is rejected by the publishers, you will be hopeless for a time, but eventually your most sanguine desires will become a reality.

If you lose it, you will be subjected to disappointment.

If you see it burn, some work of your own will bring you profit and

Books and Reading

READING

To be engaged in ***reading*** in your dreams, denotes that you will excel in some work which appears difficult.

To see ***others reading***, denotes that your friends will be kind and are well disposed.

To ***give a reading***, or to discuss reading, you will cultivate your literary ability.

Indistinct or incoherent reading, implies worries and disappointments. ◎

BOOKS

To dream of studying them, portends pleasant pursuits, honor, and riches.

For an author to dream of his works going to press, is a dream of caution; he will have much trouble in placing them before the public.

To dream of spending great study and time in solving some intricate subjects, and the hidden meaning of learned authors, is significant of honors well earned.

To see children at their ***books***, denotes harmony and good conduct of the young.

To dream of ***old books***, is a warning to shun evil in any form. ◎

LIBRARY

To dream that you are in a ***library***, denotes that you will grow discontented with your environments and associations, and seek companionship in study and the exploration of ancient customs.

To find yourself in a library for other purposes than study, foretells that your conduct will deceive your friends, and where you would have them believe that you had literary aspirations, you will find illicit assignations. ◎

BOOKSTORE

To visit a ***bookstore*** in your dreams, foretells that you will be filled with literary aspirations, which will interfere with your other works and labors. ◎

BOOKCASE

To see a ***bookcase*** in your dreams, signifies that you will associate knowledge with your work and pleasure.

Empty bookcases, imply that you will be put out because of lack of means or facility for work. ◎

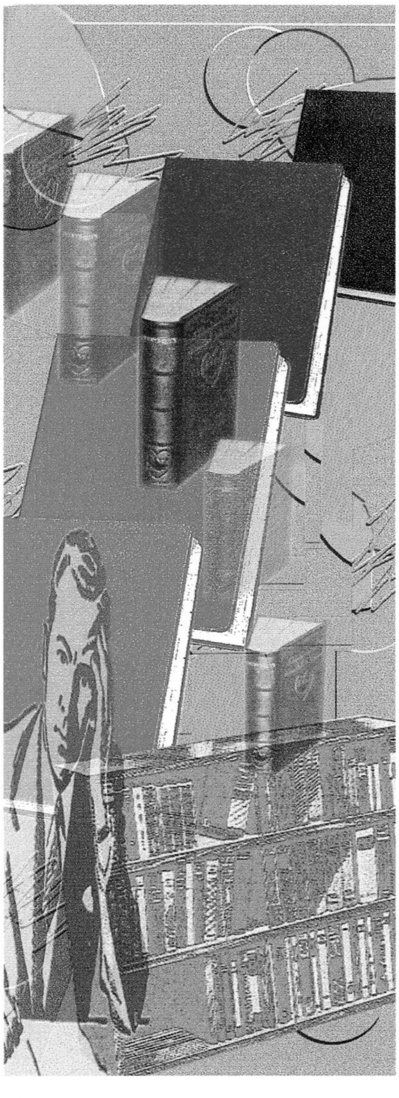

THE BOOKSTORE

TEXT *see* **MINISTER** *page 280*, **DISPUTE** *page 230* ◆ **AUTHOR** *see* **PUBLISHER** *page 234*, **ANXIETY** *page 253* ◆
MANUSCRIPT *see* **COMPLETION** *page 194*, **PUBLISHER** *page 234*, **FIRE** *page 80* ◆ **READING** *see* **INDISTINCTNESS** *page 275*,
INCOHERENCE *page 230* ◆ **BOOKS** *see* **HIDDEN** *page 270*, **CHILDREN** *page 128*, **ENCYCLOPEDIA, DICTIONARY** *page 180* ◆
BOOKSTORE *see* **STORE** *page 203* ◆ **BOOKCASE** *see* **CUPBOARD, SHELVES** *page 211*

Publishing

PRINTER
To see a ***printer*** in your dreams, is a warning of poverty, if you neglect to practice economy and cultivate energy.

For a woman to dream that her love or associate is a printer, foretells that she will fail to please her parents in the selection of a close friend. ◎

PRINTING OFFICE
To be in a ***printing office*** in dreams, denotes that slander and contumely will threaten you.

To ***run a printing office***, is indicative of hard luck.

For a young woman to dream that her sweetheart is connected with a printing office, denotes that she will have a lover who is unable to lavish money or time upon her, and she will not be sensible enough to see why he is so stingy. ◎

COMPOSING STICK
To see in your dreams a ***composing stick***, foretells that difficult problems will disclose themselves, and you will be at great trouble to meet them. ◎

PUBLISHER
To dream of a ***publisher***, foretells long journeys and aspirations to the literary craft.

If a woman dreams that her ***husband is a publisher***, she will be jealous of more than one woman of his acquaintance, and spicy scenes will ensue.

For a publisher to ***reject your manuscript***, denotes that you will suffer disappointment at the miscarriage of cherished designs. If he accepts it, you will rejoice in the full fruition of your hopes. If he loses it, you will suffer evil at the hands of strangers. ◎

Dream messages may be delivered to you via a newspaper *top* **or a printing office** *right.* **The mailman** *opposite top* **may visit you, or you may take your message to the mailman via the postal system** *opposite bottom.*

News

NEWS
To hear good ***news*** in a dream, denotes that you will be fortunate in affairs, and have harmonious companions.

If the news be bad, contrary conditions will exist. ◎

NEWSPAPER
To dream of ***newspapers***, denotes that frauds will be detected in your dealings, and your reputation will likewise be affected.

To ***print a newspaper***, you will have opportunities for making foreign journeys and friends.

Trying, but failing to ***read a newspaper***, denotes that you will fail in some uncertain enterprises. ◎

NEWSPAPER REPORTER
If in your dreams you unwillingly see them, you will be annoyed with small talk, and perhaps quarrels of a low character.

If you are a ***newspaper reporter*** in your dreams, there will be a varied course of travel offered you, though you may experience unpleasant situations; yet there will be some honor and gain attached. ◎

Advertising

ADVERTISEMENT
To dream that you are getting out ***advertisements***, denotes that you will have to resort to physical labor to promote your interests or establish your fortune.

To ***read advertisements***, denotes that enemies will overtake you and defeat you in rivalry. ◎

HANDBILLS
To dream of distributing ***handbills*** over the country, is a sign of contentions and possible lawsuits.

If you dream of ***printing handbills***, you will hear unfavorable news. ◎

NEWSPAPER BOY

THE PRINTING PRESS

PRINTING OFFICE *see* **SWEETHEART** *page 124* ◆ **PUBLISHER** *see* **HUSBAND** *page 132,* **MANUSCRIPT** *page 233* ◆
NEWSPAPER, ADVERTISEMENT *see* **READING** *page 233*

Messages and Mailmen

THE MAILMAN

MESSAGE
To dream of receiving a ***message***, denotes that changes will take place in your affairs.

To dream of ***sending a message***, denotes that you will be placed in unpleasant situations. ◎

MAILMAN
If you dream of a ***mailman*** coming with your letters, you will soon receive news of an unwelcome and an unpleasant character.

If he passes without your mail, disappointment and sadness will befall you.

If you give him letters to mail, you will suffer injury through envy or jealousy.

To ***converse with a mailman***, you will implicate yourself in some scandalous proceedings. ◎

UNITED STATES MAILBOX
To see a ***United States mailbox*** in a dream, denotes that you are about to enter into transactions which will be claimed to be illegal.

To put a letter in one, denotes you will be held responsible for some irregularity of another. ◎

Parcel Post

PARCEL
To dream of a ***parcel*** being delivered to you, denotes that you will be pleasantly surprised by the return of some absent one, or be cared for in a worldly way.

If you ***carry a parcel***, you will have some unpleasant task to perform.

To ***let a parcel fall*** on the way as you go to deliver it, you will see some detail fail to go through. ◎

LABEL
To dream of a ***label***, foretells that you will let an enemy see the inside of your private affairs, and you will suffer from the negligence. ◎

POSTAGE
To dream of ***postage*** stamps, denotes system and remuneration in business.

If you try to use ***canceled stamps***, you will fall into disrepute.

To ***receive stamps***, signifies a rapid rise to distinction.

To see ***torn stamps***, denotes that there are obstacles in your way. ◎

POST OFFICE
To dream of a ***post office***, betokens a sign of unpleasant tidings and ill luck generally. ◎

POSTING A LETTER

MAILMAN *see* **LETTER** *page 236,* **TALKING** *page 230* ◆ **UNITED STATES MAILBOX** *see* **LETTER** *page 236*

Letters

LETTER

Letters nearly always bring worry.

To dream that you see a ***registered letter***, foretells that some money matters will disrupt long-established relations.

For a young woman to dream that she receives such a letter, intimates that she will be offered a competency, but it will not be on strictly legal or moral grounds; others may play toward her a dishonorable part.

To the lover, this bears heavy presentiments of disagreeable mating. His sweetheart will covet other gifts than his own.

To dream of an ***anonymous letter***, denotes that you will receive injury from an unsuspected source.

To write one, foretells that you will be jealous of a rival, whom you admit to be your superior.

To dream of ***getting letters*** bearing unpleasant news, denotes difficulties or illness. If the news is of a joyous character, you will have many things to be thankful for. If the letter is affectionate, but is written on green or colored paper, you will be slighted in love and business. Despondency will envelop you. Blue ink, denotes constancy and affection, also bright fortune.

Red colors in a letter, imply estrangements through suspicion and jealousy, but this may be overcome by wise maneuvering of the suspected party.

If a young woman dreams that she receives a ***letter from her lover*** and places it near her heart, she will be worried very much by a good-looking rival. Truthfulness is often rewarded with jealousy.

If you ***fail to read the letter***, you will lose something in either a business or a social way.

If you have your ***letter intercepted***, rival enemies are working to defame you.

To dream of trying to ***conceal a letter*** from your sweetheart or wife, intimates that you are interested in unworthy occupations.

To dream of a ***letter with a black border***, signifies distress and the death of some relative.

To receive a letter written on black paper with white ink, denotes that gloom and disappointment will assail you, and friendly interposition will render small relief. If the letter passes between husband and wife, it means separation under sensational charges. If lovers, look for quarrels and threats of suicide. To business people, it denotes enviousness and covetousness.

To dream that you ***write a letter***, denotes that you will be hasty in condemning someone on suspicion, and regrets will follow.

A ***torn letter*** in a dream, indicates that hopeless mistakes may ruin your reputation.

To receive a ***letter by hand***, denotes that you are acting ungenerously toward your companions or sweetheart, and you also are not upright in your dealings.

To dream often of receiving a letter from a friend, foretells his arrival, or you will hear from him by letter or otherwise. ◎

ENVELOPE

Envelopes seen in a dream, omen news of a sorrowful cast. ◎

POSTCARD

To dream of receiving a ***postcard***, denotes that hasty news will more frequently be of a distressing nature than otherwise. ◎

THE LETTER

LETTER *see* **WRITING, PAPER , INK** *page 232,* **READING** *page 233,* **HUSBAND, WIFE** *page 132,* **MAILMAN, MESSAGE, UNITED STATES MAILBOX** *page 235* ◆ **ENVELOPE** *see* **POSTAGE** *page 235*

Telephony

BEEPER
To dream of hearing a ***beeper***, denotes that a crisis will soon occur.

To dream of ***using a beeper***, means someone in your life will soon become a burden. They will need constant attention and constant care. ◎

CABLE
To dream of a ***cable***, foretells the undertaking of decidedly hazardous work, which, if successfully carried to completion, will abound in riches and honor to you.

To dream of ***receiving cablegrams***, denotes that a message of importance will reach you soon, and will cause disagreeable comments. ◎

TELEGRAM
To dream that you receive a ***telegram***, denotes that you will soon receive tidings of an unpleasant character. Some friend is likely to misrepresent matters which are of much concern to you.

To ***send a telegram***, is a sign that you will be estranged from someone holding a place near you, or business will disappoint you.

If you are the operator sending these messages, you will be affected by them only through the interest of others.

To see or be in a ***telegraph office***, foretells unfortunate engagements. ◎

FAX MACHINE
To dream of receiving a ***fax***, signifies that you will soon receive unfortunate news regarding your job or business.

To ***send a fax***, is a sign that one of your business associates will disappoint you. ◎

TELEPHONE
To dream of a ***telephone***, foretells that you will meet strangers who will harass and bewilder you in your affairs.

For a woman to dream of talking over one, denotes that she will have much jealous rivalry, but will overcome all evil influences.

If she cannot hear well in conversing over a telephone, she is threatened with evil gossip, and the loss of a lover. ◎

CELLULAR TELEPHONE
To dream that you are using a ***cellular telephone***, means that a problem you are burdened with now will soon be resolved.

You will soon have more control over your own life, especially in professional matters. ◎

ANTENNA
To dream of an ***antenna***, indicates uncertain or curiosity about a relationship.

To dream of ***putting up an antenna***, denotes that you will receive responses to your queries from the particular person you have doubts about. ◎

Optical Aids

MAGNIFYING GLASS
To look through a magnifying glass ***in your dreams, means failure to accomplish your work in a satisfactory manner. For a woman to think she owns one, foretells that she will encourage the attention of persons who will ignore her later.*** ❋

MICROSCOPE
To dream of a microscope, ***denotes that you will experience failure or small returns in your current enterprises.*** ❋

BINOCULARS
To dream of using binoculars, ***signifies that you will be afflicted with disagreeable friendships.***

To dream of using binoculars to spy on others, denotes that you will be involved in unscrupulous activities. ❋

TELESCOPE
To dream of a telescope, ***portends unfavorable seasons for love and domestic affairs, and business will be changeable and uncertain.***

To look at planets and stars through one, portends for you journeys which will afford you much pleasure, but later cause you much financial loss.

To see a broken telescope, ***or one not in use, signifies that matters will go out of the ordinary with you, and trouble may be expected.*** ❋

SPYGLASS
To dream that you are looking through a spyglass, ***denotes that changes will soon occur to your disadvantage.***

To see a broken or imperfect one, foretells unhappy dissensions and loss of friends. ❋

OBSERVATORY
To dream of viewing the heavens and beautiful landscapes from an observatory, denotes your swift elevation to prominent positions and places of trust.

For a young woman, this dream signals the realization of the highest earthly joys.

If the heavens are clouded, your highest aim will miss materialization. ◎

Letters *opposite* **are extremely powerful dream images and can carry many different kinds of meaning.**

BEEPER *see* **MESSAGE** *page 235,* **NOISE** *page 276* ◆ **CABLE, TELEGRAM, FAX MACHINE** *see* **MESSAGE** *page 235* ◆ **TELEPHONE** *see* **TALKING** *page 230* ◆ **BINOCULARS** *see* **SPY** *page 271* ◆ **TELESCOPE** *see* **STARS, PLANETS** *page 84,* **BREAK** *page 265* ◆ **SPYGLASS** *see* **SPY** *page 271,* **BREAK** *page 265* ◆ **OBSERVATORY** *see* **SKY, FIRMAMENT** *page 84,* **CLOUDS** *page 74*

Wealth and Poverty

Fabulous wealth is as frequent an element in night time dreams as it is in daydream fantasies. This section covers all aspects of wealth, from opulence, inheritance, and unlooked for rich gifts to practical dreams of the earning and management of money. Taxes and property are also covered, as is the darker side of money-oriented dreams: poverty, penury, and need.

Riches

WEALTH
To dream that you are possessed of much ***wealth***, foretells that you will energetically nerve yourself to meet the problems of life with that force which compels success.

To see ***others wealthy***, foretells that you will have friends who will come to your rescue in perilous times.

For a young woman to dream that she is associated with ***wealthy people***, denotes that she will have high aspirations and will manage to enlist someone who is able to further them. ◎

AFFLUENCE
To dream that you are in ***affluence***, foretells that you will make fortunate ventures, and will be pleasantly associated with people of wealth. To young women, a vision of weird and ***fairy affluences*** is ominous of illusive and evanescent pleasure. They should study more closely their duty to friends and parents. After dreams of this nature, they are warned to cultivate a love for home life. ◎

ABUNDANCE
To dream that you are possessed with an ***abundance***, foretells that you will have no occasion to reproach Fortune, and that you will be independent of her future favors; but your domestic happiness may suffer a collapse under the strain you are likely to put upon it by your infidelity. ◎

Opulence and Excess

OPULENCE
For a young woman to dream that she lives in fairylike ***opulence***, denotes that she will be deceived, and will live for a time in luxurious ease and splendor, to find later that she is mated with shame and poverty. When young women dream that they are enjoying solid and real pleasure, but when abnormal or fairylike dreams of luxury and joy seem to encompass them, their waking moments will be filled with disappointments; as the dreams are warnings, superinduced by their practicality being supplanted by their excitable imagination and lazy desires, which should be overcome with energy, and the replacing of practicality on her base. No young woman should fill her mind with idle daydreams, but energetically strive to carry forward noble ideals and thoughts, and promising and helpful dreams will come to her while she restores physical energies in sleep. ◎

OPULENT LIVING

LUXURY
To dream that you are surrounded by ***luxury***, indicates much wealth, but dissipation and love of self will reduce your income.

For a poor woman to dream that she enjoys much luxury, denotes an early change in her circumstances. ◎

SPLENDOR
To dream that you live in ***splendor***, denotes that you will succeed to elevations, and that you will reside in a different state from the one you now occupy.

To see others thus living, signifies pleasure derived from the interest that friends take in your welfare. ◎

RICHES
To dream that you are possessed of ***riches***, denotes that you will rise to high places by your constant exertion and attention to your affairs. ◎

TREASURES
To dream that you find ***treasures***, denotes that you will be greatly aided in your pursuit of fortune by some unexpected generosity.

If you ***lose treasures***, bad luck in business and the inconstancy of friends is foretold. ◎

AFFLUENCE *see* ENCHANTMENT *page 272*, FAIRY *page 273* ◆ OPULENCE *see* FAIRY *page 273*, ENCHANTMENT *page 272*, PALACE *page 189*

Speculation

DIVIDENDS
To dream of ***dividends***, augments successful speculations or prosperous harvests.

PROFIT

To fail in securing hoped-for dividends, proclaims failure in management or love affairs. ◎

PROFITS
To dream of ***profits***, brings success in your immediate future. ◎

Property

MORTGAGE
To dream that you give a ***mortgage*** on your property, denotes that you are threatened with financial upheavals, which will throw you into embarrassing positions.

To take or hold one against others, is ominous of adequate wealth to liquidate your obligations.

To find yourself reading or ***examining mortgages***, denotes great possibilities before you of love or gain.

To ***lose a mortgage***, if in your dream it cannot be found again, implies loss and worry. ◎

DEED
To dream of seeing or signing ***deeds***, portends a lawsuit, to gain which you should be careful in selecting your counsel, as you are likely to be the loser. To dream of signing any kind of paper, is a bad omen for the dreamer. ◎

PROPERTY
To dream that you own vast ***property***, denotes that you will be successful in affairs, and gain friendships. ◎

ESTATE
To dream that you come into the ownership of a vast ***estate***, denotes that you will receive a legacy at some distant day, but quite different from your expectations.

For a young woman, this dream portends that her inheritance will be of a disappointing nature. She will have to live quite frugally, as her inheritance will be a poor man and a house full of children. ◎

Money

MONEY
To dream of ***finding money***, denotes small worries, but much happiness. Changes will follow.

MONEY

To ***pay out money***, denotes misfortune; to receive gold, great prosperity and unalloyed pleasures.

To ***lose money***, you will experience unhappy hours in the home, and affairs will appear gloomy.

To ***count your money*** and find a deficit, you will be worried in making payments.

To dream that you ***steal money***, denotes that you are in danger and should guard your actions.

To ***save money***, augurs wealth and comfort.

To dream that you ***swallow money***, portends that you are likely to become mercenary.

To look upon a ***quantity of money***, denotes that prosperity and happiness are within your reach.

To dream you find a ***roll of currency***, and a young woman claims it, foretells that you will lose in some enterprises by the interference of some female friend. The dreamer will find that he is ***spending his money unwisely*** and is living beyond his means. It is a dream of caution. Beware, lest the innocent fancies of your brain make a place for your money before payday. ◎

COUNTERFEIT MONEY
To dream of ***counterfeit money***, denotes that you will have trouble with some unruly and worthless person.

This dream always omens evil, whether you are the receiver of counterfeit money, or the one who passes it on. ◎

PENNY
To dream of ***pennies***, denotes unsatisfactory pursuits. Business will suffer, and lovers and friends will complain of the smallness of affection.

To lose them, signifies small deference and failures.

To find them, denotes that prospects will advance to your improvement.

To count them, foretells that you will be businesslike and economical. ◎

CHECKING THE DEEDS

Dreams of untold opulence *opposite* **may make you regret waking. Dreams of hard cash** *above left*, **profit** *top*, **and property** *above* **should inspire you to material success in real life.**

DIVIDENDS *see* **FAILURE** *page 258* ◆ **MORTGAGE** *see* **READING** *page 233* ◆ **MONEY** *see* **COUNTING** *page 180*, **STEALING** *page 246* ◆
COUNTERFEIT MONEY *see* **FRAUD** *page 204* ◆ **PENNY** *see* **COINS** *page 242*

Gifts and Presents

GIFTS
To dream that you receive ***gifts*** from anyone, denotes that you will not be behind in your payments, and will be unusually fortunate in speculations or love matters.

To ***send a gift***, signifies that displeasure will be shown you, and ill luck will surround your efforts.

For a young woman to dream that her lover sends her rich and beautiful gifts, denotes that she will make a wealthy and congenial marriage. ◎

PRESENTS
To receive ***presents*** in your dreams, denotes that you will be unusually fortunate. ◎

OFFERING
To bring or make an ***offering,*** foretells that you will be cringing and hypocritical unless you cultivate higher views of duty. ◎

Wills and Inheritance

WILL
To dream you are making your ***will***, is significant of momentous trials and speculations.

For a wife or anyone to think a will is against them, portends that they will have disputes and disorderly proceedings to combat in some event soon to transpire.

If you fail to ***prove a will***, you are in danger of libelous slander.

To lose one, is unfortunate for your business.

To destroy one, warns you that you are about to be a party to treachery and deceit. ◎

INHERITANCE
To dream that you receive an ***inheritance***, foretells that you will be successful in easily obtaining your desires. ◎

BEQUEST
After this dream, pleasures of consolation from the knowledge of duties well performed, and the health of the young are assured. ◎

HEIR
To dream that you fall ***heir*** to property and valuables, denotes that you are in danger of losing what you already possess, and warns you of coming responsibilities. Pleasant surprises may also follow this dream. ◎

THE RIGHTFUL HEIR

Future Money

TRUSTS
To dream of ***trusts***, foretells indifferent success in trade or law.

If you imagine you are a member of a trust, you will be successful in designs of a speculative nature. ◎

Pleasant dreams of wealth and ease may include gifts *top*, **inheritance** *above* **and fortune or just rewards in the way of hard-earned income** *opposite*.

PENSION
To dream of drawing a ***pension***, foretells that you will be aided in your labors by friends.

To fail in your application for a pension, denotes that you will lose in an undertaking and suffer the loss of friendships. ◎

LIFE INSURANCE MEN
To see ***life insurance men*** in a dream, means that you are soon to meet a stranger who will contribute to your business interests. Such a dream also indicates that change in your home life is foreshadowed, as interests will be mutual.

If the insurance men appear distorted or unnatural, the dream is more unfortunate than good. ◎

WILL *see* **DISINHERITED** *page 243* ◆ **INHERITANCE** *see* **PROPERTY** *page 239*, **DISINHERITED** *page 243* ◆ **HEIR** *see* **PROPERTY** *page 239* ◆ **PENSION** *see* **FAILURE** *page 258* ◆ **LIFE INSURANCE MEN** *see* **VISION** *page 274*

Money in your Pocket

WALLET
To see ***wallets*** in a dream, foretells that burdens of a pleasant nature will await your discretion as to assuming them. An old or soiled one, implies unfavorable results from your labors. ◎

POCKETBOOK
To find a ***pocketbook*** filled with bills and money in your dreams, you will be quite lucky, gaining in nearly every instance your desire. If empty, you will be disappointed in some big hope.

If you ***lose your pocketbook***, you will unfortunately disagree with your best friend, and thereby lose much comfort and real gain. ◎

PURSE
To dream of your ***purse*** being filled with diamonds and new bills, denotes for you associations where "Good Cheer" is the watchword, and harmony and tender loves will make earth a beautiful place. ◎

CREDIT CARD
To dream of obtaining a ***credit card***, indicates that a major change in your fortune will soon occur.

New sources of income will become available, or an inheritance may help increase your financial status. ◎

Just Rewards

INCOME
To dream of coming into the possession of your ***income***, denotes that you may deceive someone and cause trouble to your family and friends.

To dream that some of your family ***inherits an income***, predicts success.

For a woman to dream of ***losing her income***, signifies disappointments in her life.

To dream that your ***income is insufficient*** to support you, denotes trouble to relatives and friends.

To dream of a portion of your ***income remaining***, signifies that you will be very successful for a short time, but you may expect more than you receive. ◎

WAGES
Wages, if received in dreams, bring unlooked for good to persons engaging in new enterprises.

To ***pay out wages***, denotes that you will be confounded by dissatisfaction.

To have your ***wages reduced***, warns you of unfriendly interest that is being taken against you.

An ***increase of wages***, suggests unusual profit in any undertaking. ◎

FORTUNA

TAXES
To dream that you pay your ***taxes***, foretells that you will succeed in destroying evil influences rising around you.

If others pay them, you will be forced to ask aid of friends.

If you are unable to pay them, you will be unfortunate in experiments you are making. ◎

Lending and Borrowing

USURER
To find yourself a usurer ***in your dreams, foretells that you will be treated with coldness by your associates, and your business will decline to your consternation.***

If others are usurers***, you will discard some former friend on account of treachery.*** ❋

BORROWING
Borrowing ***is a sign of loss and meager support. For a banker to dream of borrowing from another bank, a run on his own will leave him in a state of collapse, unless he accepts this warning.***

If another borrows from you***, help in time of need will be extended or offered you. True friends will attend you.*** ❋

LENDING
To dream that you are lending ***money, foretells difficulties in meeting payments of debts and unpleasant influence in private.***

To lend other articles, denotes impoverishment through generosity.

To refuse to lend things***, you will be awake to your interests and keep the respect of friends.***

For others to offer to lend you articles or money, denotes prosperity and close friendships. ❋

WALLET *see* MONEY *page 239* ◆ POCKETBOOK *see* MONEY *page 239* ◆ PURSE *see* MONEY *page 239*, DIAMONDS *page 162* ◆ INCOME *see* INHERITANCE *page 240*, WANT *page 243* ◆ WAGES *see* MONEY *page 239*, INCREASE *page 127*

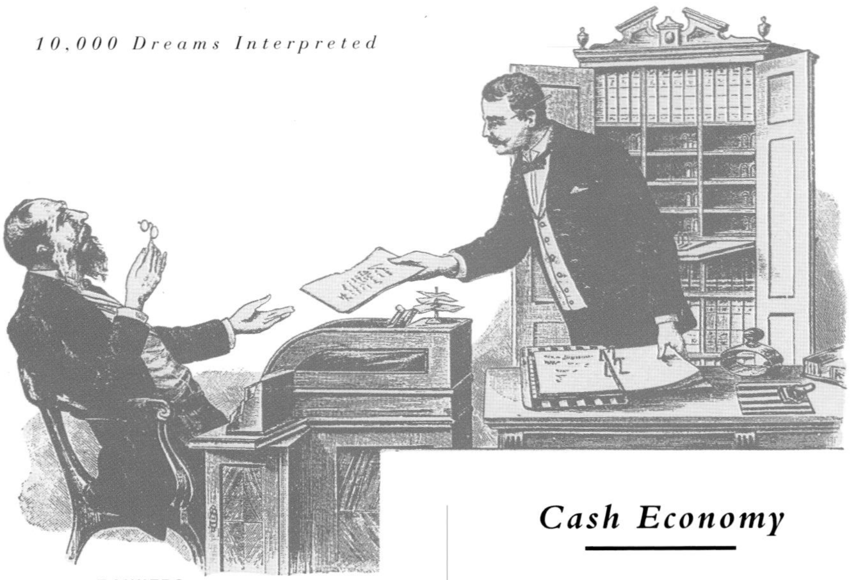

BANKERS

Bankers

BANK
To see ***vacant tellers***, foretells business losses. Giving out ***gold money***, denotes carelessness; receiving it, great gain and prosperity.

To see ***silver and banknotes*** accumulated, portends increase of honor and fortune. You will enjoy the highest respect of all classes. ◎

BANKRUPT
This dream denotes partial collapse in business, and weakening of the brain faculties. A warning to leave speculations alone. ◎

Cash Economy

CASH
To dream that you have plenty of ***cash***, but that it has been borrowed, portends that you will be looked upon as a worthy man, but that those who come in close contact with you will find that you are mercenary and unfeeling.

For a young woman to dream that she is spending ***borrowed money***, foretells that she will be found out in her practice of deceit, and through this, lose a prized friend. ◎

CASHIER
To see a ***cashier*** in your dream, denotes that others will claim your possessions. If you owe anyone, you will practice deceit in your designs upon some wealthy person. ◎

SAFE
To dream of seeing a ***safe***, denotes security from discouraging affairs of business and love.

To be trying to ***unlock a safe***, you will be worried over the failure of your plans not reaching quick maturity.

To find a ***safe empty***, denotes trouble. ◎

CASH BOX
To dream of a full ***cash box***, denotes that favorable prospects will open around you. If it is empty, you will experience meager reimbursements. ◎

TILL
To dream of seeing money and valuables in a ***till***, foretells coming success. Your love affairs will be exceedingly favorable. An empty one, denotes disappointed expectations. ◎

THE TILL

Currency

CHECKS
To dream of palming off false ***checks*** on your friends, denotes that you will resort to subterfuge in order to carry forward your plans.

To ***receive checks***, you will be able to meet your payments and will inherit money.

To dream that you ***pay out checks***, denotes that you will experience depression and loss in business. ◎

COINS
To dream of gold, denotes great prosperity and much pleasure derived from sightseeing and ocean voyages.

Silver ***coin*** is unlucky to dream about. Dissensions will arise in the most orderly families.

For a maiden to dream that her lover gives her a ***silver coin***, signifies that she will be jilted by him.

Copper coins, denote despair and physical burdens. ***Nickel coins*** imply that work of the lowest nature will devolve upon you.

If silver coins are your ideal of money, and they are bright and clean, or seen distinctly in your possession, the dream will be a propitious one. ◎

Hard cash may dominate your dreams, showing bankers at work *above left* **or a till full of money** *above*. **In contrast, you may experience dismal dreams full of the aching pangs of unsatisfied hunger suffered by those in desperate need** *opposite left* **or the bleak despair of utter poverty** *opposite right*.

BANK *see* **MONEY** *page 239* ◆ **BANKRUPT** *see* **DEBT** *page 243* ◆ **CASH** *see* **MONEY** *page 239*, **BORROWING** *page 241* ◆ **SAFE** *see* **VAULT** *page 190* ◆ **CASH BOX** *see* **MONEY** *page 239* ◆ **TILL** *see* **MONEY** *page 239*, **STORE, SHOP** *page 203* ◆ **CHECKS** *see* **FRAUD** *page 204* ◆ **COINS** *see* **GOLD, SILVER, COPPER** *page 71*

Poverty in dreams is as worrying as the real thing, and such dreams convey a powerful warning that something in your life needs careful examination. This section covers the descent into penury via want and need, through debt and the poorhouse to beggary and vagrancy.

The Poverty Trap

DISINHERITED
To dream that you are ***disinherited***, warns you to look well to your business and social standing.

For a young man to dream of losing his inheritance by disobedience, warns him that he will find favor in the eyes of his parents by contracting a suitable marriage.

For a woman, this dream is a warning to be careful of her conduct, lest she meet with unfavorable fortune. ◎

POOR
To dream that you, or any of your friends appear to be ***poor***, is significant of worry and losses. ◎

POORHOUSE
To see a ***poorhouse*** in your dream, denotes that you have unfaithful friends, who will care for you only in order that they can use your money and belongings. ◎

MISER
To dream of a ***miser***, foretells that you will be unfortunate in finding true happiness, owing to your selfishness, and that love will disappoint you sorely.

For a woman to dream that she is ***befriended by a miser***, foretells that she will gain love and wealth by her intelligence and tactful conduct.

To dream that you are ***miserly***, denotes that you will be obnoxious to others by your conceited bearing.

To dream that any of your ***friends are misers***, foretells that you will be distressed by the importunities of others. ◎

DESPERATE NEED

Want and Need

SCARCITY
To dream of ***scarcity***, foretells sorrow in the household and failing affairs. ◎

WANT
To dream that you are in ***want***, denotes that you have unfortunately ignored the realities of life, and chased folly to her stronghold of sorrow and adversity.

If you find yourself contented in a state of want, you will bear the misfortune which threatens you with heroism, and will see the clouds of misery disperse.

To ***relieve want***, signifies that you will be esteemed for your disinterested kindness, but you will feel no pleasure in well-doing. ◎

NEED
To dream that you are in ***need***, denotes that you will speculate unwisely, and distressing news of absent friends will oppress you.

To see ***others in need***, foretells that unfortunate affairs will affect yourself with others. ◎

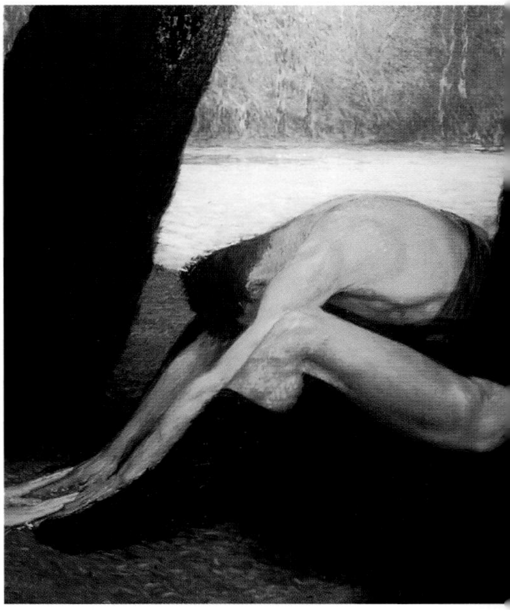

THE DESPAIR OF POVERTY

Debt and Disgrace

DEBT
Debt is rather a bad dream, foretelling worries in business and love, and struggles for competency; but if you have plenty to meet all your obligations, your affairs will assume a favorable turn. ◎

DUN
To dream that you receive a ***dun***, warns you to look after your affairs and correct all tendency toward neglect of business and love. ◎

BAILIFF
To see a ***bailiff***, shows a striving for a higher place, and a deficiency in intellect.

If the bailiff comes to arrest, or make love, false friends are trying to work for your money. ◎

DISINHERITED *see* **WILL, INHERITANCE, BEQUEST** *page 240* ◆ **POOR** *see* **PAUPER, BEGGAR, MENDICANT** *page 244* ◆ **MISER** *see* **FRIEND** *page 124* ◆ **WANT** *see* **CHARITY** *page 252* ◆ **BAILIFF** *see* **ARRESTED** *page 247*

THE BEGGAR BOY

Demands and Obligations

PENALTIES

To dream that you have ***penalties*** imposed upon you, foretells that you will have duties that will rile you and find you rebellious.

To pay a penalty, denotes sickness and financial loss. To escape the payment, you will be victor in some contest. ◎

OBLIGATION

To dream of ***obligating*** yourself in any incident, denotes that you will be fretted and worried by the thoughtless complaints of others.

If others obligate themselves to you, it portends that you will win the regard of acquaintances and friends. ◎

RANSOM

To dream that a ***ransom*** is made for you, you will find that you are deceived and worked for money on all sides. For a young woman, this is prognostic of evil, unless someone pays the ransom and relieves her. ◎

DEMAND

To dream that a ***demand*** for charity comes in upon you, denotes that you will be placed in embarrassing situations; but by your persistency, you will fully restore your good standing. If the demand is unjust, you will become a leader in your profession.

For a lover to command you adversely, implies his or her leniency. ◎

Beggars

PAUPER

To dream that you are a ***pauper***, implies unpleasant happenings for you.

To see paupers, denotes that there will be a call upon your generosity. ◎

ALMS

A dream of ***alms*** will bring evil if given or taken unwillingly. Otherwise, a good dream. ◎

BEGGAR

To see an old, decrepit ***beggar***, is a sign of bad management, and unless you are economical, you will lose much property. Scandalous reports will prove detrimental to your fame.

To ***give to a beggar***, denotes dissatisfaction with present surroundings.

To dream that you refuse to give to a beggar, is altogether bad. ◎

MENDICANT

For a woman to dream of ***mendicants***, she will meet with disagreeable interferences in her plans for betterment and enjoyment. ◎

VAGRANT

To dream that you are a ***vagrant***, portends poverty and misery.

To see vagrants, is a sign of contagion invading your community.

To ***give to a vagrant***, denotes that your generosity will be applauded. ◎

WAIF

To dream of a ***waif***, denotes personal difficulties, and especial ill luck in business. ◎

The sad sight of a beggar in your dreams *above* does not bode well. The full majesty of the law in action *opposite* is as impressive in dreams as it is in the court room.

DEMAND *see* CHARITY *page 252* ◆ PAUPER *see* POOR, POORHOUSE *page 243* ◆ ALMS *see* GIFTS, OFFERINGS *page 240* ◆ BEGGAR, VAGRANT *see* GIFTS *page 240*

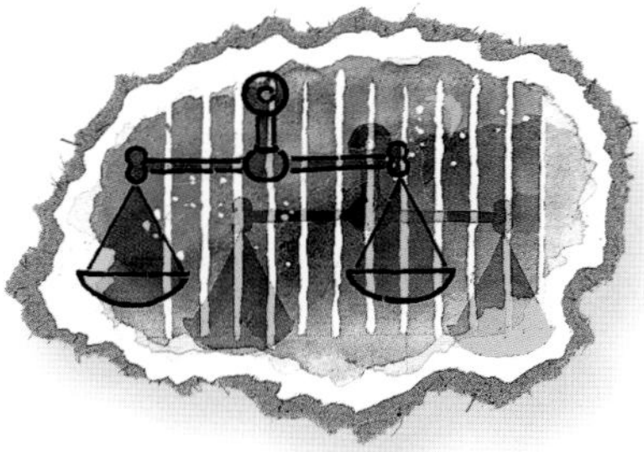

Crime and Punishment

The dreams in this section appear to be harbingers of perfidy in business and deceit in love. The section covers dreams of courtroom drama, the full panoply of the law in action, the police process, crimes ranging from stealing to murder, the kinds of punishment the law metes out, from detention in prison to exile and execution, and a glimpse of freedom in pardon and reprieve.

Legal Matters

LAW AND LAWSUITS

To dream of engaging in a ***lawsuit***, warns you of enemies who are poisoning public opinion against you. If you know that the suit is dishonest on your part, you will seek to dispossess true owners for your own advancement.

If a young man is studying ***law***, he will make a rapid rise in any chosen profession.

For a woman to dream that she ***engages in a lawsuit***, means she will be calumniated, and find enemies among friends. ◎

LAWYER

For a young woman to dream that she is connected in any way with a ***lawyer***, foretells that she will unwittingly commit indiscretions, which will subject her to unfavorable and mortifying criticism. ◎

JUSTICE

To dream that you demand ***justice*** from a person, denotes that you are threatened with embarrassments through the false statements of people who are eager for your downfall.

If someone demands the same of you, you will find that your conduct and reputation are being assailed, and it will be extremely doubtful that you will refute the charges satisfactorily. ◎

In Court

MAGISTRATE

To dream of a ***magistrate***, foretells that you will be harassed with threats of lawsuits and losses in your business. ◎

JUDGE

To dream of coming before a ***judge***, signifies that disputes will be settled by legal proceedings. Business or divorce cases may assume gigantic proportions.

To have the case decided in your favor, denotes a successful termination to the suit; if decided against you, then you are the aggressor and you should seek to right injustice. ◎

GAVEL

To dream of a ***gavel***, denotes that you will be burdened with some unprofitable yet not unpleasant pursuit. To use one, denotes that officiousness will be shown by you toward your friends. ◎

INTERCEDE

To ***intercede*** for someone in your dreams, shows that you will secure aid when you desire it most. ◎

ATTORNEY

To see an ***attorney*** at the bar, denotes that disputes of a serious nature will arise between parties interested in worldly things. Enemies are stealing upon you with false claims.

If you see an attorney defending you, you friends will assist you in coming trouble, but they will cause you more worry than enemies. ◎

NOTARY

To dream of a ***notary***, is a prediction of unsatisfied desires, and probably lawsuits.

For a woman to associate with a notary, foretells that she will rashly risk her reputation, in gratification of foolish pleasure. ◎

JURY

To dream that you are on the ***jury***, denotes dissatisfaction with your employments, and you will seek to materially change your position.

If you are cleared from a charge by the jury, your business will be successful and affairs will move your way, but if you should be condemned, enemies will overpower you and harass you beyond endurance. ◎

A BENCH OF JUDGES

LAW *see* LEARNING *page 179* ◆ JUSTICE, JUDGE *see* JUDGEMENT DAY *page 278*

Crime and Victim

CRIMINAL
To dream of associating with a person who has committed a ***crime***, denotes that you will be harassed with unscrupulous persons, who will try to use your friendship for their own advancement.

To see a ***criminal*** fleeing from justice, denotes that you will come into the possession of the secrets of others, and will therefore be in danger, for they will fear that you will betray them, and consequently will seek your removal. ◎

VICTIM
To dream that you are the ***victim*** of any scheme, foretells that you will be oppressed and overpowered by your enemies. Your family relations will also be strained.

To ***victimize others***, denotes that you will amass wealth dishonorably and prefer illicit relations, to the sorrow of your companions. ◎

ASSAULT

Rape and Pillage

STEALING
To dream of ***stealing***, or of seeing others commit this act, foretells bad luck and loss of character.

To be ***accused of stealing***, denotes that you will be misunderstood in some affair, and suffer therefrom, but you will eventually find that this will bring you favor.

To accuse others, denotes that you will treat some person with hasty inconsideration. ◎

RAPE

THIEF
To dream of being a ***thief*** and you are pursued by officers, is a sign that you will meet reverses in business, and your social relations will be unpleasant.

If you pursue or ***capture a thief***, you will overcome your enemies. ◎

BURGLARS
To dream that ***burglars*** are searching your person, you will have dangerous enemies to contend with, who will destroy you if extreme carefulness is not practiced in your dealings with strangers.

If you dream of your home or place of business being ***burglarized***, your good standing in business or society will be assailed, but courage in meeting these difficulties will defend you. Accidents may happen to the careless after this dream. ◎

PICKPOCKET
To dream of a ***pickpocket***, foretells that some enemy will succeed in harassing and causing you loss.

For a young woman to have her pocket picked, denotes that she will be the object of some person's envy and spite, and may lose the regard of a friend through these evil machinations, unless she keeps her own counsel. If she ***picks others' pockets***, she will incur the displeasure of a companion by her coarse behavior. ◎

MACE
To dream of using ***mace*** [a form of tear gas] to defend yourself against a sudden attack by muggers or thieves, foretells a danger that will shortly occur, but may be avoided if you prepare yourself against it. ◎

RAPE
To dream that ***rape*** has been committed among your acquaintances, denotes that you will be shocked at the distress of some of your friends.

For a young woman to dream that she has been the ***victim of rape***, foretells that she will have troubles which will wound her pride, and her lover will be estranged. ◎

Your dreams may lead you into a criminal underworld. You may dream that you are the victim or perpetrator of such crimes as rape *above* or assault *left*.

CRIMINAL *see* **JUSTICE** *page 245* ◆ **STEALING** *see* **ACCUSE** *page 248* ◆ **THIEF** *see* **POLICE** *page 247* ◆ **BURGLARS** *see* **HOME** *page 205* ◆ **PICKPOCKET** *see* **POCKET** *page 159* ◆ **MACE** *see* **PARTY** *page 85*

Police and Arrests

WARRANT
To dream that a ***warrant*** is being served on you, denotes that you will engage in some important work which will give you great uneasiness.

If you see a warrant served on someone else, there will be danger of your actions bringing you into fatal quarrels or misunderstandings. You are likely to be justly indignant with the wantonness of some friends. ◎

ARRESTED
To see respectable-looking strangers ***arrested***, foretells that your desire to make changes, and new speculations will be subordinated by the fear of failure. If they resist the officers, you will complete the new enterprise. ◎

POLICE
If the ***police*** are trying to arrest you for some crime of which you are innocent, it foretells that you will successfully outstrip rivalry.

If the arrest is just, you will have a season of unfortunate incidents.

To see ***police on patrol***, indicates alarming fluctuations in affairs. ◎

SHERIFF
To dream of seeing a ***sheriff***, denotes that you will suffer great uneasiness over changes before you.

To imagine that you are ***elected sheriff*** or feel interested in the office, denotes that you will participate in some affair which will afford you neither profit nor honor.

To escape arrest, you will be able to further engage in illicit affairs. ◎

DETECTIVE
To dream of a ***detective*** keeping in your wake when you are innocent of charges preferred, denotes that fortune and honor are drawing nearer to you each day; but if you feel yourself guilty, you are likely to find your reputation at stake, and friends will turn from you. For a young woman, this is not a fortunate dream. ◎

Murder Most Foul

MANSLAUGHTER
For a woman to dream that she sees or is in any way connected with manslaughter***, denotes that she will be desperately scared lest her name be coupled with some scandalous sensation.*** ❁

KILLING
To dream of killing ***a defenseless man, prognosticates sorrow and failure in affairs.***

If you kill one in self-defense, or kill a ferocious beast, it denotes victory and a rise in position. ❁

MURDER
To see murder ***committed in your dreams, foretells much sorrow arising from the misdeeds of others. Affairs will assume dullness. Violent deaths will come under your notice.***

If you commit murder, ***it signifies that you are engaging in some dishonorable adventure, which will leave a stigma upon your name.***

To dream that you are murdered, ***foretells that enemies are secretly working to overthrow you.*** ❁

HOMICIDE
To dream that you commit homicide, ***foretells that you will suffer great humiliation and anguish through the indifference of others, and your gloomy surroundings will cause perplexing worry to those close to you.*** ❁

ASSASSIN
If you are the one to receive the assassin's ***blow, you will not surmount all your trials.***

To see another, with the assassin standing over him with blood stains, portends that misfortune will come to the dreamer.

To see an assassin under any condition, is a warning that losses may befall you through secret enemies. ❁

POISON
To feel that you are poisoned ***in a dream, denotes that some painful influence will immediately reach you.***

If you seek to use poison on others, ***you will be guilty of base thoughts, or the world will go wrong for you.***

For a young woman to dream that she endeavors to rid herself of a rival in this way, she will be likely to have a deal of trouble in securing a lover.

To throw the poison away, ***denotes that by sheer force, you will overcome unsatisfactory conditions.***

To handle poison ***or see others with it, signifies that unpleasantness will no doubt surround you.***

To dream that your relatives or children are poisoned, ***you will receive injury from unsuspected sources.***

To dream that an enemy or rival is poisoned, means that you will overcome obstacles.

To recover from the effects ***of poison, indicates that you will succeed after worry.***

To take strychnine ***or other poisonous medicine under the advice of a physician, denotes that you will undertake some affair fraught with danger.*** ❁

SHERRIFF *see* **ELECTION** *page 219,* **BAILIFF** *page 243* ◆ **KILLING, MURDER,** *see* **SHOOTING. SHOT** *page 263* ◆ **ASSASSIN** *see* **BLOOD** *page 94* ◆ **POISON** *see* **RIVAL** *page 125,* **CHILDREN** *page 128,* **ENEMY** *page 260,* **MEDICINE** *page 116,* **PHYSICIAN** *page 114*

Interrogation and Torture

BAIL
If the dreamer is seeking ***bail***, unforeseen troubles will arise; accidents are likely to occur; unfortunate alliances may be made.

If you dream that you ***provide bail*** for another person, about the same conditions prevail, though they will not be hardly as bad. ◎

WITNESS
To dream that you bear ***witness*** against others, signifies that you will have great oppression through slight causes.

If others bear ***witness against you***, you will be compelled to refuse favors to friends in order to protect your own interest.

If you are a ***witness for a guilty person***, you will be implicated in a shameful affair. ◎

QUESTION
To ***question*** the merits of a thing in your dreams, denotes that you will suspect someone whom you love of unfaithfulness, and you will fear for your speculation.

To ***ask a question***, foretells that you will earnestly strive for truth and be successful.

If you ***are questioned***, you will be unfairly dealt with. ◎

INQUISITION
To dream of an ***inquisition***, bespeaks for you an endless round of trouble and great disappointment.

If you are brought before an inquisition on a charge of willfulness, you will be unable to defend yourself from malicious slander. ◎

LIE DETECTOR
To dream of being forced to take a ***lie detector*** test, signifies that you will soon be facing some sort of scandal. ◎

RACK
To dream of a ***rack***, denotes the uncertainty of the outcome of some engagement which gives you much anxious thought. ◎

TORTURE
To dream of being ***tortured***, denotes that you will undergo disappointment and grief through the machinations of false friends.

If you are ***torturing others***, you will fail to carry out well-laid plans for increasing your fortune.

If you are trying to alleviate the torture of others, you will succeed after a struggle in business and love. ◎

With Conviction

ACCUSE
To dream that you ***accuse*** anyone of a mean action, denotes that you will have quarrels with those under you, and your dignity will be thrown from a high pedestal.

If you are ***accused***, you are in danger of being guilty of distributing scandal in a sly and malicious way. ◎

CONVICTS
To dream of seeing ***convicts***, denotes disasters and sad news.

To dream that ***you are a convict***, indicates that you will worry over some affair; but you will clear up all mistakes.

For a young woman to dream of seeing her lover in the ***garb of a convict***, indicates that she will have cause to question the character of his love. ◎

Blessed Release

PARDON
To dream that you are endeavoring to gain pardon ***for an offense which you never committed, denotes that you will be troubled, and seemingly with cause, over your affairs, but it will finally appear that it was for your advancement. If offense was committed, you will realize embarrassment in affairs.***

To receive pardon, ***means that you will prosper after a series of misfortunes.*** ❋

ACQUIT
To dream that you are acquitted ***of a crime, denotes that you are about to come into possession of valuable property, but there is danger of a lawsuit before you obtain possession.***

To see others acquitted, ***foretells that your friends will add pleasure to your labors.*** ❋

REPRIEVE
To be under sentence in a dream and receive a reprieve, ***foretells that you will overcome some difficulty which is causing you anxiety.***

For a young woman to dream that her lover has been reprieved, ***denotes that she will soon hear of some good luck befalling him, and that this will be of vital interest to her.*** ❋

BAIL *see* BAILIFF *page 243* ◆ WITNESS *see* JUDGE, MAGISTRATE *page 245* ◆ CONVICTS *see* CLOTHES *page 154*, PRISON, PENITENTIARY *page 249* ◆ ACQUIT *see* JUDGE, *page 245*, MANUSCRIPT *page 233*

Imprisonment

JAIL
To see others in ***jail***, means that you will be urged to grant privileges to persons whom you believe to be unworthy.

For a young woman to dream that her ***lover is in jail***, she will be disappointed in his character, as he will prove a deceiver. ◎

JAILER
To see a ***jailer***, denotes that treachery will embarrass your interests and evil women will enthrall you.

To see a mob attempting to break open a jail, is a forerunner of evil, and desperate measures will be used to extort money and bounties from you. ◎

PRISON
To dream of a ***prison***, is the forerunner of misfortune in every instance, if it encircles your friends or yourself.

To see anyone ***dismissed from prison***, denotes that you will finally overcome misfortune. ◎

PENITENTIARY
To dream of a ***penitentiary***, denotes that you will have engagements which will, unfortunately, result in your loss.

To be an inmate of one, foretells discontent in the home and failing business.

To escape from one, you will overcome difficult obstacles. ◎

DUNGEON
To dream of being in a ***dungeon***, foretells for you struggles with the vital affairs of life; but by wise dealings, you will disenthrall yourself of obstacles and the designs of enemies.

For a woman, this is a dark foreboding; by her wilful indiscretion she will lose her position among honorable people.

To see a ***dungeon lighted up***, portends that you are threatened with entanglements of which your better judgement warns you. ◎

Death Penalty

EXECUTION
To dream of seeing an ***execution***, signifies that you will suffer some misfortune from the carelessness of others.

To dream that you are about to be ***executed***, and some miraculous intervention occurs, denotes that you will overthrow enemies and succeed in gaining wealth. ◎

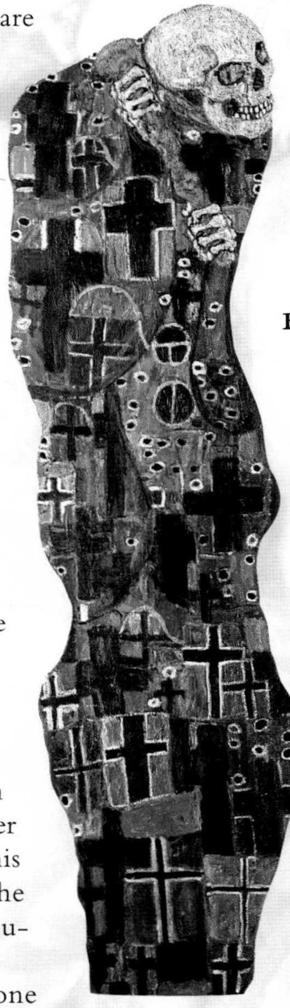

EXECUTIONER

GALLOWS
To dream of seeing a friend on the ***gallows*** of execution, foretells that desperate emergencies must be met with decision, or a great calamity will befall you.

To dream that you are ***on a gallows***, denotes that you will suffer from the maliciousness of false friends.

For a young woman to dream that she sees her lover executed by this means, denotes that she will marry an unscrupulous and designing man.

If you rescue anyone from the gallows, it portends desirable acquisitions.

To dream that you hang an enemy, denotes victory in all spheres. ◎

SCAFFOLD
To dream of a ***scaffold***, denotes that you will undergo keen disappointment in failing to secure the object of your affection.

To ***ascend*** one, you will be misunderstood and censured by your friends for some action which you never committed.

To ***descend*** one, you will be guilty of wrongdoing, and you will suffer the penalty.

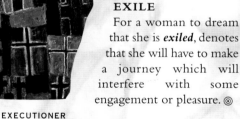

To fall from one, you will be unexpectedly surprised while engaged in deceiving and working injury to others. ◎

HANGING
To dream that you see a large concourse of people gathering at a ***hanging***, denotes that many enemies will club together to try to demolish your position in their midst. ◎

BEHEADING
To dream of being ***beheaded***, overwhelming defeat or failure in some undertaking will soon follow.

To see ***others beheaded***, if accompanied by a large flow of blood, death and exile are portended. ◎

Sent Away

EXILE
For a woman to dream that she is ***exiled***, denotes that she will have to make a journey which will interfere with some engagement or pleasure. ◎

BANISHMENT
Evil pursues the unfortunate dreamer of ***banishment***. If you are ***banished*** to foreign lands, it means that death will be your portion at an early date.

To ***banish a child***, means perjury of business allies. It is a dream of fatality. ◎

Your dreams may be shadowed by the hangman's noose or the executioner's axe *above*, the ultimate punishment that society can inflict on its criminal members.

JAIL, PRISON *see* **CONVICTS** *page 248* ◆ **PENITENTIARY** *see* **CONVICTS** *page 248*, **ESCAPE** *page 266* ◆ **DUNGEON** *see* **LIGHT** *page 216* ◆ **EXECUTION** *see* **DEATH** *page 120* ◆ **GALLOWS** *see* **FRIEND** *page 124*, **DEATH** *page 120*, **RESCUE** *page 266* ◆ **SCAFFOLD** *see* **DEATH** *page 120*, **ASCENDING** *page 268*, **FALL** *page 265* ◆ **BEHEADING** *see* **HEAD** *page 92*, **BLOOD** *page 94* ◆ **EXILE** *see* **PARTING** *page 258* ◆ **BANISHMENT** *see* **PARTING** *page 258*, **ABROAD** *page 88*, **CHILDREN** *page 128*

Vices and Virtues

Dreams of the vicious side of your nature can be uncomfortable, but may be balanced by dreams of your virtuous impulses. This section covers a modest range of sins, from the mild aberrations of vexation and idleness to the stronger emotions of rage and revenge. The dream virtues celebrate charity, obedience, and devotion among other righteous attitudes.

Vice and Temptation

VICE
To dream that you are favoring any ***vice***, signifies that you are about to endanger your reputation by letting evil persuasions entice you.

If you see others indulging in vice, some ill fortune will engulf the interest of some relative or associate. ◎

TEMPTATION
To dream that you are surrounded by ***temptations***, denotes that you will be involved in some trouble with an envious person who is trying to displace you in the confidence of friends. If you resist them, you will be successful in some affair in which you have much opposition. ◎

Bad Words

PROFANITY
To dream of ***profanity***, denotes that you will cultivate those traits which render you coarse and unfeeling toward your fellow man.

To dream that ***others use profanity***, is a sign that you will soon be injured in some way, and will probably be insulted also. ◎

BLASPHEMY
Blasphemy, denotes an enemy creeping into your life, who, under assumed friendship, will do you great harm.

To dream you are cursing yourself, means evil fortune. To dream you are cursed by others, signifies relief through affection and prosperity. ◎

Deadly Sins

VEXED
If you are ***vexed*** in your dreams, you will find many worries scattered through your early awakening.

If you think some person is vexed with you, you will not shortly reconcile some slight misunderstanding. ◎

ANGER
To dream of ***anger***, denotes that some awful trial awaits you. Disappointments in loved ones, and broken ties, or enemies may make new attacks upon your property or character.

To dream that friends or relatives are ***angry with you***, while you meet their anger with composure, you will mediate between opposing friends, and gain their favor and gratitude. ◎

RAGE
To be in a ***rage*** and scolding and tearing up things generally, while in a dream, signifies quarrels and injury to your friends.

To see ***others in a rage***, is a sign of unfavorable conditions for business, and unhappiness in social life.

For a young woman to see her ***lover in a rage***, denotes that there will be some discordant note in their love, and misunderstanding will naturally occur. ◎

CRUELTY
To dream of ***cruelty*** being shown you, foretells trouble and disappointment in some dealings. If it is shown to others, there will be a disagreeable task set for others by you, which will contribute to your own loss. ◎

ENVY
To dream that you entertain ***envy*** for others, denotes that you will make warm friends by your unselfish deference to the wishes of others.

If you dream of being ***envied by others***, it denotes that you will suffer some inconvenience from friends overanxious to please you. ◎

JEALOUSY
To dream that you are ***jealous*** of your wife, denotes the influence of enemies and narrow-minded persons. If jealous of your sweetheart, you will seek to displace a rival.

If a woman dreams that she is ***jealous of her husband***, she will find many shocking incidents to vex and make her happiness a travesty.

If a young woman is ***jealous of her lover***, she will find that he is more favorably impressed with the charms of some other woman than herself.

If men and women are jealous over common affairs, they will meet many unpleasant worries in the discharge of everyday business. ◎

HATE
To dream that you ***hate*** a person, denotes that if you are not careful, you will do the party an inadvertent injury, or a spiteful action will bring business loss and worry.

If you are hated for unjust causes, you will find sincere and obliging friends, and your associations will be most pleasant.

Otherwise, the dream forebodes ill. ◎

PROFANITY *see* **SWEARING** *page 230,* **OATH** *page 219* ◆ **BLASPHEMY** *see* **GOD** *page 277* ◆ **ANGER** *see* **FRIEND** *page 124* ◆
JEALOUSY *see* **WIFE, HUSBAND** *page 132* ◆ **HATE** *see* **ABHOR** *page 253*

Hypocrisy, Intemperance, and Betrayal

HYPOCRITE
To dream that anyone has acted the ***hypocrite*** with you, you will be turned over to your enemies by false friends.

To dream that you are a hypocrite, denotes that you will prove yourself a deceiver and be false to friends. ◎

INTEMPERANCE
To dream of being ***intemperate*** in the use of your intellectual forces, you will seek after foolish knowledge, fail to benefit yourself, and give pain and displeasure to your friends.

If you are ***intemperate in love*** or other passions, you will reap disease or loss of fortune and esteem. For a young woman to thus dream, she will lose a lover and incur the displeasure of close friends. ◎

TRAITOR
To see a ***traitor*** in your dreams, foretells that you will have enemies working to despoil you. If someone calls you one, or if you imagine yourself one, there will be unfavorable prospects of pleasure for you. ◎

Revenge

REVENGE
To dream of taking ***revenge***, is a sign of a weak and uncharitable nature, which, if not properly governed, will bring your troubles and loss of friends.

If others ***revenge themselves*** on you, there will be much to fear from enemies. ◎

Lies and Liars

LIAR
To dream of thinking that people are ***liars***, foretells that you will lose faith in some scheme which you had urgently put forward. For someone to call you a liar, means that you will have vexations through deceitful persons.

For a woman to think her ***sweetheart a liar***, warns her that her unbecoming conduct is likely to lose her a valued friend. ◎

THE LIAR

LYING
To dream that you are ***lying*** to escape punishment, denotes that you will act dishonorably toward some innocent person.

Lying to protect a friend from undeserved chastisement, denotes that you will have many unjust criticisms passed upon your conduct, but you will rise above them and enjoy prominence.

To hear ***others lying***, denotes that they are seeking to entrap you. ◎

Vexatious dreams of unsocial vices such as smooth-tongued lying *above* or indolent idling *top* may spoil your rest.

Idleness

THE IDLER

INDIFFERENCE
To dream of ***indifference***, signifies pleasant companions in your life for a very short time.

For a young woman to dream that her sweetheart is ***indifferent*** to her, signifies that he may not prove his affections in the most appropriate way. To dream that she is indifferent to him, means that she will prove untrue to him. ◎

LAZY
To dream of feeling ***lazy***, or acting so, denotes that you will make a mistake in the formation of enterprises, and will suffer keen disappointment.

For a young woman to think her ***lover is lazy***, foretells that she will have bad luck in securing admiration. Her actions will discourage men who mean marriage. ◎

IDLE
If you dream of being ***idle***, you will fail to accomplish your designs.

To see your friends in ***idleness***, indicates that you will hear of some trouble affecting them.

For a young woman to dream that she is leading an ***idle existence***, she will fall into bad habits, and is likely to marry a shiftless man. ◎

LIAR *see* **SWEETHEART** *page 124* ◆ **LYING** *see* **FRIEND** *page 124* ◆ **INDIFFERENCE** *see* **SWEETHEART** *page 124* ◆ **IDLE** *see* **FRIEND** *page 124*

Virtuous Qualities

ATONEMENT

DEVOTION
For a farmer to dream of showing his ***devotion*** to God or to his family, denotes plenteous crops and peaceful neighbors. To business people, this is a warning that nothing is to be gained by deceit. For a young woman to dream of being devout, implies her chastity and an adoring husband. ◎

CHARITY
To dream of giving ***charity***, denotes that you will be harassed with supplications for help from the poor and your business will be at a standstill.

If you dream of giving to ***charitable institutions***, your right of possession to paying property will be disputed. Worries and ill health threaten you.

For young persons to dream of giving charity, foreshows that they will be annoyed by deceitful rivals.

To dream that you are an ***object of charity***, omens that you will succeed in life only after hard times with misfortunes. ◎

A woman, after this dream, is warned of approaching disappointment. ◎

ASSISTANCE
Giving ***assistance*** to anyone in a dream, foretells that you will be favored in your efforts to rise to a higher position.

If you dream that anyone ***assists you***, this indicates that you will be pleasantly situated, and loving friends will be near you. ◎

ADVICE
To dream that you receive ***advice***, denotes that you will somehow be enabled to raise your standard of integrity, and strive by honest means to reach independent competency and moral altitude.

To dream that you seek ***legal advice*** for a problem, foretells that there will be some transactions in your affairs which will create doubt of their merits and legality. ◎

OBEDIENCE
To dream that you render ***obedience*** to another, foretells for you a common place, a pleasant but uneventful period of life.

If others are obedient to you, it shows that you will command fortune and high esteem. ◎

INDEPENDENCE
To dream that you are very ***independent***, denotes that you have a rival who may do you an injustice.

To dream that you gain an ***independence of wealth***, means that you may not be so successful at that time as you expect, but good results are promised in the future. ◎

CONSCIENCE
To dream that your ***conscience*** censures you from deceiving someone, denotes that you will be tempted to commit wrong, and should be constantly on your guard.

To dream of having a ***quiet conscience***, denotes that you will stand in high repute. ◎

ATONEMENT
This dream means joyous communing with friends, and speculators need not fear any drop in stocks. Courting will meet with happy consummation.

The sacrifice or ***atonement*** of another for your waywardness, is portentous of the humiliation of self or friends through your open or secret disregard of duty.

ASCETICISM
To dream of ***asceticism***, denotes that you will cultivate strange principles and views, rendering yourself fascinating to strangers, but repulsive to your friends. ◎

DEVOTION *see* **GOD** *page 277,* **FAMILY** *page 127* ◆ **CHARITY** *see* **ALMS, BEGGAR** *page 244* ◆ **ADVICE** *see* **LAWYER** *page 245* ◆ **INDEPENDENCE** *see* **WEALTH** *page 238* ◆ **ASCETICISM** *see* **MONK** *page 281*

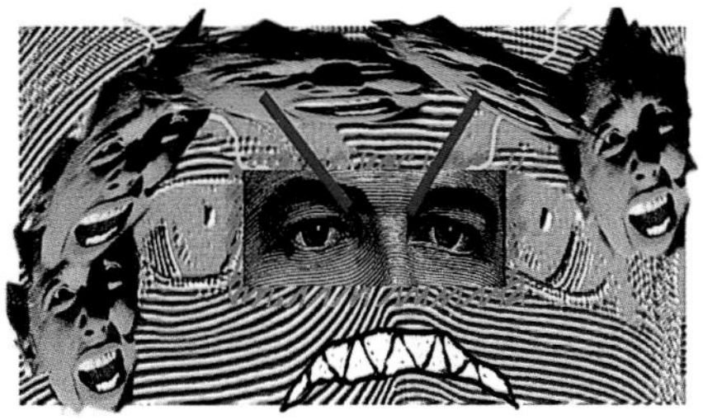

Fear and Loathing

Dreams of a powerful emotion can inflict as much mental wear and tear on the dreamer as the experience of such feelings in the waking world. Nameless dread is an emotion often felt in dreams, as is unreasoning abhorrence. This section deals with the different intensities of emotion, from fear to terror and from malice to hatred.

Fear and Terror

FEARS
To dream that you feel ***fear*** from any cause, your future engagements will not prove successful.

For a young woman, this dream forebodes disappointment and unfortunate love. ◎

AFFRIGHTED
To dream that you are ***affrighted***, foretells that you will sustain an injury through an accident.

To see ***others affrighted***, brings you close to misery and distressing scenes.

Dreams of this nature are frequently caused by nervous and feverish conditions, either from malaria or excitement. When such is the case, the dreamer is warned to take immediate steps to remove the cause. Such dreams or reveries only occur when sleep is disturbed. ◎

AFRAID
To feel that you are ***afraid*** to proceed with some affair, or continue a journey, denotes that you will find trouble in your household, and enterprises will be unsuccessful.

To see ***others afraid***, denotes that some friend will be deterred from performing some favor for you because of his or her own difficulties.

For a young woman to dream that she is ***afraid of a dog***, means she may possibly doubt a true friend. ◎

FRIGHTENED
To dream that you are ***frightened*** at anything, denotes temporary and fleeting worries. ◎

ANXIETY
A dream of this kind is occasionally a good omen, denoting, after threatening states, success and rejuvenation of mind; but if the dreamer is ***anxious*** about some momentous affair, it indicates a disastrous combination of business and social states. ◎

MORTIFICATION
To dream that you feel ***mortified*** over any deed committed by yourself, is a sign that you will be placed in an unenviable position before those to whom you most wish to appear honorable and just. Financial conditions will fall low.

To see ***mortified flesh***, denotes disastrous enterprises and disappointment in love. ◎

TERROR
To dream that you feel ***terror*** at any object or happening, denotes disappointments and loss.

To see ***others in terror***, means that unhappiness of friends will seriously affect you. ◎

Loathing and Contempt

CONTEMPT
To dream of being in ***contempt*** of court, denotes that you have committed a business or social indiscretion and that it is unmerited.

To dream that you are ***held in contempt*** by others, you will succeed in winning their highest regard, and will find yourself prosperous and happy. But if the contempt is merited, your exile from business or social circles is intimated. ◎

SPLEEN
To dream of ***spleen***, denotes that you will have a misunderstanding with some party who will injure you. ◎

To dream of virtuous impulses such as atonement *opposite* **indicate that virtue will be rewarded in real life.**

MALICE
To dream of entertaining ***malice*** for any person, denotes that you will stand low in the opinion of friends because of a disagreeable temper. Seek to control your passion.

If you dream of persons maliciously using you, an enemy in friendly garb is working you harm. ◎

ABHOR
To dream that you ***abhor*** a person, you will entertain strange dislike for some person, and your suspicion will prove correct.

To think yourself held in ***abhorrence*** by others, your good intentions to others will subside into selfishness.

For a young woman to dream that her ***lover abhors her***, foretells that she will love a man who is in no sense congenial. ◎

AFRAID *see* **JOURNEY** *page 221*, **DOGS** *page 41* ◆ **MORTIFIED** *see* **CORPSE** *page 121* ◆ **CONTEMPT** *see* **JUDGE** *page 245* ◆ **SPLEEN** *see* **ANGER** *page 250* ◆ **ABHOR** *see* **HATE** *page 250*

Bad Behavior

To dream that you are behaving badly can be exhilarating at times, although it is not so pleasant to be the object of ill manners, in your dreams or in waking life. This section examines the spectrum of antisocial behavior from the mildly reprehensible annoyance to the downright effrontery of abuse.

Insults and Annoyances

SLIGHTED
To dream of ***slighting*** anyone, denotes you will fail to find happiness, as you cultivate a morose and repellent bearing.

If you are ***slighted***, you will have cause to bemoan your position. ◎

ANNOY
To dream that you ***are annoyed*** or ***annoy*** someone, denotes you have enemies who are at work against you. ***Annoyances*** experienced in dreams find speedy fulfilment in the trifling incidents of the following day. ◎

AFFRONT
This is a bad dream. The dreamer is sure to shed tears and weep. For a young woman to dream that she is ***affronted***, denotes that some unfriendly person will take advantage of her ignorance to place her in a compromising situation with a stranger, or to jeopardize her interests with a friend. ◎

Nasty Habits

CUNNING
To dream of being ***cunning***, denotes that you will assume happy cheerfulness to retain the friendship of prosperous and gay people. If you are associating with ***cunning people***, it warns you that deceit is being practiced upon you in order to use your means for their own advancement. ◎

BOASTING
To hear ***boasting*** in your dreams, you will sincerely regret an impulsive act, which will cause trouble to your friends.

To boast to a competitor, foretells that you will be unjust, and will use dishonest means to overcome competition. ◎

OFFENSE
To dream of ***being offended***, denotes that errors will be detected in your conduct, which will cause you inward rage while attempting to justify yourself.

To give ***offense***, predicts for you many struggles before reaching your aims.

For a young woman to ***give or take offense***, signifies that she will regret hasty conclusions and disobedience to parents or guardian. ◎

ABUSE
To dream of ***abusing*** a person, means that you will be unfortunate in your affairs, losing good money through overbearing persistency in business relations with others.

To feel yourself ***abused***, you will be molested by the enmity of others.

For a young woman to dream that she hears ***abusive language***, foretells that she will fall under the ban of some person's jealousy and envy. If she uses the language herself, she will meet with unexpected rebuffs, which may fill her with mortification and remorse for her past unworthy conduct toward friends. ◎

SPITTING
To dream of ***spitting***, denotes unhappy terminations of seemingly auspicious undertakings. For someone to spit on you, foretells disagreements and alienation of affections. ◎

Bad Manners

MANNERS
To dream of seeing ***ugly-mannered*** persons, denotes failure to carry out undertakings through the disagreeableness of a person connect with the affair.

If you meet people with ***affable manners***, you will be pleasantly surprised by affairs of moment with you taking a favorable turn. ◎

TEASING
To find yourself ***teasing*** any person while dreaming, denotes that you will be loved and sought after because of your cheerful and amiable manners. Your business will be eventually successful.

To dream of ***being teased***, denotes that you will win the love of merry and well-to-do persons.

For a young woman to dream of being teased, foretells that she will form a hasty attachment, but will not be successful in consummating an early marriage. ◎

CUNNING *see* LEARNING *page 179* ◆ ABUSE *see* INVECTIVE, SWEARING *page 230,* CALUMNY *page 231*

Ruin and Devastation

The landscape of your dreams may not always be green and pleasant. This section covers dreams of dirt and filth, degradation and ruin, a spiritual and commercial wasteland, visions of collapse and disintegration. Actual dirt and decay are covered as well as dreams of symbolic ruin.

Filth and Degradation

DIRT
To dream of seeing freshly stirred ***dirt*** around flowers or trees, denotes that thrift and healthful conditions abound for the dreamer.

To see your clothes ***soiled with dirt***, you will be forced to save yourself from contagious diseases by leaving your home or submitting to the strictures of the law.

To dream that someone throws dirt upon you, denotes that enemies will try to injure your character. ◎

SCUM
To dream of ***scum***, signifies that disappointment will be experienced by you over social defeats. ◎

RUST
To dream of ***rust*** on articles, old pieces of tin, or iron, is significant of depression of your surroundings. Sickness, decline in fortune, and false friends are filling your sphere. ◎

RUBBISH
To dream of ***rubbish***, denotes that you will badly manage your affairs. ◎

GARBAGE
To see heaps of ***garbage*** in your dreams, indicates thoughts of social scandal and unfavorable business of every character. For females, this dream is ominous of disparagement and desertion by lovers. ◎

PEST
To dream of being worried over a ***pest*** of any nature, foretells that disturbing elements will prevail in your immediate future.

To see others thus worried, denotes that you will be annoyed by some displeasing development. ◎

DUST
To dream of ***dust*** covering you, denotes that you will be slightly injured in business by the failure of others. For a young woman, this denotes that she will be set aside by her lover for a newer flame. If you free yourself of the dust by using judicious measures, you will clear up the loss. ◎

GUTTER
To dream of a ***gutter***, is a sign of degradation. You will be the cause of unhappiness to others.

To find articles of value in a gutter, foretells that your right to certain property will be questioned. ◎

Laid to Waste

WASTE
To dream of wandering through ***waste*** places, foreshadows doubt and failure, where promise of success was bright before you.

To dream of wasting your fortune, denotes that you will be unpleasantly encumbered with domestic cares. ◎

RUINS
To dream of ***ruins***, signifies broken engagements to lovers, distressing conditions in business, destruction to crops, and failing health.

To dream of ***ancient ruins***, foretells that you will travel extensively, but there will be a note of sadness mixed with the pleasure in the realization of a long-cherished hope. You will feel the absence of some friend. ◎

DISGRACE
To be worried in your dream over the ***disgraceful*** conduct of children or friends, will bring you unsatisfying hopes, and worries will harass you. To be in disgrace yourself, denotes that you will hold morality at a low rate, and you are in danger of lowering your reputation for uprightness. Enemies are also shadowing you. ◎

RUBBISH

Rivers of filth *left* are as distasteful in your street of dreams as they are in waking life.

DIRT *see* **CLOTHES** *page 154,* **STAIN** *page 218* ◆ **RUST** *see* **IRON** *page 72* ◆ **GUTTER** *see* **TREASURES** *page 238* ◆ **WASTE** *see* **DESERT** *page 89,* **WEALTH** *page 238* ◆ **RUINS** *see* **BUILDINGS** *page 188* ◆ **DISGRACE** *see* **CHILDREN** *page 128,* **FRIEND** *page 124,* **MANNERS** *page 254*

Joy and Sadness

Many emotions are felt as strongly in dreams as they are in waking life. This section celebrates good cheer and covers the spectrum of moods that sweeps from ecstasy and great joy to abject despair. Failure and Adversity are also dealt with, as are the sorrow and sadness engendered by farewells, absence, and abandonment.

Good Cheer

LAUGHING
To dream that you laugh and feel cheerful, means success in your undertakings, and bright companions socially.

Laughing immoderately at some weird object, denotes disappointment and lack of harmony in your surroundings.

To hear the ***happy laughter*** of children, means joy and health to the dreamer.

To laugh at the discomfiture of others, denotes that you will wilfully injure your friends to gratify your own selfish desires.

To hear ***mocking laughter***, denotes illness and disappointing affairs. ◎

JOLLY
If you dream that you feel ***jolly*** and are enjoying the merriment of companions, you will realize pleasure from the good behavior of children and have satisfying results in business. If there comes the least rift in the merriment, worry will intermingle with the success of the future. ◎

JOLLY BOY

MERRY
To dream of being ***merry***, or in merry company, denotes that pleasant events will engage you for a time, and affairs will assume profitable shapes. ◎

Sheer Delight

LOVELY
Dreaming of ***lovely*** things, brings favor to all persons connected with you.

For a lover to dream that his sweetheart is ***lovely of person*** and character, foretells for him a speedy and favorable marriage.

If through the vista of dreams you see your own ***fair loveliness***, fate bids you, with a gleaming light, awake to happiness. ◎

PLEASURE
To dream of ***pleasure***, denotes gain and personal enjoyment. ◎

TICKLE
To dream of being ***tickled***, denotes insistent worries and illness.

If you tickle others, you will throw away much enjoyment through weakness and folly. ◎

DELIGHT
To dream of experiencing ***delight*** over any event, signifies a favorable turn in affairs.

For lovers to be ***delighted*** with the conduct of their sweethearts, denotes pleasant greetings.

To ***feel delight*** when looking on beautiful landscapes, prognosticates to the dreamer very great success and congenial associations. ◎

ECSTASY
To dream of feeling ***ecstasy***, denotes that you will enjoy a visit from a long absent friend.

ECSTASY

If you experience ecstasy in disturbing dreams, this means you will be subjected to sorrow and disappointment. ◎

JOY
To dream that you feel ***joy*** over any event, denotes there will be harmony among friends. ◎

YEARN
To feel in a dream that you are ***yearning*** for the presence of anyone, denotes that you will soon hear comforting tidings from your absent friends.

For a young woman to think that her lover is ***yearning for her***, she will have the pleasure of soon hearing someone making a long wished for proposal.

If she dreams that she lets him know that she is ***yearning for him***, she will be left alone and her longings will grow apace. ◎

LAUGHING *see* CHILDREN *page 128*, TEASING *page 254* ◆ LOVELY *see* BEAUTY *page 100* ◆ DELIGHT *see* SWEETHEART *page 124*

Lamentation and Woe

SIGH
To dream that you are ***sighing*** over any trouble or sad event, denotes that you will have unexpected sadness, but some redeeming brightness in your season of trouble.

To hear the ***sighing of others***, foretells that the misconduct of dear friends will oppress you with a weight of gloom. ◎

LAMENT
To dream that you bitterly ***lament*** the loss of friends or property, signifies great struggles and much distress, from which will spring causes for joy and personal gain.

To ***lament the loss of relatives***, denotes sickness or disappointments, which will bring you into closer harmony with companions, and will result in brighter prospects. ◎

TEARS

TEARS
To dream that you are in ***tears***, denotes that some affliction will soon envelop you.

To dream that you see ***others shedding tears***, foretells that your sorrows will affect the happiness of others. ◎

CRYING
To dream of ***crying***, is a forerunner of illusory pleasures, which will subside into gloom, and distressing influences affecting for evil business engagements and domestic affairs.

To see ***others crying***, forebodes unexpected calls for aid from you. ◎

WEEPING
Weeping in your dreams, foretells ill tidings and disturbances in your family.

To see ***others weeping***, signals a pleasant reunion after periods of saddened estrangements.

This dream for a young woman is ominous of lovers' quarrels, which can only reach reconciliation by self-abnegation.

For the tradesman, it foretells temporary discouragement and reverses. ◎

Alarm and Despondency

MOROSE
If you find yourself ***morose*** in dreams, you will awake to find the world, as far as you are concerned, going fearfully wrong.

To see others morose, portends unpleasant occupations and unpleasant companions. ◎

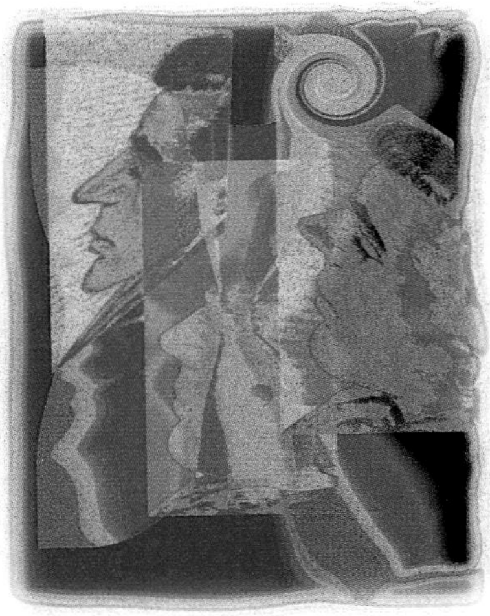

MELANCHOLY

GLOOM
To be surrounded by many ***gloomy*** situations in your dream, warns you of rapidly approaching unpleasantness and loss. ◎

MELANCHOLY
To dream that you feel ***melancholy*** over any event, is a sign of disappointment in what was thought to be favorable undertakings.

To dream that you see others melancholy, denotes an unpleasant interruption in affairs. To lovers, it brings separation. ◎

ABJECT
To dream that you are ***abject***, denotes that you will be the recipient of gloomy tidings, which will cause a relaxation in your strenuous efforts to climb to the heights of prosperity.

To see others abject, is a sign of bickerings and false dealings among your friends. ◎

Black Despair

DESPAIR
To be in ***despair*** in dreams, denotes that you will have many and cruel vexations in the working world.

To see others in despair, foretells the distress and unhappy position of some relative or friend. ◎

SUICIDE
To commit ***suicide*** in a dream, foretells that misfortune will hang heavily over you.

To see or hear others committing this deed, foretells that the failure of others will affect your interests.

For a young woman to dream that her ***lover commits suicide***, her disappointment by the faithlessness of her lover is accentuated. ◎

Dream moods may swing wildly from jollity *opposite left* **to ecstasy** *opposite right*, **and from weeping** *above* **to deep melancholy** *left*.

SIGH *see* **VOICE** *page 276* ◆ **LAMENT** *see* **FRIEND** *page 124*, **PROPERTY** *page 239* ◆ **SUICIDE** *see* **DEATH** *page 120*

Failure and Adversity

DIFFICULTY

This dream signifies temporary embarrassment for business people of all classes, including soldiers and writers. But to extricate yourself from ***difficulties***, foretells your prosperity.

For a woman to dream of being in difficulties, denotes that she is threatened with ill health or enemies.

For lovers, this is a dream of contrariety, denoting pleasant courtship. ◎

ADVERSITY

To dream that you are in the clutches of ***adversity***, denotes that you will have failures and continued bad prospects.

To see others in adversity, portends gloomy surroundings, and the illness of someone will produce grave fears of the successful working of plans. ◎

FAILURE

For a lover, this is sometimes of contrary significance. To dream that he fails in his suit, signifies that he only needs more masterfulness and energy in his daring, as he has already the love and esteem of his sweetheart. (Contrary dreams are those in which the dreamer suffers fear, and not injury.)

For a young woman to dream that her life is going to be a ***failure***, denotes that she is not applying her opportunities to good advantage.

For a businessman to dream that he has made a failure, forebodes loss and bad management, which should be corrected, or failure threatens to materialize in earnest. ◎

Final Farewells

ADIEU

To dream of bidding cheerful ***adieus*** to people, denotes that you will make pleasant visits and enjoy much social festivity; but if they are made in a sad or doleful strain, you will endure loss and bereaving sorrow.

If you ***bid adieu to home*** and country, you will travel in the nature of an exile from fortune and love.

To throw ***kisses of adieu*** to loved ones, or children, foretells that you will soon have a journey to make, but there will be no unpleasant accidents or happenings attending your trip. ◎

THE FAREWELL

PARTING

To dream of ***parting*** with friends and good companions, denotes that many little vexations will come into your daily life.

If you part with enemies, it is a sign of success in love and business. ◎

FAREWELL

To dream of bidding ***farewell***, is not very favorable, as you are likely to hear unpleasant news of absent friends.

For a young woman to bid her ***lover farewell***, portends his indifference to her. If she feels no sadness in this farewell, she will soon find others to comfort her. ◎

ABSENCE

To grieve over the ***absence*** of anyone in your dreams, denotes that repentance for some hasty action will be the means of securing your lifelong friendships.

If you rejoice over the absence of friends, it denotes that you will soon be well rid of an enemy. ◎

ABANDONMENT

To dream that you are ***abandoned***, denotes that you will have difficulty in framing your plans for future success.

To ***abandon others***, you will see unhappy conditions piled thick around you, leaving little hope of surmounting them.

If it is your house that you abandon, you will soon come to grief in experimenting with fortune.

If you ***abandon your sweetheart***, you will fail to recover lost valuables, and friends will turn aside from your favors.

If you ***abandon a mistress***, you will unexpectedly come into a goodly inheritance.

If it is religion you abandon, you will come to grief by your attacks on prominent people.

To ***abandon children***, denotes that you will lose your fortune by lack of calmness and judgement.

To ***abandon your business***, indicates distressing circumstances in which there will be quarrels and suspicion. (This dream may have a literal fulfilment if it is impressed on your waking mind, whether you abandon a person, or that person abandons you, or whether, as indicated, it denotes other worries.)

To see yourself or a friend ***abandon a ship***, suggests your possible entanglement in some business failure, but if you escape to shore your interest will remain secure. ◎

FORSAKING

For a young woman to dream of ***forsaking*** her home or friend denotes that she will have trouble in love, as her estimate of her lover will decrease with acquaintance and association. ◎

Breaking up is always hard to do, and it is no easier to say farewell in your dreams *above* than it is in real life.

ADIEU *see* HOME *page 205*, KISSING *page 125*, CHILDREN *page 128* ◆ PARTING *see* FRIEND *page 124*, ENEMY *page 260* ◆ ABSENCE *see* BANISHMENT, EXILE *page 249*, FRIEND *page 124* ◆ ABANDONED *see* HOUSE *page 188*, SWEETHEART *page 124*, RELIGION *page 277*, CHILDREN *page 128*, SHIPS *page 226* ◆ FORSAKING *see* HOME *page 205*, FRIEND *page 124*

Fame and Glory

To dream that you are famous and a figure of public recognition is almost a cliché; nonetheless such dreams have their own particular portent. This section covers the minor glories of acceptance and advancement as well as fame and adulation, and the physical accoutrements of celebrity such as medals and honors.

Favor and Adulation

ACCEPTED
For a businessman to dream that his proposition has been ***accepted***, foretells that he will succeed in making a trade, which heretofore looked as if it would prove a failure.

For a lover to dream that he has been accepted by his sweetheart, denotes that he will happily wed the object of his own and others' admiration. ◎

ADVANCEMENT
To dream of ***advancing*** in any engagement, denotes preferment and the consummation of affairs of the heart.

To see others advancing, foretells that friends will hold positions of favor near you. ◎

FAVOR
To dream that you ask ***favors*** of anyone, denotes that you will enjoy abundance, and not especially need anything.

To ***grant favors***, means a loss. ◎

IMITATION
To dream of ***imitations***, means that persons are working to deceive you. For a young woman to dream that someone is imitating her lover or herself, foretells that she will be imposed upon, and will suffer for the faults of others. ◎

ADMIRE
To dream that you are an object of ***admiration***, denotes that you will retain the love of former associates, though your position will take you above their circle. ◎

ADULATION
To dream that you seek ***adulation***, foretells that you will pompously fill unmerited positions of honor.

If you ***offer adulation***, you will expressly part with some dear belongings in the hope of furthering material interests. ◎

FAWN
To dream that a person ***fawns*** on you, or cajoles you, is a warning that enemies are about you in the guise of interested friends. ◎

Public Recognition

MEDAL
To dream of ***medals***, denotes honors gained by application and industry.

To lose a medal, denotes misfortune through the unfaithfulness of others. ◎

COAT-OF-ARMS
To dream of seeing your ***coat-of-arms***, is a dream of ill luck. You will never possess a title. ◎

SEEKING ADULATION

FAMOUS HEROES

FAME
To dream of being ***famous***, denotes disappointed aspirations. To dream of famous people, portends your rise from obscurity to a place of honor. ◎

DECORATE
To be ***decorating***, or see ***others decorated*** for some heroic action, foretells that you will be worthy, but that few will recognize your ability. ◎

In your dreams you may seek adulation *left* or already receive the prize of fame and glory from an adoring public *above*.

ACCEPTED *see* **SWEETHEART** *page 124* ◆ **FAWN** *see also* **FAWN** *page 31* ◆ **DECORATE** *see also* **DECORATE** *page 218*

War and Peace

To dream of death or glory in battle, or to witness the horror and carnage of warfare from the sidelines appears to reflect conflicts in various spheres of waking life. This section covers most aspects of the dream battlefield: how enemies are made, military strategies, the armed forces, weapons and the ultimate horror of the atomic bomb.

Making Enemies

QUARREL
Quarrels in dreams, portend unhappiness and fierce altercations. To a young woman, it is the signal of fatal unpleasantries, and to a married woman it brings separation or continuous disagreements.

To hear ***others quarreling***, denotes unsatisfactory business and disappointing trade. ◎

FIGHT
To dream that you engage in a ***fight***, denotes that you will have unpleasant encounters with your business opponents, and lawsuits threaten you.

To see ***fighting***, denotes that you are squandering your time and money. For women, this dream is warning against slander and gossip.

For a young woman to see her ***lover fighting***, is a sign of his unworthiness.

To dream that you are ***defeated in a fight***, signifies that you will lose your right to property.

To whip your assailant, denotes that you will, by courage and perseverance, win honor and wealth in spite of opposition.

To dream that you see two men ***fighting with pistols***, denotes many worries and perplexities; while no real loss is involved in the dream, yet but small profit is predicted and some unpleasantness is denoted. ◎

ADVERSARY
To dream that you meet or engage with an ***adversary***, denotes that you will promptly defend any attacks on your interest. Sickness may also threaten you after this dream.

If you ***overcome an adversary***, you will escape the effect of some serious disaster. ◎

ENEMY
To dream that you overcome ***enemies***, denotes that you will surmount all difficulties in business, and enjoy the greatest prosperity.

If you are ***defamed by your enemies***, it denotes that you will be threatened with failures in your work. You will be wise to use the utmost caution in proceeding in affairs of any moment.

To overcome your enemies in any form, signifies your gain. For them to get the better of you, is ominous of adverse fortunes. This dream may be literal. ◎

THE QUARREL

Violence

VIOLENCE
To dream that any person does you ***violence***, denotes that you will be overcome by enemies. If you do some other person violence, you will lose fortune and favor by your reprehensible way of conducting your affairs. ◎

HURT
If you ***hurt*** a person in your dreams, you will do ugly work, revenging and injuring. If you are hurt, you will have enemies who will overcome you. ◎

BLOWS
Blows denote injury to yourself. If you receive a blow, brain trouble will threaten you. If you defend yourself, a rise in business will follow. ◎

BEAT
It bodes no good to dream of ***being beaten*** by an angry person; family jars and discord are signified.

To dream that you ***beat*** a child, ungenerous advantage is taken by you of another; perhaps that tendency will be to cruelly treat a child. ◎

PUNCH
To dream that you are punching any person with a club or fist, denotes quarrels and recriminations. ◎

Dream violence may manifest itself as a domestic spat *left*, **the image of a famous war leader such as General Norman Schwarzkopf** *opposite top,* **or an old-fashioned siege** *opposite center*.

FIGHT *see* WHIP *page 33,* PISTOL *page 263* ◆ ENEMY *see* CALUMNY *page 231* ◆ BEAT *see* CHILDREN *page 128,* ANGER *page 250*

At War

NORMAN SCHWARZKOPF

WAR
To dream of ***war***, foretells unfortunate conditions in business, and much disorder and strife in domestic affairs.

For a young woman to dream that her ***lover goes to war***, denotes that she will hear of something detrimental to her lover's character.

To dream that your country is ***defeated in war***, is a sign that it will suffer revolutions of a business and political nature. Personal interest will sustain a blow either way.

If of victory you dream, there will be brisk activities along business lines, and domesticity will be harmonious. ◎

BATTLE
Battle signifies striving with difficulties, but a final victory over the same.

If you are ***defeated in battle***, it denotes that bad deals made by others will mar your prospects for good. ◎

COMBAT
To dream of engaging in ***combat***, you will find yourself seeking to ingratiate your affections into the life and love of someone whom you know to be another's, and you will run great risk of losing your good reputation in business. It denotes struggles to keep on firm ground.

For a young woman to dream of seeing ***combatants***, signifies that she will have a choice between lovers, both of whom love her and would face death for her. ◎

Tactics

AMBUSH
To dream that you are attacked from ***ambush***, denotes that you have lurking secretly near you a danger, which will soon set upon and overthrow you if you are feeling heedless of warnings.

If you lie in ambush to revenge yourself on others, you will unhesitatingly stoop to debasing actions to defraud your friends. ◎

SIEGE

SIEGE
For a young woman to dream that she is in a ***siege***, and sees cavalry around her, denotes that she will have serious drawbacks to enjoyment, but will surmount them finally, and receive much pleasure and profit from seeming disappointments. ◎

CAPTIVE
To dream that you are a ***captive***, denotes that you may have treachery to deal with, and if you cannot escape, that injury and misfortune will befall you.

To dream of taking anyone captive, you will join yourself to pursuits and persons of lower status.

For a young woman to dream that she is a captive, denotes that she will have a husband who will be jealous of her confidence in others; or she may be censured for her indiscretion. ◎

Winners and Losers

VICTORY
To dream that you win a ***victory***, foretells that you will successfully resist the attacks of enemies, and will have the love of women for the asking. ◎

YIELD
To dream that you ***yield*** to another's wishes, denotes that you will throw away, by weak indecision, a great opportunity to elevate yourself.

If others ***yield to you***, exclusive privileges will be accorded you, and you will be elevated above your associates.

To receive ***poor yield*** for your labors, you may expect cares and worries. ◎

PACIFY
To endeavor to ***pacify*** suffering ones, denotes that you will be loved for your sweetness of disposition. To a young woman, this dream is one of promise of a devoted husband or friends.

To dream that you are pacifying the anger of others, denotes that you will labor for the advancement of others.

If a lover dreams of soothing the jealous suspicions of his sweetheart, he will find that his love will be unfortunately placed. ◎

Battle Stations

FORTRESS
To dream that you are confined in a ***fortress***, denotes that enemies will succeed in placing you in an undesirable situation.

If you dream that you put ***others in a fortress***, this denotes your ability to rule successfully, whether in business or over women. ◎

FORT
To dream of ***defending a fort***, signifies that your honor and possessions will be attacked, and you will have great worry over the matter.

To dream that you ***attack a fort*** and take it, denotes victory over your worst enemy, and fortunate engagements. ◎

COMBAT *see* **FIGHT** *page 260* ◆ **SIEGE** *see* **CAVALRY** *page 262* ◆ **YIELD** *see* **LABOR** *page 194* ◆ **PACIFY** *see* **SWEETHEART** *page 124*, **JEALOUSY** *page 250* ◆ **FORTRESS, FORT** *see* **CASTLE** *page 189*

Officers and Other Ranks

SOLDIERS
To see ***soldiers*** marching in your dreams, foretells for you a period of flagrant excesses, but at the same time you will be promoted to elevations above rivals.

To see ***wounded soldiers***, is a sign of the misfortune of others causing you serious complications in your affairs. Your sympathy will outstrip your judgement.

To dream that you are a worthy soldier, you will have literal fulfilment of ideals.

Women are in danger of disrepute if they find themselves dreaming of soldiers. ◎

COLONEL
To dream of seeing or being commanded by a ***colonel***, denotes that you will fail to reach any prominence in social or business circles.

If you are a colonel, it denotes that you will contrive to hold position above friends or acquaintances. ◎

FLAG

CAPTAIN
To dream of seeing a ***captain*** of any company, denotes that your noblest aspirations will be realized. If a woman dreams that her lover is a captain, she will be much harassed in mind from jealousy and rivalry. ◎

COMMAND
To dream of being ***commanded***, denotes that you will be humbled in some way by your associates for scorn shown your superiors.

To dream of ***giving a command***, you will have some honor conferred upon you. If this is done in a tyrannical or boastful way, disappointments will follow.

To dream of ***receiving commands***, foretells that you will be unwisely influenced by persons of stronger will than your own. ◎

CAVALRY
To dream that you see a division of ***cavalry***, denotes personal advancement and distinction. Some little sensation may accompany your elevated position. ◎

SENTRY
To dream of a ***sentry***, denotes that you will have kind protectors, and that your life will be smoothly conducted. ◎

Flags

BANNER
To see one's country's ***banner*** floating in a clear sky, denotes triumph over foreign foes.

To see it battered, is significant of wars and loss of military honors on land and sea. ◎

STANDARD-BEARER
To dream that you are a ***standard-bearer***, denotes that your occupation will be pleasant but varied.

To see others acting as standard-bearers, foretells that you will be jealous and envious of some friend. ◎

War in the Air

AIR FORCE OFFICER
To dream of an ***air force officer***, foretells that you will soon be going on a short journey, or that you will be visited in the near future by some unexpected company.

To dream that you are an air force officer, means you will be promoted to a managerial position. ◎

Sea Battles

NAVY
To dream of the ***navy***, denotes victorious struggles with unsightly obstacles, and the promise of voyages and tours of recreation.

If in your dream you seem frightened or disconcerted, you will have strange obstacles to overcome before you reach fortune.

A ***dilapidated navy*** is an indication of unfortunate friendships in business or love. ◎

FLEET
To see a large ***fleet*** moving rapidly in your dreams, denotes a hasty change in the business world. Where dullness oppresses, brisk workings of commercial wheels will go forward and some rumors of foreign wars will be heard. ◎

MAN-OF-WAR
To dream of a ***man-of-war***, denotes long journeys and separation from country and friends; dissension in political affairs is portended.

If she is crippled, foreign elements will work damage to home interests.

If she is sailing upon rough seas, trouble with foreign powers may endanger private affairs. Personal affairs may also go awry. ◎

SUBMARINE
To dream of a ***submarine***, denotes that a past indiscretion will soon surface and have a negative impact on your life.

To dream of being in a submarine, means that you will inadvertently reveal some troubling news. Mayhem will ensue. ◎

You may dream of your national flag *far left*, **a life in the services** *left* **or of a fatal shot ringing out from a defender of the law** *opposite top*.

IN THE NAVY

SOLDIERS *see* **MARCH** *page 168*, **WOUND** *page 112*, ◆ **CAVALRY** *see* **RIDING** *page 33*, **HORSE** *pages 34–5* ◆ **NAVY** *see* **SHIPS, SAILOR, MARINER** *page 226*, **FRIGHTENED** *page 253* ◆ **FLEET** *see* **SHIPS, VESSELS** *page 226* ◆ **MAN OF WAR** *see* **SHIPS** *page 226*, **SEA** *page 79* ◆ **SUBMARINE** *see* **VESSEL** *page 226* ◆ **BANNER** *see* **FLAG** *page 230*

Shooting to Kill

SHOOTING
To dream that you see or hear ***shooting***, signifies unhappiness between married couples and sweethearts because of overweening selfishness. This dream is also indicative of unsatisfactory business and tasks because of negligence. ◎

SHOT
To dream that you are ***shot***, and are feeling the sensation of dying, denotes that you are to meet unexpected abuse from the ill feeling of friends; but if you escape death by waking, you will be fully reconciled with them later on.

To dream that a ***preacher shoots you***, signifies that you will be annoyed by some friend advancing views condemnatory to those entertained by yourself. ◎

SHOTGUN
To dream of a ***shotgun***, foretells domestic troubles and worry with children and servants.

To shoot both barrels of a ***double-barreled shotgun***, foretells that you will meet such exasperating and unfeeling attention in your private and public life that suave manners giving way under the strain and the righteous wrath will be justifiable. ◎

REVOLVER
For a young woman to dream that she sees her sweetheart with a ***revolver***, denotes that she will have a serious disagreement with some friend, and probably separation from her lover. ◎

PISTOL
Seeing a ***pistol*** in your dream, denotes bad fortune, generally.

If you own one, you will cultivate a low, designing character.

If you hear the report of one, you will be made aware of some scheme to ruin your interests.

To dream of ***shooting off your pistol***, signifies that you will envy some innocent person, and will go far to revenge their imagined wrong. ◎

CLINT EASTWOOD

GUN
This is a dream of distress. Hearing the sound of a ***gun***, denotes loss of employment, and bad management to proprietors of establishments.

If you ***shoot a person with a gun***, you will fall into dishonor.

If you are shot, you will be annoyed by evil persons, and perhaps suffer an acute illness.

For a woman to dream of shooting, forecasts for her a quarreling and disagreeable reputation connected with sensations. For a married woman, unhappiness through other women. ◎

The Big Guns

CANNON
This dream denotes that one's home and country are in danger of foreign intrusion, from which our youth will suffer from the perils of war.

For a young woman to hear or see ***cannons***, denotes she will be a soldier's wife and will have to bid him godspeed as he marches in defense of her and honor.

The reader will have to interpret dreams of this character by the influences surrounding him, and by the experiences stored away in his subjective mind. If you have thought about cannons a great deal and you dream of them when there is no war, they are most likely to warn you against struggle and probable defeat. Or if business is manipulated by yourself, successful engagements after much worry and ill luck may ensue. ◎

CANNONBALL
This means that secret enemies are uniting against you.

For a maid to see a ***cannonball***, denotes that she will have a soldier sweetheart.

For a youth to see one, denotes that he will be called upon to defend his country. ◎

CARTRIDGE
To dream of ***cartridges***, foretells unhappy quarrels and dissensions. Some untoward fate threatens you or someone closely allied to you. If they are empty, there will be foolish variances in your associations. ◎

BAYONET
To dream of a ***bayonet***, signifies that enemies will hold you in their power, unless you get possession of the bayonet. ◎

AMMUNITION
To dream of ***ammunition***, foretells the undertaking of some work, which promises fruitful completion.

To dream your ***ammunition is exhausted***, denotes fruitless struggles and endeavors. ◎

SHOT *see* **DYING** *page 120*, **PREACHER** *page 282* ◆ **REVOLVER** *see* **SWEETHEART** *page 124* ◆ **PISTOL, GUN, CANNON** *see* **NOISE** *page 276*

Swords and Daggers

SWORD

To dream that you wear a ***sword***, indicates that you will fill some public position with honor.

To have your ***sword taken from you*** denotes your vanquishment in rivalry.

To see others bearing swords, foretells dangerous altercations.

A ***broken sword***, foretells despair. ◎

SCABBARD

To dream of a ***scabbard***, denotes that some misunderstanding will be amicably settled. If you wonder where your scabbard can be, you will have overpowering difficulties to meet. ◎

DAGGER

If seen in a dream, a ***dagger*** denotes threatening enemies. If you wrench the dagger from the hand of another, it denotes that you will be able to counteract the influence of your enemies and overcome misfortune. ◎

POINARD

To dream of someone ***stabbing you with a poinard***, denotes secret enemies will cause uneasiness of mind.

If you attack any person with one of these weapons, you will suspect your friends of unfaithfulness. ◎

The Big Bang

EXPLOSION

To dream of explosions, ***portends that disapproving actions of those connected with you will cause you transient displeasure and loss, and that business developments will also displease you.***

To think your face, or the face of others, is blackened or mutilated, signifies that you will be accused of indiscretion which will be unjust, though circumstances may convict you.

To see the air filled with smoke and debris after an explosion in your dream, denotes unusual dissatisfaction in business circles and much social antagonism.

To think you are enveloped in the flames, or are up in the air where you have been blown by an explosion, foretells that unworthy friends will infringe on your rights and will abuse your confidence.

Young women should be careful of associates of the opposite sex after a dream of this character. ❋

DYNAMITE

To see dynamite ***in a dream, is a sign of approaching change and the expanding of one's affairs. To be frightened by it, indicates that a secret enemy is at work against you; and if you are not careful of your conduct, he will disclose himself at an unexpected and helpless moment.*** ❋

BOMBSHELL

To dream of bombshells, ***foretells anger and disputes, ending in lawsuits. Many displeasing incidents follow this dream.*** ❋

ATOMIC BOMB

To dream of the mushroom cloud of the atomic bomb, ***denotes that a catastrophic occurrence will soon affect you and your loved ones.***

To dream of a nuclear war, means that you are holding in a great deal of anger, which will soon reveal itself in a very destructive manner. ❋

Spurs and Lance

SPUR

To dream of wearing ***spurs***, you will engage in unpleasant controversy.

To see others with them on, foretells enmity working you trouble. ◎

LANCE

To dream of a ***lance***, denotes strong enemies and injurious experiments.

If you are wounded by a lance, an error of judgement will cause you annoyance.

To ***break a lance***, denotes that seeming impossibilities will be overcome and desires fulfilled. ◎

Ancient Armory

BOW AND ARROW

A ***bow and arrow*** in a dream, denotes great gain reaped from the inability of others to carry out plans.

To make a bad shot, means disappointed hopes in carrying forward successful business affairs. ◎

ARROW

Pleasure follows this dream. Entertainments, festivals, and pleasant journeys may be expected. Suffering will cease.

An old or broken ***arrow***, portends disappointments in love or business. ◎

CLUB

To dream of being approached by a person bearing a ***club***, denotes that you will be assailed by your adversaries, but you will overcome them and be unusually happy and prosperous; but if you club anyone, you will undergo a rough and profitless journey. ◎

SWORD *see* BREAK *page 265* ◆ DAGGER *see* HAND *page 97* ◆ POINARD *see* FIGHT *page 260* ◆ SPURS *see* HORSE *pages 34–5* ◆ LANCE *see* WOUND *page 112*, BREAK *page 265* ◆ ARROW *see* BREAK *page 265* ◆ CLUB *see* BLOWS *page 260* ◆ EXPLOSION *see* FACE *page 101*, SMOKE, FLAME *page 80* ◆ DYNAMITE *see* FRIGHTENED *page 253* ◆ ATOMIC BOMB *see* CLOUDS *page 74*

Accidents and Adventures

In dreams, we are the heroes of our own adventures; such dreams can be deliciously frightening and thrilling, offering excitement without real danger, like riding a roller-coaster. This section covers minor accidents, major disasters, riots and wreckage, dicing with death, rising to the challenge, and last-minute escape and rescue.

Breaks and Tumbles

ABOVE

To see anything hanging ***above*** you, and about to fall, implies danger; if it falls upon you, it may be ruin or sudden disappointment. If it falls near, but misses you, it is a sign that you will have a narrow escape from loss of money, or other misfortunes may follow.

Should it be securely fixed above you, so as not to imply danger, your condition will improve after threatened loss. ◎

STUMBLE

If you ***stumble*** in a dream while walking or running, you will meet with disfavor, and obstructions will bar your path to success; but you will eventually surmount them, if you do not fall. ◎

TUMBLE

To dream that you ***tumble*** off of anything, denotes that you are given to carelessness, and should strive to be prompt with your affairs.

To see others tumbling, is a sign that you will profit by the negligence of others. ◎

FALL

To dream that you sustain a ***fall***, and are much frightened, denotes that you will undergo some great struggle, but will eventually rise to honor and wealth; but if you are injured in the fall, you will encounter hardships and loss of friends. ◎

BREAK

This is a bad dream. To dream of ***breaking any of your limbs***, denotes bad management and probable failure.

To dream that you ***break furniture***, denotes domestic quarrels and an unquiet state of the mind.

To ***break a window***, signifies bereavement.

To dream that you see a ***broken ring***, indicates that order will be displaced by furious and dangerous uprisings, such as those often caused by jealous contentions. ◎

Appalling Accidents

ACCIDENT

To dream of an accident *is a warning to avoid any mode of travel for a short period, as you are threatened with loss of life.*

For an accident to befall stock, denotes that you will struggle with all your might to gain some object and then see some friend lose property of the same value in aiding your cause. ❁

DISASTER

To dream of being in any disaster *from public conveyance, you are in danger of losing property or of being maimed from some malarious disease.*

For a young woman to dream of a disaster in which she is a participant, foretells that she will mourn the loss of her lover by death or desertion.

To dream of a disaster at sea, denotes unhappiness to sailors and loss of their gains. To others, it signifies loss by death; but if you dream that you are rescued, you will be placed in trying situations, but will come out unscathed.

To dream of a railway wreck in which you are not a participant, you will eventually be interested in some accident because of some relative or friend being hurt, or you will have trouble of a business character. ❁

COLLISION

To dream of a collision, *you will meet an accident of a serious type and disappointments in business.*

For a young woman to dream that she sees a collision, *denotes that she will be unable to decide between lovers, and will be the cause of wrangles.* ❁

STUMBLE *see* **WALKING, RUNNING** *page 267* ◆ **FALL** *see* **FRIGHTENED** *page 253* ◆ **BREAK** *see* **ARMS** *page 97,* **LEGS** *page 96,* **WINDOW** *page 213,* **RING** *page 161,* ◆ **DISASTER** *see* **SEA** *page 79,* **SHIPS** *page 226,* **RESCUE** *page 266,* **TRAIN** *page 225,* **WRECKS** *page 266*

Riot and Wreckage

WILD
To dream that you are running about ***wild***, foretells that you will sustain a serious fall or accident.

To see others doing so, denotes that unfavorable prospects will cause you worry and excitement. ◎

WILD MAN
To see a ***wild man*** in your dream, denotes that enemies will openly oppose you in your enterprises.

To think you are one, foretells that you will be unlucky in your designs. ◎

RIOT
To dream of ***riots***, foretells disappointing affairs.

To see a friend ***killed in a riot***, you will have bad luck in all undertakings, and the death or some serious illness of some person will cause you distress. ◎

WRECKS
To see a ***wreck*** in your dreams, foretells that you will be harassed with fears of destitution or sudden failure in business. ◎

ALARM BELL
To hear a ***bell*** in your sleep, denotes that you will have cause for anxiety. ◎

DANGER
To dream of being in a ***perilous situation***, and death seems imminent, denotes that you will emerge from obscurity into distinction and honor; but if you should not escape the ***danger***, and suffer death or a wound, you will lose in business and be annoyed in your home, and by others. If you are in love, your prospects will grow discouraging. ◎

TRAP
To dream of setting a ***trap***, denotes that you will use intrigue to carry out your designs.

If you are ***caught in a trap***, you will be outwitted by your opponents.

If you catch ***game in a trap***, you will flourish in your vocation.

To see an ***empty trap***, there will be misfortune in the immediate future.

An old or ***broken trap***, denotes failure in business, and sickness in your family may follow. ◎

Deathly Danger

STRUGGLING
To dream of ***struggling***, foretells that you will encounter serious difficulties; but if you gain the victory in your struggle, you will also surmount present obstacles. ◎

SUFFOCATING
To dream that you are ***suffocating***, denotes that you will experience deep sorrow and mortification at the conduct of someone you love. You should be careful of your health after this dream. ◎

Your action dreams may see a heroic rescue *above,* **or a dramatic leap into the void** *opposite.*

STRANGLED BY UNSEEN HANDS
To dream of being ***strangled by unseen hands***, foretells that someone you feel close to is actually trying to harm you.

To dream that you are being ***choked***, means that you will soon be involved in a suffocating and exhausting relationship. ◎

BURIED ALIVE
To dream that you are ***buried alive***, denotes that you are about to make a great mistake, which your opponents will quickly turn to your injury. If you are rescued from the grave, your struggle will eventually correct your misadventure. ◎

RESCUE

Cheating Fate

CHALLENGE
If you are ***challenged*** to fight a duel, you will become involved in a social difficulty wherein you will be compelled to make apologies or else lose friendships.

To accept a challenge of any character, denotes that you will bear many ills yourself in your endeavors to shield others from dishonor. ◎

ESCAPE
To dream of ***escape*** from injury or accidents, is usually unfavorable.

If you escape from some place of confinement, it signifies your rise in the world from close application to business.

To escape from any contagion, denotes your good health and prosperity. If you try to escape and fail, you will suffer from the design of enemies, who will slander and defraud you. ◎

RESCUE
To dream of being ***rescued*** from any danger, denotes that you will be threatened with misfortune, and will escape with a slight loss.

To ***rescue others***, foretells that you will be esteemed for your good deeds. ◎

WILD *see* **RUNNING** *page 267* ◆ **RIOT** *see* **FRIEND** *page 124,* **KILLING** *page 247* ◆ **WRECKS** *see* **SHIPS** *page 226* ◆ **DANGER** *see* **WOUND** *page 112,* **DEATH** *page 120* ◆ **TRAP** *see* **MOUSETRAP** *page 40,* **RATTRAP** *page 41,* **FLYTRAP** *page 48,* **GAME** *page 174,* **BREAK** *page 265* ◆ **STRANGLED BY UNSEEN HANDS** *see* **HAND** *page 97* ◆ **BURIED ALIVE** *see* **GRAVE** *page 122,* **CHALLENGE** *see* **FIGHT** *page 260* ◆ **ESCAPE** *see* **INJURY, DISEASE** *page 106,* **ACCIDENT** *page 265*

Dreams in Action

Dreaming that you are performing a familiar action, and either doing it unexpectedly, well, badly, or at an inappropriate speed is a common occurrence. This section covers those dreams in which you experience all the physical sensations of movement that you enjoy in waking life: crawling and sliding, walking and running, climbing, and flying.

Crawling and Sliding

CRAWL
To dream you are ***crawling on the ground***, and hurt your hand, you may expect humiliating tasks to be placed on you.

To ***crawl*** over rough places and stones, indicates you have not taken proper advantage of your opportunities. A young woman, after dreaming of crawling, if not careful of her conduct, will lose her lover's respect.

To ***crawl in mire*** with others, denotes depression in business and loss of credit. Your friends will have cause to censure you. ◎

SLIDING
To dream of ***sliding***, portends disappointments in affairs, and sweethearts will break vows.

To ***slide down a hillside*** covered with green grass, foretells that you will be deceived into ruin by flattering promises. ◎

Flight

To dream of* flight*, signifies disgrace and unpleasant news of the absent. For a young woman to dream of flight, indicates that she has not kept her character above reproach, and her lover will throw her aside.

To see anything* fleeing from you*, denotes that you will be victorious in any contention. ❋

Walking Dreams

RAMBLE
To dream that you are ***rambling*** through the country, denotes that you will be oppressed with sadness and separation from friends, but your worldly surroundings will be all that one could desire. For a young woman, this dream promises a comfortable home, but early bereavement. ◎

WALKING
To dream of ***walking*** through rough briar-entangled paths, denotes that you will be much distressed over your business complications, and disagreeable misunderstandings will produce coldness and indifference.

To ***walk in pleasant places***, you will be the possessor of fortune and favor.

To ***walk in the night***, brings misadventure and unavailing struggle for contentment.

For a young woman to find herself ***walking rapidly*** in her dreams, denotes that she will inherit some property, and will possess a much desired object. ◎

WALKING STICK
To see a ***walking stick*** in a dream, foretells that you will enter into contracts without proper deliberation, and will consequently suffer reverses.

If you use one in walking, you will be dependent upon the advice of others.

To admire handsome ones, you will entrust your interest to others, but they will be faithful. ◎

Running and Jumping

JUMPING
If you dream of ***jumping*** over any object, you will succeed in every endeavor; but if you jump and fall back, disagreeable affairs will render life almost intolerable.

To ***jump down from a wall***, denotes reckless speculations and disappointment in love. ◎

LEAPING

LEAPING
For a young woman to dream of ***leaping*** over an obstruction, denotes that she will gain her desires after much struggling and opposition. ◎

RUNNING
To dream of ***running*** in company with others, is a sign that you will participate in some festivity, and you will find that your affairs are growing toward fortune. If you stumble or fall, you will lose property and reputation.

Running alone, indicates that you will outstrip your friends in the race for wealth, and you will occupy a higher place in social life.

If you ***run from danger***, you will be threatened with losses, and you will despair of adjusting matters agreeably. To see others thus running, you will be oppressed by the threatened downfall of friends.

To see ***stock running***, warns you to be careful in making new trades or undertaking new tasks. ◎

CRAWL *see* **HAND** *page 97*, **STONES** *page 68*, **MIRE** *page 90* ◆ **SLIDING** *see* **HILL** *page 90*, **GRASS** *page 56* ◆ **RAMBLE** *see* **COUNTRY** *page 89* ◆ **WALKING** *see* **BRIARS** *page 66*, **PATH** *page 222*, **NIGHT** *page 82* ◆ **JUMPING** *see* **WALLS** *page 190* ◆ **RUNNING** *see* **STUMBLE, FALL** *page 265*, **DANGER** *page 266*

Dreams of Water

DROWNING

WADING

If you ***wade*** in clear water while dreaming, you will partake of evanescent but exquisite joys. If the water is muddy, you are in danger of illness or some sorrowful experiences.

To see children wading in clear water is a happy prognostication, as you will be favored in your enterprises.

For a young woman to dream of wading in clear foaming water, she will soon gain the desire nearest her heart. ◎

FLOATING

To dream of ***floating***, denotes that you will victoriously overcome obstacles which are seemingly overwhelming you. If the water is muddy, your victories will not be gratifying. ◎

DROWNING

To dream of ***drowning***, denotes loss of property and life; but if you are rescued, you will rise from your present position to one of wealth and honor.

To see others drowning, and you go to their relief, signifies that you will aid your friend to high places, and will bring deserved happiness to yourself.

For a young woman to see her sweetheart drowned, denotes her bereavement by death. ◎

Dreams of water may find you drowning *above* rather than waving.

Rising, Climbing, and Flying

RISING

To dream of ***rising*** to high positions, denotes that study and advancement will bring you desired wealth.

If you find yourself rising high into the air, you will come into unexpected riches and pleasures, but you are warned to be careful of your engagements, or you may incur displeasing prominence. ◎

CLIMBING

To dream of ***climbing*** up a hill or mountain and reaching the top, you will overcome the most formidable obstacles between you and a prosperous future; but if you should fail to reach the top, your dearest plans will suffer being wrecked.

To ***climb a ladder*** to the last rung, you will succeed in business; but if the ladder breaks, you will be plunged into unexpected straits, and accidents may happen to you.

To see yourself ***climbing the side of a house*** in some mysterious way in a dream, and to have a window suddenly open to let you in, foretells that you will make or have made extraordinary ventures against the approbation of friends, but success will eventually crown your efforts, though there will be times when despair will almost enshroud you. ◎

ASCENDING

If you reach the extreme point of ***ascent***, or the top of steps, without stumbling, it is good; otherwise, you will have obstacles to overcome before the good of the day is found. ◎

FLYING

To dream of ***flying high*** through space, denotes marital calamities.

To ***fly low***, almost to the ground, indicates sickness and uneasy states from which the dreamer will recover.

To dream that you ***fly over muddy waters***, warns you to keep close with your private affairs, as enemies are watching to enthrall you.

To ***fly over broken places***, signifies ill luck and gloomy surroundings. If you notice green trees and vegetation below you in flying, you will suffer temporary embarrassment, but will have a flood of prosperity upon you.

To see the sun while flying, signifies useless worries as your affairs will succeed despite your fears of evil.

To dream of ***flying through the firmament***, passing the moon and other planets, foretells famine, wars, and troubles of all kinds.

To ***fly with black wings***, portends bitter disappointments.

To ***fall while flying***, signifies your downfall. If you wake while falling, you will reinstate yourself.

For a young man to dream that he is ***flying with white wings*** above green foliage, foretells advancement in business, and he will also be successful in love. If he dreams this often, it is a sign of increasing prosperity and the fulfilment of desires. If the trees appear barren or dead, there will be obstacles to combat in obtaining desires. He will get along, but his work will bring small results.

For a woman to dream of flying from one city to another, and alighting on church spires, foretells that she will have much to contend against in the way of false persuasions and declarations of love. She will be threatened with ill health, and the death of someone near.

For a young woman to dream that she is ***shot at while flying***, denotes that enemies will endeavor to restrain her advancement into higher spheres of usefulness and prosperity.

To dream of ***floating in the sky*** among weird faces and animals, and wondering all the while if you are really awake or only dreaming, foretells that all trouble, the most excruciating pain that reaches even the dullest sense, will be distilled into one drop called jealousy and inserted into your faithful love, and loyalty will suffer dethronement. ◎

WADING *see* **WATER** *page 78*, **CHILDREN** *page 128* ◆ **FLOATING** *see* **WATER** *page 78*, **MUD** *page 90* ◆ **DROWNING** *see* **SWIMMING** *page 174*, **SWEETHEART** *page 124* ◆ **CLIMBING** *see* **HILL, MOUNTAIN** *page 90*, **LADDER** *page 192*, **HOUSE** *page 188*, **WINDOW** *page 213* ◆ **FLYING** *see* **AIRPLANE, HELICOPTER** *page 228*, **MUD** *page 90*, **BREAK** *page 265*, **FIRMAMENT** *page 84*, **WINGS** *page 28*, **FALL** *page 265*, **LEAVES** *page 64*, **CITY** *page 220*, **CHURCH** *page 189*, **SHOT** *page 263*, **APPARITION** *page 274*

Fortune and the Future

Dreams of luck, fortune, and the future should never be construed as the predictions they may appear to be at first. They mostly appear to deal with how you will resolve some puzzling conflict that perplexes your waking life. This section covers dreams about good and bad luck, methods of divination, and what is written in the stars.

Good Fortune

LUCKY
To dream of being ***lucky*** is highly favorable to the dreamer. Fulfilment of wishes may be expected and pleasant duties will devolve upon you.

To the despondent, this dream forebodes an uplifting and a renewal of prosperity. ◎

UNFORTUNATE
To dream that you are ***unfortunate***, is a sign of loss to yourself, and trouble for others. ◎

TALISMAN
To dream that you wear a ***talisman***, implies that you will have pleasant companions and enjoy favors from the rich.

For a young woman to dream that her lover gives her one, denotes that she will obtain her wishes concerning marriage. ◎

LUCKY STARS

Fortune Telling

FUTURE
To dream of the ***future***, is a prognostication of careful reckoning and avoidance of detrimental extravagance. ◎

CLAIRVOYANCE
To dream of being a ***clairvoyant*** and seeing yourself in the future, denotes signal changes in your present occupation, followed by a series of unhappy conflicts with designing people.

To dream of ***visiting a clairvoyant***, foretells unprosperous commercial states and unhappy unions. ◎

PALMISTRY
For a young woman to dream of ***palmistry***, foretells that she will be the object of suspicion.

If she has her palms read, she will have many friends of the opposite sex, but her own sex will condemn her.

If she reads others' hands, she will gain distinction by her intelligent bearing. If a minister's hand, she will need friends, even in her elevation. ◎

FORTUNE-TELLING
To dream of telling your ***fortune*** or having it told, indicates that you are deliberating over some vexed affair, and you should use much caution in giving consent to its consummation.

For a young woman, this portends a choice between two rivals. She will be worried to find out the standing of one in business and social circles.

To dream that she is ***engaged to a fortune-teller***, denotes that she has gone through the forest and picked the proverbial stick. She should be self-reliant, or poverty will attend her marriage. ◎

Astrology

CELESTIAL SIGNS
To dream of ***celestial signs***, foretells that unhappy occurrences will cause you to make unseasonable journeys. Love or business may go awry; quarrels in the house are also predicted if you are not discreet with your engagements. ◎

HOROSCOPE
To dream of having your ***horoscope*** drawn by an astrologist, foretells unexpected changes in affairs and a long journey; associations with a stranger will probably happen.

If the dreamer has the stars pointed out to him as his fate is being read, he will find disappointments where fortune and pleasure seem to await him. ◎

ZODIAC
To dream of the ***zodiac***, is a prognostication of an unparalleled rise in material worth, but also indicates alloyed peace and happiness.

To see it appearing weird, denotes that some untoward grief is hovering over you and it will take strenuous efforts to dispel it.

To ***study the zodiac*** in your dreams, denotes that you will gain distinction and favor by your intercourse with strangers.

If you approach it or it approaches you, it foretells that you will succeed in your speculations to the wonderment of others and beyond your wildest imagination. ◎

TALISMAN *see* **GIFTS** *page 240* ◆ **CELESTIAL SIGNS** *see* **FIRMAMENT** *page 84* ◆ **HOROSCOPE** *see* **STARS** *page 84* ◆
ZODIAC *see* **VISIONS** *page 274* ◆ **PALMISTRY** *see* **HAND** *page 97* ◆ **FORTUNE TELLER** *see* **ENGAGEMENT** *page 130*

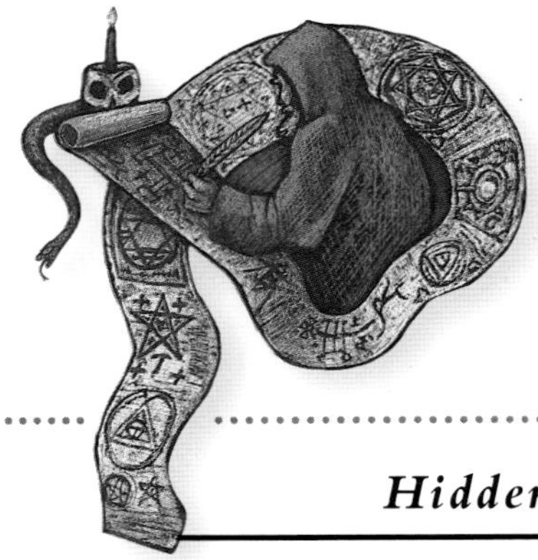

Secrets and Mysteries

Secrets and mysteries are just as intriguing in dream life as they are in reality. This section explores the everyday mysteries of unknown people and hidden objects, the man-made mysteries of secret orders and labyrinths, the political mysteries of espionage, and the arcane mysteries of the occult and the ouija board.

Hidden Meanings

UNKNOWN
To dream of meeting ***unknown*** persons, foretells change for good or bad, as the person is good-looking, or ugly or deformed.

To feel that you are unknown, denotes that strange things will cast a shadow of ill luck over you. ◎

HIDDEN
To dream that you have ***hidden*** away any object, denotes embarrassment in your circumstances.

To ***find hidden things***, you will enjoy unexpected pleasures.

For a young woman to dream of hiding objects, she will be the object of much adverse gossip, but will finally prove her conduct orderly. ◎

PRIVACY
To dream that your ***privacy*** suffers intrusion, foretells that you will have overbearing people to worry you. For a woman, this dream warns her to look carefully after private affairs. If she intrudes on the privacy of her husband or lover, she will disabuse someone's confidence, if not careful of her conversation. ◎

MYSTERY
To find yourself bewildered by some ***mysterious*** event, denotes that strangers will harass you with their troubles and claim your aid. It warns you also of neglected duties, for which you feel much aversion. Business will wind you into unpleasant complications.

To find yourself studying the ***mysteries of creation***, denotes that a change will take place in your life, throwing you into a higher atmosphere of research and learning, and thus advancing you nearer to the attainment of true pleasure and fortune. ◎

A SYBIL

LABYRINTH
If you dream of a ***labyrinth***, you will find yourself entangled in intricate and perplexing business conditions, and your wife will make the home environment intolerable; children and sweethearts will prove ill-tempered and unattractive.

If you are in a labyrinth of night or darkness, it foretells passing, but agonizing, sickness and trouble.

A ***labyrinth of green vines*** and timbers, denotes unexpected happiness from what was seemingly a cause for loss and despair.

A network or ***labyrinth of railroads***, assures you of long and tedious journeys. Interesting people will be met, but no financial success will aid you on these journeys. ◎

Obscure Portents

OUIJA
To dream of working on a ***ouija*** board, foretells the miscarriage of plans and unlucky partnerships.

To fail to work one, is ominous of complications, caused by substituting pleasure for business. If it writes fluently, expect fortunate results. ◎

SYBIL
To dream of a ***sybil***, foretells that you will enjoy assignations and other demoralizing pleasures. ◎

DIVINING RODS
To see a ***divining rod*** in your dreams, foretells that ill luck will dissatisfy you with present surroundings. ◎

OCCULTIST
To dream that you listen to the teachings of an ***occultist***, denotes that you will strive to elevate others to a higher plane of justice and forbearance. If you accept his views, you will find honest delight by keeping above material frivolities and pleasures. ◎

AURA
To dream of discussing any subject relating to ***the aura***, denotes that you will reach states of mental unrest, and work to discover the power that influences you from within. ◎

ASTRAL
Dreams of the ***astral***, denotes that your efforts and plans will culminate in worldly success and distinction. A specter or picture of your astral self brings heartrending tribulation. ◎

HIDDEN *see* TREASURES *page 238* ◆ MYSTERY *see* GOD *page 277* ◆ LABYRINTH *see* DARKNESS *page 82*, VINE *page 61*, RAILROAD *page 225* ◆ SYBIL *see* CLAIRVOYANCE *page 269* ◆ ASTRAL *see* STARS *page 84*

Spies

SPY

To dream that ***spies*** are harassing you, denotes dangerous quarrels and uneasiness.

To dream that you ***are a spy***, denotes that you will make unfortunate ventures. ◎

PASSWORD

To dream of a ***password***, foretells that you will have influential aid in some slight trouble soon to attack you.

For a woman to dream that she has ***given away the password***, signifies that she will endanger her own standing in society through seeking frivolous liasons or indulging illicit desires. ◎

CONSPIRACY

To dream that you are the object of a ***conspiracy***, foretells that you will make a wrong move in the directing of your affairs. ◎

THE WORLD OF THE SPY

Secret Societies

SECRET ORDER

To dream of any ***secret order***, denotes a sensitive and excited organism, and the owner should cultivate practical and unselfish ideas. They may soon have opportunities for honest pleasures and desired literary distinctions.

There is a vision of selfish and designing friendships, for one who joins a secret order.

Young women should heed the counsel of their guardians, lest they fall into discreditable habits after this dream.

MASONIC SYMBOL

If a young woman meets the head of the order, she should oppose with energy and moral rectitude against allurements that are set brilliantly and prominently before those of her sex. For her to think that her mother has joined the order, and she is using her bèst efforts to have her mother repudiate her vows, denotes that she will be full of love for her parents, and yet she will wring their hearts with anguish by thoughtless disobedience.

To see or hear that the leader is dead, foretells that severe strains and trials will eventually end in comparative good. ◎

ODD FELLOW

To dream of this order, signifies that you will have sincere friends, and misfortune will touch you but lightly.

To join this order, foretells that you will win distinction and bliss. ◎

Dreams of secrets and mysteries may show you the oracular activities of the sybil *opposite*; in contrast, the secrets of men rather than supernatural beings may lead you into the exciting world of spies *left* or puzzle you with the arcane symbolism of the secret orders of masons *above*.

SPY *see* **SPYGLASS** *page 237* ◆ **SECRET ORDER** *see* **MOTHER** *page 128,* **VOW** *page 219,* **DEAD** *page 120*

Magic and Myth

Most dreams have a magic of their own, but dreams about magic and its practitioners have a special enchantment. This section covers witches, wizards, and sorcery as well as mythical creatures; imaginary beasts such as dragons and unicorns, hideous apparitions such as vampires and gargoyles, and classical myths such as fates and nymphs.

Witches and Warlocks

ENCHANTMENT

To dream of being under the spell of ***enchantment***, denotes that if you are not careful, you will be exposed to some evil in the form of pleasure. The young should heed the benevolent advice of their elders.

To ***resist enchantment***, foretells that you will be much sought after for your wise counsel and your liberality.

To dream of trying to ***enchant others***, portends that you will fall into evil. ◎

MAGIC

To dream of accomplishing any design by ***magic***, indicates pleasant surprises.

To see others practicing this art, denotes profitable changes to all who have this dream.

To dream of seeing a ***magician***, denotes much interesting travel to those concerned in the advancement of higher education, and profitable returns to the mercenary.

Magic here should not be confounded with sorcery or spiritism. If the reader interprets, he may expect the opposite to what is here forecast to follow. True magic is the study of the higher truths of nature. ◎

NECROMANCER

To dream of a ***necromancer*** and his arts, denotes that you are threatened with strange acquaintances who will influence you for evil. ◎

SORCERER

To dream of a ***sorcerer***, foretells that your ambitions will undergo strange disappointments and change. ◎

WIZARD

To dream of a ***wizard***, denotes that you are going to have a big family, which will cause you much inconvenience as well as displeasure. For young people, this dream implies loss and broken engagements. ◎

WITCH

WITCH

To dream of ***witches***, denotes that you, with others, will seek adventures which will afford hilarious enjoyment, but it will eventually rebound to your mortification. Business will suffer prostration if witches advance upon you, and home affairs may be disappointing. ◎

THE DRAGON AND ST GEORGE

ENCHANTMENT *see* TEMPTATION *page 250* ◆ MAGIC *see* CONJUROR, LEGERDEMAIN *page 170*

Mythical Creatures

DRAGON
To dream of a ***dragon***, denotes that you allow yourself to be governed by your passions, and that you are likely to place yourself in the power of your enemies through those outbursts of sardonic tendencies. You should be warned by this dream to cultivate self-control. ◎

UNICORN
To dream of a ***unicorn***, signifies good fortune and happy circumstances. ◎

MONSTER
To dream of being pursued by a ***monster***, denotes that sorrow and misfortune hold prominent places in your immediate future.

To ***slay a monster***, denotes that you will successfully cope with enemies and rise to eminent positions. ◎

MONSTER

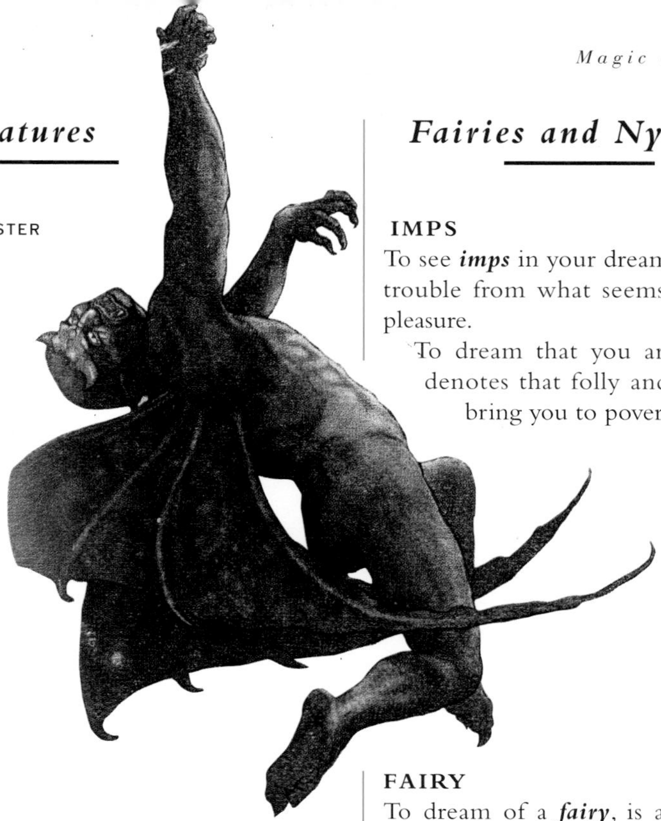

GARGOYLE
To dream of a ***gargoyle***, means that you and a close friend will soon part ways.

To dream of one coming to life, signifies that sorrow and misfortune are imminent. ◎

VAMPIRE
To dream about ***vampires***, denotes that you should beware of someone trying to take advantage of or harm you.

To dream of being attacked or ***bitten by a vampire***, is a forewarning to watch out for false friends.

To dream of seeing yourself battling or ***staking a vampire***, means that you will overcome someone who has evil or harmful intentions toward you.

To dream of someone you know well as a vampire, means that you need to be wary of such individual's intentions. ◎

Dreams that hover in the realm of myth and magic may show you St George slaying his dragon *left*, **a traditional witch** *opposite top*, **or a grotesque form of a monster** *top*.

Fairies and Nymphs

IMPS
To see ***imps*** in your dreams, signifies trouble from what seems a passing pleasure.

To dream that you are an imp, denotes that folly and vice will bring you to poverty. ◎

FAIRY
To dream of a ***fairy***, is a favorable omen to all classes, as it is always a scene with a beautiful face portrayed as a happy child or a woman. ◎

NYMPH
To see ***nymphs*** in clear water, denotes that passionate desires will find an ecstatic realization. Convivial entertainments will enchant you.

To see them out of their sphere, denotes disappointment with the world.

For a young woman to see them bathing, denotes that she will have great favor and pleasure, but they will not rest strictly within the moral code. To dream that she ***impersonates a nymph***, is a sign that she is using her attractions for selfish purposes, and thus for the undoing of men. ◎

The Fates

FATES
To dream of the ***fates***, unnecessary disagreements and unhappiness are foretold. For a young woman to dream of juggling with fate, denotes that she will daringly interpose herself between devoted friends or lovers. ◎

DRAGON *see* **REPTILES** *page 53* ◆ **MONSTER** *see* **KILLING** *page 247* ◆ **GARGOYLE** *see* **STATUES** *page 182* ◆ **VAMPIRE** *see* **BAT** *page 32*, **BLOOD** *page 94*, **BITE** *page 112*, **COMBAT** *page 261*, **ACQUAINTANCE** *page 124* ◆ **NYMPHS** *see* **WATER** *page 78*, **BATH** *page 105*

Sounds and Visions

This section discusses dreams with the double illusions of visions within dreams. It covers the contradictory dreams of sleeping; dreams of fantastic apparitions, ghosts, and phantoms; and it deals with the many kinds of strange sounds and mysterious voices that you might apprehend on the edge of your dream hearing.

Sleeping Dreams

YAWNING
If you yawn in your dreams, you will search in vain for health and contentment.

To see others ***yawning***, foretells that you will see some of your friends in a miserable state. Sickness will prevent them from their usual labors. ◎

SLEEP
To dream of ***sleeping on clean, fresh beds***, denotes peace and favor from those whom you love. To ***sleep*** in unnatural resting places, foretells sickness and broken engagements. To ***sleep beside a little child***, betokens domestic joys and reciprocated love. To see ***others sleeping***, you will overcome all opposition in your pursuit for woman's favor.

To dream of ***sleeping with a repulsive person*** or object, warns you that your love will wane before that of your sweetheart, and you will suffer for your escapades.

For a young woman to dream of ***sleeping with her lover*** or some fascinating object, warns her against yielding herself a willing victim to his charms. ◎

SOMNAMBULIST
To imagine while dreaming that you are a ***somnambulist*** [sleepwalker], portends that you will unwittingly consent to some agreement of plans which will bring you anxiety or ill fortune. ◎

NIGHTMARE
To dream of being attacked with this hideous sensation, denotes wrangling and failure in business.

For a young woman, this is a dream prophetic of disappointment and unmerited slights. It may also warn the dreamer to be careful of her health and food. ◎

AWAKE
To dream that you are ***awake***, denotes that you will experience strange happenings which will throw you into gloom.

To pass through green, growing fields and look upon a landscape in your dreams, and feel that it is a ***waking experience***, signifies that there is some good and brightness in store for you, but there will be disappointment intermingled between the present and that time. ◎

Images

If you dream that you see images***, you will have poor success in business or love.***

To set up an image in your home, portends that you will be weak minded and easily led astray. Women should be careful of their reputation after a dream of this kind. If the images are ugly, you will have trouble in your home. ❋

Revelations and Visions

REVELATION
To dream of a ***revelation***, if it be of a pleasant nature, you may expect a bright outlook, either in business or love; but if the revelation be gloomy, you will have many discouraging features to overcome. ◎

APPARITION
Take unusual care of all who depend upon you. Calamity awaits you and yours. Both property and life are in danger. Young people should be decidedly upright in their communications with the opposite sex. Character is likely to be rated at a discount. ◎

VISIONS
To dream that you have a strange vision, denotes that you will be unfortunate in your dealings, and sickness will unfit you for pleasant duties.

If persons appear to you in ***visions***, it foretells uprising and strife of families or state.

If your friend is near dissolution and you are ***warned in a vision***, he will appear suddenly before you, usually in white garments.

To see visions of any order in your dreams, you may look for unusual developments in your business, and a different atmosphere and surroundings in private life. Things will be reversed for awhile with you. You will have changes in your business and private life seemingly bad, but eventually good for all concerned. The Supreme Will is always directed toward the ultimate good of the race. ◎

SLEEP *see* **BED** *page 207*, **CHILDREN** *page 128*, **UGLY** *page 100* ◆ **AWAKE** *see* **FIELDS** *page 60* ◆ **VISION** *see* **FRIEND** *page 124* ◆
IMAGES *see* **PICTURES** *page 181*, **HOME** *page 205*, **UGLY** *page 100*, **IDOLS** *page 279*

Ghosts and Spirits

GHOST
To dream of a ***ghost*** of either one of your parents, denotes that you are exposed to danger, and you should be careful in forming partnerships with strangers. ◎

To see the ***ghost of a dear friend***, foretells that you will make a long journey with an unpleasant companion, and suffer disappointments.

For a ***ghost to speak*** to you, you will be decoyed into the hands of enemies. For a woman, this is a prognostication of widowhood and deception.

To see an angel or a ghost appear in the sky, denotes the loss of kindred and misfortunes.

To see in the sky a ***female ghost*** on your right and a male on your left, both of pleasing countenance, signifies a quick rise from obscurity to fame, but the honor and position will be filled only for a short space, as death will be a visitor and will bear you off.

To see a female ghost in long, clinging robes floating calmly through the sky, indicates that you will make progress in scientific studies and acquire wealth almost miraculously, but there will be an undernote of sadness in your life.

To dream that you see the ***ghost of a living relative*** or friend, denotes that you are in danger of some friend's malice, and you are warned to carefully keep your affairs under personal supervision. If the ghost appears to be haggard, it may be the intimation of the early death of that friend. ◎

PHANTOM
To dream that a ***phantom*** pursues you, foretells strange and disquieting experiences.

To see ***a phantom fleeing from you,*** foretells that trouble will assume smaller proportions. ◎

SPIRIT OR SPECTER
To see ***spirits*** in a dream, denotes that some unexpected trouble will confront you. If they are white robed, the health of your nearest friend is threatened, or some business speculation will be disapproving. If they are robed in black, you will meet with treachery and unfaithfulness.

If a ***spirit speaks***, there is some evil near you, which you might avert if you would listen to counsel.

To dream that you hear ***spirits knocking*** on doors or walls, denotes that trouble will arise unexpectedly.

To see them moving draperies, or moving behind them, is a warning to hold control over your feelings, as you are likely to commit indiscretions.

To see the ***spirit of your friend*** floating in your room, foretells disappointment and insecurity.

To hear music supposedly coming from spirits, denotes unfavorable changes and sadness in the household. ◎

Strange Sights

ILLUMINATION
If you see strange and weird ***illuminations*** in your dreams, you will meet with disappointments and failures on every hand.

Illuminated faces, indicate unsettled business, both private and official.

To see the ***heavens illuminated***, with the moon in all her weirdness, unnatural stars, and a red sun or a golden one, you may look for distress in its worst form. Death, family troubles, and national upheavals will occur.

To see children in the lighted heavens, warns you to control your feelings, as irrevocable wrong may be done in a frenzy of feeling arising over seeming neglect.

To see ***illuminated human figures*** or animals in the heavens, denotes failure and trouble; dark clouds overshadow fortune. If you see them fall to the earth and men shoot them with guns, many obstacles will go to naught before your energy and determination.

To see ***illuminated snakes***, or any other creeping thing, means that enemies will surround you and use hellish means to overthrow you. ◎

METAMORPHOSIS
To dream of seeing anything ***metamorphose***, denotes that sudden changes will take place in your life, for good or bad, as the metamorphosis was pleasant or frightful. ◎

INDISTINCTNESS
If in your dreams you see objects ***indistinctly***, this portends unfaithfulness in friendships, and uncertain dealings. ◎

Distant Bells

TOCSIN
To dream of hearing a ***tocsin*** sounded, augurs a strife from which you will come victorious. For a woman, this is a warning of separation from her husband or lover. ◎

BELLS
To hear ***bells*** tolling in your dreams, death of distant friends will occur, and intelligence of wrong will worry you.

Liberty bells, indicate a joyous victory over an opponent. ◎

CHIMES
To dream of Christmas ***chimes***, denotes fair prospects for businessmen and farmers. For the young, happy anticipations fulfilled.

Ordinary chimes, denote that some small anxiety will soon be displaced by news of distant friends. ◎

ILLUMINATION *see* **LIGHT** *page 216,* **FACE** *page 101,* **SKY, MOON, STARS, SUN** *page 84,* **CHILDREN** *page 128,* **FALL** *page 265,* **SHOOTING, GUNS** *page 263,* **SNAKES** *page 54* ◆ **BELLS** *see* **ALARM BELLS** *page 266* ◆ **GHOST** *see* **FRIEND** *page 124,* **ANGELS** *page 278* ◆ **SPIRIT OR SPECTER** *see* **KNOCKING** *page 276,* **FRIEND** *page 124,* **MUSIC** *page 164*

Noises in the Night

VOICE
To dream of hearing ***voices***, denotes pleasant reconciliations, if they are calm and pleasing; high-pitched and angry voices, signify disappointments and unfavorable situations.

To hear ***weeping voices***, shows that sudden anger will cause you to inflict injury upon a friend.

If you hear the ***voice of God***, you will make a noble effort to rise higher in unselfish and honorable principles, and will justly hold the admiration of high-minded people.

For a mother to hear the ***voice of her child***, is a sign of approaching misery, perplexity, and grievous doubts.

To hear the ***voice of distress***, or a warning one calling to you, implies your own serious misfortune or that of someone close to you. If the voice is recognized, it is often ominous of accident or illness, which may eliminate death or loss. ◎

INCANTATION
To dream that you are using ***incantations***, signifies unpleasantness between husband and wife, or sweethearts. To hear others repeating them, implies dissembling among your friends.

GROANS
If you hear ***groans*** in your dream, decide quickly on your course, for enemies are undermining your business. If you are groaning with fear, you will be pleasantly surprised at the turn for the better in your affairs, and you may look for pleasant visiting between friends.

CRIES
To hear ***cries*** of distress, denotes that you will be engulfed in serious troubles; but by being alert, you will finally emerge from these distressing straits and gain by this temporary gloom.

To hear a ***cry of surprise***, you will receive aid from unexpected sources.

To hear the ***cries of wild beasts***, denotes an accident of a serious nature.

To hear a ***cry for help*** from relatives or friends, denotes that they are sick or in distress.

CALLED
To hear your name ***called*** in a dream by strange voices, denotes that your business will fall into a precarious state, and that strangers may lend you assistance, or you may fail to meet your obligations.

To hear the ***voice of a friend*** or relative, denotes the desperate illness of one of them, and maybe death; in the latter case, you may be called upon to stand as guardian over someone, in governing whom you should use much discretion.

Lovers hearing the voice of their affianced should heed the warning. If they have been negligent in attention, they should make amends. Otherwise they may suffer separation from misunderstanding.

To hear the ***voice of the dead***, may be a warning of your own serious illness, or some business worry from bad judgement may ensue. The voice is an echo thrown back from the future on the subjective mind, taking the sound of your ancestor's voice by coming in contact with that part of your ancestor which remains with you. A certain portion of mental matter remains the same in lines of family descent. ◎

HISSING
To dream of ***hissing*** persons, is an omen that you will be displeased beyond endurance at the discourteous treatment shown you while among newly made acquaintances. If they hiss you, you will be threatened with the loss of a friend. ◎

WHISPERING
To dream of ***whispering***, denotes that you will be disturbed by the evil gossiping of people near you.

To hear a ***whisper*** coming to you as advice or warning, foretells that you stand in need of aid and counsel. ◎

WAIL
A ***wail*** falling upon your ear while in the midst of a dream, brings fearful news of disaster and woe.

For a young woman to hear a wail, foretells that she will be deserted and left alone in distress, and perchance disgrace. ◎

Strange Sounds

ECHO
To dream of an ***echo***, portends that distressful times are upon you. Your sickness may lose you your employment, and friends will desert you in time of need. ◎

NOISE
If you hear a strange ***noise*** in your dream, unfavorable news is presaged. If the noise awakens you, there will be a sudden change in your affairs. ◎

KNOCKING
To hear ***knocking*** in your dreams, denotes that tidings of a grave nature will soon be received by you.

If you are awakened by the knocking, the news will affect you the most seriously.

WHISTLE
To hear a ***whistle*** in your dream, denotes that you will be shocked by some sad intelligence, which will change your plans laid for innocent pleasure.

To dream that you are ***whistling***, foretells a merry occasion in which you expect to figure largely. This dream, for a young woman, foretells indiscreet conduct and failure to obtain wishes. ◎

VOICE *see* **ANGER** *page 250,* **WEEPING** *page 257,* **GOD** *page 277,* **CHILDREN** *page 128* ◆ **CRIES** *see* **WEEPING** *page 257,* **ASSISTANCE** *page 252,* **FRIEND** *page 124* ◆ **CALLED** *see* **FRIEND** *page 124,* **DEAD** *page 120* ◆ **WHISPERING** *see* **ADVICE** *page 252* ◆ **WAIL** *see* **CRYING** *page 257* ◆ **KNOCKING** *see* **KNOCKER** *page 213*

Religious Matters

Dreams about various aspects of religion are common; indeed, dreams and visions play an important role in the Judao–Christian and Buddhist traditions. However, religious dreams are necessarily conditioned by the culture of the dreamer, and so the dreams in this section are based on the concepts, hierarchies, and rituals of Western belief systems.

Religion and Revival

RELIGION

If you dream of discussing ***religion*** and feel religiously inclined, you will find much to mar the calmness of your life, and business will turn a disagreeable front to you.

If a young woman imagines that she is ***overreligious***, she will disgust her lover with her efforts to act ingenuous innocence and goodness.

If she is ***irreligious*** and not a transgressor, it foretells that she will have that independent frankness and kind consideration for others which wins for women profound respect and love from the opposite sex, as well as her own; but if she is a transgressor in the eyes of religion, she will find that there are moral laws which, if disregarded, will place her outside the pale of honest recognition. She should look well after her conduct. If she weeps over religion, she will be disappointed in the desires of her heart. If she is defiant, but innocent of offense, she will shoulder her burdens bravely and stand firm against any deceitful admonitions.

If you are self-reproached in the midst of a ***religious excitement***, you will find that you will be almost induced to give up your own personality to please someone whom you hold in reverent esteem.

To see ***religion declining in power***, denotes that your life will be more in harmony with creation than formerly. Your prejudices will not be so aggressive.

To dream that a minister in a social way tells you that he has given up his work, foretells that you will be the recipient of unexpected tidings of a favorable nature, but if in a professional and warning way, it foretells that you will be overtaken in your deceitful intriguing, or other disappointments will follow.

AT PRAYER

These dreams are sometimes fulfiled literally in actual life. When this is so, they may have no symbolical meaning. Religion is thrown around men to protect them from vice, so when they propose secretly in their minds to ignore its teachings, they are likely to see a minister or some place of church worship in a dream as a warning against their contemplated action. If they live pure and correct lives as indicated by the church, they will see little of the solemnity of the church or preachers. ◎

REVIVAL

To dream that you attend a religious ***revival***, foretells family disturbances and unprofitable engagements.

If you take a part in it, you will incur the displeasure of friends by your contrary ways. ◎

Dreams of religion *above* **may indicate that you are straying from the path of virtue.**

God the Almighty

GOD

If you dream of seeing ***God***, you will be domineered over by a tyrannical woman masquerading under the cloak of Christianity. No good accrues from this dream.

If ***God speaks to you***, beware that you do not fall into condemnation. Business of all sorts will take an unfavorable turn. It is the forerunner of the weakening of health and may mean early dissolution.

If you dream of ***worshipping God***, you will have cause to repent of an error of your own making. Look well to observing the Ten Commandments after this dream.

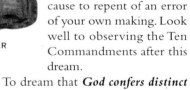

To dream that ***God confers distinct favors*** upon you, you will become the favorite of a cautious and prominent person who will use his position to advance yours.

To dream that ***God sends his spirit upon you***, great changes in your beliefs will take place. Views concerning dogmatic Christianity should broaden after this dream, or you may be severely chastised for some indiscreet action which has brought shame upon you. God speaks oftener to those who transgress than to those who do not. It is the genius of spiritual law or economy to reinstate the prodigal child by signs and visions. Elijah, Jonah, David, and Paul were brought to the altar of repentance through the vigilant energy of the hidden forces within. ◎

RELIGION *see* **MINISTER** *page 280,* **WEEPING** *page 257,* **OFFENSE** *page 254* ◆ **GOD** *see* **VOICE** *page 276,* **FAVOR** *page 259*

Angels and Heaven

ANGELS

To dream of ***angels***, is prophetic of disturbing influences in the soul. It brings a changed condition of the person's lot. If the dream is unusually pleasing, you will hear of the health of friends, and receive a legacy from unknown relatives.

If the dream comes as a token of warning, the dreamer may expect threats of scandal about love or money matters. To wicked people, it is a demand to repent; to good people, it should be a consolation. ◎

CHERUBS

To dream you see ***cherubs***, foretells some distinct joy, which will leave an impression of lasting good upon your life.

To see them looking sorrowful or reproachful, foretells that distress will come unexpectedly upon you. ◎

HEAVEN

If you ascend to ***Heaven*** in a dream, you will fail to enjoy the distinction you have labored to gain, and joy will end in sadness.

If young persons dream of ***climbing to Heaven*** on a ladder, they will rise from a low estate to one of unusual prominence, but will fail to find contentment or much pleasure.

To dream of ***being in Heaven*** and meeting Christ and friends, you will meet with many losses, but will reconcile yourself to them through your true understanding of human nature.

To dream of the ***Heavenly City***, denotes a contented and spiritual nature, and trouble will do you small harm.

To see the firmament illuminated and filled with the heavenly host, denotes great spiritual research, but a final pulling back to Nature for sustenance and consolation. You will often be disappointed in fortune also ◎.

Paradise Lost

PARADISE

To dream that you are in ***Paradise***, means loyal friends. This dream holds out bright hopes to sailors or those about to make a long voyage. To mothers, this means fair and obedient children. If you are sick you will have a speedy recovery and your fortune will ripen. To lovers, it is the promise of wealth and faithfulness.

To dream that you start to Paradise and find yourself bewildered and lost, you will undertake enterprises which look exceedingly feasible and full of fortunate returns, but which will prove disappointing and vexatious. ◎

ADAM AND EVE

To dream of ***Adam and Eve***, foretells that some eventful occasion will rob you of the hope of success.

To see them in the garden, Adam dressed in his fig leaf, but Eve perfectly nude save for an Oriental colored serpent ornamenting her waist and abdomen, signifies that treachery and ill faith will combine to overthrow your fortune.

To see or hear Eve conversing with the serpent, foretells that artful women will reduce you to the loss of fortune and reputation.

For a young woman to dream that she impersonates Eve, warns her to be careful. She may be wiser than her ancient relative, but the Evil One still has powerful agents in the disguise of a handsome man. Keep your eye on innocent Eve, young man. That apple tree still bears fruit, and you may be persuaded, unwittingly, to share the wealth of its products. ◎

Judgement

DOOMSDAY

To dream that you are living on, and looking forward to seeing ***doomsday***, is a warning for you to give substantial and material affairs close attention, or you will find that the artful and scheming friends whom you are entertaining will have possession of what they desire from you, which is your wealth, and not your sentimentality.

To a young woman, this dream encourages her to throw aside the attention of men above her in station and accept the love of an honest and deserving man near her. ◎

JUDGEMENT DAY

To dream of the ***judgement day***, foretells that you will accomplish some well-planned work, if you appear resigned and hopeful of escaping punishment. Otherwise, your work will prove a failure.

For a young woman to appear before the ***judgement bar*** and hear the verdict of "Guilty", denotes that she will cause much distress among her friends by her selfish and unbecoming conduct. If she sees the dead rising, and all the earth solemnly and fearfully awaiting the end, there will be much struggling for her, and her friends will refuse her aid. It is also a forerunner of unpleasant gossip. ◎

Commandments

COMMANDMENT

To read or hear the Ten ***Commandments*** read, denotes that you will fall into errors from which you will hardly escape, even with the counsel of wise friends and unerring judgement. ◎

MOSES

To dream that you see ***Moses***, means personal gain and a connubial alliance which will be a source of sweet congratulation to yourself. ◎

HEAVEN *see* CLIMBING *page 268*, LADDER *page 192*, CHRIST *page 279*, FIRMAMENT *page 84* ◆ JUDGEMENT DAY *see* JUDGE *page 245*, ACQUIT *page 248*, DEAD *page 120*, RESURRECTION *page 123* ◆ ADAM AND EVE *see* GARDEN *page 56*, NAKED *page 91*, SERPENTS *page 53*

Christ and the Cross

CHRIST

To dream of beholding ***Christ*** the young child worshiped by the wise men, denotes many peaceful days, full of wealth and knowledge, abundant with joy and contentment.

If he is in the garden of Gethsemane, sorrowing adversity will fill your soul; great longings for change and absent objects of love will be felt.

To see him in the temple scourging the traders, denotes that evil enemies will be defeated and honest endeavors will prevail. ◎

CRUCIFIX

To see a ***crucifix*** in a dream, is a warning of approaching distress, which will involve others besides yourself.

To kiss one, foretells that trouble will be accepted by you with resignation.

For a young woman to possess one, foretells that she will observe modesty and kindness in her deportment, and thus win the love of others and better her fortune. ◎

CRUCIFIXION

If you chance to dream of the ***crucifixion***, you will see your opportunities slip away, tearing your hopes from your grasp, and leaving you wailing over the frustration of desires. ◎

TRANSFIGURATION

To dream of the ***Transfiguration***, foretells that your faith in man's own nearness to God will raise you above trifling opinions, and elevate you to a worthy position, in which capacity you will be able to promote the well-being of the ignorant and persecuted.

To see yourself ***transfigured***, you will stand high in the esteem of honest and prominent men. ◎

The Devil and all his Works

SATAN

To dream of ***Satan***, foretells that you will have some dangerous adventures, and you will be forced to use strategy to keep up honorable appearances.

To dream that you kill him, foretells that you will desert wicked or immoral companions to live upon a higher plane.

If he comes to you under the guise of literature, it should be heeded as a warning against promiscuous friendships, and especially flatterers.

If he comes in the shape of wealth or power, you will fail to use your influence for harmony or the elevation of others.

If he takes the form of music, you are likely to go down before his wiles.

If he is in the form of a fair woman, you will probably crush every kindly feeling you may have for the caresses of this moral monstrosity.

To feel that you are trying to shield yourself from Satan, denotes that you will endeavor to throw off the bondage of selfish pleasure, and seek to give others their best deserts. ◎

DEVIL

For farmers to dream of the ***devil***, denotes blasted crops and death among stock; also family sickness. Sporting people should heed this dream as a warning to be careful of their affairs, as they are likely to venture beyond the laws of their state. For a preacher, this dream is undeniable proof that he is overzealous, and should forebear worshipping God by tongue-lashing his neighbor.

To dream of the devil as being a large, imposing dressed person, wearing many sparkling jewels on his body and hands, trying to persuade you to enter his abode, warns you that unscrupulous persons are seeking your ruin by the most ingenious flattery. Young and innocent women should seek the stronghold of friends after this dream, and avoid strange attentions, especially from married men. Women of low character are likely to be robbed of jewels and money by seeming strangers.

Beware of associating with the devil, even in dreams. He is always the forerunner of despair. If you dream of being pursued by his majesty, you will fall into snares set for you by enemies in the guise of friends. To a lover, this denotes that he will be won away from his allegiance by a wanton. ◎

HELL

If you dream of being in ***Hell***, you will fall into temptations which will almost wreck you financially and morally.

To see your ***friends in Hell***, denotes distress and burdensome cares. You will hear of the misfortune of some friend.

To dream of ***crying in Hell***, denotes the powerlessness of friends to extricate you from the snares of enemies. ◎

FIEND

To dream that you encounter a ***fiend***, forebodes reckless living and loose morals. For a woman, this dream signifies a blackened reputation.

To dream of a fiend, warns you of attacks to be made on you by false friends. If you overcome one, you will be able to intercept the evil designs of enemies. ◎

IDOLS

Should you dream of worshipping ***idols***, you will make slow progress to wealth or fame, as you will let petty things tyrannize over you.

To ***break idols***, signifies a strong mastery over self, and no work will deter you in your upward rise.

If you see others ***worshipping idols***, great differences will rise up between you and warm friends.

To dream that you are denouncing ***idolatry***, foretells that great distinction is in store for you through your understanding of the natural inclinations of the human mind. ◎

CRUCIFIX *see* **CROSS** *page 229,* **KISSING** *page 125* ◆ **TRANSFIGURATION** *see* **METAMORPHOSIS** *page 275* ◆ **SATAN** *see* **KILLING** *page 247,* **WEALTH** *page 238,* **MUSIC** *page 164* ◆ **DEVIL** *see* **JEWELRY** *page 162* ◆ **HELL** *see* **FRIENDS** *page 124,* **CRYING** *page 257* ◆ **IDOLS** *see* **BREAK** *page 265*

Holy Orders

CLERGYMAN
To dream that you send for a ***clergyman*** to preach a funeral sermon, denotes that you will vainly strive to ward off sickness and evil influences, but they will nevertheless prevail.

If a young woman ***marries a clergyman*** in her dream, she will be the object of much mental distress, and the wayward hand of fortune will lead her into the morass of adversity. ◎

MINISTER
To dream of seeing a ***minister***, denotes unfortunate changes and unpleasant journeys.

To hear a ***minister exhort***, foretells that some designing person will influence you to evil.

To dream that you ***are a minister***, denotes that you will usurp another's rights. ◎

MINISTER

CHURCH INTERIOR

PRIEST
A ***priest*** is an augury of ill, if seen in dreams.

If he is in the pulpit, it denotes sickness and trouble for the dreamer.

If a woman dreams that she is ***in love with a priest***, it warns her of deceptions and an unscrupulous lover. If the priest makes love to her, she will be reproached for her love of gaiety and practical joking.

To ***confess to a priest***, denotes that you will be subjected to humiliation and sorrow.

These dreams imply that you have done, or will do, something which will bring discomfort to yourself or relatives. The priest or preacher is your spiritual adviser, and any dream of his professional presence is a warning against your own imperfections. Seen in social circles, unless they rise before you as specters, the same rules will apply as to other friends. ◎

VICAR
To dream of a ***vicar***, foretells that you will do foolish things while furious with jealousy and envy.

For a young woman to dream that she ***marries a vicar***, foretells that she will fail to awake reciprocal affection in the man she desires, and will live a spinster or marry for convenience to keep from being one. ◎

Church Furnishings

PULPIT
To dream of a ***pulpit***, denotes sorrow and vexation.

To dream that you are in a pulpit, foretells sickness and unsatisfactory results in business or trades of any character. ◎

ALTAR
To dream of seeing a priest at the ***altar***, denotes quarrels and unsatisfactory states in your business and home.

To see a marriage, sorrow to friends, and death to old age. ◎

HASSOCK
To dream of a ***hassock***, forebodes the yielding of your power and fortune to another. If a woman dreams of a hassock, she should cultivate spirit and independence. ◎

Pilgrims

To dream of pilgrims, ***denotes that you will go on an extended journey, leaving home and its dearest objects in the mistaken idea that it must be thus for their good.***

To dream that you are a pilgrim, portends struggles with poverty and unsympathetic companions.

For a young woman to dream that a pilgrim approaches her, she will fall an easy dupe to deceit. If he leaves her, she will awaken to her weakness of character and strive to strengthen independent thought.

CLERGYMAN *see* FUNERAL *page 120*, MARRIAGE *page 130* ◆ PRIEST *see* CARDINAL, BISHOP, ARCHBISHOP *page 281* ◆ VICAR, ALTAR *see* MARRIAGE *page 130* ◆ HASSOCK *see* APPAREL *page 154*

High Priests

CARDINAL
It is unlucky to dream you see a ***cardinal*** in his robes. You will meet such misfortune as will necessitate your removal to distant or foreign lands to begin anew your ruined fortune.

For a woman to dream this, is a sign of her downfall through false promises.

If a priest or preacher is a spiritual adviser, and his services are supposed to be needed, especially in the hour of temptation, then we find ourselves dreaming of him as a warning against approaching evil. ◎

BISHOP
To dream of a ***bishop***, denotes that teachers and authors will suffer great mental worries, caused from delving into intricate subjects.

To the tradesman, foolish buying, in which he is likely to incur loss of good money.

For one to see a bishop in his dreams, hard work will be his patrimony, with chills and ague attendant. If you meet the approval of a much admired bishop, you will be successful in your undertakings in love or business. ◎

ARCHBISHOP
To dream of seeing an ***archbishop***, foretells that you will have many obstacles to resist in your attempt to master fortune or rise to public honor. To see one in the everyday dress of a common citizen, denotes that you will have aid and encouragement from those in prominent positions and will succeed in your enterprises.

For a young woman to dream that an archbishop is kindly directing her, foretells that she will be fortunate in forming her friendships. ◎

Religious dreams may be rooted in the actual rather than the spiritual; you may dream of a minister *opposite above* **or of the interior fittings of a church** *opposite*.

POPE
Any dream in which you see the ***pope***, without speaking to him, warns you of servitude. You will bow to the will of some master.

To dream that you ***speak to the pope***, denotes that certain high honors are in store for you.

To see the ***pope looking sad*** or displeased, warns you against vice or sorrow of some kind. ◎

VATICAN
To dream of the ***Vatican***, signifies that unexpected favors will fall within your grasp.

You will form the acquaintance of distinguished people, if you see royal personages speaking to the pope in the Vatican. ◎

Quakers

To dream of a *Quaker*, ***denotes that you will have faithful friends and fair business. If you are one, you will deport yourself honorably toward an enemy.***

For a young woman to attend a Quaker meeting, portends that she will, by her modest manners, win a faithful husband who will provide well for her household. ❋

Monks and Nuns

MONK
To dream of seeing a ***monk***, foretells dissensions in the family and unpleasant journeyings. To a young woman, this dream signifies that gossip and deceit will be used against her.

To dream that you are a monk, denotes personal loss and illness. ◎

NUNS
For a religiously inclined man to dream of ***nuns***, foretells that material joys will interfere with his spirituality. He should be wise in the control of self.

For a woman to dream of nuns, foretells her widowhood, or her separation from her lover.

If she dreams that she is a nun, it portends her discontentment with present environments.

To see a ***dead nun***, signifies despair over the unfaithfulness of loved ones, and impoverished fortune.

For one to dream that she discards the robes of her order, foretells that longing for worldly pleasures will unfit her for her chosen duties. ◎

CONVENT
To dream of seeking refuge in a ***convent***, denotes that your future will be signally free from care and enemies, unless on entering the building you encounter a priest. If so, you will seek often and in vain for relief from worldly cares and mental worry.

For a young girl to dream of seeing a convent, denotes that her virtue and honesty will be questioned. ◎

Martyrs

To dream of *martyrs*, ***denotes false friends, domestic unhappiness, and losses in affairs which concern you most.***

To dream that you *are a martyr*, ***signifies separation from friends, and enemies will slander you.*** ❋

CARDINAL *see* **PRIEST** *page 280* ◆ **ARCHBISHOP** *see* **APPAREL** *page 154* ◆ **POPE** *see* **TALKING** *page 230*, **MELANCHOLY** *page 257* ◆ **VATICAN** *see* **KING, QUEEN** *page 86* , **BUILDINGS** *page 188* ◆ **MONK** *see* **CLOISTERS** *page 189*, **ASCETICISM** *page 252* ◆ **NUNS** *see* **DEAD** *page 120* ◆ **CONVENT** *see* **BUILDINGS** *page 188*

Prayers, Rituals, and Ceremonies

PREACHER
To dream of a ***preacher***, denotes that your ways are not above reproach, and your affairs will not move easily.

To dream that ***you are a preacher***, foretells for you losses in business, and distasteful amusements will jar upon you.

To ***hear preaching***, implies that you will undergo misfortune.

To ***argue with a preacher***, you will lose in some contest.

To dream that you see one walk away from you, denotes that your affairs will move with new energy. If he looks sorrowful, reproaches will fall heavily upon you.

To see a ***long-haired preacher***, denotes that you are shortly to have disputes with overbearing and egotistical people. ◎

THE KINGDOM OF HEAVEN

PRAYER
To dream of saying ***prayers***, or of seeing others doing so, foretells that you will be threatened with failure, which will take strenuous efforts to avert. ◎

LORD'S PRAYER
To dream of repeating the ***Lord's Prayer***, foretells that you are threatened with secret foes and will need the alliance and the support of friends to tide you over difficulties.

To hear others repeat it, denotes the danger of some friend. ◎

CATECHISM
To dream of the ***catechism***, foretells that you will be offered a lucrative position, but the strictures will be such that you will be worried as to accepting it. ◎

BAPTISM
To dream of ***baptism***, signifies that your character needs strengthening by the practice of temperance in advocating your opinions to the disparagement of your friends.

To dream that you are an applicant, signifies that you will humiliate your inward self for public favor.

To dream that you see ***John the Baptist*** baptizing Christ in the river Jordan, denotes that you will have a desperate mental struggle between yielding yourself to labor in meager capacity for the sustenance of others, and following desires which might lead you into wealth and exclusiveness.

To see the Holy Ghost descending on Christ, is significant of resignation of duty and abnegation of self.

If you are being ***baptized with the Holy Ghost*** and fire, you will be thrown into a state of terror over being discovered in some lustful engagement.

HOLY COMMUNION
To dream that you are taking part in the ***Holy Communion***, warns you that you will resign your independent opinions to gain some frivolous desire.

If you dream that there is neither bread nor wine for the supper, you will find that you have suffered your ideas to be proselytized in vain, as you are no nearer your goal.

If you are ***refused the right of communion*** and feel worthy, there is hope for your obtaining some prominent position which has appeared extremely doubtful, as your opponents are popular and powerful. If you feel unworthy, you will meet with much discomfort.

To dream that you are in a body of Baptists who are taking communion, denotes that you will find that your friends are growing uncongenial, and you will look to strangers for harmony. ◎

Sacred Texts

BIBLE
To dream of the ***Bible***, foretells that innocent and disillusioned enjoyment will be proffered for your acceptance.

To dream that you vilify the teachings of the Bible, forewarns you that you are about to succumb to resisted temptations through the seductive persuasiveness of a friend. ◎

BHAGAVAD GITA
To dream of the ***Bhagavad Gita***, foretells for you a season of seclusion; also rest to the exhausted faculties. A pleasant journey for your advancement will be planned by your friends. Little financial advancement is promised in this dream. ◎

Dreams with a religious theme may show you the Kingdom of Heaven *left*.

PREACHER *see* NOISE *page 276,* DISPUTE *page 230,* HAIR *page 102* ◆ BAPTISM *see* CHRIST *page 279,* FIRE *page 80* ◆ HOLY COMMUNION *see* BREAD *page 146,* WINE *page 151* ◆ BIBLE *see* BLASPHEMY *page 250,* BOOK *page 233* ◆ BHAGAVAD GITA *see* BOOK *page 233*

THE DREAM DIRECTORY

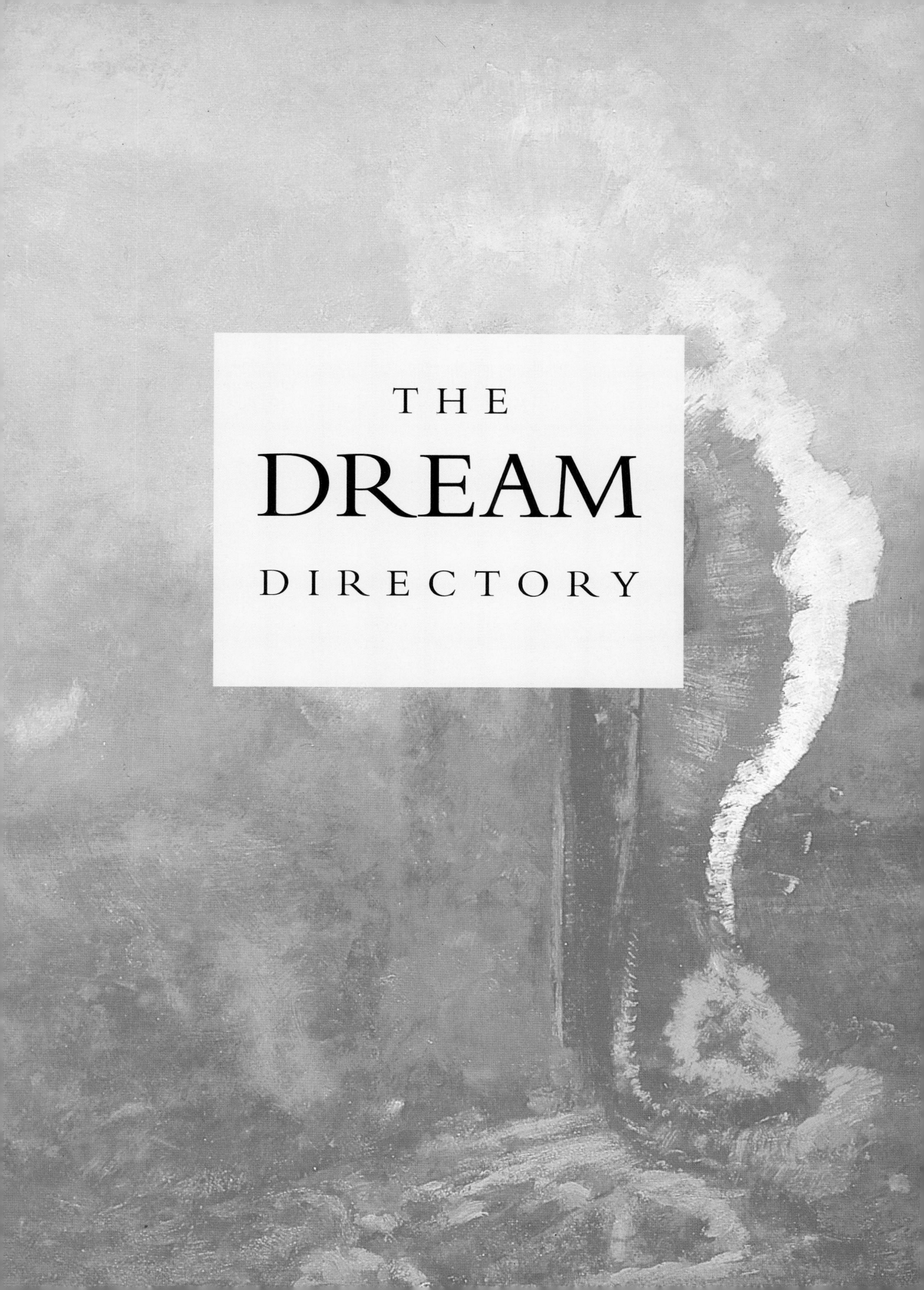

All dream entries are listed in roman type, *whether they appear as main entries, sub-entries or cross-references.*

Entries that do not refer to specific dreams in the main text appear in *italic type.*

A

B

E

I

J

K

L

M

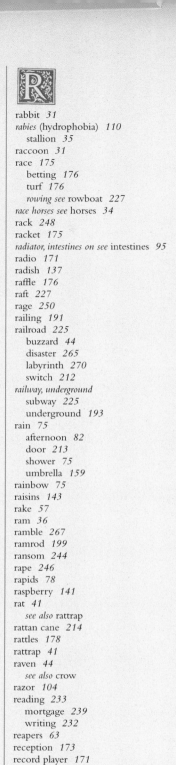

S

X

Y

Z

PICTURE CREDITS AND ACKNOWLEDGMENTS

ARCHIVE FÜR KUNST UND GESCHICHTE, LONDON: 35

CAMERON COLLECTION: 36, 57, 58, 80, 134, 231, 235, 273

THE BRIDGEMAN ART LIBRARY:
2 (Trevor Neal), 19, 26-7 (Rijksmuseum Kroller-Muller), 21 (Christie's, London), 24 (Russell-Cotes Museum and Art Gallery, Bournemouth), 25, 83 (Lauros-Giraudon), 33 (Staatsgalerie, Stuttgart), 40L (Kunstsammlung, Basel), 53, 56 (Pushkin Museum), 64 (Guildhall Art Gallery), 66, 67 (Farringdon Coll. Buscot), 69, 73 (Derby Museum and Art Gallery; Joseph Wright of Derby: *The Alchemist*), 86, 98, 99 (Rijksmuseum Kroller-Muller), 100, 101 (Hirschprungske Samlung, Copenhagen), 107B (Chelmsford Musuem), 111 (Musée Unterlinden, Colmar), 112 (Prado, Madrid), 113T, 114/15 (Giraudon), 117L (Russell-Cotes Museum and Art Gallery, Bournemouth), 118B (Wolverhampton Art Gallery), 119, 120, 122, 124/5 (Magyar Nemzeti Gallery, Budapest), 129, 130/1, 161, 170, 196, 197 (Musée d'Orsay), 206, 234 (Marseille), 241, 243, 246 (The De Morgan Foundation), 248 (The K and B New Foto, Florence), 249, 252, 274 (Musée Unterlinden, Colmar), 282

E.T. ARCHIVE: 54, 78/9, 108,131T, 177, 203, 233, 268, 280

FINE ART PHOTOGRAPHIC LIBRARY
8/9,11, 18, 23, 61, 71, 74, 76, 92, 94, 109, 110, 126, 127, 143, 144/5, 148, 149, 150, 151, 153, 155, 163, 166, 167, 178, 180, 181, 184/5, 186, 195, 200, 202, 205, 207, 211, 217, 223, 236, 240, 258, 262/3

THE IMAGE BANK 88, 229

REX FEATURES: 30, 55, 95, 103, 107T, 113, 117TR, 157, 165, 166, 168, 171, 173, 174, 182, 187, 194, 212, 219, 224, 225, 228, 230, 255, 261, 263

JEREMY THOMAS 136B, 137, 143B, 143CR, 145B, 154, 156B, 160TL

GUY RYECART 48BR, 50T, 61T, 70TR, 71R, 94B, 100BL, 102BR, 115B, 116B, 118TL, 133TR, 139, 146TL, 147BR, 149TL, 161CL,TR, 180BL, 184, 197, 201, 204T, 215

ILLUSTRATIONS

Glyn Bridgewater 173TR, 204BL, 208T, 210TL, 221B

Amanda Cameron 91TL, 174TL, 229TL, 259TL, 274TL

Jane Couldrey 68TL, 124TL, 194TL, 250TL, 260TL

Lorraine Harrison 56TL, 118TL,188TL, 245TL, 265TL

Ivan Hissey 42T, 60BL, 63T, 85TL, 89T, 102TL, 104B, 106BR, 154TL, 162BL 171TL, 198C, 201R, 220BL, 233BR, 242CR, 253TL, 256TR, 257BL, 267TL, 271BL

Katty McMurray 28TL, 106TL, 178TL, 238TL, 277TL

Tony Simpson 74TL, 126TL, 202TL, 254TL, 269TL

Jane Tattersfield 84TL, 164TL, 221TL, 256TL, 272TL

Vikki Yeates 82TL, 133TL, 218TL, 255TL, 270TL